WE MUST LEARN TO SIT DOWN TOGETHER
AND TALK ABOUT A LITTLE CULTURE:
DECOLONISING ESSAYS 1967-1984

ALSO BY SYLVIA WYNTER

Fiction
The Hills of Hebron

Drama
Miracle in Lime Lane
Shh… It's a Wedding
The Big Pride
1865 – A Ballad for a Rebellion
The House and Land of Mrs. Alba
Maskarade
Under the Sun
Rockstone Anancy

Critical Work
Do Not Call Us Negroes: How Multicultural Texts Perpetuate Racism

PUBLISHER'S NOTE

The essays in this collection were written in the heat of the struggle for decolonisation and its aftermath, and under constraints of time and resources, some quotations could not be verified against the originals. Essays varied in the extent to which they were published with endnotes and footnotes identifying their sources and, even when given, some attributions were found to be inexact. Published as they were in a variety of journals, some with limited budgets and staffing, it was evident that by no means all printer's devils escaped the proof-reader's eye. The publisher and readers of this collection owe a huge debt of gratitude to the editor, Demetrius L. Eudell, who, as a labour of love and respect for Professor Wynter, spent a couple of years checking and correcting quotations, chasing down errant references and correcting obvious printer's errors. No doubt a few have escaped us and we have possibly been guilty of a few of our own. For which, apologies.

Jeremy Poynting

SYLVIA WYNTER

WE MUST LEARN TO SIT DOWN TOGETHER
AND TALK ABOUT A LITTLE CULTURE:
DECOLONISING ESSAYS 1967-1984

EDITED BY DEMETRIUS L. EUDELL

PEEPAL TREE

First published in Great Britain in 2022
by Peepal Tree Press Ltd
17 King's Avenue
Leeds LS6 1QS
England

ISBN13: 97818452321088

Supported using public funding by
ARTS COUNCIL
ENGLAND

CONTENTS

SYLVIA WYNTER

PREFACE

With one exception, the writings that comprise this collection were published between 1967 and 1984. The first six entries, together with the last one from 1984, were originally published in the *Jamaica Journal*, established in the wake of the anti-colonial struggle. In 1962, this movement led to political independence from the British empire as well as Jamaica's formal reorganisation *cum* re-conceptualising of itself as a new nation. It is as part of this overall process of reconceptualisation that the *Journal* had its origin, with the first entry in this collection having been published in its debut issue. However, while one other contribution, involved in this same project, had been published in 1971 by the also post-colonially instituted National Trust Commission, eight others were published across several journals. These include *New World Quarterly*, published by the New World Group (Mona, Jamaica), *Savacou,* the post-colonial journal of the Caribbean Artists Movement (centred in Kingston and London), and *Caribbean Studies* (of the University of Puerto Rico). The remaining essays, with one exception, appeared in several university journals and anthologies in the United States. The previously unpublished essay "We Know Where We Are From: The Politics of Black Culture from Myal to Marley", was originally presented at a 1977 conference, hosted jointly by the African Studies Association and the Latin American Studies Association at the University of Houston, Texas. (pp. 445-498 in this volume).[1] In addition, one unpublished contribution emerged from the task of decolonising the curriculum at the University of the West Indies, Mona, where I then taught.

I mention the above as an index of what came to be the defining characteristic of the writings in this collection and my subsequent work. After returning to Jamaica from London in 1962 and in the following year beginning a teaching career at the University of the West Indies, none of these essays, except the proposal on curricular change, responded to an academic imperative. That is, they were not authored specifically within the disciplinary, in Foucauldian terms, *disciplining*, imperatives of sixteenth/seventeenth-century Golden Age Spanish Literature (a subfield of European literatures) in which I had been formally trained at the University of London. As can now be seen from a post-

Sixties hindsight, the epistemological order to which this discipline belonged had been transferred from the University of London to the University of the West Indies. This *disciplining* of a multiplicity of post-colonial Anglophone universities of the non-European world presumed that the latter were to institute themselves on the model of the former.

Nor indeed could these essays in their historico-pragmatic context have been intended to respond to the imperatives of "post-colonial studies/literary studies". As a major unintended consequence, this field has aided in the ongoing erasure of the concrete reality of the global "native" anti-colonial struggles from our fully homogenised, secular, Western and Westernised collective memory. Certainly, these struggles themselves turned out, in the end, to be Janus-faced. Unlike the earlier intra-Western European, *settler* anti-colonial struggles, in which the United States would be canonised as the iconic model, the "native" anti-colonial struggles were to be almost entirely re-pressed from recognition as a major historical turning point in their own right. Indeed, they seemingly came to be, to use Slavoj Žižek's apt terminology, one of history's now entirely, indeed hopelessly, "lost causes".[2]

Instead, all of these pieces responded to the quite different imperative of the immediacy of that anti-colonial cause which had directly arisen out of the memory of my childhood and adolescence. A profound transformation had been effected in what had been, up until then, the stable order of the colonial world of a British imperial Jamaica. This rupture occurred as the direct result of a sustained series of "native labour" strikes. These uprisings drew momentum from the marches/demonstrations by jobless crowds vainly seeking work from the British colonial authorities.[3] In the global context of the aftermath of the 1929 Economic Crash and subsequent Great Depression, a large-scale uprising in May 1938 shut down the capital city, Kingston. If only for a brief interregnum, these disturbances overturned an imperial order which hitherto had seemed, to us, its "native" subjects, to be impregnable to any such challenge. This order-overturning (i.e. *an-archical*) "movement from below" had been brutally repressed by the joint military and police forces of the colonial authorities (by the very logic of them having to act as such authorities). Nevertheless, the "sacrificial" costs paid by those who had been wounded, imprisoned, detained, shot and killed, set in motion an unstoppable dynamic of an increasingly generalised form of the anti-colonial/anti-imperial movement.

This struggle continued during a period of unceasing, island-wide turmoil, being fuelled by the activities of an organised militant "native labour" trade union mass movement with its adjunct of political parties led by Alexander Bustamante, and his cousin and rival, the barrister, Norman Manley.[4] In 1944, these disturbances culminated in the first definitive, if only then *de facto* (its *de jure* form was only to be conceded by the British in 1962) holding of elections on the basis of universal adult suffrage. This period coincided with my growing up from childhood to adolescence and gave origin, however inchoately at first in my own intellectual case, to a range of new issues. Among these questions, most centrally and recalcitrantly difficult would prove to be that of the Race/Colour Line, itself inseparable from our native labour *cum* colourised status. My attempt to come to grips with this problematic came to be *the* imperative to which the writings of this collection – as all of my later work – were to respond.

Indeed, even earlier, upon completing my studies at King's College, London University, I had set out to become a creative writer. In London, I found myself on the fringes of a group of aspiring West Indian writers. Most of us struggled, in varying ways and genres, to give imaginative reality to our regional landscape, which had up until then remained largely, if not entirely, "*unstoried, unenhanced*". We attempted to counter, imaginatively, the magma of negative stereotypes of ourselves and our peoples as "backward natives", which had been law-likely projected, in Lévi-Strauss's terms, by the mythologic of imperial colonisation.[5] Therefore, when viewed from hindsight, the major thematic of my early creative work (culminating in the 1962 publication of my novel, *The Hills of Hebron*),[6] the essays of this collection, and my later work responded to this same imperative.

As a result, the entire body of my work, then and now, had no disciplinary or "academic" end in itself. At the same time, I made full use of the insights gained from my formal discipline of literary criticism. My teaching of sixteenth-and seventeenth-century Spanish literature at the University of the West Indies enabled me to deepen, if tentatively at first, my access to the unique mode of knowledge which this literature offered. The literature of Golden Age Spain, like its contemporary counterpart of monarchical England, offered a path to understanding the objectively instituted colonial and colonising order of consciousness. It would be within the system of meaning produced by this order of consciousness that the subjects of imperial Spain and England would have been instituted and their social orders legitimated. To wit, the initial maritime explorations and imperial territorial expansions would, however conflictedly, epochally bring into existence what has become our globally incorporated, materially integrated, and hegemonically bourgeois secular world-systemic order. Consequently, the first such empire in our *human-as-a-species* history emerged on the basis of the expropriation of the habitat of the indigenous peoples of the Caribbean/West Indian islands, this followed by the large-scale trans-Atlantic importation of a *negro/negra* slave labour force from Africa.

Second, what had been up until then the traditional Euro-centred discipline of literature/literary criticism began to reformulate itself in the more globally inclusive terms of "literary studies". This was in the wake of the then ongoing successes of the global anti-colonial struggles, upon which followed an explosion of new literatures, including those of the Anglophone West Indies [and/or Caribbean]. It was in this respect that the imperative of my own overall problematic was to push me, from then on, towards what was to be a more radically far-reaching conception, beyond its present disciplinary boundaries, of literary studies itself. With all this coming to be in the wake of the Sixties' far-reaching range of social and political movements of the United States, I was invited in 1974 to teach in the new "Literature and Society of the Third World" Program at the University of California, San Diego. As part of the *multiple* intellectual challenges made to mainstream academia's then organisation of knowledge, by students as well as by some faculty, this innovative approach to knowledge resulted in one of the then few comprehensive Departments of Literature, which was in the process of reconceptualising itself in a now global, that is, trans-First World/European, sense.

The West Indian historian Woodville Marshall has perceptively pointed out that these transformations taking place as I began to teach were not only occurring in Jamaica, but in most of the former British-imperial colonies. Marshall identified this moment of great change as the "second social revolution", the successor to what had been the Anglophone Caribbean region's "first social revolution" of slave emancipation.[7] After the British Parliament passed the 1832 Reform Bill, in the following year, a legislative decree abolishing slavery was enacted, destabilising, if only temporarily, the export-oriented monoculture of the Anglo-Caribbean plantocracy.[8] This "first social revolution" nonetheless marked the emancipation of the population from their empirically-institutionalised Negro slave labour role. This subjugation of the, more precisely in the original gendered Spanish terms, *negro/negra,* had begun with the onset of Western modernity in the early sixteenth century.

Parallel to the British Parliament, the U.S. Congress played an important role in the "first social revolution" of slave emancipation in the United States, although in both instances, the agency of the enslaved was equally indispensable. Indeed, both were enacted in the context of wars, the former that of the Baptist War/Christmas Rebellion in 1831-1832 and the latter, the Civil War from 1861-1865, where the formerly enslaved like Frederick Douglass not only played a central role in the abolitionist movement, but also served as soldiers and nurses in the struggle that brought an end to "Negro" slavery.

Correlatedly, both of these "second social revolutions" were also driven by autonomous agency from below that led to large-scale social transformations in the British Caribbean and the United States. Replicating its earlier Jamaica/West Indies anti-colonial counterpart, the case of the latter was epitomised by the Montgomery Alabama Bus Boycott in 1955, when 40,000 Blacks (then Negroes) mounted a formidable challenge against the juridical and social segregation of the South. In consequence, they initiated a boycott that lasted an impressive 381 days, as they had collectively decided, in the words of the Reverend Dr. Martin Luther King, Jr., that they would rather "walk in dignity than ride in humiliation", and thereby substituted "tired feet for tired souls."[9] Then, with that initial victory won, the fight against political, educational, and social apartheid, against their overall racially inferiorised and subordinated "Negro status" was carried on by the larger Black American population with their White allies.

As an important part of this political struggle, Black students, faculty and other political activists, including poets, artists, and "public intellectuals", fought for and won, at universities across the nation, what was called, in its original founding conception, Black Studies, and this belonged to a range of new studies then being instituted. This intellectual transformation occurred in the wider political context in which Black Americans turned their backs on the "slave name" originally assigned by the West – i.e. *Negroes* – and renamed themselves *Black*.[10]

During the 1960s, the traditional Euro-centred discipline of literature/literary criticism began to reformulate itself in the more globally inclusive terms of "literary studies". This shift occurred in the wake of the successes of the global anti-colonial struggles, which, in turn produced an explosion of new literatures, including those of the Anglophone Caribbean. In this context, the imperative of my own overall problematic pushed me, from then on, to adopt a more radically far-reaching conception, beyond its present disciplinary boundaries, of literary studies itself. The Sixties' wide-ranging social and political movements in the United States led to an invitation in 1974 to teach in the new "Literature and Society of the Third World" Program at the University of California, San Diego. This innovative approach to knowledge established one of the few comprehensive Departments of Literature, seeking to reconceptualise itself in a global trans-First World/European sense. Indeed, this paradigm shift formed a part of the *multiple* challenges posed to main-stream academia by students and some faculty.

Subsequently, in 1977, Stanford University invited me to teach in one such newly-established initiative, the African and Afro-American Studies Program, which was accompanied with a joint appointment in the Department of Spanish and Portuguese. Innovative and new Black Studies programs like the one at Stanford (though named African and Afro-American Studies) had been institutionalised on the basis of a "gaze from below" perspective of the experiences of the negatively marked descendants of the formerly enslaved. Once situated in this new and contestatory field of knowledge I was able to focus on the original question of Race as it had arisen out of my earlier experience of the fundamental and close parallels between West Indian and Black American first and second social revolutions, the question of Race.

This creative energy enabled my teaching of newly devised courses built around the normally everyday repressed reality that had given rise to these movements. In both situations, however, if more rapidly so in the case of the United States, unwelcome changes had begun to occur. Already by the mid-seventies, the Janus-faced outcomes of national independence with increas-ingly negative aspects had become evident. This was in contrast to our respective existentially-lived experiences of the initial emancipatory phases of that "second social revolution" of which we ourselves had been the agents. These adverse outcomes which required additional explanatory focus, now urgently had to be brought into the equation. What in the nature and context of our respective "second social revolutions" led to these negative aftermaths? How, therefore, to account for the failure of what had been our own agency?

It should not be forgotten, that in the wake of our respective "movements from below" that tangible improvements in the lives of Blacks in the Caribbean and the United States had been achieved. This was certainly the case in Jamaica after 1944 in the context of a hegemonic Keynesian economic system functioning at the global level. Indeed, both mass parties used their control of the political State to respond to the educational and economic needs of the now politically empowered majority. In a short span of time, these political parties were able to realise more modernising improvements in the lives of a sizeable number of their voters than had been effected by the British colonial governments for a century after the complete abolition of slavery in 1838. Such was no less the case in the US, where the Civil Rights struggle had also resulted in improvements for many Blacks. However, these changes tended to privilege the incorporation of the entrepreneurial and professionally educated Black middle class as well as the technically trained lower-middle classes into the normative White middle class. These accomplishments resulted largely from Affirmative Action policies in higher-education and in a wide range of jobs, which formerly had been restricted to their White peers. At the same time, however, the Janus-faced fall-outs of both initially emancipatory projects had begun to become apparent, this even more rapidly so in the United States.

At this point, the major focus of my work unexpectedly had to come to grips with an entirely different existential dilemma. In the independent nation states of Jamaica and the Anglophone West Indies, we began increasingly to experience ourselves as resubordinated by an ostensibly objectively functioning, post-Keynesian, and globally homogenised neo-Liberal free market economic system. This was one under whose anti-statist terms, the votes of the Black and poor majority could no longer have effective leverage. Correlatedly, under this neo-Liberal mytho-logic, we found ourselves, almost overnight, and without any input, no longer imperially classified in *political* terms as "native" colonial societies, but rather were now represented in economic terminology, as "underdeveloped". As such, we were instituted as part of a new global category, the "Third World".[11] In this regard, the nation-states of post-colonial Black Africa fared even worse. Similarly, Haiti, once *the* icon of politico-military agency in the wake of its slave revolution, now has come to signify unbearable mass poverty and non-agential dependence; this before the January 2010 earthquake and, more recently, assassination of the president. All of these post-colonial nations could now be classified as the Fourth World, in effect, the Black-and-Poor World.

An even more distressing paradox emerged in this globally and externally imposed (both classificatory and empirically institutionalised) context. In post-colonial Jamaica, the descendants of the "native labour" strikers and jobless street marchers, whose "sacrificial" overturning of the colonial order in May 1938 had led to our collective political emancipation, now bore the brunt of the negative effects of this change. By contrast, those of us who were middle class – such as securely employed academics *cum* intellectuals – could often escape this economic fallout.[12] Nor was this to be any less the case, if in somewhat different terms, in the post-apartheid United States. There, the "second social revolution" led to the large majority of poorer, less formally educated Black Americans being condemned to an institutionalised neo-apartheid existence to which the now large-scale neo-plantation archipelago of the prison-industrial system remains inextricably linked.[13] This is no less the case with respect to their peers in a post-apartheid, post-Mandela South Africa. As well, many now find themselves after 1994, like their peers elsewhere, although no longer condemned to an apartheid form of secondary, low-wage, lowly-skilled migrant "native labour" (Fanon's category of *les damnés de la terre*) subjected to a new and now even more total form of the same economically determined damnation. This large-scale global joblessness is now decreed by a techno-industrially automated and mechanised consumer-driven, capitalist economic system. The logic of this externally imposed fate of large-scale joblessness produces its correlated societal underworld with communities being racked by both political and criminalised gang warfare. The latter reflects the daily performative enactment of the apprehensions of a number of its residents, who sharply perceived their always, already predestined, and systemically legitimated human expendability/disposability. All this has worsened and expanded in the wake of the 1989 collapse of the former Soviet Union's attempted alternative economic system as well as the Party-State Capitalist turn of a now post-Mao China. In China as well, large numbers of relatively more technically skilled, more highly educated (i.e. entrepreneurial, professional, technocratic) groups, have indeed been incorporated into a single Free Market economic system, in its most extreme neo-Liberal fundamentalist form. If large numbers of the country's majority lower-class population, have been, as economists exult, "lifted out of poverty", equally large numbers are now joining the ranks of the semi-jobless, jobless, and even potentially landless "migrant labour category". Those *not* lifted out of poverty represent the embodiment of China's version of the Free Market's category of the humanly expendable, condemned to techno-industrial joblessness. For a majority of the *damnés*, now part of a global "planet of the slums" inhabited by a liminally deviant "underclass", the only actualisable agency for many is that of their death-risking involvement in the criminalised drug-trade. At the same time, it is not to be overlooked that such actions remain indispensable to the normal, everyday functioning of many of our increasingly trans-First/Second/

Third/Fourth Worlds' internet-homogenised Western and Westernised, thereby hegemonically secular, middle classes, who inhabit the global *planet of suburbia/exurbia cum re-gentrified cities*. This seemingly inescapable fate has been perceptively defined by the Cameroonian scholar, Achille Mbembe, writing with specific agonistic reference to Black Africa (although it relates more generally) as "the night of the… post-colonial world" [...] which is "…trapped face to face with the terrible post-colonial closure, its deafening/dizzying affirmation of powerlessness."[14] – i.e., of *impuissance*.

My attempt to find an answer to this systemic contradiction further served to reinforce my questioning with respect to the *why* of the West's socio-hierarchic organising principle of the Race/Colour Line. I became increasingly certain that the answer to the question held the solution to our collective powerlessness (*impuissance*) with respect to the *cul-de-sac* of our ongoing post-colonial night, but I was led into an impasse. It was an impasse which meant that none of my later writings could (and increasingly so) be made to confine themselves within our present epistemologically correct boundaries (however ostensibly radical), and could thereby be made "hearable" within the terms of this epistemological order's Sixties and Seventies-identified "program" and/or "apparatus of truth."[15]

Consequently, my intuition deepened that my non-findability of an answer was itself a non-negotiable condition of the stable reproduction of our present epistemological "program" and/or "apparatus of truth". I therefore had to approach each subsequent piece of writing as a stage in a kind of *plus ultra*, or further and further developing goal. Such was in order that I could continue to focus single-mindedly on my search for the Grail of that answer – the answer as to the *why* of what has come to be the now globally extended functioning of the purely secular, and as such, originally Western world-system *cum* bourgeois phenomenon to which we give the folk-terminology name of "Race" or "Colour Line". This was finding the *why*, therefore, of the seeming incontestability of its ostensibly universally applicable (being extra-humanly mandated) *role-cum-destiny-allocating* ranking rule; a rule based on the biocentric model of the human as a purely natural organism locked within the half-mythic, half-scientific[16] Darwinian argument of the "unerring powers of natural selection" from which there could be no altering of our racial destiny.[17] As Darwin wrote:

> At some future period, not very distant as measured by centuries, the civilised races of man will almost certainly exterminate, and replace, the savage races throughout the world. At the same time the anthropomorphous apes, as Professor Schaaffhausen has remarked [*Anthropological Review*, April 1867, p. 236], will no doubt be exterminated. The break between man and his nearest allies will then be wider, for it will intervene between man in a more civilised state, as we may hope, even than the Caucasian, and some ape as low as a baboon, instead of as now between the negro or Australian and the gorilla.[18]

Our daily lived enactment of the Race/Colour Line is now being made to correlate with Darwin's encoded division between the ostensibly biologically selected global ruling class category of the wealthy bourgeoisie and the mostly Black and Poor "planet of the slums". This collection reflects the initiatory thrust to find a meta-Darwinian, and thereby meta-bourgeois, revalorising answer to this question. My central hypothesis remains that from our origins on the continent of Africa until today, the human, in meta-Darwinian terms, is a uniquely languaging *cum* story-telling, and thereby a hybridly, auto-instituting species.[19] In other words, being uniquely human is a Third level of existence, with our emergence constituting a Third Event beyond "the most decisive events" of the birth of the universe and the emergence of biological life.[20] It is therefore with the recognition of the functioning of the laws of human auto-institution, that is, of the cognitive and representational role of storytelling that enables humans to produce and reproduce our social orders, that we shall have the capacity to address effectively the negative Janus-faced outcomes, not only now of our Third/Fourth World's post-colonial *impuissance*, but that also *as-a-species* our present collective *impuissance*. These impending issues confronting us as a species have been defined by Gerald Barney as the global problematique of problems of poverty, habitat, energy and trade, among others.[21] It was with writing of the essays assembled in this collection, where I first began to lay the conceptual ground for my decolonising answer to this question of the Race and the Colour Line.

ACKNOWLEDGEMENTS

Hence my acknowledgement and sincere thanks to Jeremy Poynting, editor of the Peepal Tree Press, not only for his having proposed some years ago the publication of my earlier writings as a collection, but also for his intellectual grasp of what it was I had been attempting to do. This was then followed by his setting out to collect the material, hitherto scattered across several journals, including *Jamaica Journal*.

My acknowledgement and thanks also to Professor Demetrius Eudell, of the Department of History at Wesleyan University, for his overall collegial support and help with all aspects of the project, including tracking down one of the major entries and for meticulously documenting the sources from which my essays, papers and reviews were drawn.

This Preface must substitute for what became a book-length and much more extensive essay entitled "Prolegomena: "A Part of Some Gigantic Thing Called Colonial: The Anti-Colonial Struggle, the Urgent Contemporaneity, After our First 'False Exist' of its Seemingly 'Lost Cause.'" Although not published here, I would nonetheless like to thank those who provided me with tremendous assistance in the development of that earlier, more ambitious Preface. That work could not have been accomplished without the efforts of

Johanna Fraley and Jack Dresnick, both students of Professor Eudell, (the former from Ohio State, the latter Wesleyan), who have been intellectually engaged collaborators with me on my ongoing work. They also helped to redeem me from my computer/internet illiteracy. As well, the support of Nick Mitchell, an assistant professor at the University of California, Santa Cruz and Dorothy Antwine of the African and Afro-American Studies Program at Stanford was invaluable. Dr. Patricia Fox is also owed many thanks for editing parts of the earlier longer version of this Preface. Relatedly, I should like to acknowledge formally my sincere gratitude to Professor Debra Satz, then Senior Associate Dean of the Humanities and Social Sciences at Stanford University for a grant that enabled me to secure the editorial support of Dr. Fox. Jürgen Heinrichs, Seton Hall professor of art history, also provided substantial edits and insights on the earlier and the present versions of the Preface, as well as carefully proofreading all the essays in the collection.

Finally, my sincere acknowledgements and thanks to three groups. First, those who had been involved in the institution, conceptualising, editing and publication of the then new *Jamaica Journal*, published by the Institute of Jamaica. Specifically, among these, the Hon. E. P. G. Seaga, the then youthful Minister of Development and Welfare. Seaga's research into the village folk life of Jamaica, rural and urban, convinced him that, as he noted "this is a complete world of its own, linked by ancestral bonds to Africa and by convenient ties to the Western world". Such an insight could not be contained at the time within the disciplinary limits of anthropology. This realisation became one of the reasons for proposing the establishment of *Jamaica Journal* to provide a venue to disseminate knowledge of this world in its full complexity.[22] Complementarily, the realisation of this project was due both to its editor, Alex Gradussov and to the excellent collaboration of the professional personnel of the long-established Institute of Jamaica. This included the support of the novelist Neville Dawes, then Director of the Institute. It was Gradussov's outsider's eye for the emerging popular creativity of post-colonial Jamaica, especially that of the Rastafarians' "gaze from below" that offered a model for the process of reconceptualisation that would be a defining feature of the journal.

Secondly, my acknowledgement and thanks are due also to the New World Group, especially to two of its members, George Beckford and Lloyd Best, both scholar-economists who, as co-editors of the *New World Quarterly*, had made available a venue for the further exploration of their group's founding hypothesis with respect to the slave-labour-*plantation-as-institution*, as the explanatory key or model to the understanding of the contemporary reality of the post-1492 Caribbean, as well as of other slave-labour plantation societies such as Brazil and the US South. This was, in the terms of George Beckford's classic major work, the reality of the ongoing "persistent poverty" of the majority of the favela/ghetto/shantytown ex-slave descendants continuing as *the* major characteristic defining of all such regions. Their hypothesis asserted that the plantation was *the founding institution* of the originally post-1492 slave societies of the Caribbean and generally of the Americas, and therefore, of Western modernity itself. Their argument served to prefigure Immanuel Wallerstein's 1974 pathbreaking conceptualisation of the "modern world system".[23] Although their prefiguration had been articulated specifically from the underside positional perspective of what Wallerstein would later identify as the *periphery* slave labour regions of that world system, their work was nonetheless crucial to the gradual reorientation of my own thinking. And while, however, their emphasis, (like that of Wallerstein) had been primarily focused on the *economic* aspects of the *plantation-as-institution* model,[24] Kamau Brathwaite, a poet and literary scholar (who, together with the other members of the Caribbean Artists Group, was to publish from 1970 the journal *Savacou*), was also to open up the exploration of that model's trans-economic aspects.[25] Both approaches, taken together, served to validate the poet Aimé Césaire's ecumenically human proposal for a now redemptively humanist new "science of the word".

Taken together, all three journals (*Jamaica Journal, New World Quarterly,* and *Savacou*) were publishing spaces whose co-functioning contours made possible both the growth of my ideas, as well as the journals in which some of the major entries of this collection were to first take shape.

Endnotes

1. My thanks to Professor Anthony Bogues of Brown University, for sending me a copy of this conference paper, which had been found amongst the papers of C.L.R. James after his much-lamented death. I had the privilege of meeting James, as well as interacting intellectually with him, at a Conference that had been held in Washington, DC on the occasion of his then 70th birthday.
2. For the development of this concept see Slavoj Žižek, *In Defense of Lost Causes* (London: Verso, 2008).
3. The labour strikes that occurred in January 1938 on the Serge Island sugar estate in St. Thomas followed upon the strikes that took place the previous September on banana estates in St. James Parish. In late April 1938, on the Frome sugar estate in Westmoreland, riots broke out which were brutally repressed in early May by armed police. The news of the police brutality was carried to Kingston by labour leader Alexander Bustamente, who together with the Garveyite St. William Grant were arrested for their role in the protests. A few weeks later, dock workers on the wharves of Kingston mounted the most decisive anti-colonial action, together with the support of other city and hospital workers, which led to businesses being closed across Kingston. Advised by the barrister Norman Manley, the governor released Bustamante and his colleagues. For additional context, see in the collection here, "Jamaica's National Heroes", 300-332.
4. The Bustamante Industrial Trade Union (BITU) and its subsequent adjunct, the Jamaica Labour Party (JLP) and the Trade Union Congress, as adjunct

to Manley's People National Party (PNP). See for the role played in this rivalry between Bustamante and Manley, who were related, Jackie Ranston, *From We Were Boys: The Story of the Magnificent Cousins, the Rt. Excellent Sir William Alexander Bustamante and the Rt. Excellent Norman Washington Manley* (Kingston: Bustamante Institute of Public and International Affairs, 1989). Also to be noted, with respect to the rivalry, was their respective educational status, the one, a Rhodes scholar and barrister, the other, like Marcus Garvey, being self-taught with little formal schooling.

5. Rather than how humans think in their myths, Claude Lévi-Strauss wants to illustrate "not how men think in myths, but how myths operate in men's minds without their being aware of the fact". See *The Raw and the Cooked: Mythologiques,* Volume 1 (1969; Chicago: University of Chicago Press, 1983), 12.

6. The novel, which was originally published in 1962 by Jonathan Cape in Great Britain and Simon and Schuster in the United States, then later by Longman. It was republished in 2010 by Ian Randle Publishers, Ltd., Kingston, Jamaica. To be noted here is that the reclamation of Africa as culture sphere of origins, i.e. *inter alia,* our traditions of carving as well as for major legends, is asserted as a central epigraph and at the end of the novel.

7. Woodville Marshall, "The Post-Slavery Labour Problem Revisited," Elsa Goveia Memorial Lecture, 15 March 1990 (Mona, Jamaica: Department of History, University of the West Indies, 1991).

8. For a portrait of this slave plantation world of the then Anglo-Jamaican plantocracy, see the first essay in the collection, "Lady Nugent's Journal", 49-50.

9. King gave this speech "A Look to the Future" on September 2, 1957 on the occasion of the twenty-fifth anniversary of the Highlander Folk School in Monteagle, Tennessee. See *The Papers of Martin Luther King, Jr., Volume IV: Symbol of the Movement, January 1957-December 1958,* Clayborn Carson, Susan Carson, Adrienne Clay, Virginia Shadron, Kieran Taylor, eds. (Berkeley: University of California Press, 2000), 270.

10. See for this the fact of the far-reaching differences of meaning of the term "Black" in the sixteenth-century between Kongolese and Portuguese usage. In the Kongolese founding origin myth or cosmogony (one chartering of the encoded origin myth or cosmogony specific to their kingdom), the term "Black" (*Prieto*) was a term of hierarchical *honour,* whilst the Portuguese terms *negro/negra,* were ones equivalent only to their only enslavable groups, those stigmatised as "lineageless men and women" who were legitimately enslavable. See my *"Do Not Call Us Negros:" How "Multicultural" Textbooks Perpetuate Racism* (San Francisco: Aspire Books, 1992).

11. Originally during the Sixties, as Odd Arne Westad points out, and in the hiatus of the ongoing anti-colonial movements such as those of Algeria and Vietnam, the idea of "the Third World as the future", the concept therefore of (in French) a *tiermondiste,* i.e. *Thirdworldist,* revolutionary project had been adopted by Western student radicals and others as a progression on the orthodox Marxist-Left approach. In the wake of what might be called the post-Sixties' Counter-Reformation, however, the now hegemonic, economically determined, classificatory, hierarchical conception of the *Third World,* followed by that of the *Fourth Wourld,* would function to denote the degrees of distance or of

nearness of all ex-colonial (or ex-neo-colonial, as in the case of Latin America or China), to the norm of capitalist economic "development", as evidenced in the exemplary First World of the West's ex-coloniser countries. See *The Global Cold War: Third World Interventions and the Making of Our Times* (Cambridge: Cambridge University Press, 2005), 106-108.

12. To be noted here, however, is that with the rise of temporary and precarious academic labour, the now overwhelmingly adjunct professoriate in the United States is being increasingly governed by a logic of human expendability.

13. See in the case of the United States, for a recent update of this post-Sixties phenomenon, Ruth Gilmore's *Golden Gulag: Prisons, Surplus, Crisis, and Opposition in Globalizing California* (Berkeley: University of California Press, 2007). Michelle Alexander, *The New Jim Crow: Mass Incarceration in the Age of Colorblindness* (New York: The New Press, 2010) and Khalil Gibran Muhammad, *Condemnation of Blackness: Race, Crime and the Making of Modern Urban America* (Cambridge, MA: Harvard University Press, 2010).

14. The citation from Achille Mbembe's *Écrire l'Afrique à partir d'une faille,* is taken from Keith Walker, "Dans l'actualité du siècle qui s'annonce" ("On the reality of the century which is upon us") in *Aimé Césaire: Pour regarder le siècle en face.* Annick Thébia-Melsan, ed. (Paris: Maisonneuve et La Rose, 2000), 66. Walker suggests the following English translation of Mbembe's title as, *Writing Africa from the Perspective of a Rupture.* Personal communication.

15. See for this, Michel Foucault, "Truth and Power", in his *Power/Knowledge: Selected Interviews and Other Writings, 1972-1977,* ed. Colin Gordon (New York: Pantheon Books), 109-133. See also, even more centrally, *The Order of Things: An Archaeology of the Human Sciences,* Trans. *Les mots et les choses* (New York: Vintage Books, 1973). One of his major points here is that the disciplines of the *Human Sciences* (that is, in English), the *Social Sciences,* including centrally that of economics, although modelled on the natural sciences are not themselves sciences. For an excellent analysis of the far-reaching implications of this argument, see Gary Gutting, *Michel Foucault's Archaeology of Scientific Reason* (New York: Cambridge University Press, 1989).

16. See Glynn Isaac, "Aspects of Human Evolution" in *Evolution: From Molecules to Men,* D. S. Bendall, ed. (Cambridge: Cambridge University Press, 1983), 509-543.

17. As Hans Blumenberg notes: "Darwin justifies nature's indifference to what is alive at any given time, over thousands of generations, by appeal to the 'unerring power of natural selection' and derives from this natural right the demand (at the end of the *Descent of Man,* published in 1871) that society should open for all men the free competition that grants to the most successful the greatest number of descendants." See *The Legitimacy of the Modern Age,* trans. by R. M. Wallace (Cambridge, MA: MIT Press, 1983), 224-225.

18. *The Descent of Man and Selection in Relation to Sex,* ed. with Intro by John Tyler Bonner and Robert M. May (Princeton: Princeton University Press, 1981), 201. See also where he states: "In each great region of the world the living mammals are closely related to the extinct species of the same region. It is therefore probable that Africa was formerly inhabited by extinct apes closely allied to the gorilla and chimpanzee; and as these two species are now man's

nearest allies, it is somewhat more probable that our early progenitors lived on the African continent than elsewhere. But it is useless to speculate on this subject..." Ibid., 199. And: "The great break in the organic chain between man and his nearest allies, which cannot be bridged over by any extinct or living species, has often been advanced as a grave objection to the belief that man is descended from some lower form; but this objection will not appear of much weight to those who, for general reasons, believe in the general principle of evolution. Breaks often occur in all parts of the series, some being wide, sharp and defined, others less so in various degrees; as between the orang and its nearest allies..." Ibid., 200. For an illuminating discussion, one with respect to Darwin's 2009 Centennial year of both the epochally cognitively emancipatory nature of Darwin's overall work as well as of, especially with respect to *The Descent of Man*, etc., the profoundly real life destructive effects of its mytho-ideological aspects, see Steven Shapin's brilliant Review essay, "The Darwin Show" in *London Review of Books,* Vol. 32, no. 1. (7 January 2010): 3-9.

19. See for this, Juan Arsuaga, *The Neanderthal's Necklace: In Search of the First Thinkers*, trans. Andy Klatt (New York: Four Walls Eight Windows, 2002), 307-308, where he writes: "The first modern humans in Africa were surrounded by other populations as robust as the Neanderthals, but they *took a different evolutionary route*, an alternative strategy to solve the same ecological problems. They developed a brain specialised in the manipulation of symbols... While the Neanderthals evolved in Europe, we did so in Africa... One of [the results] is... our fabulous articulated language, at the service of a unique capacity to manipulate symbols, *or to put it another way, to tell stories and create fictitious worlds.* Creativity is our hyper-specialisation. It arose only in the African branch of human evolution and not in the European one." Emphasis added. Stories above all, as those of each group's specific chartering cosmogonies, instituting of our hitherto always *genre-specific,* and pseudo-speciating *genres of being human* as in that of our present nation-state's own.

20. See Peter V. Coveney and Roger Highfield, "Preface", *The Arrow of Time: A Voyage through Science to Solve Time's Greatest Mystery* (New York: Fawcett Columbine, 1990), 16.

21. As Barney identifies and defines this "problematique" (if perhaps missing a few other of its major connecting links)

> As we humans have begun to think globally, it has become clear that we do not have a poverty problem, or a hunger problem, or a habitat problem, or an energy problem, or a trade problem, or a population problem, or an atmosphere problem, or a waste problem or a resource problem. On a planetary scale, these problems are all interconnected. What we really have is a poverty-hunger-habitat-energy-trade-population-atmosphere-waste-resource-problem.

See Gerald Barney, *Global 2000 Revisited: What Shall We Do?* (Arlington, VA: The Millennium Institute, 1993), 25. However, while Barney's "atmosphere problem" has been highlighted by the U.N.'s Report on Climate Change by their Inter-governmental panel – i.e. in *Climate Change, 2007: Synthesis Report, an Assessment of the Intergovernmental Panel on Climate Change*: "[as] *adopted section by section at IPCC Plenary. Xxvi* (Valencia, Spain, 12-17 November 2007) [and which] "represents the formally agreed statement of the IPCC concerning key findings, and uncertainties contained in the Working Group contributions to the Fourth Assessment report" – the scientist Freeman Dyson, also emphasises, like Barney, its interconnectedness with a range of other problems, when he warns against "the obsession with [the] global warming" aspect of the overall *global problematique* – with this obsession, therefore, "distracting public attention from…[the] more serious and more immediate dangers to the planet, including the [correlated] problems of nuclear weaponry, environmental degradation, and social injustice". See Freeman Dyson, "The Question of Global Warming." A Review essay in *The New York Review of Books*, June 12, 2008, 45.

22. Edward Seaga, "A Life on a Cultural Mission", *Jamaica Journal*, Vol. 32, Nos. 1 and 2 (August 2009): 12-15.

23. See Wallerstein's *The Modern World System I: Capitalist Agriculture and the Origins of the European World-Economy in the Sixteenth Century*. (New York: Academic Press, 1974). Lloyd Best (1934-2007) was both a Professor of Economics at U.W.I. from 1957-1976, after which he resigned in order to take part in Trinidadian politics. An outstanding public intellectual and economic as well as social and political thinker, he was awarded the Order of the Caribbean Community (OCC), which earned him the title of The Honourable. Among his publications are his 1968 "Outline of a Model of Pure Plantation Economy", as well as, along with Kari Polanyi Levitt, *Essays on the Theory of Plantation Economy: A Historical and Institutional Approach to Caribbean Eonomic Development* (Mona, Jamaica: University of the West Indies Press, 2009). He was also the founder of the Trinidad and Tobago Institute of the West Indies, now known as the Lloyd Best Institute of the West Indies. George Beckford (1934-1990) was also a professor of economics at the University of the West Indies. His classic book, *Persistent Poverty: Underdevelopment in the Plantation Economies of the Third World* (Oxford: Oxford University Press, 1972), has been repeatedly republished. Best and Beckford's co-edited journal, *New World Quarterly*, was published from 1963-1972.

24. If George Beckford and Lloyd Best were to touch on other aspects of the plantation model, besides the economic – as, for example, in Chapter 3 of *Persistent Poverty*, "Social and political dimensions of plantation society", (53-83), as well as in the case of Best, in a range of his unpublished papers, nevertheless, for both, as economists, the economic aspect was to remain central, if not altogether determinant.

25. Kamau Brathwaite (1930-2020) was professor of Comparative Literature at New York University and was co-founder of the journal *Savacou*, instituted in 1970. His essay, "Caribbean Man in Space and Time" (*Savacou* 11/12 [September 1975], 1-11) put forward the conception of the "inner plantation", as a more trans-economic approach to the model of the *plantation-as-institution*.

TO CHANGE THE ORDER OF THE WORLD:
DECOLONISING CULTURE, DECOLONISING THE SELF

DEMETRIUS L. EUDELL

'You see, Miss Mullings, what we've got to have here is a staff that can uplift – you know, people, with a high sense of personal conduct, people who've adjusted themselves to their station in life and who conform to standards. We can't afford to have any disobedience here. We've got to have standards, Miss Mullings, we've just got to.'

He paused, pulled his gown around him, and went on: 'That's why I'm starting the tea club. You see, after all the classes and tutorials, we must learn to sit down together and talk about a little culture.'

Fitzroy Fraser, *Wounds in the Flesh* (London: Hutchinson New Authors, 1962), 161.

From the mid-nineteenth century up to 1920 more than 450 million people in Africa and Asia came under direct colonial rule. Britain, France, Russia, the Netherlands, and Portugal – the old European colonial powers – were followed by the newly formed Germany and Italy, by Belgium, and in a somewhat hesitant manner, by the United States. Even Japan – itself a victim of imperialist expansion at the beginning of the epoque – joined the club of aggressors.

Odd Arne Westad, *The Global Cold War: Third World Interventions and the Making of Our Times* (Cambridge: Cambridge University Press, 2005), 73.

Decolonisation, *which sets out to change the world,* is, obviously a program of complete disorder. ...Decolonisation, as we know, is a historical process: that is to say that it cannot be understood, it cannot become intelligible nor clear to itself except in the exact measure that we can discern the movements which give it historical form and content. ...It brings a natural rhythm into existence *introduced by new men, and with it a new language and a new humanity. Decolonisation is the veritable creation of new men. But this creation owes nothing of its legitimacy to any supernatural process; the "thing" which has been colonised becomes man [human] during the same process by which it frees itself.*

Frantz Fanon, *The Wretched of the Earth,* trans. *Les damnés de la terre* by Constance Farrington (1961; New York: Grove Press, 1963), 36-37. Emphasis added.

In initiating his revolution, Caliban takes language and tools and concepts from Prospero whom he must fight. All too often, his writing is accorded, or not accorded, recognition by this very Prospero. All too often in having to write *for* Prospero's approval, he negates his own intention. The writer needs to write, as Lamming does in *The Pleasures of Exiles,* addressing himself to his own audience. That at the same time he addressed himself to Prospero, too, is not irrelevant. The relationship with Prospero has not come to an end with the physical departure of Prospero. As Lamming acutely realises, since colonisation had been a reciprocal process, decolonisation must equally be so. Since it is Prospero who created the myth and assigned the respective roles, the process of demythologisation must take place between himself and Caliban. Caliban, must in a dialogue, reinvent, redefine the *relation.* If Caliban is to become a man, Prospero must cease being a myth of superman.

Sylvia Wynter, "'We Must Learn to Sit Down and Talk About a Little Culture'" (1967) – in this collection page 106.

"Race" was therefore to be, in effect, the non-supernatural but no less extrahuman ground (in the reoccupied place of the traditional ancestors/ gods, God, ground) of the answer that the secularising West would now give to the Heideggerian question as to the who, and the what we are.

Sylvia Wynter, "Unsettling the Coloniality of Being/Power/Truth/Freedom," *New Centennial Review,* Vol. 3, No. 3 (Fall 2003): 264.

In the scene from Fitzroy Fraser's *Wounds in the Flesh* noted in the first epigraph, from which the title of the collection is taken, Baldwin Sinclair, the headmaster of Rushing Heights School, is speaking with his secretary a few weeks after having closed the teachers' staffroom, a measure he took in order to control "a kingdom within a kingdom, a hotbed for conspiracy and the planning of mutiny". Originally a rebel from the humble background of the "ex-plantation village of For-A-Fip", Sinclair worked his way to the top of the social hierarchy, and now has taken on the role of upholding the governing terms of the very order that he once challenged. For instance, under his direction, the male teachers at Rushing Heights would be required to wear jackets and ties – the precise rule against which he previously revolted as a young instructor. To exert further control, not only does he bar the teachers from their lounge, but Sinclair also moved his study to the first floor so that he can more effectively keep them under his surveillance. Two of these teachers, whites from England, he intentionally hired to demonstrate to the students, whom he felt were "living in a different time", that "to be white was no longer to be a god". Perhaps, however, Sinclair himself also needed to be convinced of the non-superiority of whites, since after more than ten years, it remained difficult for him to forget that an Englishman once called him a chimpanzee, a formative experience which led him to continue to question his own humanity.

> But now with whites teaching under him, this would make them realise that he wasn't really a monkey, or that, if he was, the whites under him were rather worse than monkeys, seeing that they were under a monkey. For deep down inside him, he didn't really know if he was a monkey or not.[1]

As a response to the conflict with the teachers, Sinclair proposed to start a tea club "to talk about a little culture". Yet, rather than a dialogue, his "talk" would be a didactic monologue designed primarily to instruct the teachers in their prescribed subordinate role. This use of culture as a tool to stratify the social order, before and after colonialism, serves as a central thematic to the essays collected here.

Two decades ago, in the first publication solely dedicated to a sustained engagement with Wynter's work, Norval Edwards noted that despite being quite well known, Wynter's scholarly work had "received scant attention over the years". In his essay, also based on the title of this collection, such was even more the case with the earlier writings, which he asserted offered unique "insight into the theoretical possibilities as well as the pitfalls of West Indian nativist criticism in the first decade of independence".[2] This present collection of Wynter's work, which also coincides with her teaching at the University of the West Indies, the University of California, San Diego, and Stanford University, therefore fills in an important gap and now makes accessible in a single publication, the distinctive corpus of the original thought of Sylvia Wynter in the "early period".[3] Indeed, as Edwards perceptively argued, although the more systematic conceptualisations would follow in her later work, Wynter's major intellectual preoccupations, "such as the advocacy of a poetics of disenchantment, the emergence of Western humanism in the context of colonial expansion and plantation slavery, and the power of cognitive models to structure social and historical processes, are first formulated in this period."[4]

The five essays on which Edwards concentrated his insightful analysis can be found here in *We Must Learn to Sit Down*, as well as a number of others that build upon Wynter's seminal interventions in anti-colonial, Caribbean, and Black thinking. In addition to themes enumerated by Edwards, another illuminating area of inquiry emerged directly out of her graduate work on Golden Age Spanish literature. This line of analysis entailed a reconceptualisation of the history of Blacks in the New World as a constituent element of the intellectual and political transformations ensuing from Renaissance humanism, as these changes informed the encounters of Europeans with the peoples of Africa in the mid-fifteenth century and Indigenous populations in the Americas after 1492. Before amplification in her now canonical essay "1492: A New World View" (also an undergraduate course at Stanford), this originality of perspective can be seen from the essays included here on Bernardo de Balbuena and Bartolomé de Las Casas. Offering a novel reading that reconfigured and resituated the beginnings of the "modern world" (that is, post-1440s), the examination of Balbuena circumvents a purely hegemonic British colonial narrative by demonstrating the longer period of Jamaican history that began with Spanish imperialism. As well, her original reading of the 1550-1551 disputation (*junta*) between Las Casas and

Ginés de Sepúlveda on the nature of the being of the Indigenous peoples in the Americas, laid the foundation for a new science of human systems, or in Wynter's contemporary terms, laws of auto-institution.

Wynter has often insisted, as reiterated in her Preface, that the global anti-colonial movements played an indispensable role in the development of her thinking. These uprisings had to be mounted against a world order, which as Westad noted, mandated that "more than 450 million people in Africa and Asia came under direct colonial rule". According to Fanon, in order to understand the process of decolonisation, one must analyse the movements "which give it historical form and content". Wynter references the labour revolts in Jamaica during the 1930s, and in the United States, the Civil Rights movement against Jim Crow segregation, as helping to give historical form and content to the global movement for decolonisation/desegregation, the latter being identified as a response to internal colonialism. Between these two pivotal moments, other significant challenges to European colonial governance could be enumerated, including, among others, the movements for independence in Ghana and Algeria, the war in French Indochina, and the Pan African conference in Manchester in 1945, itself the fifth in a series of historic gatherings initiated in 1900. Another important event to be considered in this regard is the conference convened in Bandung in April 1955, where leaders of twenty-nine Asian and African countries and territories met as newly independent nations to forge peace in the midst of the Cold War.

The Indonesian President Sukarno, one of the primary organisers, recognised that Bandung was not the first such gathering of colonised peoples. In February 1927, the "Congress against Colonial Oppression and Imperialism", which evolved into the "League Against Imperialism and for National Independence", met in Brussels. This earlier gathering, which Sukarno attended, was composed of more than 170 delegates from 37 countries, representing 134 organisations, and included among others, "pacifists, communists, socialists, and trade union officials". Initially, the activities of the League focused on addressing the situation in the colonies, but then it directed "its propaganda and activities toward the 'centre'".[5] However, Bandung, by meeting in an ex-colonial nation, departed from this previous assembly, a development of which Sukarno was quite proud: "We do not need to go to other continents to confer".[6] Yet, before moving away from the centre, it held great political significance to meet in Brussels, as the attendees wanted to register their vigorous objection to the horrors that were then occurring in the Belgian Congo (previously the Congo Free State), and in fact, had chosen the name League Against Imperialism precisely to signal a critique of the failures of the League of Nations to address the colonial question in places like the Congo.[7]

At Bandung, attention was paid to the various religions, socio-cultural worlds, and "racial stocks" as these reflected the different experiences under colonialism and imperialism.[8] Nonetheless, Sukarno forcefully argued that a "multiformity of religious life" should not impede forging solidarity, which would be necessary to challenge the "modern dress" of colonialism "in the form of economic control, intellectual control, [and] actual physical control".[9] The basis of this solidarity could be found, he contended, in a "unity in desire" which contained the potential to be translated into political "unity in diversity".[10] The Final Communiqué conveyed such a unifying attempt by calling for the promotion of economic and cultural cooperation, the support of human rights, as well as neutrality and peace in the form of nuclear disarmament.

Ali Sastroamidjojo, the conference chairman and Indonesian Prime Minister, stressed that urging peace at Bandung "was not the result of some wishful thinking", but rather sprang from "the agonising tensions from which the world is suffering". This imperative led him to challenge the characterisation of those demanding peace as "unrealistic day-dreamers" and instead question whether "those who foster the illusion that the stockpiling of atom and hydrogen bombs can bring about peace?" Indeed, from Sastroamidjojo's perspective those gathered at Bandung were attempting to assume responsibility inherited from their histories of colonialism, and thus these efforts were "born out of the fulness (sic) of time which has entrusted to the independent nations of Asia and Africa their new task in the destiny of mankind."[11]

This "new task" with which *les damnés* would be charged in the post-independence context represents a central preoccupation in Wynter's scholarship, both in these essays and in subsequent work.[12] In *Jamaica's National Heroes*, she remarked upon the "seeming paradox" of borrowing from the model of the former colonial powers: "The concept and the symbols translated into our historical experience, take on meanings and implications that are in sharp opposition to those used in the imperial context" (302. Page references are to this collection). Whilst acknowledging the valiant struggles fought against tremendous odds, she insisted nonetheless that despite the significant accomplishments, these triumphs have not been without consequences: "It is their achievement that now challenges us" (330). Indeed, this very challenge remains that after having set out "to change the order of the world", the ex-colonial nations were, in the end, fitted into the origin-mythic structure of the nation-state paradigm of the West, in which they now were represented and empirically made to experience themselves as being "underdeveloped". This new designation of the former colonies enabled the ex-colonial powers to reinscribe their hegemony in different, but related, terms of inferiority and lack, a process which according to C.L.R. James occurred because "[t]hose in power never give way and admit defeat only to plot and scheme to regain their lost power and privilege."[13]

Within this framework, the fundamental insufficiency was no longer represented as the inability of the Calibans to govern themselves *politically*, as had been a substantial part of the reasoning that legitimatised colonialism, but after independence, it would be represented as a lack of economic development, now ascribed to the unerring forces of the market. Wynter has insisted that this notion of "underdevelopment" is not a purely empirical phenom-enon, but rather constitutes a "culture-systemic *telos* that orients the collective ensemble of behaviours, by means of which our present single and western-ised world system is brought into being."[14] Otherwise stated, it was an idea that enabled the production of a specific organisation of the world, both materially (economically) and symbolically (intellectually). As such, the representation of formerly colonialised nations functioned as an indispensable element in the instituting of the postwar variant of the conception and praxis of being human as *homo œconomicus* (economic man).[15] Wynter apprehended this dynamic in her initial writings, and indeed argued in "We Must Learn to Sit Down" that it is precisely this conception of being human that the transplanted Black slave experience in the Americas necessarily challenged: "The Negro with his stubborn holding on to a tribal integrated philosophy and culture, through its fragments, rhythm, dance, song... would attempt to fulfil his being, his resistance to being reduced to producer/consumer", one "producing finally the atomic bomb which waits to consume him" (103).

Wynter's reference to the atomic bomb raises another important theme in her work that converges with an exhortation to the Third World (a term coined just before Bandung),[16] made by Sastroamidjojo. Acknowledging the techno-scien-tific innovations of the West, he urged the peoples of Africa and Asia "not to be overwhelmed by the revolutionary changes resulting from atomic technology", because "we cannot enter into this atomic age with the same spirit, political or social beliefs, and moral attitudes only befitting the period which is about to draw to a close". Thus, despite the innovations and transformations which resulted from Western technology, these were accompanied with tragic effects that must also now be confronted:

> When the age of technology made its entry a hundred years ago, changing by its profound impact the lives of people all over the world, first in the west, but gradually in Asia and Africa too, it brought us steam, electricity, mechanisation, factories and many other things beneficial to the progress of all. It brought mankind also new ways of thinking and consciousness of social justice, but in its wake followed conquest, imperialism, war and destruction.

Seizing upon a contradiction that Wynter would later extensively explore, he declared that: "It looks as if mankind is not morally prepared for the fruits of its own genius."[17]

In a similar vein, invoking Aimé Césaire's "Poetry and Knowledge", Wynter maintained that "as brilliant as the feats of the natural sciences are, they themselves are half starved – because they cannot deal with our human predicament".[18] Relatedly, she has also cited Einstein's poignant statement made shortly after the end of WWII, when he declared that unleashing the power of the atom bomb changed everything "save our mode of thinking", and without a fundamental transformation in our understanding of the world, we would continue to "drift toward unparalleled catastrophe".[19] Corresponding to Sastroamidjojo's demand for a "new spirit, new ideologies and new universal morality",[20] Wynter has called for "the descendants of Prospero-slave owner, and Caliban-slave" to use "the technological knowledge acquired by Prospero from an unjust relation, mount an assault against that historical necessity, that scarcity of food and shelter, which had, in the dark and terrible ages, impelled exploitation of some by others and still impels" (139).

This collection illustrates that Wynter's more recent insistence that "the West *did* change the world, *totally*" was already a thematic focal point in her early work.[21] In this regard, she follows in the genealogy of a Caribbean anti-colonial tradition that without ressentiment acknowledged the cultural influence of Europe, whilst also maintaining a pointed critique of its hegemony. The transformative thought of C. L. R. James was emblematic in this regard as he wrote that "Thackeray, not Marx, bears the heaviest responsibility for me." James contended that English writers like Thackeray and Dickens, together with the sport of cricket, nursed his political instincts and helped him to understand the Victorian class system.[22] George Lamming deepened this thematic in his critical engagement with Shakespeare's *The Tempest,* when he proposed that the relation between Caliban and Prospero had to be reconceptualised, a process that began first and foremost with the demythologisation of Prospero. Indeed, Lamming framed his exhortation that "Caliban orders history" with Aimé Césaire's declaration from *Return to My Native Land:* "You know that it is not out of hatred for other races that I am the toiler of this unique race".[23]

This tendency is also reflected in Wynter's research and analysis as noted above, in the *Siglo de oro* of Spanish literature and thought. In the essay on Bernardo de Balbuena's *El Bernardo,* Wynter offered an analysis of one of the first works written (though not entirely) in Jamaica. Balbuena was one of the earliest abbots to be assigned to Jamaica before he moved on to become Bishop of Puerto Rico a decade later. Wynter's close reading of his epic poem serves as a reminder of the world before the arrival of the British, and underscores the significance of Spanish colonisation in Jamaica, during which time Arawaks/ Tainos and Africans were enslaved as well as the cultivation of sugar cane was introduced.

Balbuena's *El Bernardo; o, Victoria de Roncesvalles, Poema Heroyco* (*The Bernardo*) followed two decades after publishing the now highly-regarded *Grandeza Mexicana* (*The Grandeur of Mexico,* 1604). Wynter situated her explication of *The Bernardo*, a 40,000-line poem divided into 24 books, within the tradition of Greek epic poetry as well as the national and imperial epic poems of sixteenth- and seventeenth-century Golden Age Spanish literature. Using a series of allegories, the poem tells the story of Bernardo del Carpio, a hero chosen by fairies to avenge the wars and outrages of Charlemagne's warriors (Paladins or Twelve Peers/

Knights), which he duly does at the battle of Roncesvalles. Wynter argued that in a poem with direct historical references, Balbuena's utilisation of allegory produced the Brechtian alienation effect which disrupts the viewer's identification with the characters in order to think critically about what happens both on stage and in life; this to "encourage the habit of refusing to accept that things-must-be-as-they-are" (212). Such was particularly relevant in the time of great change, the end of the *Siglo de oro*, when Balbuena was writing, as the revealed truths of Catholic Christianity were being increasingly challenged both theologically and politically by the competing Christian European imperial States.

Wynter's specific engagement with figures like Balbuena and Las Casas (and later with Columbus and Renaissance/lay humanist thinkers), raised the issue of how to account for the relations between Europe and the Americas. In response to critics who disavowed the "cultural debt" of Europe to the Caribbean, Wynter affirmed the earlier analyses of Black thinkers who emphasised the foundational role of slavery in producing the wealth of Europe,[24] a line of argument she then extended to the socio-cultural realm: "The West Indian experience was 'created' by Europe; and the West Indian experience helped to create Europe as it is today. Besides to *be* West Indian is to be syncretic by nature and circumstance, by choice"[25] (118). Within this frame, it was therefore not a question of denying the history of European colonialism, but rather to challenge its self-conception: "It is the *myth* of Europe which rejects; which rejects all other experience(s), African, Indian, Chinese, which contribute to the being of the West Indian." The implication thus remained that "to be West Indian is to accept all facets of one's being" (118. Original emphasis). Moreover, as noted in her essay on the journal of the plantation mistress Lady Nugent, such a recognition included acknowledging the relation to the slaveholders: "When we read *Lady Nugent's Journal* whom do we claim as our ancestors and whom do we reject? The planters who generally revolt her, the mulattoes who disturb her, or the 'blackies' for whom she feels that pity that is sister to contempt?" (50). According to Wynter, only by laying claim to all and rejecting none, and taking "hold of our history", could the formerly colonised "transform the unjust system we have inherited, which divided us and still divides us" (51). For this reason, she argued that texts like Nugent's journal should be required reading in schools as they "might persuade us to come to terms with our own ambivalence to the past" (50).

The suggestion of including *Lady Nugent's Journal* in secondary schools demonstrates the multiple registers at which Wynter's distinctive intellectual perspective could be applied. Remaining committed to a transgressive and transformative pedagogy as much as to scholarly writing, Wynter utilised different media and genres, including radio and theatre, to convey her imaginative and provocative formulations. For instance, her play *Maskarade,* originally commissioned in 1973 by the Jamaican Information Service for a television broadcast and published in 1979 in the anthology *West Indian Plays*

for Schools, stages the Jonkunnu festival in the Jamaican hills where, like the
Maroons, refuge had to be taken for rebellious actions. The play and subsequent article on the carnival tradition illustrated her characteristic treatment
of fusing European and African traditions in the context of colonialism and its
aftermath in what Yvonne Brewster defined as "a timely, entertaining, [and]
sometimes frightening call to cultural arms".[26] As well, Wynter's adaptation of
García Lorca's *The House of Bernarda Alba* included here, can be situated in this
framework, as it too presumed similarities between aspects of Spain's then
contemporary social world with that of the Caribbean. In addition to translating Francisco Cuevas's *Jamaica is the Eye of Bolivar,*[27] Wynter translated for radio
García Lorca's play *Yerma* into Jamaican Creole, which as she recounted in her
interview with David Scott, entailed both linguistic and cultural translation:
"The play deals with the tragedy of a barren infertile woman. Because it is
based so very much on the still traditional/rural metaphysics of southern
Spain, it just can't be meaningfully translated into the English of an industrial
society. So I translated its Spanish into the Jamaican Creole as a language that
has emerged out of a parallel agrarian/rural structure."[28] This distinctive
approach sought to de-universalise the European self-conception as the
embodiment of all Being and then from a decolonising framework, re-
universalise it by situating it within a wider history of being human.

The translation of García Lorca's works into a Caribbean context demonstrates Wynter's devotion to a more expansive interpretation of the idea of
culture, a redefinition that sought to account for the experiences of both the
colonised and the coloniser. Accordingly, she challenged representations and
analyses for which the European experience remained the unproblematised
referent subject. Such an understanding was evident in Kenneth Ramchand's
description of the dynamic worlds of the Black Caribbean as a "life without
fiction" where few "cultivated the art of reading imaginative literature, and
fewer attempted to write it".[29] Here, fiction and literature take on a specific
meaning, one that views them as being generated from the creative mind of the
individual artist.

This position was embroiled in heated debates concerning the purpose and
function of literature and its criticism. One line of analysis suggested that West
Indian literature would achieve canonical status, when politics could be
minimised and the focus was placed on "human values". Within this frame, it
was argued that English novelists held an advantage over their West Indian
counterparts because they inhabited "a dense world of critical discussion" in
which they were not "forced to engage in a prolonged and painful dialogue
with itself" (110). Wynter contested this presumed universality of the Western
experience as the referent as well as the "static concept of Art for Art's sake",
both of which she contended were premised on a "fetish object called
literature" (90). Consequently, in contrast to the assertion in the vein of
Matthew Arnold that "real criticism" resulted from curiosity and the "disin-

terested love of a free play of the mind on all subjects, for its own sake",[30] she proposed a critical aesthetics along the lines of Bertolt Brecht that literature and criticism should not avoid addressing urgent social issues: "I accept Brecht's thesis that in settled periods of history, culture – and literature which is its part, with criticism as its partner – can reflect reality"[31] (90). In fact, in her adaptation of García Lorca's plays, she invoked Brecht's inquiry into natural-ness where he argued that the illusion created by theatre is only partial, "in order that it may be recognised as an illusion", thereby enabling "reality... to be altered by being turned into art, so that it can be alterable and to be treated as such" (76). Indeed, Wynter understood Brecht's approach as embodying the idea that "the twentieth century revolution must be a cultural revolution, a transformation in the way men see and feel" (139).

This dispute concerning whether the writer should be considered, in Kamau Brathwaite's terms, "an artistic *individual*, rather than an angel or agent of his *society*",[32] emerged among the discussions that arose in the aftermath of the then recent establishment in 1948 of University College of the West Indies, originally an external campus of the University of London. This issue was related to others, including questions of migration/exile and repatriation, vernacular and colonial languages, as well as the politics of identity. These polemics were not completely new issues, as some had been previously broached across the Caribbean in the 1930s and 1940s in "little magazines" such as *The Beacon* (Trinidad), *BIM* (Barbados), *Kyk-Over-Al* (Guyana), *Focus* (Jamaica), and *Caribbean Quarterly* (UWI).[33] However, in the wake of political independence, the issue of defining Caribbean literature, aesthetic and criticism logically took on more urgency.

On the one hand, this matter can be related to the broader issue of the responsibility of the intellectual to their social context. It was a debate that built on Julien Benda's 1927 *The Treason of the Intellectuals* (also translated as *The Betrayal of the Intellectuals*). Utilising the framework of Enlightenment universalism, Benda contended that European intellectuals had abdicated their responsibility by prioritising the interests of the State and capitulating to "political passions" (antisemitism, anti-proletarianism, and authoritarianism).[34] In the period of Wynter's writing in this collection, in the United States, Noam Chomsky made a similar charge in his 1967 essay "The Responsibility of Intellectuals", in which he repudiated the claims of several public intellectuals (Arthur Schlesinger, Daniel Bell, Irving Kristol) and policy experts who sought to justify the imperialism and "butchery" in Vietnam.[35] The same year, Harold Cruse casti-gated Black intellectuals for not adequately addressing the situation confronting much of the Black population: "The Negro movement is at an impasse precisely because it lacks a real functional corps of intellectuals able to confront and deal perceptively with American realities on a level that social conditions demand."[36]

In the Caribbean, the terms of such disputes were tethered to a fierce contention about how to define West Indian slave and post-slavery societies. In a series of influential writings, M. G. Smith argued that the West Indies was composed of plural societies that did not derive their integration from a normative consensus of shared common values, but rather were social orders regulated by force and coercion. From Smith's perspective, Caribbean societies could not be understood within frameworks of acculturation (as suggested by Melville J. Herskovits) or of stratification, because internal conflicts existed within each segment of a plural society that inhibited consensual integration.[35] Smith was responding, in part, to arguments, such as those by Richard N. Adams, that asserted creole cultures (of family structure, religious activities, class/ethnic relations) emerged out of the plantation communities in the Americas that were organised on the basis of racial hierarchy and enslaved labour.[38]

In his now classic *The Development of Creole Society in Jamaica, 1770-1820*, Brathwaite adopted Adams's definition of creole societies as based on a "colonial arrangement" with an accompanying "significant and powerful plantation system" to describe the British colony.[39] Subsequently, however, he deepened this theoretical formulation with his notion of creolisation, as a process of ac/culturation (where one culture is absorbed by a more forceful one) and of inter/culturation (unplanned, unstructured and osmotic exchange), where reciprocal enriching reflected the contradictory and creative potential that ensued from the originally conflictual encounter.[40] Brathwaite's thinking converged with Wynter's at critical junctures, for instance, in his review of *The Islands in Between* (a critical survey of West Indian literature edited by a British academic, Louis James) when he called for Caribbean writers to construct "an *alternative* to their imposed and inherited condition." As well, both Brathwaite and Wynter detected the inability of this collection of essays to account for the presence of African social formations in the Caribbean, what Brathwaite termed the "King James view of West Indian culture".[41] Nonetheless in their understandings of the usefulness of "creole", a perennially elusive and contested concept,[42] as an explanation for the social relations and structures of Caribbean societies, a divergence occurred. As can be discerned from the essay "Creole Criticism", which examined the writings of Kenneth Ramchand, Wynter viewed creole as a posture that in a rhetoric of "fraudulent multiracialism" systematically evaded "the African centrality in the cultural dynamic of the Caribbean peoples" (366).[43] Indeed, in her reading of Nugent's Journal, she maintained that liberal discourses of racial harmony remained ineffective in addressing the structural hierarchies that have organised the Caribbean:

> A society, reluctant to examine its premises, evasive of its past, uncertain of its identity, afraid of its own promise, worshipping its white heritage, despising its black, or at best settling for the current view of being a multiracial, multicultural 'Out of Many People One' is in danger of creating the spiritual Inferno that Mrs. Nugent pictured so vividly, in a twentieth-century setting. (67)

In fact, Lady Nugent's account revealed what Elsa Goveia, who was also responding to M.G. Smith, characterised as the "superiority/inferiority rank-

ing" principle, an integrative *and* divisive mechanism that structured Caribbean societies.[44] Nugent recounted her life in Jamaica from 1801-1805, during
which time her husband Sir George Nugent was governor of the island colony.
In the background of her journal lay the seismic impact of the slave insurrection in St. Domingue, which before 1791 was "the largest, most dynamic, and
efficient sugar plantation society", that is, as seen from the perspective of
mainstream historiography and the slaveholders.[45] The Haitian Revolution
rendered it inescapably clear throughout the Americas that slaves could
achieve their own emancipation by self-initiated means of physical revolt.
This unsettling of the colonial order led, however, to the political and
economic isolation of Haiti by European powers, until Jean-Pierre Boyer's
administration agreed in 1825 to pay France 150 million francs in reparations.
The subsequent poverty and political instability with which Haiti would be
plagued cannot be separated from this original act of coercing its leaders to be
signatories to what Charles Mills has defined as "the racial contract".[46] The
insurrection in St. Domingue can thus also be seen as a central element in
giving "historical form and content" to decolonisation, if not of having
initiated the process itself. Indeed, even if enslaved Blacks were not imagined
to be political subjects in the 1776 anti-colonial/decolonial, white North
American settler rebellion against the British Parliamentary monarchy, or in
the 1789 overthrow of the *ancien régime* by the Third Estate and their allies, the
1791 insurrection formed a central part of what Eric Hobsbawm described as
"the age of revolution" belonging to the world of revolutions that included the
French, the Industrial, and the "white settler North American". As Du Bois
noted in his 1896 dissertation "The Suppression of the African Slave Trade",
it was the rebellion of enslaved Haitians that led Napoleon to sell Louisiana to
Jefferson for a song.[47]

Given that at the time of the Haitian revolution the majority of the slaves
had been born in Africa,[48] no presupposed shared understanding of natural
solidarity could be assumed among peoples who came from different social
worlds. However, forced enslavement could certainly provide a common
experience around which to bond. Even so, there would still be a need for
stories, rituals, and customs to consolidate social solidarity, practices that
would have to challenge the dominant political and religious discourses within
which such co-identification would not be normally legitimated. Such a focus
on stories, rituals and customs was at the heart of Wynter's earlier writing. It
was on the basis of an alternative worldview, (in Wynter's more recent terms,
counter-cosmogony), one not positioned completely in opposition to the
hegemonic intellectual forms, but rather one that synthesised the forms of life,
first from different African peoples together with the dominant cosmogonies
(especially the religious imaginings of Catholicism), that the slaves of Haiti
created a completely new belief system – Vodoun. And, whilst debate has raged
as to the precise role played by Vodoun during the revolution, it has been

established that an important ceremony did occur just before the August 1791 outbreak and shortly after a larger gathering on the Lenormand de Mézy plantation had taken place.[49] Published in 1814, Antoine Dalmas's *Histoire de la révolution de Saint-Domingue* was the first to relate the secret Vodoun ceremony, presided over by the driver/coachman Boukman, where an animal was sacrificed, and during which he proclaimed that the god of the Black slaves would aid them in defeating the god of Whites.[50]

The Haitian Revolution demonstrated the presence of modes of being and behaving that were based on original African forms of life, as these were transformed in the Americas through interactions with the dominant Judaeo-Christian and European system of value and meaning. It is in this context that Wynter's distinctive examination of the ritual dances of Jonkunnu in Jamaica can be situated. Originally written in a non-academic context for a UNESCO conference on folklore, her analytical model distinguished itself from the approaches, however insightful, of both the plantocratic ethnography of Nugent and the disciplinary norms of academic anthropology, which at the time had not then fully engaged with what Michel-Rolph Trouillot later defined as the "savage slot".[51] And, although substantially influenced by historical materialist analyses, such as those of Lloyd Best and George Beckford (as noted in the preface), Wynter emphasised an examination of what Lady Nugent identified, as the "customs of the most despised part (67)". Indeed, Wynter insisted that the alternative social worlds that the enslaved helped to establish was not on the basis of *imitating* the slaveholders, but rather, as part of *creating* the basis for a completely new identity, and thus by implication, a totally new kind of society.[52]

In this regard, her elucidation of the poetics and the politics of the folkdance of Jonkunnu anticipate her subsequent elaboration of culture as that which creates humans and which humans create.[53] Wynter examined Jonkunnu "as *agent* and *product* of a cultural process" which she identified as indigenisation (238). An understanding of the African-based Black presence in Jamaica within a frame of indigenisation intervened in an original manner in the classic discussion of whether the enslaved retained or lost their "culture" once they came to the Americas. In "Creole Criticism", Wynter took Ramchand to task for his dismissal of W. G. Ogilvie's *Cactus Village* as "not of literary significance in itself" but demonstrating "how elusive African cultural survivals" are as well as "how little scope there is for the West Indian novelist who wishes to evoke Africa in these terms" (383). This debate had been forged with regard to the enslaved in the United States between E. Franklin Frazier and Melvin J. Herskovits. Often identified as having completely rejected the retention by the enslaved of forms of life from Africa, Frazier did recognise that elsewhere in the Americas, such as in Bahia, Brazil, "these Negroes were able to establish to some extent in the New World their traditional social organisation and religious practices".[54]

However, rather than emphasising ideas such as loss, acculturation and assimilation, Wynter identified the originally creative social practices, al-though she acknowledged that what Herskovits and later Brathwaite defined as acculturation "where two peoples of different cultures find culture contact points at which fusion and transformation of the one by the other is achieved" might indeed be possible (245, 275). Wynter's view, though, was to draw a distinction between the later stages of contact, where acculturation was possible, and the early phases, such as demonstrated in the history of the Maroons in Jamaica which are best seen as "largely the response of one culture to new conditions" (245). Denoting a process of indigenisation, or as she suggested in "One Love," a "neo-autochthonous blackness" (338) contains also the insight that distinguishes the changes under which the enslaved acted from those of the Indigenous peoples in the Americas, who had already established multiple worlds before the forced transformations imposed by Western European settler colonialism.

Within Wynter's conceptualisation, an intellectual path "back to Africa" can be formulated, although not from within a lens of "great civilisations" on which some Afrocentric formulations are based, but rather through the transformations created by the enslaved who re-rooted themselves in a strange new land. At the same time, as she argued in the conference talk, "Novel and History, Plot and Plantation", such traditions, despite being "a cultural guerrilla against the plantation" should not be romanticised with "a heroic folkish mythology of a Hitler". Instead, the "plot" of those marginalised can be usefully employed "as a point outside the system where the traditional values can give us a focus of criticism against the impossible reality in which we are enmeshed" (296). Indeed, given that the alternative popular forms were produced under such brutal conditions, it becomes difficult to argue in nostalgic terms for a return: "But there is no question of going back to a society, a folk pattern, whose structure has already been undermined by the pervasive market economy" (296).

Along these lines, as previously noted, Wynter joined other Black thinkers who called for a reconceptualisation of the institution of racialised slavery in the Americas, an approach which would provide the basis for a new genealogy of labour: "It is not often appreciated that West Indian man, qua African slave, and to a lesser extent, white indentured labourer, was the first labour force that emergent capitalism had totally at its disposal" (90). This reinterpretation of the history of capitalism preceded and converged with Cedric Robinson's more comprehensive elaboration of the idea of racial capitalism.[55] As Wynter noted in "One Love", the establishment of "the plantation unit became, in embryo, the modern total company town" (337). As C.L.R. James had argued, the enslaved in Haiti were close to the modern proletariat and that Blacks in the U.S. South were "semi-proletarians" or an "agricultural proletariat".[56] Wynter emphasised the ways in which aspects of sugar production, including "the vast numbers of slaves 'mechanised' in long rows to dig cane holes", as well as "the factory for the boiling of sugar after the grinding of cane", reflected "the nearest thing to a modern industrial setup that existed at that time" (337). Furthermore, she asserted that the psychic effects of the world created by the plantation system became another example of how the particularity of the enslaved experience could be generalised to understand that of the modern world: "We anticipated by a century the dispossession that would begin in Europe with the Industrial Revolution. We anticipated, by centuries, that exile, which in our century is now common to all" (90).

At the same time, Wynter always clearly delineated the structuring role of race, and not as epiphenomenal. In her examination of "the conflict between orthodox Marxism and different varieties of cultural nationalism", she argued that movements such as Garveyism, Rastafarianism, and U.S. Black Muslims implicitly challenged the "quantitative model of exploiting" often asserted within Marxism as the primary basis for social change. Drawing a parallel with the Gnostic heresies that helped to "structure the spiritual and imaginative revolutions" that hastened the end of the symbolic order of Classical Antiquity, these "popular cultural signifying systems" also "transformed the psychic structures of large masses of people"; and did so, on the basis of a "counter-signification of the self/formal system in which elements of the opposed self/formal system enter, but as elements that are now delegitimated" (468). What Wynter therefore identified in the post-slavery context as the "politics of Black culture" can therefore be seen as the foundation of her hypothesis of a new science of being human as praxis.

Such was because the "gaze from below"[57] and millenarian origin narrative of the Rastafari, formulated as "we know where we are from", fostered an understanding of a completely different destiny from that which was normally preordained from within "the cosmos of our contemporary technologically globalized order" (477). Since knowledge and praxis always function symbiotically, a new ensemble of behaviours was prescribed, that in the case of the Rastafari included abstaining from meat and alcohol. These new behavioural norms, as Wynter contended, moved beyond a simple inversion of terms, but rather, as the style of long uncombed locks illustrated, constituted a change of signs and the displacement of a semantic field (470). Moreover, this dynamic forcefully exemplified the way in which a new sense of self is always created in aesthetic terms. It is therefore precisely in such a context that the role of the anti-colonial writer/artist becomes that of effecting a parallel *disenchantment* of the dominant system of representation or what Wynter termed "mode of subjective understanding".[58] "Talking about a little culture" would therefore imply providing a new way of understanding what it means to be human, a reconceptualisation of the social Imaginary and "counter-signification of the self" already evident in the "gaze from below" (16).

> The revindication of blackness, which is in a sense the revindication of the *native*, the revindication of the humanness of Man, has taken place in

the Caribbean each time that vast movements of social upheaval have put
the articulate section of the population in touch with this "frontier zone";
however intuitively, however sketchily; however inadequately. Voodooism,
the Haitian Revolution, the Messianic Movements of the religious prophets,
Garvey's secular Messianic movement, Afro-Cubanism, Afro-Antillanism,
Negritude, Jamaican Rastafarianism, and now the Black Power Movement
in the United States and in the Caribbean, all well up from an Antaeus-
like relation with the springs of "native" and "black" feeling that are fed by
an underground cultural dynamic; a dynamic which had remained in opposition
to the colonial and neo-colonial superstructure of the society; has remained
as an alternative way of apprehending reality. (335)

As distinct, on the one hand, from the temptation of "Afro-Jamaicanism/
literary blackism", which separates "the revindication of the black mystique
from its political and economic base" (344) and, on the other, from the
"complex mimicry" of "Creole Criticism", which in the name of impersonality and objectivity, aims "to negate, destroy, diminish, disguise the African
centrality in the cultural dynamic of the Caribbean peoples" (366), Wynter
offered a different interpretation of "culture". In her formulation, the belief
system of race and its related "coloniality of being" became exemplary in
elucidating an understanding of being human in the Caribbean, but as well
beyond (a term, it has been noted, she has been apt to employ)[59] this context.
Otherwise stated, her analysis moves from the revindication of blackness and
the native, to that of the human, or in her contemporary terms, of being human
as praxis.

Precisely in this vein, the collection closes with Wynter's analysis of the
implications of the "daring conceptual leap" that the converted *encomendero* and
Dominican friar Bartolomé de las Casas made in his 1550 dispute with the
natural law, humanist, royal historian, Ginés de Sepúlveda. In refuting
Sepúlveda's neo-Aristotelian formulation that the behaviours of the Indigenous peoples (in the Judaeo-Christian genre-specific terms, "human sacrifice") reflected the natural and predetermined difference which existed between them and Europeans, Las Casas insisted that such practices constituted
not a lack of reason, but rather a specific mode of rationality, one in which what
appeared as vices to the Spaniards were considered by Indigenous peoples to
be virtues. Wynter noted that although thinking within an evangelical Christian perspective, one which continued to assume that the Indigenous peoples
mistook "their false Gods to be the true God", Las Casas nonetheless anticipated by four centuries, and in the "frame of an ongoing Copernican and
decentring revolution", the realisation of "the relativity of all human systems
of perception including our own". In other words, he could apprehend "the
reality, not of a single absolute reason, but of culturally determined modes of
reason, as the reality of the cultural-historical relativity of our own" (555).

Las Casas lost the debate with Sepúlveda, Wynter pointed out, "because he
was at once behind his time and ahead of his time." Nonetheless, his

conceptual leap, as a counter to the colonial language of expropriation, of *terra nullius* (land of no one) stipulated in papal bulls such as *Romanus Pontifex* (1454) and *Inter Caetera* (1493),[60] challenged "the system that still provides the epistemic laws for our contemporary human system in its global dimensions." In so doing, "he opened the way toward a genuine science of human systems", one that paralleled the breakthrough in understanding the natural systems, which had been effected by Copernicus, Galileo and Newton. Indeed, as she argued, "Newton's new way of seeing or *theoria*... enabled prediction and conscious control of natural forces" and thereby ushered in a new era of human history. In a corresponding manner from a paradoxical position, she asserted that Las Casas, based on an "*a priori* conviction of a universal and potentially realisable system of human co-identification" would also make "thinkable the possibility of a universally applicable law of human identification, in whose context the 'errors' of specific forms of reason and of behaviours are *lawlike* and *rule-governed*" (578, original emphasis).

The new terrain would therefore be, as Wynter has argued, a universally applicable law of human auto-institution, one that would be based on what Aimé Césaire has identified as a science of the word. From the epistemological ground of Black Studies together with thinking that arose out of the anti-colonial movements, Wynter has called for the re-enactment of "Renaissance humanism's original heresy" in order to address what she has formulated as "*aporia* of the secular", that is, "the price originally paid for the West's post-medieval *transformative mutation* effected by the discourse of Humanism in both its original Renaissance Civic-humanist and later (neo) Liberal-humanist configurations".[61] These epochal transformations had dialectical consequences, thereby giving rise to an aporia of a "humanly emancipatory process on the one hand, and humanly subjugating processes on the other" with each being "the lawlike condition of the enacting of the other".[62] The paradox therefore remain that "as Christians, Westerners could see other peoples as also having gods", even if false ones, but within the *monohumanist* charting cosomony (this in the reoccupied place of a purely *monotheistic* one), it became impossible to concep-tualise "an Other to what they call human".[63]

To re-enact this heresy of a *New Studia*, Wynter has proposed there must be an "*ecumenically human* response to the question of who-we-are" as humans, one in which we accept our roles in the production and reproduction of our social orders.[64] Such an impetus would necessarily entail the "de-extrahumanisation of all the entities and/or Agent conceptions onto which we have hitherto projected our own empirical agencies".[65] In other words, human groups have ascribed our role allocations and systemic hierarchies to forces outside of the social order, be they multiple gods in polytheistic societies, a single God in the Abrahamic monotheisms, and then in the wake of secularisation, natural law during the Renaissance, and in the nineteenth century, the bioevolutionary laws of natural selection. Within the logic of the latter, as the final epigraph notes, while no longer supernaturally guaranteed (although religion continues to play an indispensable role), the phenomenon of race has to come to replace the extrahuman ground as the principle to account for the social order and therefore to explain "who we are" as human. This new value of differentiation, in the break from the theocentric ordering of feudal Christian Europe to the new "master code" of *Man* (first in terms of natural law, then of evolution) as it expanded globally, beginning in the fifteenth century, was ascribed to "environmentally, climatically determined phenotypical differences between human hereditary variations". Du Bois termed this the "Color Line", which in effect constituted a new and secular "space of Otherness" onto which the agency responsible for the order has been projected. The creation and recreation of human societies and their correlated stabilisation call for the "inducing of the subjects of these orders to experience their own placement in the structuring hierarchies of the order,… as having been extrahumanly designed and/or determined, rather than veridically or systemically produced by our collective human agency".[66]

Before her more recent elaborations, Wynter had already redefined culture in this early writing as being "the societal machinery with which a particular society or group symbolically codes its co-identifying sense of self, with reference to which, it then acts both individually and collectively upon the world" (457). More recently, to develop this new understanding, she has borrowed a concept from analyses of the allocation of gender roles, doing so, in order to avoid the presumption of naturalness that is often embedded in the definition of culture, even when some human agency is acknowledged. Since the term culture, as Richard Waswo has noted, derives from agriculture, meaning to dwell on and to till the soil (hence, the sense of culture as being "cultivated"),[67] Wynter has replaced this concept with that of the mode of "auto-institution", in which we as humans come to know and experience ourselves in the terms of "genre-specific cosmogonies". Deriving from the same etymological root as gender, meaning kind, Wynter utilised genres of being human "to denote the fictively constructed and performatively enacted different kinds of being human, of which gender coherence is itself always and everywhere a function". Such would therefore mean that our systems of hierarchy and domination do not exist separately from our origin narratives/myths, since they "'tell the world' and ourselves 'who we are'." Thus, despite the globalisation and hegemony of the Western bourgeoisie's secular, monohumanist conception of being human as optimally as *homo œconomicus,* it is "no less cosmogonically chartered and encoded and, thereby, fictively constructed and performatively enacted *genre of being hybridly human*". This concept of hybridity can be seen as related to Jonathan Miller's explanation of the dialectical nature of human consciousness: "Although consciousness exists by virtue of some physical property of the brain… it is *not,* …an observable property of living matter."[68]

In other words, it is within the biological absolutism of this genre-specific cosmogony, "that the peoples of African and Afro-mixed descent have been lawlikely, fictively constructed as the 'Negro'/'Colored' 'Black'/'Nigger' embodiment of the ultimate *Human Otherness to Man (2)*", a conception that Wynter insisted is systemically produced by not only those who can embody the optimal Self, but as well, following Fanon's insights on self-aversion, by those instituted as Others.[69] In such a new frame, the self-alienation described by Frantz Fanon in *Black Skin, White Masks* can now be understood as being a constituent element of the "cosmogonically, mythically chartered, and thereby sociogenically encoded auto-institution" of "secular Western Man(2)'s *genre*-specific mode of sociogeny" in which Blacks were induced "to *be human* by preconceptually experiencing and performatively enacting themselves in the mimetic terms of 'White masks".[70] Thus, rather than comprehending this process in terms of a liberal humanist idea of self-hatred, Wynter has offered an ecumenically human hypothesis in which the reflex-aversively subjective experience of the *Being* of *being Black* can be identified as a "universally applicable phenomenon" in which "all human *Skins* can only *become human* by also performatively enacting them/ourselves *as human* in the always-already, cosmogonically chartered terms of their/our symbolically encoded and fictively constructed *genre*-specific Masks."[71]

Redescribing the origins and essence of being human, Wynter has asserted that unlike the Primate family to which humans partly belong, only humans remain "able to transcend the narrow, genetically determined limits of eusocial, inter-altruistic, kin-recognising behaviours" which enable the realisation of "higher levels of cooperation and organisation". In a formulation that reconceptualises the idea of culture, she has further contended that this process resulted from "the mutational co-evolution with the brain of the emergent properties of language and narrative/story-telling" which enables humans "*autopoetically to institute ourselves as symbolically made-kin* though the medium of retroactively projected origin stories or cosmogonies". In other words, humans are therefore reborn (initiated) in the terms of a genre-specific Word. Our present hegemonic Word is that of *homo œconomicus,* which emerged in in the wake of the political and intellectual movements of the late eighteenth century, and which effected a species-level transformation. However, as Sastroamidjojo asserted at Bandung and as elaborated here in this distinctive collection of writings, such a transformation has not been without major consequences for the majority of non-European peoples. Indeed, as the population group that historically has been imagined and represented as existing outside of the human species (or most negated when included as a part of it), Wynter has, from a Black Studies perspective, asserted a meta-Darwinian (i.e. meta-biocentric) and meta-Fanonian hypothesis, that this dynamic is not arbitrary but remains a function of the hybridly auto-instituting process (as a third level of existence) by means of which we as humans come to institute ourselves as species modes of the subject. As humans can only speciate and reproduce our forms of life and collective living systems through narratives, she has proposed a new conception of being human, that is, as *homo narrans*,[72] in which we begin to attempt to reconceive and recreate an ecumenically human order based on the knowledge of the story-telling precondition of our humanness.

Endnotes

1. Fraser, *Wounds in the Flesh,* 19, 158-160.
2. Norval Edwards, "'Talking About a Little Culture': Sylvia Wynter's Early Essays" in *Journal of West Indian Literature,* Special Issue: *Sylvia Wynter: A Transculturalist Rethinking Modernity,* Demetrius Eudell and Carolyn Allen, eds., vol. 10, nos. 1 and 2 (November 2001): at 12, 14.
3. Following upon the present anthology, a collection of her subsequent essays is forthcoming from Wesleyan University Press and is provisionally entitled "'That the Future May Finally Commence': Essays for Our Ecumenically Human's Sake, 1984-2015."
4. Edwards, "Talking About a Little Culture", 14.
5. Fredrik Petersson, "'We are Neither Visionaries Nor Utopian Dreamers': Willi Münzenberg, the League against Imperialism, and the Comintern, 1925-1933" (PhD dissertation, Åbo Akademi University, 2013), 136, 145. See also Vijay Prashad, *The Darker Nations: A People's History of the Third World* (New York: New Press, 2007), 16-30. Sources vary on the exact number of delegates who attended. See Michele L. Louro, *Comrades Against Imperialism: Nehru, India, and Interwar Internationalism* (Cambridge: Cambridge University Press, 2018), 34.
6. Sukarno, "Let a New Asia and a New Africa Be Born!" *Asia-Africa Speaks from Bandung* ([Jakarta]: Ministry of Foreign Affairs, [1955]), 20.
7. Prashad, *The Darker Nations,*19-21.
8. Sukarno, "Let a New Asia and a New Africa be Born!", 22. Richard Wright attended the conference under the sponsorship of the anti-Communist organisation the Congress of Cultural Freedom and, too, was struck by this diversity as something new and naïve: "It was the kind of meeting that no anthropologist, no sociologist, no political scientist would ever have dreamed of staging; it was too simple, too elementary, cutting through the outer layers of disparate social and political and cultural facts down to the bare brute residues of human existence: races and religions and continents." See Richard Wright, *The Color Curtain* in *Black Power: Three Books from Exile* (1956; New York: Harper Perennial Modern Classics, 2008), 439. On the Congress of Cultural Freedom, see Andrea Scionti, "'I Am Afraid Americans Cannot Understand': The Congress of Cultural Freedom in France and Italy, 1950-1957", *Journal of Cold War Studies,* vol. 22, no. 1 (Winter 2020): 89-124. Scionti notes that the group was funded by the CIA.
9. Sukarno, "Let a New Asia and a New Africa be Born!", 23. This "modern dress" of colonialism would subsequently be defined as "neocolonialism", which Jean-Paul Sartre had identified in the post independent relations between France and Algeria and Kwame Nkrumah in Ghana. See Sartre, *Colonialism*

and Neocolonialism, trans. by Azzedine Haddor, Steve Brewer and Terry McWilliams (1964; London: Routledge, 2001), and Nkrumah, *Neo-Colonialism, The Last Stage of Imperialism* (New York: International Publishers, 1965). In Jamaica, this development was evident in several domains, for instance in the development of bauxite production, where shortly before independence, transnational corporations were given control that carried over after independence. See George L. Beckford, "The Social Economy of Bauxite in the Jamaican Man-Space", *Social and Economic Studies,* vol. 36, no. 1 (March 1987): 1-55, esp. 13-17.

10. Sukarno, "Let a New Asia and a New Africa Be Born!", 26-27.

11. "Address by Ali Sastroamidjojo, President of the conference" in *Asia-Africa Speaks from Bandung,* 33-34.

12. As examples in later works see, "No Humans Involved: An Open Letter to My Colleagues" in *Forum N.H.I.: Knowledge for the 21st Century,* vol. 1, no. 1 (Fall 1994): 42-73 and "On How We Mistook the Map for the Territory, and Re-Imprisoned Ourselves in Our Unbearable Whiteness of Being, of *Désêtre:* Black Studies Toward the Human Project" in *Not Only the Master's Tools: African-American Studies in Theory and Practice,* Lewis R. Gordon and Jane Anna Gordon, eds. (Boulder: Paradigm Publishers, 2006), 107-169.

13. C.L.R. James, *The Black Jacobins: Toussaint L'Ouverture and the San Domingo Revolution,* 2nd ed. rev. (1938; New York: Vintage Books, 1989), 127-128.

14. Wynter, "Is 'Development' a Purely Empirical Concept or also Teleological?: A Perspective from 'We the Underdeveloped'" in *Prospects for Recovery and Sustainable Development in Africa,* Aguibou Y. Yansané ed. (Westport, CT: Greenwood Press, 1996), 299-316, qt. at 299-300.

15. The term *homo œconomicus,* "economic man", emerged in response to the work on political economy of John Stuart Mill, although it has been attributed to Mill and before him to Adam Smith. On the former, see Joseph Persky, "The Ethnology of *Homo Economicus*", *The Journal of Economic Perspectives,* vol. 9, no. 2 (Spring 1995): 222; on the latter, see Mary S. Morgan, "Economic Man and Model Man: Ideal Types, Idealisations and Caricatures", *Journal of the History of Economic Thought,* vol. 28, no. 1 (2006): 3-4. The usage here does invoke Smith's claim regarding the "propensity in human nature ...to truck, barter and exchange," in effect, the philosophical thesis that underlies our present global order, which is based on the idea that the primary motivation of humans can be ascribed to economic self-interest and profit maximisation. See Adam Smith, *An Inquiry into the Nature and Causes of the Wealth of Nations,* R. H. Campbell and A. S. Skinners, eds. (1776; London: Oxford University Press, 1976), 25.

16. Albert Sauvy, "Trois mondes, une planète", *L'Observateur,* no. 118 (August 14, 1952): 14. Sauvy modelled the concept on the Third Estate (*Tiers état*) of the *ancien régime* of pre-revolutionary France, noting that the "ignored, exploited, despised" Third World like its antecedent also wanted to become something (*veut,..., être quelque choses*), which originally referred to a non-aligned position between the Communist Bloc and the Western capitalist nations. See also Prashad, *The Darker Nations,* 6-7.

17. "Address by Ali Sastroamidjojo, President of the conference" in *Asia-Africa Speaks from Bandung,* 37-38.

18. Sylvia Wynter and Katherine McKittrick, "Unparalleled Catastrophe for Our Species? Or, to Give Humanness a Different Future: Conversations" in *Sylvia Wynter: On Being Human as Praxis,* Katherine McKittrick, ed. (Durham, NC: Duke University Press, 2015), 17.

19. This statement was made in a telegram on May 24, 1946 and cited in the *New York Times,* "Atomic Education Urged by Einstein" (May 25, 1946): 13. See Wynter and McKittrick, "Unparalleled Catastrophe for Our Species?", 18 and Wynter, "An Intellectual Argument: Against the Reduction of the Present Program in African and Afro-American Studies to Being a Unit of the Proposed Mainstream Interdisciplinary Program in Comparative Studies in Race and Ethnicity", (unpublished manuscript, May 31, 1995), 43.

20. "Address by Ali Sastroamidjojo, President of the conference" in *Asia-Africa Speaks from Bandung,* 38.

21. Wynter and McKittrick, "Unparalleled Catastrophe for Our Species?", 18. Emphasis in original.

22. C.L.R. James, *Beyond a Boundary* (1963; Durham: Duke University Press, 1993), 39, 52.

23. George Lamming, "Caliban Orders History" in *The Pleasures of Exile* (1960; London, Allison and Busby, 1984), 118-150.

24. In addition to the central argument of Eric Williams in *Capitalism and Slavery* (1944; London: Andre Deutsch, 1964), W. E. B. Du Bois noted that slavery "became the foundation stone not only of the Southern social structure, but of Northern manufacture and commerce, of the English factory system, of European commerce, of buying and selling on a world-wide scale". See *Black Reconstruction: An Essay toward a History of the Part Which Black Folk Played in the Attempt to Reconstruct Democracy in America, 1860-1880* (New York: Harcourt, Brace, 1935), 5. Frantz Fanon argued that the stolen wealth which smothers Europe "is literally the creation of the Third World". See *The Wretched of the Earth,* trans. *Les damnés de la terre* by Constance Farrington (1961; New York: Grove Press, 1963), 102.

25. In his review of *Islands in Between,* Kamau Brathwaite also made this point: "No one is claiming that European culture 'has a nationalist identity in opposition to that of the Caribbean'. What one is asking is that the mind be left open for the discussion of the possibility that the Caribbean, in spite of the operation upon it of 'The European system' in spite of – indeed, *because of* – 'the peculiar circumstances' of its history, contains within itself a 'culture' different from, though not exclusive of Europe". See "Caribbean Critics" (1969) in *Roots* (Ann Arbor: University of Michigan Press, 1993), 114. Emphasis in original.

26. Yvonne Brewster, ed. *Mixed Company: Three Early Jamaican Plays* (London: Oberon Books, 2012), 13.

27. Francisco Cuevas [Cancino], *Jamaica is the Eye of Bolivar: A Play in Two Acts* (New York: Vantage Press, 1979).

28. David Scott, "The Re-Enchantment of Humanism: An Interview with Sylvia Wynter", *Small Axe,* Issue 8 (September 2000): 119-207, qt. at 133.

29. Kenneth Ramchand, *The West Indian Novel and its Background* (London: Faber and Faber, 1970), 31. Wynter subjects Ramchand's idea of a fictionless background

to the African cultural presence in the Caribbean to rigorous critique in the essay "Creole Criticism" (365-397).

30. Matthew Arnold, "The Function of Criticism at the Present Time (1864)" in *Culture and Anarchy and Other Writings,* Stefan Collini, ed. (Cambridge: Cambridge University Press, 1993), 35.

31. In his essay "Theatre for Pleasure or Theatre for Instruction", Bertolt Brecht describes the role of knowledge and making moral arguments in his epic theatre (subsequently termed dialectical theatre). See John Willet, ed., *Brecht on Theatre: The Development of an Aesthetic* (New York: Hill and Wang, 1964), 69-77.

32. Brathwaite, "Caribbean Critics", 116. Emphasis in original. According to Brathwaite, Caribbean literature, unlike most U.S. and European literature has not "been concerned to show how different they (or their personae) are from their 'corrupt' surrounding societies. They have been exploring the communal nature of their environment, attempting, in doing so, to liberate the consciousness of the submerged 'folk'." Ibid., 117.

33. Norval Edwards, "The Foundational Generation: From *The Beacon* to *Savacou*" in *The Routledge Companion to Anglophone Caribbean Literature,* Michael A. Bucknor and Alison Donnell, eds. (New York: Routledge, 2011), 111-123.

34. Julien Benda, *The Treason of the Intellectuals,* trans. *La Trahison des clercs* by Richard Aldington (1928; W. W. Norton, 1969), 23, 45-47.

35. Noam Chomsky, "A Special Supplement: The Responsibility of Intellectuals", *New York Review of Books* (February 23, 1967).

36. Harold Cruse, "Role of the Negro Intellectual: Survey of a Dialogue Deferred", in *The Crisis of the Negro Intellectual* (New York: Morrow, 1967), 452.

37. See the collection of articles on West Indian culture, Caribbean Studies, and ethnic and cultural pluralism in M.G. Smith, *The Plural Society in the British West Indies* (Berkeley: University of California Press, 1965).

38. Richard N. Adams, "On the Relation Between Plantation and 'Creole Culture'" in *Plantation Systems of the New World* (Washington, DC: Pan American Union, 1959), 73-79.

39. Ibid., 74. Edward [Kamau] Brathwaite, *The Development of Creole Society in Jamaica, 1770-1820* (New York: Oxford University Press, 1971).

40. Edward [Kamau] Brathwaite, *Contradictory Omens: Cultural Diversity and Integration in the Caribbean* (1974: Mona, Jamaica: Savacou Publications, 1985), 6.

41. Brathwaite, "Caribbean Critics", *New World Quarterly,* vol. 5, nos. 1-2 (1969): 5-12, qts. At 10-11. Emphasis in original.

42. See Carolyn Allen, "Creole Then and Now: The Problem of Definition", *Caribbean Quarterly,* vol. 44, nos. 1/2: *Konversations in Kreole: The Creole Society Model Revisited: Essays in Honour of Kamau Brathwaite* (March-June 1998): 33-49.

43. This dynamic can also be seen, as O. Nigel Bolland pointed out, in the populist conceptions of national unity in Jamaica with "Out of Many, One People" and in Trinidad with "All o' we is One". Indeed, not only race as Bolland noted, the question of class hierarchy could also easily be elided in some creole formulations, which implied a process of cultural homogenisation. See Creolisation and Creole Societies: A Cultural Nationalist View of Caribbean History", in *Caribbean Quarterly, Konversations in Kreole,* 26. It should be noted

that Ramchand was writing from the political context of Trinidad defined by a conflictual Indo-African politics and Wynter from that of Jamaica, which also partially accounts for their varying interpretations of creole.

44. Elsa Goveia, "The Social Framework", *Savacou* (September 1970), 14. Goveia noted: "...the belief that the blacker you are the more inferior you are and the whiter you are the more superior you are, has not, by any means died out in the West Indies. It is still there in the West Indies, and it is one of the elements that still integrates the West Indian society, though it is obviously to the great disadvantage of the West Indian majority. This *divisive kind of integration* is shared by all groups in the West Indies in spite of the fact that they belong to different cultural sections of the community." Ibid., 10. Emphasis added.

45. Herbert S. Klein, *The Atlantic Slave Trade,* 2nd ed. (Cambridge: Cambridge University Press, 2010), 40.

46. Charles W. Mills, *The Racial Contract* (Ithaca, NY: Cornell University Press, 1997). Wynter has insisted that the "racial contract" is necessarily an "epistemic contract". See "Rethinking Aesthetics: Notes Toward a Deciphering Practice" in *Ex-iles: Cinema in Caribbean Society and Culture,* Mbye Cham, ed. (Trenton, NJ: Africa World Press, 1991). See also the present author's essay, "Haiti: Alpha and Omega" in *Haïti, 1804-2004: Le regard de l'Afrique,* Bernard Hadjadj, ed. (Marseille: RiveNeuve Editions, 2006), 33-50, where the argument is developed that Haiti was the first institutionally-produced "underdeveloped" nation, hence the *Alpha,* and subsequently interactions with the Western world that hindered its self-realisation on its own terms, as a harbinger of the destiny of the formerly colonised world, that is, *the Omega.*

47. Eudell, "Haïti: Alpha and Omega", 35-36. See also W. E. B. Du Bois, *The Suppression of the African Slave-Trade in the United States of America* (1896; New York: Dover Publications, 1970), 70 and Eric J. Hobsbawn, *The Age of Revolution: Europe 1789-1848* (1962; New York: Vintage Books, 1996), 69, where although Haiti is only discussed in a cursory manner, its role in the Louisiana Purchase is also noted.

48. James, *The Black Jacobins*, 55-56. Laurent Dubois, *Avengers of the New World: The Story of the Haitian Revolution* (Cambridge, MA: Harvard University Press, 2004), 40.

49. David Patrick Geggus, "The Bois Caïman Ceremony" in *Haitian Revolutionary Studies* (Bloomington: Indiana University Press, 2002), 82-83, where he states: "Taken together, I think these sources [Antoine Dalmas's, *Histoire de la révolution,* Dumsle's *Voyage dans le nord d'Haiti,* Céligny Ardouin account] prove that a vodou ceremony involving the sacrifice of a pig did take place shortly before the great insurrection" and "are the only creditable sources for a study of the Bois Caïman ceremony". See also ibid., 92.

50. Ibid. See also Dubois, *Avengers of the New World*, 98-99.

51. Michel-Rolph Trouillot, "Anthropology and the Savage Slot: The Poetics and Politics of Otherness" in *Anthropology and the Modern World* (New York: Palgrave Macmillan, 2003), 19. Trouillot noted that anthropology performed the "role played, in different ways, by literature and travel accounts" but it "did not create the Savage. Rather, the Savage was the raison d'être of

anthropology. Anthropology came to fill the savage slot in the trilogy order-utopia-savagery, a trilogy that preceded anthropology's institutionalisation and gave it continued coherence in spite of intradisciplinary shifts. This trilogy is now in jeopardy." Ibid., 19, 28.

52. Wynter cites Eric Williams's *British Historians and the West Indies* (New York: Scribner, 1966), where he critiqued Toynbee's assertion that Blacks had not brought any ancestral religions from Africa, and thus came to the Americas spiritually and physically naked, which would be covered by the cast-off clothes of the slaveholder (67).

53. Quoting Mikhail Epstein, where he argued because "culture… is what a human being creates and what creates a human being at the same time, the human being should be seen as being (simultaneously) creator and creation". See "Towards the Sociogenic Principle: Fanon, Identity, the Puzzle of Conscious Experience, and What It Is Like to Be 'Black'" in *National Identities and Sociopolitical Changes in Latin America,* Mercedes F. Durán-Cogan and Antonio Gómez-Moriana, eds. (New York: Routledge, 2001), 30-66, qt. at 33.

54. E. Franklin Frazier, "The Negro Family in Bahia, Brazil", *American Sociological Review,* vol. 7, no. 4 (August 1942): 465-478, qt. at 466.

55. See Cedric J. Robinson, "Racial Capitalism: The Nonobjective Character of Capitalist Development" in *Black Marxism: The Making of the Black Radical Tradition* (1983; Chapel Hill: University of North Carolina Press, 2000), 9-28.

56. James, *Black Jacobins,* 86 and "The Historical Development of the Negro in the United States" (1943) reprinted in Scott McLemee, *C. L. R. James on the "Negro Question"* (Jackson: University Press of Mississippi, 1996), 63-89.

57. Marcel Gauchet, *The Disenchantment of the World: A Political History of Religion,* trans. by Oscar Burge (Princeton: Princeton University Press, 1997), 108. Wynter adopted this term (or so she says very generously) from Gauchet's description of the "radical originality" of the monotheistic break of the Israelites with the polytheistic Egyptian and Babylonian empires, in which "the gaze was from below and was inspired more by the desperate determination to escape the conqueror's hold, than by the idea of revolt." See "The Ceremony Found: Towards the Autopoetic Turn/Overturn, its Autonomy of Human Agency and Extraterratoriality of (Self-) Cognition" in *Black Knowledges/ Black Struggles: Essays in Critical Epistemology,* Jason Ambroise and Sabine Broeck, eds. (Liverpool: Liverpool University Press, 2015), 186. However, before Gauchet, she already utilised such a formulation in describing such groups as ones who "move-anarchically from below-out of the place assigned to them in the dominant social order" (479).

58. For the idea of disenchantment see Wynter, "On Disenchanting Discourse: 'Minority' Literary Criticism and Beyond", *Cultural Critique,* no. 7, *The Nature and Context of Minority Discourse* (Autumn 1987): 207-244 and "1492: A New World View", 12, where she borrowed this concept of subjective understanding from artificial intelligence to convey how "humans always know and perceive their everyday world in relation to specific behaviour-orienting supraordinate goals, and their sets of subgoals or *goal-trees*", which determine "what is to be perceived and what not perceived, *with invariable* reference to one single

criterion-that of their own realisation of such goals." Emphasis in original.

59. Astutely noting the use of beyond in Wynter's titles, e.g. "*Beyond* Miranda's Meanings", "*Beyond* the Word of 'Man'" and "Minority Literary Criticism and *Beyond*", Greg Thomas has quipped: "Where ever this place, this 'Beyond...' it's clear that Wynter means to take us there!" See "Sex/Sexuality and Sylvia Wynter's *Beyond*...: ANTI-Colonial Ideas in 'Black Radical Tradition', *Journal of West Indian Literature*, 94.

60. V.Y. Mudimbe, "*Romanus Pontifex* (1454) and the Expansion on Europe" in *Race, Discourse and the Origin of the Americas,* 58-65.

61. See Wynter, "The Ceremony Found", 189-190.

62. Wynter, "The Ceremony Found", 189.

63. Wynter, "Unsettling the Coloniality of Being", 299.

64. Wynter, "The Ceremony Found", 191.

65. Ibid., 242.

66. Wynter, "Unsettling the Coloniality of Being", 315.

67. Richard Waswo, "The History That Literature Makes", *New Literary History,* vol. 19, no. 3 (Spring 1988): 541-564, esp. 550.

68. Jonathan Miller, "Trouble in Mind", *Scientific American,* vol. 267, no. 3, *Special Issue: Mind and Brain* (September 1992): 180.

69. Wynter, "The Ceremony Found", 196. Emphasis in original. Man(2) refers to the second bio-humanist phase in the late eighteenth century that followed upon the first partly secular invention of the human as *homo politicus* in the wake of intellectual revolution of Renaissance humanism.

70. Wynter, "The Ceremony Found", 198.

71. Ibid. See also where she argues: "The term 'ecumenical', while also referring to the 'universal, global Christian Church' or 'Christendom', also possesses a more generalised definition meaning 'worldwide or general in extent' or 'general, universal'. This latter definition I have adapted with the phrase 'ecumenically human' to mean the 'universal human species,' over and against our contemporary, planetarily extended referent subset ruling-group of the Western and westernised bourgeoisie, as the embodiment of the *member class* prototype of being human *Man*". Ibid., 194.

72. Ibid., 242. John D. Niles has also used this term, see *Homo Narrans: The Poetics and Anthropology of Oral Literature* (Philadelphia: University of Pennsylvania Press, 2010). Wynter's use pushes this idea.

LADY NUGENT'S JOURNAL

It is in the Big Houses that, down to this day, the Brazilian character has found its best expression, the expression of our social continuity. In the study of their intimate history, all that political and military history has to offer in the way of striking events holds little meaning in comparison with a mode of life that is almost routine; but it is in that routine that the character of a people is most readily to be discerned. In studying the domestic life of our ancestors we feel that we are completing ourselves... The past awakens many strings and has a bearing on the life of each and every one of us; and the study of this past is more than mere research and a rummaging in the archives: it is an adventure in sensitivity.

Gilberto Freyre, *Masters and Slaves*[1]

Freyre went on to lament the fact that in Brazil because, "the confessional absorbs personal and family secrets... In vain would one look for the gossip-filled diary of a mistress of the house, of the sort to be encountered with among the British and North American of colonial times." We are lucky then, to have Lady Nugent's journal. And the Institute of Jamaica is to be commended for their recent edition – *Lady Nugent's Journal of Her Residence in Jamaica from 1801 to 1805*, edited by Philip Wright.[2] The edition is illustrated with excellent photographs of drawings, paintings, caricatures, a map, etc. The notes by Philip Wright clear up references, and elucidate something of the broader background against which Maria Nugent etched in her picture of life in Jamaica between the years 1801-1805. The edition, a prestige one, (the price is two guineas) was printed in the Netherlands, is finely bound and altogether handsome.

It is clear that such an edition is intended for a select audience. It is in this intention that the Institute does Maria Nugent scant justice. Not that Mrs. Nugent (later Lady Nugent) wrote her diary to be read by anyone outside her family and, one suspects, her circle of aristocratic friends, for whom, in 1839, five years after her death, her children published a small private edition. Yet some seventy years after, Frank Cundall was quick to see her wider relevance. He published *Lady Nugent's Journal* in 1907 and other editions followed in 1934 and 1939. By this time her importance as a source for historians, for sociology scholars was undisputed.

As Philip Wright points out, "a distinguished American scholar (Lowell J. Ragatz) has described it (her diary) as giving "an utterly inimitable and imperishable picture of planter society".[3] It is interesting to note, in this context, that Maria Nugent was something of a scholar herself. We may smile today at her historical projects – she turns "the greatest part of the history of England into verse" and writes an "abridgement of French History" – but it is this determined discipline in the jungle of planter society which helps her to ask the kind of questions and come to the conclusions which the historian of today now finds invaluable.

Being a scholar was only part of Mrs. Nugent's life. And her journal goes far beyond the uses of a scholar. The limitation of the present Institute edition is that, excellent as it is, it may serve the purpose only of the historian, the researcher, and the informed and interested amateur. There is nothing wrong with this. Except that it carries bananas to Portland when the drought lies heavy on St. Elizabeth. I said earlier on that we, unlike Brazil, are lucky to have Lady Nugent's journal. And yet, in a sense, we have and we have not. We stand in an uneasy relationship to our past and avert our eyes from a confrontation. Jamaican history we feel, is a subject to be taught in school; or to be reserved like a sacred cow on academic grass. Although in a few villages of St. Thomas, the Morant Bay rebellion still lives on in obscure scraps of legend, there is, on the whole, little "popular" history. History does not move in us, nor help to consciously determine our being. We choose to remain deliberately unaware of the historical process that has made us what we are. Our choice is tacit, our conspiracy of silence instinctive. And not without its arguable reason. To rake up the past, we feel, is to exacerbate old sores. Better to let sleeping dogs lie. Yet, it is through our ignorance of the past, that we are, to quote Santayana, condemned to repeat it.

If today, over a century and a half since she wrote her journal, Maria Nugent were to return to Jamaica, one wonders what would astonish her most – that so much has changed? Or that so much has remained the same? Mrs. Nugent is, to borrow her language, alas, no more. But through her journal she has made us heir to a perspective, as impossible now to her as it is urgent to us. It is only through a proper knowledge of the past that we can find the "key to the understanding of the present". A cheap paperback edition of Lady Nugent's Journal should be compulsory reading in all advanced grades of our schools, and should take the place of, or at least find a place beside, the narcotic trash, now freely circulated in drug stores and grocery shops.

Such an edition might well require a new type of introduction, since its intention would be different and its value depend on the extent to which the editor might persuade us to come to terms with our own ambivalence to the past. To read Lady Nugent's Journal is to be faced with some difficult questions: What is a Jamaican? We are Jamaicans but who are "we"? When we read Lady Nugent's Journal whom do we claim as our ancestors and whom do we reject? The planters who generally revolt her, the mulattoes who disturb her, or the "blackies" for whom she feels that pity that is sister to contempt? The tendency amongst us is to claim and reject that portion of our ancestry, that version of the past, that bolsters our stake in the present. We slant our concept of history according to our colour and our class. For the "white Jamaican" and those who assiduously assimilate to him, the only history is the history of the English in Jamaica. And of course he clings to the fallacy that he too is "English". Those few mulattoes who do not assimilate to "white values" insist that they are the only truly indigenous and nationalist people and therefore Jamaican history begins and ends with them. For some black Jamaicans, Jamaica has no reality and no history. They prefer the illusion that they are "Ethiopian". Others, the Afro-Saxons, feel themselves involved in the history of the English in Jamaica. Others for whom "black nationalism" provides a much needed crutch or an easy ride to power, assert that history is the history of black Jamaica only. The overwhelming majority, involved with the struggle for mere survival, are uninterested in a past which the present has not yet altogether changed.

There is little discussion about this. Yet it is the consciousness of this division that makes us wary. To publicise our past, we fear, would only stir up memories of a time when we were even more savagely divided – when some of us were exploiting masters, others exploited slaves, and others uneasily balanced between. The paradox is that if we are to inform our society with that motive force which can transform the unjust system we have inherited, which divided and still divides us, if we are to become conscious of ourselves as a people, *as an entity,* then we must confront ourselves with our origins, must lay claim to and take hold of our history. How then can we resolve the contradiction? *Lady Nugent's Journal*, read in its context, may well provide an answer.

For the society which she portrays with such a terrible accuracy, a society whose economic arrangement, "like a powerful god" alienates man from man, making one the enslaved and the other the enslaver is, nevertheless, a society united by a terrible bond. It is a society whose component parts have all been torn away from a particular place, who have been disrupted from an integrated social pattern; and who, by clinging on to the "culture", the way of life that they left behind them, distort the old remembered patterns and abort the new one. Master, mulatto, slave, each in his own exile, each a displaced person, each an uprooted man. It is this tradition of uprootedness that links us all, to all of them – to the total gallery of people that Mrs. Nugent brings in their grotesque agony to our attention. More, it is the persistence of their exile in us that compels our adventure towards those new frontiers where man's psyche need no longer be sheltered by racial or cultural absolutes, and where the uprooted man may find new roots in what Conrad termed "the subtle but invincible conviction of solidarity that knits together the loneliness of innumerable hearts... which binds men to each other, which binds together all humanity – the dead to the living and the living to the unborn."[4]

In the first tour of the island which she made with her husband, the Governor, Mrs. Nugent was entertained at Prospect Penn (now Vale Royal) by a wealthy planter, Simon Taylor. On the 5th of March, 1802 she wrote in her diary:

> As there were merely gentlemen of the Party, I only brushed the dust off, and went down to dinner at 7 o'clock ... A most profuse and overloaded

table and a shoulder of wild boar stewed, with forced meat, &c as an ornament to the centre of the table. Sick as it all made me, I laughed like a ninny… and Mr. Simon Taylor and I became the greatest of friends… Mr. Taylor is the richest man in the island, and piques himself upon making his nephew, Sir Simon Taylor, who is now in Germany, the richest commoner in England which he says he shall be at *his* death…[5]

Here she puts her finger on several basic features of the society. The absence of *wives,* the profusion and yet pathetic clumsiness of the hospitality, and above all the vaulting ambition which drives men like Simon Taylor, men who, obscure outcasts from their own country, dreamt to strike it rich, and return home armed with their wealth to assault the social towers of London's exclusive society. This was their dream, the glittering prize of their exile in El Dorado. If they themselves were not to return home, then it was enough that a legitimate son, or nephew, should bear their names on gilded pennants and link them through marriage with famous names of high lineage, themselves descended from some more ancient buccaneer. For these were still the fabled days of Sugar and the London scene was lit up with the splendours of the West Indian millionaire.

"The sugar planter", writes Eric Williams "ranked among the biggest capitalists of the mercantilist epoch."[6] A very popular play, *The West Indian* was produced in London in 1771. It opens with a tremendous reception being prepared for a planter coming to England, as if it were the Lord Mayor who were expected. The servant philosophised: "He's very rich, and that's sufficient. They say he has rum and sugar belonging to him to make all the water in the Thames into punch."[7]

But fiction could not rival the fact. And the fact itself contained an enormous element of fantasy and myth, for the exaggerated claims of their fortunes put about by the West Indians were part of their stock in trade. As rich as Croesus, they bragged that they were richer. Affronted by the fact that Clive of India should have returned home from the near East with £40,000 a year as his share of the colonial loot, the Jamaican absentee planter, London merchant and Lord Mayor, William Beckford, boasted that he would leave his son, William Jnr. £40,000 a year and many thousands in cash. Whether he did or not there was no one to disbelieve it. For in spite of the fact that from 1770 there was a twenty-year depression in sugar, Lord Mayor Beckford gave splendid dinners in London where 600 dishes were served upon gold plate at a cost of £ 10,000 pounds a throw; and most famous names of the aristocracy condescended to attend. Such was the report of his wealth that the shrewd alderman was able to buy £100,000 in government loans, yet only had to put down in hard cash, one tenth. Bluff stood security for the rest.

The extraordinary career of his son, William Beckford (author of *Vathek*) was due to his determined attempt to live up to the myth that he was the "richest commoner in England". He succeeded, after squandering his West Indian fortune, in becoming the most hated one. To be fair, he had two strikes against him. He was an upstart West Indian, with pretensions to English gentility, and he was a suspected homosexual. His attempts to bribe himself into the House of Lords failed, and he had to pay a stiff sum, and carry on arduous negotiation before he could win the hand of the Duke of Hamilton for his daughter. One of the provisos was that he should not visit her in her new splendour.

But there was something unusual about Beckford that seemed to mark him out from the common run of West Indian absentees. Himself somewhat of an artist, he was a fabulous patron of the arts. Not in Jamaica, of course. Unlike Monk Lewis he never set foot in the island from which his wealth derived. Once on his way there, he couldn't bear the thought and stopped off in Portugal.

But with the wealth from this rejected island he built the Gothic splendour of Fonthill Abbey, employing artists of all descriptions and filled it with his immense collection of exquisite and precious objets d'art. Yet even his artistic feeling was contaminated by the Midas touch. Art was for him, as it still is today for the rare Jamaican who takes an interest, more an object for possession, a piece of conspicuous consumption. Hazlitt, who was not fond of Beckford, pointed out that all the items in his princely collection were "nothing more than obtrusive proofs of the wealth of the possessor".[8] It was this obtrusive proof which made him envied and hated in England, yet it was all he had to hold on to: an uprooted man coming out of the raw brigandage of an uprooted society which existed only to increase the wealth of the parent country, he could mirror his being only in his possessions. His biographer gives the following anecdote about him. It strikes to the heart of our contemporary dilemma:

> By his calculated ostentation in the West Indian tradition he sought the respects of all ranks on his precipitate return from Paris where he imagined himself slighted by his old friends, the Portuguese ambassador Marialva and the famous Count of Palmela. Back in London in his lawyer's dingy office in Lincoln's Inn he wrote: 'I came like a thunderbolt, having electrified by *sheer weight of money,* the Passporteers, Customs, the inn and post house keeper. In short everybody along the whole route; of me alone do they talk and think, to me alone do they drink.[9]

The sheer weight of money which provides the spur is matched by the sheer weight of food consumed. For eating was as much conspicuous consumption as anything else. And Creole language paid testimony to the part that food played in that variation of the Tantalus myth in which they were condemned. They lived to eat. Yet they seemed perpetually hungry. Mrs. Nugent notes that one planter said of the other – "he likes to have his keg well filled".[10] And on parting from Simon Taylor after a tour of his St. Thomas estates, she records her confusion as to his meaning:

> When I expressed my regret at parting with Mr. Simon Taylor, he said, 'I am very sorry, too, Ma'am, but good·Almighty God, I must go home and cool coppers'. I thought really he was going home, to have all the large

brass pans emptied to cool, that I had seen the sugar boiling in, and that it was part of the process of sugar making; but I found he meant that he must go home, and be abstemious, after so much feasting.[11]

From her arrival at the King's House in Spanish Town she had been horrified at the "yellow wrinkled faces"[12] of the departing Governor, a Jamaican planter, Lord Balcarres and his staff. She found her rooms in a filthy condition and soon had to "set the black ladies to work". But the table manners of Lord Balcarres and his attitude to food proved even worse. On the 31st July, 1801 she writes:

> I wish Lord B. would wash his hands, and use a nail-brush, for the black edges of his nails really make me sick. He has, besides, an extraordinary propensity to dip his finger into every dish. Yesterday he absolutely helped himself to some fricassée with his dirty finger and thumb.[13]

And a month afterwards she confesses:

> Lord Balcarres and a large party at breakfast. I behaved very ill, having placed an Aide-de-camp between me and his lordship; for really his hands, &. were so dirty, I could not have eaten anything had he been nearer.[14]

But it is during her tour of the island that she enters a Gargantuan Inferno. That she seems to have been pregnant without being as yet aware of the fact, explains some of her heightened sensation. But even so the going was pretty rough. She describes the dinner given her at Mr. Scott's Moro (Hordley Estate):

> Our dinner, at 6, was so profuse, that it is worth describing. The first course was entirely of fish, excepting jerked hog, in the centre, which is a way of dressing it by the Maroons. There was also black crab pepper-pot, for which I asked the recipe. – It is as follows; a capon stewed down, a large piece of beef and another of ham, also stewed to a jelly; then six dozen of land crabs picked fine, with their eggs and fat, onion, peppers, ochra, sweet herbs, and other vegetables of the country, cut small; and this, well stewed, makes black crab pepper-pot. – The second course was of turtle, mutton, beef, turkey, goose, ducks, chickens, capons, ham tongue, crab patties, &c. &c. – The third course composed of sweets and fruits of all kinds – I was really sicker than usual, at seeing such a profusion of eatables, and rejoiced to get to my own room..."[15]

At Nonsuch in St. Mary, she discovers "the reason why the ladies here eat a little at dinner":

> I could not help remarking Mrs. Cox, who sat next to me at second breakfast. She began with fish, of which she ate plentifully, all swimming in oil. Then cold veal with the same sauce!! Then tarts, cakes, and fruit. All the other ladies did the same, changing their plates, drinking wine, &c. as if it were dinner. I got away to my own room as soon as possible."[16]

At the Sheriff's coffee estate, she has to endure "the vulgar Mr. Murdoch, so drunk, that I called for my maid and went to bed."[17] But it is during her stay at Seville Estate in St. Ann that she begins to lose her nerve:

I ate little, and talked less. The chattering Mr. Whitehorne was on one side of me, and really wore down my spirits, and put me out of patience, by speaking with his mouth full, and obliging me constantly to change my plate. I am not astonished at the general ill-health of the men in this country; for they really eat like cormorants and drink like porpoises... Almost every man of the party was drunk, even to a boy of fifteen or sixteen, who was obliged to be carried home. His father was very angry, but he had no right to be so, as he set the example to him.[18]

In the midst of this satiety, Mrs. Nugent is starved for a little "agreeable conversation". Not that she now expected any. After the First Assembly that she gave at King's House in Spanish Town, she had remarked, after meeting the ladies and gentleman, on "a sad want of local matter, or, indeed, any subject for conversation with them...".[19] So after they had asked her how she liked the country, she sent for the fiddlers and we had a very merry dance! This determines her never to have a *conversazione* ever again but to settle instead "for Friday dances". And indeed, Balls, Grand Balls and little Balls, House of Assembly Balls and Colt's Balls, balls in honour of her first son and of her daughter, of Christmas and Easter, and a public ball for the King's Birthday are innumerable in her journal. Fortunately she liked dancing, Scotch reel and all. And at one of the Balls that she gives for the King's House slaves, she outrages and terrifies the creole Misses Murphy by dancing with a venerable old slave, exactly as she would have done at a servant's ball in England. In her frank enjoyment of dancing, and her clear-eyed realisation that being belle of the ball is due to her being "the Governor's lady", she most nearly resembles Jane Austen with whom she has quite a bit in common. In 1799 Jane Austen writes in one of her letters:

> I do not think I was very much in request. People were rather apt not to ask me till they could not help it; one's consequence you know, varies so much at times without any particular reason.[20]

In 1801 Mrs. Nugent notes in her diary: "It is wonderful how much a *high station* embellishes! – I heard it whispered on the parade this morning, that General Nugent was one of *the finest men* that ever was seen, and Mrs. Nugent, although small, '*a perfect beauty!*'"[21]

But flattery was not enough, even though she got this in lavish quantities from the ladies and gentlemen. Mrs. Pye flattered her until she "felt quite sick", and with the gentlemen flattery was a prelude to their asking some favour, some patronage, or some money-making concession. She was horrified at how indelicate both ladies and gentlemen were in their applications. Apart from this gambit the only other subjects of conversation to be had in the island was "the mountain wind, the sea breeze, slaves, plantation, the prices of different articles" as well as "debt, disease, and death".[22] And this is with the gentlemen. The creole ladies are far more rustic. Mrs. Nugent's pen is sharp as she remarks on them:

The Creole language is not confined to the negroes. Many of the ladies, who have not been educated in England, speak a sort of broken English, with an indolent drawling out of their words, that is very tiresome if not disgusting. I stood next to a lady one night, near a window, and, by way of saying something remarked that the air was much cooler than usual; to which she answered, 'Yes, ma'am, *him rail-ly too fra-ish*'.[23]

As for the content of what they have to say –

The extent of Mrs. Israell's travels has been to Kingston, and she is always saying, 'When I was in town'; she says, too, that frost and snow must be prodigious odd things.[24]

And even more incisively:

Mrs. C. is a perfect Creole, says little, and drawls out that little, and has not an idea beyond her own Penn.[25]

Mrs. Nugent soon discovers the range of interests and the occupation of the Creole ladies – gossip, spoiling their tyrannical children, dressing, flirting, laughing in the carriage at the church door during the service loud enough to be heard inside, and most of all scolding their servants. She writes of the ladies at Seville Estate:

… they appear to me perfect viragos; they never speak but in the most imperious manner to their servants, and are constantly finding fault.[26]

The only custom, in fact, of the Creole ladies that Mrs. Nugent approves of, and that she too in fact indulges in is the custom of *creolising*. "After breakfast, the usual routine," she notes, "writing, reading, and creolising". Philip Wright inserts this explanation:

Creolizing is an easy and elegant mode of lounging in a warm climate; so called because much in fashion among the ladies of the West Indies: that is, reclining back in one arm-chair, with their feet upon another, and sometimes upon the table.[27]

When creolising with the ladies, she puts them to stringing beads or keeps her ear to the ground by listening to their gossip.

The dominant theme of this gossip is the relationship of the gentlemen, their creole husbands, brothers, sons, fathers with "the brown and black ladies". Soon after her arrival Mrs. Nugent records "the ladies told me strange stories of the influence of the black and yellow women, and Mrs. Bullock called them serpents."[28]

On her first visit to Simon Taylor at Prospect Penn, Mrs. Nugent says after dinner, "I took tea in my own room, surrounded by the black, brown and yellow ladies of the house".[29] As Simon Taylor is an old bachelor, she assumes that he "detests the society of women". At his Golden Grove Estate, however, she soon discovers that Simon Taylor, like every other white man in the colony, conforms to the sexual pattern of the society:

> A little mulatto girl was sent into the drawing-room to amuse me. She was
> a sickly delicate child, with straight light-brown hair, and very black eyes.
> Mr. T. appeared very anxious for me to dismiss her, and in the evening,
> the housekeeper told me she was his own daughter, and that he had a numerous
> family, some almost on every one of his estates.[30]

After this she accepts the fact that the planters had harems, and for "political"
reasons as well as from her own curiosity and kindness, receives the "wives"
unofficially in her rooms whenever she is a guest at any of the estates. Only on
very rare occasions does she meet any "creole ladies" in the drawing rooms.
White wives are scarce. Where the "creole ladies" are present, Mrs. Nugent
meets with their resentment when she insists on giving private audience to
their black and brown rivals.

The jealousy of the creole ladies is intense. The easy availability of other
women reduces their status. They are intended to breed legitimate heirs and
little else. The brown and black ladies, well aware that to be a white man's
mistress is the only avenue of social and economic mobility open to them,
work hard at being mistresses. It becomes their occupation, their profession.
They are good at their jobs, and all throughout the journal Mrs. Nugent refers
to the power and fascination which they wield over the white men. To have
children by white men, too, is to make sure that their children will rise in status
and that their own position will be more secure. When she visited the Hope
Estate (of which the present Hope Gardens was a part) she writes:

> The overseer, a civil, vulgar, Scotch officer, on half pay, did the honours to
> us… The overseer's *chère amie*, and no man here is without one, is a tall
> black woman, well made, with a very flat nose, thick lips and skin of ebony,
> highly polished and shining. She shewed me her three yellow children,
> and said, with some ostentation, she should soon have another. The marked
> attention of the other women, plainly proved her to be the favourite Sultana
> of this vulgar, ugly, Scotch Sultan, who is about fifty, clumsy, ill made, and
> dirty. He had a dingy, sallow-brown complexion, and only two yellow
> discoloured tusks, by way of teeth…[31]

Mrs. Nugent disapproves strongly of this type of ménage. She is too fervent a
Christian, too secure in her own integrated pattern of social behaviour not to be
shocked at the kind of liaison that threatened Christian marriage. As we shall
note later on she consistently advocates Christian baptism and marriage for the
slaves. Her dislike of miscegenation, although perhaps based on some racial
ground, is most concerned with it being a "social mistake". In 1804 she enters:

> In my drive this morning, met several of the unfortunate half-black progeny
> of some of our staff; all in fine muslin, lace, &c. with wreaths of flowers in
> their hats. What ruin for these worse than thoughtless young men![32]

She remonstrates with the young officers attached to King's House, "her
family", "upon the improper lives they lead" and "the horrid connections they
have formed". She listens to their histories, to their troubles in which "the brown

ladies, as usual concerned". But seeing that her efforts are useless she concludes: "This is indeed a sad immoral country, but it is of no use worrying myself".[33]

She sympathises with the creole ladies, "ninnies" as they are, and as a wife aligns herself on their side. She speaks with distaste of the efforts of the President of the Legislative Council to get her to patronise a "decayed" mulatto milliner of "bad character". And she is very funny about Captain Johnson's determined efforts to prove that his "ugly mulatto favourite" was not guilty of stealing a pair of shoes, even though the shoes were "found in her pocket".[34] In a more serious vein she announces "the death of poor wretched Captain Dobbin. He died without seeing his children, and it is said has left all he is worth to his black mistress and her child. This is, I am afraid, but too common a case in Jamaica".[35]

She also tells about a *crime passionnel* centring once again on a devastating brown lady:

> ... all the conversation about a sad affair that has just taken place. A Mr. Irvine, in a fit of jealousy, having murdered one of his servants. It seems the favourite was a brown lady; and to, mend the matter, Mr. Irvine is a married man, and his unfortunate wife has been long nearly broken-hearted, as his attachment to this *lady* had occasioned his treating her often with the greatest cruelty even.[36]

Yet the fact that she "receives" the black and brown ladies, makes it clear that she realises that the force of long habit and necessity had brought into being this type of union, and that her own standards of morality and immorality could not here prevail. For what was at work in the society was the response to an economic system. Whilst she saw the effects, she was unable to relate them to their root cause. As Freyre has insisted,

> In reality neither White nor Negro in himself was the active force in the sexual and class relations that developed. What was given expression in these relations was the spirit of the economic system that like a powerful god, divided us into enslaver and enslaved... There is no slavery without sexual depravity. Depravity is the essence of such a regime. In the first place, economic interests favour it, by creating in the owners of men an immoderate desire to possess the greatest numbers of *crias* (children). From a manifesto issued by slave-holding planters, Nabuco quotes the following words so rich in significance. – 'The most productive feature of slave property, is the generative belly'... The masters of these slaves favoured dissoluteness in order to ... increase the herd.[37]

The effect of this system was to create in the women a pride in their "generative belly" and in their physical appearance which was a *sine qua non* to the attainment of this ambition. Their lives centred about the bed, about dressing, and external adornment. The mind was not cultivated, nor the intelligence. These would have been drawbacks. For the secret of their success with their men lay in their passivity, in their acceptance of a slave status which augmented feelings of masculinity.

The effect on the men was to develop in them an excessive pride in their virility. The capacity to breed, like the capacity to absorb food and drink, and to acquire money was what marked out the men from the boys. Mrs. Nugent neatly notes this quality of boastful "machismo":

> ... for the Inn [the Ferry Inn] is situated on the road, between Kingston and Spanish Town, and it was very diverting to see the odd figures and extraordinary equipages... Then a host of gentlemen, who were taking their *sangaree*, in the piazza; *and their vulgar buckism amused me very much.*[38]

It is no wonder that in a society such as this, someone like Mrs. Nugent should have felt herself in a place of exile. In spite of her journal, her husband, her children, her sketching, writing poetry, practising French – in spite of the balls, the grand balls, the Assemblies, the levees, the wining and dining, the incredible beauty of the island with its "lilac-coloured mountains" the hollowness at the heart of the life lived here catches hold of her. At first she attributes this only to the climate:

> I cannot tell what it is, but this climate has a most extraordinary effect upon me; I am not ill, but every object is, at times, not only uninteresting, but even disgusting. I feel a sort of inward discontent and restlessness, that are perfectly unnatural to me. – At moments, when I exert myself, I go even beyond my usual spirits; but the instance I give way, a sort of despondency takes possession of my mind. I argue with myself against it, but all in vain. ...but till the malady of the spirits has taken its departure, all these considerations, and even religion, are of no avail.[39]

Increasingly she notes the lack of personal and social relationships, the impossibility of personal happiness in a society totally geared to one purpose – making money. She soon gives up the friendship of Mrs. Pye, because the latter, anxious for status, makes known to all far and wide her closeness to the "Governor's Lady", and the latter is criticised for "favouritism". General Nugent as Governor finds it impossible to rely on the discretion of many members of the Legislative Council. To enhance their status, they are apt to drop inside knowledge, and to make economic use of it. Bribery and corruption is an essential feature of the society. Even Mrs. Nugent is not averse to giving gifts to the wives of Members of the Assembly to "secure their vote". She notes how sweet smiles are bestowed on her by the gentleman who hopes to be appointed Chief Justice, and learns that Lord Balcarres had accepted 1,000 guineas as a "douceur" from the former Chief Justice (who had not been a lawyer) for the appointment. Absentee public officials living in England rent out their posts as Collector of Customs to merchants, etc. Dishonesty is the accepted practice. Attorneys are soon owners of the estates left in their charge.

Religion also worships the Golden Calf. The clergymen are in some cases ex-overseers who purchased their livings. In one church the sacrament is administered only three times a year, and some gentlemen argue with Mrs. Nugent that religion is a farce. Kingston merchants do active business with the

French forces assaulting Santo Domingo, whilst England and Jamaica are at war with the French. Every other consideration is secondary to the "greed for gain". At the end of her first tour in the island, Mrs. Nugent writes:

> In this country it appears as if everything were bought and sold. Clergymen make no secret of making a traffic of their livings… It is indeed melancholy, to see the general disregard of religion and morality, throughout the whole country. Every one seems solicitous to make money, and no one appears to regard the mode of acquiring it.[40]

On leaving Jamaica Mrs. Nugent comments on how different she feels now "from what I did on my first arrival". And one cannot help detecting a lessening of her *joie de vivre* across the years. To have remained longer in the colony would have infected her own relationship with her husband. Their frequent escape to Government Penn and Port Henderson is an attempt not only to go to somewhere cooler than Spanish Town, but to keep up that adult friendship between husband and wife which is unknown in the prevailing mores of the society. She observes that the ladies and gentlemen are surprised that at a ball, she and General Nugent are content to sit out dances and converse with each other. Increasingly she longs for "dear England, and our domestic comfort there".[41] When she is safely back, she enjoys at the home of the Buckingham's, with the relief of one suffering from thirst, "music and much agreeable conversation". But before her longed-for departure she confesses to her journal:

> The people here are so uncongenial to us, that I am often reminded of the complaint of the poor French émigré, that I met with in some late publication – "Toutes les pages du livre de ma vie semblent effacées." [All the pages of my life seem to be blotted out.][42]

On the voyage coming out, Captain Noble, whistling one minute, dies of a stroke the next as Mrs. Nugent tries to aid him. On the voyage going home, "the carpenter was found dead in the very act of putting up his tools, last night".[37] These sudden and violent deaths, from yellow fever, apoplexy, help to create the feeling of despair that shadows her journal. She tries to steel herself not "to lament as I am apt to do", for "the usual occurrence of a death".[44] She fears for the health of her own husband and children. She gives a picture of Doctor Robertson, lately married to a young wife, afraid of the climate and yellow-fever, wanting at all costs to be sent home, finally breaking down as he pleads with General Nugent:

> It was quite shocking to see the state he was in, crying and sobbing like a child; and with such a robust figure as his, made the scene altogether most deplorable.[45]

She is horrified at the lack of feeling shown by the creoles for the suffering of others, or for those recently dead. Gentlemen even make jokes about the dear departed and draw her anger upon their heads. She perceives the brutalisation of their spirit, but does not admit its provenance. The wealth of the West Indian, by the time it arrives in London to help support the genteel society of which she forms part and in which she cultivates her capacity to feel, is made here on the sugar estates. On the sugar estates, unlike England, no magic wand of good breeding can waft the horror away. She has a glimpse of this inferno on her visit to New Hall estate belonging to *King* Mitchell ("a coarse looking man, but humane")[46] near Spanish Town. She is being shown the "whole process of sugar making". In the boiling house she observes some of the slaves "with a large skimmer upon a long pole, constantly stirring the sugar and throwing it from one cauldron to another". She continues:

> I asked the overseer how often his people were relieved. He said every twelve hours; but how dreadful to think of their standing twelve hours over a boiling cauldron, and doing the same thing; and he owned to me that sometimes they did fall asleep, and get their poor fingers into the mill; and he shewed me a hatchet, that was always ready to sever the whole limb, as the only means of saving the poor sufferer's life! I would not have a sugar estate for the world![47]

And these slaves are kept at their cauldron by the practise and threat of violence. The whites who must practise this violence must brutalise their spirits, and they do. They accept it as natural that they should live in an island where a gun fired at five starts the day; and at eight, concludes it; where the guns look out to sea against the covetous enemy anxious to get the wealth of sugar and slaves that the island possesses; and where the guns are ready to swivel round upon the slaves, the most valuable property of all at any such time that they may revolt against being a mere commodity. During Mrs. Nugent's stay in Jamaica, a relative handful of miles across the Caribbean, the first successful slave revolt in history was already working out, under Toussaint and after Dessalines, its paradoxical destiny.

Santo Domingo, soon to be called Haiti, was the biggest problem that General Nugent had on his plate during his Governorship of Jamaica. He seemed to have carried on British policy very successfully, and was in fact rewarded with a baronetcy after his return home. The priorities of Nugent's policy as Governor was to make sure that the example of Haiti did not spread to Jamaica. In this he was successful and wrote in a despatch to London: "the Island of St. Domingo is no more talked of here, than if it was in the East Indian Seas".[48] His second policy was to foster good relations with Toussaint with whom the British had signed a trade convention, after their effort to capture the island for themselves had failed. The important thing for Nugent to see to was that the rich sugar-producing island of Haiti did not fall once more into the hands of the French, and enable them to recapture the sugar market from Britain. At the same time, fearful of the example of the Black Republic, Britain would not do anything to prevent Napoleon's troops from recapturing the island, especially if its cane fields would be devastated in such an attempt.

Nugent, helped by Mrs. Nugent, carried out this tortuous and tricky policy superbly. Lady Nugent received magnificent dresses from Pauline Leclerc, Napoleon's sister, and wife of the General in charge of the French troops attacking Santo Domingo. But they give the French neither aid nor comfort, and carry on their trade negotiations with Toussaint and, after he had been captured, with Dessalines.

Early on, when she has only recently arrived in the island, Edward Corbet, the British agent in Santo Domingo, gives her a good account of General Toussaint and she remarks: "He must be a wonderful man, and intended for very good purposes".[49] Later on, an Aide-de-camp, of one of the "brigand generals", a mulatto named Captain Dufour comes on a mission and she is surprised by him: "He is a much more gentleman-like sort of man than I expected... I was surprised at the good language he spoke".[50]

But she does not take the Jamaican black or mulatto with quite the same sort of consideration. It would be difficult for her to. The Haitians are free men who have won their freedom. Except towards the end, when she begins to be fearful of a black revolt in Jamaica, her attitude towards the "blackies" is one of a benevolent paternalism. One suspects that she likes "the blackies" more than her own white servants. Certainly she sees little difference between them and is indignant about the airs her white servants gives themselves in dealing with the Negroes. She lambasts the lower orders for "considering the negroes as creatures formed merely to administer to their ease, and to be subject to their caprice; and I have found much difficulty to persuade those great people and superior beings, our white domestics, that the blacks are human beings, or have souls."[51]

Mrs. Nugent is certainly convinced that they have souls. She is determined that all the King's House domestics should be made Christians and properly baptised before she leaves. She labours at this, instructing them in the duties of a Christian before Baptism. She goes as far as drawing up a catechism with which to instruct them. She approves of Mr. Wilberforce and his efforts on their behalf and sends him a copy of the catechism she has drawn up. She is worldly wise enough to keep her opinion of Wilberforce to herself, seeing that this would do the slaves no good with the planters and make more difficult her husband's task of putting through measures in the House of Assembly which were mere favourable to the British interest than to the Jamaican planter.

She takes care of their welfare, however, whilst she waits on Mr. Wilberforce to do the rest. Time and time again she gives them extra indulgences. On Boxing Day, one of the traditional slave holidays, she writes:

Nothing but bonjoes [sic], drums and tom-toms, going all night, and dancing and singing, and madness, all the morning... Some of our blackies were most superbly dressed... in the masquerade... gold and silver fringe, spangles, beads, &c. &c. and really a most wonderful expense altogether. General N. gave the children money, and threw some himself among them from the gallery, and in the scramble all the finery was nearly torn to pieces, to my great vexation. However, they seemed not to mind it, but began dancing with the same spirit as if nothing had happened, putting their smart clothes into the best order they could. We gave them a bullock, a sheep and a lamb with a dollar to every person in the house... Perhaps, however, it is more than is usually done; but, for the short time we are with them, we will make them as happy as we can.[53]

She looks on the slaves "drunkenness" after the holiday with a more benevolent eye than she does on their masters. Altogether she is rather "amused" by their antics and indulgent to their "baby-like pleasures".[54] She is rather worried about the fact that her household slaves do not exert themselves: "...the poor blackies...They are all so good-humoured and seem so merry, that it is quite comfortable to look at them. I wish, however, they would be a little more alert in clearing away the filth of this otherwise nice and fine house."[55]

But rather sensibly, she concludes: "Reflect all night upon slavery that the want of exertion in the blackies must proceed from that cause".[56] She is glad at a banquet to be able to get away from "the smell of the blackies and of hot meats",[57] and amused at entering Seville Great House at night to find about a dozen black heads "popping up" from the floor. In the feudal relationship of the great House the household slaves slept on the floor in the corridors etc.

Her favourite black servant is her young attendant, Cupid, who carries out her chair, and is to serve as valet de chambre to her first child. She baptises him, and when she is departing leaves him money to buy a keepsake, and during her confinement, she reports that he pined and refused to eat until she was safely recovered. There are only a few other "blackies" who stand out as individuals to her in the journal. At Golden Grove Estate she records – "One little black girl came to beg that I would take her with me. She was remarkably thick-lipped and ugly, but intelligent child."[58] And in 1805 she writes –

> ... we met a gang of Eboe negroes, just landed, and marching up the country... I bowed, kissed my hand and laughed; they did the same... One man attempted to shew more pleasure than the rest, by opening his mouth as wide as possible to laugh, which was rather a horrible grin. He shewed such truly cannibal teeth, all filed as they have them, that I could not help shuddering. He was of Herculean size, and really a tremendous looking creature.[59]

Sometimes, as at New Hall sugar estate, she glimpses the less "happy" side of slavery. At Mr. Shirley's estate Spring Gardens, "two poor negroes, who had been in chains nearly a year, came to General N., to ask him to intercede for them".[60] And whilst at Government Penn, she records that "Many negroes came to make complaints of their masters". At another time Lord Balcarres's slaves also lay a complaint. And on January 10th whilst still at the Penn she records that a carpenter from Spanish Town came to beg General Nugent to intervene on behalf of a young slave who was due to be hung the next morning. The boy had entered a house and stolen a watch. She explains: "The law of the land is, it seems, that three magistrates [that is, planters] may condemn a slave to death... General N. made every exertion, but in vain, to save the life of the boy, and to send him out of the country; but it appears that it could not be done, without exercising his prerogative very far, and giving great offence and alarm to the white population. – This law of the three magistrates appears to me abominable…".[61] She sits in, too, and listens to a case involving some slave merchants and is distressed by the revelations that she hears.

Yet, from her vantage point of Governor's lady at the King's House, she is shut away from the grosser realities, and is so enabled to make that accommodation of conscience to profit which is the reverse side of Protestant piety. As Wright points out, she backs her reasons for marriage of the slaves, with an argument "addressed to the slave owners' material interest":

> Amused myself with reading the Evidence before the House of Commons, on the part of the petitioners for the Abolition of the Slave trade. As far as I at present see and can hear of the ill treatment of the slaves, I think what they say upon the subject is very greatly exaggerated. Individuals, I make no doubt, occasionally abuse the power they possess; but, generally speaking, I believe the slaves are extremely well used. Yet it appears to me, there would be certainly no necessity for the Slave Trade, if religion, decency, and good order, were established among the negroes; if they could be prevailed upon to marry; and if our white men would but set them a little better example. Mrs. Bell told me to-day, that a negro man and woman of theirs, who are married, have fourteen grown up children, all healthy field negroes.[62]

But except for these few instances when she advances, according to Wright, on "dubious grounds", she feels herself on the "side" of the slave, and never fails to note whatever is exotic or colourful in their appearance. In Barbados, the sight of Negro slaves running behind their master's horses holding on to the horses' tails, "amuses" her greatly. Her descriptions of the John Canoe bands, of the Sunday Negro market where the slaves sold the excess from their provision grounds, her account of the "blackies'" use of the English language, of the old black woman who peeps in at her at the St. Thomas bath, the old negro midwife with her handful of herbs during her confinement, are vivid. She has a sharp eye for the ridiculous – "Mr. Wilkie" looked like "a man who has been buried and dug up again";[63] Mr. Scott before and after he had been struck by lightning; the bride in tears before her wedding because there was no white satin ribbon to be had in Kingston – nor sage and onions to stuff the duck; the Jews of the militia attending a Christian Sunday service so as not to lose their five shillings a day pay; Mrs. Cummins the white nursery maid who after she married an officer, "has in consequence, thrown off her cap, and been dressed in her own hair"[64] – informs her pen with regard to "herself and the blackies":

> ... myself, in the sociable, with our two black postillions, in scarlet liveries, but with black ankles peeping out of their particulars, and altogether a rather novel sort of appearance...[65]

But half way through her journal, a different note, as far as the "blackies" are concerned, begins to be heard. Santo Domingo is not yet sealed off. The French prisoners and refugees, planters and slaves and mulattos in Jamaica are supposed to be stirring up trouble. France is taking a leaf from England's book and is prepared to use a slave insurrection to defeat their crafty Anglo-Saxon enemy. On the 17th of June, 1803 Mrs. Nugent cautiously notes:

> It is said that much mischief is brewing in the country, and that it is connected with the St. Domingo French &c.; but all this is secret information, and must be enquired into privately.[66]

From hereon she becomes fearful that "this wretched country is devoted to the same destruction that has overtaken St Domingo".[67] She tries to "keep my mind at ease!" But in the rest of the country the rising hysteria, the fear of the blacks, begins to come to a crescendo. A Slave Court is held in Kingston and two slaves are tried and found guilty of "forming a rebellious conspiracy". They are hanged by the neck at the Parade, and their heads severed from their bodies. As a warning their heads are put on poles one on Slipe Pen road, the other on that adjoining the city leading to Windward. That Sunday Mrs. Nugent regrets having to go to Church "for we were obliged to pass close by the pole on which was stuck the head of the black man who was executed a few days ago."[68]

In July, several Negroes "disappear" from different estates. Agitated, Mrs. Nugent prays: "God preserve us from the horrors of an insurrection!".[69] Almost a year later there has been none, but she is still haunted by the possibility. She notes that when there is talk of the bravery and success of Dessalines in Haiti among her dinner guests "the blackies in attendance seem so much interested, that they hardly change a plate, or do anything but listen".[69] When in April 1805 a large French fleet is expected to attack Jamaica, and General Nugent declares Martial Law and sends Mrs. Nugent and his family off to Port Henderson, she needs the comfort and courage of her "white maid, Margaret Clifford". In Spanish Town, the Negroes "appeared to be inclined to riot... when the troops marched out, but they were soon dispersed by the militia". She argues with herself that perhaps the Negroes' commotion will be only temporary, "for, like children, they are fond of fuss and noise, and have no reflection".[70] Later, out for a walk with her children, she has an encounter in which she sees for the first time in the apparently happy and acquiescent slave, the instinct for freedom; an instinct which must by nature of her involvement in its captivity, pose a threat to her very existence. And she writes:

> We met a horrid looking black man, who passed us several times, without making any bow, although I recollected him as one of the boatmen of the canoe we used to go out in, before we had the *Maria*. He was then very humble, but to-night he only grinned, and gave us a sort of fierce look, that struck me with a terror I could not shake off.[71]

The French did not make their expected attack and the slave revolt did not take place until some twenty-five years after Mrs. Nugent had left Jamaica. But in 1804, a year before the Nugents left Jamaica, the golden bubble of sugar began to burst. In England William Beckford, the once "richest commoner" in

England finds that his fortune made from slaves and sugar is vanishing like Cinderella's finery as sugar's clock strikes midnight. He is forced to sell his magnificent folly, Fonthill Abbey.

He sells it to a Scottish millionaire of humble origin who "had, in the modern manner, made his money out of gunpowder, depression in the Funds and real estate".[72] In 1825, with a symbolic crash, the main tower of Fonthill Abbey collapsed. Jamaica and the society that had financed this golden tower collapsed more slowly, but even more surely. The Scottish millionaire wrote off his loss, sold the land at Fonthill as building lots. Some time after, a great part of the Abbey was demolished and used as building materials. Only the northern end of it now stands. As with Jamaica, only the ruin remained.

Now that the island's gold mine had been exhausted, the greedier took their departure. As the island became less wealthy, less of a prize, a sense of fair-play came dimly into being. The mulatto gentlemen, who in Mrs. Nugent's time had been excluded from office, from society and from the voter's list, from the House of Assembly, and from the King's House, fought and won the right to all. Mrs. Nugent had met several mulatto women who were the daughters of members of the House of Assembly. One year before she came to Jamaica, the Speaker of the House of Assembly, Kean Osborne, whom she frequently entertained, and whose estate at Woods she visited and wrote about in her journal, had an illegitimate son by a woman of colour. The Assembly and Island politics was dominated by this mulatto Robert Osborne and by another Edward Jordon, until the Morant Bay Rebellion of 1865 and the imposition of Crown Colony Government. Another mulatto, George William Gordon, son of a former Scotch overseer turned planter and member of the House of Assembly, was to challenge the power of a British Governor in a way that General Nugent had not been challenged, even by the most recalcitrant planter, and to pay for his challenge with his neck. And above all, the "blackies" rebelling in 1831, impatient for freedom, will finally get it in 1838. Those of the creoles committed to their exile by force of circumstances or by attachment will fight a rearguard action to keep their former power and influence. But as the society changes and the free black peasant and landless labourer begins to assert his right to citizenship, the old bases of power begin to be replaced, but not until freeholders like Paul Bogle and hundreds of others had paid with their lives for challenging the pattern.

If Mrs. Nugent were to return to Jamaica today she could still see recognisable traces. The plantation system, although less profitable and less dominant, has not been displaced. A "greed for gain", a new and yet old goldrush has begun to replace, in a different context, the sugar bubble. A society, reluctant to examine its premises, evasive of its past, uncertain of its identity, afraid of its own promise, worshipping its white heritage, despising its black, or at best settling for the current view of being a multiracial, multicultural "Out of Many People One", is in danger of creating the spiritual Inferno that Mrs. Nugent pictured so vividly, in a twentieth-century setting. For it is a society where the majority are still exiles in their own country. They are exiles because for too long they have been made to deny one part or the other of their heritage.

And yet it is in her description of the customs of the most despised part that Mrs. Nugent gives a clue, and points a finger, without being aware of doing so, at a significant and hitherto missing link. For in our tormented tossing about for an identity, our labelling ourselves Afro-Jamaican, Euro-Jamaican, Afro-Saxon, Chinese-Jamaican, etc., we have missed a truth because so many of us may have subconsciously wished to evade it. And this is a truth that has been obscured by the myth fostered by British historians and sucked in with our mother's milk. It is the myth that Eric Williams in his book *British Historians and The West Indies* tilts an angry lance at when he quotes the great historian Toynbee to this effect:

> The Negro has not indeed brought any ancestral religion of his own from Africa… His primitive social heritage was of so frail a texture, that every shred of it was scattered to the winds at the first impact of our Western civilisation. Thus he came to America, spiritually as well as physically naked; and he has met the emergency by covering his nakedness with his enslaver's cast-off clothes.[73]

To this Eric Williams remarks, "With all this it was possible for Toynbee, with his tremendous scholarship, to ignore completely the civilisation of Africa before the European slave trade".[74] But what is even more to be wondered at is that Toynbee should here choose to ignore the theory of history that he has given the world – the theory of "challenge and response". Recent and numerous studies have shown the dominance of African religions, their persistence in the New World. Freyre has in fact insisted that in Brazil, it "was Europe reigning without governing: it was Africa that governed".[75] But perhaps what is most significant is that of all the uprooted men who came to the New World, the African was the only one who through force of circumstance lost contact for centuries with his point of origin, and lost contact with the touchstone of orthodoxy. He was forced to cover the resultant "nakedness" not with the "enslaver's cast off clothing", but with a new cultural creation of his own. For the African in the New World became a Negro, and the Negro is the world's first uprooted race. He is the only race who is not tied to a land mass. The African belongs to Africa. The European to Europe. The Negro has no such territorial cradle.

He was fortunate in that the African religions which he remembered and transmitted emphasised a world view that was embracing rather than exclusive, a cult rather than a sect. This prepared him to accept all gods and all influences, to borrow equally from all. From the European, what Toynbee calls "the cast off clothing", from the Indian, from the Chinese, from the Moslem. In Guyana, Negroes play drums at the Festival of Hosein and Hassan; at a shango ceremony in Trinidad, St. John speaks through the mouth of a Negro medium in the voice of an Indian businessman. And San Philomene sings to the worshipper a snatch of a Hindu song. In Jamaica, the Indian Maid is featured in the Pocomania bands. In Haiti, Catholic Saints and Legba and Damballa are not incongruous together. Out of their remembered African music joined together with hymns and Protestant tunes, the American Negro created jazz. And jazz is the music of twentieth century uprooted man.

In her description of Christmas Day, December 1801, Mrs. Nugent gives us a picture of an early indigenous theatre in the making. It was this indigenous theatre in the American South that first gave the Christy Minstrels the idea of their parody. And it is significant that the "white" minstrel shows effectively helped to conceal the fact that the Negro, instead of *imitating* his master – Gentlemen pray be seated – was *creating;* to conceal the fact that of all the peoples who came to the New World, the Negro as a group, has been the most creative culturally. He has been because he has had to be. It is the rhythm of the negro – not of the African, not of the European – that informs the popular music of the New World – jazz, Afro-Cuban, and in Jamaica, ska and rock steady. What happens in Trinidad every carnival, happened in a more coherent form on Christmas day 1801 in Spanish Town, Jamaica. Mrs. Nugent writes:

> All night heard the music of tom-toms, &c. Rise early, and the whole town and house bore the appearance of a masquerade. After Church, amuse myself very much with the strange processions, and figures called Johnny Canoes. All dance, leap and play a thousand antics. Then there are groups of dancing men and women. They had a sort of leader or superior at their head, who sang a sort of recitative, and seemed to regulate all their proceedings; the rest joining at intervals in the air and the chorus. The instrument to accompany the song was a rude sort of drum, made of bark leaves, on this they beat time with two sticks, while the singers do the same with their feet. Then there was a party of actors. – Then a little child was introduced, supposed to be a king, who stabbed all the rest. They told me that some of the children who appeared were to represent Tippoo Saib's children, and the man was Henry the 4th of France. What a *mélange!*[76]

Then as now the Negro was the syncretic mixing force of the society. When the creole lady answered Mrs. Nugent about the coolness of the air – "Him rail-ly too fresh", she merely gave back the *mélange* that the Negro, fusing his former speech habits with the English language, had made. This *mélange* of language, habits, customs, peoples, is what constitutes the single most important factor of our identity. It is only when we accept and explore the implications of this – when we lay claims to all and reject none – and consciously continue the process of creative fusion already begun, that we shall begin to take on that identity which lies far beyond the horizons of race or place. The paradox of the Jamaican, or Caribbean identity, is that it will defy definition. Balanced, perhaps, between the impossible and the absurd. To be found, who knows, at one of the few estates that Mrs. Nugent did not visit. So we will let her have the last word:

One place that we passed was called Paradise, and a Mr. Angel was the inhabitant.[77]

Endnotes

1. *The Masters and the Slaves: A Study in the Development of Brazilian Civilization* (New York: Alfred Knopf, 1946), xxxvii-xxxviii.
2. *Lady Nugent's Journal* (Institute of Jamaica, 1966; reissued Kingston: University of West Indies Press, 2002). Hereafter abbreviated as *LNJ*, xi.
3. Wright. *LNJ*, xi, quotes from Ragatz, *The Fall of the Planter Class in the Caribbean* (1928; New York: Octagon Books, 1963), 486.
4. Conrad, T*he Nigger of the Narcissus: A Tale of the Forecastle* (1897; New York: Doubleday, 1919), viii-ix.
5. *LNJ*, 5 March 1802, 64-65. Emphasis in original.
6. Eric Williams, *Capitalism and Slavery* (1944; London: Andre Deutch, 1964), 85.
7. George Cumberland, *The West Indian* (1771; London: J.M. Dent, *Eighteenth-Century Plays*, ed. John Hampden, nd.)
8. William Hazlitt, *Criticism on Art: And Sketches of the Picture Galleries of England*, Second Edition, edited by His Son (London: C. Templeman, 1844), 289.
9. The source of this quotation cannot be located. However, some similar information can be gathered from Cyrus Redding, ed., *Memoirs of William Beckford*, vol. 1 (London: Charles J. Skeet, 1859), 65-66.
10. *LNJ*, 11 Aug 1801, 15.
11. *LNJ*, 12 March 1802, 71.
12. *LNJ*, 29 July 1801, 10.
13. *LNJ*, 31 July 1801, 11.
14. *LNJ*, 30 July 1801, 11.
15. *LNJ*, 24 August 1801, 17.
16. *LNJ*, 11 March 1802, 70.
17. LNJ, 25 March 1802, 79.
18. *LNJ*, 28 March 1802, 80-81.
19. *LNJ*, 7 August 1801, 14.
20. Jane Austen to Cassandra Austen, 8 January 1799 in *The Letters of Jane Austen*, Sarah Chauncey Woolsey ed. (Boston: Little, Brown, and Company, 1905), 49.
21. *LNJ*, 4 June 1801, 4. Emphasis in original.
22. *LNJ*, 2 October 1801, 29 and 5 December 1803, 184.
23. *LNJ*, 24 April 1802, 98.
24. *LNJ*, 10 February 1802, 58.
25. *LNJ*, 15 January 1802, 52.
26. *LNJ*, 27 March 1802, 80.
27. *LNJ*, 10 September 1802, 117.
28. *LNJ*, 31 July 1801, 12.
29. *LNJ*, 5 March 1802, 65
30. *LNJ*, 10 March 1802, 68.
31. *LNJ*, 1 October 1801, 29.
32. *LNJ*, 28 September 1804, 214.
33. *LNJ*, 10 August 1803, 172 and 23 November 1803, 183.

34. *LNJ*, 26 and 27 August 1803, 173.
35. *LNJ*, 17 May 1805, 234.
36. *LNJ*, 17 November 1803, 182.
37. Freyre, *Masters and Slaves*, 324.
38. *LNJ*, 13 June 1803, 163. Emphasis added.
39. *LNJ*, 29 August 1801, 17-18.
40. *LNJ*, 24 April 1802, 97-98.
41. *LNJ*, 31 December 1801, 49.
42. *LNJ*, 30 August 1801, 18.
43. *LNJ*, 5 July 1805, 246.
44. *LNJ*, 30 August 1801 and 2 September 1801, 18.
45. *LNJ*, 1 January 1805, 191.
46. *LNJ*, 10 December 1801, 45.
47. *LNJ*, 24 February 1802, 62-63.
48. *LNJ*, 21 October 1801, 33.
49. *LNJ*, 22 August 1803, 173.
50. *LNJ*, 24 April 1802, 98.
52. *LNJ*, 26 December 1804, 219.
53. *LNJ*, 28 December 1801, 49.
54. *LNJ*, 4 August 1801, 13.
55. *LNJ*, 6 August 1801, 14.
56. *LNJ*, 13 April 1802, 90.
57. *LNJ*, 10 March 1802, 69.
58. *LNJ*, 22 January 1805, 220.
59. *LNJ*, 17 March 1802, 74.
60. *LNJ*, 4 January 1802 and 10 January 1802, both on 51.
61. *LNJ*, 8 April 1802, 86.
62. *LNJ*, 1 February 1802, 55.
63. *LNJ*, 2 June 1805, 238.
64. *LNJ*, 13 September 1804, 213.
65. *LNJ*, 17 June 1803, 163.
66. *LNJ*, 18 June 1803, 164.
67. *LNJ*, 26 June 1803, 165.
68. *LNJ*, 3 July 1803, 166.
69. *LNJ*, 4 March 1804, 198.
70. *LNJ*, 1 April 1805, 226.
71. *LNJ*, 2 April 1805, 227.
72. The source of this quotation could not be located. The Scottish millionaire was John Farquhar who had made his fortune as a British government contractor selling gunpowder in Bengal.
73. Eric Williams, *British Historians and the West Indies* (London: Andre Deutch, 1966), 196.
74. Ibid., 197.
75. Freyre, *The Masters and the Slaves*, 5.
76. *LNJ*, 25 December 1801, 48.
77. *LNJ*, 21 April 1802, 95.

AN INTRODUCTORY ESSAY
TO AN ADAPTATION OF FEDERICO GARCÍA LORCA'S
THE HOUSE OF BERNARDA ALBA
AND AN EXTRACT FROM THE ADAPTED PLAY
THE HOUSE AND LAND OF MRS. ALBA

"This requires reflection on the notion of translation itself. Where the meaning of the original work is not external to its language, translation can no longer be conceived as the reproduction of meaning in a more or less transformed linguistic setting. With the abstraction of meaning from the particular universe in which it constituted itself, the meaning is no longer that which it was."
Samuel Weber[1]

Edoh... edoh. edoh... oh oh oh oh!
Edoh, edoh
House an' land a-buy fam'ly on!
Edoh you no hear me on,
Me no have nobody on!
House an' land a-buy Fam'ly oh!
(A *Jamaican folk-song, whose theme is exactly that of García Lorca's original play.*)

A NOTE ABOUT ADAPTATION

The adaptation sets out to make correspondences clear. Not to translate the play from one language into another. It is an attempt to solve an almost insuperable difficulty that of making García Lorca's play "live" in an English version. So far, there have been two types of translation of the Lorca drama. One, the most widely used, translates the Spanish of the original into a realist urban language. Although actable, these versions capture only the surface events of the play, and leave their audiences puzzled as to what all the fuss is about. What's this Lorca kick? is the immediate reaction of many a theatre-goers after seeing an English version of any of the plays.

Much of the power of Lorca resides in his language. His choice and use of language respond to a definite intention – that of writing plays immediately reachable by the most educated and the most illiterate of Spaniards. García Lorca was born in the South of Spain and grew up amidst a rich folk tradition. He took part in the investigation and research into the folk poetry and folk songs of Spain, and in his plays recreated rhythms and cadences of speech familiar to the people. With this type of language he was able to deal with problems at once familiar and obscure – sexual frustration, fear of change, family ties that were as stifling as they were necessary. He did this not through realist reportage but with a lightning poetic intuition.

Lorca wrote for an audience still involved in an oral tradition. The associational impact of his language and imagery struck sparks from the unconscious level of response. The sun, the rain, drought, flood, are understood by the people of a traditional unindustrialised society, as economic forces. Their living depends on these forces. Natural forces, in the imagery of the people and of Lorca, play something of the part of an all powerful Fate. The people to whom such imagery is meaningful tend to accept the nature of their society as something decreed and comparable to the irrational inevitability of drought or flood.

To the man in the city, on the other hand, rain or drought is a mere inconvenience; water comes from the tap, bread from grocery store. The city itself, and the industrial process constitute an assault on the concept of an all powerful Nature. Its force is no longer inevitable. Language in such a society loses something of its elemental quality; it becomes a processed affair, instant, ready mixed. To translate a Lorca play into this kind of English is, in a way, a negation of translation. One has merely put certain English phrases and sentences in the place of Spanish phrases and sentences. Substituted a one-dimensional prose for the total response of Lorca's poetry.

Roy Campbell, on the other hand, has made some excellent poetic translations of Lorca's plays. But in his translation the plays are poetry, not drama. Like the realist translations, the poetic translations transfer Lorca's plays into a world where English is spoken, but a world which exists in a vacuum. Neither of these two types of translations transfer Lorca's plays to an *equivalent* world where the language spoken is determined by *equivalent* conditions and circumstances.

I have therefore made this adaptation somewhat along modified Brechtian lines. That is, I have examined the play in the original in order to identify the social, historical and economic determinants of the characters and their society. I have then put the play back together in a Jamaican locale and period where the determinants are roughly equivalent to those of the original play. In the 1930s when Lorca wrote his plays, Spain was, in relation to the rest of Europe, a traditional underdeveloped country. Wealth was still substantially based on land, agriculture. Yet the landowners were threatened with change, with industrialisation, political democracy, the rise of trade unionism, communism, socialism, republican and anarchist ideas. The society of the Albas is on its way down. The crisis of the daughter's lack of suitors is an economic crisis; it shows that the landowning class is short of cash.

In a traditional society the daughters have no "option" of a "career" or a role outside marriage. The tragedy of their situation lies in this fact. In the ordinary translations it is difficult for modern audiences to understand the lack of an alternative *life* for these girls. Too often then, the character of Mrs. Alba can seem mainly perverse. When in fact, she too is conditioned by economic and historical forces. Her class is in the grip of their long dying. Industrialisation is on the march.

To make the conflict explicit and possible I have placed the adaptation in a Jamaican locale in the early nineteen-twenties. Jamaica was then (and still is to a certain extent) an underdeveloped static agricultural society. Its stagnant colonial society is equivalent to the Spanish provincial society. I have used some of the elliptical qualities and cadences of the Jamaican dialect speech. A speech whose rhythms are still largely moulded in the context of an oral tradition.

In the adaptation I have imagined Mrs. Alba and her family to belong to the Jamaican plantocracy. This plantocracy is the descendant of the rich sugar barons of the eighteenth century when "Sugar was King" and Jamaica an extremely profitable and highly prized colonial possession. This class started its slow decline with the British Sugar Duty Act of 1846 which repealed the special position of Jamaican sugar on the British market. A few landowners still hang on to their land and the remnant of their power, but it's all rather motheaten. The society suffers the economic stagnation of all colonies. Things have not changed much, but with the First World War come and gone, the beginnings of change hover on the horizon.

As with Lorca's society – so with the Jamaican – relations between Mrs. Alba and her servants are still largely feudal. Yet the servants are beginning to express their resentment of a power which no longer seems to them as absolute as before. The landowning class is beset with falling prices. The land is losing its value and they face the erosion of their economic dominance, and therefore of their prestige. The values of their class, once underpinned by their economic supremacy, are no longer valid. They fight to maintain a façade. They brandish their outmoded values like banners, but their defeat is imminent. They and their values can no longer justify their existence.

Mrs. Alba then is depicted as, to borrow Lukács term, a "world-historical individual".[2] Her personal intransigence, her exaltation of the past, are gestures, not of an individual, but of an entire class. At the same time I have retained something of the peculiarly Spanish outlook. I have made the Alba family descendants of refugees who fled to Jamaica from Santo Domingo during the nineteenth century. Jamaica had been a traditional place of refuge for exiles from Cuba, Haiti, Santo Domingo, during the nineteenth century. Many of these families remain in Jamaica today.

They assimilated quickly to their equivalent class – the planter class. In the static colonial society of the twenties, the badge of the planter class, is the "whiteness" of skin which it shares with the occupying colonial power. Since there is little economic or social mobility, whiteness of skin becomes *the* status symbol. It is the visible symbol of the planters' power and glory. As the power vanishes and the glory with it, the symbol gets an even more desperate value placed upon it. To remain "white" is to assure oneself that nothing has changed, that the plantocracy is still in the saddle. Pride of caste in the original play is made more complex by pride of colour in the Jamaican context. Both spring from similar roots.

For the original Bernarda, a sense of honour is the patrimony of the well born. One fulfils the duties and traditional obligations of one's traditional class. One acts up to one's accepted value of oneself. The Jamaican equivalent of "honour" is the Victorian respectability which lingered much longer in the colonies than in Britain. Respectability is the mark of anyone who is not of the lower order. Virginity before marriage is the badge, *sine qua non*, of this respectability. A professed sensuality is taken to be the "curse" of the lower orders, the "black people", the "common canecutter". Respectability, like colour, was taken to be an end in itself. It marked out the "chosen" from the "damned"; separated the sheep from the goats.

Today in our more mobile society, the automobile, education, a degree, a profession, the house in the suburb, clothes bought in Miami, conspicuous consumption, honours awards are the status symbols. But "respectability", (i.e. saying, the expected platitudes) and "colour" are still valued as means to reach the room at the top. What is more dangerous, the presupposition that the "top" is white and the "bottom" black is still widespread. This confusion of values acts as a divisive force. It represents a dead value system which remains like yesterday's hangover. Our apparently easy and permissive society is shot through with private personal tragedies that spring from a confusion about colour, sex, a sense of identity. Yet there is little open dialogue about all this. In fact, there is a compulsive secrecy. A compulsive fear. To admit that these tragedies exist is to admit that there is something wrong with the system. To admit that there is something wrong is to take the first step towards changing it. And our society is gripped in a common post-independence paradox, the paradox of a people who having made certain fundamental changes in their way of life, are reluctant to push these changes to their logical conclusion. So they hang on to the recent status quo.

Our fear of dialogue is most marked when it centres about the confusions of colour and shade. We have taken political power away from the plantocracy. But we have not negated their value system in regard to the supremacy of white skin. In that way we have not been able to free ourselves from the legacy of the past. Because we are not free from the dead wood of the past we have not been able to utilise what was good and useful in it. We have remained then in an uneasy relationship to our past and to the remnants of this plantocrat class that remains. We secretly resent their presence at the same time as we worship their exploded values.

We make a convenient division into "them" and "us". They are the descendants of the oppressive slave-owning class, "we" are the descendants of the oppressed. We ignore that in the present arrangement of society, we carry in ourselves the oppressed and the oppressor, the exploited and the exploiter, the settler and the colonised, the master and the slave. The contradiction can only be resolved when we decide to change the present, to eliminate the difference. Once this decision is taken then we can look at the past and accept jointly the guilt and the glory. The victim is no less responsible for oppression than the oppressor. One oppresses, the other accepts his oppression. Both are joined together by a common landscape, speech, country, by a common set of historical circumstances. By the personal tragedies that afflict us through our acceptance of these circumstances. Our fear of examining them. Our refusal to change them.

The function of the theatre is to explode fears by bringing them out into the light of day. Lorca's play tapped the roots of the frustration of his Spanish audiences. It is to be hoped that this adaptation can perhaps reach through to the deeper areas of conflict of our own.

A NOTE ON THE CONCEPT OF PRODUCTION, SETS ETC.

The adaptation is, of course influenced by the theories of Brecht.[3] It accepts his view that there is no such thing as a "fixed and unalterable human nature".[4] That in fact, human consciousness is determined by social being, a social being that each individual helps to create. He helps to create this social being by his acceptance of, or revolt against, the particular economic and social arrangement of society which exists at the given period in which he has his being. He is himself conditioned by this arrangement of society. But he has free will to change the arrangement which conditions him. With the development of technology, as Brecht points out, this is even more true. Science "is in a position to change Nature to such an extent as to make the world seem almost habitable, man can no longer describe man as a victim, the object of a fixed but unknown environment. It is scarcely possible to conceive of the laws of motion if one looks at them from a tennis ball's point of view"[5]

Man, can use science to change the nature of his society, and the nature of his social being, and the nature of his consciousness. Because for various reasons he is reluctant to do so, he takes refuge in the outmoded and dead belief in the fixity of human nature determined and predestined by unseen forces. He relinquishes his free will in order *not* to respond to its challenge. He must therefore blind himself with illusion, in order to refuse to take that path from bondage to freedom, from ignorance to consciousness which is the central challenge of the century of technology. The theatre of the past, and even of today, Brecht insists, with its accent on "naturalism" is one of the avenues which Man uses to *escape* the truth. The theatre then, both in production and writing must seek to escape this flight to an illusion. As Brecht puts it:

Too much heightening of the illusion in the setting, together with a 'magnetic' way of acting that gives the spectator the illusion of being present at a fleeting accidental 'real' event, create such an impression of naturalness that one can no longer interpose one's judgment, imagination, or reactions, and must simply conform by sharing in the experience and becoming one of 'nature's' objects. The illusion created by the theatre must be a partial one, in order that it may be recognised as an illusion. Reality, however complete, has to be altered by being turned into art, so that it can be seen to be alterable and to be treated as such.

And this is why too we are inquiring into naturalness; we want to alter the nature of our social life.[6]

More than that, in writing and in production and in acting, the theatre must seek to uncover the prevailing laws of motions of the society which causes the individual to "be" what he is – whether he accepts this "being" or "rebels" against it. The theatre of the past tended to see things only from the tennis ball's point of view. The theatre of today must make explicit the forces which puts the tennis ball in motion. Naturalism in the theatre sets out to describe every tiny movement of the tennis ball. Therefore when it loudest proclaims truth, then it is being most untruthful. The movements of the tennis ball only have real meaning when it is seen in the context of the other tennis balls, and in the context of the society in which the tennis balls have their relative being. The society too must be seen in the context of the forces which keeps it in motion.

The alienation effects which Brecht advises then, tend to this particular purpose. To go behind the apparent surface of windmills to the deeper truth which lies behind. As he says:

...whereas in relatively stationary ('quiet') periods artists may find it possible to merge wholly with their public and to be a faithful 'embodiment' of the general conception, our profoundly unsettled time forces them to take special measures to penetrate to the truth. Our society will not admit of its own accord what makes it move. It can even be said to exist purely through the secrecy with which it surrounds itself.[7]

The main changes in the adaptation of the play have been made in response to these ideas. The social relationships of the characters, so magnificently brought out by Lorca, have been made more explicit. The social circumstances, the economic arrangement of the society which conditions these relationships are shown as a partial agent which causes people to act and react in a certain way. Because of this, the actions themselves explore and throw light on the relationships not only in the microcosm of Mrs. Alba's house, or in that of the island, but in the larger concept of the change-over from an agricultural to an industrialised society, from the value system that springs from the ownership of money.

This is the main aim of the build up of the past by Poncia and the Servant in Act One. Through them we establish the history of the economic and social forces in which the Alba family now finds itself enmeshed. For here, in the adaptation, it is these forces that are imagined to play the part of Fate. Mrs. Alba is tragic because she is ignorant of the economic forces which have entrapped her daughters. But she is also ignorant because it suits her self-interest to be ignorant. Thus, at one stage in the play when Poncia suggests to her a course of action which would avert the tragedy – i.e. that she should take a mortgage on her house and land as dowry for Adela – she insists that "that is the way things are". That is, she accepts predestination because it suits her self-interest to accept predestination. Later on, when Adela argues that the pearls in Angustia's engagement ring signify tears, she insists that "things turn out the way we want them to turn out". Here, in direct contradiction, she insists on "free-will" because it suits her self-interest to do so. She is then blinded by her own self-interest in an outmoded value system, and in an economic arrangement of society which stifles her daughters' lives. She accepts society and her own actions as given. She has and wants to have no idea of the effect of her actions and decisions on her daughters' lives. She prefers an illusion to true consciousness of circumstances that are to her unpalatable. She holds on to a past that has vanished but a past in which she was able to exercise an egotistic power. In the name of this ritual she sacrifices her daughters. Her blindness is none the less tragic because it is wilful. Modern tragedy springs from the wilful blindness of individuals to the responsibility that they have for events. A refusal of the consciousness of one actions, is a refusal of this responsibility. Modern tragedy springs from self-interested ignorance, from the refusal of a society to "admit what makes it move", since it owes the prevalence of its arrangement to the "secrecy with which it surrounds itself".

A SUGGESTION ABOUT SETS

The material objects in Mrs. Alba's house are the reality, the human beings and the props. Yet the material objects must be shown to be made and manipulated by the human beings in the first place. To show this, or to intimate it rather, I have imagined the acting area of the stage divided into three parts. A vestibule area, a central living room area, at a raised height if possible, and a pantry area. The vestibule area in which the play opens has the suggestion of an altar. When the area is lit up, the objects of veneration of the Alba family are crowded and piled on top of one another in the centre, pushed there whilst the servant cleans.

These objects are a rococo mirror in a heavy gilt frame, a large elaborate Hope Chest, and an antique chair. But although the objects are themselves solid, more solid than the people, although they are supposed to represent the solidity of the objects of those whose wealth and power come from the land, one must at the same time show that they are created by man; and received their value from the value he attaches to them. If they dominate his house and his life it is because he wants them to. Because of this, instead of a real mirror, a painting of such a mirror and a stand on which to hang the mirror are seen for what they are. When the Servant cleans and puts up the stand and hangs up the mirror as she talks, we see the household gods being put into position and manipulated by one of their victims. Her acceptance of their dominance is then seen. She is implicated by a sin of omission in their tyranny.

In the central living area, the portrait of Don Bernardo in its gold frame is equally a painting of a painting. And in this painting the gun which he holds can be outsize and out of proportion to the rest of the picture. The gun then and the cane can be real. But the importance given to the gun in the painting [an outsize papier-mâché gun in the manner of a modern painting which makes use of real, discarded objects stuck on to canvas] is to suggest the implication of a fate that springs from the structure and organisation of an ex-slave colonial society whose law and order must rest on the gun as its final authority. The gun with which Don Bernardo defended his power and wealth in Santo Domingo is the gun which leads to the death of his great-granddaughter. Built on violence, the family is destroyed by self-inflicted violence.

When we first see the living-room area, the furniture and painting and the stand on which it is to hang are pushed to the centre of the room and covered with a dust sheet. As Poncia tells of the past, she replaces the furniture, hangs up the painting and creates the present living room as she creates the past that led up to it.

The use of doors and windows are important to the set. But the important thing in this production would not be the walls which can be imagined, but the key door in the living room area, through which Miss Josie tries to escape, and one jalousie window which Bernarda opens and closes. These can be isolated. A pantry window in a frame from which they look out can also be used, but is not necessary. What must be conveyed is the very insubstantial quality of the house which so substantially dominates their lives. The claustrophobia can be suggested by the use of lighting to avoid the apparent truth of walls and reach for the deeper truth. The walls that close them in are not of wood nor stone but of a value system. Which its prisoners accept and to which they subscribe.

These are of course only suggestions. There are many more ways in which sets and production can be conceived. The point is to avoid in production as in acting that effect which Brecht describes as:

> a complete fusion of the actor with his role which leads to his making his character seem so natural, so impossible to conceive any other way, that the audience has simply to accept it as it stands, with a result that a completely

sterile atmosphere of *'tout comprendre c'est tout pardonner'* is engendered as happened most notably under Naturalism.[8]

Although then, I have kept closely in my adaptation to the original Lorca whose poetry achieves some of what Brecht's theories outline, I have made additions and changes. It is these additions and changes that compel a new approach to the usual Lorca production – a new approach which can keep in mind the guiding principles formulated by Brecht and along which I have attempted, however tentatively, to base my adaptation. These are:

> My whole theory is much naïver than people think... I wanted to take the principle that it was not just a matter of interpreting the world, but of changing it and apply that to the theatre.[9]
>
> The modern theatre mustn't be judged by its success in satisfying the audience's habits but by its success in transforming them. It needs to be questioned not about its degree of conformity with the 'eternal laws of the theatre' but about its ability to master the rules governing the great social processes of our age; not about whether it manages to interest the spectator in buying a ticket – i.e. in the theatre itself – but about whether it manages to interest him in the world.[10]

LIST OF CHARACTERS

In order of appearance

THE SERVANT: In her thirties. Thin. Black.

THE OLD WOMAN: Old enough to be almost beyond age. Black.

PONCIA: In her fifties. Sambo colour. Formidable, her will to power more subtly disguised than her mistress'. A devious malice underlying her identification with Mrs. Alba and her family.

THREE YOUNG WOMEN: Pre–1914 young women. They make brief appearance. Roles can be doubled by the three young women who come in as mourners.

MRS. BERNARDA ALBA: In her late fifties. White with some admixture of Negro. The harsh weather-beaten face of the tropical plantocracy. A most formidable woman.

ANGUSTIAS: Almost thirty. White. The daughter by Mrs. Alba's first husband.

THREE OLD LADIES: Range between white and near white in the familiar Caribbean spectrum of shades. In their sixties.

THREE YOUNG WOMEN: Somewhat darker shades than the old ladies but managing to appear white with powder etc. In their twenties. The mourners.

MAGDALENA: The second daughter of Mrs. Alba. The first by Mrs. Alba's second husband. Magdalena and her other three sisters are clearly darker than Angustias, with a Lena Horne colouring. Twenty-seven years old.

AMELIA: Twenty-five. The third daughter, insignificant.
MARTHA: Twenty-four. Hunchbacked. Sallow. Thin.
ADELA: Twenty. The beauty of the family.
VOICES OFF: The lead singer and the chorus of the canecutters. A labourer.
    The crowd.

ACT ONE: Early afternoon, the house of Mrs. Alba.
ACT TWO: Half an hour later. Same place.
ACT THREE: One month later. Late afternoon. Same place.
ACT FOUR: One week later. Mid evening. Same place.

The play is imagined to take place in the house of Mrs. Alba in a backwoods
parish of the backwoods island of Jamaica in the early nineteen-twenties.

Short Summary of the Plot of the Play
After the funeral of Mrs. Alba's second husband, Angustias, the only daughter
of Mrs. Alba's first marriage and the only one to have a considerable dowry,
receives a proposal of marriage from Peter Romans, a handsome but
impoverished fair young man. The jealousy of the four daughters of Mrs.
Alba's second marriage, and particularly the love of the youngest daughter,
Adela, for Peter, leads to Adela's tragic death. Mrs. Alba hypocritically
hushes up the "scandal" and refuses to admit the tragedy of the situation.

ACT ONE

The lights go up on the vestibule acting area of the stage. The chest is in
the centre of the acting area. On the chest is piled the stand, the painted
mirror. The straight-backed chair is pushed up beside the chest. The effect
is that of furniture piled up in the centre of a room, whilst the room is
cleaned. There are brooms, a bucket with water, and several rags and dusters
scattered about.

THE SERVANT is down on hands and knees shining the floor with a coconut
brush. She is tall, thin. Sexless, in a shapeless smock, her hair tied with a
faded rag. Barefeet. She works and moves with the weariness of one who
suffers from chronic malnutrition, yet she shines the floor with a piled-
up rage and resentment. Her face is set in a constant grim complaint even
when she is alone. Her eyes are bitter, but veiled by the hypocrisy of the
forcibly subservient. Mrs. Alba and the system affects them all with the
quality of cruelty.
    She is shining the spot where the mirror and chest is to go. She finishes
and gets up, putting her hand to her back and groaning as she does so.

She takes the stand off the chest and places it erect: she talks to the audience as she works:

SERVANT: This is Mrs. Alba's house. *She takes up the mirror.* Outside is Mrs. Alba's land. (*She gestures with a sweeping gesture*). Everywhere your eye fall on. Every corn stalk, cane stalk, guinea grass blade! Hill and gully, ruinate and cultivate. Everywhere your eye rest on, attach by law to Mrs. Alba's name. *She hangs the mirror on the stand.* This mirror with its gold frame is one of her household gods. *She pushes the chest to stand under the mirror.* And this mahogany chest in which her daughters guard their hope. Like dead flowers pressed in a book. *She positions a chair.* And this is a chair. An antique one. Too good for the likes of me to rest my worn-out body on.
She kneels. Rubs a piece of beeswax on her brush:
I am Mrs. Alba's servant. You see me often enough in my cap and apron. Or like this in my few rags when I clean. But as far as you are concerned you don't see me. You see a servant. You don't know my name. As far as you are concerned I don't need one. I am a servant and my name lies in my purpose. To serve Mrs. Alba's house, attend her gods. And when I die, manure her land.

She bends over and begins to shine the floor. Off, church bells toll for a funeral. The bells are cracked and tinny. The OLD WOMAN enters R. She is about ninety. Dressed in a collection of disparate rags. Bare dusty feet. Small wizened face and body, grey hair sparse and loose, the expression on her face between ecstasy and despair. She is an old beggar woman, yet not a typical old beggar woman. Grotesque, not picturesque nor folksily quaint.

Her shadow falls on the floor. The servant looks up and kneels back on her ankles. Her face is harsher, about to enjoy her display of power:

SERVANT: What you want? Who call you in here?
OLD WOMAN: I am hungry.
SERVANT: I am hungry too. That don't say I can walk into people's house as I have the mind. Look how you track up my polish floor with your dirty foot!
OLD WOMAN: I am on a long journey...
SERVANT: Then what you stop for? Keep on... Move!
OLD WOMAN: I am tired.
SERVANT: There's a grass bank outside the gate. Help yourself. But get out of Mrs. Alba's yard before I loose the chain and set the dog on you.
OLD WOMAN: I am a stranger here.
SERVANT: Go back to where you come from then.
OLD WOMAN: It's so long now I forget where...
SERVANT: Ask God. He will tell you where...

She rubs more beeswax on her brush, her reactions automatic.

OLD WOMAN: I can't find Him anywhere.

SERVANT: Find who?

OLD WOMAN: God.

SERVANT: God?

OLD WOMAN: I go up and down. To where the earth end. I ask and I ask. Nowhere I can find him.

SERVANT: Then what you want to find him for? What business you have with him?

OLD WOMAN: I want to ask him the meaning...

SERVANT: Which meaning? *She sucks her teeth, then sticks her finger in her mouth, pries out something from her teeth, wipes her finger on her dress, then leans over and continues shining the floor.*

OLD WOMAN: I wasn't always as you see me now. Long time back it wasn't so my life situate.

SERVANT: Long time back, long time gone.

OLD WOMAN: You should a-see me then.

SERVANT: I don't even care to see you now.

OLD WOMAN: I did have a piece of land. Narrow but it long. And a man. And children to care my old age. And a neighbour to give me good morning. To pass the time of day. A breadfruit tree. Coco leaf. Fat in the rain. St. Vincent and mosella yam. Till one day God lift his Hand.

SERVANT: The Lord giveth and the Lord taketh away. Blessed be the name of the Lord. (*She has been waxing her brush. Now she leans over and begins to shine the floor.*)

OLD WOMAN: One by one God lift His Hand. One by one I bury them. Till the ground full right up with the grave of my dead.

SERVANT: (*Sings as she shines*) Oh death where is they sting?
Oh grave thy victory?

OLD WOMAN: (*Angry*) Where I was to plant and sow? I was to eat bread that grow from their bone? Grief and hungry put it in my heart to find out...

SERVANT: To find out what?

OLD WOMAN: To stand face to face with God and ask him say: Why you do it? What reason you lay your hand heavy on me. Take away my generation from me – my sons of my sons? You leave me here, an old woman. Alone. With the pain in my back. The ice in your wind, the nail in your sun. Death to come catch me with not a soul to shut my eyelid, to weigh them down, to hold a wake and mourn for me?

SERVANT: And you ask Him?

OLD WOMAN: I start out to ask Him. I cut down trees and piled them on top. I climb up and up. All I see is johncrow wheel-a-wheel their shadow over me. All I see is that.

SERVANT: You can't miss that. Life is a dungle. Man is garbage. I can tell you that for a fact. And free of charge.

OLD WOMAN: But I climb down back. I fall down. I faint. My head spin like a top. But I hold on. And I walk and I walk to the end of the earth and to where the sea stop. And all the walk I walk, I ask. And all the ask I ask for God, not a soul could tell me where God was. I ask all the people and put my case. And all the people say: Eh, eh! Who you think you is that God should answer you, when he don't give answer to the rest of we? You think you know grief? Just listen to this... And this... (*Pause*) What you waste your eye water for, old woman? What make you different? So much time you bruise your mouth on the slammed door, you don't learn your lesson yet? Old woman, the All Besetting One sits on the back of all us. (*Pause*) And we cannot shake him off.

SERVANT: You didn't have to go the end of the earth to hear that... (*She straightens, kneeling and puts more wax on her brush*).

OLD WOMAN: I never obtain my desire. I never find God to answer my question. And the answer that man give break my heart.

SERVANT: Die then. It's easier.

OLD WOMAN: No. Not till somewhere in the world I find a man to answer my question.

SERVANT: And if God can't help you, is man you going turn to?

OLD WOMAN: Only he I have. (*The servant goes back to her polishing.*) Only he know my condition. (*The servant polishes with more vigour.*) I ... don't taste bread to my mouth since... since I don't even know when.

SERVANT: I don't taste none to mine neither, God see and know...

OLD WOMAN: Even a bread crust to mash between my gum, bring spit to my mouth...

SERVANT: Any bread crust I have is for my girl-pickney. She have to live. She young.

OLD WOMAN: I am old. And alone.

SERVANT: Dogs are alone. And they manage.

OLD WOMAN: Your heart is hard.

SERVANT: Life is hard. What's more I have my work to do. So just come off my polish floor, get out of Mrs. Alba's yard before I fling the bucket of dirty water over you. Move!

The old woman goes. The servant takes a cracker from her apron pocket, picks pieces of fluff from it then pushes it whole into her mouth. She chews with the gesture which comes from the relationship of a constant hunger to food. As she chews and shines the floor she talks to herself.

SERVANT: Damned mad woman! As if God have time to waste with her. With her damn fool question. No wonder black people always down and out. Look at Mrs. Alba. The only time she give God good morning is when she go to Church to marry, christen, bury or bow down before the Golden Calf of her house and land. Only black people sing psalms on Mount Zion with their naked back out of doors. Is only one answer God have for black people and is only one answer he should give them. So let me shut my mouth and break my back cleaning Mrs. Alba's floor. Until the day Death release me from bondage as he just done release the old wretch husband! (*Pause*) Want to find God! God!

She puts a hand to her forehead and groans with a deep grievance. Then she catches sight of Poncia who comes across from the pantry.

Poncia sambo-coloured. In her fifties. Long black dress, old fashioned cut even for the period. She wears a Jippi Jappa hat with a black band. She has a hunk of bread and a large piece of saltfish in her hand. She tears at these with a sharp hunger. She looks at the servant with an ironical eye. The latter is at once subservient, quick to excuse herself.

SERVANT: It's those bells Miss Poncia. They beat like a hammer in my head.
PONCIA: The funeral should be over in the next half hour. And Miss Bernarda will be on spot. So go on. Try!
She seats herself on the antique chair and eats between spurts of talk.
PONCIA: The church service went on and on. That long mouth parson beat his lip up and down. As soon as I saw my chance I slipped out. A big funeral though. The church look pretty with all the wreaths, the bunches of flowers. And pack! People from all over!
SERVANT: White people?
PONCIA: Or as near as they can manage. Plenty old women. Their skin crease and yellow like linen that fold away in a drawer and forget come out to sun themself like lizard. Cry into their handkerchief for the occasion. And the old men them. (*Pause*) Their few white hair paste on their brown skull. Prop over on their stick and flinging their spit as they sing the hymn and warm their old eyes on the young women's breasts. Mourn for the old days that no power can bring back... (*She kicks off one shoe then uses her foot to ease the shoe off the other. The servant shines away.*) Another funeral. Another old family gone. Another planter pass on without a son to come after to carry on the land. And the mortgage that the land stumble under.
SERVANT: They have land to mortgage. We have none.
PONCIA: We have a hole in the ground. Six feet long.
SERVANT: The only land we'll ever have.
PONCIA: We have our hands. We can eat bread by the sweat of our brow.
SERVANT: And how much so bread we get?
PONCIA: Enough. We wash it down with sweet water. Not with aloes. And sleep sound.
SERVANT: On a bed of bones.

PONCIA: With a man to warm our back.

SERVANT: Then walk off leave us with children to put food in their mouth.

PONCIA: But at least we know what it feel to hold our own flesh in our hand. (*She has finished eating, brushes crumbs away from her mouth, takes off her hat.*) All those high and mighty young ladies, drive up today in their broken-down buggies, you think they will ever know how it feel to hold baby to their breast? You should see them kneel in church. Their hands clasp under their dry face, their eyes open wide to search for a husband.

SERVANT: They find?

PONCIA: Find what? Which of the planters not married, ugly, old, bald or fat? Which of their sons don't run away from the land and the mortgage that the land carry like a hamper on its back? Which of them don't go away to England these days, get their education and never set a foot back?

The lights go down on the vestibule area until Poncia and the servant remain in the half dark. The lights come up on the living room area. The vestibule area is to the right corner of the central living room area which is raised. Three steps lead up from the vestibule to the living area. The pantry area is on the same level as the vestibule area and in the left hand corner, directly opposite to the vestibule. The exits and entrances from vestibule and pantry are imagined to lead from the vestibule to the front gate, from the pantry to the kitchen and the back gate.

In the living room area a door catacornered upstage R. is imagined to lead onto a front verandah. This is the door which signifies freedom to Miss Josie, the door through which the mourning guests enter. To the R. further downstage is the jalousie window, which is imagined to give on to the verandah, on to the street, and the outside door. Another door catacornered upstage left leads to a long passage, the bedrooms.

When the lights go up on the central living area all the props and furniture are piled up centre and covered by a dust sheet. Poincia comes up on to the living room, takes out a small table, and a small old-fashioned gramophone which she puts on the table, winds, opens, and puts the needle on the record. The record is cracked. It plays, but not too loudly, soldier's voices singing "It's a long way to Tipperary". Poncia hums the tune as she comes to sit on the step which leads from the living area to the vestibule. The servant continues her polishing:

PONCIA: How many of the planters' sons
Went off to fight in France?
How many of them?
How many of the young gentlemen?
To put the Kaiser in his place
To see that only British trade
Followed the British flag?
To guard the land... ?

Three young ladies dressed in 1914 styles, finery and fluttering ribbons from their hats, run gaily into the living room area. They carry Union Jacks in one hand, and knitted bags dangling from ribbon straps in the other. They wave the Union Jacks, then flutter it like a handkerchief at a departing ship. The music plays on:

PONCIA: The day that they left
The band played on...
The *Gleaner* newspaper
Praised them as heroes...
The young ladies waved them off
From the wharf...
Their fiancés were off
To the wars...
Glory filled their eyes
With salt!

The young ladies dab at their eyes with their Union Jacks, then go and perch primly on the dust sheet.

Determined they would
Do their part
To keep the home fires burning,
They rolled bandages...

The young ladies rip their Union Jacks in two, then roll them into bandages.

Until one by one, the telegrams
Rolled in...

The young ladies take telegrams from their bags. Open them, weep into the bandages.

The commanding officer
Sent his regrets
For a gallant young gentleman
Who would not come back
And sent back his effects
And a photograph
He had taken in France
Just before his death...

The young ladies take out framed photographs of young soldiers from their bags. They are draped in black crepe.

For the young ladies
To drape in black
And dust with the Union Jack...

The young ladies dust the photograph with the bandages, then kiss the photograph. The lights go entirely off the central living area, and come up on the vestibule where the servant polishes with her brush.

PONCIA: How many of the young gentlemen
Went off to fight
For King and country?
To keep the world map
Red with blood
To guard the land?
How many of the young gentlemen
Stayed on
Under the mud...?

The servant is squatting back on her heels. Rubbing wax on her brush.

Endnotes

1. Samuel M. Weber, "Translating the Untranslatable", Introduction to Theodor W. Adorno, *Prisms*, trans. by Samuel and Shierry Weber (1967; Cambridge, MA: MIT Press, 1981).
2. György Lukács, *Lenin: A Study on the Unity of His Thought* (Cambridge, MA: MIT Press, 1971).
3. John Willet, ed. *Brecht on Theatre: The Development of an Aesthetic* (New York: Hill and Wang, 1964), 37.
4. Brecht states, the human being "is alterable and able to alter", "The Modern Theatre is the Epic Theatre", ibid.
5. Brecht, "Can the Present Day World Be Reproduced by Theatre", in ibid., 275.
6. Brecht, "From the Mother Courage Model", in ibid., 219.
7. Brecht, "Building Up a Part: Laughton's Galileo", in ibid., 164.
8. Brecht, "From a Letter to an Actor", in ibid., 235.
9. Brecht, "Notes on Erwin Strittmatter's play *Katzgraben*", in ibid. 248.
10. Brecht, "A Little Private Tutor for my Friend Max Gorelik", in ibid., 161.

WE MUST LEARN TO SIT DOWN TOGETHER AND TALK ABOUT A LITTLE CULTURE

REFLECTIONS ON WEST INDIAN WRITING AND CRITICISM

CRITICISM CONSULTED

Wayne Brown, "The Novelist in an Unsettled Culture", *Impact* – A Publication of the Guild of Undergraduates, U.W.I.

W.I. Carr, "Roger Mais: Design from a Legend", *Caribbean Quarterly*, vol. 13, no. 1, March 1967.

Louis James, ed., *The Islands in Between – Essays on West Indian Literature*, (London: Oxford University Press, 1968).

T.W. Adorno, *Prisms*, trans. by Samuel and Shierry Weber (1967; Cambridge, MA: MIT Press, 1981).

George Lamming, *The Pleasures of Exile* (London: Michael Joseph, 1960).

I

For colonisation is a reciprocal process; to be a colonial is to be a man in a certain relation; and this relation is an example of exile.

George Lamming, *The Pleasures of Exile*

The article, "The Novelist in an Unsettled Culture", is written by Wayne Brown, a final year student of English at the University of the West Indies. The essay on Roger Mais, published in the *Caribbean Quarterly*, was written by W.I. Carr, a former lecturer in English on the Mona Campus. The collection of essays – *The Islands in Between* – is edited by Louis James, also a former lecturer in English there. The essayists are for the most part West Indian. Both Louis James and Carr are Englishmen. All, West Indian or Englishmen, are connected, in one way or the other, with the University of the West Indies. John Hearne, a writer who functions in this context as critic, runs the University's recently built Creative Arts Centre. But my concern is not with labels – English or West Indian, writer or critic – my concern is with connections. The first connection to be made is that the critical writing of the English-speaking Caribbean, as a body, is centred at and diffused from the university.

The second connection to be made is that this critical exploration is con-ducted, for the most part, under the guidance and within the perspectives of

English criticism. This itself reflects the fact, that the University, like the society, is a "branch plant industry of a metropolitan system".[1] In all such systems, the creators of original models, i.e. the writers, must cluster at the centre if they are to have the freedom and the opportunity to create. The third connection follows from this last – that whilst the critics are safely "home and dry" at the university, the writers are scattered, in exile. Already, in 1960, George Lamming foresaw the inevitability of his own exile. He wrote then:

> I am still young by ordinary standards (thirty-two to be exact) but already I feel that I have had it (as a writer) as far as the British Caribbean is concerned. I have lost my place or my place has deserted me.[2]

Even more recently, C.L.R. James said in an interview, in Paris, with the French newspaper *Le Monde*:

> The majority of us (writers in exile) keep on talking about the only subject which really explodes in our hearts – our native land. But as it becomes more and more of a dream, its contours fade, and when our people at home read what we have written about them, they cannot recognise themselves any more. They (the writers) will cut my throat for having said this, but it is the truth, as much for me as it is for them. I, who am old, have lived through this calvary, but they who are young, are only now undergoing theirs. Until my last breath, I shall refuse to accept that this exile will not have an end.[3]

These are naked statements. They are statements to which attention must be paid. To attend them, I must reveal my own connection, declare my interest.

I write, and writing is the impulse of my life. I am neither writer nor critic, neither playwright nor novelist. I am a Jamaican, a West Indian, an American. I write not to fulfil a category, fill an order, supply a consumer, but to attempt to define what is this thing to *be* – a Jamaican, a West Indian, an American. I believe that this definition is the beginning of awareness; the 'taking of consciousness' of being, as modern Latin American writers express it. Lamming, in the *Pleasures of Exile* worked towards this kind of awareness. He wrote,

> ...unawareness is the basic characteristic of a slave. Awareness is the minimum condition for attaining freedom.[4]

The Mexican writer Leopoldo Zea [Aguilar] sees the importance of this type of awareness at the national level. Up till now, he writes, Mexico was involved in action. But in action that was not aware of its origin or intention. Now Mexico had to enter into an awareness of its reality. To be aware of reality means that,

> we shall have to make ourselves aware of the springs which have moved hitherto irrational forces in order to direct them better. In this way we shall not fall for yet another Utopia.[5]

I share in this intention. I therefore cannot regard what I write as a fetish object called literature – a being in itself – to be deified under the static concept of Art for Art's sake. Like Roland Barthes, I cannot accept that culture is a piece of inexplicable magic, to be created by the artist, unconsciously, as medium, with the critic as High Priest and conscious interpreter.[6] I accept Brecht's thesis that in settled periods of history, culture – and literature which is its part, with criticism as its partner – can reflect reality. But that in traumatic times like ours, when reality itself is so distorted as to have become impossible and abnormal, it is the function of all culture, partaking of this abnormality, to be aware of its own sickness. To be aware of the unreality of the inauthenticity of the so called real, is to *reinterpret* this reality. To *reinterpret* this reality is to commit oneself to a constant revolutionary assault against it.

For me then, the play, the novel, the poem, the critical essay, are means to this end – not ends in themselves. Yet they are means which are at one and the same time, self-contained cells, and part of a dynamic living process. This process marks the path for the West Indian from acquiescent bondage to the painful beginning of freedom. Freedom means the rejection of "white lies" and the acceptance of the "black truth" of his condition. Our condition is one of uprootedness. Our uprootedness is the original model of the total twentieth-century disruption of man. It is not often appreciated that West Indian man, *qua* African slave, and to a lesser extent, white indentured labourer, was the first labour force that emergent capitalism had totally at its disposal. We anticipated by a century the dispossession that would begin in Europe with the Industrial Revolution. We anticipated, by centuries, that exile, which in our century is now common to all.

The exile of the writer, then, not only from the Caribbean, but from Latin America and from many other neo-colonial territories, is part of a general negation. It is part of a process of negation in which culture itself has been dispossessed. The Brazilian critic, Clarival do Prado Valladares, writing on the concept of Negritude, recently, commented:

> Whilst Western civilization considers art as a distinct activity which tries to reflect in the object, the interiority of the individual artist... tribal art, according to William Fagg, 'is completely integrated in tribal life and society'. It is a functional element of the social machinery and not a means of escape from the social machinery, as art is today, in all the rest of the world.[7]

He went on to consider the present state of tribal art in Africa. Now that the artist of Africa was drawn into "the culture industry" of the West, he had begun to lose the "virility of his motivation". This motivation had been to create art which expressed the collective thought and feeling of the tribe. Now instead the artist turned out traditional models of fecundity as "bibelots" for Europeans; and for the new European oriented elite-bourgeoisie of Africa. Even when a group of traditional craftsmen use old tools, and traditional musical instruments to create traditional arts, its excellence was negatived, because,

> . . .all this was being done through the motivation not of tribal but of tourist

art. The product, rightly called folkloric art was authentic up to a certain point. Beyond that point it lost its motivation, its aesthetic reason, and became marked with the travesty of the touristic object, which recalls an exotic origin, but which at the same time, serves the requirements of and responds to the imposition of the taste of the buyer.[8]

Tribal art in Africa and elsewhere is merely undergoing the dispossession of art and culture everywhere today. In the West, and the "free world" over which the West exercises dominance, culture has become a mere appendage to the market mechanism; another industry among others. In the Soviet Union, and the "fraternal" countries over which the Soviet Union exercises dominance, culture is a mere appendage to the mechanism of the established order. The Communist world makes this emphatically clear. Hence the "trial" of writers. The "free world" resorts to more subtle methods. It accepts its writers, encourages their heresies, acclaims them, pays them. It understands that the logic of the market mechanism tends to make the writer, as it makes what he writes, irrelevant.

Like the tribal artist today, the writer writes not for the tribe, but for the market. He produces not for man but for the consumer. By accepting the part of the man as the whole, the writer, and the artist, deny the humanity of man. In denying the humanity of man, he denies his possible brotherhood, his possible coming together as one. A multitude of consumers constitute not a group, to borrow Sartre's distinction, but a series of consumers, each waiting in line at the supermarket for their packaged cultural product. A multitude of consumers are the negation of a multitude of men. Art which accepts man as a consumer belongs to what Malraux calls, "the appeasing arts".[9] These arts, as Malraux points out, are not inferior arts. They are anti-art. Art is a vital and functional element of the dynamics of a society, that which unites men – the more than bread by which they live. Anti-art, whether expressed in the James Bond novels, or the French anti-novel, the very latest avant of the avant garde, helps men to escape from the reality of a society which they have fashioned; which now fashions them; and which they can no longer endure. "Good art", said Tolstoy with prophetic insight, "is that which serves the religious perception of our times – that of the unity of mankind".[10] "Bad art" is that which disserves it. The appeasing arts, says Malraux – the cinema, the soap opera, the television serial, invite men to escape to an illusion.

The appeasing arts are not confined to the lowest possible denominator. Just as there are consumers of all grades – Top people take the Times and a bold new breed wears buffalo jeans – so there are "appeasing arts" of different brands and different quality. In art, as in other goods produced for the market, the connoisseurs are those who recognise "fine" art by its delicate bouquet, its esoteric genealogy, its abstruse rationale. The top grade consumer-connoisseur is deadly opposed to the inferior brands of the appeasing arts which constitute mass culture. He may have accepted James Bond, because although the masses accepted him too, James Bond was in his way a connoisseur, too. A lowbrow in ideas but with highbrow consumer tastes in food, women and cars. To accept James Bond was the most complex and U form of inverted snobbery. The highbrow, who slummed for a while with Bond in high-class beds, could return to highbrow ideas in volumes tooled for the anti-philistine. And of course, the middlebrow consumer has his middlebrow brand and line all nicely catered for. The essential factor was that both high and middlebrow could be made to feel that they belonged to an elite. Nothing tops silvertop gin and only the elect of the intellect could savour it without sin. The writer who consciously sets out to write for an elite is as much involved in the appeasing arts as the writer, who, wanting to write "for the people" falls into the trap of writing for the consumer.

The concept of "people", better expressed by the Spanish "pueblo", is fast vanishing. The writer who returns from exile at the metropolitan centre to "write for his people"; to seek with them to "break out of identity imposed by alien circumstances", and to find a new one, must come face to face with the fact that his "people" has become the "public". And the public in the Caribbean, equally like the public in the great metropolitan centres, are being conditioned through television, radio, and advertising, to want what the great corporations of production in the culture industry, as in all others, have conditioned them to want. Returning from exile at the metropolitan centre, the writer all too often finds that he returns only to another example, another facet of exile. Yet by not returning, the writer continues to accept his irrelevance.

I returned. I returned because I had no choice. I could not write, my talent did not suffice, except I could return to the lived experience of my own corner of reality. I accepted that writing would have to be done in the interstices of my time. For my writing was not a marketable product in the "branch plant society" to which I returned. My interpretation of one aspect of European literature could be sold. I had the Good Housekeeping label of a metropolitan university. If the label had been marked English literature rather than Spanish, I would be able to function in my own society as an interpreter of West Indian literature rather than of Spanish literature. But within the "branch plant" arrangement of my society and its university, I (and others infinitely more gifted than I am) would have no possibility to function as the *creator* of any such writing.

Given my particular position, I cannot pretend to objectivity nor impartiality in my approach to these critical essays. Nor can I pretend to function purely as a critic in relation to them. I prefer to bear witness to my own reaction on reading what is after all a feedback report on the body of writing now labelled West Indian. And my first reaction on reading these essays was that this critical body of work confronted us with a paradox, at once so simple and so complex, that it staggers the imagination; until one remembers that in the upside-down reality in which we have our being, paradoxes are "normal". For what they show us, these essays, is that the books, as the products of the writers, have a function, at least in academic circles. There they are transformed into texts. West Indian books have a function in West Indian society. West Indian writers have none.

Since the texts are there, to be explained, interpreted, accepted, dismissed, the interpreter replaces the writer; the critic displaces the creator. Yet in displacing the creator, he diminishes his own validity. Criticism is a part of culture and not its instant powder substitute. When the creative instinct is stifled or driven into exile, the critical facility can survive only as maggots do – feeding on the decaying corpse of that which gives it a brief predatory life. The exclusion of the West Indian writer from West Indian life has even more far-reaching implications than the agony of exile undergone by the writer himself. It implies the acceptance by us all of a "bewitched reality". It implies our acceptance of an arrangement of society in which the writer, in order to find a way of functioning, must go to the metropolitan centre. It implies our complicity with the commissars of the market system. The Communist commissars send their dissident writers to prison. The market commissars, by inducing writers to find outlet and function only at the metropolitan centre, send them into exile. We come to terms with our "branch plant" existence, our suburban raison d'être.

To be a colonial, says Lamming, is to be a man in a certain relation. A suburban is a man without a being of his own; a man in a dependent economic and cultural relation with the metropolis. To be in that relation is an example of exile. The air of inauthenticity which pervades the West Indian University springs from the fact that the university, like its society, only much more so, is in exile from itself. Like Caliban, as Lamming sees him in the *Pleasures of Exile*, the university has no self which is not imposed on it by circumstances. Many of these critical essays, which embody the University's criticism of West Indian writing reflect, and parallel, this inauthenticity. Some do not.

II

We have met before. Four centuries separate our first meeting when Prospero was graced with the role of thief, merchant and man of God.

Lamming, *The Pleasures of Exile*[11]

In his long and detailed introduction to *The Islands In Between,* Louis James, as editor has only this to say about the exile of the West Indian writer:

Seen against the various tensions of the area, it is not surprising that many creative Caribbean writers moved away from the West Indies to see their predicament in perspective... V.S. Naipaul – who entitled an account of his visit to his ancestral homeland *An Area of Darkness* (1964) – and Samuel Selvon, left permanently for England. Into exile in London too, went many other creative West Indian writers, including George Lamming, Wilson Harris, Andrew Salkey and Edgar Mittelholzer.[12]

Why does Louis James accept and pass over, as a given fact, a connection without which West Indian writing cannot be properly explained? For James cannot be accused, as W.I. Carr can be, of refusing to see literature in the context of a given time and place. Indeed much of his introduction is given over to a historical sketch of the area which produced West Indian writing, and of the circumstances which helped to define it. Yet this historical sketch is distorted by James' essentially "branch plant" perspective – a perspective that views the part for the whole; that adjusts new experience to fit an imported model, with a shift here and a shift there; that blinds its horizons in order not to perceive the logical and ultimate connections that would invalidate the original model that had formed his being and distorted his way of seeing. The "branch plant" perspective is the perspective of all the "appeasing arts", and of their corollary, "acquiescent criticism".

What do we mean by this? James does not hesitate to point out the colonial background to West Indian writing. No West Indian, however passionate and anti-colonial, could fault him on this. He says all the right things, makes all the right genuflections. He praises the British presence in the Caribbean,

> Only an extremist would deny the positive contributions to West Indian social and political life made by England. They are ubiquitous, and deeply ingrained, far more so than in Africa or India. English education opened up a cultural heritage which reached beyond England to Europe, beyond Europe to Asia and Africa. It provided a highly developed tool of language with which a writer like Walcott could explore his own unique predicament, just as the British liberal traditions formed the basis for the struggle for independence from England.[13]

Louis James is quick to adjust the balance with this:

> At the same time the English traditions could be destructive. Petrified within the social structure as the standards of respectability they could also, as we have noticed, divide class from class, and constrict the evolution of national ways of life.[14]

If we examine both the praise and the dispraise, we shall find that James has really evaded the issue. He has, to use a just phrase of T.W. Adorno "parries by not parrying".[15] No one, in reading both accounts could fail to see on which side the balance tilts in favour of England and her "positive contributions". Yes, an English education provided Walcott with a highly developed tool of language to explore a "unique predicament" which England's economic interest had created, a predicament which had profited her. If British liberal traditions formed the basis of the West Indian's struggle for independence, it was the British anti-liberal tradition which, by making him colonial, caused him to have to struggle in the first place. From this long and anti-liberal tradition England also profited. Her "destructive English traditions" which divided class from class, were there to serve a purpose; to continue an economic and political arrangement which profited her. The more they profited her, the less they profited the West Indies. The end result is an arrangement by which, with independence attained, the majority of the West

Indians were illiterate. The writer wanting market and audience had to go to England; as the West Indian emigrant wanting a living wage had to go to England. As the West Indian University, wanting skilled personnel, had to turn to England. The presence of Louis James in the Caribbean and the absence of the writer in London are part of the same historical process.

The distortion of Louis James's perspective comes from his avoidance of this connection. He sketches the history of the Caribbean from an Archimedean point outside the historical process. Yet it is a process in which he is as involved as is the West Indian. This pretended objectivity and detachment is the common stance of what I call, for convenience, the "acquiescent critic". In attempting to write from outside the process, in pretending detachment, the "acquiescent critic" accepts the status quo, by accepting his own fixed point outside it. He falls into the trap of which Adorno spoke:

> He, the cultural critic speaks as if he represented either unadulterated nature or a higher historical stage. Yet he is necessarily of the same essence as that to which he fancies himself superior. The insufficiency of the subject... which... passes judgement... becomes intolerable when the subject itself is mediated down to its innermost makeup by the notion to which it opposes itself as independent and sovereign.[16]

James, as an English teacher teaching in a West Indian university, passing judgement on West Indian writing, is mediated to his bones by the colonial experience, by the colonial myth in which he is as involved, though in a different role, as is the West Indian.

It is Lamming the writer and the West Indian, and not James the critic and the Englishman, who sees this vital connection. James's criticism, in the final analysis, is there to reinforce the status quo; Lamming's is there to question it. Lamming, the questioning critic, cannot take fixity as his stance; he knows himself and his perspective moulded by a historical process imposed on his being. He writes from a point of view inside the process. He knows that he does. Awareness is all. In the *Pleasures of Exile*, he begins his historical sketch of the Caribbean quite differently from James. He speaks to James, not at him. "We have met before," Lamming tells him. "Four centuries separate our first meeting..."[17]

III

"Behind everything is imperialism," Edgar said.

"Forget imperialism," Capleton snapped. "We don't have any guns, or planes."

"Why forget imperialism," Ramsay thought.

Neville Dawes, *The Last Enchantment*[18]

History was built around achievement and creation and nothing was created in the West Indies.

V.S. Naipaul, *The Middle Passage*[19]

Mouche affirmed that there was nothing here worth looking at or studying; that this country had neither history nor character.

Alejo Carpentier, *The Lost Steps*[20]

In *The Pleasures of Exile* Lamming performs the highest function of criticism. He *opens* for us Shakespeare's play, *The Tempest*. He reveals extensions of meaning that have hitherto avoided us. He does this by involving himself, a twentieth-century Barbadian Negro, within the context of the play. He brings "immanent criticism" to a new height; that is he reveals the qualities that the play has as "an end in itself" by paradoxically placing it firmly within the context of the adventure of its time. He says:

> I see *The Tempest* against the background of England's experiment in colonisation… And it is Shakespeare's capacity for experience which lead me to feel that *The Tempest* was also prophetic of a political future which is our present.[21]

Lamming places *The Tempest* within the process of England's creation of Empire. *The Tempest*, he shows us, was as much the cultural expression of England's adventure, as were the voyages of Drake and Hawkins its economic expression. It is the measure of Shakespeare's genius that at the height of England's – Prospero's – intoxication, he should have been aware of the dimension of Caliban's tragedy: "That when I waked,/ I cried to dream again".[22]

It is the measure of Lamming's critical insight that he sees this as the beginning of a *cultural* connection that was not separate from the economic, but lay at its very heart. To elucidate this connection Lamming begins to chart for us "the triangular course of that tremendous Voyage which swept Caliban from his soil and introduced him to Heaven through the long wet hell of the Middle Passage." This is the beginning of an African's history as Caliban; and of Hawkins's as Prospero. Both, after that voyage, had suffered a sea-change and had been transmuted into something terrible and strange. The history of neither Caliban nor Prospero can be understood from now on, outside of that relationship.

Lamming points out that from the start it was a relationship based on violence in the name of commerce. He does this merely by quoting Hakluyt:

> … and got into his possession, *partly by the sworde, and partly by other meanes, to the number of 300 Negros at the least, besides other merchandises which that countrey yieldeth. With this praye he sayled over the Ocean sea unto the Iland of Hispaniola and arrived first at the port of Isabella.*[23]

Thus we had "the Middle Passage". A triangular trade spelling profit for all those of Prospero's race who survived the crossing. And spelling loss far all of Caliban's – for those who died, in their millions, for those who survived to inhabit a brave New World, for those who remained behind to wage inter-necine war, to trade their kith and kin in exchange for Prospero's symbol of power, his magic wand – the gun.

I have quoted Naipaul's statement about history in the West Indies. It is an often quoted statement. Louis James begins his historical introduction with this statement. W.I. Carr, in his long and illuminating article on Roger Mais, also quotes the statement, and comments:

> I used to feel that this summed it all up, and I partially reject it now, because it seems to me too much of a comment upon the present, or upon the effort possible in the present. Naipaul seems to be inviting one just to get up and go away.[24]

The quotation by both these critics of a judgement made by Naipaul in his travel book the *Middle Passage* is a comment as much on the critics as it is on Naipaul. But a distinction must be made. James begins with this comment which, when examined, really implies a division pointed out by Sartre:

> Not so very long ago, the earth numbered two thousand million inhabitants; five hundred million men, and one thousand five hundred million natives. The former had the Word; the others had the use of it.[25]

Louis James contradicts this division later in the section headed "Unconquerable Spirit", and in the quotation from C.L.R. James which he uses:

> One has to hear with what warmth and with what volubility and at the same time with what precision and accuracy of judgement this creature, heavy and taciturn all day, now squatting before the fire, tells stories, talks, gesticulates, argues, passes opinions, approves and condemns both his masters and everyone who surrounds him.[26]

That is Louis James opposes to the dangerous division of Naipaul – *Men* make history; *Natives* don't – a section in which he sketches the development and the creation from African beliefs and fragments of the "coherent" culture which at first he denies. What gave coherence to this culture was its revolutionary intention. If in the day Caliban laboured and worked in order to create the economic base for the dazzling progression of "achievements" of Prospero, at night he became a man once more. His folk songs, his folk dances, his calypso with its satiric intention, his dances, imitating the white dances, transforming them with the heavy rhythm whose survival assured the existence of his being, constituted a nightly revolution against the reality to which he was condemned. One sees the acuteness of Adorno's comment that because culture "arises in men's struggle to reproduce themselves…" it "contains an element of resistance to blind necessity".[27] This Caliban, transformed at night before the fire, talking, singing, involved in ritual and religion which was still arranged around a spiritual altar of African gods, created the culture out of which the Haitian revolution, fused into an equally revolutionary European cultural tradition, sprang. The night gathering about the fire had tremendous relevance. Around the fire the Native took hold of the Word. And it was His Word in his own mouth, fired by his own dream. By making use of the Word, as Lamming shows, Caliban had initiated his first act of revolution against Prospero. He had appropriated Prospero's language, as Prospero had appropriated his labour, thinking to appropriate his being. But his being survived and returned Prospero's language, changing for ever its meaning. The cultural tradition out of which the West Indian, who is fed by the Caliban culture of the West Indies, writes, is an inherently revolutionary one. That was always its intention.

Louis James has glimpses of this. But by the arrangement of his material, he sees as subsidiary that which is really central. Because of this he misses certain implications. He quotes Brathwaite at the head of his introduction:

> For we
> who have cre-
> ated nothing,
> must exist
> on nothing...[28]

He uses this to reinforce Naipaul's statement, rather than seeing it as an ironic comment on it. For Naipaul's concept of history is nothing more than a reflection of Naipaul's terrible enchantment by what Louis James himself calls "the brilliant myth of Europe".[29] Gordon Rohlehr, in his excellent essay on Naipaul, uses the critical approach of Lamming. He explains Naipaul in the context of Trinidad. But he points out this retrogression in sensibility and interprets the connection between the man and his world. He sees the *Middle Passage*, compared to *Biswas*, as revealing "a sensibility which is itself a part of the colonial experience in which Naipaul had been, and is still, involved."

> Naipaul is a Trinidad East Indian who has not come to terms with the Negro-Creole world in Trinidad, or with the East Indian world in Trinidad, or with the greyness of English life, or with life in India itself where he went in search of his roots.[30]

The validity of Naipaul, even in a maimed book like *The Middle Passage*, comes from his own personal involvement in the "horrors" which he describes. His sense of unreality, his revulsion in India as in Trinidad, is his intuitive and terrible response to the colonial experience. The fact that India and Trinidad and the rest of the Caribbean are now "free"; that they have a flag and an anthem, are not any proof to Naipaul that things have changed. Indeed, in a sense, they have got worse. Naipaul's value is his true and certain geiger response to a situation. His danger lies in another facet of the colonial experience – his constant misinterpretation of this unreality, and its source. On his return to Trinidad, Naipaul was caught up in an increasing "poverty of culture" which Oscar Lewis had recently shown is endemic to the early states of industrial capitalism. In this sense, although Trinidad had made more economic progress since independence than in all her British years, she too, like the rest of the Caribbean, like India, like England herself, has entered a vast dispossession.

Naipaul's insights into this dispossession, whether in travel book or in his novels, are acute. His honesty impels him to experience this dispossession through his own being, and not alone describe it in others. Yet his animus against the Negro sharpens his eye for the Negro's dispossession. In spite of himself, this revelation has a revolutionary intention. His portrait of Eden in *The Mimic Men* takes us back to the implications of Lamming's analysis of the relation between Prospero and Caliban. In *The Mimic Men*, Ralph Singh, a Trinidadian Indian and failed politician, takes refuge in London. His escape is merely the conclusion of a flight that had begun long ago in Trinidad when, by changing his name – Ranjit Kripalsingh to Ralph Singh – he had denied his being and accepted a basement bargain status in the "white-Christian Anglo-Saxon-educated, rich" continuum of Prospero, his flight conditioned by the cultural myth through which Prospero exercises his domination; the cultural myth which had taught Singh (and Naipaul) nothing but reverence for Western power and the psychological basis of Western power, referred to by Sartre as "that other witchery of which I have already spoken, Western culture".[31] Now, refuged in his London hotel, Singh recalls the past with a dry telling of the beads. The most successful part of the book is this evocation of the past – of days at school when four boys, one of whom was Singh, had tried to escape from the stereotypes which the cultural myth of Prospero had used to keep them in happy subjugation. One of the four boys was Eden.

> Eden was something of a buffoon. He was the blackest boy in the school and for some time was know as Spite… His reputation as a buffoon and his special relationship with Deschampsneuf had been established early… Eden had fixed on Asia as the continent he wished to travel in; he had been stirred by *Lord Jim*. His deepest wish was for the Negro race to be abolished; his intermediate dream was of a remote land where he, the solitary Negro among an alien pretty people, ruled as sort of a sexual king.[32]

The myth, devised by Prospero, as the magic to prop up his power, had sold to Eden the emasculation of his spirit. The myth, by emasculating his spirit, conditions his compensatory dreams and fantasies. Once his dreams have been conditioned, Prospero grants him freedom of speech; Prospero grants him the vote, a national flag, an anthem. He is sure now that Caliban will speak only to deny himself; vote only to abolish himself. Yet the system breeds its contradictions. For Eden, leaving school, becomes envious when Deschampsneuf gets a job in a bank and he can't. The rage at not being able to handle money, the new magic wand, the new gun, festers. It is forgotten in the daily round. Until Ariel, in the person of Naipaul, in *The Mimic Men* returns Eden-Caliban to himself. Eden, once made aware of his emasculation, will grope back to his pristine dream of freedom. When he gives tongue to his dream it will be the more terrible for having been denied so long. Eden will speak then with the voice of the young black American, Eldridge Cleaver,

> We shall have our manhood. We shall have it, or the earth will be levelled by our attempts to gain it."[33]

The Calibans, their past appropriated, their present distorted, are determined to have the future. They have a right to it. The Cuban poet Retamar writes:

> You were right Tallet. We are men of transition.
> Between the whites…
> And the nocturnal blacks, blue at times, chosen through
> Terrible proofs; only the best survived
> The only superior race on the planet.[34]

The history of the Caribbean is a history of survival. It is only the "racist humanism" of Europe, as Sartre calls it, that sees history in European terms only – history as achievement and creation. Yet as Alejo Carpentier shows in his novel *The Lost Steps*, the creation of Beethoven's Ninth is an essential *corollary* of the negation of Auschwitz. Naipaul accepts the racist definition of history with the part of his intellect that is crippled by it. As Rohlehr says:

> It (Naipaul's Englishness) manifests itself, rather, in his unconscious acceptance of a typical European view of Third World inferiority… It shows itself in his contemptuous rejection of all things West Indian…[35]

Naipaul's self-hatred, foisted by the cultural myth which he has accepted, ugly in some of its manifestations, is yet an essential part of his talent. His own torment provides him with a scalpel with which he dissects, with the precision of a Fanon, if without his understanding and clear intention, the state of Caliban's and Ariel's descendents. *Biswas* is essentially a tragedy of dispossession. The disintegration of Hanuman House is the disintegration of the last decaying remnants of Hindu culture. Distorted as Tulsidom is, struggling to survive in a new world where the sole economic motive has made irrelevant all the customs and traditions by which the Indian had affirmed his being in his exile, it yet provided a shelter for many of the others, who, unlike Biswas could not make the adjustment to "creole" culture and the competitive ethic. Hanuman House, stagnant and evil, is swept away as Biswas enters his house. It is not accidental that Naipaul kills him off. Like Don Quixote, with his madness gone, Biswas might have woken up to find his house a cage. With the house and the Prefect car, Biswas has entered suburbia. The Tulsis, the human enemy, have been replaced with the remote gnomes of Zurich, and the vast and all embracing Hanuman Headquarters in which all the Biswases are now imprisoned.

In this new Hanuman House, it is Caliban who is still subversive. For Biswas has learnt to write. He is now a journalist, and has the Word, even if that Word is conditioned by the consumer, Biswas has taken his place as the Ariel of the system. Caliban cannot. Even in this new house, he is still on its lowliest floor. He is the base on which the superstructure is erected. His is the negation that makes possible the dazzle of the culture industry. Lamming shows the beginning of the myth and its reality in Shakespeare's *Tempest*. At the heart of the myth is what Adorno calls "the original sin"[36] of all culture: *the separation of mental from physical work.* It is the original sin at the heart of the relationship between Prospero and Caliban. Caliban is not himself without guilt. Caliban, a version of cannibal, was for Shakespeare, the original Carib in the New World. Ariel was perhaps, the Arawak, the innocence of the younger stages of a culture when progress and advance is not bought at the expense or the negation of others. The Caribs, on the other hand, were predators. They kept young boys whom they captured from other tribes, castrated them, and brought them up as slaves until they were fat enough to be eaten. It is interesting to note that some observers on Columbus's first voyage found the Caribs, i.e. the cannibals, the predatory, warlike, warmongering tribe to be

> in some ways more civilised than the inhabitants of other islands even though they did not appear to possess any gold. Their houses were better built, their weapons very well made, and their cotton was just as skilfully woven as the best Spanish cloth.[37]

Caliban's mother had enslaved Ariel. The advanced culture of Caliban, like the advanced culture of Greece and that of Western civilisation, has been created at the expense of slaves and helots of all times and all races. The more "advanced" the culture, the more its original sin. Prospero enslaves Caliban; as the representative of a more powerful and advanced culture, his enslavement of Caliban is more total. His culture depends on Caliban's labour. To get Caliban to accept this conversion of himself into brawn, muscle, body; to get him to consent to this division of labour which gave brainwork and the fabrication of cultural myths to Prospero and manual work to Caliban; even more, in order to rationalise to himself this inherent injustice, Prospero creates a stereotype and sells this stereotype to himself, Miranda and Caliban. Lamming notes the constant sadism with which Prospero brainwashes Caliban.[38] He quotes Prospero's speech:

> But as 'tis
> We cannot miss him; he does make our fire
> Fetch in our wood and serves in offices
> That profit us. What ho! slave! Caliban
> Thou earth, thou! Speak![39]

Prospero wants only answers to his summons, respectful obedience to his orders.

By calling Caliban "earth", as Adorno shows in his analysis of culture's guilt, Prospero, the anti-Philistine, throws on Caliban the guilt of his own oppression. He distorts Caliban into pure body. As pure body, Caliban performs his first revolutionary act. He attempts to rape Miranda. Mervyn Morris, a West Indian and a writer, in one of the most "acquiescent" and depressing essays in *The Islands in Between*, dismisses the *Pleasures of Exile* in almost the same tone and language with which the English critics destroyed Lamming once he broke out of the pattern, analysed the West Indian scene through its relationship with England; and the English scene through its relationship with the

West Indies. It is the connection that is at the heart of the imperial myth. Once the connection is clear, the myth is in danger.

Morris, mediated to his bones by the limiting pragmatism of modern English criticism, by the pragmatism of "decent" modern English prose which accepts "reality" and makes no attempt to explore its contradictions, dismisses *Pleasures of Exile* as "a rag-bag collection" of essays,[40] and has this to say:

> ... the discussion of *The Tempest* scarcely illuminates the play, assuming without evidence that Caliban is black, eagerly discussing whether he did try to lay Miranda, and inquiring into the absence of Prospero's wife.[41]

The discussion of Caliban's attempt to rape Miranda is at the heart of the racial myth which is shattering the world today. Lamming discussed it in 1960 and was a precursor of what is now a commonplace. But what particularly condemns Morris and his easy dismissal is the terms in which Lamming discusses this rape. He points out that Caliban, still involved in his dream of freedom, wants to rape Miranda with a positive intention. His motive is not revenge. "I had peopled else", and Lamming quotes, "this isle with Calibans".[42]

His issue would have been the reunion of body and brain – the reunion of two stereotypes, the white man with his burden and the black man with his minstrel song. The reunion would have shattered the stereotypes, the division between mental and physical work, the original sin at the heart of all society, all culture. Caliban's dream impelled him towards wholeness: "... that, when I waked, / I cried to dream again".[43] It is this dream that Morris, locked in his too-English, neat, not garish, language and *Weltanschauung*, forgets. It is this forgetting that inhibits Morris's exploration of his own talent.

Morris, like Naipaul, comes to too-quick terms with the "brilliant myth of Europe"; with its concept of what is culture and what is history. W.I. Carr is perhaps the most subtle and consistent propagator of the concept of culture through which the cultural myth of Europe exercises its dominance. As we shall see, Carr belongs to the kind of cultural criticism that Adorno identifies:

> But the greatest fetish of cultural criticism is the notion of culture as such. For no authentic work of art and no true philosophy, according to their very meaning, has ever exhausted itself in itself alone, in its being-in-itself. They have always stood in relation to the actual life-process of society from which they distinguish themselves.[44]

In his essay on Mais, Carr sets out to disassociate Mais from the material processes of life. By accepting culture as a deified object, enthroned in ritual, whose communal sustaining belief has long since vanished, except for a handful of the elite who believe with their intellects, this kind of critic, like Spengler,

> ... severs culture from man's drive to survive. For him it becomes a game in which the soul is its own playmate.[45]

Morris, although to a lesser extent than Carr, accepts this concept of culture. So does Louis James, although with some reservations, and so does Cameron King who is co-author with James of the essay on Derek Walcott. Hearne, in his essay on Wilson Harris, is a clear exponent of this concept, almost in spite of himself. Wayne Brown in the article in *Impact* shows himself a disciple of Carr, with the imagined consequences – although here and there an original and thinking mind tries to break through the "witchery" called Western culture, sold to him by Carr. These are for me essentially "acquiescent" critics – critics who reflect and parallel the inauthenticity of the university and its society. Against these, Lamming's *Pleasures of Exile*, Rohlehr on Naipaul, Creary on Mais, move towards genuine criticism – and therefore towards illumination rather than that mystification which is at the heart of the "brilliant myth of Europe".

The poem of Césaire which is the manifesto of Negritude, which Lamming quotes, and which Brathwaite echoes – and James quotes without perceiving its implications – is an attack on the concept of man as a producer-consumer. The Negro with his stubborn holding on to a tribal integrated philosophy and culture, through its fragments, rhythm, dance, song, would fit in, like the Catholic with his medieval memory, uneasily. We who have created nothing is *not* a negative statement, as is Naipaul's. It is the very negation of what Naipaul has said. History is not a building, fixed in place and time, its bricks the dates of each achievement, the records of things created, its cement the blood of victims and victimisers; history is the history of man's attempt to fulfil his being, his resistance to being reduced to producer/consumer, producing finally the atomic bomb which waits to consume him. "Eia for we who have created nothing",[46] like Caliban's attempted rape of Miranda, is an assault against all culture which accepts as the price of its existence the negation of any part of man's being. It is, like Caliban's attempted rape, a move towards wholeness. Negritude, unlike its current yet necessary distortion, *Black Power*, *is* essentially syncretic and inclusive and whole.

"White Power" is the trap that Prospero fell into when, in order to free Ariel, he enslaved Caliban, then found that freeing Ariel and enslaving Caliban paid off. Prospero's magic, his culture, his poetry, soured into white power and imperialism. Black Power is its negation. Negritude, in the sense in which Caliban understood it, and the Brazilian Clarival do Prado Valladares defines it, contains their solution and resolution. Commenting on the sculpture of the Brazilian Agnaldo Manoel dos Santos, which won first prize at Dakar, he points out in the work, "the links of the ancient African art and medieval Catholic art... the syncretism of two cultures, African and Iberian", and concludes:

> This ought to be the true path of Negritude... I think that the character of a culture is more important than its racial contingency. The universal presence and dimensions recognizable in Negritude are the result of the first of these attributes.[47]

Even more than the fusion of races or the fusion of cultures, the task that faces Caliban, if he is to put an end to exile, is the fusion once more of the body and the brain – the refusal to accept the separation between physical and mental work which is culture's sin; the refusal to be an elite, the brain, to a mass, the brawn. In accepting the consumer role for the mass, we accept their separation in the same way as we accepted and continue to accept that some men must be hewers of wood and drawers of water. There is need for a cultural revolution of this kind of magnitude. For it is only with an end to the division between body/brain, consumer-mass/technocrat-elite that the world will have a chance to break out of the Spenglerian rise and fall of civilisations. Adorno tells us that the concept of Fate has always been the reflection of the domination of one group of men over another. The end of such domination is the end of the concept of Fate, and of its more refined extensions in the cultural myths by which men of all races, of all brilliant civilisations, have used to dominate other men, whose negation underpropped their brilliance. Adorno quotes James Shotwell:

> The civilizations that have come and gone have been inherently lacking in equilibrium because they have been built upon the injustice of exploitation. There is no reason to suppose that modern civilizations must repeat this cataclysmic theory.[48]

There is no reason to believe this, although there are many indications that we will. The concept of culture as a fetish object, justifying the negation of others, the concept of history as something which excludes the "natives", the contempt implicit in Naipaul, his quoters, and Mouche, the Western culture addict, whom Alejo Carpentier shows in her sterility,[49] passing judgement on a culture more valid and more whole than her tourist *object d' art*, are psychological barriers that must be battered down if we are to survive. The "appeasing arts" come to terms with these concepts. "Acquiescent criticism" bolsters them. The imperial way of seeing has not disappeared with the imperial flag. Its manifestations are more subtle; because more subtle, they are more dangerous. It was easier to fight "manifest unfreedom" in 1938, as Mais fought, than to grapple with "seeming freedom" as we must do now.

IV

BEATIE: "…It does work, it's happening to me, I can feel it's happened, I'm beginning, on my own two feet – I'm beginning…"
(… BEATIE stands alone, articulate at last –)

Arnold Wesker, *Roots*[50]

It is remarkable that the Negro ever writes at all. In order to endure he must be cunning and silent. Jazz is a mode of silence.

Neville Dawes, *The Last Enchantment*[51]

In Mexico, the word is used not to reveal but to conceal… the true use of

language would commit us to a daily and permanent revolution...
Carlos Fuentes[52]

To write at all was and is for the West Indian a revolutionary act. Any criticism that does not start from this very real recognition is invalid. The hostility that Carr speaks of, in his essay on Salkey in *The Islands In Between,* the hostility that the writer meets with at the hands of the educated sections of the West Indian public springs from this fact. The hostility that the West Indian writer meets with from university students, for example, comes directly from the concept of literature sold to them by educators like Carr. These educators, the moulders of generations of West Indians, are, in the large majority, as English as they are West Indian. They are a cultural, not a racial product. They worship at the shrine of a graven idol called culture. They come out of the same all embracing mould, the same formation. As Baldwin Sinclair, the rebel turned headmaster, discovered when he read up on the etiquette of proper English and headmasterial behaviour, there's no escaping the mould.

> It was indeed hard to argue against six standard textbooks. But, obviously, all of them belonged to the same school of thought, to the same stable of knowledge, and fed on the same fodder of belief.[53]

Lamming points out that the higher up the West Indian moves in the social scale, the more educated he is, the more the cultural myth indoctrinates him through these standard text books.

Naipaul's concept of history is the result of this indoctrination. Yet Naipaul's novels, as Rohlehr points out, are an assault on this concept. In *Biswas*, Rohlehr tells us, Naipaul who says that the West Indies has no history, himself writes, "in the history of West Indian underprivilege".[54] Biswas, safe from too much education, like Lamming's Papa in *The Castle of My Skin,* does not, as Carr would like him to do (in his essay on Mais, Carr accuses the Jamaican of being unable to ponder his own limitations) ponder his limitations. These limitations are imposed on him by colonial circumstances. He might not know this; and certainly does not care. Both Biswas and Papa assault these limitations. The assault on these limitations is what gives meaning to their lives. They come within the category of men who live their lives and fulfil their being. They are men, to borrow Alejo Carpentier's terms, who "work out a destiny for themselves" against all possible odds. In a world where Carpentier sees "many faces and few destinies",[55] they are men through their struggle against circumstances. Both, in a profound sense, fail. Their failure is important. The failure of the men and women in West Indian novels is a witness to the impossible odds against which they are pitted.

To see Roger Mais's *The Hills Were Joyful Together* and *Brother Man,* Carew's *Black Midas,* Lamming's *Castle,* the way many reviewers do as "the triumph of the human spirit" is to deliberately and wilfully misread the message. For what these books and others – Ramsay's failure in *The Last Enchantment,* Baldwin

Sinclair's failure in *Wounds of the Flesh,* and so many more, all failures, attest to, is the total deprivation of all the Calibans by Prospero's machinery of power. The heroic survival of the few, their heroic failures are only matched by the squalid and innumerable failures of the many. Patterson's *Children of Sisyphus* showed honestly and remorselessly the failure of all. The West Indian writer, shows clearly a society in which,

> what keeps the mechanism creaking along is human deprivation under conditions of insane sacrifice and the continual threat of catastrophe.[56]

In showing this society, however ineptly, the struggle of Caliban to realise himself against the brutality of Prospero's arrangement of society, the West Indian writer attacks that concept of culture by which:

> The precarious and irrational self-preservation of society is falsified and turned into an achievement of its immanent justice and "rationality".[57]

The West Indian writer is therefore involved in what Fuentes calls "a daily revolution". This is the reason for his exile, from Latin America and from here. Prospero's arrangement sees to this. This is too, in many cases, the reason for his failure as novelist, as poet or what have you. In initiating his revolution, Caliban takes language and tools and concepts from the Prospero whom he must fight. All too often, his writing is accorded, or not accorded, recognition by this very Prospero. All to often in having to write *for* Prospero's approval, he negates his own intention. The writer needs to write, as Lamming does in *The Pleasures of Exile,* addressing himself to his own audience. That at the same time, he addressed himself to Prospero, too, is not irrelevant. The relationship with Prospero has not come to end with the physical departure of Prospero. As Lamming acutely realises, since colonisation had been a reciprocal process, decolonisation must be equally so. Since it is Prospero who created the myth and assigned the respective roles, the process of demythologisation must take place between Caliban and himself. Caliban, must in a dialogue, reinvent, redefine the relation. If Caliban is to become a man, Prospero must cease being a myth of superman. Once this dialogue has really begun, the historical process which placed Louis James in the Caribbean and Lamming in London can be meaningful.

Lamming, seeing the connection between coloniser and colonised, examined *The Tempest* against the experience of England's early adventure in Empire. Louis James, in spite of the many subsidiary excellencies of his comments, does not see West Indian literature against its necessary background – England's late adventure in the dissolution of Empire. What do we mean by this? For James, unlike Carr, reveals the connection between West Indian writing, the use of dialect etc., and the upsurge, beginning in the thirties, against colonial rule. But he keeps his analysis, with no more than a brief reference, firmly in a West Indian compartment. He does not see West Indian literature as the expression of the breaking out of all the Calibans, not only all over the British Empire, but at the heart of Empire itself.

That was what the English angry generation was about. E.R. Braithwaite's *To Sir, with Love* was significant in that it showed that Prospero had enslaved Caliban of his own race as he had enslaved others. Since the enslavement rested on a system which divided mental and physical work, body and brain, Braithwaite's hero, black but educated, was a Prospero representative to the Caliban East End children. His refusal to accept that these children should be excluded from all the props of Prospero's humanity, his struggle against the colonial circumstances imposed on these East Enders, comes from his own memory and still present experience (through his black skin) of the Caliban torment. The book is valid because of this connection.

Arnold Wesker's *Roots* is even more illuminating. What Wesker shows us in *Roots* is a Beatie, a twentieth-century Caliban's mate, condemned to waitressing; bludgeoned, bruised, dehumanised like the rest of her family by the Telly, the radio, the advertisements, slick and sick; by shoddy programmes, shoddy clothes, shoddy amusements, shoddy personal relationships, the shoddy ideas and evasions, the shoddy view of the rest of the world. What Wesker shows us in *Roots* is a Beatie breaking out through pain and hurt, to grasp the Word, the Word as liberator, and not as a prison cell. Jimmy Porter in *Look Back in Anger* breaks out from the place of silence in which the imperial system, in which he was at once coloniser and colonised, had imprisoned him, to which he had acquiesced. His railing in *Look back in Anger* was the beginning of his revolt. What has happened to this anger now? How was it stifled, channelled safely into avenues of conformity?

In *The Pleasures of Exile,* Lamming used *The Tempest* to show us the origin of Caliban's imprisonment by the word. Miranda, reflecting her father's teaching, addresses Caliban indignantly:

... when thou didst not, savage,
Know thine own meaning, but wouldst gabble like
A thing most brutish, I endow'd thy purposes
With words that made them known...[58]

Each time Caliban writes, he reveals his purpose. His purpose, by the nature of his enslavement, cannot be a purpose acceptable to Miranda and Prospero, by the very nature of their domination and exercise of power. Caliban, by writing at all, is groping towards his own choice of words. This is to grope towards his own purpose. To speak for himself is to make Miranda's interpreter role irrelevant. Since this role is a key guardian role in Prospero's system, then Miranda, as interpreter, must defend it. To defend this role, she welcomes Caliban's speech, encourages his purpose, and straining his purpose through the spectrum of her own, ends up confusing his intention. In England, the angry generation having rebelled, like Baldwin Sinclair in *Wounds in the Flesh,* against the system, have been made headmasters, been caressed by power and given upholstered places on a modern chromium fence. They have come to acquiesce;

their works have begun to take their place within the appeasing arts. Their anger provides a new thrill, a new frisson, a sort of superior James Bond.

In his latest novel, *Season of Adventure,* Lamming creates, in the character of Charlot, an angry young Englishman, who after anger experiences only a sense of futility. Lamming analyses why:

> The second achievement of England's corpse was the effect of the pantomime on his generation. They were angry. But it was not the potent anger of a man unfairly dispossessed, [even when dispossessed in England, Charlot felt himself the dispossessor in relation to the West Indian, the African, and profited to however small a degree in his role as dispossessor] a man whose silence might contain a dangerous future. The anger of Charlot's generation had no precise details. It was not about poverty or hunger or waste... Hunger and poverty and waste had equal urgency with the activity they called the Arts. Literature among the more attentive was an organism with all its parts complete. They could dissect it like a knee, and put it up again. They checked its pulse, charted the course of its veins, and listened for the mortal pause of its heart, like a patient far gone in cancer. Their anger was an atmosphere in which they moved; a burning faith which showed their futures raped. In anger everyone, because they had been deceived, not simply by parents and teachers. They had been deceived by the very assumptions that had once made their country great.[59]

When their anger "had started to pay off and all their intentions had assumed a different role", in spite of themselves; when "without any change of attitude without betrayal of the heart, they had suddenly won the approval of their enemies",[60] Charlot packs his bag, and leaves for San Cristobal to teach history. In doing this,

> He had wanted to undermine the monotonous strength of his own inheritance. Europe had become the name of some erratic growth of moss or weed which totally imprisoned all his hopes.[61]

But San Cristobal puts an end "to all his notions of adventure". In his pupil Fola he sees "a perfect example of his own displacement". In seeing Fola's displacement, a displacement even more total than his – he is aware of his. She can scarcely afford to be aware, lest her precarious being, fragilely cotching, be swept away – in accepting the blunting of his anger by the power of England's myth, still potent in her corpse, Charlot has only one reaction left:

> Guilt was their last privilege. Their sole atonement became a daily exercise in the rebellious posture.[62]

This penetrating analysis of Charlot gives us an insight into the critical attitudes of a W.I. Carr. These attitudes are important and are worthy of attention. To discuss these attitudes is to initiate the dialogue between Caliban and Prospero – West Indian and Englishman – that we consistently avoid. Fearing confrontations, we take refuge in claptrap phrases like "racial harmony". Racial, and, even more important cultural harmony or cultural fusion can only come out of a high degree of awareness. Awareness calls for honesty of intention and expression. To be aware of Prospero's attitudes and of our own is to set in motion that demythologisation which for both is extremely difficult and, as Lamming insists, painful. For both West Indian and Englishman, their critical attitudes whether conforming to or reacting against, spring from the seeds of their colonisation,

> which has been subtly and richly infused with myth. We can change laws overnight; we may reshape images of our feeling. But this myth is most difficult to dislodge... it is there, a part of the actual texture of behaviour itself.[63]

Where, as in the faculty of Arts and particularly in the Department of English, West Indian and English lecturers are busily engaged in interpreting the literature of Prospero – the cultural myth which at once enchains and at once holds out the possibility of liberation – as well as the emerging literature of Calibans which at once rebels against (as Héctor Murena puts it "America is the child of Europe and we must assassinate her historically in order to begin to live")[64] and at once fulfils the potential of freedom that is implicit in Prospero's charms, then this degree of awareness must be of a very high order indeed. The dangers of acquiescent criticism spring not only from a lack of awareness but from a deliberate rejection of such awareness.

V.

> But what makes cultural criticism inappropriate is not so much lack of respect for that which is criticized as the dazzled and arrogant recognition which criticism surreptitiously confers on culture. The cultural critic can hardly avoid the imputation that he has the culture which culture lacks... When the critics... permit themselves to be degraded to propagandists or censors, it is the old dishonesty of trade fulfilling itself in their fate. The prerogatives of information and position permit them to express their opinion as if it were objectivity. But it is solely the objectivity of the ruling mind. They help to weave the veil.
>
> Adorno, *Prisms*[65]

At the beginning of his article "The Novelist in an Unsettled Culture", Wayne Brown quotes a statement about England made by W.I. Carr. Brown uses this statement as a measuring rod with which to assess the West Indian cultural experience. Carr wrote and Brown quotes:

> The novelist in England inhabits a dense world of critical discussion, of weekly reviews, of shared exchanges. He has the great advantage of relative anonymity in a culture, or rather in a social context, which is not forced to engage in a prolonged and painful dialogue with itself... He is not obliged, by the conditions of his living to explore the nature of his Englishness. It is present for him in the achievement of his predecessors. And at the same time the English novel is so evidently a product of a high degree of social awareness.[66]

It is plain from this that Carr sees England through different spectacles to those with which Lamming's young Englishman, Charlot (in the novel, *Season of Adventure*) sees it. Carr shares Charlot's feeling of guilt, is trapped in the same rebellious posture, but lacks the latter's disillusioned awareness that his posture is a posture.

Instead, Carr weaves a myth about present-day England in much the same manner as the narrator's father in Alejo Carpentier's novel *The Lost Steps* weaves a myth about a Europe he, too, had long since left. Carr sells his illusion of present day England to Brown as the narrator's father sells his dream of a distant and magnificent Europe to his son. The father instills in his son a view of the world, a Manichean view, in which, as Professor Coulthard expresses it, the world is a battle field between the light of "recorded (European) culture, and the darkness of original animality, (America)".[67]

In Europe, the narrator's father tells him, working men partake of German *Kultur*, enter libraries and read devoutly, attend concerts and listen with raptness to the music of Beethoven. In America, however, there was only the barbarous killings of Pancho Villa and his men. America was the continent of "little history" in which darkness had its being.

For the son, drunk on his father's myth, the *Ninth Symphony* of Beethoven comes to symbolise all the light of a great and unparalleled civilisation. When his father dies, he goes to Europe, and still seeing it through his father's eyes, he is "dazzled and enthralled by the music, architecture and painting of the Old World". During the war, he hears the German concentration camp guards singing the chorus from Beethoven's *Ninth*:

> *Freude, schöner Götterfunken*
> *Tochter aus Elysium*[68]

He begins to question his father's myth of a *Kultur* in which million of men are burnt to a scientific ash in ovens, while their burners sing the chorus from the *Ninth*. Along with the myth, he questions the entire gamut of what Sartre calls "our precious set of values"; and on closer scrutiny, he, too, sees that there isn't one "that isn't stained with blood".[69] He sees through "the striptease of humanism", comes face-to-face with the underlying reality, sees it "naked, and it's not a pretty sight". He is haunted now by the sickness of his father's dream which is his heritage; by that "fine sensibility" of Europe, part and parcel of that supermanhood, which to realise itself as Prospero's dominance, had created Caliban – slaves in America; and in Europe had created of its own kith and kin, Caliban-monsters, transforming the "cultured" workmen of his father's dream into the alienated Nazi mass, alienated – like today's London dockers marching for Enoch Powell, North America's blue-collar workers clamouring for George Wallace – from that very humanist being that the *Eroica Symphony* sets out to celebrate.

He returns to America where the cities are a tired reflection of the European sickness, other victims of the super-culture myth. He gets the chance to travel into the interior of Peru to search for some primitive musical instruments. In a settlement, hacked out of the jungle, he falls in love with a girl, Rosario, a "girl mixed of all the great races of the world, the most differentiated, the most separated who for millenniums had remained ignorant of their common existence on the planet."[70] There he begins to make a discovery of a culture which, unlike the Western one, had not yet separated magic from reality by the use of reason, a culture in which Nature was not there to be exploited, but to be cohabited with. A culture in which, for Rosario who inhabited it, herbs were living beings in a mysterious world which existed alongside the apparently "real one"; where the woods had its one-legged genie, and nothing that grew under the shadow of a tree could be plucked except one left a coin in payment, a coin paid with a ritual gesture, a ritual asking for permission. Carpentier knows that he cannot return to inhabit this culture. One cannot appropriate a way of life; one must live it from one's first breath. He knows that he and Rosario are separated, and that which separated them

> were the thousand books read by me, and that she knew nothing of; her beliefs, customs, superstitions, notions that I was ignorant of, notions which supported a reason for living as valid as mine.[71]

His illumination comes from his break-out from a Euro-centred world – his realisation of the possibility of "other" states of being, of an endless variety of potentiality and possibility. In the end he leaves. The artist cannot stay in the past nor even entirely inhabit the present; his concern is to go towards and to help create the impossible, which is tomorrow.

In the Caribbean, as in the backwoods of America, the potentiality of another "culture" has always existed; and still exists, although now going down before the assault of a worldwide negation of culture brought by modern industrial "civilisation". It was this culture – fragile, makeshift, temporary, but *valid* – out of which Lamming wrote *In the Castle of My Skin*. It had been a culture created by the village. Once the village breaks up at the end of the novel, Lamming says goodbye not only to the village, but to this other culture that had given him heroes like Papa, and a set of values that were humane because they never thought of humanity, but of the mutual survival of one another. The destruction of the village erases the culture, but not its memory. And not its echoes. It is that which gives such meaning to the last sentence of Lamming's *Castle*:

> I had said farewell; farewell to the land.[72]

Carr is ignorant of this culture; or rather he does recognise it as one. In his analysis of Mais's *The Hills Were Joyful Together,* he does not see the singing of the folk song at the fish-fry, for what it is – a carry-over from the culture of the land, when food, like the fish, had come manna from the hand of a fixed and certain God. Carr is more concerned with the fact that,

Mais' explicitness at the end of the episode nearly over points it: 'And they all laughed, and bright tears stood in the eyes of some, to witness that they still understood the meaning of miracles'.[73]

He is far more concerned with the fact that Mais almost departs from an artistic norm than that Mais, by echoing the passage reveals that a people have been expelled from a way of life which, however poor, they had shared a communal being. Out of that being they had created a folk song. Now they no longer create. They only remember.

Jean Creary knows of this culture. Her comment on the fish-fry points to the dispossession of the people, rather than to Mais's departure from a norm:

These rhythms, both communal, and within Mais's artistic eye, culminate in the choreographed meeting point of the fish fry, where the imprisoned spirits of the slum-dwellers erupt into a rhythmic celebration of life and fellowship... But the pattern is asserted so that it may be denied. There is no ultimate escape from the disintegrating forces of poverty.[74]

The poverty of slum culture has replaced the culture of village. Even the echoes have almost entirely disappeared by the time Patterson meets the *Children of Sisyphus*. This is the real "unsettlement of culture" in the Caribbean context, but it plays no part on Wayne Brown's horizon. The "unsettling culture" of his title is obviously supposed to compare and contrast with the "settled culture" of an England which Carr has portrayed.

Yet, the problems of the new novelist of England parallel to some extent, the problems of the West Indian. For the new English novelist must, like the West Indian, come to terms with his own kind of dispossession. England is still a metropolitan centre, and the English novelist is assured of a market and a market function. It is true that, as Carr says, the young English novelists still have a dense world of critical discussion of weekly review, of shared exchange. But this exchanges the narcissistic one of a closed world from which the reality of the transformation which England is now undergoing, in change over from colonial power to colony, is deliberately excluded. The writers for the most part, even when they chronicle portions of the new reality, of the change, refuse for the most part to see and accept the implications. The few who do, like Lamming's character Charlot, and feel their inadequacy to cope with problems of such magnitude, get the hell out. What in fact a W.I. Carr sells to a Wayne Brown as a "shared exchange" is in fact, a masturbatory exercise. Charlot realises this, when from the distance of a West Indian island he recalls his London friends,

... charting through dead lakes of coffee the origin and end of every well-known failure.[75]

As for the "nature of his Englishness" which, according to Carr, the English writer can take for granted, because "it is present for him in the achievement of his predecessors", it is precisely here that the English writer finds himself in a dilemma as paradoxical, in its way, if not more so, than the dilemma of the West Indian writer. The new English writer, a Sillitoe, an Osborne, a Braine, a Kingsley Amis, descendants of classes dispossessed from "Englishness" – in the Shakespearian context – by the Industrial Revolution, must now come to terms with a Caliban history of deprivation, an Oliver Twist past that the memory of a Dickens can only partially redeem. Far more terribly, any exploration of "Englishness" would lead him to an admission of involvement in another type of exploitation where he was no longer the exploited, but the exploiter; where to anchor himself in the achievement of his predecessors he would have to accept the guilt, not only of the past, but of the continuing present. He would have to admit with Sartre:

> You know well enough that we are exploiters. You know too that we have laid hands on first the gold and metals, then the petroleum of the 'new continents' and that we have brought them back to the old countries. This was not without excellent results, as witness our palaces, our cathedrals and our great industrial cities; and then when there was the threat of a slump, the colonial markets were there to soften the blow or divert it. Crammed with riches, Europe accorded the human status *de jure* to its inhabitants. With us, to be a man is to be an accomplice in colonialism, since all of us without exception have profited by colonial exploitation.[76]

To explore the nature of Englishness with the perspective with which Sartre explores the nature of Frenchness *would* commit the English novelist to changing its name and nature.[77] It is not, as Carr puts it, that the English novelist, is not "forced to engage in painful dialogue", it is simply that until now, he has not had the necessary courage to begin to do so. Here too, he parallels the West Indian. For the culture which Englishman and West Indian share, is a culture permeated by what Wilde calls, "the careless accuracy of facts",[78] a culture which uses pragmatism as its shield against the "black truth"; a culture which survives through its power of evasion. English "culture" is settled, but as Lamming points out, with the stillness of a corpse. If and when the "painful dialogue" with itself begins, it will be a long delayed sign of new life.

This dialogue must, by its very nature, threaten the present social context which Carr sees as a standard of excellence; and the "structure" which supports this social context; a structure in the final analysis controlled "by the gnomes of Zurich", and which, at second-hand remove, controls us. Lamming, the West Indian, has begun the dialogue that the English, given their ambivalent role – exploiter and exploited, puppet and part puppet-master – must avoid. This is the main difference between the West Indian writer and the English. The West Indian has little to lose by questioning – and thereby threatening Prospero's cloud-capped towers. By the mere fact of being a West Indian, Brown breaks out of Carr's distorted perspective when he argues:

> But one looks for the object of satire in the West Indies and finds that he must look to history and a mother country 4,000 miles away in the throes

of its own death or to the economics of modern capitalism and Big Brother U.S.A. if he is to apportion blame.[79]

Looking even further one would end up with the super-culture myth which underpins this economic octopus. Brown, impelled by his own circumstance, here contradicts the myth purveyed by a Carr. He does not as yet pursue this contradiction to its logical conclusion. When he does so, it will become clear that Carr's role as critic in the system of Prospero is that of an *agent provocateur;* the louder he shouts against it, the more he fulfils his function as guardian of the system.

VI.

His vanity aids that of culture: even in the accusing gesture, the critic clings to the notion of culture, isolated, unquestioned, dogmatic. He shifts the attack. Where there is despair and measureless misery, he sees only spiritual phenomena, the state of man's consciousness, the decline of norms. By insisting on this, criticism is tempted to forget the unutterable, instead of striving, however impotently so that man may be spared.

Adorno, *Prisms*[80]

"You see Miss Mullings, what we've got here is a staff that can uplift – you know, people… who conform to standards… We've got to have standards, Miss Mullings, we've just got to…"

Fitzroy Fraser, *Wounds in the Flesh*[81]

Lamming's Charlot, coming to terms with his own displacement, shares displacement with his West Indian pupil, Fola. Their relation is one of equality. Carr, by refusing to accept his own, sees himself still in the interpreter role of Miranda. What Carr cannot forgive the West Indian is that he should become his own interpreter, his own saviour. For this threatens Carr's role and sense of purpose, a sense that is being increasingly challenged as sterling totters, and recovers, pulled by strings from Zurich. Because he refuses to see the apparatus which controls his and the West Indian's common condition, he must hold on for relevance to a well-known and recognised role. In his long and illuminating essay on Roger Mais, he sets out to destroy any West Indian writer who too clearly, by making certain connections that Carr must avoid, diminishes this role. The essay on Mais is as much in dispraise of these West Indian writers as it *is* in praise of Mais, who, safely dead, can be erected into a fetish object, and whose anger can be disguised under the name, and throne of Art.

The list of writers dispraised therefore has its significance. I am included, although the connections I made were so confused and ill-made, as hardly to have seemed worthwhile meriting Carr's guns. Certainly not when compared to his dismissal of Eric Williams's *Capitalism and Slavery*. It is interesting to note that Williams's book – prepared as a doctoral thesis for Oxford University –

could not, for quite a few years, find a publisher in England. It was first published in the United States of America and has since become a classic.[82] *Capitalism and Slavery* exposes the close connection between the growth and expansion of capitalist enterprises in England and the U.S.A., and the profits made from the slave-trade on what has come to be known as the Middle Passage.

It is logical that a Naipaul, although using the title *The Middle Passage* for his travel book about the Caribbean, should avoid making mention of the economic connection and implications. Nor, in fact, does he seem ever to have bothered to read Williams's book. Steeped in the English interpretation of their own history, he is able to criticise the "lack of culture" in Trinidad, measuring it against an English "norm"; and without ever understanding that the lack of the one and the norm of the other are equally the results of a single and common historical process. He averts his gaze from the guilt of the strong and concentrates his contempt on the degradation imposed on the victim by the aggressor.

It is also logical that Carr should quote Naipaul with approval. If he finally rejects Naipaul's view of history – "History was built around achievement and creation and nothing was created in the West Indies" – he does so not on rational grounds, nor from an intellectual rejection of an inherently Fascist statement, but because the acceptance of this statement would invalidate his own emotional attachment to a Messianic role and function, that of redeeming the Caribbean's lack. He criticises Naipaul for his statement, only because such a statement "seems to be inviting one just to get up and go away".[83] Which, of course, is scarcely the point. Especially as, in his Mais article, he supports Naipaul's thesis when he maintains that the history of the West Indies is not a history but merely an "agglomeration of wicked incidents".[84] He refuses to see any *human* purpose behind the incidents; any logic however haphazard. We are to place the blame for what happened on some vast impersonal force called History. History belonged to England and History is the arch-knave. Here Carr quotes one of the High priests of Western culture, T.S. Eliot, with approval:

> History has many cunning passages, contrived corridors
> And issues, deceives with whispering ambitions,
> Guides us by vanities…[85]

Carr then uses Eliot's mystic utterance to demolish the connection made by Williams that Carr refuses to admit:

> The politician and the propagandist will hardly recognise themselves here, neither perhaps will the historian. One remembers, for example, the frigid determination with which Eric Williams gives us the facts of West Indian history in his *Capitalism and Slavery* but denies us any experience of its texture.[86]

In the name of an artistic norm and imperative called "texture", the revolutionary insight of Williams's books, the connection and interdependence of English and West Indian history is avoided. We note that Carr sees

Capitalism and Slavery as being only about "West Indian history"; the far-reaching insights into England's economic history made by Williams are irrelevant. He goes further. As the "cultural critic", having "the culture which culture lacks" he points out, with forbearance, Williams's basic shortcoming:

> What the reader will question will not be Dr. Williams' knowledge nor his professional competence. It will be his relationship to the past and the present.[87]

The shortcoming of course, is Carr's. It is his relationship to the present, which makes it imperative to dismiss Williams's connection. Such a connection reveals the present relationship between a Carr and a Williams through the past connection between them – "We have met before", Lamming wrote, "four centuries separate our first meeting when Prospero was graced with the role of thief, merchant and man of God."[88]

These are the kind of insights a Carr must evade, if he is to maintain an illusion, rather than acquire a true knowledge of his own past – and ours. With Hawkins's first raid on Africa, his first Middle passage to the West Indies with Africans as human merchandise on board, the nature of being an African and the nature of Englishness had changed. In the place of African and Englishman there was now only a relation – slave dealer and slave. Our common history is the history of that relationship; our common destiny is its negation.

In *The Pleasures of Exile* Lamming explores some of the cultural aspects of the economic relation revealed by Williams. Lamming also must be dismissed and demolished. Dealing with writers rather than with a historian, Carr justifies his dismissal not on lack of "texture", but on clumsiness of technique, vulgarity, imprecision, vindictive cliché. He uses the notion of culture "isolated, unquestioned, dogmatic" to disqualify those writers whose insights are unpalatable; and of course bases his disqualification on the basis of the "decline of norms". He is the typical *Kulturkritik* assessed by Adorno; in order to *censor* those writers whose views he rejects, he will serve as propagandist for Roger Mais, now dead and helpless to reject his sponsorship. Unlike Mervyn Morris, Carr is too acutely aware of the danger which Lamming's analysis constitutes to casually dismiss it. Rather, he whittles away in a crablike approach, whittling Lamming down to size through condescension. He will accord to *The Pleasures of Exile*,

> ... if not always the strictest relevance, at least the advantage of convenience. The blurred insistencies, if only by the density of their accumulation, manage to draw attention to contours of feeling with which people are familiar. And so we concede an order of attention.[89]

The point having been made, the attention is reserved for another significant attack on Lamming.

Several West Indian novelists, those who attended elementary schools, rather than secondary schools, experienced with a kind of edged clarity the Empire Day ritual. Several have felt impelled to exorcise the shame; once, looking back, and seeing the incongruity of the situation, they realise how happily they had assented to their own degradation. Austin Clarke deals with it, and so does Neville Dawes, in *The Last Enchantment*. Dawes, also one of Carr's pet hates – he deals among other things with the connection between West Indian and English man, the West Indies and England – is dismissed with the characteristic aside which Carr prefers to use – the sly knife rather than the blunt hatchet.

> They [Mais's characters] are not the cardboard product of predictable views of race or social and cultural background, and not puppets controlled at the behest of vindictive cliché as they are in, say, Neville Dawes' *The Last Enchantment*.[90]

The mention of race, thrown in casually, is important. For in the prevalent myth of "racial harmony", which until the timid appearance of Black Power this year, ruled as a graven idol even more on the Mona campus than in the rest of Jamaica, black writers who discuss race are to be shunted aside. Naipaul's racialism vis-à-vis the black man can be discussed not as a neurosis, as Gordon Rohlehr firmly terms it, but as Art. Neville Dawes's exploration of his own feelings of blackness in a white world must be dismissed as "vindictive cliché".

This determined avoidance and distaste for "race" is not confined to Carr. Louis James, in an otherwise excellent and sensitive interpretation of Vic Reid's *The Leopard*, makes the, to me, astounding statement:

> It still remains true, however, that on the level that dominates the book, the emotional, the story is one-sided and INTENSELY ANTI-WHITE.[91]

The statement seemed astounding until, reading the essay by James and Cameron King – "In Solitude for Company" – I came upon this other statement. It is intended as an answer to what the authors say is a common accusation made against the poet Derek Walcott – that he turns "to European culture and experience" in preference to West Indian culture and experience. The reply from James and King does Walcott even more of a disservice than the original accusation, and reveals an attitude of the critics that is part and parcel of the apparently objective approach. James and King argue with some heat,

> ...the concept that 'European' culture has a nationalist identity in opposition to that of the Caribbean has the dangerous elements of racial mythology. The 'literature of England' reaches backwards and outwards to the cultures of Greece, Rome and medieval France. It touches the thought and civilisations of Europe, the new world, even Asia and Africa. Its preoccupation is with man as a human being, and for this reason a culture that becomes isolationist and inward looking can paradoxically cut itself off from the means of knowing itself.[92]

Granted that the original "accusation" against Walcott is confused and imprecise, the reply to the accusation is itself a clear example of that "racist humanism" of which Sartre speaks. It is clear that James and King see European culture as being the super-culture which embraces all other cultures, and obliterates as it absorbs. To deny any part of "European culture" is to deny "humanity"; is to be involved in "racial mythology". What James and Cameron peddle and what Walcott is at times trapped by, is the "cultural myth" rather than the cultural reality of Europe. The cultural myth underprops the economic and political power of Europe based on its exploitation of non-Europeans; the cultural reality of Europe consistently attacked and opposed this dominance, this concept of Europe as a super-culture, as the end product of Man's glorious March towards "humanity". The cultural reality of Europe sees the ambivalence of its own power and glory and embodies its real creativity best when it is most self-critical. It is this reality that speaks with Sartre to answer the dangerous myth-making of mediocre minds. [He quotes]:

> ...Leave this Europe where they are never done talking of Man, yet murder men everywhere they find them, at the corner of everyone of their own streets, in all the corners of the globe. For centuries they have stifled almost the whole of humanity in the name of the so-called spiritual experience.[93]

If Walcott has not yet realised the full range of his talent, it has nothing to do with his either accepting Europe or turning his back on Europe. He has no choice. The West Indian experience was "created" by Europe; and the West Indian experience helped to create Europe as it is today. Besides to *be* West Indian is to be syncretic by nature and circumstance, by choice. It is the *myth* of Europe which rejects; which rejects all other experiences, African, Indian, Chinese which contribute to the being of the West Indian. What is important is whether Walcott accepts the myth of Europe for its creative reality. The myth of Europe will alienate him from himself in much the same way as it has alienated European man. The creative reality will give him a complex, if painful, mirror in which to reassemble all the divided fragments of his still indeterminate identity. The dilemma of being either West Indian or European is a false one. To be a West Indian is to accept all the facets of one's being. The overemphasis on the European facet is a hangover of the myth; and implies a rejection of the others. The swing of the pendulum, now in vogue, will redress the balance towards the myth of Africa. One then hopes that the West Indian and Walcott will work through to the reality of both.

Louis James and Cameron reject anything in the West Indian experience which seems to exclude, or criticise too acutely, the West Indian's "cultural debt" to Europe. Pretending to objectivity, they are critics whose objectivity is the *objectivity of the ruling mind*. In his article on Mais, Carr sets out to reject anything in West Indian writing which brings the West Indian into a too sharp confrontation with the European, and here, specifically, the English colonial power. Any such confrontation brings too sharply into question his own position and involvement. Since the importance of Mais both as man and writer is part and parcel of the Caribbean anti-colonial, and anti-British movement of the 'thirties, Carr goes to great lengths to prove his thesis that to see Mais against the background of political turmoil, and to interpret his work in the light of this turmoil, is to diminish Mais's validity *qua* writer. It is in the context of this thesis that he drags in Lamming's evocation of the Empire day scene in his first novel, *In the Castle of My Skin*. Not only does he damn the writer for writing about this scene, he damns the West Indian reader for reacting with emotional acuteness to Lamming's passage. He puts his condemnation in brackets, to show it as a pretended careless aside, the last academic refuge of the destructive:

> (... I am thinking, for example, of the kind of automatic and literal-minded acceptance of the Empire Day scene in George Lamming's *In the Castle of My Skin*. We have there all the dreadful *décor* of the West Indian setting not so very long ago – the meaningless blare of the British national anthem, the suits, the sycophantic bullying teachers etc. No West Indian could read the episode without responding to the deadening pressures of the occasion. But in fact he is importing his own experience into the book. As a piece of writing it is strained, factitious, derivative.)[94]

Lamming was the first "British-colonial" to chronicle that experience. He did it well enough for a Carr to get the point of how many psychological crimes had been committed in the name of British "democracy". As a passage it is derivative, derived from Lamming's life. Lamming has imported a terrifying experience into his book. For all West Indians of his generation, the passage of writing is not only "telling" about an occasion, it creates a mnemonic pattern which dredges up associations at an unconscious level. It is powerful enough to make a Carr feel uncomfortable. It is a passage of writing by a West Indian writer who had lately come out of the culture of a village which was largely oral – like the African tribal culture, like the medieval European's. It is written for ear and eye, and that is its achievement. It is not Carr's concept of what writing should be. It must therefore be dismissed.

Coming to Mais himself, Carr's thesis that "to assign to art a predominantly political and social context is to misunderstand the nature of art", is best answered by Jean Creary's review of Mais's works – in the essay, "A Prophet Armed" in the collection, *The Islands In Between*. She shows that to interpret the social and political background through art and art through the social and political background, is to give truer insights into the nature of each; when the interpretation is based on the desire to illuminate rather than to obscure. Yet it would be naive not to see that Carr's posing of a false dilemma, his attempts to "rescue" Mais from the kind of political tribute paid him by Norman Manley – for example, "Roger was a product of that moment of history and drew from it the direction and power and purpose which his writings reveal..."[95] – has its purpose. To accept that Mais's work owed something to the mass movement of the Jamaican people to break out from colonial non-being, is to accept that confrontation that we have mentioned before, and that Carr is at such pains to avoid.

To admit the validity of the anti-colonial experience would be to admit that the West Indian Caliban first found his being when he broke into his own speech to assault the structure of values of which Carr is the purveyor. Because of this evasion, he chooses to see Mais's work as some sort of "inexplicable magic", understandable only in terms of Mais's peculiar genius.[96]

He therefore begins by isolating Mais. Mais could not have come out of Barbados (can anything good come out of Nazareth?) because,

> ...its flat overbred topography is alien to the bracing, symbolic framework of Mais' imagination.[97]

Having got in a side swipe at Lamming, Carr then goes on to dismiss Trinidad and its "nervously inspired anarchy". Finally, giving the Jamaican hills the credit of producing Mais, Carr then gets in his blow at the Jamaican people, whom, apart from a rather selectly dropped list of names, Carr doesn't care for. Mais, Carr argues, is too good to be a "Jamaican possession". Since the West Indian is a mythical rather than an actual entity, Carr allows Mais to be "a deeply significant West Indian possession".[98]

To rub in his point, Carr selects as a "Jamaican possession", the poet, J. E. Clare MacFarlane. MacFarlane, Carr suggests, is good enough for Jamaica and Jamaicans; Mais is too good for them. The malice is almost neurotic. Louis James, in his introduction to *The Islands in Between*, made a distinction between the different generations. Men like MacFarlane were pioneers in West Indian writing. They wrote at a time when for a black man to write at all was itself a miracle. They borrowed from English models, sensibility, metre, attitude. Their faults were the faults of their circumstance. But, as Fanon has pointed out, we must learn not to underestimate the efforts of our forefathers. They fought with the weapons that they had. Carr sees and wishes to see only that these men seem ridiculous. And he passes on to his West Indian pupil, Wayne Brown, the destructive quality of his contempt. Carr laughed at the spectacle of a Clare MacFarlane being crowned Poet Laureate at the Ward Theatre in Kingston. Brown selects as his object of ridicule A.J. Seymour of Guyana. Seymour, a later and better poet than MacFarlane, is quoted by Brown as saying:

> I would say that the time has come for a novel to be published which placed emphasis upon the qualities of dignity, discretion, superiority and timelessness in the West Indian scene.[99]

Brown mocks Seymour's concept of dignity, contrasting it with the "dignity" of Naipaul's Biswas:

> It is a story, (a fable as Mr. Carr calls it) that has something, everything to do with 'dignity', though not we are afraid, 'dignity' as Mr. Seymour pronounces it; an unconscious pathetic, heroic assertion of identity in a situation where history has contrived to make it impossible for identity to matter.[100]

Yet, it is clear, that dignity for Biswas had come to mean – not as in the mystification of Carr's interpretation, the struggle to be what he is, for his personal identity, like some little private property of the soul – but a house and Prefect car. Dignity, equally for a MacFarlane and a Seymour, had come to mean a literature which could portray the black man, not only as minstrel clown, but as man. The concepts of "dignity" of a Biswas, a MacFarlane, a Seymour were all "reactions imposed on them by colonial circumstances". All three, in different ways, attempt to break out of a degrading stereotype imposed on them by the British cultural and colonial myth. We can dismiss their concepts of dignity, only if we accept that by their struggle, all three can make this claim upon our imagination – that we acknowledge their "unconscious pathetic, heroic assertion of identity in a situation where history has contrived to make it impossible for identity to matter."[101]

Fitzroy Fraser in his novel *Wounds in the Flesh* – also dismissed by Carr – tells of the conversion of the rebel Baldwin MacDonald Sinclair into the headmaster, striving to conform to the English norms of being a headmaster, trapped like his former English friend, Jonesy, in the English traditions of Headmastership; both wanting to be different, but both influenced and controlled by the mould and manners of the headmaster of the top school where they had both taught. Baldwin wants to bring to his little country school all the missionary light of Europe that the "top school for top people" enjoys. In his efforts to do this he clashed with an English couple, both teachers, both hustlers, indifferent and on the make. They blackmail Baldwin into granting their request, by confronting him and throwing in his face the passes that Baldwin had made at the wife. Baldwin, confronting them, pretends that he gives in of his own accord. He wouldn't use force he says, to hold them to their contract. These were not colonial times, he says, looking at the "ex-coloniser, the "ex-user of force". But the ex-colonisers couldn't care less; all they want is out. Baldwin, the black Baldwin, must now take upon himself the white man's burden. He begins his missionary mission. He appoints a regular afternoon where the staff should meet for tea. He is determined that the staff shall hold on to the standards of the ex-coloniser. He earnestly implores them:

> "We must learn to sit down together and talk about a little culture."[102]

It is not the intention, but the crassness of it, the reductio ad absurdum of his own, that offends Mr. Carr.

It is, in a more sophisticated dress, Baldwin's concept of culture that Carr peddles in his article on Mais. In attempting to detach Mais from the whole "material process" of his country's life, Carr gives us a portrait of Mais which is anti-Mais, and anti-the whole meaning of his struggle against circumstance. Carr contradicts Manley's statement that Mais and his art were a product of a moment of history:

> But, although Mr. Manley's pages are a generous tribute to the memory of

a dead friend, it seems to me his emphasis is a misleading one. It doesn't help us to come at a sense of Mais' quality as a writer, and although it points to the content of the fiction, it can't help us in trying to define its underlying tragic metaphysic. Anyone who has read *Black Lightning* with attention is surely entitled to feel that Henry James might be more usefully invoked than George Lamming, or even Vic Reid. But Henry James, alas!, is not likely to be a welcome guest.[103]

Miss Creary's title "A Prophet Armed" is the best reply to Carr's assessment of Mais. For no one could call Henry James a prophet. If Mais, in *Black Lightning*, which for all its occasional excellences is a flawed and incomplete book, echoes James, then it is a mere moment in a vast gamut of feeling. Henry James is all that Mais is not – the culture symbol that proves that America, "that super-European monstrosity",[104] had achieved her European potential. She had got herself "a great writer". But Mais is far more than a writer. This is what Miss Creary brings out. Mais was gardener, journalist, painter, politician, poet, dramatist, novelist, talker, lover, bon vivant, good companion. All the facets of his being reinforced the "wholeness of the man". His life, in spite of Carr, was not reduced to writing books. He was a prophet, descending from England's William Blake, like him concerned with "building Jerusalem".[105] That was what he was talking about, that was what he was making the bricks for – in life, love, politics, writing, painting, facing death. His only West Indian parallel is José Martí.[106] Mais's writings like Martí's, were essentially confrontations with power. They were not protest "writing", nor "protest painting". Protest accepts the inevitability of that which it protests against and asks for adjustments to suit the protester and those on whose behalf the protester pleads.

Mais, like Martí, realised that political liberty was nothing if the liberty of the spirit was unattained. This was the revolutionary intention behind *Brother Man* – a rare character in all literature, except perhaps in the Russian. Mais, like Martí, accepted that the poet and the writer should be "the footstool of the *pueblo*"; that the artist's mission was to write for the people and to paint for the people, even if in doing that one loses those felicities of style that adorn the art of those who create for an incestuous elite. Mais's books were in no sense of the word belonging to "the appeasing arts" – elite or mass. In the *Hills are Joyful Together* and *Brother Man,* he took the "native" out of the darkness behind the Word, and drew him into the light world of print – the light that had been confined only to *men*. In both these first two books – *Hills* and *Brother Man* – and in his third book, in another manner, Mais was talking about *Jerusalem,* to a people in exile in another *Egypt*.

Black Lightning is not, as Carr asserts, a better book than the other two. The question of being better or worse is, in a final analysis, irrelevant. Carr's choice of *Black Lightning* corresponds to his own concerns. *Black Lightning* seems to him a more "private" book; and this is why he prefers it. Miss Creary points to its achievements, and suggests the reason for its failure:

> Moving and impressive as *Black Lightning* for the most part is, the sense of an incompletely formulated statement persistently haunts one.[107]

Even more acutely, she goes to the heart of the matter when discussing *Brother Man*. Mais was a prophet. And a prophet deals in visions. The areas of failure in all Mais's books, in his paintings, in his life itself, occur in those areas where there was, to borrow Miss Creary's term, "a limitation of his vision".

The limitation of his vision in *Black Lightning* cannot be removed from the limiting conditions of the colonial experience of the late 'forties and 'fifties. The exhilaration and release which had come from facing the "enemy" in a direct confrontation were replaced by the tortuous and dangerous subtleties of a "limited experience" in self-government. West Indians were being taught by their former master who had governed them arbitrarily, how to govern themselves with a democratic procedure; they were being taught how to reconcile political independence with economic and cultural dependence on the "master", now transmuted into a peaceful and lovable Big Brother; they were being initiated into the world of Pilate's diplomacy, where the two-party system, by making each party identify the other as the enemy, caused them to avert their eyes from the powerful neo-colonial apparatus. It was a sad and miserable time. Worse than now. The confidence trick was not even suspected then. The failure of the artist in *Black Lightning* was the failure of the bright promise of a New Day which Mais had prophesied and helped bring about – a day whose high noon faded in the semi-darkness.

But Mais's "failure" is creative; it is a triumph of failure, as Eduardo Mallea, the Argentinian writer, puts it. In the unreality of our times, success would have meant the negation of that reality for which one fought. And prophets always come before their time; they are warners of the future; or of the end. *Black Lightning* is important for quite other reasons than Carr gives to it. In *Black Lightning* Mais is saying that even in the personal illumination of a Brother Man and a Minette, their love is not enough. The vision must be made into song. The song must be communicated through areas of feeling that have scarcely been tapped; that the colonial experience, except in the candour of a Brother Man, buries, distorts. Mais in *Black Lightning* came to understand that the artist was locked and lost with his "personal vision", which could become the egotism of pride in his power of knowledge, in his creative hands, making like God. His vision had to be transmuted into the substance of the lives around him if it is not to perish in blindness. Mais was a Samson who dreamed that the enemy was not the poor maligned Philistines, but myths which divided Jews and Philistines.

As Jake the sculptor carved, Samson became Christ, the eternally crucified, holding potential seeds of violence within himself, and potential seeds of liberation. Blinded by his vision, afraid of the conclusions, Jake withdraws into himself and learns about friendship and love that is humble through Amos, the hunchback, who plays sweet music on his accordion, as David played to Saul. In the end, in the time of the long rains, when Jake gives his carving to be burnt for firewood, he has pulled down the whole temple, the whole superstructure which has enthroned a graven idol called culture. The statue is used to warm the bones of men and women since it could not, through the incompleteness of the artist's vision, warm their spirits. Where the Nazi concentration camp guards incinerated men and women and children in gas ovens to strains of the *Ninth Symphony*, thinking to "purify" the culture which had produced such a fetish masterpiece, Jake-Mais gives his masterpiece to be incinerated so that men may live. Mais's whole life was a life dedicated not to preserving artistic norms *à la* Carr, but a life dedicated, "to striving, however, impotently so that men may be spared." Mais differs from all other West Indian writers in the way that José Martí differed from other Cuban writers. Both had fulfilled their being as, in the phrase of Martí "a man among men and not a wolf among wolves"; both had lived a life directed at the impossible. Both have entered the element of myth.

VII.

In the union on the bluff over the river, the students' steel band was practising and the plangent drone butted steadily into the yielding texture of the night. It was monotonously arresting as a pulse beat: the unworked rhythms of a people who have only realised music as a social adjunct and not yet as an art... All the way down the long shallow hill into Queenhaven, bursts of remembered music seemed to gather themselves like small waves inside me and break open uncontainably:

Freude, I sang,
Freude, schöner Götterfunken
Tochter aus Elysium.

John Hearne – *Land of the Living*[108]

The West Indian who comes near to being an exception to the peasant feel is John Hearne.

(Lamming – *The Pleasures of Exile*.)[109]

Barrie Davies – "The Seekers" – a critical essay on John Hearne, falls midway between acquiescent criticism, as exemplified in Carr, and challenging criticism exemplified by Lamming, Rohlehr, Creary. They are not hard and fast categories, and the categories are my own, and arbitrary rather than impartial. Challenging criticism seems to me to relate the books discussed to the greatest possible "whole" to where they belong. Acquiescent criticism either refuses to do this altogether as in Carr, or does it imperfectly, as in James and Cameron King; or relates to a background which is mythical rather than real, as in Hearne on Harris. The aspects of Hearne's criticism which we shall look at in a while, parallel aspects of Hearne as novelist. Lamming has accused Hearne of lacking the "peasant feel" which is basic to many other West Indian writers. He has also attacked him for idealising a kind of colonial squirearchy in his novels. And, by implication he removes

Hearne from the revolutionary intention of other West Indian writers. The West Indies, Lamming says, "belong to that massive majority whose leap in the twentieth century has shattered all the traditional calculations of the West, of European civilisation…" [110] He excepts Hearne from this peasant feel. Yet, this is, I think, a simplified view.

In his article on Harris, John Hearne, begins:

> It is from Yeats's great phrase about the 'unity from a mythology that marries us to rock and hill' that we may, justifiably, begin an examination of Wilson Harris's singular exploration of his corner of the West Indian experience. To Harris, this sacramental union of man and landscape remains the lost, or never established, factor in our lives. We enjoy, we exploit, we are coarsely nourished by our respective Caribbean territories – but illegitimately. We have yet to put our signatures to that great contract of the imagination by which a people and a place enter into a domestic relationship rather than drift into the uncertainties of a liaison.[111]

This is a significant statement about Hearne's own work, and attitudes. On the one hand, he justifies Lamming's stricture about not having the peasant feel, by his total blindness to that ambivalent "we". Who *is* we? For the West Indian peasant, by the mere fact that he is a peasant, has already entered into that "sacramental union of man and landscape". His folk song, his folk culture, fabric or beliefs about herbs, superstitions, relationships to trees – no Jamaican peasant can quite come to terms with cutting down a tree, except out of dire necessity – are the signatures that he has put to that "great contract of the imagination with which a people and a place enter into a relationship". The relationship began illegitimately – the African slave who in the middle of the seventeenth century was given a plot of ground to cultivate on Saturdays and Sundays, to help feed himself and so keep the labour power for the canefields and the mills in good condition, did not choose his plot of ground nor choose to labour on it. But soon he saw it as a source of memory – the continuance of a relationship that he had known in Africa; and soon he saw it as a source of freedom.

For soon he came to see his relationship to this plot as that which preserved his being. In the interstices of the slave system, he entered into a union; it was sacramental in its profoundest sense. On this plot he buried his dead, so that the souls of his ancestors as they had done in Africa remained in close union with the living. The clump of breadfruit trees today mark his plot of ground and his union with it, as the ruined Great House marked the European's domination of the land. Hearne's failure to grasp this, justifies Lamming's criticism. Yet such a failure is understandable. The colonial provisions in our society were marked and deep. Lamming, growing up in a village, had this instinctive knowledge. But for Hearne, urban and with several generations of a middle-class background, there is no intuitive grasp of this fact. It is a necessary but difficult act of apprehension.

What Hearne intuitively grasps is that the people who lived in the Great

Houses had also entered into a contract with the land. It was a proper marriage rather than an illegitimate one. And like all marriages, the land, the woman, was subjugated and dominated by the male. The subjugation, and the exploitation of the union, was carried on through the labour of slaves, but the relationship between the master and the land was still there. With the end of slavery, those few planters who remained, settled down to a less violent domestic relationship. Hearne's instinct to create Brandt's Pen and Carl Brandt was the same as Lamming's to recreate Papa and his house and "the corner where Papa who keep goats does live."[112] That Hearne gives us an idealised version of Carl Brandt and of the Pen is true enough. But Carl Brandt and his like needed an idealised version of themselves to evade the reality of injustice that would otherwise press in too closely on them. And as Hearne shows, Brandt lives up to this ideal. His relationship with his workers is feudal, but it is charitable and protective and still human. Brandt is a Prospero in his paternal authoritarianism, but his lack of Prospero's intelligence and ambition makes him kindlier, more generous in spirit. Brandt's Pen and Carl Brandt are Hearne's ideal, even though the Pen does not provide the setting for the majority of the novels. But the ideal is always there, imagined, serene and gracious in the distance. Except in *Land of the Living* where, as Davies points out, no reference is made to the Brandts at all. Davies is good on the significance of Brandt's Pen:

> The one area of safety appears to be the spacious middle-class life of Brandt's Pen which, significantly, embodies values and beauties from a life that has really past, that of the old plantocracy. Even Roy McKenzie, feels its attraction:
>
> > 'And this is the thing that could really corrupt me. Not the wealth of it… but it's the closeness of it that could change me. This incestuous, happy, kindly closeness where every personal contact is never let go, and where every one fits into his place like a cork into a bottle.'
>
> …Brandt's Pen is a 'womb with a view'. One cannot but feel that the tension between Hearne's own emotional attraction to it and his intellectual rejection unbalances these novels.[113]

Yet the area of the "heart's country" to which Hearne has dedicated himself, is not Brandt's Pen, but the Suburbaville of Queenshaven in Cayuna. Brandt's Pen is the fleeting vision of the Eden from which Suburbaville residents have been displaced. Andrew Fabricus, a former Brandt type, cast out of planter life through his father's inadequacy, spends his life working until he has saved enough to buy a property and reinvent the past in a modern setting. Rachel Anscomb and Jojo Rygin measure their own climb to the top through the possessions and the money with which they can match the careless luxury of a Brandt's Pen. Which of course, they can never do; Brandt's Pen is the culmination of two centuries of practise in gracious living: Davies quotes Hearne:

> In the big, high dining room, where the long, deep-gleaming mahogany

sideboard was bright with silver and crystal, Elvira had laid two places on large squares of coarse, starched, white linen. Two centuries of polish had brought the table to a texture where the cloths looked as if they were floating on black water. There was grapefruit, cut and cored, with clear amber crystals of brown sugar soaking into the pale green flesh. While they were eating these, she brought in a heavy tray of ham and eggs on a thick, bone white, blue-flowered dish...[114]

Davies criticises Hearne here, for not knowing "when to limit, to select, to stop". But he misses the point of the accumulation of adjectives and objects. The ritual of food in the Caribbean, in the country planter's house, or among the peasants in the village, is part of the contract they have entered into with the land. Freyre shows this brilliantly in his *Masters and Slaves* where he examines the food patterns of Brazil, and the fusion of dishes, and ceremony. Just as Lamming describes in detail the making of "cuckoo", cornmeal turned with okras, as the special feast the boy gets when going away,[115] so Hearne describes the meal, not only as a fact but as a ritual pattern of behaviour, of being.

The ritual, transferred from eating, from taste, from pleasure in order and in the security of traditions, extends to all the areas of the senses. This is Hearne's original contribution and that which includes him in those writers with a revolutionary intention. For his captation of "the quality of life in the Caribbean, qualities of experience recorded through heightened senses",[116] provides for the middle-class West Indian readers an assault on the vision of snow and spring and flowering cherry trees which, like the Empire Day ritual, had filled their consciousness, through books, alienating them from that "contract with the land" from which the peasant had never wandered. Davies pinpoints Hearne's very real achievements:

Eye, ear and nose are indefatigably awake. An orange peel is a ring of 'blazing yellow'; beer bottles sweat icily; beer slides glacial down throats gummed with heat. In bathing in the sea each variation of sensation is observed.

The water was pale blue and it felt smooth and clinging, like warm milk. But when they swam out and dived to the white sea-bed, it was cool and there was a dim, glassy blue light around them, and coming to the surface again they could feel the salt stinging their eye-rims, as they blinked the water out of them.

Hearne is portraying a state of feeling, a heightened awareness he sees answering and penetrating the intense light and colour of the West Indian environment. In the process, he has provided masses of data about the quality and density of the Caribbean experience. He has been doing what James Fenimore Cooper, faced with similar imaginative problems in America, called illustrating 'the land and water which is their birthright.'[117]

This is Hearne's significant contribution. It is a quality most marked in his first three novels; it continues in the others but not with the same force. As Hearne gets further away from the "established order", the feudal ideal of

Brandt's Pen that he hankers after, he enters the more shifting reality, the spiritual placelessness of Cayuna's Suburbaville, on the fringes of Brandt's Pen. Outside Suburbia, outside the neat fences and the clambering bougainvillea, change waves threatening fists of, "the background of meaning-less blue". For Suburbaville separates the terror of Tiger Johnson's hell, of Henneky's inferno from the serene order of Brandt's Pen; Suburbaville is caught in between, a buffer between the base and the superstructure. Outside Suburbaville, the slums begin. And in the slums live the strangers.

In his second novel, with I am sure unconscious irony, and without meaning to, Hearne portrays as the real "stranger at the gate", not the cultured (presumably Haitian) communist, Étienne, a black man castled in the very Western values whose political and economic bases he has set out to over-throw, but the Cayunian slum-king, Tiger Johnson. Johnson and the nameless murderer of Mark Lattimer in *Voices*, and Sonny in *Autumn Equinox*, and Henneky in *Land of the Living*, are the real strangers in Hearne's novels. The gates of Brandt's Pen, and the gates of Suburbaville are shut fast against these strangers; and to a great extent – and it is here that Lamming's criticism has point – so too are the gates of Hearne's imagination. Lattimer's murderer is seen through the eyes of a Lattimer, a Tiger Johnson through the eyes of a Mckenzie, Henneky through the eyes of a displaced Jew, Stefan Mahler. To reverse this angle of seeing will be very much Hearne's Rubicon.

Davies is good on the political aspects of Hearne's novels. He points out that,

> The communist activities exist at the level of those in a James Bond novel. We suspect that they mean little as politics, to Roy McKenzie or to Jim Diver. For them to be a Communist is to be alien and romantic; they have no rational programme.[118]

To illustrate this, Davies shows how Mckenzie, the Communist, "finds fulfilment by hurling himself to death against the front of a police car to enable Étienne to escape"; and how, in *Autumn Equinox,* Jim Diver sacrifices himself, although with no assurance that his sacrifice will have any effect, only perhaps, "to prove something to himself". From this Davis concludes that "it would be hard to see a consistent political philosophy in these novels".[119] Having come to this conclusion, Davies goes on to argue that

> Human commitment... in unselfish love is of more importance to Hearne than political commitment. Rachel throws herself in the way of the bullet Jojo intended for Michael. It is a heroic gesture which in its very completeness destroys all possibility of realising the values that it asserts. Mark Lattimer's love for Brysie is cut short by a casual machete stroke; and Jim Diver's for Eleanor by the anti-Castro thugs. The fatalistic tragedy cuts short human and political aspirations alike.[120]

And here we begin to wonder. Has Davies here, without quite realising it, not put his finger on what he says the novels lack – a consistent political philosophy? Can it not be argued that Hearne's political philosophy is one founded on a world view which accepts the dominance of Fate in order *not* to change circumstances? The most curious observation to be made about Hearne's Cayuna is its essentially static nature. The more things change, the more they remain the same. Not that Hearne's politics are the politics of *reaction,* the politics of a Brandt, say, who by striving to retain the old way of life, by opposing a total concept of the past to the present, in reacting from change, can in fact help to precipitate change. Hearne's political philosophy, and this is what I find disturbing in a man of his generation, seems to me to be the far more dangerous "liberal" politics of the present status quo. By at all times asserting the primacy of individual choice over the needs of the whole, by in fact, assuming a dichotomy between the two, Hearne seems to me to share and to accept that world view, which Adorno analyses in an essay on Spengler:

> The return of what is always the same, in which such a doctrine of fate terminates, is, however, nothing but the perpetual reproduction of man's guilt towards man. The concept of fate which subjects man to blind domination, reflects the domination exercised by men. Whenever Spengler speaks of fate he means the subjugation of one group of men by another… In reality the inexorability of Fate is defined through domination and injustice…[121]

Are Hearne's characters really interested in changing society? Or only in acting out roles, in making gestures about changing it, changes which are doomed from the start? In *Voices Under the Window,* the changer of the system, Mark Lattimer, is doomed, and the author dooms him by an accident of Fate, a casual machete stroke rather than by the logic of his circumstance. For Lattimer's socialism is, from the start, like its author's, of the head rather than the heart. Although his political commitment begins with his punching a sailor who uses the term "nigger", one suspects that after this brief emotional flurry, (he himself is part, a small part, black) Lattimer begins to act through an intellectual imperative, committing himself as his Czech communist friend had advised him, to the "destiny of the poor". But he commits himself without every having really felt what José Martí termed the "slap on his own face" that the poor feel every day, the total sense of outsidership.

And it is here perhaps that Hearne confuses the issue. For, if he had shown us that the political commitment of his hero was as much an upper middle-class privilege, as much a product of the social and political arrangement of his society as was his colour of skin, quality of hair, of education, of feeling, of conscience; if he had shown us that in taking over the running of the system Lattimer was merely coming into an inheritance, and that in chanting the slogans and seeking the destiny of the poor he was in fact fulfilling nothing but his own private destiny, easing nothing but the private property of his conscience, then his death, at the hand of an unknown murderer, would not have been by accident, but the result of a terrible logic. For then the unknown murderer would have been seen also as a logical product of the same system; a man who kills aimlessly in an aimless existence which is his lot of inheritance. But Hearne draws back from such a conclusion. It would have made Lattimer's murderer as important as Lattimer himself. It would have shown both as the result of the same historical process, a process in which Lattimer had an ineluctable appointment with his murderer; an appointment decreed not by Fate, not even by History, but by Man's unjust arrangement of his society.

The pattern of *Voices* is repeated as novel follows novel and all the potential threats to the basic arrangement of Cayuna society are eliminated – white Roy McKenzie with his romantic and upper middle-class Communism; black Jojo Rygin, threatening the system with his grasping after black economic power; Rachel Anscomb, rocking it with her brown body power, her outsider's sharp aggressive brain; Henneky, finally assaulting the implicitly accepted values of "white power, white religion and white culture" on which the system is based. All these seekers after change Hearne condemns to death or frustration.

Yet the Brandts do not fail. They live on, serenely. The inhabitants of Suburbaville do not fail – the Olivers and the Sybils; Andrew Fabricus, buying his estate, taking his modernised place in the system, effortlessly defeating in Parliament the corrupt black politician Littleford, does not fail; nor does his wife Margaret, painting Leda raping the swan, creating a classical oasis of Art in a society whose suburbs, by their acceptance of privilege, do violence to the slums of a Tiger Johnson, day after sour day. The Brandts and the inhabitants of Suburbaville embody for Hearne, those "human values" which "politics" can only destroy; and come hell or high water these human values must be preserved by the few who can afford them. So these few do not fail; nor does the Jew Stefan Mahler, wounded with the memory of Nazi Holocaust and therefore supposed to "understand" the wounds of the black outsider, Henneky, fail. At the end of the *Land of the Living* Henneky dies, but boy gets girl – Stefan gets Joan.

Here Davies makes his most acute observation:

> And yet, in the present social situation of Cayuna, Henneky's death remains a dramatic aberration. There is little hope of a moral resurrection. There cannot even be real contact between the white Mahler and the Negro Henneky, no mutual recognition that 'they have been wounded by the same accident'.[122]

There can be no real contact because Mahler, the Jew, even after the Nazi experience, fails to see the connection that Alejo Carpentier's narrator saw; instead, Mahler happily sings the chorus from *Beethoven's Ninth*, opposing it to the music of the steel band which he, and his author, mentally dismiss as being "a social adjunct" to people's lives which had not yet become "ART". One sees that Mahler, like Hearne, is still imprisoned in a European scale of reference, a very arrogant Euro-centred view which had justified the massacre of all the *Untermenschen*, who had not *as yet* become Aryans, did not *as yet* participate in European *Kultur*; who in fact were perhaps forever shut out by race and blood and breeding from any real progression to an imagined cultural Valhalla.

Mahler, coming to Cayuna, takes his top place in the system, a place accorded to him by his whiteness of skin; he is now the Aryan and the black Henneky, the exiled Jew. If he is to live as a man, Henneky must destroy the system. Mahler, like Hearne, wants to keep the system, making a change here and a change there, but making sure that the "human values" which are important to them are not thrown overboard. Yet because these values are reserved only for the few, the more than equal, they partake of the sickness of all privilege, of all injustice, and they constitute a daily slap in the face to the poor who have no share in them.

In order to avoid this connection, Hearne with the eye of the evader – Davies points out that Hearne's eye cannot "adjust to record the more shadowy aspects of his panorama. We never really see the seething poverty in the slums of the Queenshaven Jungle –"[123] takes refuge in the concept of Fate. In a world supposedly dominated by Fate, the individual can only "accept" his destiny; he cannot create it; can only make "gestures" of change, he can never really change it. In such a world, the poor are only props to be used by the few who can afford the luxury of private lives and a liberal conscience. The world of Hearne's novels resembles the world of Graham Greene's *A Burnt-out Case,* set in the Congo, and that of *The Comedians* set in Haiti.[124] In Greene's novels, Africans and Haitians are there only as background crowds, to provide the setting for the spiritual wrestling of the burnt-out liberal European intellectual, or for the sexual wrestlings of the played-out European comedians. In Hearne's Cayuna, the poor serve as the background crowd. The body of a Bernice in *The Land of the Living* is there to recharge Mahler with feeling, so that he can fulfil this feeling in his relationship with Joan – as Africa is there to recharge Greene's intellectual, and Haiti to rekindle both the conscience and the sexual capacity of his comedians – the black horror in the background provides the stimulus for both.

Whilst Henneky and Bernice die hunted tragic deaths, Mahler remains once more at ease. A little anguish to be carried over into his relationship with Joan, whose drunken and unhappy soul he has redeemed, can hardly atone for the death of a Henneky and a Bernice, for the acceptance of their continued exclusion from the possibility of happiness. Davies glimpses this and asks:

> Is the cosy adjustment into middle-class domestic life any answer to a challenge posed by the life and death of Henneky?[125]

Yet Davies fails to see that in choosing this "cosy adjustment into middle-class domestic life", in choosing "human commitment to unselfish love" as being of more importance than "political commitment", Hearne has himself *made* a political commitment. For in asserting that politics destroy "human values", Hearne accepts that these values are a fetish object, like culture; that like culture, or Brandt's Pen, they are timeless and static. He disassociates the creation of values from particular societies at particular stages of existence, as he disassociates "culture" from the "material processes of existence". "Human values" are not there to serve Man, but to be served by him. Under Greek values, Greek culture, Hearne avoids seeing Greek slavery as their base; he evades also the logical connection between the "timeless world" of Brandt's Pen and the terror of the Queenshaven slums. And he evades these connections by concentrating on sex as "a serious human issue".

In concentrating on the private life of individuals at a time when private life has become "a mere appendage to the social process", Hearne distorts his perspective. Even the most all-embracing bed can scarcely today contain the powerful forces that determine the private life down to its very marrow. It is no longer sex that impels society, but society that impels and distorts and confuses sex. The trivial tragedy of a drunken Joan Culpepper and the deeper tragedy of a Henneky are dictated by the same forces. By exalting private personal *gestures* as an end in themselves, rather than as symptoms of the same sickness, Hearne defends the immanent rationality and justice of the system. Ritual replaces belief, and prevents any genuine action springing from such belief.

It is this basic distortion which lies at the failure of the later novels of John Hearne. In his first novel, *Voice Under the Window,* Hearne is still aware of his own temptation: he makes Lattimer's politically conscious friend tell him:

> Love for your generation, is only interesting and important if it takes place inside a much wider frame than two people together can make. The same with everything else; every private thing has a responsibility to something bigger than seems to enter into every corner of your lives. Even when *you* aren't aware of it as you aren't, Mark, it lies on your conscience.[126]

In *Voices* some sort of a balance was kept between the private love and "the much wider frame"; this was also to some extent true in *Stranger at the Gate.* But in Hearne's third novel, *The Faces of Love,* "love" made of the island and people of Cayuna a convenient frame in which to work out its private destiny; the "something bigger" became only a stage setting in which the lovers could do their own thing. Because of this imbalance, Hearne's characters have become trapped in trivia.

Land of the Living, which Davies sees as Hearne's best book, seems to me to be his most alienated: an intellectual exercise in which Hearne sings the blues for Auschwitz and Henneky's crucifixion, only to solve it in the success story of Joan Culpepper's bed. There is a certain barbarity in such a resolution. *Land of the Living,* like *Autumn Equinox* belong essentially to what Malraux calls "the appeasing arts";[127] they provide an escape to an illusion, which alone keeps the unjust reality creaking along; they provide the pleasures of romance which, as Malraux shows, does not unite men but separates them by the very human values that Suburbaville can afford and Queenshaven can't.

Both Hearne's return to his island, and his long silence since *Land of the Living* are hopeful signs. But the danger of returning home is not, for Hearne, as Davies suggests, the danger of "intellectual isolation". The world of the Mona campus – at the University – where Hearne co-administers the Creative

Arts Centre – can keep one well in the vanguard of "intellectual thought", especially that of England. Yet it is, paradoxically, this "intellectual thought" that can be the danger. The Argentinian, Eduardo Mallea, has described two Argentinas: "an invisible Argentina, and a superficial Argentina of men who had substituted appearances for reality".[128]

Here too there are two Jamaicas, and the Mona campus for the most part belongs to the "superficial" Jamaica which has substituted appearances for reality. What Hearne as a writer may well be in need of is not only a return from exile in the metropolitan centre, but a new kind of exile, one which Mallea describes:

> Without exiling oneself one cannot get anywhere. The path of creation is the path of exile; and there is a time for rejecting this and a time for accepting; there is a time for choosing to remain tied to surrounding fiction and a time for exiling oneself. And such an exile in our country, means going and living in the invisible nation with its invisible sensitivity, living in the heart of the nation.[129]

This is an exile whose actual distance can perhaps be measured as the distance from the Mona Campus to August Town, yet whose spiritual distance is incalculable. It *is* an exile into a new way of seeing, of feeling. And the exile cannot be fitful, a mere slumming, like Mahler's; nor a slogan-like commitment to the "destiny of the poor". It is, instead, a commitment to one's survival as a human being and a writer. One can only hope that Hearne's next novel – continuing his evocation of landscape, his "marrying of our emotions to rock and to smell, and taste and sound, his genuine gift as a story teller, that ancient gift, common to all cultures, will break new ground, out a of creative exile in the invisible... heart of nation". For it is only there – not a place, but a new gamut and range of feeling – that Hearne will cross his Rubicon; will learn, through a new emotional identification, how to see the white Mahler through the black Henneky's eyes; how to define the "insider" Lattimer through the outsider's eye of a Tiger Johnson. This new kind of eye, the outsider's eye, will mean that Hearne, having paid his dues, will have learnt how to really sing the blues for a Henneky; he would then have no need of a borrowed suffering. To sing the blues the writer must be haunted by the same sickness; and the same wound. Our wounds must haunt us, in our exile in the invisible nation, every minute of our waking day. If we don't sing the blues for our own pain, who will sing the blues for them? It is in this sense that Hearne needs a new type of exile, into outsider territory; that he needs a blacker *Weltschmerz*.

VIII

I am not much interested in what the West Indian writer has brought to the English language... A more important consideration is what the West Indian novelist has brought to the West Indies.

Lamming, *The Pleasures of Exile*[130]

Once the mind is no longer directed at reality, its meaning is changed despite the strictest preservation of meaning.

Adorno, *Prisms*[131]

They wished to renew Western music, imitating rhythms which had never had a musical function for its primitive creators.

Alejo Carpentier, *The Lost Steps*[132]

If John Hearne, in his latest novels, enters the middlebrow world of the "appeasing arts", Wilson Harris, of whom Hearne writes with approval and ritual mystification in the essay – "The Fugitive in the Forest", takes his place, with his novels, and in spite of the sincerity of his stated intentions, in the highbrow context of the appeasing arts. To see the validity of this, one has only to read a short story – "Kanaima"[133] – written by Harris and published by Kenneth Ramchand in his collection of West Indian narrative. Ramchand, addressing this narrative to West Indian readers and to West Indian school children, edits and simplifies Harris's story, with the motive of communication. The result is a powerful story, in which Harris *recreates* a myth believed in by both Negro and Indian, by the folk over whom Kanaima exercises dominance; and provides that element of the unattainable that man, capitalist or communist or Third World, ignores at his peril. In this story Harris shows us a fusion between the belief and the believer; and the believer through belief becomes consciously aware, in the light of Harris's interpretation and re-invention, of his own tenuous and fragile journey up the rockface supported by the moulding of the face of Kanaima, his own projected dream creating the reality of Kanaima. In this story, Ramchand as editor pares away the narcissistic accretions of Harris, the writer qua writer, and reveals the validity of Harris as creator, as the re-interpreter of collective fear and hope. There is then, in this short story, the "virility of motivation" with which the artist communicates, by establishing that reciprocal relation with his audience which is the basis of all art that sets out to give meaning, however impossible and difficult, to existence; rather than providing an escape from an existence accepted to be meaningless. This "virility of motivation" is lacking in the novels of Harris.

It is this lack which betrays the revolutionary intention of Harris; without this primary and compelling motive of communication – even of the incommunicable – the writer floats in a free fall of obfuscation. This is not to deny Harris's insights – his opposition to the concept of the "individual character" as portrayed in Hearne, for example; his shattering of the established images of feeling, in order to shatter the distorted reality which these images project and support. What one objects to is that he replaces existing reality with another *arbitrarily* created one out of his own imagination; not in opposition to, nor as a contrasting illumination of reality as it exists, but one so totally unrelated, that it ends up by being escapist. Whilst denying the fixity of the "individual character" – Hearne points out that Harris argues that the problem of character in the West Indian novel is one of *fulfilment* rather than *consolidation* – Harris in fact establishes in his novels the primacy of the unrelated individual imagination.

It is this paradox that explains the fascination that a Harris has for a Hearne, in spite of the very profound differences between them. But it is this paradox, too, that makes it impossible for Hearne to grasp the very real insights of Harris, and therefore to understand where the insights, put into practice, have failed to come across. Yet Hearne's essay here and there gives us clues to Harris's failure. In discussing Oudin, one of Harris's "characters", Hearne points out that at the end of the novel, the reader can see Oudin, stripped of his magic realism; see him,

> …as just another old Guyanese peasant dead on the floor of a hut on the coastal savannahs.[134]

By the very careless and casual contempt implicit in this statement – a contempt totally absent from the intention of a Harris – one sees that the "reality" of the peasant has been exploited as a symbol for a literature, which, in ostensibly reinventing him, totally excludes him; since its meaning is foreign to him. He has been used to create a myth in which he neither partakes nor believes – it is Harris's rather than Guyana's myth.

In his first novel, Lamming tells how he first came upon its title:

> I first came across the phrase 'castle of my skin' in a poem by the West Indian poet, Derek Walcott. In a great torrent of rage, inseparable from hate, the poet is addressing some white presence… 'You in the castle of your skin, I among the swineherd'. This phrase had coincided with my search for a title, and I remembered that night and knew that in spite of his Age, meaning Skin, Papa could never see himself among the swine. Nor could the village. So I thought that it was correct, and even necessary to appropriate that image in order to restore the castle where it belonged.[135]

In Harris's novels, and in areas of the later ones of Lamming, the "castles" of the West Indian people are being continually appropriated, either to build the peacock palace of Harris' private vision, or to strengthen the walls of Lamming's now distant village, continually rebuilt, exquisite and nostalgic, fading from reality, out of lingering echoes. Lamming's awareness of his dilemma, his linking of the reality of Papa's hut and village to the present reality of his London centre, enables him to provide moments of illumination about a new relation.

Harris on the other hand, inhabits a closed palace, whose jewelled walls reflect only themselves. There Harris achieves what he sets out to achieve – the attainment "of an inward dialogue and space" in a world where language and being has been emptied of meaning. But his dialogue is a monologue which begins and ends in a cul-de-sac. In one of his essays, Adorno explains the dilemma of a Harris:

> For it is only in the process of withdrawing into itself, only indirectly that is, that bourgeois culture conceives of a purity from the corrupting traces of the proletarian disorder which embraces all areas of existence... Only in so far as it withdraws from Man, can culture be faithful to man. But such concentration on substance which is absolutely one's own, contributes... at the same time to the impoverishment of that substance. Once the mind is no longer directed at reality, its meaning is changed despite the strictest preservation of meaning. Through its resignation before the facts of life, and, even more through its isolation as one 'field' among others, the mind aids the existing order and takes it place within it.[136]

Despite his conscious intention, the novels of Harris end up as a highbrow consumer product, accessible only to the initiated, and alien to its own audience. In striving to perfect a *theory* Harris strives to achieve *artistic norms* and turns his back on the other striving – that striving which his own short story "Kanaima", so well illustrates – the striving, "however impotently, that man may be spared".[137] Because of this, the artistic norms of Harris's novels are achieved in a vacuum – excellent, like Narcissus, in love with, and reflecting only itself.

But the core of Harris's confusion can perhaps be found in an essay, "The Writer and Society", in which he makes a "far-reaching" distinction between "social character, that is, social species or species of convention", and "primordial character".[138] To make his point he uses illustrations from Greek myths and from the Haitian vodun, or voodoo. Speaking of the experience of the "possessed" dancer in voodoo, he says:

> Remember at the outset the dancer regards himself or herself as one in full command of two legs, a pair of arms, etc., until, possessed by the muse of contraction, he or she dances into a posture wherein one leg is drawn up into the womb of space. He stands like a rising pole upheld by earth and sky or like a tree which walks in its own shadow or like a one-legged bird which joins itself to its sleeping reflection in a pool. All conventional memory is erased and yet in this trance of overlapping spheres of reflection a primordial or deeper function of memory begins to exercise itself within the bloodstream of space.[139]

One cannot help but feel here that Harris has never attended, and knows very little of the Haitian voodoo ceremony. Apart from the almost ludicrous disparity of the description, the fundamental point that the "primordial consciousness" of the individual possessed dancer is achieved by means of a complex ritual and technique, a ritual and technique created, and participated in by the social group, is missed; and therefore that primordial and social character are complementary, rather than distinct entities.

The individual possession of the dancer is attained, not only through individual effort alone, the individual dance, but by the "work" (to use the Jamaican Pentecostal term) "the labouring in the spirit" on a collective journey travelled by the group, and on this journey every landmark is a communal possession. The journey to possession by the Unconscious is a *conscious* one. The primordial revelation is attained through an elaborate, extremely logical and *social* ritual. It is paradoxical that Harris, who in general seems to be well aware of the *logic* that underlies all so-called primitive art, should miss such a basic corollary. His mistake seems to be one shared by many European artists, whose predicament, the Cuban novelist Carpentier describes, when he says that they took fetish objects like African masks and attempted to use the *objects* in their assault on Cartesian reason. They failed because they were unaware that these objects had their own rationale; that they were in fact not only manifestations of a reasoned and logical belief, but of a belief, and of a reason which had not separated itself from the way of life which created it and which it created. As Carpentier writes:

> They looked for 'barbarity' in objects which had never been barbarous when they fulfilled their ritual functions in primitive rhythms. They wished to renew Western music imitating rhythms which had never had a musical function for its primitive creators...[140]

In his novels Harris attempts to evoke a primordial consciousness, without providing the social keys, the communally recognised landmarks which would invite the reader's participation in the "work of the spirit" on the journey. Without this the journey does not take place; there are gestures of movement rather than movement itself; without a common belief, ritual degenerates into a solitary exercise in a cell. Perhaps Harris's comment on modern American poets best describes his own novels, novels in which,

> ... one may only point to the symbol of an overwhelming ordeal without release.[141]

IX

> He went and sat down beside the wall he was building, high enough now to give a little shade from the sun. The building was still in its earliest stage. He knew it was to be part of the new University College but he couldn't imagine the ultimate shape and he felt excluded from its social meaning...
> Neville Dawes, *The Last Enchantment*[142]

> How often is Art in all its forms and fancies going to make friends with the multitude? National galleries sheltering the best, or municipal ones sheltering the worst, aren't much good to the common man, passing through the common hours...
> It is useless to say that the artist can sit safely in his ivory tower, looking scornfully down from a lancet window at the people below. He can't, for sooner or later sturdy shoulders pressing against it will send the ivory tower toppling. The artist may live on for a while, hearsed in honour from a few; but when the few go, the end of the artist comes.
> Sean O'Casey, "The Arts Among the Multitude"[143]

In the first part of this essay we pointed out that the body of critical writing which we are discussing has come out of the University of the West Indies. As the only institution of comparable size that the Caribbean territories will be able to afford, it is clear that the University must commit itself to the cultural destiny of our territories. If we borrow Eduardo Mallea's distinction once more, we may well ask – to which Jamaica, which Caribbean, is the University of the West Indies to belong? To the inauthentic, making gestures, and in particular the gesture of "silence", which is, according to Mallea, the most typical gesture of those who refuse to explore their reality? Or to that other, "that invisible heart" which compels exploration and awareness. The critical essays show that the University is still poised between the choice – and leaning more towards the older, the easier, the gesture of silence. Silence – and in silence we include slogans and formulas borrowed from the metropolitan centre and applied without relevance – is more "academic", conforms to "established standards". Silence is more liveable with. With silence, the descendants of Prospero and Caliban, ex-colonial master and ex-colonised, can pretend that the multiple flags waving in place of the Union Jack have bewitched away the past. Yet we can realise our common present only by the exploration of our common past. To replace this exploration by silence as we have mainly done so far, is to give to silence the sound of the school yell that Dawes describes in *The Last Enchantment*:

> The unity, the oneness of the same school yell, was superficial, and the much-vaunted 'great harmony among the different races' was an inaccurate interpretation of a very precarious compromise.[144]

Above all, this kind of silence, of the unsaid, has deprived the University, as it does some of these essays, of a genuine sense of purpose. To avoid the past connection between Prospero and Caliban, is to ignore what *unites* them in the present: the unity of a *common purpose*. Without the realisation of this purpose, with our continued pragmatic acceptance of "just getting on with the job", we shall continue to turn out an elite technocrat class (some with liberal slogans, some with Black Power slogans) all seeking to take an "elite" place in any order (liberal, Communist, Black Power) which is based on an elite. We shall continue to turn out the "brains" prepared to direct the "brawn", and thereby prepared to continue the sickness and injustice of an ancient separation. What then is this common purpose?

Our purpose begins to formulate itself with our awareness of the University as the logical result of a common history stretching over some four centuries; as a place where the descendants of Prospero-slave owner, and Caliban-slave, can, by using the technological knowledge acquired by Prospero from an unjust relation, mount an assault against that historical necessity, that scarcity of food and shelter, which had, in the dark and terrible ages, impelled exploitation of some by others and still impels it. Our purpose is stated by Adorno in an essay:

The only adequate response to the present technical situation which holds out the promise of wealth and abundance, is to organize it according to the needs of a humanity which no longer needs violence because it is its own master.[145]

And what, one may well ask, has all this got to do with "talking about a little culture?" Injustice, based in all its forms on a concept of elitism, continues not because the technological means are not available to provide food, shelter, and freedom from material want for *all*, but because minds, which have for centuries been moulded and preformed to come to terms with the *actuality* of scarcity and therefore of injustice, elitism and division, find it difficult to come to an awareness of the distortion of their own barbaric formation. This formation had been imposed on us through long centuries by the blind necessity of material existence and this formation continues to dominate us through the power of the very cultural myths which we had devised as our avenue of escape, our illusionary flight from this necessity. And that is why the twentieth century revolution must essentially be a cultural revolution, a transformation in the way men see and feel. To paraphrase Brecht: "The Barbarians had their cultures; it is time now that we had ours."

It is not, of course, going to be as easy as all that. The Argentinian writer, Ezequiel Martínez Estrada, discussing among other things, the cultural failure of the Russian Revolution, also pinpoints the reasons for the failure of the nineteenth-century independence movements of Latin America:

> Neither here nor elsewhere is there any public awareness of the fact that cultural emancipation is not any easier, although it may be less bloody, than political liberty; and a great part of the failure of our independence movements was due to the fact that our liberators were not liberated from themselves... Mentally freed, they were subconsciously in chains, because they continued to accept the structure of European cultures, changing only their forms and a small part of their content, in the same way as they had done with their political institutions...[146]

This is an exact analysis of our situation, both as society and University today. This situation is reflected in the imitative solutions which we devise to all our problems. This is not to deny that our cultural distortion is a reflection of a power situation in which we are still economically dominated, as was nineteenth-century Latin America, by metropolitan centres. As a University, we have attacked the distortion of this *economic* dominance; yet we continue to reflect in our goals, curriculum, "standards" the cultural corollary of this economic arrangement. The refusal of our society to take us seriously may well spring from the fact that "culturally" we reflect the very untruths that we denounce. We need a new awareness of our own paradox, and this awareness should be diffused through our praxis, however inadequate rather than through our sermons.

The cultural image of the University can be said to be embodied in its critical writing and in its Creative Arts Centre, not in its writers nor in its creative artists. It may be argued that it is the policy of the Centre to invite down writers to become West Indian versions of the English Universities "writers-in-residence" for the period of exactly one year. Yet it is clear that the writer-in-residence, brought-down-for-a-year, can be there for no other purpose than for that of being a piece of cultural display – there for his advertising value rather than for the reality of his function. The writer-in-residence-for-a-year is the appeasing gesture used to disguise the fact that, as a University and a society, we *acquiesce* in the arrangement by which West Indian writers must continue to live in metropolitan centres and thereby be rendered impotent to take part, not "in the talking about culture", but in its creation. And for that, the University and its society need the writers as much as the writers need them.

If it is argued that there is no place in the present arrangement and curriculum of the University to provide the writer with a function, it can be answered that this may very well be where the change in the arrangement and curriculum ought to begin. It is not by accident that the uprising of the 'thirties threw up writers and artists at the same time as it threw up politicians; both are at one and the same time prophets and technicians of change. The failure of a society can depend on the limitations of the vision and the skill of both. The exile of the one or the other creates an imbalance for the society as a whole. The exile of the writer from the University, which as an institution is itself the result of the upheaval of the Thirties, is a serious lack; it is the writer and not the academic who is best able to link the University to that "invisible heart of the nation". The link is of the imagination rather than of the intellect; and it is this link which can include Dawes's worker-politician Edgar within "the social meaning from which he is so far a stranger". Without writers to give flesh to its intention, without *functioning* artists, the Creative Arts Centre remains but another appeasing gesture, another Ark for the faithful in which the elite and the highbrow can contemplate their intellectual navel, whilst the floods of proletarian disorder sweep over the multitudes outside.

A new "culture" for us is not a luxury, not and no longer the playmate of an elite soul; it must be instead the agent of man's drive to survive in the twentieth century.

Adorno is right when he says:

Today, adjustment to what is possible no longer means adjustment; it means making the possible real.[147]

Endnotes

1. The exact quotation cannot be located.
2. "On the Occasion for Speaking", *The Pleasures of Exile* (London: Michael Joseph, 1960), 50.
3. Dominique Desanti, "Le Père des Jacobins Noirs le Jamaïquain C.L.R. James",

Le Monde (April 4, 1968): http://www.lemonde.fr/archives/article/1968/04/06/le-pere-des-jacobins-noirs-le-jamaiquain-c-l-r-james_2489779_1819218. html?xtmc=le_pere_des_jacobins_noirs&xtcr=1. C. L. R. was, of course, not from Jamaica, but Trinidad.

4. Introduction to *The Pleasures of Exile*, 12.
5. Leopoldo Zea Aguilar (1912-2004) was a Mexican philosopher who applied the ideas of logical positivism to systems of thought in Latin America. We cannot locate the source of this quotation but the concept of utopia is discussed in his *El torno a una filosofía americana* (México: El Colejo de México, 1945).
6. Roland Barthes, *Mythologies*, trans. by Annette Lavers (1957; New York: Noonday Press/Farrar, Straus & Giroux, 1972), 82-83, 133.
7. Clarival do Prado Valladares, "Negritud o mundo negro", *Mundo Nuevo*, no. 4 (Octubre 1966), 68.
8. Ibid., 69.
9. André Malraux, "Art, Popular Art, and the Illusion of the Folk", *The Partisan Review*, vol. XVIII, no. 5 (September 1951): 487-495.
10. Count Lev N. Tolstoi, *What is Art?*, trans. Aylmer Maude (New York: Thomas Y. Crowell and Co., 1899), 182-183.
11. *The Pleasures of Exile*, 12.
12. *The Islands in Between* (London: Oxford University Press, 1968), p. 4.
13. Ibid., 25.
14. Ibid.
15. T.W. Adorno, *Prisms*, 19.
16. Ibid.
17. Lamming, *Pleasures of Exile*, 12.
18. Dawes, *The Last Enchantment*, 27.
19. V.S. Naipaul, *The Middle Passage: Impressions of Five Societies – British, French and Dutch – in the West Indies and South America* (1962; London: Andre Deutch, 1978), 29.
20. Alejo Carpentier, *Los pasos perdidos* (1953; New York: Penguin, 1998), 131.
21. Lamming, *The Pleasures of Exile*, 13
22. Ibid. and *The Tempest*, Act 3 Sc II, ll. 134-135.
23. Ibid., 12.
24. "Roger Mais – Design from Legend", *Caribbean Quarterly*, vol. 13. no. 1 (March 1967), 13.
25. Jean-Paul Sartre, "Preface" to Frantz Fanon, *The Wretched of the Earth*, trans. *Les damnés de la terre* by Constance Farrington (1961: New York: Grove Press, 1966), 7.
26. *The Islands in Between*, 11. The quotation is from C.L.R. James in *The Black Jacobins* (1938; New York Vintage Books),18, quoting De Wimpffen on the West Indian slave.
27. Adorno, *Prisms*, 69.
28. Quote is from Edward Brathwaite, *Rights of Passage* (Oxford University Press, 1967), cited in *The Islands in Between*, 1.
29. *The Islands in Between*, 4.
30. Gordon Rohlehr, "The Ironic Approach: The Novels of V.S. Naipaul", *The Islands in Between*, 122.

31. Sartre, Preface to Fanon's *The Wretched of the Earth*, 17.
32. V.S. Naipaul, *The Mimic Men* (New York: Penguin, 1967), 162, 180.
33. Eldridge Cleaver, *Soul on Ice* (New York: McGraw Hill, 1968), 61.
34. Roberto Fernández Retamar, *Poesía reunida, 1948-1965* (La Habana, Cuba: Ediciones Unión/Bolsilibros, 1966), 324.
35. Rohlehr, "The Ironic Approach", *Islands in Between,* 121-122.
36. Adorno, *Prisms*, 26.
37. The source of this quotation cannot be located. However, the "Letter of Dr. Diego Álvarez Chanca on the Second Voyage of Columbus" offers a similar perspective: "These islanders appeared to us to be more civilized than those that we had hitherto seen; for although the Indians have houses of straw, yet the houses of these people are constructed in a much superior fashion… They had a considerable quantity of cotton, …so well woven as to be no way inferior to those of our country." Julius E. Olson and Edward Gaylord Bourne, eds. *The Northmen, Columbus and Cabot, 985-1503* (New York: Charles Scribner's Sons, 1906), 289. Later in the letter, the alleged castration and cannibalism of the Caribs, that Wynter mentions, also appears: "When they take any boys prisoners, they cut off their member and make use of them as servants until they grow up to manhood, and then when they wish to make a feast they kill and eat them." Ibid., 290-291.
38. Cited in Lamming, "A Monster, a Child, a Slave" in *The Pleasures of Exile*, 98.
39. *The Tempest*, Act. I, Sc II, ll. 310-314 [Norton ed.].
40. Mervyn Morris, "The Poet as Novelist", *The Islands in Between,* 83.
41. Ibid., 83-84.
42. *The Tempest,* Act I, Sc. II, lines 420-421, cited by Lamming, "A Monster, etc.", 102.
43. *The Tempest*, Act III, Scene 2, ll. 137-138.
44. Adorno, *Prisms*, 23.
45. Ibid. Adorno references Clarival do Prado Valladares "Negritud o mundo negro", in *Mundo Nuevo*.
46. Wynter references Aimé Césaire's, *Cahier d'un retour au pays natal* (1956; Paris: Présence Africaine, 1983), 47. Wynter's translation of "Eia pour ceux [those] qui n'ont jamais rien inventé".
47. Valladares, "Negritud o mundo negro", 70 (Wynter's translation).
48. Adorno, *Prisms*, 71.
49. Alejo Carpentier, *Los pasos perdidos* (1953; New York: Penguin, 1985).
50. Arnold Wesker, *Roots* (first performed 1958), (London: Penguin Books, 1959), 148.
51. Neville Dawes, *The Last Enchantment* (London: McGibbon & Kee, 1960), 181. Now available in Peepal Tree Press, Caribbean Modern Classics, 2009, 214.
52. The source of Carlos Fuentes' quotation could not be located, but elsewhere he states: "Permanent revolution is the daily conquest of the outer limits of truth, creativity, the disorder that must always oppose the orthodox." *A Change of Skin*, trans. by Sam Hileman (New York: Farrar, Straus & Giroux, 1968), 289.
53. Fitzroy Frazer, *Wounds in the Flesh* (London: New Authors, 1962), 136.
54. Rohlehr, "The Ironic Approach", 122.
55. Carpentier, *Los pasos perdidos* 249, 270.
56. Adorno, *Prisms*, 38.

57. Ibid.

58. *The Tempest*, Act I, Sc. II, ll. 354-357.

59. George Lamming, *Season of Adventure* (London: Michael Joseph, 1960), 38.

60. Ibid., 38-39.

61. Ibid., 27.

62. Ibid., 27, 39.

63. "The Occasion for Speaking", *The Pleasures of Exile*, 26.

64. Héctor Murena, *El pecado original de América* (1954; Buenos Aires: Editorial Sudamerica, 1965), 34.

65. Adorno, *Prisms*, 19-20.

66. Wayne Brown, "The Novelist in an Unsettled Culture".

67. George Robert Coulthard, "The Spanish American Novel, 1940 - 1965", *Caribbean Quarterly*, vol. 12, no. 4 (December 1966), 10-11.

68. Carpentier, *Los pasos perdidos,* 102-103.

69. Sartre, Preface to *The Wretched of the Earth*, 21-22.

70. Carpentier, *Los pasos perdidos,* 88.

71. Ibid., 114.

72. George Lamming, *In the Castle of My Skin* (1953; New York: McGraw-Hill, 1954), 312.

73. Carr, "Roger Mais", 20.

74. Jean Creary, "A Prophet Armed: The Novels of Roger Mais", *The Islands in Between*, 54.

75. Lamming, *Season of Adventure*, 36.

76. Sartre, Preface to *The Wretched of the Earth*, 22.

77. Brown, "The Novelist in an Unsettled Culture". In *Encounter*, John Wain points out that George Orwell, did just this. Orwell argued that the English "… do not wish to recognise… that their own fine feelings and noble attitudes are all the fruit of injustice backed up by force. They do not want to learn where their incomes come from." John Wain, "Orwell and the Intelligentsia", *Encounter*, vol. 81, no. 6 (December 1968): 72-80. Orwell was even more explicit, arguing according to Wain "that, since the British Empire was a system for exploiting cheap coloured labour, the true "proletariat" of England had dark skins and lived thousands of miles away."

78. Oscar Wilde, "The Decay of Lying", in *Intentions* (Boston: Brainard, 1909), 14.

79. Brown, "The Novelist in an Unsettled Culture".

80. Adorno, *Prisms*, 19.

81. *Wounds in the Flesh*, 161.

82. The first publication of *Capitalism and Slavery* was by the University of North Carolina Press in 1944.

83. Carr, "Roger Mais", *Caribbean Quarterly*, 13.

84. Ibid., 11.

85. Ibid., 13. And see T.S. Eliot, "Gerontion", *The Complete Poems and Plays* (London: Faber and Faber, 1969), 38.

86. Ibid., 12.

87. Ibid.

88. *The Pleasures of Exile*, 12.

89. Carr, "Roger Mais", 3.

90. Ibid., 8.

91. Louis James, "Of Redcoats and Leopards: Two Novels by V. S. Reid", in *Islands in Between*, 72. Emphasis added.

92. Cameron King and Louis James, "The Poetry of Derek Walcott" in *Islands in Between*, 89-90.

93. Sartre, Preface to *The Wretched of the Earth*, 8.

94. Carr, "Roger Mais", 9.

95. Norman W. Manley, "Introduction: Roger Mais – the Writer" in *The Three Novels of Roger Mais* (London: Jonathan Cape, 1966), vi.

96. Like Louis James, Carr makes "anti-colonial genuflections". Colonialism was for Mais as all other writers, he admits, a "primary nullification". But his "colonialism" is again seen as a vast impersonal force, without connection or relatedness with England. And he rejects any notion of the creative quality of the awakened anti-colonialism of the West Indian people. Carr, "Roger Mais", 10.

97. Ibid., 4.

98. Ibid.

99. Brown, "The Novel in an Unsettled Culture".

100. Ibid.

101. Ibid.

102. Fraser, *Wounds in the Flesh*, 161.

103. Carr, "Roger Mais", 4.

104. Sartre, Preface to *The Wretched of the Earth*, 22.

105. "...building Jerusalem" probably refers to Blake's epic poem *Jerusalem: The Emanation of the Giant Albion,* and to the poem which is the Preface to *Milton: A Poem in 2 Books,* whose last stanza conveys the sentiment suggested by Wynter: "I will not cease from Mental Fight,/Nor shall my Sword sleep in my hand:/Till we have built Jerusalem,/In Englands greens & pleasant Land." See *The Poetry and Prose of William Blake,* David V. Erdman, ed. (Garden City, NY: Doubleday and Company, Inc. 1965), 95.

106. Born in 1853, Martí was a journalist and a lawyer, apostle of, fighter for Cuba's independence from Spain. He died in 1895 but lives on as Cuba's national hero.

107. Creary, "A Prophet Armed", 61.

108. John Hearne, *Land of the Living* (London: Faber and Faber, 1961), 61.

109. Lamming, "The Occasion for Speaking", 45.

110. Ibid., 36.

111. John Hearne, "The Fugitive in the Forest: Four Novels by Wilson Harris" in *The Islands in Between*, 140.

112. Lamming, *The Pleasures of Exile*, 226.

113. Barrie Davies, "The Seekers: The Novels of John Hearne" in *The Islands in Between*, 117.

114. Ibid., 114.

115. Lamming, *In the Castle of My Skin*, 280-283.

116. Davies, "The Seekers", 112.

117. Ibid., 113.

118. Ibid., 117.

119. Ibid.

120. Ibid.
121. Adorno, Prisms, 70.
122. Davies, "The Seekers", 119.
123. Ibid., 114.
124. Graham Greene, *A Burnt-out Case* (New York: Viking Press, 1961) and *The Comedians* (London: Bodley Head, 1966).
125. Davies, "The Seekers", 120.
126. John Hearne, *Voices Under the Window* (London: Faber and Faber, 1955), 85.
127. Malraux, "Art, Popular Art...," 487-495.
128. Eduardo Mallea, *Historia de una pasión argentina* (Buenos Aires: Editorial Sudamericana, 1968), 66.
129. Mallea, *Historia*, 197.
130. Lamming, *Pleasures of Exile*, 36.
131. Adorno, *Prisms*, 23.
132. Carpentier, *Los pasos perdidos,* 270.
133. Wilson Harris, "Kanaima" in *West Indian Narrative: An Introductory Anthology*, Kenneth Ramchand, ed. (London: Nelson, 1966), 196-205.
134. Hearne, "The Fugitive in the Forest" in *The Islands in Between,* 142.
135. Lamming, "Journey to an Expectation" in *The Pleasures of Exile,* 228.
136. Adorno, *Prisms*, 23-24.
137. Adorno, *Prisms*, 19.
138. Harris, "The Writer and Society" in *Tradition, the Writer and Society: Critical Essays* (London: New Beacon, 1967), 48-64.
139. Ibid., 51.
140. Carpentier, *Los pasos perdidos,* 270.
141. Harris, "Art and Criticism" in *Tradition, the Writer and Society,* 10.
142. Dawes, *The Last Enchantment,* 147.
143. Sean O'Casey, "The Arts Among the Multitude" in *The Green Crow* (New York: G. Braziller, 1956), 163-164.
144. *The Last Enchantment,* 29.
145. Adorno, *Prisms*, 93.
146. Ezekiel Martínez Estrada, *En Cuba y al servicio de la revolucíon cubana* (Habana: Unión de Escritores y Artistas de Cuba, 1963), 133.
147. Adorno, *Prisms*, 94.

MORITAT FOR A LOST LEADER

I

I did not go to take my place
In your death procession,
The Mardi Gras of mourning
Must fill my empty space
With words that try, yet fail to say,
Why, hearing you were dead
I wept for yesterday.

Through hills dressed in drought and bronze
You played your piper's song,
Came to our tawdry Samarkand
Crying wares for our pain
Selling a step or two of a dance.
Your melody was rare.

The hills are avenues that lead
Into sky and air,
The trees are circuses that move
From fair to fair.
Death like a monkey doing tricks –
For peanuts, nothing to it
Turns somersaults on the bridle track
Where the moon's up.

In some drowned Atlantis where the sun
Filters shadows on the floor
We shall tell your legend when the sea
Sings against the bone.

On the mound of a hill, Ulysses sits
And stares into the dark
A juke box in a Church of God
Decorates a temporary halt.

The words you used as instruments
Long lost their cutting edge,
Words are the mess of pottage:
They've tricked us in the end.

Yet words must be your monument
For how you used them!
Beyond a politician's promise
Into the poetry of a prophet.

The fire died down
The ashes grew cold
The dogs lay among them and gnawed
The dead bones.
The Word became not bread, but a stone.
Yet once the words were wings that took us up
To where the earth was small to Icarus:
What mattered, fat
Town Councillors with the power of their purses?
Their pomp and circumstance and glory?

What mattered if the wings were wax, and we flew
Too near the sun?
What if the slogans we spat
At the sky fell back to blind our eye?
What if we woke up to find we'd come
To the disenchanted end of the story?
What mattered if the dream was circumscribed by facts?
The flight to the impossible was enough.
All went down
With the flood,
Yet our dance traces the sun on the sea-floor
And, in the still palace of the drowned
Music sounds.

II

The clock in the dragon's den strikes one p.m.
Death fields a catch at silly mid-on:
Death goes in to bat, hits a six, cracks
The stained glass window of the sun.

You played the piper's song but fat
Town Councillors still called the tune:
You could not reach up for the moon, they said.
You bowed your arrogant head, compelled
Got things done and well, slowed down
To the compass of their circumstance.
Worms ate our innocence
We mocked to show our loss.
Was this the end of Eden then?
Was this the promised Zion?

We cried aloud, we wailed upon the water:
The seeds are brown, the taste is sour
The communion wafer
In our mouths hints of gall and vinegar
Where is yesterday?
What rutted side-tracked turning did it take?

We who took up the bed of ourselves
And walked,
Into what cul-de-sac did we dance
To find ourselves
High walled in Babylon?

Death fields a catch at silly mid-on
Death cracks
The stained glass window of the sun.

III

> *Come let us mock at the great*
> *That had such burdens on the mind*
> *And toiled so hard and late*
> *To leave some monument behind.*
>
> YEATS.

Come then, let us take stock
Credit the profit, debit the loss
Of this good merchant who sold us
A step or two of a dance, and
Exchanging charity for power
Which he wore like a flower in his lapel,
Lead us along, piped us a song
In our tawdry Samarkand.

One worshipped, or reviled, your shrine:
Not for you the hail-fellow smile,
Back-slapping joke, alert male pride:
The intelligence of the scribe lit
The sea water of your eyes.

Virtue came easy but you found it
Difficult to cross the great divide
To where the publican cotched outside:
Charity took you by surprise.

A gaulin, your wings
Hovered over the salt grass
Over the bemused cattle straying
In the scrub and alien country
Of the wretched of the earth.

You stooped to alight, and came
To know what failure is, to taste its ashes;
Learnt to come to terms with
The intricacy of grief.

The broken ones for whom you were a crutch
To lean upon,
Shall guard your memory; the angry ones
For whom you played your role as scapegoat
Someone to fix the blame upon:
Satan in their asphalt slums.

Men have need of Satan,
Where God has taken flight
Or, at least, does not advertise.
I am that which I advertise I am.

Before we go down to the dark
Before all language is lost
All meaning is gone, and men speak in neon signs:
Before all the aches of the heart
Are dulled by aspirin, and the tears of things
Catered for by pep-up pills,
Before all grief is institutionalised,
Passion shunted aside, come then:

Let us celebrate this man
Who, in our tawdry Samarkand
Sold us a dream and a song
And a step or two of a dance!

And so, o lost leader, we sing your funeral rites
Words must be your monument, lyrical as light
No Trojan Hector; No tamer of horses
In a dim Mycenian myth
No Alafin of Oyo's vanished kingdom.
In Africa, that gold land of night
And still
The pyre burns bright.

The sons of Priam are gathered as one
They put out the fire with their tears
They wrap the clean bones in cloth
They put the bones in a casket
And the casket in the earth:
The words you spoke print echoes on the air.

O Trojan Hector, how compare
Your remembrance in the hearts of men?
O Alafin of Oyo your shadow cast on water
In a patterned bowl – all that remains of a man
Which is his soul – where is it now?
Your mourning song – where has it gone?
Which spirit mouth now chants the words,
Which spirit flute, the tune?

Under the seagirt earth
In the core of the bronze hills
A man goes there to find not what he said or seemed or did
But the dream that he dreamed of himself which was him.

IV

Politician, statesman, lawyer, patriot:
The last time I saw you, you'd shrugged
Those skins aside:
Arrogance's interregnum and all pride:
Now, the rare smile, poet, old man, child.

We thanked you for the care you'd had for us:
But as we spoke, I knew you'd slipped away from us
Gone to find your crown, o great Prince,
In Death's doomed Kingdom:

The river stopped for a while to give a drink
To death so that without hurrying
You could catch him up.
The hills humped their backs.

Down in the town a bar door swings
Open, closes on brown lips laughing:
The glass jar has spilt its flowers
The feather in the lady's hat is bent.
Death passes.

Two golden birds drowse in your eyes:
Death walks with you, conversing
Along the bridle track.
The moon rises over a staccato of rock:

Death comes alive
In the illuminated wonder of your mind.
The moon weaves a processional of light.

BERNARDO DE BALBUENA
EPIC POET AND ABBOT OF JAMAICA 1562-1627

With my pen, to reach the heights that I desire,
There, with Homer second I to be the first would then aspire.[1]

Now its author can say that he is newly come into the world again, from
the *soledades* (desert place/ solitudes) of Jamaica, where all this while he
has lived as one *encantado* (bewitched /enchanted).

> Bernardo De Balbuena, writing from Puerto Rico, 1623 –1624.[2]

I had never wanted to stay in Trinidad. When I was in the fourth form I
wrote a vow... to leave within five years. I left after six; and for many years
afterwards in England, falling asleep in bedsitters with the electric fire on,
I had been awakened by the nightmare that I was back in tropical Trinidad.

> V.S. Naipaul, writing from England 1960 – 1961.[3]

Two voices across three centuries, one, a poet and a Mexican-Spaniard, the
other a novelist and Trinidadian-Indian, yet both moved by the same compulsion – the urge to escape from a reality which seems bewitched to the first, and
a nightmare to the second. Spain, in her conquest and settlement of the New
World, transplanted, her laws, system of government, military-feudal complex, above all her dominant religious motif, and the culture based on it. In the
early seventeenth century, a Balbuena only had to leave Jamaica for Puerto
Rico to find himself in touch, however tenuously, with what was, to him, a
civilised reality. With the later British colonisation of the New World, a
colonisation whose raison d'être was purely economic, the twentieth-century
Naipaul, to find a cultural metropolitan centre, had to go thousands of miles
to London, to sit and shiver beside an electric fire.

Bernardo de Balbuena was not the first abbot to feel anguish at the thought of
the years he had spent – or misspent – in Jamaica. His predecessor, Francisco
Marques de Villalobos, wrote his King, Philip III of Spain, pleading that he be
sent elsewhere, that he be no longer allowed "to suffer in this exile". His letter
was dated March, 1606. By August, purgatory was ended; Marques de Villalobos
was dead. He was buried at the hour of high mass, at one side of the main altar
of the principal church which stood in the Plaza Mayor (the main square) in Villa
de la Vega, today's Spanish Town. In his will, Marques de Villalobos left to a

friend who had cared for him in his last illness all that he had to leave – his twenty-four years of service to the King as Abbot of Jamaica. After twenty-four years of a kind of martyrdom, not even his bones would lie in his beloved Spain again. Worse than that, with the English occupation of the island, and the consequent erasing of the Spanish presence, the English would build their Cathedral on the site of his faith and altar and temple. They would bury their dead and erect their tombs, and mingle his reluctant dust with their heretical own.

In quite a few respects, Bernardo de Balbuena was to be far luckier than his predecessor. He got out of Jamaica to become Bishop of Puerto Rico. When he died there a few years later (1627) his worldly goods were substantial enough to lead to a violent scene about his deathbed. Church and state, the Dean of the Cathedral and the Governor of Puerto Rico, wrangled as to which should inherit his possessions, as to whether the will that the dying man had just signed was valid or not. Had Balbuena survived his sickbed, he might have converted the scene into literature. He came of a culture and at a time when the commander of a Spanish squadron, at the height of a terrible storm which wreaked havoc with ships and crew, could turn to a fellow-hidalgo, and show him with pride a new sonnet written by Lope de Vega, Spain's Shakespeare, a sonnet which he said Lope de Vega had given him just before he left the Court in Madrid. After reading the sonnet aloud, with the winds shrieking, he followed this with a critical appraisal, as if, his fellow-hidalgo narrates, "he had been criticising it in a serene academy of letters".[4] What men dreamt and wrote, and what they lived, coexisted side by side. Literature realised itself in life, and life surprised itself as literature, in what a famous critic has called, "the literaturisation of life".[5]

For in another, and more fundamental sense, Bernardo de Balbuena differed from his predecessor; Balbuena was a poet. And this was the *esse* of *his* being. Not only was he a poet, but he aspired to rank himself among those poets who wrote what was, in his culture, the culture of Western Man, the noblest form of poetry, the epic. In this respect too, Bernardo de Balbuena, was lucky. In 1624, three years before his death, his epic poem *El Bernardo* (*The Bernard*, literally) was published in Madrid. A copy of the princeps edition can be seen in the Institute of Jamaica where it bears the proud inscription: "The earliest book published by a resident in Jamaica."

How did a poet, and an *epic* poet at that, come to be a resident in Jamaica? The explanation is inseparable from the manner of the Spanish conquest and settlement of the New World. In his epic poem, a form of poetry which, even as late as the end of the seventeenth century, Dryden could class as "undoubtedly the greatest work which the soul of man is capable to perform",[6] Balbuena gives the elevated and poetic facts about his father's emigration to Mexico. In the prologue to his *El Bernardo,* he engages in one of the most passionate debates of his age, the validity of poetic truth as distinct from historical truth. This tension between poetic truth and reality was basic to the Spanish experience in the New World, and his own.

His father, of the same name – Bernardo de Balbuena – is believed to have been born about 1522 – one year after Cortés had conquered the city of the Aztecs – Tenochtitlán, the centre of their great empire, razed it to the ground, and began the rebuilding of what is today's Mexico City. Some of his family – that is, of Balbuena's father – are supposed to have gone out to Mexico in the early days of raw adventure. Their patron was Nuño Beltrán de Guzmán, who had been appointed President of the Royal Audiencia, a Council consisting of magistrates through which the Government was carried on. Nuño Beltrán de Guzmán was also Governor of Pánuco; he left behind him a legend of cruelty that was surpassed by few. A terrible hunter of gold and of Indians to sell as slaves, his name became a byword even in a desperate age. But Spain sent two kinds of conquistadores to the New World – the conquistadores of the flesh, and those of the spirit. Those who came to conquer with the gun, and those who came to conquer with the Cross of Christ. There were times, even in the early stage, when these bolstered and supported one another. There would be a later time when the Cross would take it for granted that it would survive in the gun's shadow. But there was a heroic age, an epic age of Spanish missionary priests, such as Bartolomé de Las Casas, Motolínia, and the Franciscan Zumárraga of Mexico, as well as others, who saw the New World not as a source of gold nor slaves, but of souls waiting to be garnered for God, to be brought into the brotherhood of Christ. The New World was for these conquistadores the prefiguration of what a later Spanish soldier/poet would write of with rapture:

> O great, oh most rich conquests
> Of the Indies of God, of that great world
> Hidden from human eyes[7]

But for Cortes and the other conquistadores, the issue was simple and the issue was different. They had endured incredible hardships, performed unimaginable feats of valour to get and capture a land whose name would now become the synonym for earthly riches.

"I came", said Cortés, "to get gold, not to till the soil like a peasant."[8]

The get-rich-quick attitude would win out; Midas would, in the end, if not defeat Christ at least, keep him cornered. But in the early days, the missionaries fought back. Don Juan de Zumárrága y Arrazola was able to get a Nuño Beltrán de Guzmán recalled as Governor and President of the Audiencia, for his brutality to the Indians. But Beltrán de Guzmán returned as a private citizen, and the Balbuena family stayed on. When the young Balbuena-senior, came out to New Galicia in Mexico, he too had come not to till the soil like a peasant. That was what Indians were for. Possibly through the influence of his family, who were now settled as landowners, he obtained a post in the Chancery of New Galicia, the then name for the province of Mexico which today comprises Jalisco, Aguascalientes and part of Durango, Zacatecas and San Luis

Potosí. He eventually became Secretary to the Audiencia, or Chancery of Compostela in 1548. There was, then, factual truth in the verse in which Balbuena the epic poet, having created for himself in Book XIX of his heroic poem, *El Bernardo* a most noble and magnificent family tree, refers to his father as one branch of a famous Christian and warrior family, one who,

> ...where the sun gilds itself with gold
> When, on this land, it does not, as yet reverberate
> With the power, grand and great, of the imperial seal,
> To Jalisco will go, there to establish a royal Chancery.[9]

But the epic poet selects his truth. He would owe his being born in Spain to a series of sordid facts, which epic poetry would have had to transmute into allegory. In *El Bernardo*, one of the constant allegories is that of the power of Avarice. Balbuena-senior was a man of his times, and of the frontier gold rush atmosphere. As part of the Spanish organisation of the New World, it was customary for all administrative officers, at the end of their term of office, to submit to a *"residencia"*, i.e. an investigation into the conduct of their particular office. During this investigation, all persons who had grievances could make formal complaints. In 1557, many charges were presented against Balbuena-senior, and some of his colleagues.

According to these charges, Balbuena-senior had been negligent, avaricious and unjust in his conduct of office. As a magistrate, he was said to have delayed and deferred cases in favour of his intimate friend and fellow magistrate, Contreras. Not only did he charge excessive fees for his services, but he neglected to perform these services, spending days and nights in the house of his friend, Contreras, playing at cards and chess. In fact, as one witness put it, "he seemed to have cut his navel string in the house of Contreras".

Besides his official post, Balbuena-senior owned a property at San Pedro Lagunillas where his son would later be parish priest. Some witnesses accused him of having used the Indians, who had been officially designated to work on public projects in Compostela, as additional labour on his property. In addition, he was accused, as a citizen, of brutal treatment of those Indians who had been allotted to him to work under the *encomienda* system.

Under this system, groups of Indians were placed in trust to each "settler", and were to work for the settler who should see to the wellbeing of their soul and body. But the *encomiendas*, a system which had been used by Spain in her reconquest of Spanish territory from the Moors, did not have the checks and balances and the immediate royal and governmental presence. It meant only outright slavery in the Indies. Urged by the missionary priests, the Crown in Spain promulgated, in 1542, a whole code of new laws, "for the governing of the Indies, and the protection of the Indians". But as Peter Martyr, humanist Italian settled in Spain, a member of the Governing Council of the Indies and a precursor of the poet Balbuena as Abbot of Jamaica, clear-sightedly wrote:

All these instructions have been thought out by prudent and humane juris consults, and sanctioned by religious men. But what of that? When our compatriots reach that remote world, so far away, and so removed from us, beyond the ocean, whose courses imitate the changing heavens, they find themselves distant from any judge. Carried away by love of gold, they become ravenous wolves instead of gentle lambs, and heedless of royal instructions.[10]

Balbuena senior was like all the others, carried away by love of gold. One of the charges brought against him was that he had left his job and gone off with some thirteen or fourteen neighbours to look for rich mines in Jocotlán. He nearly paid with his life. Some Indians attacked the group. Only Balbuena-senior and a Negro slave of his escaped.

Balbuena had also been closely connected with the founders of the city of Zacatecas, capital of the province, which was rich with mineral wealth. In a document in which some of these founders take possession of a mine in that city, Balbuena-senior was the notary. Why should he not, too, own a mine for himself? The wealth of the region and the proliferation of its mines was to figure in the heroic poem of his son. In one of the most interesting passages of *El Bernardo,* the magician-enchanter, Malgesi, with two companions, Reinaldos, a French paladin and Orimandro, King of Persia, make an aerial voyage in a flying boat over Europe and Spain, to the moon, and then over to the, as yet undiscovered, New World, across the "deep dark immensity of the sea" to the lands which, the author prophesies, one day will pay:

... tribute to Spain, and pour out cheaply,
Turned into silver, the blood of its veins.[11]

Among other places, over which they fly marvelling, the poet speaks of the wealth and treasure of Zacatecas, still buried in its earth. Balbuena-senior failed to get the quick treasure that he sought. The poet, his son, found in poetry the Midas touch where all the wonder of the New World could be turned into epic verse.

Avarice and neglect and cruelty to his Indians were not the only charges brought against Balbuena-senior. He was also accused of living in concubinage with a certain María de Jaramilla, an Indian woman and of having had a mestizo son called Pedro with her. In fact, his accusers said he was seeking to marry this María. It is possible that like many others, Balbuena-senior may have left a wife in Spain. In 1557 he was found guilty of all the charges laid against him and suspended from office, together with his cronies, including Contreras. In 1560, he went off to Spain to fight against the judgement on behalf of his friends and himself. Whilst there, he had an affair with Francisca Sánchez de Velasco. From this union, Bernardo de Balbuena, the poet, was born in Valdepeñas, in the province of Ciudad Real somewhere between 1561-1562. Like his mestizo half-brother, Pedro, he was of illegitimate birth. His illegitimacy was to have a profound influence on his life. His inordinate ambition, his almost physical hunger and thirst for honour and position in life, for fame and renown, can be traced to this deep wound. Always Balbuena would want to prove himself beyond the best, against the best, and like Icarus, to soar beyond the sun. Both as cleric and as poet Balbuena aimed at nothing but the top.

II
A SWAN WILL SPRING WITH TENDER WINGS

In 1564, Balbuena-senior returned to Mexico. We know that he returned to public office so his representations in Spain must have borne fruit. We do not know at what date Bernardo the poet came to Mexico, but he came as a child, separated from his mother, and spent his childhood and adolescence in Guadalajara, Compostela and San Pedro Lagunillas where his father had property and employment. Yet, as we shall see, the landscapes of these places are important to him only in so far as they attest to the greatness of Spain. Bernardo had cut his navel string in Spain, and the New World had importance for him only in so far as it was her reflection across the seas. He began his studies in Guadalajara, and in 1580 went to continue studies in Mexico City. Balbuena's love for Mexico City and its "culture", as opposed to the "*soledades*" of the rural areas and provincial towns, was due to the fact that in Mexico City he found himself in a culturally transplanted Spain.

In the New World, the Spaniards followed the Roman imperial tradition, by using the city – *urbs* – as the unit of imperial expansion. This of course responded to the Spanish reality at home, where the city-state with its municipal cabildo or town council governed a considerable surrounding area. But the speed with which the intellectual and cultural life of Spain was brought to Mexico City was remarkable. With the coming of the first Viceroy, Antonio de Mendoza, in 1535, schools were at once set up and a printing press began operation in 1536. By 1553 courses had begun at the University of Mexico, an exact replica of those in Spain. First rate humanists and theologians came out, and first rank was given to the Chair of Scholastic Theology. Apart from the University there were Dominican and Jesuit colleges, and the latter in particular offered their students a Christian humanist education. It is believed from what Balbuena tells us in his first published book – The Grandeur of Mexico (*La Grandeza mexicana*) – that he studied at one of these Jesuit colleges and attended classes at the University. Certainly he graduated with a first degree.

Balbuena was born and grew up in that era when Roman Catholicism, which saw itself as the universal religion, found itself on the defensive against the attacks of the growing Protestant spirit. Spain spearheaded the resistance to this heresy. The militant order of the Jesuits, founded by Loyola, was one of the weapons with which Catholicism fought back in the movement known as the Counter-Reformation. One of the results of this movement was that letters and learning were seen to be only valid in so far as they strengthened the

Catholic faith; in so far as they were not an end in themselves, but subserved the salvation of man, directing his life on earth to its eternal end in Heaven. Since "humanism" itself had come to flower in the expanding economy of the commercial city-states of Italy where a professional class of writers, turning back to intensive study of the Greek-Roman world and of the pagan thought of the ancients, had brought about that change of perspective in which man sought to achieve moral perfection on earth for its own sake; and since the very idea of humanist studies and disciplines sprang from the belief that such perfection could be found in the study of the letters and philosophy of the ancient world, there was bound to be a paradox and a tension in the very concept of Christian humanism. Yet out of this tension much of the literature of Spain's Golden Age would spring. In this tension and paradox, as Christian priest and humanist poet, Balbuena himself would write and live.

The basic idea of humanist studies was to give an education that would enable the student to conform to an ideal human type. In such an education the study of the Greek epic poems of Homer, and the Latin epic of Vergil was a *sine qua non*. In the Christian-Catholic interpretation, the heroes of Homer and of Vergil could be studied as ideal types of human behaviour, *before* the coming and revelation of Christ. Just as the Greek and Latin pagan gods were transformed during the Middle Ages into allegorical myths to explain the Christian mysteries, so now the epic heroes of the past were studied as prefigurations of Christ, who was now the ideal and model for all human behaviour. It was impossible then to receive such an education and not come to believe that the greatest aspiration of a writer would be to write an epic at once Christian and humanist, to fulfil the dual purpose of moral perfection on earth, and eternal salvation in Heaven. For a Balbuena, as for the men of his age, an epic poet imitated God the creator; and an epic poem, as Dryden expresses it, could have no nobler end:

> The design of it is to form the mind to heroic virtue by example; 'tis conveyed in verse, that it may delight, while it instructs.[12]

To be an epic poet was no light matter. It was a vocation, a calling, needing years of study, practise and dedication, both moral and literary. It was a destiny. And, in the epic poem itself, as Malgesi and his companions travel in the flying-ship over Spain, Balbuena's birthplace is pointed out, *(Bk.XVI)* prophetically, his poet's stable, marked if not with a star, with a poetic verse:

> From that most pleasant valley, ringed with cliffs
> Where humble shepherds' huts now stand
> Where the river Javalon, the thick foliage
> Dresses with roses and with radiant flowers
> A swan will spring with tender wings
> Which, if with time, extend their reach
> Fame will make of them, in memory
> Of your valour, an immortal history.

His poet's destiny is to straddle two worlds with his poetry as his magician
Malgesi is able to do with his magic.

> And as the height and crown of my desire
> I see him cross two worlds – the Old and New
> Yoking from both, for his grave verse,
> All that is best for his substance and his source.[13]

III

> Everything ends with the different
> ebb and flow of Time – fine robes, gold
> rich jewels, treasures of all kinds
> Not that immortal name which poetry bestows…[14]

Balbuena, translating Ovid, in *The Grandeur of Mexico*, published 1604.

The literary competition – in Spanish, *certamen* – was a part of the literary life
of Spain, which had been transplanted to Mexico City. These competitions,
springing out of the chivalresque concept of life and literature, were modelled
on the idea of knightly tourneys or jousts. But they were the arts of peace, and
not of war and were promoted by State and Church. These festival-competi-
tions began in Mexico City from the very earliest times. We have a description
of one which was held in the sixteenth century.

Promoted by the Royal Chancery, the festival was held with pomp and
circumstance. A herald, carrying the arms of the City of Mexico, went through
all the streets, blowing a trumpet. As he went along, he announced the themes
of the competition, and the prizes to be given. The presidents of the festival were
members of the chancery. The judges included a representative of the Archbishop, one of the Chancellors of the University, and, in his own person, a
professor of philosophy. Each judge privately judged the entries, then wrote a
report, justifying his judgement and signed it. When they met, the secretary of
the competition, usually a Jesuit theologian, counted the votes in their reports,
and the winners were decided upon. On the day of the prize-giving, sometimes
held in the hall of the Jesuit College of St Peter and St Paul, the walls were
decorated with the poets' entries. The four top prizewinners, selected for the
elegance of their style and the thought and knowledge displayed in their content,
were crowned with laurel before the audience and were proclaimed in the name
and by the authority of the Royal Chancery to be "poets laureate".

Balbuena's poetic vocation was proclaimed with his entries in several
literary competitions. From 1585, whilst still studying in Mexico, until 1590
– when he had already graduated, been ordained a priest and was already filling
his first post – he entered four competitions, and won a prize in each. His
prizewinning entries[15] were published in his first book – *The Grandeur of
Mexico*. In the same book, he tells us that in 1586, in the competition held as

part of the celebrations to welcome the new Viceroy of Mexico, he received first prize from among a field of "three hundred entrants, all exceedingly talented in the poetic art, and who could compete with the best in the world".[16]

A man would find fame through poetry, but he could not live by it in Mexico. Nor for that matter in Spain. Geniuses like Cervantes and Lope de Vega had to turn their hands to several things to make ends meet. Balbuena's bread-and-butter official career had, in a sense, been decided for him. For the bureaucracy of the Church was the one career open to a man of talent, and of illegitimate birth.

And so, somewhere about that time, he began his priestly career as Chaplain to the Chancery of Guadalajara, no doubt due to his father's influence. His life in the small towns and villages, which he was to loathe, the "*soledades*" in which he felt himself bewitched, began. He did not cut his literary ties with Mexico City, however. In 1590, on the arrival of a new Viceroy, Don Luís de Velasco, he entered a laudatory poem about the Viceroy which won the prize. The same year he won another prize with a virtuoso acrostic-type poem.

His stay in the capital would have increased his discontent with the provincial town of Guadalajara. But worse was yet to come. In 1592 he was promoted to be parish priest of San Pedro Lagunillas, and Minas del Espíritu Santo, two small villages to the north of Guadalajara.

Balbuena must have felt despair closing in on him; the same despair which the Guyanese writer Edgar Mittelholzer pictures so vividly, feeling himself trapped in drowsy provincial New Amsterdam, behind God's back. And like Mittelholzer, Balbuena never ceased his efforts to escape the trap. In the same manner that Mittelholzer posted off manuscript after manuscript to English publishers, so too did Balbuena, open fire on two fronts. To escape the provinces, the backwoods and oblivion, he could use one, or both paths: his priestly and his literary vocation. So, in 1592, he filed an application for a post in Mexico City. His application was filed at Guadalajara, from where it was sent on to Seville, the centre of colonial administration in Spain; where it was registered, gathering dust for many years. According to the conventions of what was called the royal *patronato* the King, through the Council of the Indies, made all appointments to the administrative positions in the Church of the New World.

From 1592-1602, with the exceptions of a few trips to other places, and perhaps to Mexico City, Balbuena remained in, what was to him, exile in the remote places of Mexico. In the *Grandeur of Mexico,* the contrast between his enthusiastic praise of Mexico City, and his contempt for the provincial places could not be more pronounced. In his panegyric about Mexico City, a classical form widely practised in Renaissance and post-Renaissance Europe, he starts off in praise of the city:

> Of famous Mexico I sing the site
> The origins and grandeur of its buildings

> Its horses, streets, manners, courtesy,
> Letters, virtues, variety of calling...[16]

In contrast, in the same book he describes the provincial milieu in which he had lived as

> ... this narrow and small world, large in land, and small in people. And outside of this rich city (*Mexico City*) almost a desert, almost the end of the world in what pertains to learning and letters, good taste, cultured intercourse and the play of the mind... The urge for profits from their lands, and greed for gain, having tyrannised and claimed the best minds (or thoughts) for their own...[17]

Some three hundred and fifty years later, Naipaul, in describing Trinidad, pictures the same cultural bankruptcy, the same misdirection of talent and the mind. His description of Trinidad can easily make do for Jamaica, as could, so long ago, Balbuena's Mexico. In *The Middle Passage* Naipaul writes:

> I knew Trinidad to be unimportant, uncreative, cynical... and the most successful people were commission agents, bank managers and members of the distributive trades.[18]

Where Naipaul goes on to say:

> Power was recognised but dignity was allowed to no one... Every person of eminence was held to be crooked and contemptible. We lived in a society which denied itself heroes.[19]

Balbuena says it in verse,

> In little narrow towns all is strife
> All is gossip, rumours, evil tales,
> Lies, envy, hate – all pertaining to that life.[20]

And yet, it was out of Trinidadian society that Naipaul was to write *Biswas*. And it was in these little narrow towns that Balbuena was to have the most creative period of his life.

He wrote there his pastoral novel – *The Golden Age in the Woods of Erifile* – whose importance for our purpose lies in several aspects. One, that he was, as always, in touch with and following the literary vogues of contemporary Italy and metropolitan Spain – though always with that delay in fashion which is the fate of all provinces, doomed, to borrow Lévi-Strauss's phrase, to be "not so much exotic as out of date".[21] By the time Balbuena published his novel in Madrid, in 1608, the vogue for the pastoral had passed its peak, but was not entirely dead. His wide and assiduous reading of the latest publications in Italy and Spain are attested to in the widespread evidence of influences from Italians and contemporary Spaniards in his work. As critics have pointed out, Balbuena displays a facility of invention and a talent for versifying not inferior to other practitioners of the art. It is clear, therefore, that in the isolation of these remote places, he lived with books and could have said, as did the somewhat younger, greater, Spanish poet, Quevedo:

> Retired in the peace of these deserts
> I live conversing with the dead
> And listen with my eyes to men who're gone
> Yet, who in silent counterpoint of harmony
> Awake, cry out to the dream of life...[22]

But a Quevedo, living at the heart of Empire, had no illusions about the defeat of the dream of Empire and the crumbling away of its reality. For him the *soledad* outside the centre and the court alone held peace. For Balbuena, the court, the city, the Centre of Empire alone held glory.

The pastoral was an aristocratic mode of literature which pictured in poetry, prose, or a mixture of both, the idealised life of aristocratic lovers disguised as shepherds, singing of the pains of love and its joys – never, of course, tending sheep. In the commercial expansion of Europe, with its rapid social mobility for the rising bourgeoisie, anxious to identify with the leisured pastimes of the aristocratic class, the pastoral form became a must. In the pastoral, there is a pretence of despising the corrupt, agitated life of the Court and therefore valuing life in an idealised, tamed and idyllic natural setting: a "cultured" imaginary *soledad* in fact redeemed by art. Balbuena, caught by the difficulty of idealising the nature of Mexico that surrounded him, perhaps subconsciously aware that the Indian, unlike European rustics, could not be transmuted into a literary shepherd, since the forest and the trees were still too newly spattered with their blood, set his pastoral in a valley of his beloved Spain, near his birthplace. Only one interlude is imagined to take place in Mexico. The artifice works in a form that is completely "artificial". But if this had been his only work, Balbuena would have only just managed to survive oblivion.

According to his Mexican biographer[23] in the pastoral novel Balbuena shows his love for Dona Ysabel de Tobar, whom he had known in his student days, who later married, and then was left a youngish widow. It is possible that he did genuinely love her, or it might be that she was, according to the custom of love poets of the day, a literary excuse for some rather fine love sonnets. The fact that she came from a powerful and influential family would not have hindered his taking her as his earthly muse. To survive in a society based on power, largely outside or on the margin of the law, one had to know how to keep a weather-eye open for those friendships which could help to keep one afloat.

Above all the pastoral poem served as a preliminary exercise for the epic poem which was in the process of being written in those ten years. At the end of the poem, a warlike figure called Selvaggio announces that if the divine breath fills his flute with power enough to make the sun stop in the sky, he will sing a song of Mars and War, a song of Spain's valour that will astonish the world, from the Indian to the Moor. It is a song that will cause Time to conserve his memory and bring him an envied glory, dealing as it will with,

The Arms of that New Achilles
The great Bernardo, honour, glory exemplar
Of gallant deeds and noble hearts![24]

C.S. Lewis quotes Goethe who, in speaking of the epic, pointed out that the formalised diction of the epic is a "Language which does your thinking and poetising for you".[25] The poet, moving within the tradition of the epic, approaches what they called the "universal truth" of poetry. He is compelled by his form, by its accumulated tradition, to see things *sub specie aeternitatis*. The treatment of the enemy, for example, beginning with Homer, is significant. The nobility of the enemy is showed to the same extent as that of one's own side, or rather of the side from which one is singing one's song.

Baseness is on both sides. The cheap and vulgar nationalism of history would be, for epic poetry, the original sin. The enemy in the epic is each man's potentiality for baseness; the hero, each man's potentiality for greatness.[26] Not only the human beings, but the landscape comes within the epic context. In Homer, for example, the sea had always been Poseidon the great god, "the shaker of earth", the constant, the enduring reality against which man cast his shadow, doomed to mortality. So, Balbuena, in his epic poem looked at the landscapes which he had loathed, and forgot the small petty accidents which had bruised his spirit, remembering only the essence, that which remains when everything passes.

Thus, as the magician Malgesi and the others fly over Mexico, the poet describes what they see with an epic eye: the high mountains of Jalisco and Jala, full of sweet honey, the gardens of the valleys of Vanderas, the sea breaking on the wild shore. And the great volcano of Jala – today called Ceboruco in the state of Nayarit – flaming with fire was, the poet admits, the torch by whose light he wrote his poem, catching epic grandeur from the sight. Here in the peace and quiet, the small fountain began that would end in the river of his poem – here where his desire for fame first urged him on.

In 1602, finding himself forty years old, with nothing published, and still only the parish priest of two remote villages, he had had enough. He decided to cut his losses and leave for Mexico City. Before leaving he went north to San Miguel de Culiacán to say goodbye to Dona Ysabel de Tobar. She had decided to take the veil and enter a convent. Before leaving, he promised her to write and tell her about the city of Mexico as she had requested. With this as his literary excuse, Balbuena after arriving in the city, wrote and published in 1604 his first book, *The Grandeur of Mexico*. From now on, everything that he did would be directed towards the twin goals of advancement in one career, and fame in the other. He was determined to get out of the "small narrow world"[27] in which he had lived until now. The publication of his book was one manoeuvre in the battle to escape; in that same year, he took his second degree and became a licentiate of the University and began to prepare an application asking for a position or canonry in the churches of Mexico City or Tlaxcala.

In its basic intention then, *The Grandeur of Mexico* was to be a bread-and-butter-singing-for-supper and a position in the church hierarchy. But the poetic end, here and there, goes beyond the prose purpose. Much of the material of the book is designed to show Balbuena's academic learning and therefore to prove to his peers his fitness for high position in the Church. In the first edition, besides the customary laudatory sonnets from his small learned circle of friends, the book contains first a Letter to the Archdeacon of New Galicia, Doctor Don Antonio de Ávila y Cadena; the letter itself consists of a short prologue in prose, a poem in praise of the new Archbishop of Mexico,[28] a gloss or learned explanation in prose on the poem dated October 1602, a few days after the arrival of the Archbishop in Mexico. After this comes the main text of the book written in the Italianate verse of the terza rima, and in the form of a poetic letter – epistola – to Dona Ysabel de Tobar. In the first twenty tercets, he praises Dona Ysabel as a flower born to blush unseen; he also praises her noble lineage, pointing out her distant kinship to the Duke of Lerma, the powerful and corrupt favourite of Philip III of Spain.

Balbuena's Mexican biographer – Rojas Garcidueñas – points out that at the end of the XVIth century the Tobar family was important in Galicia, and that some of its branches may have been related to the Balbuena's. And as Rojas Garcidueñas remarks, Balbuena had an almost servile respect for power. But this servility was a constant of his time, and Balbuena was in all respects, except in his epic poem, a conventional man who wanted to get on.

He therefore praises the Duke of Lerma as he who,

> ... today serves as base and column
> to the great weight of the world...[29]

As van Horne says,[30] this poem, *The Grandeur of Mexico* is the one in which Balbuena most nearly approaches "realism" as we know it today. In his pastoral novel, Dona Ysabel appears only as the beloved nymph, from whom her shepherd must part, each one after that "to inhabit strange and distant kingdoms". In the epic she appears as the nymph, inseparable from and elevated into his Muse, (Bk. XIX)[31] whilst Culiacan is seen from the aerial heights of the flying ship (Bk XVIII) as the place which, "created the flower of the world's summer".[32]

In *The Grandeur of Mexico,* under all the blandishments, she appears as a possible weapon in his search for patronage. Already his eyes were fixed on Spain, the centre of power, where the Duke of Lerma and the Count of Lemos were two of those who exercised this power and dispensed shares in its benefits.

The second edition, which came out in Mexico City and also bears the date 1604 on its title page[33] was most likely intended to have been published in Spain. It is dedicated with a long poem to "the most excellent Count of Lemos and Andrade Marquis of Sarria, President of the Royal Council of the Indies".

This poem also had brief explanatory notes or glosses in prose. Also in both editions, coming at the end of the book, is an essay entitled "An Apologetic Compendium in Praise of Poetry". Van Horne has called all of this additional "apparatus" the "essence of pedantry", the kind of pedantry mocked by the genial Cervantes in his Prologue to *Don Quixote*, whose first part appeared in 1605. In his Prologue, Cervantes ironically speaks of the author's despair at his lack of learning, and therefore at the academic bareness of his work:

> My book will lack all this; for I have nothing to quote in the margin or to note at the end. Nor do I even know what authors I am following in it; and so I cannot set their names at the beginning in alphabetical order, as they all do, starting with Aristotle and ending with Xenophon.[34]

But a friend consoled him, advising him to make up his own quotes, write his own verses, and make up too, the learned names of their authors, for even if

> ...some pedants and graduates turned up to snap and growl at you behind your back in the name of truth, you need not bother about them a bit, for... they cannot cut off the hand you wrote it with...[35]

It was all very well for Cervantes to laugh in his Prologue, in real life the pedants and graduates, firmly ensconced as they always are, in the higher branches of the bureaucracy can cut off the limbs, on which an aspirant, especially a New World upstart, tries to sit. Balbuena, living in a cultural colony, haunted by that self-contempt and fear of inadequacy which is inherent in our marginality, was determined to show with the best of them his wide reading from A to Z. With his enormous energy he puts on display his humanist classical learning, as well as his theological knowledge and ortho-doxy. Van Horne quotes only some of the names our poet cites – amongst them, Strabo, Ovid, Horace, Vergil, Martial, Macrobius, Tibullus, Propertius, Juvenal, Seneca, Lucan, Aristotle, Justin Hyginus, Herodotus, Varro, Vitruvius, Diodorus Siculus, Pindar, Homer, Hesiod, Solinus, Lactantius, Bernard, Gregory, Basil, Jerome etc. Some critics have termed this effusion bad taste; some have slyly pointed out that he could have culled his quotations from several encyclopedic manuals that were common at the time. But whatever the case may be, the quotations made his point.

The long essay in praise of poetry at the end of the book, also full of pedantry, had a further point to make. It set out to defend poetry against those academic theologians who considered poetry inferior to theology, philosophy and history; condemning it as a flighty occupation. He set out to justify the seriousness of poetry to justify his own seriousness in writing it, and to argue the point that there was nothing to prevent a poet sharing in the plums of office as a high church dignitary.

As with every form of writing that Balbuena practised, his "Apologetic Compendium in Praise of Poetry" was neither new nor original. Originality as such was not accounted a virtue in the cultural climate in which he moved. The

Aristotelian doctrine of "imitation" came to mean, for the theorists and the writers of the Renaissance and the post-Renaissance, the imitation of the ancient classical models or of modern writers who, by their excellence, had attained the rank of classics. We would not begin to understand the formation and the structure of Balbuena's epic poem if we did not bear in mind, stretching behind him, both as model and sources, the Greek Homer, the Roman Vergil, Italians of the fifteenth and sixteenth century such as Boiardo, Ariosto, Tasso, Girolamo Vida, and other Spanish contemporaries or near contemporaries. The citing of names also showed that Balbuena was a disciplined and studious poet who had studied in order to imitate.

In his "Praise of Poetry",[36] Balbuena, therefore, expresses ideas that had sprung from the fusion made by Italian theorists, in the 1550s of the theory of poetics of the Greek Aristotle, with those of the Roman Horace. Out of this they had come up with a basic maxim that poetry should both delight and instruct. This had helped to dispel the uneasiness of Christian theologians who had felt it difficult to accommodate the truth of poetry – which was "fiction" – with the truth of Christian doctrine which they held to be absolute. Spain did not acclimatise this theory until the 1590s. Before that there had been defences of poetry, but as one critic points out, they tended to be strident, since they lacked cogent arguments as to the "high seriousness of poetry". With the doctrine of teaching and delighting, poetic fiction could be made to illustrate Christian truths; or, in countries where the secular notion of truth was gradually replacing that of religious truth, poetry could still be made to illustrate universal and absolute truth.

All over Europe, apologies for and defences of poetry appeared, based now on the doctrine of delight and instruction. Sidney in England writes his *Apology* (1595) of poetry praising that delightful teaching which is the end of poetry.[37] Balbuena's arguments are the commonplaces of his time, and as usual he was provincially behind the vogue.

But Balbuena, unlike his European counterparts, had to fight his battle on two fronts. He had to defend poetry and assert the existence of poetry in its own right, in a society for whom the only poetry was gold, silver and the products of the land. In his *Grandeur of Mexico*, Balbuena had pointed out how greed for gain in the smaller places led to a lack of care and concern for culture. Even, in his praise for Mexico City itself, we divine a canker of doubt. Whilst he lauds to the skies the wealth and thriving commerce of Mexico, and the culture and cultivation of letters that is based on it, there is a certain ambivalence as far as the wealth is concerned.

For Balbuena, within the conventional form of the Renaissance panegyric, gives us a new reality, and his description of Mexico City, vivid, acute, breaks out of the idealised form of the panegyric, as if it suspects that it is describing the beginning of a process whose end will make idealism, once and for all, irrelevant. Mexico City's raison d'être, as Balbuena describes it for us, is the private interest, the self-interest of each citizen. The lawyer, the arrogant quack of a doctor, the actor acting, the beggar begging, the prior preaching, the merchants in the shops, all buying or selling – all moved by self-interest – the self-love which is the city's motor. In the Scholastic theology in which Balbuena had been indoctrinated, "the institution of property, and the transactions of the marketplace" must all, in Tawney's words "justify themselves at the bar of religion".[38] Economic man was rapidly replacing religious man all over Europe, and in all the places touched by Europe's imperial expansion. But in Europe and particularly in Spain, the strength of tradition and of the religious motive made the transition not quite so naked, not quite so transparent. In the New World, a man touched god in order to turn to gold; then diverted his best energies into transforming everything into a commodity that paid off.

No one, says Balbuena, having money in his pocket can pass a bad day in that city. But the great sin, which once, in the Scholastic context, was the *appetitus divitiarum infinitus* – the excessive appetite for riches – is not now a sin. The sin is poverty and this is how Balbuena describes her:

> Poverty wherever it lives is in the skin of an old woman
> Wretched, miserable and savage
> With ugly face and uglier manners...[39]

Van Horne takes Balbuena seriously and with a straight face when in the letter to the Archdeacon he argues that to be rich is to be a worthy man and to be poor is dishonourable. Without being able to see the exact text, it seems to me that here he has his tongue in his cheek, as did Sancho Panza's grandmother when she said that there are two classes of people in the world, the haves and the have nots; and like a contemporary anonymous Spanish pamphleteer who wrote that men call the rich man honourable because he has enough to eat. It was a world which foreshadowed our own, a world in which already, as Marcuse puts it,

> ... they bring these realms of culture to their common denominator – the commodity form. The music of the soul is also the music of salesmanship. Exchange value, not truth value counts. On it centres the rationality of the status quo, and all alien rationality is bent to it...[40]

In a world in which this process had already begun, Balbuena set out to defend poetry and, repeating an old commonplace in a new reality, to insist that the cosmos itself is nothing else than a line of harmonious verse that, in fact, to paraphrase the universe itself, was a line of verse.

His basic line of argument was that poetry was as old as the world, that it could be traced back to the ancient biblical prophets, back to the psalms of David and therefore had a legitimate origin since it was a divine gift. All men shared in poetry, even the Aztec Indians had poetry for their joy and comfort, and poetry had always been and could be a stimulus to virtue. It is the fault of bad poets that poetry bears an ill-name, for poetry properly handled could be a path to salvation.

Poetry is like music, not earthly music alone, but like the imperishable music of the spheres. Here he uses a worn metaphor, based on the Ptolemaic concept, that the universe consisted of a series of concentric spheres which, revolving around the fixed earth in the centre, harmonise in a divine music which man could hear not with his senses, but with his reason. Poetry, therefore, was far too lofty to deal with light matters like love. It should concern itself with "serious subjects, complete, wise and full of morality and philosophy".[41]

He praises poets who have done this, naming among them Don Alonso de Ercilla y Zúñiga, whose epic poem *Araucana,* published in two parts in 1569 and 1589, was already highly acclaimed. Ercilla was a Spaniard of noble birth at the time of the Conquest and fought in the campaigns against the warlike Araucanian Indians. He returned home to Spain, and wrote his epic poem in which the bravery of the enemy, was as great, if not more, than the bravery of the Spaniards. In fact he had been sharply criticised by some Spaniards for what they considered his overpraise of the Araucanians, and his neglect of his own countrymen. Balbuena, whilst mentioning him with praise, hastens to insist how different his epic subject will be. Van Horne has pointed out how intensely Balbuena embraces the motif. In contrast to the first wave of Spanish who had enthusiastically seized on the themes of the New World, Balbuena, with a certain disdain, turns his back on these. He vows in his poem to the Count of Lemos that:

> No longer will my pen be busied
> To raise up shadows, sketch the greatness
> Of this most desert region......
> Nor of the brute barbarians, the ferocious courage,
> Let others sing the bravery of the Araucanians.

He will sing instead, he promises,

> ... the ancient prowess
> The deeds and victories of your Spanish Bernardo.[42]

Unlike the first generation of Spaniards, Balbuena was a Spaniard overseas, a spiritual "colon", for whom Spanishness was a necessity, of survival. As a young Argentinian writer has said of Luis Borges:

> What could he be except an Argentinian? He is a typical national product Even his European is national. A European is not Europeanist. He is simply a European.[43]

The nostalgia for somewhere else, the backward glance, the idealised mythical cultural home is a constant of the New World experience. The hordes of Caribbean and Latin American writers at present living metropolitan lives, shivering besides fires, despising the *soledades* they have left behind, bears this out. Among the complex meaning of the Spanish word, *soledad* is one which is equivalent to the Portuguese *saudade*, indicating separation from the desired place, and the consequent longing for that place. Distant from one's country, one's *tierra,* one lives in a state of *soledad,* spiritual and physical. When one's home country becomes a hated nightmare, as it has for Naipaul and so many other New World writers, then one is indeed trapped in placelessness. One can have nostalgia for nowhere.

In 1606, Balbuena, having failed to get any reply to his application for a post in the churches of Mexico or Tlaxcala sailed from Mexico City for Spain. His father had died in 1593, and he left his affairs in the hands of a half brother, Francisco de Balbuena y Estrada, who seems to have been a legitimate son. Balbuena, not oversupplied with funds, took with him, as his only servant, a nine-year-old mulatto boy, not a slave, but free[44], called Christopher. (Black men, Negroes, free and enslaved, had accompanied Cortés in his conquest of Mexico and the African presence had early begun its at once agonised and formidable infiltration of the New World reality.) He had gone in search of fame, and a post in a civilised part of the Empire. He was going now from the remote confines of the New World to the very centre of that Christian Dominion whose king he had saluted in *The Grandeur of Mexico,* as, "Sacred, Catholic, Royal Majesty, whom God has made a Deity on earth".[45]

There at the centre, he was determined to make his way to the top. But the way to the top is fraught with ironical twists and turns. Balbuena would go to Spain and obtain a post, but his post would be on the island of Jamaica, surely the most remote *soledades* of them all.

PART 2

A man studies and studies. Then, with favour and good luck he finds himself a wand in his hand or a mitre on his head when he least expects it...

Cervantes, *Don Quixote,* Part II. Ch. 67.[46]

He (i.e. Balbuena) was elected Abbot of Jamaica, on 29th April, in the year 1608.

Gil González Dávila, *Ecclesiastical Theatre of the Primitive Church of the West Indies,* Madrid, 1649.[47]

Cervantes, creator of Spain's immortal hero of failure, Don Quixote, knew in his own lifetime, little of favour and less of luck. As a soldier, he had his left hand maimed from the wars, had been captured by pirates and imprisoned in Algiers. Ransomed at last, he had to return home to Spain and to the struggle of managing to make both ends meet. He shifted and scuffled from one job to the next, trying to get a safe post in the administrative bureaucracy of the Crown. He applied for, and hoped to get a substantial post in the Indies. But the competition and scramble for these places was fierce. He was turned down in 1590. This refusal may have added a certain acidity to his comment in one of his shorter novels that

... the passage to the Indies is the refuge and protection of all the desperate
men in Spain, the safe hiding place of those in revolt ... the will of the
wisp of the many and the private hope of the few.[48]

Bernardo de Balbuena was determined to be one of the favoured few. He
had had enough of what he himself had termed "the small and narrow world"
of provincial Mexico. His sights were set on a position in the important
Churches of Mexico City or Tlaxcala, or, failing that, in the other New World
centre, in Lima, in the Viceroyalty of Peru.

And of course, as a writer, he had also come to the most important cultural
centre – Spain – in search of greater fame and recognition. For one thing, such
fame and recognition could be set to work for him in the more tangible down-
to-earth search for a job. He carried with him in his luggage, one published
book of poetry – *The Grandeur of Mexico*[49] and the manuscript of his heroic
poem, *El Bernardo*, which, whilst still in manuscript, was to be instrumental in
obtaining him his first important post – as Abbot of Jamaica.

On 16th October, 1606, Balbuena and Christopher disembarked at Seville,
the port that was the hub of and gateway to the Indies. Balbuena at once set
about the business of being a "*pretendiente*", that is a man on the make for a job.
Unlike Cervantes, Balbuena belonged to the educated elite – the *letrados* – a
kind of intellectual aristocracy who had studied at the University, and who,
with the customary arrogance of academics, tended to despise the lay genius
– the *ingenio lego* – of writers like Cervantes. But Balbuena besides being a poet
as well as *letrado,* held as yet only the licentiate degree from the University of
Mexico. And he knew that a doctorate was an essential part of the equipment
of survival and success. In much the same way as today, a doctorate was not so
much the mark of a scholar, as the bureaucratic rung of a ladder. He applied
himself with diligence. One year after his arrival, in 1607, he obtained the
doctorate in theology from the University of Sigüenza, and acquired among
other fringe benefits the right to wear the *borla blanca*, the white tassel which
proved that he had made it.

The Count of Lemos, a powerful grandee, was President of the Council
which governed the Indies. As such he was the source and fount of all
patronage. In his campaign to tap this source for a post, Balbuena, whilst still
in Mexico, had dedicated his second edition of *The Grandeur of Mexico* to the
Count. He had also sent on for publication in Spain the manuscript of his
pastoral novel, *The Golden Age in the Forests of Erifile*[50]. In the same year in which
he got his doctorate – 1607 – Balbuena had this pastoral novel published in
Madrid. This book, too, was dedicated to the Count. Already, in the long poem
of praise, which Balbuena had inserted in the second edition of *The Grandeur
of Mexico*, the poet had promised the Count to celebrate his name and lineage
in his forthcoming heroic poem, *The Bernard*. This poem, like all epic poems,
long in preparation, is again heralded at the end of Balbuena's pastoral novel
as a new song to be sung to trumpets, one that would startle the world and its

peoples from "the Indian to the Moor". Now, the poem itself, still in manuscript, began to play its part and to win not only fame for its author but that "favour" and "good luck" which would ensure him bread and a place at the table. From Balbuena himself we learn that the Count of Lemos, in recognition of the two books already dedicated to him, took time off to read the manuscript of *The Bernard*.[51] Even in an age in which adulation was common, he could hardly have failed to have been flattered.

At the beginning of the heroic poem in the second stanza[52], the Count of Lemos is made central to the poem. He is proclaimed the lineal descendant of the legendary hero of the poem, and not only *any* descendant, but one whose own heroic deeds and acts have brought it about that

> Fame now promises the House of Castro
> Laminas of gold, statues of alabaster.

More to the meat of the matter, the Count is praised in his role as President of the Council of the Indies, and Governor, so to speak, of the New World:

> The New World, unworthy of your favour
> Adores you with the voice and livery of man
> Your noble blood, descended from a thousand kings
> Sends just laws and honours to that land.[53]

The Count is praised in the epic dimensions of a hero – his wisdom is compared to that of Nestor in Homer's epic, the *Iliad*; his prudence to that of Homer's epic hero, Ulysses. His magnanimity and generosity is compared to that of the Roman Emperor Augustus, who was the real life patron of Vergil, the Roman epic poet of the *Aeneid*. The implied correspondence is clear. Augustus had been Vergil's patron; so also had been Maecenas, Augustus's adviser, whose name has become a synonym for patron. Their financial bounty made it possible for writers to live for their art. In exchange, the writer, Vergil, glorified the Emperor as the lineal descendant of his epic hero Aeneas, whom he makes the founder of Rome, and glorifies too, the Empire over which Augustus rules. In a literal as well as in a poetic sense, Vergil saw his patron – Augustus – as the source of inspiration, the begetter, the muse of his poetry. So, too, Balbuena praises the Count as equal to the gods Apollo and Bacchus, as the fountain and source of his song. The Count will smooth the rough path to Mount Parnassus, at the top of which the poet will achieve excellence and fame – since the Muses have their dwelling place there. The Count will honour Balbuena's work with spiritual and practical help, since as Balbuena reminds him in the poem, he is,

> ... a new Augustus who showers
> Honours on men of letters... [54]

In return, as quid pro quo, Balbuena's poem will record the Count's fame, and eternalise his name.

What might seem to us today like outrageous flattery was commonplace in those ages when writers had to depend on the personal patronage of the rich in order to live. The rich, too, came to need the poets. They wanted to survive their mortal bodies through the survival of their name in the permanence of the printed page. Some did it through elaborate tombs with suitable epitaphs, and who could write these better than a poet? And where too would it live as long on stone but on the printed page? In his defence of poetry, Balbuena's near contemporary, Sir Philip Sidney warned rich and powerful men who did not patronise poets with their money that their memory would "die from the earth for want of an epitaph".[55] Edmund Spenser, too, warned patrons that they should provide poets with the wherewithal while they lived, since the poet's verses "steel in strength in time and durance shall outweare"; and the rich and the great who could not sing for themselves would be sure, except they paid a poet to sing for them, to "die in obscure oblivion".[56]

The Count of Lemos and his kind were the antecedents of Foundations like Ford and Guggenheim and others. Henry Ford may have called history "bunk",[57] but he would not have been averse to having his own role in it recorded. Balbuena, like any modern aspirant for a foundation grant, made his application in the prescribed manner according to the prescribed formula. His poetry was good enough for its purpose. Lemos saw that his name would live as long as Balbuena's poem about Spain's legendary, but mythical national hero – Bernardo del Carpio – survived. He would not gamble with his own immortality by ignoring the poet who could ensure it. So this time, Balbuena hit the bull's eye. When the Council of the Indies met to consider the applicant for the vacant post of Abbot to the Church of Jamaica, Balbuena's name was not even on the short list of eight that came up for consideration. But the Count exerted his influence, and the official Chronicler and historian of Spain, González Dávila records that: "He (i.e. Bernardo de Balbuena) was elected Abbot of Jamaica on 29th April, in the year 1608". One cannot help thinking, that, relatively speaking, the Count of Lemos ensured his immortality at cut-price.

Cut-rate or not, a post was still a post. And, as abbot, Balbuena would be quite some way up in the hierarchy of the Church, even if his rung on the ladder was in Jamaica, and somewhat remote. Yet it was to be some two and a half years or more before the abbot would arrive to pursue his vocation in Villa de la Vega, today's Spanish Town. Balbuena ran into trouble when he tried to obtain the customary Bulls from the Pope, confirming his appointment. This trouble had to do with his illegitimate birth. In a letter, the Spanish emissary in Rome wrote to the authorities in Spain pointing out not only that Balbuena was illegitimate,

> ... by the papers that have come it is clear that the aforementioned Doctor is the natural son of his parents, not legitimate nor legitimised by subsequent matrimony.

but that he seemed to have tried to evade the implications of his illegitimacy:

> He says that he has no obstacle in this Abbacy, whereas being illegitimate, he needs dispensation which His Holiness will grant. But please advise if he needs it as is certain, unless he has already had it for such offices, which I doubt.[58]

It is possible that in Mexico, Balbuena through the influence of his family connections, had been able to hold his priestly office without papal dispensation. In the New World, as Eric Williams comments about Spanish Trinidad, illegality was the rule that proved the exception of metropolitan law.[59] But even in Mexico, his illegitimacy may well have been the bar to his advancement. This was his buried hurt, his secret wound which gave an added quality of ferocity to his ambition both for a high Church position and for success as an epic poet. As we shall see later, Bernardo de Carpio, the national hero of his poem, was himself of illegitimate birth. The choice of his subject was an attempt to auto-create himself, through the celebration of this hero. Meanwhile, he had to live. Depending on the Count of Lemos's influence he had evidently evaded any reference to the problem of his illegitimacy in applying for the Bulls from Rome. This evasion can be understood when we realise the extent to which birth, lineage, the mania for rank and titles of nobility, and the peculiar and all pervasive obsession of Spaniards of the time with the problem of *limpieza de sangre* – purity of blood – formed and dominated the very structure of Spanish society in which Balbuena lived. The need to be well born, to be of Christian descent, unmixed with Jewish or Moorish blood, to be the legitimate son of verifiable descent, of "someone" (*hijo d'algo* i.e. hidalgo) was part of a psychological compulsion comparable in terms of our own society to the need to be as "white" as possible; and to deny "black" blood as the original taint. We shall see how Balbuena used his heroic poem in this context as a literary and psychological justification of his illegitimacy; how he used his epic poem to make legitimate his outsidership in relation to the structure of a society to which he was devoted, and to whose values he paid full allegiance.

For the moment, however, Balbuena concerned himself with the strictly practical issue of survival. Survival had to do with money, or rather, Balbuena's lack of it. His stay in Spain, getting his doctorate, his time in Madrid as a *pretendiente* in search of a post, greasing the necessary palms, and paying living expenses for himself and his servants, seemed to have eaten into the money which he had taken with him from Mexico. The obtaining of the Bulls also cost money. And, whilst the Pope in Rome was prepared to grant the needed dispensation, he could not make the slow and rusty wheels of the papal bureaucracy move any faster. Also, in addition to the dispensation procedure, there was another hold-up. For purely technical reasons, the papal bureaucrats had to search in the Papal Archives for the Bulls that had been issued to Balbuena's predecessor as Abbot of Jamaica – Marques de Villalobos – before they could issue the new Bulls to Balbuena. The latter waited and waited in

Madrid. His money began to run out. One year after his appointment in 1609, he sent in a petition to the Council of the Indies. In this he asked that the income accruing from the Abbacy of Jamaica should be given to him, until the matter of his appointment was confirmed. Because of the delay in this, he wrote, "… he has been delayed here for a year, so impoverished that he can no longer support himself in the capital."[60]

He got no answer to this petition. He fired off another, requesting that he be allowed to go to Jamaica and to act there in his post until the bulls were issued. In May, 1609, this second petition was granted, but Balbuena did not leave. He may have been reluctant to do so without the official bulls, knowing what difficulties the ecclesiastical appointees could have with the civil authorities in places like Jamaica if their appointments offered a loophole for attack, through not being fully confirmed.

He may have been waiting too, on the publication of his poem, *The Bernard*. In February, 1609, through the influence of the Count of Lemos, Balbuena had obtained for his poem the necessary ecclesiastical approbation, and by June he had also managed to obtain the license to print and publish his book.[61] The printing press, and the power of its influence had been early recognised by the Church. The Inquisition, among its other manifold duties, kept a watchful eye to see that literature remained orthodox in matters of faith and fulfilled a social and moral responsibility within the limits laid down by the Catholic faith. Control was strict, as for example, in Soviet Russia. Yet, in Spain, literature flourished rather than otherwise. But the author had to go through quite a process in order to get his book published. He had to obtain the license or *privilegio*, a kind of copyright which he could sell outright to the printer-dealer; and of course the ecclesiastical approval which testified that the work deserved to be printed for its excellence, and above all because, as the censor said of *The Bernard*: "there is nothing in it against the Catholic Faith and good morals…"[62]

Yet, for some reason or the other his poem was not published; nor was it to be for many a long year. Whilst he waited for the bulls to arrive from Rome he seems to have survived by borrowing money. On coming to Spain he had returned to Valdepeñas where he was born and to Viso del Marques from where his father had originated. A cousin of his in Valdepeñas, a certain Martínez Castellanos, recorded in his will that,

> Likewise I declared that I advanced money to my cousin Don Bernardo de Balbuena, Bishop of Puerto Rico, and according to his letters, he offers me very good expectations; especially now that he has taken possession of that office, he writes to me and offers me good payment with interest.[63]

This, of course, was written when Balbuena, after his long stay in Jamaica as abbot, had at last received promotion (1619) and taken up the bishopric of Puerto Rico (1623).

Balbuena may have managed to survive, too, through the help and charity of Spain's Shakespeare – the prolific dramatist, poet, lover and priest, Lope de Vega y Carpio. Although about this time he was usually impecunious, Lope was known for his generosity. He and Balbuena struck a friendship, not least of all because their common obsession with the theme of the mythical Spanish hero, Bernardo del Carpio, and the manner in which, one in his plays and the other in his epic poem, both used it for similar psychological ends – the auto-creation of themselves, transforming their lowly births through the magic wand of fiction. In 1625, Lope de Vega was to praise Balbuena among other Spanish poets, and in 1627, the year of Balbuena's death, Lope de Vega testifies in a letter to the fact that Balbuena, then Bishop of Puerto Rico, had sent him eight hundred reales[64] through his agent in Seville. Was Balbuena sending this money as a gift in recognition of past favours – Lope de Vega, had earlier on been valet-Secretary to the young Count of Lemos and might have been instrumental in helping Balbuena to win the Count's favour – or was he repaying money he had borrowed from the great poet and playwright during his time of indigence?

By February 1610, the Bulls had arrived from Rome. Although Balbuena had received his clearance papers for himself and his party to proceed to Jamaica in May 1609, another decree was made out in February 1610 to allow them to "pass to the island of Jamaica". His party consisted of – according to the records which were kept as a corollary of the strict watch and control exercised over those travelling to the Indies – his servants, Christopher now about thirteen or fourteen years old and described in the clearance papers as free mulatto, native of Mexico; a married couple and a single man, both from Balbuena's native Valdepeñas; one other single man, also from Madrid, who listed himself as a *hidalgo* i.e. gentleman, although he was going out as Balbuena's servant. Van Horne conjectures that they went out as intending emigrants as well as servants.[65]

They all had to swear – except Christopher of course – that they were of old Christian blood, untainted with the intermixture of Jew or Moorish blood, and therefore unlikely to be heretics and therefore subversive to the State which was based on the Catholic-Christian faith.

One other cleric went with him, Father Gonzalo Sanabria. And, in the permission which had been granted him in 1609, sandwiched between the servants and the goods that he was allowed to carry with him, three Negro slaves were listed. Like the goods "to the amount of 1,000 ducats, jewels worth 500 ducats and books connected with his studies, worth 200 ducats",[66] the Negro slaves, considered but another and more profitable kind of goods, were to be admitted into Jamaica free from the usual tax which the King and the State collected as their cut of the profitable African slave-trade. Although, according to Catholic practice, the slaves would have been baptised, and would be theoretically classed as men – they were supposed to have, like everyone else, immortal souls – they came within the Aristotelian definition, accepted by some

theologians, of inferior men with implicitly "inferior souls" who occupied the
status of a "living tool". In the final clearance papers, they were not listed among
the passengers; their records remain mute among the goods.

The actual date on which Balbuena and his party sailed from Seville is not
known. But we know that, as very few ships of the "flota" – or regular sailing
fleet which went to the Indies under heavy escort – went directly to unimpor-
tant outposts like Jamaica, they sailed to Santo Domingo. From there they
arranged the trip across to Jamaica. Their final permits were dated in June
1610, and they may have sailed soon after. They then stayed in Santo Domingo
some three months, while Balbuena met the important dignitaries, with an eye
to future promotion in the far more important centre of Santo Domingo; and
tried to hire a small vessel in which to cross over to Jamaica. He found a ship
jointly owned by its Captain and co-pilot, Francisco Coldera and Manuel Luis,
and rented it from them for the excessive price of 400 silver pesos, each one to
the value of eight *reales*. The price was high because of the riskiness of the
venture. Armed contraband traders of other nations, who broke the prohibition that no one but Spaniards should trade in the Indies, were thick in
Caribbean waters and especially frequented the deserted ports of Jamaica.
Even worse, fortune-seeking pirates of all nations had established their
dominion over the Caribbean seas. The passage, also, could be stormy and
rough. On top of all this, the inflated prices which are part of the unhappy fate
of all colonies, came into play. In addition to the money he paid for the hiring
of the vessel, Balbuena, as was customary, had to find food and drink for his
party on the crossing. They could not have eaten very well – if they ate at all.
Balbuena himself later wrote that he had difficulty scraping up the money to
pay his passage on the ship to Jamaica.

Somewhere towards the end of 1610, they arrived at Port Caguaya – today's
Passage Fort. The Abbot and his party were met by the dignitaries of the town
of Villa de la Vega. They proceeded in a stately manner by road to the town
which was some seven miles from the disembarkation point. When he arrived,
the Abbot, to borrow a nice phrase of the historian of Spanish Jamaica[67] in
regard to another incumbent[68] – looked at Villa de la Vega, and Villa de la Vega
looked at the Abbot.

> When Your Majesty bestowed this Abbacy on me, and while preparing to
> come out to serve my Church, the Count of Lemos, at that time, President
> of Your Royal Council of the Indies, directed me to observe carefully the
> things that in this island appeared to me to be worthy thereof and in a faithful
> and brief report to give the same to Your Majesty and to your Royal Council.
> Balbuena in a letter from Jamaica, July 1611[69]

We are left in no doubt as to what the Abbot saw as he looked at Villa de la Vega
towards the end of the first decade of the seventeenth century. In a letter written
to the King, about a year and a half after his arrival, he gives a picture of Spanish
Jamaica, of its religious, social and economic life. In his epic poem, too, Spanish

Jamaica makes its appearance in a more idealised form. The two descriptions illustrate two kinds of truth – the truth of history and historical facts, and that of poetic or universal truth. In the Prologue to the Epic poem, a prologue which Balbuena wrote in Jamaica in 1615, he discusses the relative validity of these two kinds of truth. There, as first and foremost a poet, Balbuena comes down with vehemence on the side of universal and poetic truth. As Abbot, however, as an ecclesiastical administrator, he had to deal with historical facts, as he encountered and contended with them, in his task of ministering to the immortal souls of the people of Jamaica.

As one of his first acts as Abbot, Balbuena wrote in his letter, he had ordered confessions to be taken throughout the island with "particular care". From these confessions, he fixes the total number of inhabitants at 1,510. Of these he lists 523 as Spaniards, including men and women. Children number 173. There are 75 "foreigners" – these most likely refer to Portuguese settlers, among them Portuguese Jews, some of them merchants. Of the original inhabitants, the Arawak Indians, "natives of the island" as Balbuena lists them, there are only 74. The class of the free Blacks was fairly heavily represented. There were some 107 "free Negroes". And the number of slaves of African origin was relatively large – 558, in Balbuena's confessional census.[70]

The number given for the European inhabitants must have been nearly accurate. There most likely were more Arawak Indians and African ex-slaves in the island, however, refugees in the fastness of the mountains. The Maroon tradition in Jamaica sprang from both an Arawak and an African resistance to forced labour. With the first settlement of Spaniards in the island, during the early decades of the XVI century, the sharing out of the Indians to settlers in the system which later became standardised as the *encomienda* system, the resistance to forced labour, and to the whole work-money-Christian God ethos of the Spaniards, had led to mass suicides with cassava poison or to escape into the inaccessible regions of the Blue Mountains. The escape of African slaves, too, to these regions, began almost at once and at the same time. Arawaks and Africans would have joined forces.

The present day Maroon memory and legend that they are descended from the Arawaks as well as from the Africans has recently been denied, in a controversy in the press[71] by someone who claims to deal with historical facts. But his historical facts are based on insufficient information in this case, on English records alone. The earlier Spanish records show that as late as 1601, the Spanish Governor of Jamaica, Fernando Melgarejo Córdoba, sent an expedition to attack and subdue and bring in a settlement of Indians entrenched in the Blue Mountains; and at the same time to search for gold. The expedition does not seem to have succeeded in either venture. It is clear, though, from the records that the tradition of a guerilla defence in the mountains was, in its early stage, a fusion of Arawak and African actions. The Maroon myth belongs, then, to that species of truth, of universal truth, in this case, the resistance of men to being reduced from manhood to slavery, which lives on in what Balbuena terms "the common tradition" in the prologue which he wrote in Jamaica. It is this kind of truth which, like Sir Philip Sidney in his *Apology for Poetry*, Balbuena defends in his prologue, exalting it against historical truth based on facts. The historian, hampered by what Sidney terms "the cloudy knowledge of mankind"[72] can never be in possession of all the facts; therefore his so-called factual dogma is always open to error. The myth or the legend, on the other hand, does not claim that its facts are true; only that its underlying essence could have been true.

The Maroon legend, which lays claim to both African and Arawak antecedents is true, not in its detailed and fallible fact, but in its core. The question as to how much of racial fusion there really was is irrelevant; what is important is that the myth itself, which embodies "the self-consciousness and memory of mankind"[73] has sprung from the deeds of both peoples; a myth that pays tribute to the invincibility of the human aspiration to be free. The Maroons are factually the mythic descendants of Arawaks and Africans – as Balbuena, in his epic poem, would make the mythical Spanish hero Bernardo del Carpio the ancestor of his patron, the Count of Lemos; of the glory and heroism of Spain and the patriotism of the Spaniards; and of the moral choice needed in the search for the true and ideal destiny of Man.

A considerable nucleus of the total population lived in the town of Villa de la Vega.[74] In his letter to the King, Balbuena does not describe the town in detail. He tells us, that "a river of good water"[75] passes through the town – this was of course, today's Rio Cobre. From his account of the main buildings and principal functionaries, it is clear that the town itself was laid out on the typical plan which the Spaniards translated from Spain to all areas of the New World. The life of the town was centred around the main square – the Plaza Mayor – with the principal Church and the Town Hall as the focus of community life. The streets had been laid out in an orderly manner by Alonso de Miranda, the Governor, who welcomed Balbuena when he arrived. The same Governor had also repaired the Town Hall or Cabildo. Although Balbuena does not tell us this, we know from a later record that there were some two hundred houses in the town itself. These were built low, without lofts, as a protection against earthquakes and hurricanes. The roofs were covered with tiles, the walls were made of mud, although some were of wood, and a few of the principal ones made of brick.

There were common lands in and near the town for the benefit of all the citizens. But in 1604, the citizens of Villa de la Vega had complained that the then Governor – Melgarejo Córdoba – had allowed many of the free Negroes to build their huts on a part of this common land. Balbuena himself tells us of the "many hunting grounds" outside the town, these occupied by horned stock, "in which the colonists have their shares similar to the ranches they formerly had stocked with tame cattle from which have sprung those that are now wild in these grounds".[76]

The economic life of the town and the island then centred to a large extent on the export of hides and tallow, as Balbuena tells the King, on the "killing of cows and bulls, leaving the meat wasted". In addition, lard, which was obtained from "the large herds of swine raised in the mountains, which are common to who may wish to hunt them" was another export commodity.[77] Jerked pork, in the manner of the Carib Indians, was plentiful – that method has been handed down to us today, mainly through the Maroons.

Farms growing cassava, maize and vegetables, and sugar mills, cocoa walks and cowpens surrounded the town, according to a later description. Balbuena himself tells us that the "land is abundant and suitable for growing all the seeds and grains that are cultivated in Spain". Cassava, the Arawak food *par excellence*, was planted in fairly large quantities. Balbuena writes that the "bread eaten here" is made from cassava and can be "preserved for many months". He tells the king, too, of the groves of cedars, brasil trees, mahogany and other woods.[78] As we shall see later, the woods of the island feature among the measures that he suggests to the King for the island's benefit and improvement. For what appals the goodly Abbot, above all else, is, in spite of the great natural advantages that the island possesses, the state of neglect and the general misery; a misery which affects the state of the Church and of religion, as much as everything else, and is almost unbelievable.

There was a root cause for the neglected condition, the condition which would cause him to look back from Puerto Rico, and regard Jamaica as the "*soledades*" in which he had been as one bewitched (*encantado*). The root cause of the neglect of Jamaica had to do with the fact that, as Balbuena says early, in his letter, the island of Jamaica "now belongs to the estate of the Admirals of the Indies, the Dukes of Veragua".[79] The Admirals of the Indies and the Dukes of Veragua were the heirs and descendants of the great Discoverer, Christopher Columbus. Jamaica, in between bouts of litigation, belonged to them. It was their island estate; to borrow an English phrase, it was their "plantation". How had this come about and what effect did this have on Jamaica, on Balbuena and on his epic?

The magnificent titles, powers, lands that had been granted to Christopher Columbus as part of the package deal that was his reward for discovering the New World had been, through the intrigue of his enemies, and the ingratitude of kings, gradually diminished. He died in Spain in relative obscurity in 1506. His son, Diego, who had married into a powerful grandee Spanish family, contested these rights of his father with the Crown. After his death in 1526, his wife Doña María de Toledo returned from La Española to Spain to fight for these rights on behalf of her son Luis, who was still a child. Her son, she claimed, should be Admiral and Viceroy of all the Islands and the Mainland; he should obtain among other perquisites, ten per cent of all treasure found in the Indies. After years of stubborn litigation, a settlement was reached in 1536. Columbus's grandson was to have a relatively small part of what was claimed for him: land on the mainland for a Dukedom which would entitle him to be called Duke of Veragua, and as his entailed estate (*mayorazgo*) "the island of Jamaica". At the time of the award, the President of the Council of the Indies[80] had argued with harsh commonsense that Jamaica should be given to the Columbus heir,

> ... because it is small, and up till now has been of no advantage whatsoever, seeing that it possesses neither gold nor silver nor pearls nor anything else, besides cattle pens.

The President went on to recommend, "This should be given to him as his with the title of Duke or Marquis, the King remaining the Supreme Authority".[81]

Jamaica then was to be, at one and the same time, the private property of the heir of Columbus *and* part of the Spanish empire overseas. From this divided role, and because of the dual authority, much of the neglect which the island suffered was to ensue. Much of the factionalism in Church and State politics was to spring from this cause. One was either a Columbus-family man; or a King-and-Crown man. Balbuena was appointed by the Count of Lemos[82] acting for the King at a time when the Columbus family was busily litigating among themselves. After the death of one of the heirs of Columbus – Don Cristóbal de Cardona y Colón – two branches of the family went to law to settle which branch should succeed to the title and estates.

The right to appoint both abbots and governors belonged to the Columbus heir. During the litigation, however, the King and the Crown temporarily took over this right, until the issue of the rightful heir was concluded. And so, an abbot like Balbuena's predecessor – Marquis de Villalobos – was a King's appointee; so was the Governor, whom Balbuena met when he arrived in Spanish Town. That Governor left shortly after.[83] This may have been due to the fact that in the year 1608 the inheritance lawsuit had finally been settled in favour of Don Nuño Colón. This was also the very year in which Balbuena had been appointed as abbot by the King. Our abbot must have been placed in a precarious position. Would Don Nuno Colon insist on his right to appoint his own abbot? Was this one of the reasons why Balbuena had to delay his departure from Spain? Certainly, we know that Don Nuño insisted on appointing, in 1610, his own man to be Governor of Jamaica – Espejo Barranco – and that, after Balbuena was promoted to the bishopric of Puerto Rico in 1619, Don Nuño insisted to the King on his right to appoint the next abbot.

What exactly took place we do not know. Perhaps Balbuena, with that suave tact and prudence which was to mark his performance both as abbot and bishop, met the agent of Don Nuño, or Don Nuño himself in Madrid, and made it easier for them to accept his appointment to the Abbacy of Jamaica as a *fait accompli*. And, either in Madrid or in Jamaica, Balbuena wrote Don Nuño Colón into his epic poem, praising him along with his great ancestor – the Discoverer. In praising Don Nuño, he praised the island which was the marquisate, the estate of the Columbus family. There is no doubt that in this case, as in others, Balbuena used his pen to good effect, to assure his survival in a sea of uncertainty. The island of Jamaica may have entered epic poetry in a somewhat tortuous manner. Be that as it may, Balbuena was left undisturbed in his abbotship.

His epic description of Jamaica is condensed into a single stanza in the XIXth Bk. of *The Bernard*. But his praise of Don Nuño, and the prophecy about himself as Abbot of Jamaica, expands the Jamaica reference into three stanzas. The action of *The Bernard* is imagined to take place in the 9th century, so the praise of Columbus's discovery of the New World, of Don Nuño and Jamaica, is praise which is given as a prophecy, by the great magician, a Tlaxcalan Indian who is visited in Mexico by the French magician Malgesi and two other characters in a flying boat.

The Tlaxcalan magician first foretells to them the discovery of the New World by Columbus, and the consequence which it will bring in its train. Columbus, transforming men into dolphins, will reach the shores of the unknown world; he will meet with people, concealed and hidden from the eyes of his world until then, and take some of them back to Spain. The Golden Age will then be reborn again, as the rich earth of the New World yields up its treasures which will load the ships for Spain. The Christian faith which Columbus brings – almost one feels, as a *quid pro quo* – will transform the Indian gods, graven idols without souls, back into the stone from whence they came. Columbus will give to Castile and León a New World. He will give to them vast new peoples still hidden in the shadows of the West.

In exchange, the Colón family would be given the right to use a heraldic shield, which Balbuena describes in his poem, which will bear testimony to the ducal Crown which Columbus and his successors will wear.

But the Tlaxcalan magician, addressing Columbus still to be born, prophesies that avaricious ingratitude will diminish the honours and titles which he would leave to his descendants.[84] In spite of this, however, his memory will be preserved in the eternal flow of time, and among his successors one, in particular, and that Don Nuño Colón – who else? – will add lustre to that memory. From stanzas 83-85, Balbuena sings with dignity for his abbotship and his supper. In the first stanza of these three, the Tlaxcalan magician tells Columbus that time will repay the great debts owed to his solicitude, and

> In Don Nuño Colón, reborn again
> The grandeur which your heroic spirit found
> Will become in him the fiery forge of Spanish honour:
> Great Lord Admiral and Duke of Veragua.

In the next stanza Jamaica comes into its epic own: Don Nuño is the

> Marquis of the hidden Jamaica
> Abounding in precious woods
> Green pastures, rich metals,
> If cursed with a careless and an idle people;

> In whose spacious earth the gleaming gold
> Multiplies for tomorrow's world;
> Which now, with glittering rays, spreads out
> Haloes of light along the Rio Cobre's shores.[85]

Jamaica is of course, "hidden" because the Tlaxcalan magician is prophesy-ing of the New World long before it became "revealed" through Columbus to Europe. The myth of the presence of gold in Jamaica had begun with Columbus himself and had been often repeated. In fact, Balbuena's predeces-sor as abbot, Marquez de Villalobos, had written to the king in November 1582, urging him to take over the island from the Columbus family, who, he implied, mismanaged it. Worse than that, since in the terms of the agreement made with the Crown, the Columbus family were not permitted to put up fortifications on the island – the Crown was not anxious for the Columbus family to fortify themselves on the island and set up an independent kingdom as many of the early conquistadores had been tempted to do, because the coasts of Jamaica were infested with corsairs, contraband smugglers and buccaneers. In fact the settlers complained that they lived a "frontier" life. To encourage the King to take over the island, Villalobos stated categorically that there were mines of gold and copper, and there were seabeds with oysters which had yielded pearls to a few fortunate inhabitants.

The more cautious Balbuena does not mention the existence of gold as a fact in his letter. Only in his epic poem does he insist on the gold which lay buried in the earth, signs of which were to be found in shining grains on the Rio Cobre's shores. His letter goes into details instead about the "precious woods". He uses these woods as the bait with which he tactfully implies to the King that he should take over the island. He does not openly state this. Mail and letters were opened by the State authorities, who were Columbus family partisans, and, if necessary, intercepted. Villalobos had complained to the King about this fact. But Balbuena walked more carefully. He points out the possible usefulness of Jamaica to the Spanish Navy. The island is "surrounded with ports with very secure harbours and rivers of fresh water that flow from the mountain ridges". From the abundance of woods, among them, one called red ebony, "granadillo" – which is "incorruptible and not quite as black as ebony"; another called thorn – *espino* – "of variegate colours", and, in addition, cedar, mahogany and brasil wood. Balbuena points out that the island would be most suitable for shipbuilding:

> ... and so convenient for this that if Your Majesty should desire some ships or galleons to be built there, any such work, would from the natural fitness of the country, the great abundance of woods and cheap provisions ... prove much cheaper and more profitable than those that have been done, and are going on in other parts of the world...[86]

Had his advice been followed and Jamaica become a naval centre for the Spaniards, the essentially seaborne power of England, some forty years later, would have found it impossible or at least more difficult to capture Jamaica.

The cheapness of food was partly due to the historical role that Jamaica had played in the early part of the sixteenth century. The island had provided provisions and horses for conquistadores like Alonso de Ojeda, Diego de Nicuesa, Gil González Dávila on their expeditions to the mainland. The island had even provisioned Balboa, discoverer of the Pacific, who, incidentally, forgot to pay for the provisions sent him.[87] But at the same time she emptied herself of her settlers, since all the more enterprising got out to search for the rich El Dorado on the mainland. Meanwhile the island had been well stocked with cattle and pigs as a provisioning base, and soon many were running wild. But, denuded of its men, the island slipped into a remote backwater – a *soledad*, as Balbuena would call it – and became even more so as the "historical axis" of discovery and settlement shifted entirely to the mainland.

The island, and Villa de la Vega fell into a drowsy inertia. With all the advantages that the island possesses – "all these good possession" – yet, Balbuena writes, "because of their natural laziness", the settlers are so poverty-stricken, that "they can hardly manage to feed themselves with cassava and beef which are the cheapest commodities here". In an earlier part of his letter he was even more trenchant. In spite of the fertile soil and good climate, "the people are so lazy and indolent and opposed to work that through this fault it (i.e. the island) generally suffers great misery".[88]

Not even in the epic vision and idealised language of *The Bernard* does Balbuena retract the charge of laziness on the part of the inhabitants. In his epic poem, Jamaica is "cursed with a careless and an idle people".[89] The Abbot seems to have tried to encourage some show of activity on the part of the settlers. In his letter he tells of a new venture that has been made in brasil wood. Cargoes had been sent to Spain for the first time that year, that is, the year in which he was writing. The wood has been sent to be used to make dyes, and, the Abbot adds, "Here, experiments have been made with it, and it gives three different dyes, all very fine, both for wool or silk".[90] If the venture turns out well, Balbuena hopes, it could mean great wealth for an island, rich in woods and oppressed by poverty.

The poverty of the people and the island was reflected in the state of the Church. Balbuena must have been rather dazed that first morning after his arrival, when he went through the prescribed ceremonial with which a prelate was greeted. The ceremony for the arrival of a high-ranking churchman paralleled that of the Governor. The latter, on first arriving, presented his credentials then walked through the town hall, and its several rooms, opening and closing the doors as he did so. Similarly, Balbuena had to go to the Church in the Plaza Mayor in Spanish Town, pray, open and close the doors, ring the bells, and walk through the Church, taking possession in the Lord's Name. Balbuena performing this ceremony, could hardly have avoided feeling that if this was what he had come to be abbot over, then the Abbacy of Jamaica was not much.

In his letter to the King, after sketching something of the religious organisation in general –

> There are some clergy born in the island with a lot of chaplaincies but these are poor like the people in general. There are two monasteries, one of Saint Dominic and one of Saint Francis, and at present, three monks in each and among them two preachers.[91]

He describes the state of the principal church itself, the Church dedicated to Our Lady of Expectation. He found the church, Balbuena reports, "so poor, ruined and roofless, that when it rains it cannot be entered to say mass". The Church is "bare and despoiled of vestments by incursion of enemies who have sacked it three times". These enemies, pirates and privateers of Spain's enemies, attacked Jamaica with impunity because of its undefended state. They grabbed all they could get; and as rich ornaments were to be found in the Church – in 1604, for example, the King had given 2,000 ducats to the Church to repair it and to buy ornaments – they always made sacking the Church a priority. They also came either to plunder the settlers of provisions for their ships or, more ordinarily, to trade manufactured goods in exchange for dried pork, meat, bread. One of the attacks to which Balbuena referred had been led by Sir Anthony Shirley – called by the English a "*gentleman*" adventurer, and by the Spaniards, a pirate – who in 1596 landed with his men, attacked the town and demanded a large ransom, including provisions from the inhabitants, as a ransom not to set fire to their houses. Villalobos, who had retreated to the Cayo de la Legua in company with the other priests, whilst the bulk of the people hid in the mountains, was surprised by Shirley in his hiding place, and forced to flee in his nightshirt. Shirley and his men seized on the Abbot's jewels, ornaments taken from the Church for safekeeping, his books, clothes, linen etc. Church and Abbot remained poorer than ever. And Villalobos may well have died out of a feeling of futility and sheer despair.[92]

In the four-year interval between the death of Villalobos and the coming of Balbuena, things went from bad to worse. Balbuena, like his energetic predecessor, set about at once to try and mend matters. He and the Governor, he tells us, "went from door to door to beg for such an urgent need" but that "it had not been possible to get anything worthwhile". As the people of the island "were incapable of repairing it with their alms" he himself had tried to improve the Church as best as he could by "making among other things a neat frontal…" Unlike Villalobos, Balbuena did not find the Baptismal Book with "leaves torn out"; but he found all other Church matters "confused and out of order". He undertook at once his visitation and inspection of the Abbacy and its Church. At the time of writing the letter he was in the process of holding a synod which, it seemed to him, did not appear to have ever been held before. All in all, he writes, he is busy attending to the necessities of the Church, spending his own money with "what my necessities could afford".[93]

We know earlier on from Villalobos that the tithes which supported the Church were not much, amounting only to 600 ducats a year. Balbuena develops this theme. It was the practice for the collection of tithes to be leased out to one individual who paid an estimated lump sum and then collected it back with some profit to himself. Balbuena points out that only some 710 pesos[94] had been paid for the year and a half after Villalobos' death – 1606-1607. For 1609-1610, Balbuena insists that the amount has been less. This means that with the share of the tithes that fell to the Abbot, he did not have much money to play around with to repair the Church and even to repay his expenses. With acumen, he now suggests two ways in which the Church can be repaired and properly kept up.

The more routine suggestion for the benefit of the Church had to do with the fact that Villalobos, on arriving in Jamaica, had collected all the tithes that had accrued during the interim vacancy and, at his death, had ordered this sum – 1,100 pesos – to be restored to the Church, or to the "person to whom they might belong". For five years now this money had been lodged with a private person. Balbuena asked that the matter might be examined and, if just, that the money "might be applied to assisting the necessities of the Church which are so great." His second suggestion gives an interesting insight into the way the country was run or rather, misrun, in the interests of the Columbus family by Governors who only came out to the island to make a quick killing before they sighed with relief and left it.

The island was the private fief of the Dukes of Veragua and the Marquises of Jamaica. In fact, as far as Spanish law is concerned, it has never ceased being so. Morales Padrón, the historian of Spanish Jamaica, comments with a certain grim complacency: "The Marquisate of Jamaica, existed and still exists, nominally, in the person of Don Cristóbal Colón de Carvajal y Maroto".[95] As such it existed only to contribute to the upkeep of the feudal and aristocratic splendour of a Spanish noble house. The governors and the abbots appointed by the Columbus family acted in fact as majordomos, or stewards, for the absentee owner. Like the later attorneys of English Jamaica, they enriched themselves as quickly as possible at the expense of the citizens and of the owners. One of the ways in which the fleecing of the citizens was done is exposed by the Abbot Marquez de Villalobos in an angry letter to the King. As a King's Abbot – he had been appointed by the conscientious Philip II of Spain – Villalobos clashed fiercely with the Columbus faction. They were not accustomed to Abbots gainsaying their will; but this time they had met their match in the intelligent well-born prelate who took his duty seriously.

In urging the King to take over the island he revealed that a Governor sent out by the Columbus heir, a certain Lucas del Valle Alvarado[96], had, after clearing out all the money that he could from taxes etc., left Jamaica, leaving in charge a Creole-Jamaican settler, one Pedro López, who had paid the Governor a sum of money for leaving him to act in his place[97]. Pedro López had at once set out to make his authority work for him. Soon he had a very good piece of speculation going. He brought in from Santo Domingo, the centre of Spanish Government in the Caribbean, some 500 pesos worth of copper coins called quartos. Each peso was the equivalent more or less of 13 silver reales. In 1582, when Villalobos was writing, each silver real was worth twenty-five quartos in Santo Domingo. Pedro López had all the quartos brought from Santo Domingo marked with an "S". He then used his authority to legally decree that the silver real in Jamaica could be bought for only eleven stamped quartos. He and his cronies then bought up all the silver reales in Jamaica, sent them to Santo Domingo, changed them into quartos, had them stamped and repeated the process all over again. It meant that Pedro López had bought a position which was in effect a license for making money at the expense of the citizens who had to sell their products for the devalued real, or for quartos which only had value inside the island. By the time Balbuena arrived, the situation was such that he complains in his letter to the King that: "What little silver it has had the foreign merchants have been bleeding it off little by little, so that now there is not a real in it".[98]

By the time he came to the island, the position had become legitimised. The quartos were now brought to the island through the special permission of the Royal Audiencia in Santo Domingo, and were still stamped in Jamaica. But the discrepancy had widened. The silver real in Santo Domingo was bought for fifty-one quartos, but in Jamaica for only seven. Whereas Villalobos had clashed openly with the Columbus faction over the issue – to the point where he had even threatened excommunication, (only to be told by the authorities that his appointment by the King was not valid since he had not brought his Bulls of confirmation by the Pope), and been insulted by Pedro López, a "choleric" man – Balbuena's approach was much more subtle and effective. Balbuena does not confront openly either the speculators or speculation. Instead he suggests that the speculation should be used for the good of the Church and the island in general, rather than for the advantage of the unscrupulous and ruthless few. Speculation could be made to improve the general well-being, spiritual and material, rather than creating a paradise for profiteers.

He approaches the matter in a crabwise manner. Insisting on the ruined condition of the Church, he tells the King that:

> I am grieved to see the so noticeable need of this Church, and I have no money, or strength to remedy it. I am so anxious about it and my soul is so full of these cares, that a means had occurred to me...[99]

This means, he explains to the King, it would not cost the Royal Treasury a single quarto. All he asks is that the King should give to the Church the license to bring from Santo Domingo a thousand ducats worth of quartos. Whatever profit was made from the deal would then be used for the repair and adornment of the Church, "which the heretics – (i.e. pirates and gentlemen-adventurers) had left so ruined". The majordomo of the Church would handle and account for the money. The speculation would benefit the country, too, seeing that "the chief cause of its poverty is lack of money, and a way of bringing it in".[100] He goes on to explain that the island does its main trade in products with the mainland and with Spain, but the products of the island are paid for in merchandise and not in money. Silver reales have disappeared. The introduction of a substantial amount of new quartos, stamped and therefore usable only in the island would "help to open up the trade of the country". It seems clear from what Balbuena says that the so-called idleness of the people had much to do with the fact that because of the scarcity of money, the economy was mainly a barter one, where people had adjusted to little more than a mere sufficiency of their basic needs.[101]

Balbuena knew that such a licence granted to the Church would outlaw the speculation of the Marquis' henchmen, who shared the profits with the Marquis himself. He hints delicately, begging the King to grant the license to the Church since although the island,

> is the territory of a private owner, in the end Your Majesty is the sovereign prince on whom it is more fully incumbent to see to the welfare and conservation of your subjects.[102]

But it was not to be as simple as that. The Marquis had powerful strings to pull at Court, to block any suggestions that might cut against his interests. One year and a half after he had written, the Abbot had still not received a reply to his letter and to his suggestions. In December, 1612, he wrote off to Spain again, asking this time that the Church be granted license to import 2,000 ducats worth of quartos.

From a document that Van Horne found in the Spanish Archives, he suggests that the petition was either granted, or was on the verge of being granted, when it seems to have been stopped by representatives of the Marquis. Balbuena was never allowed to put his scheme into operation. It is rare in the history of Jamaica that the private interests of the greedy have been subordinated to the interests of the needy many.

It was not only the civil authorities who saw the island primarily as a place for making a quick profit with little effort. Nor was it only the governor who represented the Marquis. Two of most energetic and intelligent governors appointed by the Crown – Melgarejo Córdoba and Alonso de Miranda – whilst doing some good for the island did even more for themselves. But in an era in which salaries were paid irregularly and in which gifts and perquisites were an accepted form of rewarding the new bureaucracy called into being by the sudden extension of the Spanish Empire, these attitudes, and a certain amount of chicanery, was understandable. Had they been accompanied by a measure of competence on the part of the Governor and his officials, Spanish Jamaica might have been a more prosperous place. But all too often the ability to be corrupt was the only criterion of office. All too often the Governorship of the island was seen as a pair of shears with which to shear the island sheep. Nor was this attitude restricted to the State bureaucrats. From the earliest days, the bureaucracy of the Church, too, had tended to regard the Abbacy of Jamaica as a financial perquisite rather than a religious obligation.

PART 3

> The sacred pastoral staff will here await
> The author of this history,
> Here, in shadows of eternal spring
> He'll sit and sing, noising your fame abroad,
> And, in hope of better things, will gird
> A precious mitre on his brow.
> Balbuena, *The Bernard*, Bk. XIX[103]

In Balbuena's epic poem, *The Bernard*, the Tlaxcalan magician, after describing Jamaica, prophesies that the author of the poem – i.e. Balbuena – will serve in Jamaica both as poet and ecclesiastic. Jamaica is the destined place in which he will write in some parts of his poem – "he'll sit and sing" – but it is also the place where he will wear "a precious mitre on his brow", and carry a "sacred pastoral staff". The mitre and the staff are the signs of office of a Bishop. How did Balbuena come to claim and make use of these episcopal insignia whilst only an abbot? Not the least part of the answer lies in the fact that when the Abbacy of Jamaica was first set up, the then Spanish King, Ferdinand, gave the post of abbot as a financial sinecure to his chaplain, the Canon of Seville, and Treasurer of the House of Trade of the Indies – *Casa de Contratación* – Don Sancho de Matienzo.

In 1511, bishoprics had been established in Santo Domingo and Puerto Rico. They were subordinated to the Church in Seville. Because of the smallness of the population in Jamaica, only an abbacy was set up there. It was to be supported out of the tithes of the congregation; and as from 1516, out of these tithes, Don Sancho de Matienzo, who had no intention of setting foot in his abbacy, was to be paid. It is possible that in order to make it easier for Don Sancho to collect his cut, the abbacy, instead of being made to depend on either of the bishoprics of the other islands, was put directly under the Archbishop of Seville. The Abbot of Jamaica was therefore termed a *Magnus Abbas* – a Great Abbot – and was to enjoy, within the island area of his jurisdiction certain privileges belonging to a bishop. There he could wear the mitre, carry the bishop's crozier, wear the bishop's ring and other pontifical insignia, set up an ecclesiastical court, and, this was important for abbots who intended to be absentees, appoint a vicar to act for him. He could not, however, administer confirmation, ordain priests, nor consecrate the Holy Oil. This was one of the problems whose consequences a Balbuena would later have to cope with.

The first Great Abbot, Don Sancho Matienzo, set a pattern of absenteeism and a purely mercenary approach which was to be followed either in both, or in one aspect, by most of the Abbots of Jamaica, with a few outstanding exceptions. The Abbacy, such as it was in the early days, was situated at New Seville on the North Coast, where the first major settlement had been established by the Spaniards. The settlers were a tough-minded lot. If Don Sancho had no desire to take up his duties in a rough provincial outpost, the settlers had no intention of paying him his tithes. His constant appeals to the King and the King's letters to New Seville ordering that Don Sancho should be paid his portion of the tithes, left the settlers unmoved. One notes, with some satisfaction, that in the end Don Sancho died, unpaid. After his death, between 1522-24, two other abbots, one of whom was a distinguished Hieronimite priest, and a Protector of the Indies, did not manage to reach Jamaica, the Hieronimite priest having died before he sailed.

The fourth abbot, although an absentee, was one of the few to add lustre to the Abbacy of Jamaica. He was Peter Martyr of Anghiera, an Italian humanist who had settled in Spain, taken orders there, and had been appointed Director of the Palace School for young nobles. Like Balbuena he was a writer, although not a poet. He listened to first-hand accounts of the New World from Columbus and his men, and from these accounts compiled his famous *Decades of the New World*. In the Eighth Decade he gives a rhapsodic account of the island which he had never seen, but whose beauty had struck Columbus. Jamaica, Martyr in effect wrote, was an Eden, without winter or summer, fertile with clear rivers and perpetual spring and autumn. It was an earthly paradise, one of the hidden places where God had made the first man from clay, breathing life into his soul. There was no land whose climate was more "beautiful and benign". He was her Abbot and she was his "bride, the happiest of all".[104]

Peter Martyr, to prove his love for his "bride" determined to adorn her. The settlers in New Seville had built a provisional church of wood thatched with straw. He would build one of stone which would endure and commemorate his name. In this he was a true humanist as was Balbuena. Fame was their chief preoccupation. Central to the epic poem of *The Bernard* is the choice between gold and fame. Peter Martyr did not hesitate. The emoluments due to him from his Abbacy were to be used to help towards the building of the Church. He asked the King's help and Charles V gave him first a sum of 800 pesos. After work began in 1525, King Charles gave him another 100,000 maravedis in 1526. A group of Indians who had been assigned to the King to be used for the building of public works was put to the building of the new Church. Peter Martyr sent out an emissary to see to the building of the Church and to collect his tithes for that purpose.[105]

From a seventeenth-century description of the ruins of the unfinished church it has been deduced that it was most likely planned as a Gothic building with three naves featuring buttresses. The ground plan was roughly some thirty *pasos* – footsteps – long by thirty wide. There were two rows of pillars. The naves as well as the chapel were vaulted, a kind of church unusual in the Antilles, and the plateresque facade with its intricate decorations showed the relative luxury it was intended the church should have.[106]

Above the door of the church, the heads of Christ, the Virgin, and a coat of arms was carved. A stone inscription below pointed out, that after the first church of wood had been destroyed,[107] the new church had been built by Peter Martyr, Abbot of Jamaica and a member of the Council of the Indies. Peter Martyr had begun his stone church[108] expecting his name to endure. But from the beginning he had trouble in the building of the Church from powerful men like the Treasurer Pedro de Mazuela, who was more interested in gold than in immortality.[109]

The emissary that Peter Martyr had sent out to supervise the building of the Church soon wrote back about the lack of cooperation he was getting. The Treasurer, Mazuela, had in fact taken away a group of Indians assigned to work on the Church and was using them on his private work. What was this private work? As early as 1519, the Treasurer Mazuela, who was de facto second to the Governor and who acted as such after the Governor, Garay, left for the Mainland in 1523, had written to the King asking that the settlement should be transferred from New Seville to the south coast. Among the many reasons he gave was that he had on the south coast a "sugar mill and twenty Portuguese labourers" settled there, since the land and the climate and the flat plains were more advantageous. This permission was finally given and the capital transferred in 1534.[110]

The remains of a sugar mill have been recently discovered on the site of New Seville. The mill is, most likely, one of the two which the Governor, Francisco de Garay, owned and operated in partnership with the King of Spain.[111] After Garay's departure for Mexico in June 1523, and his later death there, Mazuela and another official took over Garay's possessions, including the two sugar mills, one of which was said to have produced 300,000 lbs of sugar a year.[112] It is not improbable therefore that the Indians allotted by the King to work on building the Church and thereby ensure Peter Martyr's fame, were put instead to, among other things, produce sugar for Mazuela and his island partner.[113]

Be that as it may, Peter Martyr was forced to complain to the King, who wrote Mazuela ordering that the Indians should be put to work on the Church at once. The work continued. Then Martyr died in 1526, and once again the work was neglected. The King, in 1533, urged that the work on the Church should go on and that the chapel should be finished.[114] But the following year Mazuela had his way and the settlers transferred to the South Coast, to Villa de La Vega, the town built near Mazuela's "ingenio" or sugar mill. The mill prospered. The church fell into ruins. The inscription which should have preserved Martyr's name was lost as the ruins crumbled. With one of those supreme ironies of history, some months ago, after some 400 years in which sugar and its gold and the economic motif had dominated the history of Jamaica, the broken stone of the inscription was found by a researcher into the ruins of New Seville – in a butcher's shop. The name of Peter Martyr engraved on stone had won out and endured after all – the desire for fame had outlived Mazuela and the greed for gold. This moral lesson would have pleased and justified the author of *The Bernard*.

In 1546, the New World Church was separated from the Church in Seville, Spain. An Archbishopric was established in Santo Domingo and the Abbacy of Jamaica was now to be subordinated to it. But a de facto situation had, in the meanwhile, sprung up. In 1518, three years after the establishment of the Jamaican Abbacy, a Bishopric was set up in Santiago de Cuba. Although the Abbacy still depended directly on Seville, in the hierarchy of things it was still, in a secondary manner, subordinated to the Bishopric of Santo Domingo. When the Bishopric of Santiago was established, the Pope, Leo X, had attached the Abbacy of Jamaica as a dependency to that diocese. In 1522, after the death of Don Sancho Matienzo, the first Abbot of Jamaica, the first Bishop of Santiago de Cuba, laid claim to the dependency of Jamaica. He accused certain interested parties – one understands by this Don Sancho Matienzo – of having "by devious paths" frustrated the true destiny of the Abbacy as part of the diocese of Santiago de Cuba. It seems clear that the Bishop of Santiago resented the lessening both of his area of jurisdiction and of the part of the tithes which would accrue to him, for certain episcopal services. But the Abbacy of Jamaica had been set up by Ferdinand, that is by the Royal power of Spain. The fact that the Bishop of Santiago claimed that the Pope had granted the dependency meant that the new King and Emperor, Charles V, anxious at all times to limit the papal intervention in the imperial Church, decreed that there was no reason why, in fact, the Abbacy of Jamaica should be annexed to the Bishopric of Santiago de Cuba.[115]

However the Bishops of Santiago de Cuba did not give up. After the death of Peter Martyr, for the first and only time one person was appointed both as Bishop of Santiago and Abbot of Jamaica, with a half of the tithes of the latter being apportioned to him. This was the Dominican priest, Fray Miguel Ramirez. He was the first to visit the island. He had come for one purpose – to make money. He passed through the town like a tempest, taking over groups of Indians to work for him, some of the Indians even belonging to the King. Such was his greed that a Spanish bureaucrat said of him that he would cause Spain to lose Jamaica. His fortunate death in 1535 freed Jamaica from his unfortunate attentions. From then on, different incumbents were appointed to the Bishopric of Santiago de Cuba and to the Abbacy of Jamaica – in spite of the fact that the geographical nearness of the two would have made their fusion logical.[116]

After 1536, the Columbus heirs had the right to appoint abbots. But this right was not exercised until after 1539. In 1534, the King had appointed the Licentiate Don Amador de Samano as Abbot. He was the first to actually take up residence in Villa de La Vega. With him was initiated that clash between Governor and Abbot, between State and Church, which was to be a feature of island life. In the clash between Samano and the acting Governor, Pedro Cano, one of the clergy, a brother and close relative of the acting Governor, Juan Cano, supported the latter against the Abbot, claiming that the Abbot had not brought Bulls of confirmation. In the bitter struggle and rivalry that ensued, Samano reported Juan Cano to the Bishop of Santiago asking that he be investigated and punished. The acting Governor Pedro Cano, however, was called to answer for his conduct to the Abbot before the Royal Audiencia of Santo Domingo.[117]

From there on, a constant conflict ensued between Santiago de Cuba and Santo Domingo as to whose jurisdiction the Abbacy of Jamaica fell under. From 1539, the Marquis of Jamaica and Duke of Veragua begin to designate the abbots, and with the exception of one – the licentiate Mateo de Santiago, they can all be included in the general description that Villalobos made of them to the King when he wrote that they were men who as abbots had never had "…any order or care for anything… since they were more anxious to acquire property than to fulfil their duties". The independent and strong-willed Villalobos, appointed by the King, had a very strong sense of the role of the Abbacy and was all for it being independent of the Bishopric of Cuba. He points out in a letter to the King that when during the Abbacy of Mateo de Santiago (1573-78), the King had ordered the Bishop of Santiago de Cuba to make a pastoral visit to the island for purposes of confirmation, the Abbot Mateo de Santiago had complained that no one had been confirmed on the island since it had been discovered; the power of confirmation not being permitted to an abbot, even a great abbot, and that all the Bishop of Santiago de Cuba, Juan del Castillo, had come to do was to extort some 1,500 ducats for himself. Even after he left, he sent an emissary to collect a further 1,000 ducats. Villalobos then began to do battle, writing letters to the Archbishop of Santo Domingo to annul the attachment of the Abbacy to Santiago de Cuba, which had been de facto confirmed by the pastoral visit of Juan de Castillo. The matter was sent to the Council of the Indies. Villalobos succeeded in putting off any further visitation to the Abbacy by the Bishop of Santiago, but in 1593, the King decided that whilst the Abbacy of Jamaica was included in the ecclesiastical Province of Santo Domingo, it was still attached to the Bishopric of Santiago de Cuba. So the matter remained until Villalobos died and Balbuena arrived in 1610.[118]

In his letter to the King of July 1611, the new Abbot makes it clear that like his predecessor he rejects the subordination of the Abbacy to Santiago de Cuba. He described the Abbacy in this fashion:

> Two leagues from the sea in this place is the Collegiate Church of this Abbacy, which is *nullius diocesis*. Its Abbot had episcopal jurisdiction, suffragan to the Archbishop of Santo Domingo in whose district it is, and subject in temporal matters to the Royal Audiencia…[119]

As the anomalous position of the Abbacy, and the problems from which the island suffered became clear to him, Balbuena, an idealist as an epic poet, but a pragmatist as Abbot, made two recommendations to the King, either of which would improve the existing situation.

In his long petition sent to Spain, dated December 1612, Balbuena set out the problems that beset the religious life of the country through the anomaly of the Abbacy. He includes in his petition evidence from his vicar, Andrés de Segura, a long established resident in Jamaica, and from Juan de Cueto, member of a Jamaican settler family, and a priest who had applied for the position of Abbot at the same time as Balbuena got it. All three point out the disadvantages which spring from the isolation of Jamaica. The distance between Jamaica and Santiago de Cuba was short. Yet the storminess of the passage, and the prevalence of corsairs and pirates in the undefended parts of Jamaica and about her coasts, make the visit of a Bishop from Santiago not only costly – Balbuena, with perhaps some exaggeration, puts the cost at about 1,500 ducats – but dangerous because of "the peril that there is from enemies".[120]

Since the Great Abbot could not consecrate the Holy Oil, the island many a time was without this precious spiritual commodity. Andres de Segura points out in his evidence that the consecrated Holy Oil had to be sent to Jamaica by sea, and as the consecration was only valid for a year, the oil had to be sent annually. Because of the difficulty of getting to Jamaica, the oil was not sent in some years. Worse, at times when the oil was sent, the ships transporting it were captured by Protestant and heretical pirates, some of them with a blasphemous turn of humour. As Andrés de Segura tells it, although the faithful bearers tried to cast the vessels of oil into the sea, the heretics,

> ...pulled up the urns and finding the Holy Oils, impiously poured them out and anointed themselves with them, making mockery and scorn of our holy ceremonies.[121]

Since only Bishops could ordain, the Jamaicans who wanted to enter the priesthood had to leave their island to be ordained elsewhere. Both Segura and Cueto maintain that it took the one six years, and the other eight years, of wandering from Cuba, to Santo Domingo to Panama, to achieve ordination. Cueto, too, remarks that his wanderings had caused him to return home "very much worn out and broken in health".[122] Without the presence of the Bishop too, confirmation could not take place.

Balbuena and his witnesses therefore strongly propose two courses of action. The one which they support strongly is that the Abbacy should be promoted to a Bishopric. Naturally Balbuena was interested. But he was pragmatic enough to go on to argue that if this was not done, then the best thing as alternative would be to abolish the Abbacy together and put the Church of Jamaica under the jurisdiction of the Bishop of Santiago de Cuba. That Bishop would then receive the main portion of the income. This would make it to his advantage to place a vicar there, and to make regular visits out of the income that he would be assured of. In the Church, as elsewhere, zeal was not enough.

But the wheels of the Spanish imperial bureaucracy moved very slowly. The petition was referred back to the Governor and Chancery of Santo Domingo from Seville sometime after March 1616. It was in this petition that Balbuena had again argued for a license to import money from Santo Domingo into Jamaica. It is improbable that the Duke of Veragua would have wanted such a high Church dignitary as a Bishop in Jamaica. Some Bishops took their religious vocation very seriously indeed and could prove as inconvenient to the State Power as a St Thomas a Beckett or a Villalobos. In all the arguments adduced for the reasons of the decline of the Spanish Empire and the quick rise of the Dutch, French and English Empires, little attention has been paid to the fact that the strong and powerful presence of the Spanish Church, with all its large areas of venality and self-betrayal, nevertheless constantly held out an ideal of spiritual perfection, subversive to the purely Machiavellian *realpolitik* of state power, and sometimes produced men of the calibre of a Las Casas to actualise the potentiality of the ideal. The "black legend" of Spanish imperialism is owed to the exposé made by Las Casas of the Spanish conquest. Too often the Church, both Catholic and Protestant, had been the accomplice rather than the accuser of the crimes committed in the name of Empire. It was not until the appearance of Baptist missionaries in the slave-and-sugar English society of Jamaica that the tension between the dictates of economic man and the lofty moral claims of religious-directed man would once again begin the process that would lead to the black legend revelations of the horrors of slavery. Nor is it fortuitous that the very core to the African resistance to slavery would have been mainly centred around African religious leaders like Boukman in Haiti, and Native Baptist deacons like Samuel Sharpe.

This petition of December 1612 was the same petition which the agents of the Columbus family had blocked. Van Horne speculates that both the license to be granted to the Church to import money, and the idea of a Bishopric and a powerful Church presence was displeasing to the Marquis and his faction. Like many another, Balbuena, seeing the logical and necessary reforms that he asked for unanswered year after year, would gradually have to content himself with these piecemeal measures, which always implies an acceptance of the status quo. These measures by their very inadequacy merely patch up and help to maintain an improbable and unreal status quo. And slowly, for an intelligent and imaginative man, the rust of inertia begins to eat away at one's soul. Before one knows it, one has become woof and warp of the very fabric which one had set out to recreate. But the process, by its very slowness, is imperceptible. It was only after he had left Jamaica that Balbuena would look back on his years there as years in which he had been *encantado* – bewitched.

How did Balbuena perform his daily duties as abbot? From a document drawn up between 1611 – 1612 we learn that it is the opinion, at least of some of the citizens of Villa de La Vega that, as van Horne paraphrases it, "he preached very well, giving evidence of great learning in his sermons; and that in his private life he set a good example to the citizens of the island".[123]

The Captain of the ship which took him to Jamaica from Santo Domingo, Francisco Coldera, also gives evidence to the effect that for the five months he was in Jamaica, before loading up for his trip back to Santo Domingo, he observed from the actions of the Abbot that he was "a most Christian man, full of virtue and learning".[124]

We have already seen how actively he took up his duties as to confession, holding a synod etc., getting the church repaired as best he could, begging for alms to help towards the repair. In his first letter to the King he shows himself concerned about the degree of incest – or incestuous relationships within the Roman Catholic definition – to be found among the Spanish population. The Spanish population of the island, he points out, is descended from only three families. All are inbred by marriage, all related. The entire country is "stained" with it, the sin is "so widespread and deep-rooted" that there seems to be no practical remedy for it. Even more important, this type of relationship is to be found in the highest places. To root out such a general sin, he says with realism, would not only depopulate the country, but would lead "to the injuring of many reputations". Attacking the sin and censuring it, Balbuena argues, would serve more as "hindrances than as a remedy".[125] The crusading spirit of a Las Casas was not that of Balbuena. If, as epic poet, he moved in a world of ideal moral choices, as Abbot in the real world of Villa de La Vega, as in the narrow places of provincial Mexico, he had come to terms with the greyer world of compromise, of the acceptance of certain brutal realities of a frontier-type existence, where the patterns and traditions of the old world no longer had relevance, where some form or the other of illegality was the norm.

Balbuena makes no special mention of his African or Indian flock. The latter, the Arawak Indians, the remnant that was left, were by now all nominally Roman Catholics, although with memories of their old religion which subtly coloured and restructured the new. Theirs had been a gentle religion, one which had caused Las Casas to say that he knew of no people more fitted for Christianity – the Christianity of Christ in its pristine meaning. Modern scholars have pointed out that the Arawaks believed in a Supreme Being, of whom carved objects found in isolated huts – zemis – were representations. Their Supreme Being was the "Spirit of Cassava and the sea, Being without antecedent".[126] Cassava and sea food formed the basis of their subsistence and structured the peaceful pattern of their lives. As José Juan Arrom points out, their God was not harsh and vindictive like Jehovah, nor a warrior like Odin. Instead he was a generous being who ruled the "creative forces of land and sea". He reflected the mildness of the Caribbean climate, the fruitfulness of its soil, the lack of an aggressive and competitive spirit.[127] But equally this God could not stand up to the challenge of a religion which had adopted on the one hand the humility of Christ, and on the other the terrible fighting sword and spirit of St. James of

Santiago – St. James the Moorslayer, the mythical twin brother that Spanish Christians had created for the Saviour, so that they could spread Christian power, and peace and love, by means of a Christian sword.

The African religions brought to the New World by the slaves and the freed Negroes persisted. Responding to the more complex organisations of African societies, the religions were more complex. One Abbot, Mateo de Santiago, had written to the Council of the Indies complaining about the neglect in which the African lived as far as Christian instruction was concerned.

The Spanish settlers who wanted slaves to work rather than souls to be saved resented his zeal and complained to the Marquis of Jamaica. Dispersed and spread out in ranches over the island, the Africans transplanted such patterns of life as were compatible with the new conditions. When the Abbot Mateo de Santiago complained that they lived together without sacrament of marriage "Bringing up their children and their chickens as if they were man and wife",[128] they were carrying on, in a simplified manner perhaps, part of the original African patterns. The availability of land on which they could plant food and rear stock made this transition even more possible. The Catholic apparatus of Saints made the accommodation of the polytheistic religions of the Africans easier. The Christian God, His Mother and the retinue of Saints were given a central place in the range of gods transplanted from Africa.

But a Balbuena, imaginative as he was in his own cultural pattern, could not extend his mind to comprehend this far more basic spiritual deviation. To him the revelation of the Christian God to Indian and African had been enough, as he said in *The Bernard* for the "false" gods of other people, their graven idols, to turn back into the lifeless stone from which they had been made. Even though in his prologue he would defend the power of legend, of the "common tradition", it was not possible for him to see how the "common traditions" of other faiths could live on, subtly infiltrating a dominant Christianity.

Paradox and irony edged Balbuena's career. He had gone to Spain to find a post which would get him out of the backwoods places in which he had served till then. He ended up as Abbot of Jamaica. He took his post with cheerfulness, seeing it as the first rung on a ladder. On his way out to Jamaica, he had remained long enough in Santo Domingo to make important friendships among the Church hierarchy there. About one year after he got to Jamaica, he drafted a long testimonial in which he gives power of attorney to Baltasar López de Castro y Sandoval and Juan Ortiz de Sandoval to act on his behalf. The substance of his application as van Horne paraphrases it was this:

> that Balbuena suffered great expenses and privation in travelling to Jamaica; that his income as Abbot was very small; that he was meritorious in character and intellect; that he would like the Crown to make up the difference between his actual income and the 500,000 maravedis that were guaranteed to many American prelates, or transfer him from Jamaica to a good office in Mexico, in Tlaxcala, or in Lima.[129]

With this "memorial" Balbuena encloses evidence from witnesses as to his character; and got the endorsement to his application from many of the high Church dignitaries in Santo Domingo. This endorsement is signed May 15, 1612. It was dispatched to Seville, but it was not until some six years later that some bureaucrat finally exerted himself enough to read the application and make a summary of its contents. Meanwhile as Balbuena prophesied in his own poem, he waited "in hope of better things". It was obvious that his heart was set on being appointed to a high position in his own adopted home, Mexico City; failing that Tlaxcala; failing that Lima, Peru. In his poem, too, he had foretold that whilst he waited for better things, i.e. promotion, he would "sit and sing". Whilst it is obvious that Balbuena corrected parts of the manuscript of his heroic poem *The Bernard* in Jamaica, and even perhaps wrote in the verses we have quoted with reference to Jamaica, we have no proof that he wrote any significant original poetry there. For a poet not to write may well be the final and absolute sign of his being like one "bewitched", and it is in this sense that the cultural unreality of a remote backwater may have come to catch him by the throat, to make him feel that he was trapped in a sluggish nightmare in which time itself had stopped. Even today, this particular angst still haunts our island – the one that Columbus had called "the most beautiful one of all those that he had seen", and yet the one in which, shipwrecked on the North Coast, stranded there for over a year, he was to undergo his "dark night of the soul"[130] and to write his tragic and famous letter from Jamaica.

"The wealth that I have discovered," Columbus wrote, in his terrible and farsighted prophecy, "will stir up all mankind to revenge and rapine".[131] And, as Balbuena himself said of the provincial places of Mexico, the best minds are occupied with greed for gain. In Jamaica, the sloth of the spirit, *accidie*, one of the deadly sins, was all pervasive.

Man's high adventure was reduced to sleeping, eating, making money the easiest way – by trick and fraud. Books were closed to the vast majority. And apart from the Africans and the Indians, relatively little memory remained of an oral culture. And from these – African and Indian – Balbuena was separated by a wide gap unbridgeable by his Christian Catholic imagination. Faced by these brutal facts, Balbuena, sitting down to write the Prologue of his poem *The Bernard*, in the year 1615, sensed that for the sake of his own spiritual survival, he could not accept the facts-as-they-are, the facts of history, when the history in which he was involved seemed like one of these unbelievable enchantments in which the heroes of the popular sixteenth- and seventeenth-century romance of chivalry often found themselves, trapped by malignant magicians or enchantresses. Instead, coming down on the side of poetic truth, of ideal and universal truth, Balbuena gave to the already fairly stereotyped theory his own sense of urgency. His heroic poem, in the face of the daily pettiness, the little intrigues that constituted the reality that surrounded him, became more than just a poem; it was his escape into the wide realms of the imagination that, once published, would become the magic wand that would disenchant him, the epitaph in print that would cause his name to survive the flesh and its inevitable oblivion.

> There are some… who will have already brought to my notice the fact that this victory at Roncesvalles and the death of the Twelve Paladins there is commonly held to be fabled and untrue, according to the scrupulous diligence of the most serious historians of Spain… I answer, therefore to these objections, that what I am writing is a heroic poem, which is supposed to be the imitation of a human action in some lofty personage, where by the very word imitation, true history is excluded… For poetry must be, not truth itself, but the imitation of truth, where one writes of events, *not* as they happened, but as they *might* have happened…[132]

It is from his prose Prologue, and not from his poem, that we can deduce the historical dates in which Balbuena wrote both poem and prologue. Most critics before van Horne had assumed that the Prologue had been written in Puerto Rico sometime after he arrived there in 1623, and before the publication of the poem in Madrid in 1624. Van Horne, however, points out that in the Prologue Balbuena says that his poem had been finished for a little under twenty years, although he had gone on correcting and giving it that perfection, a process which is never-ending. The poem, he goes on, could have been published long before this, especially as he had received a ten-year license to print and publish it. Of this ten-year license, six years, he says, or a little over, have already expired. We know that the license to print was given in Madrid in 1609.

Six years after the license was given – that is in 1615 – Balbuena seems to have made final and definite arrangements for the poem to be published at last. But not being in Madrid and able to insist on seeing things through himself, the publication of the poem did not take place. As he was to comment with some bitterness in the new dedication that he wrote to the poem, in 1623, writing from Puerto Rico, the long delay in publication had been due to "the difficulties with which matters left to the care and diligence of others usually meet".[133] It was not until 1624 that he found the kind of agents who brought about the poem's publication. This was the crown and apex of his poetic career, as being promoted Bishop of Puerto Rico was the apex of his Church career. Neither his epic poem nor his rank as Bishop quite attained to that soaring excellence of which he dreamed. Balbuena was not destined to be the Homer nor the Vergil of Spain, but his *The Bernard*, whilst making use of various well-worn sources and influences and devices, had the quality of a sea change, induced perhaps by the imaginative impact of the New World, an all-pervasive strangeness, difficult to define, that edges with more complex meanings the phrase of the seventeenth-century ecclesiastical censor who wrote inter alia: "and I think that all intelligent Spaniards who are given to reading poetry, will not find in their language, a poem such as this one."[134]

What was *The Bernard* about? How does its pattern fit in with the precepts which Balbuena set out in the Prologue, which he sat down to write in Villa de La Vega some three hundred and fifty years ago? Did he write by day, in the shadow of the church bells, whilst the heat simmered and John-crows specked the steel-blue sky? Or at night, when some coolness descended, caught in an arc of light, whilst brilliant moths flattered in out of the dark? As he sat there, confident now that the book was about to be published, beginning his first paragraph with the excuse that, although the publication of a book of poetry might not be in accord with his office and dignity, his priestly vocation, and theological studies, yet the poem had been written in his youth with the imaginative fire and fury of that age; that although time altered things in such a manner that what had seemed brilliance and talent then, might now be judged otherwise, still what had once been considered a virtue could not now altogether be considered a vice. Did he, under his sedate prelate's exterior, still hope for that acclamation as poet that had so far drawn him on like a will-o'-wisp? Did he sense that if *The Bernard* did not make it, did not bring him fame, this would be the end for him as poet, since all the wellsprings of his talent, expended on its 24 Books, and some 40,000 lines of verse, had now dried up? Was he swept by that apprehension, peculiar to middle-age, of futility and failure? He had invested all of himself in *The Bernard.* If his credit failed, he would be bankrupt of that immortality through fame which was his obsession.

The writers of imperial Spain produced a rash of epic poets and poems in the sixteenth and early seventeenth century. These poems were all self-consciously national and imperial. There was the feeling abroad that Spain had been chosen, with the discovery of the New World, to continue where Rome had left off. As politically they continued a tradition of Empire, so too in poetry they continued to develop the tradition of the heroic or epic poem. To understand something of the influences that went into *The Bernard*, it is necessary for us to look briefly at the original Greek epic and its multifaceted literary descendants.

Epic poetry in its oral form is common to all civilisations. The masterpieces of Greek epic poetry – *The Iliad, The Odyssey* – which have survived, are believed to have belonged originally to a cycle of oral epics dealing with a civilisation which collapsed and died somewhere in the eleventh century before Christ. Two centuries after, or so, it is supposed that a blind singer of poetry from the island of Chios pieced together these two books from the sagas which had been handed down. The telling and handing down of these sagas was done by a specialised minstrel class, versed in the Arts of Memory, a vital art, in societies without writing. The minstrel occupied a quasi-oracular role. He was the repository of the communal memory. He alone could give his people a sense of identity by retelling for them the great deeds of the past. His feats of memory and storytelling came from his ability to be possessed by a god. He was therefore a man marked down and set aside for a special role – he was at once prophet and poet.

His memory was selective; and so was the community's. The innumerable historical facts that writing can record had to be left out. Instead, the poetic truth of the origin and continuance of the tribe or people were fashioned into myths and legends and stories which held at their core the historical constants of their particular culture. But it was, through the telling of the deeds of particular great men – heroes – that the memory of the people of itself was carried on. Heroes were heroes, not only through their deeds, but by the fact that what they did or said was destined by the gods to remain in the memory of men as songs, poems, legends. This destiny was ambivalent. It often brought tragedy in its wake and, more commonly, the onerous life and fate of those who are destined to be more than other men. In this original oral epic – C. S. Lewis has termed it the primary epic – the marked characters do not feel that this destiny has been laid upon them for a "great cause", such as the cause of country or religion. They lack the sense of mission which will come later with the Roman Empire and Vergil's *Aeneid* and which *The Bernard* will share: a sense of mission whose debased equivalent in our day and age has been known as "the white man's burden".

C.S. Lewis points out that characters in the original primary oral epic know that they will leave the world and its affairs "much as they found them". They live out their "human and personal tragedy" against a "background of meaningless flux".[135] The meaningless flux is saved only by the song that will live after them. But it is the song, of which they are the subjects, that will live on in the memory of their descendants. They and their particular substance are doomed. In the *Iliad*, Helen, (wife of Menelaus, who caused the Greek-Trojan war by running off with Paris, a Trojan prince), says to Paris's brother Hector as the Greeks besiege the ill-fated Troy: "On us two Zeus set a vile destiny; so that hereafter we shall be made into things of song for men of the future."[136]

In the *Odyssey*, as the minstrel honoured in the great hall has finished his song about Troy, the war, and its fatal end, King Alcinous says: "The gods made this doom; it was they who fated this destruction of men, so that even among later generations there should be a song of it."[137]

The epic hero, then, in the primary sense, accepts the destiny laid down for him by the gods. By living up to this destiny through the exercise of his will, he performs deeds which will be the stuff of which songs are fashioned. The minstrel who remembers and refashions them and passes on his songs, also accepts his destiny and fulfils it. Both, the man of deeds, and the man of song, complement each other. Together they make the kind of song that will cast a creative shadow of excellence for their descendants; and will inspire them, in their turn, to great deeds and great songs. The heroic song is man's salvation from oblivion. The fashioning of the heroic poem is no less difficult than the heroic deed. The heroic poet is no less destined than the hero. One with deeds, the other with words and music – or as in the later epic, with verse alone – will fuse together in a heroic poem which, as Balbuena had earlier stated, will "exalt the spirit of those who read".[138] As Sidney rounds it off, "so the lofty image of such worthies most inflameth the mind with desire to be worthy".[139]

From the Greek epic, Balbuena retained the idea of the heroic poem as the supreme ambition of any poet. From the Greeks, too, he took models of ideal behaviour and in his prologue he proudly states that his hero Bernardo del Carpio is the equivalent of Achilles, whilst his French enemy, the great Roland, is the equivalent of Hector. He cites other parallels, too, although there is in general little detailed correspondence in their adventures, there is resemblance in their basic types.

When, however, Balbuena says that he is writing a heroic poem to celebrate the greatness of his "patria" through the deeds of a famous hero, the essentially patriotic and national concept comes not from the Greek epic, but from the Aeneid of Vergil. It belongs to the tradition of what C.S. Lewis defines as the "secondary epic". This kind of epic which began with Vergil is literary, rather than oral. Although the Roman poet, Vergil (70-16 B.C.) modelled himself closely on the Greek epics, he wrote at a different time and under different circumstances. Because of the different conception of heroism and human greatness[140] which prevailed in the Roman Empire of Augustus Caesar, Vergil celebrated in Aeneas a very different kind of hero. As a professional writer in a far more sophisticated society, Vergil's relation to his public was far different from the prophetic-minstrel role of the earlier bards who had their function and being in an oral culture.

Vergil altered "the very notion of the epic". In the Greek epics, the great events like the Trojan war, served as the background for the working out of the personal destinies of Achilles and Hector. Both men fight for their own survival, and for that of their two bands of men, of their different cities, but they carry no historical mission, no imperial destiny upon their shoulders. Whilst each will take booty from whoever is defeated, will capture their enemies' families as slaves etc., neither feels that it is his duty to subjugate the other, and establish imperial rule. Their patriotism to their respective territories or cities is, as C. S. Lewis has described it, the relationship of a man to his wife, his home, the piece of earth which sustains him "...the tie of a mutual belonging."[141] The *Iliad* ends not with the fall of Troy, but with the funeral rites for the Trojan Hector. The Odyssey ends with a man's return to the poor island which he calls home.

The abstract concept of the nation and of empire in the national and imperial epic begins with Vergil. Aeneas carries a great destiny – the destiny not to be the stuff of a song, but to found city called Rome and lay the basis of its future greatness. The fall of Troy had been the background to Achilles and Hector. In Vergil, Aeneas is the destined instrument of the creation of Rome – and of Roman power. He escapes from burning Troy carrying the household gods and the past in the figure of his father Anchises on his back, and goes to Latium, where he defeats the heroic Turnus, model of the old tradition of heroism, in order to establish a new kind of greatness, the epic of expansion and conquest, rather than that of survival. The new ideal is not that of Turnus, nor of Achilles to "give my life in barter for glory", – but to be *pius*, responsible, to submit to and serve the destiny of a nation and Empire. The new imperial ideal is proclaimed by Vergil:

> Do thou, man of Rome, remember to govern the nations –
> These shall be thine arts – to establish the custom of peace
> To spare the vanquished and break in battle the proud.[142]

As one critic puts it, the personal ideal of the Homeric hero is replaced by the social ideal. Yet it would be more exact to say that the old ideal – through which man fulfilled his *own* destiny himself – is replaced by a national imperial ideal in which he becomes the *instrument* which helps to fulfil the national destiny willed by the gods. Aeneas is first and foremost "the man of destiny, guided by Heaven's clear will". And so is Bernardo del Carpio, the hero of Balbuena's poem.

The breakdown of the Roman Empire, and the succession of attacks by the Germanic tribes, was an historical event that lead to a new body of epic poetry. This poetry was, in turn, to lead to the myths, legends, ballads and epic poetry written about Balbuena's hero, Bernardo del Carpio. The era of the Frankish invasion of Northern Gaul in the fifth century and the constant fighting and counter-fighting caused the creation of a body of epic poetry centred around the Frankish hero Hruodland – who became in European literature Roland or Orlando. As the Frankish Emperor Charlemagne became the symbol to early medieval Europe of Christian resistance to the Moorish and the Viking invasions, legends spread and multiplied. The Moslems overran Spain from 711 onwards, but were stopped near Poitiers by Charles Martel who defeated them in 732. The Spaniards were to take almost eight centuries to drive out the powerful invaders. The French epic which sprang up about Roland/Orlando, in which Charlemagne and the French warriors were seen as Christian paladins waging war against the Mohammedans, heralds of the Anti-Christ, became popular in Spain where the war against the Mohammedans continued as a reality for centuries. The climax of the French epic is the death of Roland at Roncesvalles, in a famous battle, a rearguard skirmish against the Moorish enemies. Spanish versions of the French epic soon began. A chronicle supposedly written by the heroic Archbishop Turpin, who had also perished with the "flower of French" chivalry at Roncesvalles, glorified the deeds of Roland, Charlemagne and the French, against the Mohammedans, even more.

Since it was the Spaniards who were doing the actual fighting against the Moors, this became a little hard to take. A counter-myth and counter-legend was therefore created in the form of the very Spanish Bernardo del Carpio. The battle of the myths began, and out of this battle Spain's legendary hero was born. His creation was a fact of importance. Just as the Spaniards had created the legend of the warrior St. James of Santiago to match the fighting faith of the Moors, so now they begin to assert themselves against the arrogant pretensions of the French Christians. A Spanish historian points out that,

This instance [i.e. the case of Santiago] in which a belief owes its origin to polemical motives is not unique. Everyone knows that the fabled Bernardo del Carpio emerged in opposition to Roland and Charlemagne who were glorified in poems humiliating to Spain. About 1110 the Monk of Silos protested in his Chronicle against the French epic stories that tried to convert Charlemagne into the liberator of Spain: the Emperor did not conquer the Moors, nor did he rescue the road to Santiago from their control; the Spaniards owed nothing to Roland and his Lords. Towards the end of the twelfth century, a Spanish minstrel launched Bernardo del Carpio against the arrogant French, in a Battle of Roncesvaux – conceived from a Spanish point of view – Roland perishes and Charlemagne flees.[143]

The old poem of the patriotic Spanish minstrel has not survived. But as the Spanish epic poems were fragmented into short popular ballads, worked and reworked by generations, Bernardo de Carpio took on a life of his own. In the Spanish ballads, popularised and spread out during the struggles of the feudal nobles against kings, still struggling to establish their monarchical power, Bernardo del Carpio is seen more in his role as the young, noble son of the Count of Saldana, whose illicit love affair with Alfonso the Chaste's sister, a love affair from which Bernardo was born, had lead to the Count's lifelong imprisonment and the King's sister's forced retirement to a convent. In the ballads, Bernardo wins lands and fame and challenges the King, time and time again, for his parents' freedom. In the ballads, his role against Roland was secondary.

But from the time of Balbuena's birth (1562) until when he had finished writing the first draft of his poem about 1595, France was the chief enemy and challenge to Spain's empire and greatness. Balbuena instinctively turned towards the Bernardo of the anti-French tradition. Several other epic poems, of relatively little value, had been written on the same theme. None could match the ardent patriotism which causes Balbuena, in the interpretation which follows Book X of the poem, to insist on "the natural duty which a man owes to his country".[144] At the beginning of Book X itself, he attacks those who sing the greatness of other nations and neglect their own. He vows that throughout his lofty tale, he will sing the valour of unconquerable Spain, destined by heaven, it seems to him, to be the crown and apex of Europe.

PART 4

It is in times of struggle that humanity ascends from one idea to the other and the intellect does not triumph except the fantasy is shaken up; when an idea has triumphed and unfolds itself in peaceful practise, the epic no longer exists, only history. The epic poem can therefore be defined as the ideal history of humanity in its passage from one idea to the other.
De Sanctis, *The Theory and History of Literature*[145]

...to weave together the episodes of such a long poem...
Bernado De Balbuena, In the Prologue to the *Bernard*, written in Jamaica, 1615[146]

Many of us Jamaicans, cut off from the experience of a large part of the New World, have no Spanish. Even if we had, *The Bernard*, epic poem, out of date and time, and immensely complex and tangled, is difficult to read.

It is not easy to give an outline of *The Bernard*. Divided into 24 Books, with some 40,000 lines of eleven-syllabled verse, plus an allegorical commentary at the end of each book, the poem presents a bewildering maze of incidents. Balbuena follows the poetic dictates of his time that the epic should begin in the middle. In his prologue he argues in support of this convention that there are two kinds of relation, the natural and the "artificial" – artificial does not have its modern meaning of falsity, but rather of artifice, something that is made by art, and that whilst the natural way of relating things, beginning from the beginning, is natural and historical, the "artificial" way which is poetic, begins in the middle, so that novelty will be added. This novelty, will of course, spring from the disruption of the time sequence, a disruption which attracts the interest through admiration, one of the reactions which the good writer should endeavour to produce. This kind of "admiration" means more nearly, surprise, a strangeness of things which the inventive qualities of the author can subtly create. In all this, Balbuena is merely reinterpreting the commonplaces of the poetic theories of his time.

He begins his story, as he himself tells us, not with Bernardo's birth, but in the middle of things – with war between France and Spain threatening, and Bernardo, a grown young man ready to begin his adventures. This is poetic truth versus historical truth. History would have had to record all the details of Bernardo's life; poetry can begin with him at a time when his life begins to take on its poetic significance. Poetry can select, choose, discard. History cannot. The poet is a maker, a creator; the historian merely records. Hence the supreme contempt with which a Balbuena, and even more a Sidney, regards the historian – and the historian's arrogant dismissal of the truth of poetry.

Unity of action, centred on the hero, is demanded of the epic poem. Balbuena points out that he has made the central action, that action which leads to the fight between the two heroes and their two forces at the pass of Roncesvalles. But this central action is a leisurely one in which Balbuena is able to branch off into a complicated series of side-issues. He accepts and defends the theory that poetry should instruct and delight; to do this, he tells us, he will relate the ancient deeds of Spain, the histories of her noble families; he will describe varied places, mountains, fountains, rivers, castles, and sumptuous palaces; in fact he will throw in for good measure "an almost universal geography of the world";[147] besides all this, he will tell of the strange customs of other peoples which are worthy of being remembered.

He will weave episode after episode together, breaking off each episode, much in the manner of a modern soap-opera, "at the moment of greatest danger, and at the most exciting part of the plot" as he puts it.[148] At once he will hurl the reader into another equally exciting adventure, breaking off that one again, and so on, with the effect that the reader will be anxious to find out what happened and so will keep on reading. As for the more improbable adventures, he says, the author will make sure that they are related by characters in the poem, rather than by the author himself. For, he argues, improbable stories pass from mouth to mouth, and people tell and retell them, believing them to be true. It is this common belief in their truth, Balbuena implies, that gives these stories verisimilitude – the likeness of truth. Balbuena was, in effect, arguing that the power of belief creates its own truth.

But the poet must not only delight. He must also teach. One can teach best by arousing in the reader compassion and sympathy for the distress of others. Balbuena has made sure to move all readers to pity by describing "many pitiful deaths, tragic events, destruction of peoples, the rise and fall of Kingdom's princes".[149] The plethora of Balbuena's imagination had been lightly described by one critic as being like the thick and foliaged forests of the New World.

The summary of the action which follows is therefore the merest outline:[150]

The hero is born after a love affair between the Count of Saldana and the King's sister. The King imprisons the Count, puts his sister in a convent. The boy Bernardo had been singled out by the fairies who, in the system of marvels used by the poet, control the affairs of earth. Two fairies, Alcina and Morgana, angered by the constant wars and outrages of Charlemagne, Roland and the other French paladins, plan to overthrow the might of France at the moment when France thinks that she is at the height of her glory. The boy Bernardo is given into the care of Orontes, a wise man and magician, to be educated and reared. He is taught all the knightly virtues and the craft of war. The fairies have chosen him to be the instrument of their vengeance. He is to kill and destroy the powerful and enchanted Orlando/Roland and defeat the French at Roncesvalles.

But before he can do this he must prove himself in a succession of adventures. As an unknown young man he saves his uncle, King Alfonso, from an ambush; an invisible power guides him to a boat, he embarks, the boat takes off and meets with a ship; on the ship is the King of Persia and Angelica, a Princess of Cathay; the Persian King dubs him a knight; he fights the King to free Angelica, wounds the king, helps to cure him. Then he goes off on his destined quest to find the arms of the famous Greek warrior Achilles.

On an island he sees a lovely woman rising from the sea in a pearl chariot. On shore, the chariot changes to a doe with golden horns. Bernardo follows it into a forest, comes to a cave, sees the ubiquitous Angelica in the arms of a serpent who flees into the cave. Bernardo enters the cave, then comes to a meadow and sees two giants. One has killed the serpent, the other is dragging off Angelica by her hair. Bernardo follows them. One giant squares up to Bernardo with a mace. Whenever Bernardo wounds him, wasps, instead of blood, come from the wound. When he strikes the wasps, they change to gold. Bernardo cuts the giant in two. The lower half sinks to the ground in the form of blood, the upper half flies into the air. Bernardo follows the other giant into a flame, without singeing a hair. A spirit conducts Bernardo to a boat which cuts through dark water thick with serpents. At daybreak he finds himself in bed in a hall crusted with precious gems and treasures. He comes upon two castles, one of Youth and Beauty, the other of Ugliness. Ugliness attacks Young Beauty which defends itself with roses – rather like flower power. He sees Angelica at a window of the Castle of Beauty and tries to rescue her. Evil spirits attack him, but he captures one, who in exchange for her freedom, tells him how to catch and bind Proteus the prophetic sea-god with pearl chains and compel him to tell him the future. Bernardo goes into the cave and tries to grab hold of Proteus, who changes into many shapes. But Bernardo holds him fast. He gives up and tells Bernardo what he wants to know – who are his parents, what is his ancestry, what victories he will win in the future. One thing Proteus also predicts is that Bernardo will never gain the freedom of his father and mother, whose fate he has learnt for the first time. But our hero now knows his past and something of his destiny.

Proteus disappears. Bernardo finds himself clad in Achilles's armour entering a garden, where he is welcomed by two beautiful female forms who tell him that the armour was reserved for him – and that he is in Alcina's garden. After this, in a series of adventures fighting pirates at sea, he joins forces with the King of Persia to try and rescue Angelica; goes to the aid of some hapless maidens who are taken to Crete as human sacrifices; and meets and falls in love with Arcangelica, the daughter of Angelica and Mars, the god of War. Arcangelica is dressed in a Knight's armour and has come to rescue her mother; she, in turn, falls in love with Bernardo. They are parted and he goes in search of her. He is cast ashore on an island where, on the banks of the river, stands the Castle of Themis, the goddess of law, wisdom, equity. He enters the Castle and sees two women, one lascivious and sexy, the other most virtuous and wise, the goddess Themis herself. Men keep appearing out of a fountain; the majority of them go to the sexy lady, drink from a gold cup which she holds in her hand and are changed to beasts. A few, through good luck rather than deliberate choice, stumble across to Themis, drink from the cup which she holds and are changed from beasts back into men. Themis tells Bernardo that her cup has all the intelligence of the world; the other cup holds ignorance and deceit. He follows the way of Themis and is given light by her. He now wears the armour of Achilles and has wisdom from Themis. He leaves and climbs to the top of Mount Parnassus, after defeating the forces of ignorance.

There Apollo predicts that a poet, i.e. Balbuena, will sing his fame.

Illuminated with wisdom and the pre-knowledge of his own fame he returns to his true destiny – Spain. At the mouth of the Ebro River he meets a dragon with a wide mouth, wide enough to swallow him down. In the dragon's stomach he has many adventures. He meets a giant Moor with whom, of course, he fights. He wounds the giant and draws blood, or at least what should have been blood. Instead, out of the giant's veins, comes not blood but money. From each coin that falls there springs an arm with a sword. A maiden, quite at home in the dragon's stomach, is seated close by, holding a magic sword, the sword of Achilles, the one piece of equipment that Bernardo had not got before. The giant Moor grabs the sword from her and wounds Bernardo in the side. Bernardo fights back. The giant dissolves into thin air. Bernardo suddenly finds himself in a palace, with a beautiful lady, Iberia. In the palace there is a fountain from which each man gets that which he most desires. Bernardo's choice is Fame. The sword of Achilles, wet with his own blood, is now his; it has been imperfect until plunged in royal blood. All of the adventures of Bernardo have lead up to his securing this sword, and being prepared to undergo the ordeals, make the right choices, respond to the challenges. Iberia explains to him whose are the great Spanish names and lineages that are woven on the tapestries that hang on the walls. Among the lineages there is a description of the lineage of the family of our poet, Balbuena.

Famous now, and armed with a sword which can cut through all the enchanted armour of Orlando/Roland, the French paladin, Bernardo has his first encounter with the French hero. In the meanwhile, Orlando/Roland has been having a series of adventures like Bernardo, but without the same purposeful sense of destiny with which Bernardo had been doing his thing. One significant adventure of Orlando's was his entry into the Castle of Avarice. There, all his companions through their greed had been turned, in a Midas episode, into gold. They had disregarded the written warnings on the walls as to the evil power of avarice. Orlando stops, just in time, and reflects on the folly of pursuing filthy lucre. He tries to free his companions but everything that he inserts into the room is at once turned to gold. Only later on will another French paladin learn through a Mexican magician how to disenchant his companions, who are bewitched by their lust for gold. Reinaldos will put the dead body of the famous King Arthur of the Round Table before them. Only the thought of death can make men lose their love of money, remember their virtue and honour and make themselves remember that,

> ... gold is but dust
> Man, a lofty and celestial treasure.
> (Bk. XVIII, 182).[151]

In his first encounter with Orlando/ Roland, Bernardo unhorses the great paladin who is dazed with the shock of his defeat; but the duel ends inconclusively. It is but a preview for the encounter at Roncesvalles. In the meanwhile, Bernardo reaches the climax of his adventure with his entry into the enchanted castle of Carpio. He is told that his missing love, Arcangelica, had entered the Castle. Bernardo, declaring that enchantments can be conquered by a determined knight, enters the Castle amidst flames and the earth quaking. He does not see Arcangelica, but is attacked by a Bull whom he fights. They fall into a pit of water. He loses consciousness. He awakes to find himself embracing a beautiful woman. She tells him that the magician Clemes from Africa, of the Carpio family, was buried here by Hercules; that he built this palace and a magic mirror in which the future could be seen.

Bernardo looks into the mirror and sees that he is not destined to marry Arcangelica, but the princess Crisalba whose hand he won at a joust in Acaya, but whom he had left to follow Arcangelica, who had jousted evenly with him dressed in knight's armour. Now destiny lays it down that he is to forget Arcangelica and marry Crisalba, suitably a Christian. From this union will spring a succession of famous Spanish families, chief among them the Castro family who would be Counts of Lemos. Having accepted his destiny, Bernardo sees all the music and the flames and the apparatus disappear. He is now left the owner of the unenchanted and very real Castle of Carpio. In the castle he finds Orontes, his old wise teacher, together with three hundred armed knights. With these he leaves for Leon to ask the King's pardon for his father who has been imprisoned all his life. He joins the King who is going to meet the attacking French army at the pass in the Pyrenees mountains – Roncesvalles. The battle is fought after many omens have predicted the French defeat. In true epic manner valour is shown on both sides. Bernardo and Orlando/ Roland meet in a truly prodigious battle. Bernardo, helped by destiny, wins and the poem ends:

> Roland fell dead, but alive remained
> The fame of his eternal name, his soul
> Snatched away, flew swift to its sphere,
> And at the feet of the great Bernardo
> His gallant body lay.[152]

Having given what purports to be the outline of *The Bernard*, it is only fair to say that this outline is a straight line cut through a morass of other happenings and a profusion of other characters who all have their own adventures and do their own thing. We have had to leave out, for clarity's sake, the various adventures of Orlando/Roland; of Ferragut, the Spanish Moor, who having been told of the Fame of Bernardo and the glory that he will acquire, burns to emulate him and gets entangled with the seductive enchantress Arleta, who, once embraced, becomes an old hag. Also omitted are the adventures of the noble Goths, Teudonio and Gundemaro; of Morgante King of Corsica; of the tricky Garilo; the conferences of the French King at Court; the innumerable tales that characters tell; the saintly miracles, and the conversion of Moors to Christianity that occur; the discovery of the eighth-century King Rodrigo of Spain, still doing penance one hundred years after, for having lost Spain to the Arabs through his seduction of a young girl; the story of Estordian who turns into a silkworm, and of his love weeping for him, who turns into a fountain; the battles, the duels, the clashes, the enchantments of magicians like Malgesi, the French enchanter; of the Dutch Arnold of Espurg, with the magic ring of Angelica with which he turns the thief Garilo into a cat; the Tlaxcalan magician of Mexico who conjures down out of the air the flying boat of Malgesi in which the latter and two companions, the King of Persia, Orimandro and Reinaldos, a French paladin have taken a trip to the Moon and are now viewing the as-yet-undiscovered New World; the Tlaxcalan's prediction of the events of the New World in which Jamaica as the future Abbotship of the prophesied poet Balbuena – of *The Bernard* – comes into its epic destiny. All these episodes and personages flash in and out of the complex serial story that would have staggered Walt Disney's imagination, all woven around the central conflict of the French-Spanish national clash through the fight of their two chivalric heroes.

The ecclesiastical censor, Mira de Amescua, points out that Balbuena had practised the theory of imitation of good models by imitating from the Italian Ludovico Ariosto[153] the "variety of the happenings and the episodes". Whilst Balbuena does not mention Ariosto's name in his Prologue, he does mention an earlier Italian writer, Boiardo[154]. These two Italians perfected the type of epic poem that came to be known as the Romanesque epic, a hybrid of the epics of Homer and Vergil and of romantic chivalresque tales. This type of epic began in Italy with Pulci[155], and reached perfection with Boiardo, Ariosto, and Torquato Tasso,[156] during the Renaissance. But the romantic tales had sprung up before that, with the fusion of the Carolingian sagas about Roland and the Breton cycle of stories of Celtic origin, which were adopted into French literature in the twelfth-thirteenth centuries. The Breton cycle brought in the elements of magic, the mysterious and fantastic unknown world filled with the terror of the Celtic imagination, the enchanted forests, and wilderness – *soledades*; the encounters with incredible monsters, the description of weird castles and sumptuous palaces that appear and disappear. The greatest of all magic was the magic of love. The Breton cycle, the Arthuriads, had been elaborated for the increasingly luxurious feudal courts of France, for the refined tastes of the ladies and their knights, where the chivalresque ideal of Courtly love, of the perfect gentle knight submissive to his lady, and suffering the torments of unrequited love, would begin that obsession with "romantic" love that was to haunt the European imagination for centuries. It is only in our day that this fevered concept of love has begun to give way before the advances of technology, and the elimination of all magic, including that of love. But at the time it constituted a revolution in sentiment.

When the Italian Boiardo borrowed the theme of Orlando/Roland in his *Orlando Innamorato*, the fusion of the fighting epic with the love and other magical elements of the Breton cycle, plus the reflective ironic attitude of humanist-classical learning, entirely changed the original concept of the warrior knight devoted to fighting the Christian cause against the Moors. The title itself – *Orlando In Love* – is suggestive of the change. The superman-warrior finds himself helpless with love for Angelica, a pagan princess of Cathay who leads him a merry dance. Orlando/Roland is brought to the state of losing all for love – even his mind. It is this aspect that the greatest writer on this theme, Ariosto, takes up as he continues and develops the theme and story in his *Orlando Furioso*. Whilst all the paladins fight over Angelica and perform incredible deeds for her sake, she falls in love with a wounded and handsome Moorish foot soldier, Medoro, and goes off with him to Cathay. Orlando goes mad with love.

The Italians are playful, humorous, light of touch. From them Balbuena borrows their variety and complexity of incidents, their sheer storytelling art. From them, too, he borrows the apparatus of gods and semi-goddesses, and fairies who can control events, in the manner of the old epics. And, Balbuena tells us, he does this because he does not want to use the "heroic majesty… of the Christian religion" to provide the supernatural machinery that the poem demands. For there is a seriousness of purpose in Balbuena that is lacking in Boiardo and Ariosto. This seriousness of purpose, Balbuena shares with the majority of the Spanish epic writers, and with the Italian Torquato Tasso who wrote the epic poem of the Christian crusade to capture Jerusalem.

In his approval of the poem, Mira de Amescua praises "the truth of the action and the weaving of the story".[157] This, he says, is an excellent imitation of Tasso. As we have pointed out before, to imitate great models was the mark of a good writer, above all of a serious writer who took his craft seriously. Yet, what, we might well ask, does Mira de Amescua mean by the "truth of the action"? From the barest summary of the adventures of Bernardo and the others, it would be quite impossible for us to accept "the truth of the action" in our twentieth-century version of reality. The "truth" that the censor refers to here is another kind of truth – poetic truth, universal truth. It is the validity of this truth which Balbuena discusses in his Prologue; and which Sidney does far more trenchantly in his *Defence of Poetry*.

Balbuena, like all other literary theorists of his day, bases his arguments mainly on the poetics of Aristotle – at least on that part which serves his purpose. Aristotle, Balbuena says, advised that epic subjects should have some slight historical basis, "a spark of truth" from which the poet could create delight and verisimilitude. He had, therefore, chosen the theme of Bernardo del Carpio because, even in the chronicles of historians there were only brief accounts of him; the poet would not therefore be hampered by too many historical details.

In the sixteenth and early seventeenth century there were two 'schools' of epic writing in Spain: the "historical" and the "fantastical."[158] The "historical" writers, who came, by and large, earlier in time, when the Spanish Empire was in a process of rapid expansion, defended the historical truth of their epics. Balbuena, coming at the end of the epic vogue, at a time when Spain was now on the defensive, defends the "fantastical" type of epic writing. He attacks those poets who had boasted that their poems were true histories. This could not be so, he argued, because as Aristotle said, poetry must be the imitation of an action and not the action itself.

He uses this same argument to answer Spanish historians who, with the rise of rational enquiry in the seventeenth century, had begun to dismiss the story of Roland and of Bernardo del Carpio as fables and myths. Even if they were not true, he says, even if the "common tradition" which handed them down "from memory to memory until our own days" should prove to be doubtful, it would still not affect the poetic truth of his poem. For poets are supposed to deal with events not as they happened, but as they might have happened, as they ought to have happened. Poets, he implies, must be concerned with the moral truth of their poems. Sidney, using the same line of argument, points out that historians cannot deal with moral truth because, since they are "captivated to the truth of a foolish world", and since the facts show that the majority of times evil men have succeeded, and good men have failed, then their recording of these facts can lead to immoral action on the part of their readers. History can deter men from "well-doing", and encourage them "to unbridled wickedness".[159]

The poet, however, because he is free, "having all from Dante's heaven, to hell under his pen" can create and recreate events, to exalt virtue and to punish vice to make the hero more heroic, the villain more villainous. With a "tale which holdeth children from play and old men from the chimney corner" the poet can instruct men "in moral doctrine, the chief of all knowledges", and in the kind of moral doctrine that leads to moral action. The poet does not, like the historian, deal with particular events such as, for example "Alexander and Darius when they strave, who should be cock of this world's dung-hill". The poet, instead, deals, as Aristotle says, with the "universal consideration and the history... with the particular".[160] Poetry is therefore more philosophical and serious than history. As Aristotle pointed out, the particular only marks what this king did or said, or suffered. The universal deals with moral values rather than pragmatic realities. It weighs what "is fit to be said or done, either in likelihood or necessity". The truth of its action must therefore depend on the truth of its moral values.[161]

It is this kind of truth that Mira de Amescua is talking about. When he compares Balbuena to Tasso, he is aware that both writers placed at the end of each book of their poem, allegorical keys which would give the underlying moral purposes even to those adventures that might seem merely entertainments to pass the time. Balbuena does not express his ideas as clearly and as vigorously as Sidney. In fact Sidney expressed what Balbuena tries to say in his prologue far better than Balbuena does. But he states clearly that his poem set out, not only to "... give pleasure, to move the soul and the passions but also to instruct the reader in moral virtue through the concealed morality and allegory" which lies in the poem.[162]

His characters, too, he tells us, are designed to represent exemplars of virtuous or evil actions. In the person of Bernardo, an epic prince, we are to see the model of a generous man, invincible by evil powers, full of heroic virtues; in Angelica we see a rather loose-living lady, whom age is beginning to wither;

in King Alfonso a prudent and Catholic King, and so on. He concludes, with a moral drawn from the theme of "vanity of vanities, all is vanity" (Ecclesiastes 1:2), that the "main action shows how little men can trust and believe in the fickle favours of Fortune".[163] Time changes all things. Nothing is certain. The soul, he implies, must look to its eternal salvation, and not trust in the apparent favours of our temporal lives.

As many critics have pointed out, the allegory of Balbuena is not entirely consistent as far as some of the episodes are concerned. In the basic outlines, however, the allegorical conflict is clear. And certain episodes only take on significance when one reads the key which accompanies them. Twentieth-century man does not possess an allegorical turn of mind. He inherited this loss from the "rationality" which began in the seventeenth century, and which has become overwhelming in our technological age. Facts are facts. Pragmatism is the answer. One does not look for hidden meanings. But increasingly, as the rational factual world around us becomes more and more intolerable, the more difficult it is for us to accept an insane world as a fact, so too there has been the movement in art and literature away from the mere reproduction of a so-called reality. The alienation effect which the dramatist Brecht called for in drama[164] brings into focus the purpose of allegory in Balbuena's day. Brecht's effect is intended to destroy the viewer's identification with the characters on stage, in order to make him develop the habit of critical thought about what happens on stage, and in life, and encourage the habit of refusing to accept that things-must-be-as-they-are. This should lead to the recognition that both on stage and in real life, things can be arranged differently; to the viewer's non-acceptance of the passive consumer attitude, to his critical involvement as a participant towards change, and change in favour of a better arrangement of reality. Whilst Balbuena, as did his readers, accepted Catholic Christian moral values as the revealed truth, he yet sensed that the world that was engulfing them increasingly denied these truths. To write a heroic poem about a hero who, in adventure after adventure, in allegory after allegory, chooses Fame, the religious ethic and the old heroic virtues, instead of gold, money and the new and dominant values of the economic ethic, was to approximate to what the most contemporary writer on the role of art and literature has described as "The Great Refusal" which art can make to the existing reality.

> ... art contains the rationality of negation. In its advanced positions, it is the Great Refusal – the protest against that which is. The modes in which man and things are made to appear, to sing and sound and speak, are modes of refuting, breaking, and recreating their factual existence.[165]

Balbuena was hankering in his poem, and in his allegory, after an idealised past that had had its own cruelties and brutalities. As Marcuse says, this idealistic mainly feudal-aristocratic art was a privilege and an illusion, a product and possession of the leisured classes. But as Unamuno pointed out[166] the man who hankers after an ideal, even an ideal that might seem to belong to the past, helps to propel reality into the future. The true reactionary is the man who remains content with the present and the facts as they are. Sidney, in a new context, in his attack on historians as men "captive to the truth of a foolish world" is startling in his urgent contemporaneity. And so, more haltingly perhaps, is Balbuena. The truth of an action lies not in the truth of its facts, but in the truth of how men choose to arrange them. The choice, and the arrangement, is in any society, at any time, a moral and an ethical one. Moral choices are implicit in the arrangement of facts. The poet or artist must continually make this choice in the arrangement of his fiction. And the moral choice that they make, and present in their work, is a constant criticism of the society that refuses to do the same in the arrangement of the quality of its life. That is why art has moved back to abstraction, and literature must grope towards a new kind of allegory now that language itself is being emptied of content by the pervasive dominance of the pragmatic and of unrelated facts. The contemporary refusal to arrange and interpret facts is itself an acceptance of moral chaos.

In Bernardo's quest, we note that time after time he comes upon a situation in which he must make a choice. Many of the choices are subtle; he can choose not to act in many of his situations, since there is nothing that compels him to. When the pearl chariot carrying the beautiful lady rises out of the sea, and changes into a doe with golden horns and plunges into the enchanted forest, he can choose not to follow it. Yet this leads him to the armour of Achilles. His most constant temptation, then, is to be passive, to let adventures pass him by. But he never hesitates in this choice. The more difficult and strange and frightening the ordeal, the more rapidly he embraces it. In the end he goes through the flames and the quakings into the Castle of Carpio, in pursuit of his lost love, Arcangelica. Yet when he gets in, he never finds her. In fact, he is told that he is destined to lose her and to marry someone else. He accepts his destiny. But when we read the key to the allegory we see that this is more than a passive acceptance of fate.

In the allegory, Arcangelica daughter of Mars and Angelica, represents the spirit of revenge, or vengeance. Beautiful and courageous, Bernardo falls in love with her. Yet as the spirit of Vengeance, she would have impelled him to seek revenge on his King for having imprisoned his father and his mother and to force the King to release them. In fact, he would have remained the ideal hero of the old feudal nobility, who kept the country in a state of anarchy – from the viewpoint of a Balbuena – by asserting their rights.

Most of the popular ballads stress this aspect of Bernardo. In the epic poem, he enters the Castle of Carpio and wrestles with the bull, which seems to represent the passion which he feels for Arcangelica. In this wrestling with himself, no one wins. He falls with the bull into water. Then wakes up to find himself in the arms of the beautiful girl who shows him his true destiny in a magic mirror. Even here he could have made the choice whether to accept or to go once more in search of Arcangelica. Instead, he chooses to marry Crisalba, a Christian princess, giving up the pagan Arcangelica and the old thought of vengeance. This acceptance leads him to his new destiny. With his armed knights, he rides, not to seek revenge, but to ask pardon of the King for his parents. But even this recedes into the background. With Spain threatened, he puts his personal interests aside and rides to defend her at Roncesvalles.

It's a bit hard on his father and mother, but the point that Balbuena is making is that within the values of the monarchical system, the national interests must come before the private interests – the good of the whole must come first. Like Aeneas who sacrificed Dido to the destinies of Rome, so Bernardo forgets his parents in the interests of his country. That this has not been easy is shown by the real love which he feels for Arcangelica. But the theologian in Balbuena insists that the spirit of vengeance is pagan and non-Christian. Whatever its other virtues, it remains a dangerous temptation in the context of a national-Christian destiny. The point of the allegory is that the reader sees not only the surface romance of the story, but, in figuring out the moral struggle that Bernardo must undergo, exercises his own sense of right and wrong, of moral choice. We must remember that Balbuena still wrote at an age, and in a culture and religion, where men watched the state of their souls with as much anxiety as they now watch their spreading waistline or their receding hair. Then, exercises were designed for the soul, in much the same way that exercises keep the body beautiful and trim and fit today. Men, then, read about how to win virtue and influence their salvation as now they read how to win friends and influence people. At the end of his first book, Balbuena states that the ultimate purpose of his work is in the teaching of morality and good habits, and that the allegory which does the teaching is not an accessory to his story, but its principal intention. He has not given all the keys to his allegory, but anyone who reads with attention can figure it out for himself, because there is no part of his book where one cannot discover, "under the sweetness of its veil of fable, the doctrine and teaching necessary to virtue".[167]

The flight of the magician Malgesi to the New World is peculiar to Balbuena, even though the side trip that they take to the Moon is imitated from Ariosto's *Orlando Furioso*. In Ariosto's poem, one paladin goes to the Moon to recover there the lost senses of his friend Orlando. He finds it in a flask and carries it back and restores Orlando to sanity. The trip to the Moon, and to the New World has a different purpose for Balbuena. As he explains in his allegory, Malgesi the French magician represents "the contemplative soul, when with its three powers, Understanding, Memory and Will, it raises itself to the contemplation of higher matters, beginning with the weakness and little substance of inferior things, and working upwards".[168] The King of Persia represents Understanding. The French Paladin Reinaldos represents Memory, and Morgante, King of Corsica, represents the Will. We find each of these three at times involved in adventures that reflect little credit on them. In the beginning, for example, Malgesi is trapped by Orontes and figures in an undignified episode. Balbuena explains in the allegorical key that when the contemplative soul leaves his quietude for action, he suffers humiliation and travail. When Orimandoo, King of Persia, tries to force his love on Angelica, we note that he is separated from the others. This implies that Understanding, or Will or Memory, or the contemplative soul, whose powers these are, when not in relation to one another, are vulnerable to different temptations. In the flying boat, harmoniously functioning together, they are able to conquer Nature, to reach the Moon and do so without arrogance. Once there, they are filled with humility. Their own skill seems insignificant compared to the grandeur of God who created such a magnificent Universe.

In one of those occasional startlingly beautiful lines of his, Balbuena describes the stars as the flying boat draws close. They are not now stars but numberless,

> Islands of gold sown by the wind
> *Islas de oro sembradas por el viento*[169]

Balbuena has them flying so high that the earth hangs low beneath them. The moon appears to them as "hollow mountains filled with light". There are silvered cliffs and lakes on whose shore the shadows of cold night live. A sleeping giant is guarded by a beautiful lady who strings pearls together, and whose white face men call the moon, who holds in her hands the reins of the sea. From the moon they look back on the globe of the earth, surrounded by the sea. Technology has made Balbuena's fiction come true. And part of the allegory of Balbuena still remains valid: contemplation, understanding, memory and will have played their parts in putting men on the Moon. But so, too, has that massive accumulation of gold which, time after time, in allegory after allegory, Balbuena was to warn against.

When the three travellers come to the New World, however, Balbuena sees the New World as paying its tribute in gold and silver to Spain which will bring her, in turn, the religion of Christ and the Catholic Church. The New World becomes for him an allegory of the contemplative life. The great flight of Malgesi and his companions, he explains, is an ascent of the soul from the contemplation of earthly things to that of heavenly things; and this contemplation brings to the soul,

> the great happiness of the New World which is the great blessedness promised to man, as the Indies have been promised to the Monarchy of Spain.[170]

For Balbuena, the destiny of Spain in the New World will be nothing less than the revelation of the Kingdom of God in history. And his hero Bernardo, through the choices that he makes, will help to create the kind of Spain that will fulfil this destiny as he fulfilled his. Spaniards, like the Jews had once been, were now the Chosen People. This was not, of course, how things were to turn out. The destiny of the New World would be, and still is, to negate the very concept of a chosen people, a chosen race, a chosen faith, to negate, with agony and technology, the very concept of destiny, the inevitability of fate.

The most persistent allegory has to do, as far as Bernardo is concerned, with his desire for Fame. In the Castle of Themis he chooses intelligence rather than self-deception. When he leaves, he is therefore able to climb up to Mount Parnassus, defeating the squadrons of the ignorant who would hold him back. He reaches the top of the mountain, and there, in a palace, Apollo explains the carvings and tapestries that immortalise Spanish feats. This allegory, Balbuena explains, shows the difficulty man has both to acquire virtue and human knowledge. The vast squadrons of ignorance keep back the pilgrim soul. But the heroic and famous prize of virtue is that one arrives, like Bernardo, at the Temple of Immortality. There he sees his own tomb, and his fame is predicted. His great deeds will once again be sung after eight hundred years of oblivion, and his heroic name will once more astonish the world as the deeds wrought by his sword now astonish it. From a branch of laurel, a pen will spring a poet – i.e. Balbuena – who will record the full compendium of his deeds. Then, what the Fates have already destined for him will be resung, resurrected, taken from oblivion, and both he and the poet who sings his deeds, will become famous:

> You shall be the first and he the second
> Both of one name, of one obsession – Fame
> You with your sword will perform wonderful feats
> He with his humble pen, will sing of them.[171]

Balbuena's Fame is involved with that of his hero.

We have mentioned before the fact that Balbuena's choice of hero served a very personal purpose. Balbuena, like his hero, was of illegitimate birth. The emphasis on lineage and nobility of birth was so powerful in the Golden Age of Spain, that writers like Lope De Vega, genius though he was, could not altogether come to terms with the fact that he was the son of a humble craftsman. Lope's full name was Lope de Vega Carpio. With that imagination which he displayed in his writing, he set out to autocreate himself. He wrote several plays on the theme of Bernardo del Carpio, in which Bernardo wins fame and castles by his deeds. Lope's Bernardo wins these castles from the Moors and hands them over to the King. When the King offers to reward him, he asks for the right to put on his shield the heraldic device of the nineteen castles that he had won.

Lope then proceeded to have, in real life, the reward that his dramatic creation Bernardo had asked for. On the publication of one of his books – a pastoral novel – he had these nineteen towers, the heraldic device, printed on the title page.[172] This lead to an outburst of mockery and derision on the part of his fellow writers and in particular to a satirical poem written by Lope's rival poet, the well-born and famous Gongora.[173] The nineteen towers that Lope had inscribed and their arrangement on his shield, was unknown in heraldry.

But Lope, in spite of being laughed at, kept his shield with his nineteen towers. His genius, he felt, was enough to create its own aristocracy, its own law of heraldry. As he said in a play:

No man should boast
Of his noble birth
Only he who, of a humble father
With valour for his mother
Engendered himself anew.[174]

Balbuena believed like Lope. It is more than probable that the heraldic device which first appeared on the title-page of his *Grandeur of Mexico* was as fraudulent as was Lope's. And the noble lineage which he traces for the Balbuena family at the end of Book XIX, although not investigated by his biographers, seems to belong to one of those fabricated lineages so common in the Spain of the time. On one side, Balbuena in his poem seems to claim descent from Charles Martel of France,[175] one of his ancestors therefore having on his shield the "bars of Aragon and the lilies of France".[176] The castle and the lion on the shield which Balbuena used usually represent two states of Spain: Castille and Leon. They may also refer to Bernardo del Carpio, who was supposed to be from Leon, and who won castles. All in all, Balbuena's heraldic shield and lineage are most probably part of an auto-creation à la Lope.

But to achieve Fame as a poet would justify all this. The obsession with Fame, both for his hero and himself, is constant.

In Book Two, he describes the Castle of Fame, and shows how difficult it is for the dead-in-spirit to enter. He prays that the heroic flight of his humble pen will put him high above the unstable wheel of Fortune, so that Time, with its voracious moths, will not consume his name. And when writing his poem, his spirit falters, a goddess appears to him in a chariot and takes him on her flight through the skies. She prays to Heaven to give him strength as a reward for his having hungered for knowledge of the Truth, in a world which is the stage and theatre of the ignorant, who set themselves up as the Muses and Apollos of earth, a world where Avarice tempts most men to give up for gain "the sovereign majesty of man". Everyone drinks in this world of the cup of deception, and virtue is mocked. But he, although his strength sometimes falters, has tried to follow virtue and striven to write a poem which will give him trophies of immortality. To help him with his poem, she shows him all the marvels of the earth.

But it is at the beginning of the Book XX that we get one of the most intimate and moving pictures of his yearning for perfection in poetry, for Fame. He gives a stylised picture of himself writing beside a river under a tree. As he writes, an eagle swoops down, takes the paper in his claws, and flies off. He follows it with his eyes. The thought strikes him with anguish. Does this mean that all the work that he has put into his epic poem all these years will be swept away by the swift and cruel harpy of Time in an hour's span? Will the eagle take his poem from people to people? Or will he lose it, dropping it from his claws? Only Time will solve the enigma. In the meanwhile, he will write on with faith. After all, if the bird took the paper, it left his pen. The eagle is the king of birds and this means that his Fame will outlast Time, and will be spread from nation to nation. Fame has been his guide, his goal. He has tried for the best. He will put away servile fear and once more return to his task. It is not only his name, but Spain's that he celebrates. Fame is his spur.

The Midas allegory is central to the poem. Orlando's companions are trapped in the Castle of Avarice, and turned into Gold. Malgesi and his three companions are pulled down in their flying boat because of the power of the appetite for the buried wealth of the earth which the Mexican magician arouses in them. In the allegory to Book XIX, Balbuena speaks of the "power of money, and how at times it can buy favours and armed might, which makes it able to buy the justice that it could not get in any other way."[177] In Bernardo, the poet celebrates the man who time after time turns his back on gold and seeks an immortal name. In Book XIX when Bernardo wounds the giant, and money pours from the gaping wound, Balbuena writes that any other man would have been tempted to leave off fighting and gather the flow of gold coins.

> But he, who only honour nobly inclines,
> Wealth cannot disturb his mind;
> For the man who seeks an immortal name
> Gold is a poor metal to substitute for Fame.[178]

Fame conquers all in the ideal world of *The Bernard*. Gold is rejected with disdain. But in the real world of Jamaica, Fame was irrelevant. In the real world of Jamaica, it must have seemed to Balbuena that the eagle who had taken away his paper was reminding him that his Prologue and his poem belonged to the scrap heap of the past. A new world was in the making where the only Fame that a man would care for would be the Fame of his possessions – the amount of gold coins in his chest, his acres of land, his sugar mill, the number of his slaves. After sending off his Prologue to Spain, Balbuena turned to the harsh reality of Villa de la Vega once again. As Marcuse in our own time noted in *Negations*:

> The purport of idealism, viz, the realisation of the Idea, dissipates. The history of idealism is also the history of its coming to terms with the established order.[179]

The Puerto Rican chronicler, Diego de Torres Vargas, in his account of the island and city of Puerto Rico, published in 1647, said about our Abbot:

> To the aforesaid Don Pedro de Solier, succeeded Doctor Bernardo de Balbuena, native of Valdepeñas in La Mancha, Abbot of Jamaica from whence he came wealthy.[180]

How true was this last statement? Did Balbuena, like quite a few others, use the years spent in our island to enrich himself? Or did he perhaps come into some inheritance from his family in Mexico? There is no clear evidence one way or the other. In the application that Balbuena sent in 1611-1612 asking either for a new post, or for a guaranteed sum to help out with his salary, he claimed that he arrived in Jamaica flat broke. We may have dismissed this as the kind of judicious exaggeration used in an age when salaries were paid, and expenses refunded so irregularly that the harassed official had to point up the urgency of his claim. But we do know that whilst in Madrid he had had to borrow money. And that later on, from Puerto Rico, he sent quite a substantial sum to Lope de Vega, his friend, the poet. From there, too, he offered to begin paying back the loan he had received from his cousin. It is true that his salary there was far better than that in Jamaica. Appointed to the Bishopric in August 1619, he did not arrive until the beginning of 1623, but in the meantime, he had applied from Jamaica asking that he be given one half of the income from his Bishopric during the time that the post was vacant. This, a common petition in those days, was granted.

But Balbuena himself tells us that this money was not much. Even less was the amount he earned officially in Jamaica. From his application for another post, we know that the privilege of collecting the tithes was farmed out to the highest bidder each year. But only the fourth part of this amount was paid to the Bishop, or, one assumes, to the Great Abbot. Two ninths was retained for the King. All the rest was assigned to the Cathedral Chapter to the priests of the episcopate, and the hospitals etc. of the diocese. In his application, Balbuena listed the income to the Jamaican Abbacy that had accrued since Villalobos' death in August 1606. Between then and the end of 1609, the income accrued had been roughly some 1045 silver pesos. That is for three and a half years. The yearly amount, then, was not much more than the 400 pesos that Balbuena had had to pay for his voyage from Santo Domingo to Jamaica. Of course, apart from the tithes, he would be paid for the saying of masses and other such functions. Yet would this have been enough to send him away "wealthy from Jamaica"?

Life and food was cheap. In his letter (1611) to the King, Balbuena wrote:

All the products of the country are cheap, so that while a silver real is worth thirteen quartos, they give for one quarto four pounds of beef at the butcher".[181]

Bread also, made from cassava, was dirt cheap. Also, although Albuena may have lacked immediate capital when he arrived, he took with him goods amounting to 1,000 ducats, jewels to the amount of 500 ducats and books to the amount of 200. Amongst the goods were three Negro slaves. He took with him also, as we have noted, "several servants from Spain", some of whom may have been his relatives from Valdepeñas. Did he and they use the slaves to go into the cattle business? Did they export products including dye woods? His indefatigable biographer, Van Horne, found amongst the Archives of the Indies two business entries which refer to Balbuena. One refers to,

100 hides of cattle, bulls and cows, dry and in good condition, with the outside mark of fire on the head and of red ochre on the sides.[182]

These had been carried from Jamaica in a ship, the *Magdalena*, whose Captain was a certain Martin Romero. Another entry refers to a ship whose Captain was Sebastian Lope, which arrived in Seville in 1614. His ship carried 70 hides for Balbuena,

> salted, dried and in good condition except one that was rotted on the loin, with the mark outside of red ochre on the sides.[183]

Both entries were consigned to an agent, Manuel del Río of Seville. But it is clearly stated in the documents that the hides were part of the Abbot's portion of the tithes. We already know of the scarcity of money in Jamaica; and from other documents we know that payment of tithes was frequently made in products. Later on in Puerto Rico, Balbuena, asked to contribute funds to the Royal treasury, contributed 100 arrobas[184] of white sugar. Van Horne thinks that these – i.e. export of hides – "may not have been the only transactions in which Balbuena took part". And from the letter of Lope de Vega in which he grants power of attorney to a bookseller of Seville to collect from a merchant of that city, Senor Don Pedro Rodríguez de Loayssa some 800 reales which the Bishop of Puerto Rico – i.e. Balbuena – had sent him, we know that this merchant looked after the financial affairs of Balbuena. Lope de Vega concludes that the Bishop had sent instructions to the merchant "who administers the financial affairs of the said Lord Bishop".[185] Did Balbuena make a profit, over and above his income, out of his stay in Jamaica? Did the lust for money, against which his hero struggles so hard in *The Bernard*, take hold of its author?

Van Horne points out that in his letters, both as Abbot and as Bishop, we see the "customary struggle" to get the income due to him and whatever increment that was going. He was not unusual in this. The great ideals were all very well, but a man had to survive. And it was not wise in Villa de la Vega to be at the mercy of one's neighbours. In fact, in a world where all were out to get as much as they could, one was not respected for honesty or cheerful poverty. In fact, as van Horne points out, his neighbours would have thought him incapable and stupid. Altruism was not, and is still not, admired. The "ginal", the sharp dealer, was the hero; not Bernardo, the ideal warrior, the Christian crusader. Except for his epic poem, Balbuena was not a crusader. The compromise that he rejected in his poem came to play an important part in the reality of his circumstance.

In his first letter to the King written from Jamaica in 1611 he points out that his "income is meagre". Later on, in his application he made more explicit his demand that as Abbot he should be included amongst those Bishoprics where, if the post did not carry an income of 500,000 maravedis, then the rest was to be made up from the Royal Treasury. This request was never granted him in Jamaica, although it was done in Puerto Rico. But even there, Van Horne tells us, in spite of innumerable requests from Balbuena to the King, and from the King to the authorities in Puerto Rico, the extra sum had still not been paid by the time he died. And Balbuena died a reasonably well-off man. How did this come about? In July 1611 he had written to the King pleading the greatest poverty, pointing out that after the expenses of his voyage, "I am in great need as I have no income with which to pay and support myself."[186] In the same letter, he had pointed out that whilst other prelates had additional income beside their salary, he had none.

Was this true? We know that Balbuena had kept up his family connections with Mexico, that indeed he arranged for a nephew of his, one Juan de Balbuena, to come to Jamaica, to Villa de la Vega, as a priest and serve there for some time. Juan de Balbuena seemed to have returned to Mexico and gone from there to Spain. After getting his doctorate, he returned to Puerto Rico in 1623, where his uncle's influence and recommendation got him the post as Cathedral prebend in San Juan. After Balbuena's death in 1627, the Dean of the Cathedral stated that he had left some 21,400 pesos "which he had brought as his patrimony (i.e. as inherited money)".[187] Balbuena's father had died before he left Mexico in 1604. Of his poverty while in Madrid, there can be no doubt. Although, whilst in Puerto Rico, he still wrote letter after letter clamouring for increases to his income – in one he pointed out that his income from the Bishopric was only 600 ducats, whilst the expenses of travel had cost him 3,000 ducats, although he argued that he could not support himself on that, we do not get quite the same tone of desperation that we got in his first letter from Jamaica.

There is no doubt about the fact that he was comfortably off in Puerto Rico. Torres Vargas tells us that he wanted to found a convent for nuns in Viso in Extremadura in Spain, from where the Balbuena family came. He sent much money and goods to this end to Spain. But almost all the ships were lost – perhaps in a storm, perhaps captured by pirates or enemy privateers. Balbuena, Torres Vargas then tells us, decided that God wished him to spend the money in that part of the world where he had earned it. So he started to occupy himself with a project that the Town Council had in mind – that of building a convent for the many unmarried daughters of Spanish settlers, who, without a dowry, could not find a husband. The convent was built almost two decades after his death, in 1646.

This all seems to lead to the conclusion that either Balbuena lied about his extreme poverty, having an income from Mexico when he claimed to be broke, or that, perhaps through judicious management of his business affairs, per-haps, who knows, through a little speculation here and there, he managed to make a quite considerable profit out of his stay in Jamaica. With his prudence and tact, he was able to get on with all factions in Villa de la Vega. He even made a friend out of Juan de Cueto, a Jamaican priest, who, like Balbuena, had applied for the position of Abbot. Cueto belonged to one of the principal families. He had been applying for the position as Abbot since 1598, bringing his application up to date from time to time. It would be expected then that he would have resented Balbuena. But Balbuena, in applying for another position in 1611-1612, allowed Cueto to include in this petition a document setting out his own claims to the Abbacy. It was high time, he argued, that a native should be given the Abbacy, since this had in fact been recommended by the Emperor Charles V (1st of Spain).

Once Balbuena was appointed Bishop of Puerto Rico he recommended strongly that Juan de Cueto should succeed him, But this was not to be. The Marquis of Jamaica insisted on appointing his own protégé – Mateo de Medina[188] – as Abbot. But since Balbuena had no disgruntled enemies, there do not appear to be any letters of complaint against him through which we could have known whether or not the wealth which went with him from Jamaica had been acquired there (and through the rather dubious methods that were customary), or whether it had in fact come to him from his paternal estate in Mexico. Certainly, in real life Balbuena came to terms with the reality of the power of money, and, as his letters show, was tenacious in claiming as much as he could get from the tithes of the faithful, and from the Royal Treasury.

Did the bureaucrat drive out the poet in Balbuena? He wrote his Prologue in 1615. He was appointed Bishop of Puerto Rico in 1619. But for various reasons he did not leave Jamaica until 1622. We know that he got the information of his appointment in the middle of 1620. In 1621 he received a letter instructing him to attend a Provincial Council called together both by the Pope and the King, to be held in Santo Domingo beginning in 1622. Apart from the Prologue and the rewriting of a stanza here or there, we have no evidence to show that Balbuena wrote any poetry in the eleven years of his stay in Jamaica. We cannot be absolutely sure, as many of Balbuena's papers and books were to be destroyed in Puerto Rico. But from the letters Balbuena wrote as Bishop from Puerto Rico, Van Horne points out that we see only the routine acts of a functionary, the constant struggle to claim and obtain pay and perquisites. All signs of poetic inspiration – which touched his letter-description of Jamaica with vigour – has disappeared.

Balbuena was a man pushing fifty when he arrived in Villa de La Vega. If he arrived flat broke in that society, a society which then, as now, regarded a man's possessions as his only criterion of manhood and honour, he must have determined at that middle turning of his life that, to borrow an English king's later phrase, he would not go poor on his travels again. He tried for reform in Jamaica, but when reform was blocked he came to terms with the status quo. While he hoped for a better position in Mexico, and for release from the soledades of Jamaica, he made sure to survive in a reality in which his epic hero Bernardo could not have lasted a day. The wiles of Ulysses were more apt. Fame was all very well, but Balbuena, like Don Quixote – and unlike Villalobos who had died poor and wretched – came to accept the middle-aged fact that inns are not enchanted castles, that innkeepers are not magicians, that for the price of a night's lodging, a life's keep, one had to take not shield or lance, but sufficient money in one's purse. Yet what one gains on the swings, one loses on the roundabouts. To come to terms with survival in the world of Villa de La Vega, and later in San Juan, Balbuena had to turn his back on the ideal world of poetry, had to learn how to inhabit the world of prose. In his Prologue he pointed out that his epic poem had been written in his youth; a time when the *furor poeticus* banishes all else that can exclude the divine creative breath: worldly honours, gold, position, rank. But middle-age tends to settle for less. Balbuena left Jamaica well supplied with cash, but with nothing to show except an occasional rewritten stanza and, of course, his Prologue. So far as we know, nothing new of any merit, not one original line of verse – that verse which, as he had written when he was young, was the simulacrum and image of the Universe. Jamaica had indeed been a *soledades* where he had been as one bewitched. He left it, but carried in his spirit something of the desolation, of that aridity of the soul which comes upon those who give up verse for rank and gold; poetry for prose. Even though he could now proudly sign himself, as he did after his promotion, time and time again: Abbot of Jamaica, Bishop-Elect of Puerto Rico.

Puerto Rico may have been a more civilised cultural reality for Balbuena, but it was still a frontier outpost. And the whole Caribbean was by now an outlaw frontier territory where pirates and privateers and all of Spain's enemies swooped like vultures on a weakened prey. In order to attend the Provincial Council in Santo Domingo, Balbuena began the long, tiring and dangerous journey by sea and land. He seems to have sailed first to Cuba, and from there to Santo Domingo. He escaped hurricanes and pirates and arrived safely. But he must have had an anxious time at sea. Whilst at Santo Domingo, at the Council he would have sighted the forty enemy ships that at one time threatened to attack. After the Council, early in 1623, he sailed to Puerto Rico, travelling overland to the capital and visiting areas of his diocese. He was now over sixty years old. He wrote to the King after his arrival in San Juan that he would have to postpone some of his duties, "through lack of health caused by the hardships of such a long route".[189]

After he recovered, he took up his duties, holding examinations for the clergy, planning a synod, recommending worthy priests, including his nephew, for posts, writing a description of the island of Puerto Rico; laying claim to the different districts which should be included in his diocese etc. All his actions are the actions of a prudent bureaucrat, actions which could in no way disturb the established tenor of island life. After his death, the Cabildo of the Cathedral of San Juan was to speak of "his wisdom, his peacefulness and prudence".[189] The compelling mediocrity of the island societies reduced him to their level in the end. Only three incidents were to break the monotonous and placid surface of Balbuena's life in Puerto Rico – the publication of his poem, the attack by a Dutch privateer force on San Juan; and his deathbed scene, which was to take place in circumstances that could have come straight out of the most bizarre episode of his *The Bernard*.

In 1624 at last, some 15 years after Balbuena had first arranged to publish his poem, *The Bernard* appeared in Madrid. The royal license is dated 9th July, 1624. On the title page he is called Abbot of Jamaica, but the document which fixes the price and which is dated 28th September, 1624, refers to him as Bishop of Puerto Rico. The poem appeared when the vogue of the epic had passed. Spain was now clearly on the defensive; the high confidence of the sixteenth century was passing away. We know that Lope de Vega, his friend, was to praise it. Cervantes (1547-1616) in his *Viaje del Parnaso* had praised Balbuena's poetry in *El Siglo de Oro*. But now he was long since dead. Mira de Amescua, priest, censor and playwright, had in 1609 praised *The Bernard* – still in manuscript – as unique. Nicholas Antonio, the seventeenth-century (1617-1684) Canon of Seville who compiled a catalogue of Spanish writers from the earliest times up until 1684 referred to *The Bernard* with great praise, singling out perceptively Balbuena's descriptive ability, his talent in presenting things with vividness, the rich variety of his work, his geographical and astronomical references,[191] his style and use of language. But in spite of this high praise, Balbuena's poem remained forgotten and ignored. Even Nicholas Antonio had lamented its sparse popularity. No new edition appeared until the early nineteenth century. But the reason and circumstance of this new edition would dearly please our patriotic Abbot.

The second edition of *The Bernard* appeared in 1808 when the Napoleonic invasion of Spain had awakened the most fervent national feelings in the majority of Spaniards. The edition was prepared by Manuel José Quintana, the fervently patriotic Spanish poet, writer and critic. He saw *The Bernard* as a poem which could help stimulate and exalt the patriotism of Spaniards in their struggle against the newly arrogant France of Napoleon Bonaparte. Bernardo del Carpio, and his poet Balbuena fulfilled their destiny at last providing a model of patriotism to the future by recalling the great deeds of the past. Critical opinion since then has praised the poem. Its excessive length, its extravagance, its pedantry and complicated plots and language are not enough to obscure something new and strange – springing not only from the baroque tension between the ideal heroic world of the poet and the increasingly materialist reality of the new age, but from the tension between the old world and the new, from the amorphousness of a sea-change that creates an at once monstrous and powerful atmosphere. As Mira de Amescua said, the poem is unique. Its uniqueness defies analysis precisely because it is a new potentiality breaking out of old traditional forms. There is something unfinished about *The Bernard*, something like the vast American Continent itself, still waiting to be fulfilled.

Pirates had abounded in the world of *The Bernard*. Now reality caught up with the poet and Bishop. The Dutch privateers had helped to win Holland's independence from Spain, and to lay the foundations of the expansion of Dutch commerce and the Dutch Empire, through their pitiless sacking, burning and looting of Spanish towns and Spanish islands. Just as Villalobos had had to flee in his nightshirt from an English "gentle-man-adventurer" so now it was Balbuena's turn to be threatened by the depredations of a strong Dutch privateer force. In the latter part of 1625, three years before the famous Piet Heyn was to capture the Spanish treasure fleet off Matanzas in Cuba, a Dutch privateer fleet of 17 ships lead by Bowdoin Hendrick[192] – in the Spanish documents, Balduino Enrico –attacked the city of Puerto Rico. They laid siege to the city of San Juan in September. The garrison left the city and blockaded themselves in the Castle, El Morro. The Dutch burnt part of the city[193] whilst the Spaniards made sorties against them. The Dutch looted and wrecked part of the city, sacked and burnt the Bishop's palace, looted his books and papers. They entered the Cathedral and took away the bell, an organ and the greater part of its ornaments. They burnt the images, the songbooks, the reredos, and partly damaged the Cathedral. The rebellious Protestant fury, the lust of vengeance, which Balbuena had allegorised in the beautiful Arcangelica, had transformed itself into reality. And the reality held terror for those who were its victims. The allegory of his poem stormed into Balbuena's life. Unlike his hero, Balbuena fled.

Reality was not chivalresque. Balbuena was an old man, weak from illness and nearly blind. Not even the armour of Achilles could prevail against the gun and its new and ruthless ideology. Balbuena and his Canons, in fact all the clergy, fled to the country outside San Juan. Only a Prior, of the order of the missionary preachers, Antonio de Rosas, remained in the city, whilst the soldiers defended the garrison and together with some of the citizens made armed sorties against the Dutch. The citizens were later to write that whilst the Bishop and all the others fled the city and "the soldiers were left alone, fearing death",[194] Antonio de Rosas with the Cross of Christ in his hands went about in the thick of the fire, from soldier to soldier, confessing, praying, exhorting, giving the last sacraments and burying the dead. Those who lived, he encouraged to fight on for the cause of their King and their Faith and their God.

The Dutch were finally forced to withdraw. The next year, 1626, they anchored off Negril in Jamaica intending to attack. But they contented themselves with capturing a small vessel loaded with hides, jerked pork and lard and sailed off without attacking. In the meanwhile, Balbuena had returned to the desolate city of San Juan. His books, among them most likely several copies of the princeps edition of *The Bernard*, and all his papers had been destroyed. Nor had he emerged with credit from the confrontation with the heretic. But the fighting he could not do in reality, he could recreate on paper. He took up his pen to praise the valorous deeds of a certain Captain of Infantry, Juan de Amézqueta y Quijano. In the thick of the fight, Balbuena wrote, the Captain fought magnificently against the Dutch. Indeed, one day, had the others gone to his help and responded to his call and followed his lead, he would have cut off the heads of the enemy, and captured all their trenches. He, therefore, recommended the Captain for promotion.[195] As we read his letter we think of the tremendous blows of Bernardo and Orlando, and the cuts and thrusts of their magic swords which could fell giants. So he erased the discordant reality with the magic power of his pen. And the magic pen of Lope de Vega was to give Balbuena the last word. In his *Laurel de Apolo*, in which Lope lists the poets of his time, he immortalises Balbuena and his frontier experience in these words:

> Sweet may your memory remain
> Oh generous prelate
> Most learned Bernardo de Balbuena
> Who held the pastoral staff
> When the rebel Dutchman, fierce Enrique
> Stormed Puerto Rico
> Sacked your library
> But your genius no, that he could not touch
> Even with all oblivion at his command.
> How well you sang our Spanish Bernardo!
> How well portrayed our Golden Age![196]

But the Golden Age was drawing to its close. Already, the sun was setting on the brief splendour of Spanish imperial grandeur. *The Bernard* was a piece of heroic defiance in the teeth of apprehensions of mortality. Now the poet himself was to breathe his last hour upon the stage. His deathbed scene could have served as a magnificent allegory of the power of Codicia – the greed for gain, the lust for gold. Death was not unexpected. In a letter of July 1626 written to the King, he tells of his broken health which prevents him from carrying out his duty and visiting the more distant parts of his diocese. He became ill the next year and, on the last day of his life, Tuesday, 11th October, 1627, was involved in an incredible scene. Three days before his death, Balbuena made his will. In this will he left all that he had to the Church. On the day of his death the public notary was sent for to confirm his will and make it official. The Governor of Puerto Rico – Juan de Haro[197] – being informed of this, took a group of officials and soldiers with him and went to the Bishop's house. He posted the soldiers around the house, entered, and with his officials surrounded the deathbed of Bernardo de Balbuena. He ordered the Dean and the Church officials out of the room, demanding to know what they were doing there. A clash of words ensued. The notary was caught between two stools. Balbuena handed his will to him and said that it was his last will and testament. He wanted the notary to witness it. He had destroyed the one he had made six months earlier. This new one should be made valid. But the Governor glared at the notary, and the notary, intimidated, refrained from signing and validating the will.

At least, this is the version that the Church was later to give. And it seems that this version was closer to the truth. If Balbuena were to die intestate his goods would revert to the State Treasury. In the rather free and easy atmos-

phere of the times, the Governor and his officials would have helped themselves to a share. If the money were willed to the Church, then it would be out
of the Governor's reach. To be fair, the Governor may have suspected that a
high Church dignitary or two might have helped themselves, too. But there
can be no doubt that the Governor was using force to extort money for himself,
even though he later wrote to the King that he had been trying to protect the
interests of the Royal Treasury. As Church and State wrangled over the dying
Bishop's bed, the news spread throughout San Juan. The Bishop had already
received the last sacrament and, his soul at peace, he may have remembered,
as he watched the altercation, the powerful lines with which he had explained
the allegory of Book I of his epic poem:

> lust of the flesh and the appetite for riches are the two passions most yoked
> together in the human heart; and even in the wide course of the heavens
> the rich man seeks to have dominion.[198]

And so the Bishop died. But the wrangle continued. The Dean wanted to
make an on-the-spot inventory of the Bishop's possessions. The Governor
refused to allow this. The Notary later complained that the Governor ordered
him out of a room where he was taking the inventory of a large quantity of
silver plate. The Dean excommunicated the Governor. The Governor arrested the Dean. Then he took over the possessions of Balbuena, and helped
himself liberally. That is according to the Dean. According to the Governor,
Balbuena had died intestate, and it had been his duty to take over the dead
man's possessions and put them in the royal deposit. He had posted guards
about the house to see that the Bishop's possessions were not stolen. But who
could guard the guardians?

The matter was put to litigation and the Church won. Torres Vargas tells
us that the Bishop of Puerto Rico was given a splendid funeral and buried in
the chapel of the Cathedral of San Juan, a chapel which was built and dedicated
to the Saint of his name, and who knows, to the hero of his epic "both with the
same name and the same obsession – Fame". From his will he had left money
to pay for the oil to keep a lamp burning in the chapel and for Masses to be said
on the first Sunday of each month for his soul; as well as for an extra Mass with
a sermon and a Vesper Service to be performed on his Saint's day. In poetry and
in religion he had tried to perpetuate his memory and his name. He had done
all that he could towards this aim – had compromised with life and aimed high
with his verse. In an absolute sense he had failed, but *The Bernard* remains as
the record of his flight towards the impossible. At the end of his Prologue he
had quoted with pride a line of his poem, which he thought, demonstrated his
technical skill.[199] We might place it as his epitaph, accepting as he did all human
experience as but a striving towards one inevitable and final outcome:

> Which is good, which is ill, which is life, which is death, which is the end.

Endnotes

1. Freely translated – as indeed are all translations from his poetry in these articles [i.e. from the series in *Jamaica Journal*] – from Del Doctor Bon Bernardo de Valbuena, *El Bernardo o Victoria de Roncesvalles* in *Biblioteca de Autores Españoles, desde la formación del lenguaje hasta nuestros días,* vol. 1, Don Cayetano Rosell y López, ed. (Madrid: Ediciones Atlas, 1945), 175. Hereafter referred to as *El Bernardo.*

2. Ibid., 139.

3. V. S. Naipaul, *The Middle Passage: Impression of Five Societies – British, French and Dutch – in the West Indies and South America* (1962; London: Andre Deutsch, 1974), 41.

4. Source not located.

5. The critic to whom the term "literaturisation of life" is attributed is Italo Svevo (né Aron Ettore Schmitz). See Livia Veneziani Svevo, *Memoir of Italo Svevo* (1950; Vermont: Marlboro Press, 1990), 120.

6. John Dryden, "Æneïs – To the Most Honorable John, Lord Marquis of Normandy..." (1697) in *The Works of John Dryden,* Vol. XIV (Edinburgh: Archibald Constable and Co., 1821), 127.

7. Francisco de Aldana, "Carta para Arias Montano", in *Poesías Castellanas Completas* (Madrid: Ediciones Cátedra, 2000), 450.

8. George Cubitt, *Cortés: Or, The Discovery and Conquest of Mexico* (London: John Mason, 1848), 57.

9. *El Bernardo,* 347.

10. Peter Martyr, *De Orbo Novo,* Book VII, ix. (1530).

11. *El Bernardo,* 304-305. ibid., 331.

12. Dryden, John Dryden, "Æneïs...", 127.

13. *El Bernardo,* 331.

14. Scindentur vestes gemma frangentur et aurum,
    Carmine quam tribuent fama perennis erit.
    (Ovid, 10th Elegy Bk)
    Todo se acabara con los diversos
    cursos del tiempo, el oro, los vestidos,
    las joyas y tesoros mas validos,
    y no el nombre inmortal que dart los versos.
    John van Horne, ed., *La Grandeza Mexicana de Bernardo de Balbuena* (Urbana: University of Illinois Press, 1930), 166

15. These entries were: 1) a poem in which Christ consoles the Soul, written for Corpus Christi (1585); 2) a poem written on the theme of the psalm – Super flumina Babylonis – (i.e. Psalm 137) "By the Rivers of Babylon, I sat me down and wept. How shall I sing the Lord's song in a strange land?" This was written for the arrival of the New Viceroy. The other two entries are mentioned in the text.

16. Source not located.

17. *La Grandeza Mexicana,* 82.

18. Ibid., 78.

19. Naipaul, *The Middle Passage,* 41.

20. Ibid.
21. *La Grandeza Mexicana*, 104.
22. C[laude] Lévi-Strauss, *Tristes Tropiques,* trans. by John Russell (1955; New York: Criterion, 1961), 91.
23. Francisco de Quevedo, "Desda la Torre" in *Obras Completas,* vol.1: *Poesía Original,* José Manuel Blecua, ed. (Barcelona: Editorial Planeta, 1963), 105.
24. José Rojas Garcidueñas, *Bernardo de Balbuena: la vida y la obra* (México: Instituto de Investigaciones Estéticas, Universidad Nacional Autónoma de México, 1958).
25. Ibid., 82. See also *La Grandeza Mexicana*, 90.
26. C. S. Lewis, "The Technique of Primary Epic" in *A Preface to Paradise Lost* (1942; London: Oxford University Press, 1956), 23.
27. We see in Balbuena's own work, this contrast between the "historical" fact and the epic fact. As a second/third generation settler, Balbuena's attitude to the Indians of Mexico, as can be deduced from his most "factual" book, *The Grandeur of Mexico*, is one of contempt for the *"incluto"*, the brute man. Here he seems to accept the line of argument that was based on Aristotle's statement that some men are naturally inferior. In this his first published book he presents an image of an Indian pursuing a wild beast, and says that "the beast was less intractable and ferocious than the soul that was pursuing it". Yet in the epic, *The Bernardo*, the Tlaxcalan Indian magician whose magic and wisdom are powerful enough to pull down the French magician Malgesi's flying boat from the air and down into his cave, is shown as the equal if not the superior of Malgesi. Of course, Malgesi was French, not Spanish; and the Tlaxcalan Indians, a powerful tribe and the traditional enemies of the Aztec empire, were the allies who made it possible for Cortés to conquer Mexico. But the contrast between "the savage Indian" of *The Grandeur of Mexico* and the "wise and powerful Indian" of the epic is still there.
28. Rojas Garcidueñas, his biographer, surmises that the poem to the Archbishop would have been recited aloud by the children of the Cathedral Choir when the Archbishop was formally welcomed. The poem to the Archbishop begins with a gloss on an ode of the Latin poet Horace – *Laudabunt alii claram Rhodam*
    "Let others sing the sacred place of Delphos/ Of great Thebes its walls and edifices, And of rich Corinth the two seas... ". He sings the greatness of the lineage and of the person of the Archbishop, concluding that Mexico City, blessed with its new Shepherd, can now compare itself with all the famous cities of Greek and Latin Antiquity. Here we see the fusion of the Christian actuality with the pagan classical ideal. Rojas Garcidueñas, *Bernardo de Balbuena*, 176.
29. *La Grandeza Mexicana,* 81.
30. John van Horne, "Introducción," *La Grandeza Mexicana,* 14, 17-18. See also van Horne, *Bernardo de Balbuena: biografía y crítica* (Guadalajara: Imprenta Font, 1940), 115-116, 125.
31. *El Bernardo*, 340
32. *La Grandeza Mexicana,* 79-80.
33. van Horne believes that although the title page of the second edition holds the date 1604, it might not have appeared until 1606 when, with the death

of the Archbishop, Balbuena would have lost hope of patronage from that quarter and therefore dedicated it to Lemos instead.

34. Miguel de Cervantes Saavedra, *The Adventures of Don Quixote,* trans. by J. M. Cohen (New York: Penguin Books, 1950), 26.

35. Ibid., 27-28.

36. "Compendio Apologetico en Alabança de la Poesia" [sic] in *La Grandeza Mexicana,* 143-166.

37. Sir Philip Sidney, *An Apology for Poetry or The Defence of Poesy* (1595), Geoffrey Shepherd, ed. (London: Thomas Nelson and Sons, 1965), 101.

38. R. H. Tawney, *Religion and the Rise of Capitalism: A Historical Study* (1926; London: J. Murray, 1948), Preface to 1936 edition, xii.

39. *The Grandeza Mexicana,* 103.

40. Herbert Marcuse, *One-Dimensional Man: Studies in the Ideology in Advanced Industrial Society* (Boston: Beacon Press, 1964), 57.

41. *The Grandeza Mexicana,* 165.

42. Ibid., 26.

43. Ernesto R. Sábato, *Sombre héros y tumbas* (Barcelona: Editorial Planeta, 1968), 187.

44. van Horne points out that the records of disembarking passengers at Seville, in this case wrongly, describes him as being an *esclavo,* i.e. slave. Van Horne, *Bernardo de Balbuena,* 66. See also Garcidueñas, 21.

45. *La Grandeza Mexicana,* 81.

46. Cervantes, *Don Quixote,* 899.

47. "[Gil] González Dávila." *Teatro eclesiastico de la primitiva iglesia de las Indias occidentales, vidas de svs arzobispos, obispos y cosas memorables de sus sedes* (Madrid: Diego Diaz de la Carrera, 1649) cited in van Horne, *Bernardo de Balbuena,* 59.

48. In *El celoso extremeno,* i.e. The Jealous Extremenian. "… que es el de pasarse a las Indias, refugios y amparo de los desesperados de Espana, Iglesia de los alzados engano comun de muchos, y remedio particular de pocos. In van Horne, *Bernardo de Balbuena,* 59.

49. Published in Mexico in two editions, both dated 1604 on the title page, although the second may have been released as late as 1606.

50. *El Siglo de pro en las selvas de Erifile.*

51. The Count of Lemos died in 1622. Balbuena, in 1624, rewrote the dedication of *The Bernard* to the Count's heir and brother, Don Francisco Fernandez de Castro etc. Balbuena told the new Count that his predecessor "with the agreeable kindliness of his most noble condition did not disdain to pass his eyes over it." *El Bernardo,*139.

52. The poem is written in 'octaves', a stanza consisting of eight lines, each of 11 syllables, with a regular rhyme scheme. Adopted from Italian into Spanish poetry the octave form was used for formal, solemn and serious poetry.

53. *El Bernardo,* 143.

54. *El Bernardo,* 363.

55. Sidney, *An Apology for Poetry,* 142.

56. Edmund Spenser, *The Shepherd's Calendar,* W. L. Renwick, ed. (London: Scholartis Press, 1930), 160.

57. Charles N. Wheeler, "Fight to Disarm His Life's Work, Henry Ford Vows," *Chicago Daily Tribune* (25 May 1916): 10.
58. van Horne, *Bernardo de Balbuena,* 62
59. Eric Williams, *History of the People of Trinidad and Tobago* (London: Andre Deutsch, 1964), 14.
60. Although the exact wording could not be located, both van Horne, *Bernardo de Balbuena,* 50 and Rojas Garcidueñas, *Bernardo de Balbuena*, 31-32 support this interpretation.
61. The ecclesiastical censor was in this case Mira De Amescu, also a priest and writer, a well-known playwright of Spain's Golden Age. Like Balbuena, he was of illegitimate birth, and his illegitimacy also influenced his choice of career, and his attitudes.
62. ". . .no ay en el cosa contra la Fe Catolica, y buenas costumbres".
63. van Horne, *Bernardo de Balbuena*, 64.
64. An eighth part of the well-known silver piece of eight. One real was worth 34 maravedis, the basic Spanish money denomination.
65. van Horne, *Bernardo,* 69 and Roja Garcidueñas, *Bernardo,* 30.
66. See van Horne, 'Bernardo de Balbuena in Jamaica', *The Daily Gleaner* (June 21, 1934): 11.
67. Francisco Morales Padrón, *Jamaica Española* (Sevilla: Escuela de Estudios Hispana-Americanos, 1952), 176.
68. Marques de Villalobos, the predecessor of Balbuena.
69. Letter to the King, 14 July 1611 has been reprinted in van Horne, "Documentos del Archivo de Indias Referente a Bernardo de Balbuena", *Boletín de la Academia de la Historia,* vol. 96 (January-March 1930): 865.
70. Ibid., 866.
71. *Daily Gleaner,* Barker & Harris controversy.
72. Sidney, *An Apology,* 124.
73. George Lukács, *The Theory of the Novel: A Historico-Philosophical Essay on the Forms of Great Epic Literature,* trans. by Anna Bostock (1920; Cambridge, MA: MIT Press, 1971), 125-127.
74. In a later document – see Morales Padrón – referred to as Santiago de la Vega; hence the English referred to it as St. Jago later as Spanish Town.
75. Balbuena, Letter to King, 14 July 1611, 865.
76. Ibid., 866.
77. Ibid., 867.
78. Ibid., 868.
79. Ibid., 865.
80. Fray García de Loaysa, Bishop of Siguenza and President of the Council of the Indies.
81. Morales Padrón, *Jamaica Española*, 107-114.
82. The fact that Balbuena, in writing to the King, in his descriptive letter of July 1611, states that the Count of Lemos asked him to write such a letter, makes it almost certain that Balbuena had been appointed through Lemos's influence.
83. Alonso de Miranda was Governor between 1607-1611. During Balbuena's stay in the island, some three other Governors were appointed – Pedro Espejo

Barranco, Andrés González de Vera, Sebastian Lorenzo Romano.

84.   In 1556, the privileges of the Columbus heirs were whittled away even more. They lost all rights to Veragua, kept only the ducal title; kept their title of Admiral, but only honorary, without pay. Only an income of 17,000 ducats, and Jamaica were left. After Jamaica was captured by the English, only the income, and the nominal title of Marquis of Jamaica remained as the legacy of the Discoverer.

85.   The belief that Jamaica had deposits of gold caused King Ferdinand to appoint an official, Juan López de Torralba, to supervise the gold mines etc. The latter went to Barcelona around 1519, carrying samples of Jamaican gold which Morales Padrón guesses might have been gold washed down by rivers. Clinton Black in his historical guide to Spanish Town, surmises that the Rio Cobre may have got its name from deposits of copper found on the river bank. But the belief in gold, as expressed by Balbuena, might have lead to quote Black "to the myth of the Golden Table which, legend says, lies hidden somewhere in the Rio Cobre's depths". Before the river diverted to irrigation, it is believed, that if one stood on the riverbank at a certain spot, at noon, a Golden Table rose out of the river, and hung glowing on the air for twelve seconds. Balbuena would have loved this myth which could have come straight out of the enchanted landscape of *The Bernard.* *El Bernardo,* 340. See also Clinton Black, Spanish Town: The Old Capital (Spanish Town: Parish Council of St Catherine, 1960), 60.

86.   Letter to King, 14 July 1611, 867.

87.   Vasco Nuñez de Balboa. He died on the gallows, accused of being a traitor, before he remembered.

88.   Letter to King, 14 July 1611, 868, 865.

89.   *El Bernardo,* 340.

90.   Letter to King, 868.

91.   Ibid., 866.

92.   Ibid., 868-869.

93.   Ibid., 870-871.

94.   Treasure from America was expressed in *pesos* which means 450 maravedis worth of gold and silver. It was equal to 1.2 ducats.

95.   Morales Padrón, *Jamaica Española,* 114.

96.   Lucas del Valle Alvarado, appointed as Governor in 1583.

97.   Villalobos's opinion of Pedro López was low. By appointing him to act as Governor he charged that the real Governor had made the feet become the head.

98.   Letter to King, 870. The draining away of the silver *reales* remained a constant feature until the capture of the island in 1655. Clinton Black, in his historical guide to Spanish Town, quotes Edward Long "...large quantities of (copper coins) have been dug up in Spanish Town, the hills adjacent to it and other parts; but no gold or silver coin was ever found, that I have heard of". Edward Long, *History of Jamaica,* vol 1 (London: T.Lowndes, 1774), 584.

99.   Ibid., 869.

100. Ibid., 870.

101. There seems to be a discrepancy in Balbuena's letter: earlier on in the letter

he seems to suggest that the *real* is worth thirteen quartos. This is from the translation made by Pietersz and Cundall, the translation used throughout this article. See Frank Cundall and Joseph L. Pietersz, Jamaica under the Spaniards: Abstracted from the Archives of Seville (Kingston: Institute of Jamaica, 1919), 35.

102. Letter to the King, 870.
103. *El Bernardo,* 340.
104. *The Decades of the New World,* 1555; *De Orbe Novo: The Eight Decades of Peter Martyr D'Anghera* (1555), by Francis Augustus MacNutt (New York: G. P. Putnam's Sons/Knickerbocker Press, 1912), 346. See also Morales Padrón, *Jamaica Española,* 166.
105. Ibid., 201-202.
106. Morales Padrón, ibid., 204-205. The treasurer's name has more recently been rendered as "Pedro de Mazuela". Irene Wright employs Pedro de Maçuelo, which nonetheless still included the "de". See Wright's insightful article regarding Martyr's building of the church, which reprints original documents, "The Early History of Jamaica, 1511-1536", *The English Historical Review,* vol. 26, no. 141 (January 1921): 70-95. The town itself – New Seville, also called in early maps Sevilla d' Oro, i.e. Golden Seville, seemed to have been planned on the same scale. William B. Goodwin – in his *Spanish and English Ruins in Jamaica* (Boston, 1946) – maintains that there are indications that the town "comprised a theatre, a church, a monastery, an Abbey and governmental buildings of quality". He adds: "We have found that artisans of all kinds were brought from old Spain and that the city as planned would have been something that never survived in any part of the Spanish regime in America". Goodwin lists some of the surviving ruins, among them two of the flanking towers of the fortified townsite of Seville, just west of the present town of St. Ann's Bay; and the foundations of Peter Martyr's Cathedral Church.
107. Two churches, built of wood and straw had been destroyed, by fire, one of them, Goodwin surmises, having been a monastery.
108. The King of Spain in January 1525 ordered that the same skilled Indians who built the fort which defended the town should be put to work on the Church, and the leftover bricks and lime from the fort should be used for the Church.
109. Morales Padrón, *Jamaica Española,* 202-203.
110. Ibid., 45-46, 269.
111. There had been early attempts at settlements on the South Coast which had the great advantage of being nearer to the Mainland. The Plate Fleet which took supplies of water, meat and foodstuffs on its annual voyages between Vera Cruz, Jamaica and Havana touched on the South side to refit. Mazuala's sugar mill and Portuguese settlers were therefore only contributory although powerful factors in the decision to move the capital from Seville to Spanish Town.
112. See Morales Padrón, *Jamaica Española,* 95. Francisco de Garay had signed a contract with King Ferdinand to exploit land and livestock that the King owned in Jamaica to the profit of both, and with the intention of provisioning the expeditions of discovery and conquest of the Mainland. Garay had come the

New World with Columbus and was one of the earliest settlers in Hispaniola.

113. The site of the present-day Gray's Inn sugar estate is said by Goodwin to be one of the sugar plantations which the King and Garay owned and worked. It may have been also the site of another sugar mill.

114. Garay died in 1526, but it is most probable that Mazuela took advantage of his absence after 1523, to move in early on the sugar mills. In 1532, the son of Garay, now grown to manhood, began a battle for his inheritance, which was finally won for the Garay heirs who then settled in Spanish Jamaica.

115. Strictly speaking it was Queen Juana, the wife of Philip II who ordered in 1533 that a Chapel should be built for the Blessed Sacrament and that the Cathedral Church of Seville should be finished.

116. Morales Padrón, *Jamaica Española,* 163-164.

117. Ibid., 166-167.

118. Ibid., 169-171.

119. Ibid., 173-181.

120. Letter to King, 865.

121. Balbuena did not exaggerate. The Governor wrote in 1603 that the corsairs – Dutch, French and English – had become so bold that they had built 'trading ships' on shore and there held a 'game of bowls'. Morales Padrón, *Jamaica Española*, 78.

122. van Horne, *Bernardo de Balbuena,* 75.

123. Ibid., 76

124. Ibid., 78.

125. Ibid., 70.

126. Letter to King, 866.

127. José Juan Arrom, "El mundo mitico de los taínos: Notas sobre el ser Supremo", *Thesaurus: Buletín de Instituto Caro y Cuervo,* vol. 22, no. 3 (1967): 378-393, qts. at 386, 393.

128. Morales Padrón, *Jamaica Española,* 174.

129. van Horne, *Bernardo de Balbuena,* 114.

130. *The Life of the Admiral Christopher Columbus by His Son Ferdinand,* trans. by Benjamin Keen (New Brunswick: Rutgers University Press, 1959), 132.

131. Ibid.

132. *El Bernardo,* 141.

133. Ibid., 139.

134. van Horne, *Bernardo de Balbuena,* 160.

135. C.S. Lewis, "The Subject of Primary Epic" in *Preface,* 30.

136. *Iliad,* Book VI. 357-358.

137. *Odyssey,* Book VIII. 578-580.

138. *El Bernardo,* 140.

139. Sidney, *An Apology for Poetry,* 119.

140. C. M. Bowra *From Vergil to Milton* (London: Macmillan, 1963).

141. Lewis, "Technique of Primary Epic," 23.

142. *Aeneid,* Book VI. 850-852.

143. Américo Castro, *The Spaniards: An Introduction to Their History,* trans. by Willard F. King and Selma Magaretten (Berkeley: University of California Press, 1971), 406-407.

144. *El Bernardo,* Book X, 253.
145. Francesco de Sanctis, *Teoria e storia della letteratura* (Bari: Laterza Gius, 1926.
146. *El Bernardo*, 142.
147. Ibid., 141.
148. Ibid., 142.
149. Ibid.
150. For this summary, no easy task, I have made use of summaries made both by van Horne and Balbuena's nineteenth-century editor, Quintana, simplifying the story line even more.
151. *El Bernardo*, 335.
152. Ibid., 313.
153. Ludovico Ariosto (1474 -1553) brilliant poet of the Italian Renaissance.
154. Mateo Maria Boiardo (1430 - 1494) Italian poet.
155. Luigi Pulci (1432 -1494) Italian poet.
156. Torquato Tasso (1544 -1595) Famous Italian epic poet.
157. According to Martín Zulaica López, this phrase, "an ekphrasis", could be found below the title of the poem [although it does not appear in any volume consulted by the editor]. See his "'Obra toda tejida de una admirable variedad de casas': la écfrasis en El Bernardo de Balbuena", *Hipogrifo*, vol. 4, no. 1 (2016): 174.
158. A distinction made by Marcelino Ménendez y Pelayo, in van Horne, *Bernardo de Balbuena*, 152.
159. Sidney, *An Apology for Poetry,* 111.
160. Ibid. 111, 113, 120, 116, 109.
161. The entire paragraph summarises Sydney's rather than Balbuena's arguments. Sidney says what Balbuena wants to say rather better.
162. *El Bernardo,* 142.
163. Ibid.
164. Bertolt Brecht, "Alienation Effects in Chinese Acting", in *Brecht on Theatre: The Development of an Aesthetic*, ed. and trans. by John Willet (New York: Hill and Wang, 1964), 91-99.
165. Herbert Marcuse, *One-Dimensional Man* (Boston: Beacon Press,1968), 63.
166. Miguel de Unamuno (1864-1936), *Del sentimiento trágico de la vida* (Madrid: Renacimiento, 1930), 312-313.
167. *El Bernardo,* 154.
168. Ibid., 335.
169. Ibid., 315.
170. Ibid., 335.
171. Ibid., 320
172. Lope de Vega Carpio, *Arcadia: prosas y versos con una exposición de los nombres historicos y poéticos* (1598) (Madrid: Gregorio Rodríguez, 1645).
173. Luis de Góngora y Argote (1561 - 1627). He mocks Lope de Vega in the sonnet beginning: "On your life, Little Lope rub out for me/ Those nineteen towers on your shield".
174. In the play *La Hermosora A borrecida*, (i.e.Beauty disdained). Lope de Vega, *La Hermosura Aborrecida* in *Obras de Lope de Vega: obra dramáticas,* v. 6 (Madrid: Tipographia de Archivos: Olózaga, 1928), 249-287.

175. Charles Martel, a Frank who defeated the Moors at Poitiers in 732 and prevented Christian Europe from being overrun by the superior strength and civilisation of the Mohammedans.
176. *El Bernardo*, 347.
177. *El Bernardo*, 295.
178. Ibid., 347, 341.
179. Herbert Marcuse, *Negations: Essays in Critical Theory*, trans. by Jeremy J. Shapiro (Boston: Beacon Press, 1968), 92.
180. Alejandro Tapia y Rivera, ed., *Bibloteca historico de Puerto-Rico que contiene varios documentos de los siglos XV, XVI, XVII y XVIII* (Puerto-Rico: Imprenta de Marquez, 1854), 463.
181. Balbuena, Letter to King, 14 July 1611, 867. There seems to be some confusion here. Earlier on in the letter he seems to say that a silver *real* is worth seven quartos.
182. van Horne, *Bernardo de Balbuena*, 81.
183. van Horne, ibid.
184. An *arroba* is a Spanish weight of about 25 lbs.
185. See Angel Franco, *El Tema de américa en los autores españoles del siglo de Oro* (Madrid: 1954), 34.
186. Letter to King, 14 July 1611, 871.
187. van Horne, *Bernardo de Balbuena*, 110.
188. Don Mateo de Medina Moreno was Abbot of Jamaica, 1622-1650.
189. Letter to King, 22 November 1623, in "Documentos del Archivo", 872.
190. van Horne, *Bernardo de Balbuena*, 112.
191. Before the Discovery of the New World and even after that, the Antipodes were held to be inaccessible. Even after the Spaniards had proved the torrid zones to be accessible to ships, old myths persisted that the torrid zones were uninhabitable. In Book XVI, the King of Persia (i.e. Understanding), asks whether it is true as wise men say that there are no Antipodes? Is it true he asks that of the five parts of the World, there are only two that are habitable – that the other three burn up with too much heat or are frozen with ice? That in the other parts of the world, people walk upside down, and that other areas are inhabited by pygmies, centaurs and dragons? The magician Malgesí takes them to the new World to prove that all this is not true. Although Balbuena takes for granted and used the Ptolemaic system, which saw the earth as the fixed centre of the Universe, in Book XVIII, the Tlaxcalan magician brings in the Copernican system in this verse:

> Men suspect that that light (i.e. the sun's)
> Which is of all lights the most bright
> Is not as the world now judges, on the height
> But is instead at the fixed centre of the sphere
> And all the immense multitude of golden stars
> Revolves, with entire revolution around it
> And the earth also which appears to stand still
> Itself revolves around the sun. *El Bernardo*, 334

192. There had been a truce between Spain and the Dutch after 1609 when the independence the United Provinces was recognised. In 1621 hostilities broke

out again. This privateer force of Boudewijn Hendricksz was therefore also part of the official Dutch forces. In the letter which Hendricksz sent to the Governor Juan de Haro, calling him to surrender, he refers to himself as, " ...I Bowdoin Hendrick, general of the forces, in the name of the States General and his Highness the Prince of Orange..." See R.A. van Middeldyk, *The History of Puerto Rico: From the Spanish Occupation to the American Occupation* (New York: D. Appleton, 1903), 126.

193. van Horne, *Bernardo de Balbuena,* 106

194. On the 21st of October, Hendrick sent a letter declaring his intention to burn the city, if the defenders would not come to terms. Juan de Haro replied that the island had enough building material to build another city, and that he only wished that the whole army of Holland were there to watch Spanish valour and bravery. The day after, some 100 houses were burnt by the Dutch. The city's archives as well as Balbuena's palace and library were burnt. Middeldyk, *The History of Puerto Rico*, 127.

195. The Captain lead many a sortie and night attack before the burning of the city. After the burning of the city, Amézqueta, together with another Captain, Botello and some 200 men, attacked the enemy front and rear. So furious was their charge that they drove the Dutch from their trenches, and pursued them into the water as they tried to reach their launches. This kind of exploit discouraged the beseigers who withdrew on the 2nd of November, leaving 400 dead and one of their larger ships stranded. Balbuena's letter of praise had its effect. Captain Amézqueta and Captain Botello received 1,000 ducats as a reward. Amezquita was later appointed Governor of Cuba. Ibid., 127-128.

196. Lope Felix de Vega Carpio, *Laurel de Apolo* (1630; Londres: Leclere y Campañia, 1824), 31-32.

197. This was the same Governor who had so successfully defended Puerto Rico from the Dutch attack. For his valour he had received a grant of 2,000 ducats; and been made a Chevalier of the Order of Santiago, a chivalric military Christian Order. But the reckless bravery and courage were the comitant of the lust for quick money, and quick reward as compensation for the hazards of a frontier life.

198. *El Bernardo,* 155.

199. To make the line of the verse more sonorous and rich, Balbuena tried to use as many words as possible, words whose sounds could run together, so that in a line with 14 words, and 18 syllables, with the sounds telescoped into each other (*synalepha*) the line still remained 11 syllabled: "Que es bien, que es mal, que es fin,que es vida y muerte". Ibid., 142.

JONKONNU IN JAMAICA:
TOWARDS THE INTERPRETATION OF
FOLK DANCE AS A CULTURAL PROCESS

We have for a long time cherished the desire to bring to the eyes of the Haitian people the value of their folklore. By a disconcerting paradox, these people who had... the most moving history in the world... that of the transplantation of a human race unto a stranger soil, in the worst possible biological conditions, now display a badly concealed embarrassment, even shame, to hear speak of their distant past.[1]

Jean Price Mars on Haiti writing in 1928

To touch on any aspect of folklore in Caribbean societies is to touch on a complex subject; and one that has been, until now, relatively little researched. The English-speaking Caribbean, even more than the other islands, has ignored to a large extent the need for any such study. It is part of the complexity of the subject that the tacit avoidance of serious investigations itself posits certain fundamental assumptions with regard to folklore – assumptions which are themselves part and parcel of the tragic ambivalence of our societies. The very act of considering Jamaican folklore to be in need of specialist research in related fields, is itself an approach both to the awareness of, and possible resolution of this ambivalence.

The magnitude and importance of our theme forces us to delimit the areas to be examined in this article. We propose to:

a) Offer a thesis with regards to, and attempt an interpretation of, the Jonkonnu folkdance as *agent* and *product* of a cultural process which we shall identify and explore as a process of *indigenisation*.

b) Tabulate the survivals of folkdance in Jamaica, briefly relating them to the cultural process.

But before we examine these areas, we propose by way of introduction to place our subject in a general context of cultural change.

Professor G.R. Coulthard, in several books and articles, has explored the cultural movements known as *Négritude* and *Indigenismo*. In his book *Race and Colour in Caribbean Literature* (1958) he identifies Price Mars, the Haitian ethnologist, as the source and fount of the movement which would be known as *negritude*. He writes:

In 1927, there appeared a book which was to leave a profound and lasting imprint on Haitian culture... I refer to "Ainsi Parla l'Oncle" of Jean Price Mars. Price Mars's purpose in this book was to rehabilitate and revalue the African elements of Haitian life. To this end he first analyses the civilisations of Africa, correcting the idea that the Africans were savages, and afterwards explored popular beliefs, folk-dances, folk tales and Haitian superstitions – all of African origin.[2]

The book was a cultural breakthrough of great significance. For the first time young Haitian writers tore their eyes from France and, in looking at their own folklore, saw with surprise the roots of their being. It was in examining their Haitian roots that they crossed time and space, breaking through the curtain of silence and shame behind which their African heritage had been concealed. The most fiery prophet of the new movement – *Négritude* – Aimé Césaire of Martinique, in his famous *Discourse on Colonialism,* related the degradation and destruction of cultures to the European process of colonisation. Africans, of French Africa, led by the Senegalese writer-politician, Léopold Sédar Senghor, saw, too, that the same process of destruction through contempt had taken place on that continent. As Césaire was to put it, the Europeans had used culture and the idea of culture as part of the technique which they employed to exploit the non-Europeans of the world. "The idea of the savage black", Césaire said, "is a European idea".[3]

What Césaire was in the intellectual and cultural field, Marcus Garvey of Jamaica was in the political-agitational field. His great organisation based in the United States and his massive plans for a physical return to Africa comprised the corollary of the spiritual and intellectual return of the *Négritude* movement. While his movement failed, it had shaken up the fantasy and stirred the imagination of millions of black folk in the United States and the Caribbean. His movement awakened an awareness of Africa, a revaluation of Africa, and a sense of pride in the past, whose myth had been used to keep black people in servitude and self-contempt. This started the process which has led in a direct line to the present Black Power movement. But *Négritude* was a movement of artists and intellectuals. It has survived in the present Black Power movement in those aspects which lay stress on Black Studies; the need for a revaluation and renaissance of black culture.

It is this aspect that ties up with the paradox that lies at the heart of Price Mars's thesis – the paradox that concerns us most nearly. For Price Mars's thesis implies that the study of the African heritage in Haiti does not make a Haitian an African, but paradoxically returns him to his Haitian roots. And he singles out with amazement a cultural process which has been taken for granted, or largely ignored. How can Haitians, he asked, not glory in such a history, a unique history, "the transplantation of a human race unto a stranger soil, in the worst possible biological conditions"?[4] That this transplantation had taken root and grown was the clearest testimony to the strength and creativity of African cultures. Yet it was this very creativity and strength on which young Haitians, in fief to the values of the Western world, turned their backs.

After Haiti's successful war of Independence against the French, she was faced with the problem of founding a new state based on free labour, of creating a new nation. The easiest way out was to copy the model of her former masters. She succeeded.

Haitians became magnificent coloured Frenchmen, says Price Mars, but by an implacable logic "to the same degree we unlearnt how to be Haitians, that is to say, how to be men born in determined historical conditions, having garnered in their souls, a complex psychology, which gives to the Haitian community its specific physiognomy." In unlearning how to be Haitians, Haitians came to regard themselves with European eyes. And, in these eyes, according to Price Mars, "the Negroes were the refuse of humanity, without history, without morals, without religion... in whom it was necessary to infuse... new moral values, a new human investiture." With this premise, the conclusion was inevitable: "From then on," says Price Mars, "all that is authentically indigenous – language, customs, feelings, beliefs, became suspect stained with bad taste in the eyes of the elite..."[5]

The official culture of free and independent Haiti excluded, with contempt, Haitian folklore. To revalue Haitian folklore was to strike at the heart of the official and elite ideology. Price Mars was aware of the danger. The reader, he said, would see clearly how dangerous it was to discuss Haitian folklore with a Haitian audience; nor was he sanguine that a creative and thorough revaluation would ever take place. He saw his book as a beginning, rather than a solution. And he argued that the study of Haitian folklore had its importance for mankind as a whole. The Haitians are a handful of people, he says, "but our presence on a spot of that American archipelago which we have 'humanised', the breach which we made in the process of historical events to snatch our place among men" was worthy of study, in order that it could be situated "within the common life of man on the planet".[6] Folklore was the record, the living testimony of the roots that the Haitian people had put down in a "stranger soil" which, by reason of these roots, was now theirs.

Price Mars's book "opened the flood gates of the Africanisation of Haitian art", as Professor Coulthard puts it.[7] Which was, far more fundamentally, the Haitianisation of Haitian art. The Haitian version of African religions – voodoo, was revalued by writers like Lorimer Denis and François Duvalier, Christianity with its sole claim to revelation, was attacked. But, because of the peculiar conditions of Caribbean history, a cultural revaluation trapped by past racial definitions of Europe, now itself became trapped in racial – and ultimately *reactionary* – categories of thought and language, and entered a blind alley. The cultural revolution bogged down.

The cultural problem of folklore, and its revaluation, extends far wider than the Caribbean. "The words 'négritude' and 'indigenismo'... do not lend themselves to an easy one-word translation into English. They are, in fact convenient labels used to summarise complex racial, cultural phenomena which have emerged from non-English speaking societies."[8]

Both movements spring from "colonialisation and the assumption of racial and cultural superiority of the colonisers". The main function of both, Coulthard suggests, is the "loosening of the stranglehold of European or 'Western' (and this includes the United States) culture, weakening the prestige of European civilisation with its claims to exclusive cultural tutelage, and the affirmation of a new and distinctive cultural perspective based on native and often racial foundations."[9]

Coulthard traces the conquest by Spain of the main indigenous Amerindian civilisations of the American continent. He examines the imposition of the Roman Catholic religion, and the total condemnation of all other 'native religions' as works of the Devil. And he quotes an early Spanish theorist – Ginés de Sepúlveda – who argued that the Spaniards had a right to enslave the Indians because the latter were culturally inferior. The quotation from Sepúlveda is paradigmatic of the whole complex line of justification which the followers of Christ would use in order to deny his teachings. Above all, for our purposes, it illustrates the use of "culture" as a weapon of domination; and defines the posture of European civilisation in relation to all oral cultures. Above all it foreshadows that total dismissal of folklore as "culture"; a dismissal which is still widespread, and which indeed is part of the ambivalence of Jamaicans towards their folklore. The assumptions of Sepúlveda are still widely acceptable.

"Now compare," Sepúlveda writes, "those gifts of prudence, sharpness of wit, magnanimity, temperance, humanity and religion (of the Spaniards) with those of those little men ('homunculi') in whom you will hardly find a trace of humanity. They have no culture, no system of writing (nor do they) preserve monuments of their history; they have the vaguest obscure memory of facts recorded in certain pictures, they lack written laws and have barbarous institutions and customs."[10]

Culture and humanity resided in writing. Without writing there was a void. The oral culture of the indigenous civilisations was "barbarous" i.e. Non-European. By a process of repetition "humanity" came to be synonymous with Europeans, and European culture.

The Spaniards did to the Amerindians in their own continent, what many European nations did to the Africans in theirs. In both countries then, an approach to independence was at once linked with the revaluation of their indigenous cultures. Senghor, ardent exponent of Négritude, which began in the Caribbean, was at the same time part of the indigenist movement of Africa. Both peoples had been alienated from their cultures, their roots and their being in their own lands. Both movements, in Latin America and in Africa, would begin with a rehabilitation of ancient Amerindian and African cultures.

Caribbean men and the American Negro represented a more complex phenomenon. Alienated from Africa, their movement of Négritude was a spiritual return to Africa, a gathering together of all the peoples of the black diaspora whether alienated in space, time or degree. This is the movement which Césaire spearheaded; and in which he was joined by Senghor and many others. But Price Mars represented more clearly, with his study of folklore, a Négritude which was indigenist. For the more total alienation of the New World Negro had occasioned a cultural response, which had transformed that New World Negro into the indigenous inhabitant of his new land. His cultural resistance to colonialism in this new land was an *indigenous* resistance. The history of the Caribbean islands is, in large part, the history of the *indigenisation* of the black man. And this history is a cultural history – not in "writing", but of, those "*homunculi*" who humanise the landscape by peopling it with gods and spirits, with demons and duppies, with all the rich panoply of man's imagination.

Folksongs tell the human story in a way which the historian never learns.[11]

But then even history has been partly trapped in the conflict between the official culture of the Caribbean, and the unofficial and excluded culture. To a large extent, history has dealt with the official culture in official categories of thought. History has mainly been about the European superstructure of civilisation. Yet, in the interstices of history, we see, in glimpses, evidences of a powerful and pervasive cultural process which has largely determined the unconscious springs of our beings; a process which we shall identify and explore as the process of *indigenisation*, a process whose agent and product was Jamaican folklore, folksong, folk-tales, folk-dance.

II

Ohonam mu nni nhanoa
The spirit of Man is without boundaries.

Akan/African proverb

First of all get a house and a woman and an oxe for the plough.

Hesiod, *Works and Days*[12]

When a planter hath purchased some 20, 30 or more Negro slaves, he first gives to each man a wife without which they will not be content or work. Then he gives to each man and his wife an half acre of land for them to plant for themselves... maize, potatoes, yam etc.; which land they cleare (in their Leisure hours) and build them a wigwam on it, and then plant it as fast as they can...

John Taylor, Writing from Port Royal, Jamaica in 1685[13]

From John Taylor's seventeenth-century description of the slave pattern in Jamaica, it is clear that the process of adaptation from one peasant society in Africa to another, part similar, part different, was already established. To persuade the African to fulfil his purpose of growing cane and making sugar, the planter was being forced to make certain vital concessions to the former cultural pattern of the latter. True, the observant Taylor goes on to point out that the Planter was dominated by an economic motive.

The development of this pattern, where the slave became part-slave in relation to the European plantation, and part-peasant in relation to the plot of land on which he fed himself and his family, was, in Jamaica, the crucial factors in the indigenisation process.

If we examine the circumstances of this process we shall understand something of the complexity and contradiction that still remain at its heart. What Elder calls the *"Negro struggle to sing and dance"*[14] was central to this process of adaptation. Why was this so?

III

The indigenous race is a race of agriculturalists
                                                    Mariategui[15]

But what is Culture? In effect it is the result of a double effort of the integration of Man with Nature and Nature with Man.
                                        Leopold Sédar Senghor[16]

Senghor, in his *Essay on the Problem of Culture*, argues that Man adapts himself to his physical milieu, and this milieu helps to inform not only his social and economic structures, but even his art and philosophy, but, by an inverse movement, Man also transforms Nature by adapting it to his own exigencies. It is this double, dual relation that lies – or rather *lay* – at the heart of the creation of all cultures, until the unique Western experience. For, Senghor seems to imply, the great expansion of Western civilisation, "an economic and instrumental civilisation, could make us believe that one part of the process, the transformation of Nature by Man is the very essence of Culture."[17]

We propose that this break in thought, attitude and relation, by which a dual and oscillatory process was replaced by the single-minded conquest of Nature by Western Man, began with the discovery of the New World. Or, if it did not begin, a quantitative change brought a qualitative change in emphasis. For it is with the discovery of the New World and its vast exploitable lands that the process which has been termed the reduction of Man to Labour and of Nature to Land under the impulsion of the market economy[18] really had its large-scale beginning. For the European, alien to the New World, Nature became land; and land, if it were to be exploited, needed not *men* essentially, but so many units of labour power.

Slavery was not new. What was new was a relation. In the ancient world, the Mediterranean, Asia, Africa, America itself, slavery was a long established fact. But there, "Even when defined as chattels and cruelly treated, slaves were looked upon as a normal class within the body politic".[19] They were part of the social order. And the social order took precedence over all else, including the economic motive. In America, and even more especially in British America, the economic motive became the impulse of the society.

This new economics, which reached its peak with the Industrial Revolution, was created on the blank palimpsest of the New World, especially on the islands of the English Caribbean. The societies created in Jamaica by the planters and merchants were societies created only as "an adjunct to the market". The relation of the planters and merchants to Nature in the Caribbean was a relation only of dominance. It was not white man, black man, or Indian man, but labour that mattered. Taylor tells us of the brutal treatment meted out by planters in seventeenth-century Jamaica to white indentured servants. Every ounce of labour was dragged out of them. Since they would be free after four years, they were cared for worse, and fed worse than the Negro slaves. They were deprived of all customs that could have social significance, of traditions that had given them significance as men.

If the European presence in the New World represented the techniques of civilisation by which Nature is utilised; by which Nature, becomes "an instrument of the will to power", by which man enters into a relation of land-labour-capital, the African presence represented a paradox and contradiction. For in the scheme of the European relation he represented both labour and capital. His labour would make the European civilisation a reality. In the three things which Hesiod points out as necessary to the peasant – a house, a woman and an oxe for the plough, we see that, as Taylor told us, the house, the plot and the woman were provided. In this sense the African slave was peasant. His relation with Nature would remain that of peasant from time immemorial.

It would be the double relation in which he adapted himself to Nature and transformed Nature. Out of this relation, in which the land was always the *Earth,* the centre of a core of beliefs and attitudes, would come the central pattern which held together the social order. In this aspect of the relation, the African slave represented an opposing process to that of the European, who achieved great technical progress based on the primary accumulation of capital which came from the dehumanisation of Man and Nature. In general, he remained a transient, a frequent absentee, his society without roots in the new soil. The African presence, on the other hand, *rehumanised Nature,* and helped to save his own humanity against the constant onslaught of the plantation system by the creation of a folklore and folk-culture. On the other hand, he himself served as the *ox* for the *plough* of the plantation system which brought about the technical conquest of Nature. He was, therefore, involved in a dual role, ambivalent between two contradictory processes.

The history of folk-culture in Jamaica is the history of this ambivalent relation. Folklore represents the attempt to prolong and recreate a system in which the community and the society and the social order is primary; folklore is not only the relation of Man to Nature but of Man to himself. Folklore was the cultural guerilla resistance against the Market economy.

The folklore of the Jamaican sprang out of the slave's attempts to grapple with a new Nature, in a new and complex relation "on a stranger soil... under the worst possible biological conditions". What he retained from his African experience, and what he transformed, and what he recreated, was determined by this attempt and struggle.

Africans came with the earliest Spanish settlers of the island. As in the other islands, they became hunters, worked for the Spaniards, yet also planting their plots and keeping their stock, following the old African pattern of life, as one Spanish Abbot of the island lamented, without the Christian sacrament of marriage – "bringing up their children and their chickens as if they were man and wife".[20] But whilst some Africans, coming, as Herskovits has pointed out, "from a social order (in Africa) whose economy was sufficiently complex to permit him to meet the disciplinary demands of the plantation system without any great violation of earlier habit patterns",[21] that is, from relatively complex agricultural societies, adapted to the transplanted pattern, others, and especially the Kromanti – i.e. the Ashanti, Fanti – many coming from a highly specialised military caste, began that pattern of guerilla warfare, of resistance, which is part of the dual pattern of adaptation/resistance, central to our history.

The escape into the mountainous interior of the island by those slaves – especially the Kromanti – who were to become famous as the Maroons, began early under the Spaniards. Indians, too, ran away to avoid forced labour, and there, in the mountainous interior as the two peoples mingled in a common resistance, it is more than possible that the process that Herskovits defines as *acculturation* took place i.e. where two peoples of different cultures find culture contact points at which fusion and transformation of the one by the other is achieved.

But increasingly as the Arawak Indians died out, the Maroons humanised their mountainous interior with adaptations of their own culture. It is difficult then to speak of *acculturation* since it was largely the response of one culture to new conditions. The use of the word by some Western anthropologists has given a secondary meaning to the term which we must discard in the early stages of the Jamaican cultural process. As Redfield points out, to many of these scholars the term acculturation was seen as a label for "the modifications of the indigenous life under influences from the white man's world."[22]

And whilst in the later stages such a term can be used, it is our contention that the early stages of the process involved the rooting of the African in the New World; and therefore the process of *indigenisation*.

The English attack and capture of the island in 1655, and the joint Spanish-African resistance over several years, solidified the Maroon reality as the indigenous people, now waging a war against the English invaders. And from details of English clashes with the Maroons, we see that the latter were organised in settlements which were almost exact replicas of the pattern of their lives in Africa. The land was tilled, crops cultivated, religious feasts celebrated with song and dance. There, they retained African customs,

246 WE MUST LEARN TO SIT DOWN TOGETHER AND TALK ABOUT A LITTLE CULTURE

folklore; later, their settlements served as a place of escape for slaves from the plantations. Linking them together, across space and distance, was the drum from Africa, and the abeng or horn, both of which were the media of communication. The Drum, central to African religion and belief, became a focal point of physical and cultural resistance. Already in the seventeenth century Sloane tells us of

> Drums made of a piece of hollow tree covered on one end with any green skin and stretched with Thols and Pinns – an instrument forbidden on the Plantation because used for war in Africa...[23]

The meaning of the drum was tied up with song and dance; with African religion and African philosophy and an African world view:

> All art is born from religion... And... without a previous and clear idea of the consubstantially religious and magical character which verse, song, music and dance has... among Negro-Africans, their art cannot be understood, neither in its multiple manifestations, nor in its instruments, nor in its history.[24]

IV

> The *Indians* and *Negroes* have no manner of religion by which I could observe of them. It is true that they have several ceremonies, as dances, playing etc., but these for the most part are so far from being acts of adoration of a God, that they are for the most part mixed with a great deal of Bawdry and Lewdness...
>
> Sir Hans Sloane[25]

The Europeans used writing. Their observations of the religious practices of the slaves are the only written records that we have. The slaves passed on their religion through the cultural media of communication which they brought with them from Africa – through the complex drum script, which was the African equivalent of the alphabetical script. The alphabet preserves information longer; the drum spreads it more quickly and across physical space. The proscription of the drum came about when it was realised that the drum rhythms were part of the unifying force of revolts.

The dance is a central cultural medium of the African religious pattern. It was this pattern that Sloane saw. But to observe the dance and the customs through the eyes of Sloane, who denies the Africans any religion at all, is to begin with one of the causes of the paradox and conflict which we shall explore. Here we see the clash that always takes place between monotheists and polytheists. The African religion has what has been called a "monotheistic superstructure", that is to say, a basic belief in one Absolute Creator who is over all. Yet under him are many lesser gods. Because of this the Africans were prepared to accept Christianity, and the concept of the Trinity – seeing its three heads as new and leviathan gods with a powerful place in their world view. The

Christian missionaries, like all monotheists who conceive God as a jealous God, saw the African world view as a dangerous and pagan heresy. Whilst the African religious view could accept Christianity, Christianity rejected the beliefs of Africa. Subtly, a Manichean accommodation would evolve through contact; to the Christian world view the African Gods would become identified with the Devil.

This confrontation and accommodation has endured up until today.

V

Their songs when they dance on feast days are all bawdy, or tending that way...

Sir Hans Sloane[26]

They have Saturdays in the afternoons and Sundays, with Christmas holidays, Easter called little, or Pickanniny, Christmas, and some other great feasts allowed them for the culture of their own plantations to feed themselves from potatoes, yams and plantains etc. which they plant on ground allowed them by their masters...

Sir Hans Sloane[27]

These negroes have a great veneration for the Earth...

John Taylor[28]

The earliest descriptions of folk dances are related to religion, and the feasts and festivals connected with this religion. The pattern of duality between the plantation and plot, is seen in the fact that holidays are conditioned by the seasonal demands of the sugar crop; so the slaves transfer African festivals and African meanings to Christmas and Easter and crop-over. But side by side with this process of adaptation was one of continuity. Feasts related to the culture of their own grounds were also celebrated. They lend themselves to myth and legend. It is the provision ground on which the cultural pattern was established. The plantation was the property of the master: mere land; as the slave was the property of the master: mere labour. The relation of the slave to the provision ground was a relation of a man to the Earth. While the plantation ideology, the official ideology, would develop as an ideology of *property*, and the rights of property, the provision ground ideology would remain based on a man's relation to the *Earth*, which linked a man to his community. The first would give rise to the superstructure of civilisation in the Caribbean; the second to the roots of culture.

The dance was an expression of, and a strengthening of Man's relation with the Earth. John Taylor tells us of a series of slave revolts in the last part of the seventeenth century and points out that the binding oath among the conspirators was affirmed by their kissing the Earth. This came from their "great Veneration for the Earth".

It has been widely recognised that although slaves came from many parts of Africa to the New World, the majority came from the areas of West Africa with interrelationships of cultural attitudes. The concept of the Earth was general. To the African the Earth is not property or land. The Earth is the base of the community, and is concerned with the common good. Cultivation plots of individuals are but parcels of land cut from the limitless earth. The technical power of the Earth is universal and all men show this in the ritual observances by which they show their respect. The dance plays a central part in these ritual observances. The aim of all ritual measures is to preserve the benevolence of the Earth to the community. The forces of the Earth are part of the vital universal force, the concept of which is central to African philosophy.

Man receives life from the Earth, in the crops which he reaps. The feasts and festivals acknowledge and strengthen the tie between the life of Man and that of the Earth. The elaborate funeral ceremonies which the African transplanted to the New World are also part of this relation. Taylor and Sloane describe the funeral ceremonies about the grave. The significance of these ceremonies cannot be overestimated both in the African and the Jamaican cultural patterns:

> This is not only because the dead are laid to rest inside the earth, but also because interring the dead is an act of crucial social and personal importance, charged with ritual meanings of great intensity. It is one of the points at which Man's life and the mystical powers of the Earth come into contact in a way that is fraught with the deepest affective and social meaning for the individual and wide consequences for the organisation of the society. Thereafter one who was human becomes a spirit...[29]

As a spirit, he does not cease to play his part in the life of the others. The relation of Man to his ancestral spirits is a historical and an actual living relation. The ancestral spirits are numerous and extended aspects of the life force. Dance in the Caribbean will focus on two main aspects:

a) the strengthening of the forces of the Earth, the fertility of Earth and Man.

b) the reaffirming of the ties with the ancestral spirits and the community, and the Earth, through possession in the dance.

It is these aspects that will be emphasised. The 'bawdry' and 'lewd' quality that Sloane noted, was related to the fertility concepts – to the religious veneration of the Earth. The circumstances of the transplantation to the New World cause these 'bawdy' rites to take on a central significance of resistance and response.

VI

The dancer is possessed when he depicts an event, and he is possessed when he disguises himself... Among the ancient Germans the ecstasy began at the moment when the dancer put on an animal skin. The skin was sufficient to blot out the self and to admit the animal spirit. This ecstasy of mummery accompanies religious life through all the stages of its development to the belief in gods. Osiris, Dionysius, Siva and the deities of old Mexico – God has descended upon the earth and becomes flesh in his dancer. And out of the deified dancer is formed retrogressively the beautiful conception of the dancing god who creates the world and keeps it in sacred order.[30]

The Jonkonnu or John Canoe festival had its beginning in a cultural process that Sloane witnessed and described in the seventeenth century. Today the Jonkonnu is still celebrated in the country parts of Jamaica. The celebrations steadily decrease in effectiveness and meaning, but attempts are being made to revive the dance through the National Festival. Also, the externals of Jonkonnu have been utilised by formal dance groups. The Jonkonnu is, therefore, useful as a central focus towards an interpretation of the origins and meaning of Jamaican folkdance.

Sloane writes:

They have likewise in their dances Rattles ty'd to their legs and wrists and in their hands with which they make a noise, keeping time with one who makes a sound answering it on the mouth of an empty Gourd or Jar with his Hand. Their dances consist in great activity and strength of Body and keeping time, if it can be. They very often tie Cows Tails to their Rumps and add such others to their bodies in several places as gives them a very extraordinary appearance.[31]

Already in this description the basic elements of what is to become the Jonkonnu festival are apparent. The array of musical instruments, in particular the use of rattles, and the emphasis on rhythm and percussion; the acrobatic quality of the dances and "the Cows Tails on their Rumps".

Orlando Patterson, in his *Sociology of Slavery,* has pointed out the close connection of the Jonkonnu festival with the Yam Festivals of Africa. The Yam Festival was an important festival of the Ashanti, who came to Jamaica in great numbers. These *"feasts",* as Sloane refers to them, were continued in relation to the provision grounds of the slaves. 'Monk' Lewis, writing in the early nineteenth century, mentioned the general harvest of yams each year by the slaves, and Patterson quotes sources who in 1824 referred to September as "the time of yams". Patterson also traces the Jonkonnu back to culture areas of West Africa, and in particular to the institution of the secret society, whose functions was to take "a central part in the seasonal festivals and recreations of the tribe, to which they belong".[32] The rites for the yam harvest, which usually took place between September and October, involved the invoking of the gods and the ancestral spirits, all of whom were connected with the strengthening of the life force.

Patterson suggests three clusters of origins for the Jonkonnu:

> These were: the yam festival activities of the Mmo secret societies of the Ibo peoples; the recreational activities of the Egungun secret society of the Yorubas; and the Homowa harvest festival of the Ga peoples.[33]

All three have to do with the impersonation of ancestral spirits by masked dancers at festivals, usually connected with agricultural activities. The primary annual festival of the Egungun of the Yoruba is "a masquerade performed by male members of the Egungun cult in order to make visible the ancestral spirits and to command their power."[34]

The Homowo festival of the Ga links elaborate yam feasts with "drinking and dancing in lament and remembrance of the dead".[35] The focal point is the relation to the earth. The dead, although not living human beings, although lessened life forces, still retain "their *higher*, strengthening, fathering life force".[36] The dead are not the negation of life, but part of the life force. The festival which celebrates the earth and its fertility – the harvest festival – is, therefore, intimately linked to the evocation of the ancestral spirits; and of the gods or forces of Nature. The folkdance of the living is made more alive by the presence of the spirit of the dead.

Here we come to the central importance of the masks in the Jonkonnu procession; of the "Cows tails tied on their Rumps" as Sloane saw it. It must be clear that the mask here, as in Africa, is not just the face and headdress, but the entire costume. And the mask itself in African religious thought is of incalculable significance. As Franco Monti explains:

> The mask is the medium. It is the link between the supernatural and the human; it speaks a complex and symbolic language which can only be interpreted by the initiates who are in a position to translate the messages which it emits into humanly comprehensible terms...

But above all:

> The mask is almost always closely connected with the fundamental element of African life, the dance – so much so that it seems difficult to talk about them both as separate entities. Rhythm, according to many African myths, existed at the beginning of time and was often thought to have been the absolute Creator of the worlds and their inhabitants...[37]

Rhythm is the universal life force. On donning the mask the dancer enters into this force, the god possesses him, and in a modern Jamaican cult term informed with the same meaning, the dancer *delivers* himself by patterning the steps of the god, or ancestral spirit.

Rhythm is part of the dance, and the dance is a part of rhythm. The theme is set by the drum controlled by the sacred rattle which determines the different beats. The music and dances Sloane saw and describes, the rattles, the percussion, was 'creating', therefore, what Monti terms "the very essence of the universe, the hidden fluid that runs through all beings – human, animal and vegetable – the magical point of contact of participation of men with nature".[38]

What kind of mask does the "Cow tail on the Rump" represent? It is only when we ask this, that we can ask – What kind of dance?

As Patterson points out, Jonkonnu dances initially played their central role in the yam festivals in Jamaica. Yams were connected with the provision grounds. Even today a variety of yam called *afu yam* traces its etymology to Twi *Afuw* – a plantation cultivation ground. The mask that Sloane saw was an animal mask; and the dance designed to increase the fertility of the earth and to pay ritual respect, was the seventeenth century version of today's Jonkonnu.

Cassidy and Le Page, in their *Dictionary of Jamaican English,* give a definition of Jonkonnu as:

> The festival or celebration centring about John Canoe. Originally that was African, but elements of the English [M]orris dances and especially of the French carnival 'sets'... were absorbed into it, and certain stock characters from all these sources became established...[39]

Long is the first to mention the term *Jonkonnu.* As Cassidy and Le Page point out, the pronunciation and spelling of the name is varied. They suggest a possible derivation:

> By folk-etym from some such form as Ewe *dzono* sorcerer and *kúnu* i.e. something deadly, a cause of death.[40]

The quality of fear which was always attached to this original Jonkonnu points to the basic significance of the masked dancer who "lends" himself to the spirit who dances through him. Beckwith, in her investigations into Jamaican folk life, speaks of the survival of the Jonkonnu mummings in remote districts of Jamaica in the 1920s. She commented:

> The ox-head has been forbidden because of the fear it inspired...[41]

A Jamaican informant speaking of what Jonkonnu meant to him as a child, shows how in the later Afro-Christian cultural pattern the "spirits" of the African ancestral cult became the "devils" of Afro-Christian Jamaica. Among the participants of the Jonkonnu includes:

> Satanic hosts, some with tusks, some with the heads of donkeys and horses but with the feet of men.[42]

An Ashanti charm, *suman*, which is described by Rattray is cited by Simpson for the interesting parallelisms to be found with Jamaican folk religion. We see here many implications for the fear inspired by the oxhead mask. The charm was a priest's headgear, with a foundation of 'woven grass' matting:

At the back and the front were ram's horns. At the front and between the horns was a wooden *afona* (sword) at the back a *sepow* (knife). On the outside of the horns, on each side were small knives representing the instruments used by executioners to cut off heads... The horn means, 'I shall butt you', the knives, 'I shall cut off your head'.[43]

But if the oxhead inspired terror, horsehead, another Jonkonnu character, inspired only contempt in twentieth-century Jamaica.

Cassidy quotes a *Gleaner* "Letter to the Editor" in 1951 which refers to Jonkonnu as commonly called "horse-head"; and objects to reviving the festival because the dances were "demoralising and... vulgar". The police had managed to succeed in suppressing it in his district, "and many people were taken to court for it".[44]

The horsehead, so strenuously objected to, represents the earliest *acculturation* between the original African Jonkonnu described by Sloane and elements from English Morris dancing. Since the English Morris dance celebrated a pagan rite, its culture contact points with the African Jonkonnu were numerous; the English Morris dance elements, therefore, entered both the *religious* aspects of the Jonkonnu; and its parallel *secularisation* process which developed in the nineteenth century, as we shall see. How did this acculturation come about?

In the eighty or ninety years after Sloane wrote, and by the time of Long's description, the plantation system had established itself is Jamaica. The rise of sugar on the world market made Jamaica a sugar society. Each estate was an enclosed world and although the refusal of the Jamaican planters to Christianise their slaves (for economic motives) prevented the later acculturation that would take place, there were points of contact between the English, Scotch and Irish indentured servants, and particularly the bookkeeper class. It was through this class, poor, cut off from much contact with their fellow-whites, living in concubinage with African, creole, and mulatto women, that some sort of cultural fusion must have occurred.

The Morris dance is part of the Spring festival, where young men dance for the renewal and continuance of life. It is, in effect, "medicine dance" handed down through the European counterpart of the secret societies "which practised the medicine-religions that conditioned life in Europe before Christendom".[45] Among its customs was a hunt, the flesh of the prey being eaten, or a lamb which, after leading the procession all day, was killed and eaten by the dancers. Each Morris group had a leader. There were several characters who made up the group. The hobbyhorse, which became the Jamaican horsehead was only one of several animal men. In some groups the horse is the central character or Mask. In others, the fools wearing animal masks divert and distract while the dancers carry on their vital task of "distilling the medicine and spilling it out over the people and places they visit". The dance distils the medicine "in rhythmic waves which reach the trees and animals and houses and people, quickening to life, washing them clean and making them whole". Another type of Morris dance; the horn dance, was a fertility medicine dance.

Apart from the Spring rites, there were midwinter rites. It is in these rites that we find the "Sword dance-cum-Play" which was to become one aspect of the Jonkonnu. Like the Morris Dancers the swordsmen are seen as actors who once disguised themselves, blacking their faces or covering them with masks. They, too, had the same retinue of characters: hobbyhorse, clown, the woman, a Dirty Bet, of sometimes a king or queen, lord or lady and often a quack doctor, and his man Jack. There were other characters with smaller roles.[46]

The Egungun secret society of the Yoruba is a cult dedicated to numerous spirits, designed to foster sentiments of reverence for the ancestors. An Egungun, which is, in effect, a Jonkonnu as mask, dancer and leader of the group, is seen as the embodiment of the spirit of a deceased ancestor who returns from heaven to visit his people. This spirit is called *Ara-Orun* i.e. a citizen of heaven. The Mask, i.e. the costume, must entirely cover the dancer. He carries a whip and speaks in a ventriloquial voice. A Jamaican description of Jonkonnu in Westmoreland (1925) says:

> There is no talking at all – not a word of dialogue. If they have to speak at all reach other they whisper and disguise their voices.[47]

From Long's description the sword is in his hand, rather than the whip, and the fact that the dancer bellows out as he dances "John Connu" may suggest the influence of the English Sword-dance-cum-Play. The sword is also important in Ashanti rituals, however. The numerous crowd of drunken women who follow him and refresh him with aniseed water finds a replica in the band of women who escorts the chief masquerader Egungun-Oya. Oya, the river goddess, is here supposed to assume the form of man and so the women are her escort, Could the aniseed water be an offering to the river goddess?

Different guilds have different Egunguns. The word *Egungun* itself means "masquerader"; in the Jonkonnu celebration described in 1925 the group referred to themselves as "masqueraders", rather than Jonkonnu.

During the Egungun festival in June, a festival, which could be termed the Yoruba, "All Souls", is held. It is a mourning for the dead and yet a joyful festival. Large numbers of Egunguns appear and the whole town is in fete. There are processions and plays. Each Egungun guild puts on its own play. (The term "play" in Africa referred to singing and dancing as well as to the pantomime and "drama", and also to all those included. It came to have the same meaning in Jamaica, as we shall see)

There could be much rivalry, even fighting, between the different Egungun groups. This feature was continued in the rivalry between the different Jonkonnus. Long writes:

In 1769 several new masks appeared: the Ebos, the Papaw having their respective Connus, male and female who were dressed in very laughable style.[48]

The guilds of Africa now became the tribal groups in Jamaica. Later on they came to represent crafts and trades. The common features are there. The animal masks, the male and female Connus, respond to the Egungun claim that in performing the Egungun play they have the power to metamorphose themselves into animals and to change their sex.

The plays, like the English folk doctor-play had the power of transformation of reality. Whilst we have as yet found no definite mention of the "death and rebirth theme" as part of the Egungun plays, plays about death and resurrection were a feature of many other cults taken to the Caribbean. Patterson mentions the "Resurrection" rite of the Mawu Lisa ceremonies performed on initiates as the first test for entry into the Sky cult of Dahomey. As we shall see later the *Myal Dance* is the Jamaican reinterpretation of the African and English patterns.

There is a fusion of procession and doctor-or-cucumby's play, which makes it an interesting parallel with the Jonkonnu, as writers after Long described it. The death and rebirth "doctor-play" features as part of Jonkonnu by 1801 when Lady Nugent described it. On Christmas Day, she writes, "the whole town bore the appearance of a masquerade". There are many "Johnny Canoes" and many "strange processions" and groups, made up of "dancing men and women". Apart from the processions, "there was a party of actors. Then a little child was introduced… a King who stabbed all the rest… some of the children… were to represent Tippoo Saib's children and the man was Henry IV of France. After the tragedy they all began dancing with the greatest glee…"[49] The tragedy was the "doctor-play" mock duel at the end. Arthur Ramos (*The Negro in Brazil, 1939*) describes the Brazilian equivalent of the Jonkonnu – the Maracatu as having two parts – The richly clothed procession and the *Cucumbys* play, both African-inspired. The pattern of the latter play – King/Queen/Prince/Sorcerer/Congo King: Queen sends ambassadors to Congo King's Court: Conflict occurs: Prince demands apology. Fight takes place when none is given. Prince killed. Sorcerer uses incantations, chants which chorus repeats. Prince revives. All dance and sing – is the pattern of the Jonkonnu play.

Two other writers, Barclay and De La Beche, described part of a play, Richard III:

> The Joncanoe men… were the two heroes, and fought not for a Kingdom, but a queen, whom the victor carried off in triumph. Richard calling out A horse, A horse, etc. was laughable enough. The piece, however, terminated by Richard killing his antagonist, and then figuring in a sword dance with him.[50]

This fight or confrontation is also present in the description that Lewis gives of the Jonkonnu festivities.

It is obvious from these descriptions that the version of the Sword-Dance-Play that had become popular in the Jamaican Jonkonnu was the version with the duel at the end, in which the two protagonists fight with swords; one is killed, but, revived by the music, gets up and dances – whether a sword dance between the two contenders, or a general dance. Excerpts from Shakespeare and other plays were then performed, but according to Belisario – whose sketches and descriptions of Jonkonnu are invaluable – these excerpts were all fitted into the pattern of the folk play: their ending kept the same ritual and significance.

Whatever might have been their performance, says Belisario:

> Combat and Death invariably ensued, when a ludicrous contrast was produced between the smiling mask and the actions of the dying man. At this Tragical point, there was always a general call for music – and dancing immediately commenced – this proved too great a provocation usually to be resisted even by the slain, and he accordingly became resuscitated and joined the merry throng.[51]

What happened to the other version of the doctor-play, in which the mock doctor with his assistant was called in to revive the dead protagonist? We suggest that as the festival continued a dual process was set up. In the nineteenth-century acculturation between African cultural patterns and European civilisation came to a peak. In this development Jonkonnu secularised itself, taking on more European elements. The Combat-to-the-Death version of the doctor play took part in this process, which we can label as one of "creolisation". But in another parallel process – that of indigenisation – Jonkonnu kept its religious significance. It was in this other process, we suggest, that the 'Doctor' version of the English and Scotch doctor-play had its role.

Let us look at the two processes of Jonkonnu:

> Reds and Blues, sometimes also going by the name of 'Johnny Canoeing'. On the north side of the island it is a splendid affair, but on the south side it is just the reverse. In the latter instance, the negroes dress themselves in bulls' hides, with the horns, on into which they are sewn, and go bellowing about the streets, butting all the people they meet. This is the remnant, most probably, of some superstitious African ceremony.[52]

The description that "Monk" Lewis gives of the Jonkonnu festival, in general shows the high point of European influence. But Lewis's description of the procession shows that much of the original element of Jonkonnu is now interpreted in terms of European symbols; and the procession he saw resembles nothing so much as a modern Victory Parade-cum-float.

From Lewis's account the planters and their families were as involved – as financial backers and spectators – as the slaves:

> First marched Britannia; then came a band of music; then a flag; then the Blue King and Queen – the Queen splendidly dressed in white and silver

(in scorn of the opposite party; her train was borne by a little girl in red); his Majesty wore a full British Admiral's uniform, with a white satin sash, a huge cocked hat with a gilt paper crown upon the top of it. These were immediately followed by 'Nelson's car' being a kind of canoe decorated with blue and silver drapery and with 'Trafalga' written on the front of it; and the procession was closed by a long train of Blue grandees... all Princes, Dukes and Duchesses, every mother's child of them.[53]

The terms *"Blues and Reds"* Lewis explains as springing from the rivalry for the favours of the Brown Girls – the mulattoes and quadroons who were the traditional housekeepers i.e. concubines of the planter, attorney and overseer class – between the English and the Scotch Admirals and other Navy personnel at the Kingston Naval Station. Both gave balls for the Brown Girls. In the Sets the Brown Girls declared their allegiance to the English (The Reds) or to the Scots (The Blues). English and Scots planters and their wives etc. vied in rivalry, the wives lending jewellery and helping with the finery of the different sets; and being fiercely partisan.

Belisario tells us that the concept of the competing sets and Set-Girls was brought to Jamaica from Haiti by the French refugees and their slaves and servants who accompanied them when the Haitian War of Independence began. In Haiti, the French Catholic Carnival, itself a rite similar in some concepts to the Jonkonnu, with pagan elements reinterpreted in Christian-Catholic terms, set the dominant patterns; but already infiltrated by African elements, such as the use of drums and rattle.

The drums are the type of drums that are still called in Jamaica the Gumbay drums. The characteristic of this drum is that it is always played with the fingers. The name of the drum has given its name to one of the surviving dances of African origin which still exist today – the Gumbay dance. The importance of the drum and drummers, link the Jonkonnu, for all its European elements, with its African origin. The drums, for example, play a central part in the Yoruba Egungun procession, and in the dramatic presentation of the Egungun 'plays'.

Through the French Set-Girls, the Creoles (i.e. Negroes born in Jamaica) began to dominate the Carnival. The Jonkonnus were still part of what Chambre terms the "Johny Canoeing" on the north side of the island, which was a "splendid affair" but they were a subsidiary part in Lewis's account; and even the costume of the Jonkonnu chief masked dancer was creolised in some aspects. "Monk" Lewis describes the Jonkonnu chief dancer as "a Merry Andrew dressed up in a striped doublet and bearing on his head a kind of pasteboard houseboat filled with puppets, representing some sailors, others soldiers, others again shown at work on a plantation."[54] Lewis was one of the earliest writers to describe this "houseboat" mask.

It is this mask which links the creolisation process of Jonkonnu with the second process, the indigenisation process. Whilst the creolisation process represents what Kerr has termed as a more or less "false assimilation" in which the dominated people adopt elements from the dominant one in order to obtain prestige or status, the indigenisation process represents the more secretive process by which the dominated culture survives; and resists. Not only do we have Chambre's account of the south-side Jonkonnu, with the horned African bull mask, the bellowing and butting of people in the streets, but his statement that it was the survival of some superstitious i.e. religious African ceremony. A description of 1826 brings out the religious aspect even more clearly:

> First came eight or ten young girls marching before a man dressed up in a mask with a grey beard and long flowing hair, who carried the model of a house on his head. This house is called the Jonkonoo, and the bearer of it is generally chosen for his superior activity in dancing... The girls also danced... All this ceremony is certainly a commemoration of the deluge... The custom is African and religious although the purpose is forgotten. Some writers says the house is an emblem of Noah's ark, and that Jonkonoo means the sacred boat or the sacred dove...[55]

The houseboat "mask" is linked with religious symbolism. As we saw before, African religions were used as a binding force in slave revolts. Conspirators were sworn with an oath which involved kissing the Earth – Asase Afua was the Akan goddess of the Earth; her name survives in the word for plot, cultivated land, and in the yam called Afoo yam. African religion then played a central role of resistance. The Jonkonnu as the cultural manifestation of African religious beliefs was therefore involved in this resistance. It was also the more "public", "secular" manifestation of a syncretic cult religion which played and was to play an important part both in the Jamaican religion and folk culture. As Curtin comments on Jonkonnu:

> ...the John Canoe dance was in fact closely associated with survivals of African religion and magic. The figures represented in the houseboat headdress, the phraseology of the songs, the instruments – all were very similar to those of African cult groups that were otherwise driven underground.[56]

VII

And whereas it had been found by experience that rebellions have been often concerted at negro dances and nightly meetings of the slaves of different plantations... be it therefore enacted that if any overseer... or other white person... shall knowingly suffer any slaves to assemble together and beat their military drums, or blow horns or shells every white person offending shall... suffer six months' imprisonment...
  Laws for the Government of Negro Slaves, Jamaica, 1787, Clause 21[57]

Oh amba you! Edooooo oh! Amba you!
You should a brought 'a fiah to us now
Oh amba you! Edoeeeeeedooodo Amba you!

Should a buried a crossroads, Look
O amba you! Edoeee doo-do! O Amba you!
            Myal/Jonkonnu song, collected in St. Elizabeth by Beckwith[58]

Let us look first at what Curtin terms the "survivals of African religion and magic" with which the Jonkonnu dance is linked. The houseboat headdress is important in this connection. From Belisario's sketches and descriptions of the Jonkonnu band, just before the festival in its more elaborate form disintegrated, it is obvious that the houseboat mask was a very special mask for the leader. The mask of the other characters such as Cowhead, and Horsehead were animal masks borrowed from the African and the English folk ritual. The mask of Koo-Koo or Actor Boy, whilst elaborate does not seem to have any particular symbolism. In fact the mask seems to be a "secular" mask corresponding to the "profane masks" that the Egungun cult used for processions similar to those of the Jonkonnu, when they satirised groups such as prostitutes, policemen, Europeans, Hausa, etc. These "profane masks" were used by the cult when the purpose of their parades was merely to entertain. Yet the sacred is never quite separate from the profane in the African context. The name Koo-Koo which has given rise to a most ingenious explanation recorded by Belisario, nevertheless seems most likely to derive from the Yoruba word – ku, which means "a luminous spirit", i.e. that which a good man becomes after death. The word ikoko, related to the same root refers to the food, drink and meat offerings that is put on the graves in pots. This food is supposed to belong to the *Kas* or spirits of the dead. Koo-Koo is most likely related to both these words, since the Egungun cult was an ancestral cult; and in this context Actor Boy would embody the ancestral spirit. His pantomimic gestures in the Jonkonnu procession which seemed to refer to his hunger, would perhaps be intended to remind that the "spirit" must be fed; and perhaps by implication that the group must be rewarded with good tips.

    Actor Boy, Belisario also tells us, some ten years before (i.e. before 1837) played one of the main parts in the Combat-till-Death version of the doctor plays. He most probably played the part of the younger protagonist who gets killed, is restored to life, and joins in the dancing. But the creolised version of the Jonkonnu began to lose much of its original meaning, and by Belisario's time Actor Boys were "reduced to displaying their finery" and "to the performance of certain unmeaning pantomimic actions".[59] The significance of most of the other characters sketched by Belisario had also become confused. Yet a character like Jack-in the-Green who stands with the set girls in one sketch, carried religious connotations in both his English and his African meaning.

    The Jonkonnu houseboat also carried religious connotations, as both Williams and Chambre indicate. The horned mask, the oxhead mask and its symbolism was clear. Why did this mask give way to the houseboat? Did the Jonkonnu figure sketched by Belisario, in "mask, wig and military jacket, posing upon his head the house-shaped cap glittering with mirrors and tinsel and topped by a tufted dome or peak"[60] still carry a religious connotation, in spite of his secular and European type dress? Was the houseboat an African mask in an original form? Or has an old artistic form and function – the mask – been translated to the New World to create a new mask for a new reality? This calls, as so many other areas of Jamaican folk life, for detailed research.

There are several suggestions that can be made. One is that the houseboat mask, however adapted, was made from an original African mask, or several related masks from similar rituals of different tribes, rituals which assimilated to each other and syncretised in the New World experience. Beckwith points out that in Bermuda a similar precession to that of Jonkonnu existed. This was called the Gumbay Parade. The men are masked with heads and horns of animals, but some carried on their heads "beautifully made imitations of houses and ships, both lighted by candles. The houses were termed 'gumbay' houses. When the men came near the houses they danced a special dance and shouted: Gombay relay, Gombay relay."[61]

It seems possible that like the Jonkonnu described by Long, the Bermuda masked dancers are involved in a 'medicinal' purification ceremony similar to that of English folk rites. The Gumbay dance as it survives in Jamaica today is danced to exorcise evil spirits.

Beckwith did not succeed in tracing the houseboat mask to an African original. She cites Mohammedan parallels but admits that links between those and the Jonkonnu houseboat are improbable. There is however one possibility which needs to be explored. Monti tells of a mask which is built on the model of "the house with several storeys which is the prerogative of the hogon"[62] – the supreme political and religious chief of the Dogon tribe of Sudan. This mask is called the *sirige* mask. It patterns the face of the hogon's traditional house with its eighty niches corresponding to the number of the original ancestors. The mask is very tall and, at the top, are two small figures who represent the mythical ancestral couple. The complex religious concepts of the Dogon express the relationship of man to his kinship group, Man to Anima, the God/creator, and to Nommo, the Universe. It expresses this relation in physical and symbolic terms. The plan of the village itself replicates this relationship. The big house of each lineage, of each kin group, with its layout of rooms again patterns this relationship.

The house of the hogon, paramount chief of the Dogon, is also built so as to present a model of the Universe. The hogon's mask which he wears on feast days again patterns this model. The Dogon then lives physically within their myths; ritually enclosed by their symbols.

Does the houseboat copy this mask? Or did some transported "African" master of the masks, design the houseboat mask taking into consideration the Great House of the slave masters; placing his ancestral toy figures within, still working on the plantation in death as they did in life? Did the Haitian African or Creole groups introduce this mask into Jamaica? The first description we have of it, seems to be "Monk" Lewis's in 1816. What connection is there between the Jonkonnu house of Jamaica, and the Gumbay house of Bermuda? There is interesting research to be done here.

The aspect of the Jonkonnu that is most to our purpose is the connection that Beckwith established between the Jonkonnu houseboat mask, and dance, and Myal ceremonies in St. Elizabeth; between the Jonkonnu songs, drums, and drum rhythms and the Myal songs, drums and drum rhythms. In remote districts of St. Elizabeth she claimed that the Jonkonnu dancers and houseboat were connected with *obeah*, i.e. Jamaican religio-magical practises:

> White says that before 'building' the house-shaped structure worn in the dance, a feast must be given consisting of goat's meat boiled without salt, together with plenty of rum. As the building progresses, other feasts are given. On the night before it is brought out in public, it is taken to the cemetery, and there the songs and dances are rehearsed in order to 'catch the spirit of the dead,' which henceforth accompanies the dancer until, after a few weeks merriment during which performances are given for money at the great houses and at village crossroads, it is broken up entirely. For 'as long as it stays in the house the spirit follow it.'

We can deduce that the houseboat mask was seen as an ancestral mask. The Jonkonnu dance and parade in St. Elizabeth still fulfilled part of its African meaning, by evoking the 'ancestral' spirits, or at least community spirits. Miss Beckwith notes the "Similarity to and in some cases their identity" between "a group of avowedly Myal songs from the Cockpit Country of St. Elizabeth neighbouring the Maroon settlement of Accompong with the John Canoe songs from Lacovia and Prospect..."

She notes that the man who leads the group of Lacovia dancers, "an oldish man named Ewan who wore a houseboat mask headdress similar to the original was a notorious Myal man in the district, who held communication with the spirits of the dead." She noted the use of the special Gumbay drum. She also observed that in the Jonkonnu songs "a good deal of Jamaica witchcraft is mixed up with the words". Informants also told her that the Jonkonnu/Myal Man of Lacovia took his houseboat headdress to the graveyard and danced the special dances with special songs among the dead. From all this she concludes that there was a close link between Jonkonnu and Myalism and that in this part of Jamaica at least, "the John Canoe mask and dance is associated with the invocation of the spirits of the dead". Jonkonnu is linked to Myalism through meaning, song and dance. 'Myalism' was the cult that "had been driven underground".[63]

VIII

Not long since, some of these execrable wretches in Jamaica [sic Obeahman] introduced what they called the *myal dance*, and established a kind of society, into which they invited all they could. The lure hung out was, that every Negroe, initiated into the myal society, would be invulnerable by the white men...

Long, 1774[64]

"When you dance the Myal, if Death loves you and you deal with him, he will give you one..." (i.e. an Amber Talisman).

Jamaican Myal Man to Beckwith, 1921[65]

Already by the time Sloane wrote, certain drums had been forbidden in the plantation, because of the planters' fear of the central part the drum played in the planning and psychological preparation of the slaves for revolt. Revolts from the earliest times were a constant feature. Writing in the 1680s, Taylor describes four that had taken place within the span of a few years. Not only were drums part of the whole ritual of revolt; so also were dances. We know that war-songs still exist among the Maroons. Many of the Maroons are of the Ashanti tribe, for whom the warrior ancestors were of far more significance, than for example the agricultural gods. Many of them came from a powerful military caste. In Africa, dancing is the special preserve of warriors since dancing is a ritual and physical preparation for war.

Whilst the war dances would have remained in their African form on Maroon territory, on the estates the war dances had to be adapted or transformed, once the planters suspected their purpose. As the Slave Laws show, the planters came to learn that "negro-dances" were the occasion for the planning of revolt. Any meeting of the slaves from different plantations was also, at once, suspected. For a long time therefore the slaves largest area of freedom for assembly was at funerals. The mortality rate of slaves was high. Funerals, always central to the African world view, took on an added significance. The very rate of death, which occasioned the funerals and therefore frequent meetings at the graves of their dead, would have increased their instinct for revolt.

It was the custom, too, at funerals to dance war dances. Both Edwards and Phillippo describe the custom of "martial dancing" by Negroes at the grave. As late as 1816, "Monk" Lewis relates that a funeral ceremony was used as a place and time for plotting rebellion. In Haiti police decrees forbade funerals and also the water-mumma dance in which the leader went into a trance during which he worked out the revolt plans given to him by his tribal god.

Jamaica too had its water-dance to the water spirit, or river goddess. This spirit known as "Rubba Mumma" was supposed to: "Inhabit every fountain-head of an inexhaustible and considerable stream of water in Jamaica". The slaves, in times of drought, used to persuade their master to sacrifice an ox at the fountainhead of the water turning the mill. The water spirit was supposed to materialise like a mermaid at noon, combing her long black hair. Fish from such were held to be her children and were never eaten. But above all: "Mial songs and dances were done for her".[66]

The dance of the "Rubba Mumma" seems then, to have been linked to the Myal cult. Above all it had a common purpose. The trance of the leader, who comes out of his possessed state with instructions from his god, these instructions then having the power and force of a god's backing, helped to make revolt against many times impossible odds, seem more feasible. But the dance of the Water Mumma had one drawback – with so many different tribal gods, and slaves of different origins, the god of the leader did not bind all the slaves. But tribal divisions still continued; each tribe had its own Connu. As revolts after revolt failed, it became clear, that to face the monolithic power of the planters and the whites, the slaves would have to evolve a general Jamaican cult religion as opposed to tribal ones. We suggest then that Myalism was to pre-Emancipation Jamaica what Voodoo was to Haiti. Patterson summarises the Myal dance ceremony:

> ...the myal dance was meant largely to exhibit the magical powers of the cult leader, usually called 'Doctor'. The chosen initiate was placed within a circle formed by the Doctor and his assistants. The Doctor then sprinkled him with several powders,... then blew upon him and danced around him frantically. He was then whirled rapidly around until he fell into a deathlike trance. The Doctor then departed, with loud shrieks, to the woods from which he returned a few hours later with different kinds of herbs, the juice from part of which was squeezed into the mouth of the entranced initiate and the remainder rubbed on his eyes and finger tips. At the same time pieces of glass-bottle, snakes, reptiles and other particles were produced under the guise of coming from beneath the skin of the initiate. This was accompanied by a chant, to which the assistants, holding hands, danced in a circle around both Doctor and initiate, stamping their feet in time with the rhythm of the chant. When, sometime later, the initiate dramatically recovered, a miraculous resurrection was proclaimed.[67]

Long recognised above all that the purpose of the cult was directly political; and that it set out to serve as a unifying force. A myal man he recounts, tried to persuade a fellow slave to "be of their party" and to do this in a rebellion "gave him a wonderful account of the powerful effects produced by the myal infusion, and particularly that it rendered the body impenetrable to bullets".[68]

The Kromanti rebellion of 1760, Long also tells us, was fomented by men who sold medicine to make the rebels invulnerable. The concept of medicine, the fact that the Myal cult leader was known as "Doctor", that Martha Beckwith was able to collect Jamaican versions of old English and Scots Folk Doctor-Plays from informants in St. Elizabeth and in the Cockpit Country – that is territory near to the Maroons, suggests that one version of the Sword-Dance play – the version in which the quack doctor comes in, provides comic relief, charges a lot of money, but revives his dead patient who has been killed in a duel survived in the more secret process we call indigenisation. Tolstoy has pointed out that folk art is the only universal art. Certainly it seems clear that the pagan folk rites of England and Scotland, remnants of a pagan folk religion that had been banished by Christianity had survived to influence the syncretic Myal cult; itself centred about the medicine dance common to all folk rite influenced by different folk rituals, resisted the purely economic impulse of the plantation system, an impulse which attacked the very concept of religion itself. Resistance to slavery would draw its strength from a folk rite of considerable power. Later, Myalism, was to strike up alliance with the Baptist religion. This alliance was a natural one. It was through this alliance and fusion that elements of Christianity would become an indigenous – rather than a merely creole part of Jamaican folklore

The survival of both the Doctor Play and Myalism in the environs of the Cockpit Country would suggest that the Myalist cult got its first powerful impulse from the Kromanti tribe, the majority of the Maroons. The Maroons, although having a base of interrelated tribes, still had to face the problem of welding different tribal groupings into a whole. From the description of a Kromanti memorial anniversary dance held for the dead that Edwards gives, it is clear that they solved this problem by extending their ancestral kin to include deified heroes of their guerilla warfare. The Spanish Jamaican guerilla leader Ysassi who fought with the Maroons against the English invaders, for example, became a deified ancestor and tutelary saint, side by side with African Maroon heroes like Accompong and Ikboa.

This flexible and pattern then spread out. Although the Maroon impulse was most likely the strongest, the widespread quality of the Myal cult suggests a process of assimilation between different tribal rituals. The frequency of funerals served its purpose; fusion would begin there. Fetish specialists who came from Africa, especially the more adaptable ones, became guiding forces in the cult. The Creole Negroes, in their ambivalence between acceptance and rebellion, when they chose rebellion had to create a cult that was no longer tribal; since they themselves were detribalised. Former rituals like the Rubba Mumma dance would have been absorbed into the Myal ceremony. The Dahomey sky cult with its Death and Resurrection rite and other similar death, rebirth motifs would have reinforced the central concept of the Myal dance as the "good medicine" which gives life.

We suggest that as the purpose of the Myal "medicine" dance was to bind together people not now of the same family but of the same belief, conviction, cause; its ritual of death and resurrection was in effect a war dance, a war ritual, an extension of the "martial dances" danced at funerals, of the binding force of ancestors worship. Now it was not only the dead ancestors that would rise up. It was their descendants, who through the power and courage of their leader who "dealt with Death" would be enabled to rise up, like the sword dancers at the end of the English folk play or the initiate in the Dahomean resurrection rites. Bullets had no power against them; reality was transformed by the dance.

We suggest also that the Myal cult was "driven underground" because the planters realised the danger of such a unifying dance, ritual and religion. The laws of 1774 prescribed the death sentence for anyone attending the Myal ceremonies. Jonkonnu on the other hand, was tolerated, and its more creolised versions even encouraged by the planters who looked upon it as "harmless fun". But we suggest also that since the separation between the sacred and the secular is a matter of emphasis rather than of opposition in the African world view, both Myalism and Jonkonnu contained elements of each other. We suggest, too, that both passed on elements of their rituals, beliefs and dances to the surviving dances and version of folk religion – that exist today. On the more African side of the Afro-Christian continuum, *Convince, Kumina;* in the middle of the continuum, *Pukkumma*, and on the more Christian end, *Zion Revival*. Gumbay which survives in St. Elizabeth is itself the lineal descendant of Myalism, but a Myalism which had undergone transformation through the Great Myal Procession in the 1840s. We suggest, then, that Jamaican folkdance has been a continual cultural process, which both in Jonkonnu and Myalism transformed mainly African and some English elements into the first Jamaican cult religion; and in the first and only Jamaican folk festival.

IX

Las' yeah me turn out
I hope you well.
You went a war, edo edo
You went a war,
Me no gone 'way yet
I hope you well,
Till we meet a Canoe-lean-a-hill
Kia-money dead, I hope you well...

Johnkonnu song: collected Beckwith[69]

What of the descriptions of the actual dancing of the Jonkonnu festival? The Jonkonnu, as we have seen, had its beginning in the yam festival rites of Africa. Since all African dance has a "meaning and a sense", the dances were closely related to the purpose of the Jonkonnu festivity at the beginning of the cultural process. The "great activity and strength of Body",[70] to which Sloane referred, was a central feature of Jonkonnu dancing. The chief Jonkonnu – the central dancer who "wore" or carried the houseboat "mask" – was "generally chosen for his superiority in dancing". The Jonkonnu "saluted his master and mistress and then capered about with an astonishing agility and violence". The girls who accompanied him "also danced, without changing their position, moving their elbows and knees, and keeping time with calabashes filled with small stones".[71]

Long's description shows the Jonkonnu masquerader with a wooden sword in his hand, "Whilst he dances at every door bellowing out John Connú! with great vehemence".[72] Lady Nugent noted that all the "Johnny Canoe" figures "dance, leap and play a thousand anticks".[73]

"Monk" Lewis, writing about 1818, shows the process by which in the creolisation of the Jonkonnu, the Set-Girls dominate the procession whilst Jonkonnu figures are subsidiary. In Lewis's version these once central figures no longer "make part of the procession i.e. of set-girls". They go about from house to house "tumbling and playing antics to pick up money for themselves".[74] Another account of 1826 shows two "Joncanoe-men" who now are a part – but a mere accessory part of the Set-Girls. They accompany the girls from house to house giving "a display of buffoonery" after which they collect money.[75] Two years later Jonkonnu has a wife and the two "dance without intermission, often wheeling violently round, and all the while singing". Chambre shows the Jonkonnu ox-head mask "bellowing about the street butting all the people they meet".[76]

In the account of the Bermuda Jonkonnu (i.e. Gumbay Parade), the group of Gumbay men, as they come to each house, "dance a breakdown and shout: 'Gumbay ra-lay'."[77] The emphasis is on agility, powerful leaps, acrobatic dancing on the part of the men dancers.

Curt Sachs has pointed out that the leap dance is the mimetic dance in all cultures in which the dancer identifies with the planted. The taller the leap, the taller the yams, the more flourishing. Long strides, vigorous dancing is involved in the same process of fertility and growth. The stilt dance also "aims at... fertility".[78] In Belize, British Honduras, the stilt-dancer who appears in a parade at Christmas is called "John Canoe". And in Barbados a central figure of the Christmas masquerade used to be a stilt-dancer who controlled the dance with a tin rattle. The quality of the dance of the Jonkonnu figures shows its origins as fertility dances connected with the yam festival.

As we have seen, however, the rites were also a memorial for the dead: the ancient spirits possessed the Jonkonnu and through him the spirits danced, strengthening the life forces – danced "good medicine" to increase the fertility of the Earth and his descendants, to renew the life force.

Sachs has pointed out that side by side with this serious sacred purpose, as an antidote, there is also "a roistering troop of clowns". And beside "the divinely inspired dancer walks the jester – a child of the dance".

Some descriptions, especially those when the Jonkonnu's original purpose had been overlaid by the creolisation involved in the introduction of the Set-Girls, stressed the antics, tumbling and buffoonery of the Jonkonnus. To Lady Nugent, the Jonkonnus' dancing and leaping took its place among the "thousand antics" that they played.

But there is no doubt that by the 1820s and 1830s the more secularised festival had increased the role of Jonkonnus as *jesters* and reduced their role as "divinely-inspired" medicine men. The introduction of the Set-Girls led to this reduction. As Cassidy points out, the Sets had absorbed the Jonkonnus by 1833; worse, it had set up a new relation in which the more African element of the festival was now considered inferior,

> ...his part was no longer separate but had become merely the grotesque element of the whole.[80]

The distinction between the Set-Girls and the Jonkonnus was marked by the fact that the former

> sought elegance in costume, dancing, singing, and general behaviour, whereas the Jonkonnu was grotesque, wild, farcical and often disordered.[81]

The Creoles have triumphed over the Africans, imposing their Creole standards; and interpretation. And creole standards approximated as closely as possible to the dominant European "high standards" of "excellence". On his own ground, the folk festival, Jonkonnu – in both his African and pagan English connotations – had been disinherited.

The new social order of Emancipation was accompanied by the break-up of many of the large estates. Many planters reluctant to give up slavery, lamented this breaking-up as the end of "civilisation". Jonkonnu changed, too; it was saved and converted it into a peasant festival. With the settling of the ex-slaves on the land, the creation of "free" villages, a peasantry in the full sense of the word now existed. Jonkonnu ceased to exist in the creolised form and became the preserve of the peasant. The dancers of Lacovia whom Beckwith saw, who leapt and danced, retained the dance in it original form even though they may have forgotten much of its true meaning.

Later descriptions of the Jonkonnu Christmas parade, however, prove that the Jonkonnu, during the creolisation process, had drawn into its original form influences from the creole class – in a description given in 1951, "two men in women's clothing did a Quadrille".[82]

How did the Quadrille – a European folkdance adapted into high society, become a part of the indigenous folkdance of Jamaica, entering the folk pattern of the Jonkonnu?

X

> Is nuttin I lub as de square katreel,
> I out fe dance till me two-foot peel.
> R.M. Murray, 'Poem on the Quadrille', 1961[83]

> There is another Set, denominated 'Housekeepers' who never dance in their progress through the streets.
> Belisario: Plate 2 1837[84]

The "creolised" Jonkonnu of the Set-Girls patterned the power structure of the society. Slave society was hierarchical. The hierarchy was based on the biological concept of race. The room at the top was spacious and white, that at the bottom, cramped and black. In between, on the middle rungs of the ladder, one was graded according to one's shade. Culture, too, was reduced to a racial concept. European culture was white: African culture was black. In this concept the Jonkonnu dance became mere "antics"; and grotesque.

On the other hand, Belisario depicts the Set-Girls, splendid in their finery, matched in the colours of their dresses, shoes etc., arranged in order with four Grand Masters to protect the Set-Adjutant bearing flag, hand-drum, singer, tambourine, Commodore – with their queen and their maam at their head, danced through the streets, to the rhythm of their rattles (i.e. maracas). But the Set-Girls were graded not only according to the colour of their costumes, but also to that of their skins. Black girls did not dance with brown girls:

> ...blacks and browns never mingled in the same sett. The creole distinction of brown lady, black woman was in those days of slavery of social distinctions strictly observed...[85]

Creole black Sets, in their turn, did not mingle with African (i.e. slaves born in Africa) Sets; and for a while tribal divisions, as Long informs us, resulted in each tribe having its own "Set" or Connu.

But Jonkonnu also satirised the power structure. One Set poked fun at the "housekeeper class", which, although it accommodated courtesans, regarded itself as superior. Dancing also played its part in the distinction. The more African sets danced more vigorously – the more European in a more restrained and elegant manner. The housekeepers would not condescend to dance in the streets at all. They only danced in the houses of the whites.

This satire brings out another aspect of the Jonkonnu: not only did it pattern the power structure, but at least as far as blacks and whites were concerned, it served to ritually reverse the usual order of things, and behaviour. Especially on the estates, where the browns did not exist as a class (they belonged to the towns), the Jonkonnu, very much in the manner of the European Carnival with its mock king, broke down – again ritually – some of the barriers between black and white. Stewart tells us that during the Jonkonnu festival,

> the slaves appeared an altered race of beings". They showed themselves off in 'fine clothes', trinkets; in a 'more polished mode of speech'; they spoke to their masters 'with greater familiarity'; they entered the Great House and 'drank with their masters' and altogether '...the distance between them appear(ed) to be annihilated for a moment, like the familiar footing on which the Roman slaves were with their master at the feast of the Saturnalia... They seem a people without the consciousness of inferiority or suffering.[86]

They changed their names for that day, and took on ones of power and authority, that of prominent whites – Admiral Rowe, General Campbell. They called these "gala-day" names. They sang satirical phillipics against their masters – i.e. calypso – and in general took over the society.

Patterson has elaborated on the function of the Jonkonnu in slave society as an example of "ritual license"[87] which helps the society to a certain level of functional integration.

Although the influence of the Haitian-Catholic Carnival might have reinforced this aspect of the Jonkonnu, this original reversal-of-authority-function was part of the Yoruba tradition. Both the Egungun cults – with which Jonkonnu has many parallel – and, in particular, the Adimu festival, reveal this pattern and social function. In this festival a masked dancer is escorted by a group of followers all wearing a distinctive hat with an appropriate badge. Adimu, the chief masker, is escorted by a strong force which clears the way before him and prevents others from coming too close. A figure of respect, all must pay obeisance, even the Chief. After the festival, the costume was burned "and the relic of power is over". The Adimu, possessed by a god, is paid respect by all during the day of his reign; but, afterwards, he becomes once more an ordinary person. The Jonkonnu figure, therefore, incorporated both the Egungun and the Adimu Cult characteristics.

The society – with its numerous and bitter divisions – found a precarious integration in a festival whose framework and function was African in origin. This framework and function was able to fuse with the Haitian-Catholic Carnival influences, since, in spite of its overlay of civilisation and Christianity, the European Catholic Carnival was itself a reinterpretation of pagan folk rite. It was with this ritual remnant that the Jonkonnu, in its indigenous aspect, found culture contact points; thereby absorbing elements into its own structure. Both folk elements provided the only cultural release in a society where culture was expendable.

One other festival also provided the opportunity for cultural assimilation. The crop-over festival on many estates was a time when whites and blacks came close together. We have pointed out previously that the bookkeeper class, mainly Scots, with little prospect of a return to Scotland, and very close in custom to the folk patterns of Scotland (and some of England) – were the transmitters of the British folk cultural patterns in so far as they became a part of Jamaican life. Celebrations took place at different times on different estates. They were, in effect, Harvest festivals; and, whatever the economic motive of the planter-owners and merchants in London, there would have been a feeling of satisfaction among men who had worked in a common endeavour. Patterson quotes from the early novel, *Marly*:

> As soon as the crop was over, the Negroes assembled in and around the boiling house, dancing and roaring for joy to the sound of the gumba.[88]

Provisions were given to the slaves for a feast, and the overseer and the whites had one by themselves. In the evening the fiddlers from the Negro village were summoned. The rest of the slaves assembled at the Great House. The fiddlers began to play; the "whites left the table, and on choosing their stable partners, the reels commenced". They danced together and, later in the evening, "the whites resumed their place in the room when country dances commenced, in which the Negro girls performed their parts extremely well".[89]

The Scotch-reel was to become part and parcel of the Jamaican folkdance. Like many other European folkdances, it would play its part in that ambivalence and duality which is at the heart of the dance as a cultural process.

European folkdances were not only passed on through "crop-over" celebrations, but were very much a part of high, or planter, society. And if the planters had no other form of cultural life, they certainly had balls. Lady Nugent, in her diary, tells of her disastrous attempt to hold a *conversazione,* only to find that the planters and their ladies had one lack in common: "the sad want of ... any subject of conversation with them". So she sent for the fiddlers and "we had a merry dance". She decides, from then on, to settle for "Friday dances".[90] From that point, balls fill the pages of her diary during her few years stay as the Jamaican Governor's wife: Grand Balls, Little Balls, House of Assembly Balls and Colt's Balls, balls in honour of her first son and daughter, of Christmas and Easter, for the Kings Birthdays, etc. Amongst the dances performed by Lady Nugent was the Scotch-reel, which has entered Jamaican dialect as the "Katreel". This word is, also, and more often, used to refer to the quadrille.

Plantation Jamaica observed the dances that England danced, and, in the nineteenth century, the metropolitan high society adopted, besides the Scotch-reel, the quick waltz, the polka, the Mazurka and the Alpine country waltz. But the quadrille, formally identified as such in the nineteenth century, was in origin an English country dance which the French transformed into the cotillon at the beginning of the eighteenth century. This dance spread to England, and, one would imagine, to planter society (such as it was) in Jamaica. Out of the cotillon came the "firmly fixed series of six figures", which became known as the quadrille. As early as 1817 there was another variant – the *quadrille à la cour* or The Lancers with its five sets. Towards the end of the first two decades of the nineteenth century, it was being danced by high society.

Lady Nugent's reference to "fiddlers" makes it clear that slaves, from early, were taught the use of more European-type instruments, and could play at planter balls. This was to be one of the few genuine culture contact points between the planter class and the slaves. So balls became, also, the custom and tradition of the brown and creole-black elements among the slaves. Many of these were house slaves, who, approximating to the dominant pattern of the whites, tried to imitate them in all they did. We call this process creolisation, rather than indigenisation. (Nor can we properly call it acculturation since it was not a culture that was responded to, but its techniques – its status power; whilst the other culture that was necessary to the culture fusion was avoided.)

The majority of the browns and the creole-blacks in nineteenth-century

Jamaica accepted the value system, which meant that the closer they came to the whites in customs and habits, the closer they came to the top. This implied, and meant, a turning back upon as many "African customs" as possible. The brown class and the creole blacks, far then from representing a mixture of cultures as is generally assumed, represented – and represent still – rather the attempt to shed one culture and achieve the other. They were – and are – in fact 'cultural half-castes', and have been, as a result, an uncreative and frustrated class. Or, rather, they have been uncreative to the extent to which they succeeded in their conscious desire.

In the first half of the nineteenth century, there was a clear indication of the triumph of European dances. Patterson notes:

> In 1825 De la Beche spoke of the 'old school' and the 'new school' among the Negroes, stating that the former still clung to the 'goombay and African dances', but that the latter much preferred the fiddles, reels and other music and dances of the whites. A year later Barclay wrote that African dances were being replaced by Scottish ones and the Gumbay by the fiddle. This tendency had, of course, been long prevalent among the mulatto slaves and the free people of colour.[91]

But whilst the tendency of 'creolisation' tended to abandon the more African type dances for the European ones, and the conservative slaves still hung on to their "goombay and African dances", the process of indigenisation drew in from the European-type dances and instruments any elements that would function in the original established matrix.

Already by 1720 the banjo was being used by the slaves in their dances, and by 1818 it featured with the drum in the Jonkonnu. By 1826 a fiddler, also, played with the band. In 1951 the fife blended with the drum as two men dressed as women danced the quadrille in the Jonkonnu masquerade. For the quadrille had been originally a folkdance. In Jamaica, it suffered a sea-change to become a folkdance once again.

But there was another dance in 1951 – one performed by a Sailor and a Whore Girl "who dance(d) vulgar all the time".[92] This was the same one danced in the Jonkonnu Parade at Portland as late as 1969 – and termed by the citizens who watched it with shocked delight: "a real dirty dance". Apart from the Whore Girl, there was another character called the Wild Indian. In this dance, both these principals are men, but Whore Girl is dressed as a woman. He/she lifts his/her dress, holding it at both sides to show the underwear, bends back with knees open and bent before, and does a dance which is an exaggerated form of the hip-sway and pelvic roll. The Wild Indian straddles his/her hip, and, lifting one leg and changing the other, does a backward-and-forward movement of the pelvis, known in Portland as "the forward jam". This dance, openly sexual, lasts for only a short while.

In this dance, we suggest that the Whore Girl satirises the prostitute – as the Egungun cult satirised prostitutes and policemen. One character in the

Portland masquerade is a policeman who arrests both dancers. If the crowd pays pennies to bail them out, they are set free and the dance continues – the parody of the couple dance, a fertility dance intended to "promote growth in the tribe – and in Nature".

XI

Hipsaw my dear! You no shake like a me
You no wind like a me
Hipsaw my dear you no do like a me
You no jig like a me you no twist like a me
Hipsaw my dear...!

A Slave in the Eighteenth Century Explaining her Dance in Song and
Dance

Me wi dance de shay shay
Me will dance the kachrill...
Me wi dance till the whole
a mi foot-bottom peel.

Folk Song[93]

As we pointed out before, the leap dances of the central Jonkonnu were performed to increase the fertility of the Earth. But the fertility of Nature and that of Man were interlinked. Fertility rites – involving phallic symbols and simulated intercourse – form a part of all pagan religions. Among the Indians of northwestern Brazil, a special phallic lance is seen almost as a medicine dance which carries fertility into very house, field, to the woods etc. "They jump among the women, young and old, who disperse shrieking and laughing..."[94] The butting of the women – still performed by the Cowhead character in the Jonkonnu – is a mimetic extension of this fertility rite: horns symbolise fertility.

We suggest that the dance performed by the Wild Indian and Whore Girl, with its obvious sexual connotations, is the remnant of the fertility dance which has lost its meaning – and one very closely connected to the dance which Beckwith describes as an "erotic dance to jazz music", and which she calls the shay-shay.

The shay-shay is described by de Lisser as a dance derived from the Cuban *chica*. His description of it as a dance "which consists of slow movement of the body... the dancer never allows the upper part of the body to move as she writhes or suffers over the ground",[95] and a couple-dance always performed to song – shows that whilst it is similar to the *chica*, it is a courtship dance that has long existed in Jamaica.

Long's 1760 descriptions of this courtship dance – the music both grave and gay, the male dancer "all action, fire and gesture" his body "vigorously turned and writhed every moment" and "his limbs agitated with… lively exertions"; the female dancer coy, retreating, keeping the "upper part of her person steady"[96] as she moves her hips – is repeated again and again by other writers.

Stewart tells what a central part this dance played in the lives of the slaves. (This dance, and the others, they called *plays,* since all the dances in the African context have a context and a sense.) His description of the circle around the couple, and of the female singing leader and chorus songs – links this dance to the calinda described by Moreau de Saint Méry. The *calinda* and the *chica*, like other Afro-Cuban and Caribbean dances, spread out to Europe from the sixteenth century, giving rise to dances like the *sarabande, chaconne, pasacalle, folia* and *cumbe*. The *fandango* had its origin, too, in an Afro-Cuban dance, even though it was further stylised. From the fandango a succession of other dances were derived, including the *bolero*.

The next description that we have of the dance which de Lisser called the shay-shay, and Long described in 1760, Stewart in 1823 – is from Williams. The dance is performed as part of the Christmas celebrations, although not as a part of the Jonkonnu festival. The dance is the same, but Williams compares it to a bolero and tells us that the slaves call it "the love dance". The dance has obviously been 'creolised': the gentleman-dancer wipes his lady's face with a hankerchief and she wipes his.

The European influence is obvious. The original love-dance was of African origin; and, dancing in couples in Africa, as Janheinz Jahn points out, is "conceivable only as the fulfilment of the fertility dance". This fertility dance was related not only to the couple who performed but to the fertility of the earth as a whole. Each couple represent a strengthening of these forces, a paradigmatic representation. They are not in the isolated couples of European dance. But when Europe took over dances such as the *chica* and the *calinda*, since "Europe… because of its tradition as well as its social structure, adopts foreign dances only in the form of dances for couples…"[97] the African dances were assimilated as much as possible to the "norms of European morality". In a moment of extension and return, the slaves now take over the "personal relationship" of the couple, a feature, as mentioned before, of the European dance.

The movement of the Whore Girl, as she leans backward with legs open and the upper portion of her body steady as she hipsaws and winds and twists, is a parodied and more explicit motion of the original African courtship dance. (Janheinz Jahn prints a photograph of a similar dance in the Lake Chad area.) But, at the same time, the fusion of the original African pattern and the European individual couple context, causes the dance to seem indecent both in its Christian/ European context, and in its African religious context.

Common to all these African courtship dances was a movement of mimed climax which, in its original context, is supposed to last but a brief moment if the meaning is to be retained.

To both the spectators and the dancers – Wild Indian and Whore Girl – the meaning has been lost. Because of this, what should, or was originally, a brief moment – is prolonged, as in the cabaret-type dancing performed to achieve sexual excitement for sexual excitement's sake. The *bamboula,* too, danced by the older people in the Virgin Islands to the sound of the Ka drum – the drum used in Jamaica both for *Kumina* and the *Tambu* dance.

Yet, because dance and song can pass on meanings – independently of conscious thought – the dirty dance of the Jonkonnu Wild Indian and Whore Girl still retains echoes of its original significance. Its symbolic character is inherent in the fact that a man dresses up as a woman, puts on the mask or costume of a woman. He therefore represents the female – Wild Indian, also costumed, the male. The forward jam movement is the explicit prolonged version of the *vacunao* or climax. The prolongation is due to the European couple idea where the dancers perform personal motions, relating to their own stimulation.

But even here, the moment is kept relatively brief by the invention of the policeman who arrests them until they are bailed out by the crowd. And the fact that the dance is performed by Whore Girl, parodies its own obscenity as the members of the Egungun cult did when they, too, wore profane masks. But as it parodies obscenity, it celebrates the life force; and vice versa; the Jester and the god-possessed dancer always side by side. As Janheinz Jahn points out: in the integrated African world "there can be no strict separation between the sacred and the profane... Everything sacred has... a secular component, and everything secular a relevance to religion". Dance, as the cultural medium par excellence which expressed and transmitted this religion, was not easily divided into these categories. In African philosophy, all dance, all art "is the embodiment of a singular universal life force" and the only difference between dances would depend, in the original African context, as to whether or not each dance "symbolises more or less of the universal life force".[98] The "Doctor Play" of the Jonkonnu, for example, symbolised a lesser amount of the life force than the myal doctor ceremony. In this sense the Jonkonnu "Doctor Play" was more secular, the myal dance and ceremony were "religious".

But the religion was African, and pagan and black. Increasingly, as Jamaica became more Christianised and monotheistic, the African gods were exiled – along with the culture in which they were involved. By 1825 we are told the practice of Jonkonnu had begun to fall off very much as "most of those who had become Christians were ashamed to join in it".[99] Transformed "indigenised" folkdances became the more respectable" dances. Shame and extreme reticence was displayed towards dances of African origin. Jonkonnu – and the courtship dance which formed a part of the same cultural complex – was exiled to the remoter country areas. To rise on the social scale, one danced the quadrille – but turned one's back on the shay-shay. One claimed all that was Europe – and denied Africa. Africa would *not* be denied. The African gods were too pervasive, too tangled with the unconscious roots of our being. They were the roots.

XII

The question is: are we prepared to accept what is originally ours, and not be afraid because it is simple and given to Cottons and no silk? Or are we afraid because most of the vital expression of our folk material is of African origin?

Beryl McBurnie, on "West Indian Dance", 1955[100]

The Christian middle-class widely holds particular views of revivalists; pagan, superstitious, comical in ritual behaviour, tolerant of dishonesty ... The ambivalent attitude of the middle-class towards their African heritage contributes to the contempt.

Edward Seaga, writing on Revivalist Cults in Jamaica, 1969[101]

Both Martha Beckwith in the 1920s and Earl Leaf in the 1940s found the Maroons willing to dance polkas and quadrilles, but reluctant to dance dances of African origin. Colonel Rowe, head of the Maroons, spoke of Obeah to Leaf as part of the "African arts and sciences"; but in front of the Presbyterian parson, referred to Obeah as "witchcraft and paganism". The Presbyterian parson, according to Leaf, "disapproved of Maroon dancing, because of its affinity to Africa and Afro-Jamaican religious lore".[102]

The problem is not a simple one nor the opposition either/or; Christianity has become inextricably mingled with Jamaican folklore and Jamaican folk religion. As Cassidy points out, both doctrinal and ritual elements of Christianity are fused with the remains of African religions in the Revivalist cults of today. How and why did this come about?

Redfield discusses the theory that all religions and cultures have a "high" or "learned" tradition as well as a "little" or "folk" tradition. The first is carried on by the learned or reflective few, whether in oral or in written cultures. The second, the little tradition, is carried on by the people through song, dance, legends, stories, myths, plays, ritual. There is a constant interaction between the two. Sacred epics, for example, can arise as stories among the people, be taken up by the high tradition, refashioned and returned to the people. The Bible is a perfect expression of this. The ethics of the Old Testament, for example, arose, "out of tribal peoples and returned to peasant communities after they had been the subject of thought by philosophers and theologians".[103]

Redfield describes the process by which the high traditions adopt variants created by the people and fit them into the framework of orthodoxy as a process of *universalisation*. The opposite process by which the people take fragments of the high tradition, and adapt it to new and local purposes, forgetting its original framework of interpretation, he calls *parochialisation*. The kind of civilisations where the high and the little tradition are related to one another – as in China – is called a "primary" civilisation. The second type where an invading civilisation displaces the high tradition of another culture and people, and replaces it, is called a "secondary" civilisation. The civilisation of Islam, for example, although an invading civilisation, was able to re-root itself in the folk tradition of the invaded countries by allowing them local variants of the Mohammedan religion.

In Jamaica, the African religions suffered a discontinuity. The folk and little traditions, carried on through the drum, song and dance, persisted and remained creative. But the high tradition carried on by priests in Africa who had to undergo years of initiation and reflection, could not survive under conditions of disruption and forced labour. Whilst, therefore, religious myths survived, they suffered a distortion. Anancy, for instance, is known only as Anancy the trickster, and not as Anansi, the God Creator.

The Christianity of the plantation system functioned as a branch plant extension of the Anglican Church in England. The Non-Conformist religions, on the other hand, and in particular the Baptist religion, was adopted by the Christianised slaves as their 'high tradition'. The Bible became the Book, the high tradition into which they could feed the living roots of their religious impulse. The culture contact points with the Baptist and the former African religions were numerous. In particular the symbolism of total immersion in water; and the leader system by which former Myalist cult leaders were able to be responsible for classes. After Emancipation, with the psychological pressures of the new order, with the rigidity of the orthodox Baptists who put a ban on dancing, for example, numerous Myalist cults with Christian elements and Native Baptist cults with Myalist elements, began to attract converts from Orthodox Baptist sects. The high tradition was now only the Bible; and numerous leaders were free to interpret it as they wished.

In these re-interpretations the powerful African survivals infused themselves. The African gods came back as angels, and some as emissaries of the devil. For the Christian Manichaeism, the division into absolute good and absolute evil, God and Satan, was one of the most powerful borrowings. The African world view in which good and evil are not separate but are twin aspects of the same reality, had to fight a hard battle for survival. But, as Herskovits points out, the African concept in which conquering African peoples had absorbed the gods of the conquered, and vice versa, made possible the fusion and transformation.

The official Baptists were unable to accept the transformation. A new separation and discontinuity occurred. After Emancipation the strain and pressure of adaptation lead to an outbreak of "Obeah". The newly freed men, in a society where no preparation had been made to adapt them to the new order or vice versa, attributed their problems to enemy "Obeah". They retaliated. Enemies retaliated. The Myalist cult became "Obeah pullers" of the society. It was believed that an Obeahman stole the shadow or personality of his victim for evil purposes and nailed it to a cotton tree. The Myalist evolved an elaborate sacrificial ritual in which dancing by members of the cult around a cotton tree made it possible to retrieve and restore the stolen shadow to the victim. As once the Myal dance had returned life to the dead, so the new dance now returned the lost personality. This concept responded to the complex African belief in the different souls that each man possesses.

In the 1840s, in response to severe problems and difficult conditions, the Myalists, now fused with Christian elements and phraseology, began and carried out the Great Myal Procession. The Myalists saw themselves as "medicine men" sent to "pull all the obeah" and cleanse and purify the earth in preparation for Christ's second coming. Many Native Baptists, and even Orthodox Baptists, joined in the Procession. They went from estate to estate, church to church, held meetings, danced, became possessed, whirled, with additional rites of self-flagellation and prolonged fasting. The Procession had aspects reminiscent of the English medicinal folkdance rites, which had already become part of Myalism. Many Myal leaders had worked in the hospitals on the estates – and afterward set up as "medicine men". They saw themselves as "angel men" dancing the medicine of Christ, in much the same way as Jonkonnu danced fertility medicine, and as the English folk rite danced "medicine' – with dancing men, disguised as animal men and Jacks-in-the-Green, who danced dispensing medicine by the touch of green boughs, or handkerchiefs, with broom dancers, sweepers, sword-bearers, clearing and purifying the way. In the Great Myal Procession, Christianity, Indo-European and African paganism fused at the moment in a cultural contact that created a new entity, neither Christian, Indo-European, nor African – a new reality. This was the moment when the "culture" of Europe as distinct from the mere techniques of its civilisation became an integral part of the Jamaican reality. The fusion took place on the unofficial excluded level – the creative level, the level of the people.

The Great Revival of 1860-61 began by Orthodox Christian Missionaries following the example of the Revival movement in the United States and Britain, was soon taken over by Native Baptists and Myal groups. The example of Pentecost and the missionaries' appeal to "get the spirit" and be "reborn" again was a culture contact point which lead to the transformation of Myal and Native Baptist groups into the Revivalist cults of today. The devotees became possessed by angels through deep trances, visions and above all through the power and force of the dance. They prayed as they danced, read the Bible, purified themselves by flagellation. The Great Revival became more 'African as it progressed' and:

> ... the attitudes of present-day cultists reflect this situation. Talented and experienced cultists can 'work the '61 order of revival' whilst lesser figures can get up only to the '60 order![104]

The religion of an invading civilisation – Christianity – had come into a relation of cultural continuity with the invaded culture. Revivalism which sprang out of orthodox Christianity and Myalism, became heir to all the accumulated traditions of dance and song and healing ritual – seen in the proliferation of Revival "balmyards where Mothers heal with herbs and psalms".[105] The Myal took on a new life in the Revival cults, while its more secular partner, the Jonkonnu, would contribute its pattern, as we shall see. Out of this comes the paradox that it is Revivalism, whose cultists, whilst mostly racially unmixed, are the true syncretisers of the Jamaican cultural tradition, the *culturally* mixed, accepting all influences within the basically Afro-Jamaican matrix.

One other folk rite was to become a part of Jonkonnu; and later of the Pukkumina Revivalist cult, and the more African Kumina. After emancipation Indians were brought as indentured labourers to work on the sugar estates. Many came from Bombay, and a substantial portion of them were of the Shiite sect of the Mohammedan religion. They brought with them the annual festival of the commemoration of the death of Hosein and Hassein, the sons of Ali. In Jamaica this festival became known as the Hussay Festival – although variants: Assay, Hossay Wuse, are also used. There were many culture contact points. A pattern of near ancestral worship, sacrifice to the Tajeh – or Hussay – the model of a temple in which the two martyrs are supposed to reincarnate themselves, the model made like a Jonkonnu mask, all glitter and splendour; and above all the processions of each group with its Hussay; the fighting between them, the music, the dancing, the stick and sword fighting; the concept, also, that those who followed the Hussay and took part would receive atonement for their sins and be purified. In the Hussay, too, the spirits of Ali's son reincarnated themselves as the ancestral gods did behind the Jonkonnu mask.

The Jonkonnu drew in elements of the Hussay Festival. In a description of Jonkonnu in 1925, we read:

> They have several tricks this year, as for instance a woman with a broom who swept the path ahead of them. She was quite new as also were the two 'habbres' or 'coolies'... East Indians...[106]

The little traditions of Africa, England, Scotland and India fused. The influence of Indian folksongs are evident in some Jamaican folk songs. The Indian order plays an essential role in the Pukkumina cult. But after the Great Revival, the little tradition whilst remaining ceaselessly creative, and provided with a high tradition in the Bible, was once more devoid of a learned interpreter caste related to its roots, able to provide it with a universal meaning. The little tradition remained "parochialised".

The learned have been taught to look with contempt on all practices that are non-Christian and *ipso facto* non-European. Even those who carry on the little tradition are ambivalent towards it.

In the Revivalists cults, the dance is still used as a cultural means by which cultists *experience* through *possession* that creative life force whose names are many, but which remains the same. Yet, in the value-system of Jamaica, these dance religions are despised; or looked upon with mocking contempt, rather like a more ridiculous form of Jonkonnu. The upper classes base their claim to being upper on the continued retention of European values; and the denigration of African ones. To the middle classes and the aspiring middle classes, both the dance religions and the Jonkonnu are seen as frontal assaults on their painfully acquired "Western" and, *ipso facto*, Christian status.

To a very broad cross section of the Jamaican people, including many Zion revivalists, all the African heritage, including Jonkonnu and Pukkumina must be avoided – since the African heritage belongs "to the days of darkness". Yet Africa exists powerfully in Jamaica today – in the Revival cults, Kumina, Convince, the funeral-going even of the middle class, the fervour of orthodox Christians' singing and hand-clapping, the easy rhythmical movements of all Jamaicans, in the Jonkonnu – but it exists without interpretation of meaning.

And without its framework of meaning it repels the more Christian element who sees it only as one more example of the "sexual licence" and immoral lack of restraint of the "lower classes". Meaningless, it reinforces their attitude of rejection and contempt which is, since this is a part of their cultural being, self-rejection and self-contempt. This attitude extends to the dances which have become "parochialised", a means of interpretation of a religion whose wider meaning is lost. Whilst the religion is constantly experienced and expressed through the dance, its universal elements and significance are obscured.

The "gods" remain in the revivalist cults – the "parochial gods" of the little tradition. Christian Jamaica sees them as pagan and idolatrous; progressive Jamaica sees them as a drawback to "progress" and "modernisation", those new absolute and unquestioned gods. By both, the little tradition is spurned and denied.

Folklore and folkdance belong to the little tradition of Jamaica. Hence the danger which Price Mars spoke about that one faces in dealing honestly with the problem. Colonel Rowe of Accompong, caught between the official tradition of Christianity and the powerful traditions of his history, had to deny the latter. This conflict and ambivalence is at the heart of cultural creativity in Jamaica; or rather of its frustration.

TABLE OF FOLK DANCE SURVIVALS

A. RELIGIOUS
B. SOCIAL

A. RELIGIOUS
(1) MORE PURELY AFRICAN SURVIVALS
   a) KUMINA
   b) CONVINCE
   c) GUMBAY

(2) MORE AFRO-CHRISTIAN SURVIVALS
    a) ZION REVIVAL
    b) PUKKUMINA

B. SOCIAL

(1) MORE SOCIO-RELIGIOUS
    a) NINE-NIGHT DANCES
    b) RASTAFARIAN DANCING

(2) MORE SECULAR
    a) MORE RURAL: QUADRILLE/MENTO
    b) MORE URBAN: SKA/REGGAE

(3) PRESENT-DAY REMNANTS OF JONKONNU
    a) BRUCKINS
    b) JONKONNU

NOTES:

A. RELIGIOUS

(i) *Kumina, Convince* and *Gumbay*: these are more purely African survivals, all descended from original Myal cult. First two reinforced in African elements by contact and involvement with Maroons – preserved the more African Myal after absorption in the Great Revival. Elements strengthened by the arrival of African immigrants after Emancipation to work sugar estates, particularly St. Thomas, where both cults found.

Gumbay – a remnant of Myalism – of the great Myal Procession. Found only in remote area of St. Elizabeth, uses drumming and dancing to exorcise evil spirits – or to "tame them" when one moves into a new house. Among drums, special one-headed square goatskin drum played with the fingers as shown in Belisario's sketch of the Jonkonnu, roughly same drum sketched by Miss Roberts in the 1920s. Drum used both by Jonkonnu dancers and Myal practitioners; usually same people. Myal and Jonkonnu rhythms and songs similar.

Kumina ancestral cult uses *gomba (i.e.* gumbay) drums – a set of three drums, two *bandas* or *bass* drums and a playing drum, to evoke ancestral spirits and gods. Gods are termed "African gods" and two types "earthbound gods" and "sky gods".

Myal term used to refer to "the possession dance of a dancing Zombie". Zombie is either an African god or ancestor once possessed by a god.

Kumina worship – a religious dance ceremony held on occasion of birth, betrothal, and Nine-Nights.

At Nine-Nights the KUMINA QUEEN in a special dance invokes spirit of deceased, and speeds it to its rest. Most important Kumina dancing takes place at the memorial for deceased about a year after death. Dance ceremonies help member of cult engaged in lawsuit. Dance invokes the gods and spirits – "power" to ensure other party in court case withdraws or disappears. Cultist dance around in circle whilst dancers – in the Myal – dance inside circle. Among dances – (a) courtship dance between Queen and two men (b) possessed dance of Queen alone, dancing with glass of water on head, lighted candle in hand – at times climbs fence or rolls on ground, entranced. (c) Possessed dance of men – climb trees, hang from feet, head downwards, still dancing. (d) Mimed weapon dance between cult leader and another man. (e) "Coolie-man" dance, possessed by an East Indian spirit. (f) Mimetic fertility dances – "distinctly sexual".

Convince cultists believe in Christian deities, but these are remote. *Convince* deals instead with ghosts of relatives, ancestors; and by extension, those of the ex-members of cult; also ghosts remembered from oral history. Dance invokes power of ghosts, behaviour amoral. Ghosts not Christians, cultists argue; outside Christian concept of sin. Each ghost with prescribed dance and dance step, prescribed costume. Songs, special for different spirits. Only handclapping used. Hymns sung to call ghosts. Ghost uses body of cultist violently, driving him to climb trees etc. Through body of the cultist, it drinks, smokes, uses special and rather blasphemous language, attempts sexual intercourse. Lends power to cultists to "pull obeah" , or "set obeah".

(2) AFRO-CHRISTIAN SURVIVAL
a.) Zion Revival
b) Pukkumina

Two Revivalist cults, heir to all elements that entered Jamaican folklore: Zion Revival belongs to more Christian side of Afro-Christian continuum; Pukkumina, influenced by Kumina, more African-oriented cult.

Jonkonnu parade with its different "Characters" influenced cults –principal "Spiritual Dancers" dance roles – called "posts" in Zion Revival, and "portions" in Pukkumina. Myal Procession and Great Revival influenced by concept of "dancing in circle, labouring in the spirit" and "groaning" in order to attain deeper order of possession – deepest '61 order – the Great Revival year.

The concept of "spiritual journey" on which dancers travel, central to Pukkumina – same origin. Both cults exist in all parts of Jamaica – Zion Revival tends to replace Pukkumina in rural areas. In Kingston, Pukkumina holds its own in more poverty-stricken areas. Pukkumina and Zion cults increase in response to rural influence – changes in social order – advent of technology – increasing modernisation and subsequent feeling of disruption from kindlier rural pattern. Both cults offer refuge of communal urban framework. Both cults "danced religion" – to both possession and possessed dancing sign of the saved.

For both these, the spirit world is divided into three categories:

a) Heavenly spirits

b) Earthbound spirits

c) Ground spirits

Zion Revival deals only with first two, Pukkumina excludes none – particularly fond of "ground spirits", i.e. ghosts. Nearer ancestral cults like Kumina – both cults, God remote. Jesus for Zion Revival nearer to man. His death and Resurrection fuses with original Myal ritual.

He comes to be seen as "a 'curing' spirit, the ultimate source of all healing forces".

Zion Revival, with proliferation of "balm yards" where they heal with herbs and psalms – true heir to Myal in healing aspect. Jesus pours out healing spirit through Holy Ghost as at Pentecost. The Holy Ghost passes on these gifts through messenger angels, who "teach" them through spirit possession and spiritual dancing. One of these gifts – "unknown tongues". Pukkumina tend to use African and Hindustani words in songs. Angels in Zion, ghosts in Pukkumina allot to their converts both "posts" and "portions", i.e. roles they must dance in spiritual dancing; and costumes they must wear. Both angels and ghosts give their converts moral advice – cults function as source of morality. Cults also function as mutual aid, through partner insurance, loan and burial societies, spiritual dancing and religious concept provide cohesion.

MAIN CHARACTERISTICS OF DANCING

1. Both cults adhere to main pattern of choral circle, dancing around the "SEAL" or consecrated ground.

2. Zion Revival use drums which play especially *before* procession.

   Both cults use rhythmic "groaning" to achieve varying depth of intensity of possession. Groaning: "a series of deep guttural sounds, made by rapid inhalation and exhalation of breath through the mouth".[107]

   Zion Revival breathing polyrhythmic – the cultists use sidestep movement, body lifts on one foot, then lowered with a stamping sound on other – which at same time travels ground with small hop. Continues movement and sound coalesce in unified whole. Circle "labours" i.e. dances in unison to achieve harmony through similar depth of possession. When this attained, angels send messages which leader interprets by singing – this called "rich area of folk-music".

3. Whilst for Zion Revival "spiritual dancing" used to summon spirits, in Pukkumina "ground" spirits possess devotees – violently knocking them to ground. Pukkumina breathing pattern in "groaning" – one-two beat, marked by the movement. This a "genuflecting or bowing motion in which the upper half of the body bends forward, while at the same time, the knees are bent, resuming an erect position ... with this movement dancers travel sideways towards 'the light of the spirit'."[108]

Each special "portion" of each cultist devised to be danced to cope with hazards and dangers of "journey". Spectacular dance of "River Maid" to take "bands" across river. Colourful dance of the Indian order leads "bands" through India. Technological terminology noteworthy: "locomotive", leads "train" assisted by "engineer", "brakemen", "coalman" etc. Shows urban emphasis of cult.

4. Both cults use "Tables" – spiritual ceremonies combining religious service and feast as in "thanksgiving", "uplifting", mourning, "sacrifice" and "destruction" (particularly secret, as connected with popular dread of Obeah). New "tables" devised for new needs. (Destruction Tables' movement reversed from normal counter-clockwise to clockwise; foot-stamping also reversed, left foot being used first.)

Revivalists through spiritual "labour" and "work" deny brute facts of everyday existence by their transcendence in super-reality. They establish in dance "a putative society" in which they are the elect, the elite. Dance turns world upside-down, liberating participants. Challenge and response syndrome leads to fact that dance as a vital and meaningful reality found mainly among dispossessed.

B. SOCIAL
(1) SOCIO-RELIGIOUS

NINE-NIGHT DANCES: Kumina/Tambu/Buru/Dinkie minie/Calimbe/Combolo/Etu

Ritual connected with death plays special part in Jamaican folklore. *Kumina* dance, like original *Tambu Buru, Etu, Dinkie minie* – dance associated with speeding the dead. All counterparts of the Haitian *Banda*. Both *Buru* and *Dinkie minie became* associated with wild eroticism – reference to fact that fertility dances, in all folk cultures, performed at wakes etc. to reduce power of Death, by opposing life force. Description of *Dinkie minie* danced in Eastern Portland, shows this: "A peculiar jumping dance to drums... involving vertical heights in the jumps... the dancer bends on one leg at the knee and makes a long series of high leaps all on the other foot."[109] Parallels leap/ fertility aspect of Jonkonnu.

Nine-Night dances spread out their purpose and meaning to purely social functions. Meanings changed. *Dinkie minie* now associated with ring plays at Nine Nights. *Buru* kept an association of violence and eroticism. Both war dances and fertility dances originally danced at wakes etc. Name, dance and association of *Buru* taken over by Rastafarians. *Calimbe and Combolo* terms which survived regular performance of their dances. *Calimbe* a dance in which two men hold pair of sticks while third dances upon it. Dance represents death of third dancer as vegetation spirit – lifted up and then lowered, life restored to him. *Combolo* an alternative term for similar dance with erotic implications.

Tambu Etu – in isolated areas – still danced at social functions in particular those connected with funerals and weddings.

RING PLAY and the dances accompany song and action.

Games played in circle to pass time at wakes and Nine-Nights. Dance actions accompany songs and game, among them:
   a) A shuffle step, one flat foot, one toe; feet always on ground in a slow turn called "riding".
   b) Wheel by which player selects his partner.
   c) Bows and curtseys and hopping steps to imitate animals.
   d) Exhibition dancing steps in which player shows his motions.

Many ring-plays influenced by English children's games and some songs adapted from English folk tunes. But African antiphonal form also dominant. The Ringplay with its integrated song, dance, words and mime, the indigenous form – only one in which dance as conscious art form can meaningfully develop.

b) RASTAFARIAN DANCING

A millenarian movement, which sees Ethiopia as both Heaven and Fatherland on earth; the Emperor the black Christ. Bible, interpreted in "black" terms – is "high" tradition of sect. Called "Black Israelites". Nostalgia for lost and distant Africa – reject prevalent value-system of society. Assimilate instead, all "despised" African elements of folkculture. Nyabingi Order, or Locksmen, more fanatic members of sect, vow not to cut either hair or beard. This Order adopted *Buru* and *Kumina* dances and drumming from semi-religious cult. Both used to welcome fellow cultists from prison. Nyabingi dances, with Nyabingi drumming on a set of three drums called *akete* i.e. Maroon war-horn – dances of fire and power, with emphatic footwork, jerky taut arm movements, stamping and abrupt turns, sudden stops and starts, fierce mime. Both dancing and drumming impressive. Through their longing for Africa, Rastafarians stumbled on their Jamaican roots.

(ii) MORE SECULAR

a) *More Rural*
   European folk-dances, after they died out in Europe, took on own life in Jamaica. Quadrille, like mazurka, polka, jog, schottische etc. became widespread and indigenous. In quadrille slight but pervasive hip movements introduced. Quadrille, in remote European past, danced as fertility charm.
   Mento very much a dance of African origins, featuring hip-sway and pelvic roll and connected with original courtship-fertility dances. Influenced by stateliness and more suave quality of quadrille, especially as danced by older rural folk. In midst of quadrille figures, mento movements will be introduced and folk tunes played both as mento and quadrille. In towns and especially in cabaret dancing, more erotic aspects of mento degenerated into belly dance. Even here not altogether lost vitality of original meaning. Mento, perhaps *the*

national folkdance. Gentler than Trinidad calypso, somewhat like Cuban rhumba but without fast footwork, mento, danced with shuffle step over small space, ripples whole body in up-and-down, side to side movement.

b) More Urban

More urban and modern dances: *Ska* and the *Reggae,* – response of rural folk, alienated from ancient folkways, confronted with rapid urban and technological change. Source of both dance and song heavy marked beat of Pukkumina and Zion Revival. Part of dance movement of ska taken from "portion" of Pukkumina cultist's "train". Body bent forward, back almost horizontal one leg placed forwards, slanting outwards. Arms held straight out, loosely doubled in fists, move backwards and forwards in pumping movement which jerks head and shoulders forward. Change over to other leg takes place by straightening back and putting other leg forward. Second part of dance owes origin to jockey's dance in today's Jonkonnu – riding and whipping part. Arms bent from elbow, and fists held in front holding "reins". Whole body moves forward and back in jogging motion. Knees bent, "riding" motion controlled from pelvis. One hand goes backwards to "whip" horse, swings forward to crack whip, with a sudden and dramatic movement. Then the 'riding' resumed.

Reggae, more honed down, energy more reined-in, also, in essence, the Jockey's dance. Only body held straight, and arms, one on belly, other stretched out to side, alternates as head and body keep up a muted tight rocking back and forth, from taut pelvis rather than from knees. Feet move, going forward change slant of rocking body. Dance of city streets, all excess rural energy stripped away. Movement used in Revival cults by those cultists who are rocking themselves into getting the spirit.

Reggae secular purpose, only enjoyment. Young urban dispossessed known as "Rudies" associated with these song and dances. Rudie at once *macho* (very masculine) and violent – assertion of manhood by circumstances deprived. Walk weapon dance – weapon – rachet knife. When society affords him manhood, both transformed into art; into the dance. Dance expresses new tension of new transitional social order.

PRESENT-DAY REMNANTS OF JONKONNU*

a) Bruckins

Bruckins survives in Portland – originally celebrates Abolition of slavery 1838. Many "play" patterns of Jonkonnu contained in Bruckins as shown in songs dealing with abolition; songs with dance use swords. Dancers wear costumes

---

* Revival of Jonkonnu as a folk dance entry in National Festival gives it both new lease of life and "official" acceptance. Whole Festival itself needs to take reinterpreted shape and format of Jonkonnu, the original "Carnival" form of Jamaica.

to match songs and dances, sometimes, words used. Similarity with Brazilian *quilombo* celebrating important Negro events and with Trinidadian *Cannes Brûlées* [Canboulay] which celebrated Emancipation. Sword dance in Bruckins represents fusion of African and English folk elements as seen in Jonkonnu.

Bruckins movements today – dancer steps forward on alternate feet, bending over from the waist with movement forward of head and arms – arms jerked back as body straightens. (Similar step in Portland Jonkonnu – rhythmn different – by "masquerade queen"). Queen strides forward, arms held regally, stiffly by side. Step called "bruckins" – queen said to "bruk" when performing movement. In *Abolition,* "bruckins" dancers use shoulders, arms and head for the bruckins – faster tempo used.

b) Jonkonnu

Now only Queen performs "bruckins" step. *Jockey* does riding step; *Pitchie-Patchie* in multicoloured rags, shakes rags and body telling crowd to "dress" i.e. make way. *Masquerade Queen* wears crown and veils face; also John Crow feathers and Jamaica beads. *Warrior* wears tallest headdress and carries hatchet – same as Yoruba *Shango* – and sword. Dance consists of great leaps crossing sword and hatchet over head. Then bringing hatchet down on hop of one leg onto ground telling crowd to "dress". *Devilman* prances and capers, dressed all in black (tightfitting) pants and shirt, mesh wire mask of tarred black mask with cow-tail beard and moustache. Wears bell in place of tail moving constantly with pelvic motion making bell ring. Carries a two-pronged fork. *Belly-Woman:* man dressed as pregnant woman with outsize stomach which slips as she/he dances, in jigging step – fertility symbol: makes crowd laugh. *Policeman* costumed as real policemen. *Whore Girl* (man representing her) dressed with strings of beads and feathers, wire-mesh face mask and silk panties and stockings. *Wild Indian* – headdress of feathers and beads. All headdresses decorated with small mirrors. All dances satirical (*Whore Girl, Wild Indian* and *Policeman* dance previously discussed). No central Jonkonnu. Band headed by fife player in charge. Tourism induces weekly performances for cruise ships. Jonkonnu at nadir. *Whore Girl* and *Wild Indian* now similar to belly dancer. Vestige of original meaning lost.

WHEN FOLK BECOMES CONSCIOUSLY FOLK, ITS "INSOLUBLE CORE" DISAPPEARS. IT BECOMES "FOLKSY" AND PARODIES ITSELF. THE JESTER DANCES ON. BUT THE GODS ARE GONE.

MAIN REFERENCE WORKS

Beckwith, M., *Black Roadways: A Study of Jamaican Folk Life* (Chapel Hills: University of North Carolina Press, 1929).

Beckwith, M., *Christmas Mummings in Jamaica* (Poughkeepsie, NY: Vassar College Folklore Foundation, 1923).

Beckwith, M., *The Hussay Festival in Jamaica* (Poughkeepsie, NY: Vassar College, 1924).

Cassidy, F.G., & Le Page, R.B., *Dictionary of Jamaican English* (Cambridge: Cambridge University Press, 1967).

Cassidy, F.G., *Jamaica Talk: Three Hundred Years of the English Language in Jamaica* (London: MacMillan, 1961).

Coulthard, G.R., *Race and Colour in Caribbean Literature* (Seville 1958; London: OUP, 1962).

Coulthard, G.R., "Parallelisms and Divergencies between 'Negritude' and 'Indigenismo'", *Caribbean Studies*, vol. 8, no. 1 (April 1968) 31-55.

Elder, J.D., *Evolution of the Traditional Calypso of Trinidad and Tobago. A Socio-historical Analysis of Song Change.* Unpublished Ph.D. Thesis, 1966.

Griaule, M, Dieterlin, G., "The Dogon", in *African Worlds*, ed. Daryll Forde (London: Oxford UP, 1954).

Herskovits, M., The *Myth of the Negro Past* (Boston: Harper and Brothers, 1958).

Hogg, D.W., *Jamaican Religions. A Study in Variations.* Unpublished PhD thesis, Yale University, 1964.

Jahn, J., *Muntu: An Outline of the New African Culture* (London: Faber and Faber, 1961).

Kennedy, D., *English Folk Dancing, Today and Yesterday* (London: G. Bell, 1964).

Leaf, E., *Isles of Rhythm* (New York: A.S. Barnes, 1948).

Monti, F., *African Masks* (London: Hamlyn, 1969).

Ortiz, F., *La Africanía de la música folklórica de Cuba* (1954; La Habana: Editorial Letras Cubans, 1993).

Patterson, O., *The Sociology of Slavery* (London: MacGibbon & Kee, 1967).

Ramos, A., *The Negro in Brazil*, Trans. Richard Pattee (Washington: Associated Publishers Inc., 1939).

Redfield, R., *Peasant Society and Culture: An Anthropological Approach to Civilization* (Chicago: University of Chicago Press, 1956).

Roberts, H.H., "Some drums and drum rhythms of Jamaica", *Natural History*, vol. 24, no. 2 (March-April 1924), 241-251.

Sachs, C., *World History of the Dance*, trans. by Bessie Schönberg (London: George Allen & Unwin, 1937).

Seaga, E.P.G., "Revival Cults in Jamaica. Notes Towards a Sociology of Religion", *Jamaica Journal*, vol. 3, no. 2, 1969.

Senghor, L.S., *Négritude and Humanism* (Paris: Éditions du Seuil, 1964).

Simpson, G.E., "Jamaican Revival Cults", *Social and Economic Studies*, I.S.E.R. vol. 5, no. 4 (December 1956): i-iv, 321-442, v-vii.

Endnotes

1. Jean Price Mars, *Ainsi parla l'oncle* (1928; Ottawa: Éditions Leméac, 1973), 43.
2. G. R. Coulthard, *Raza y color en la literatura antillana* (Sevilla: Escuela de Estudios Hispanos-Americanos, 1958), 145-146.
3. Aimé Césaire, *Discours sur le colonialism* (Paris: Présence Africaine, 1955), 30.
4. Price Mars, *Ainsi parla l'oncle*, 43.
5. Ibid., 44-45.
6. Ibid., 46-47.
7. Coulthard, "Parallelisms and Divergencies between 'Negritude' and 'Indigenismo'", *Caribbean Studies*, vol. 8, no. 1 (April 1968), 49.
8. Ibid., 31.
9. Ibid.
10. Coulthard is quoting Sepúlveda here, ibid., 32
11. Jacob D. Elder, "Evolution of the Traditional Calypso of Trinidad and Tobago: A Socio-Historical Analysis of Song Change" (Ph.D. dissertation, University of Pennsylvania, 1966), 111.
12. The source of this translation could not be located, but a contemporary one of Hesiod's Works and Days is by M.L. West (London: Oxford Classics, 1988), 49.
13. *Jamaica in 1867: The Taylor Manuscript at the National Library of Jamaica*, David Buisseret, ed. (Kingston: University of the West Indies/Mill Press/National Library of Jamaica, 2008), 267-268.
14. Elder, "Evolution of the Traditional Calypso", 83.
15. José Carlos, *Mariátegui, Siete ensayos de interpretación de la realidad peruana* (Lima: Empresa Editora Amuata, 1965), 44.
16. Léopold Sédar Senghor, "Le problème de la culture" in *Liberté I: Négritude et Humanismse* (Paris: Éditions du Seuil, 1964), 93.
17. Senghor, "Le problème de la culture", 93-94.
18. Karl Polanyi, *The Great Transformation: The Political and Economic Origins of Our Time* (1944; Boston: Beacon Press, 1957), 130-131. Here Wynter paraphrases Polanyi.
19. David Brion Davis, *The Problem of Slavery in Western Culture* (1966; Ithaca: Cornell University Press, 1975), 45.
20. Francisco Morales Padrón, *Jamaica Española* (Sevilla: Escuela de Estudios Hispano-Americanos, 1952), 174.
21. Melville J. Herskovits, *The Myth of the Negro Past* (New York: Harper and Brothers, 1941), 293.
22. Robert Redfield, *Peasant, Society and Culture: An Anthropological Approach to Civilization* (Chicago: University of Chicago Press, 1956), 21.
23. Hans Sloane, *A Voyage to the Islands of Madera, Barbados, Nieves, S. Christophers and Jamaica...* vol. I (London: printed by B.M. for the author, 1707), lii. [paraphrased]
24. Fernando Ortiz, *La Africanía de la música folklórica de Cuba* (1954; La Habana: Editorial Letras Cubans, 1993), 139.

25. Hans Sloane, *A Voyage,* lvi.
26. Ibid., xlvii.
27. Ibid., lii.
28. *Jamaica in 1687,* 272.
29. Meyer Fortes cited Freda Wolfson, ed. *Pageant of Ghana* (1958; London: Oxford University Press, 1965), 232.
30. Curt Sachs, *World History of the Dance,* trans. *Eine Weltgeschichte des Tanzes* by Bessie Schönberg (London: George Allen and Unwin Ltd., 1937), 79.
31. Sloane, *A Voyage,* xlix.
32. Orlando Patterson, *The Sociology of Slavery: An Analysis of the Origins, Development and Structure of Negro Slave Society in Jamaica* (1967; Rutherford: Fairleigh Dickinson University Press, 1975), 244.
33. Ibid., 245
34. Ibid.
35. Ibid.
36. Janheinz Jahn, *Muntu: An Outline of the New African Culture,* trans. by Majorie Grene (1958; London: Faber and Faber, 1961), 106.
37. Franco Monti, *African Masks* trans. *Le Maschere Africane* by Andrew Hale (1966; London: Hamlyn, 1969), 17.
38. Monti, *African Masks,* 23.
39. F[rederic] G[omes] Cassidy and R[obert] B[rock] Le Page, eds., *Dictionary of Jamaican English* (Cambridge: Cambridge University Press, 1967), 249.
40. Ibid.
41. Martha Beckwith, *Black Roadways: A Study of Jamaican Folk Life* (1929; New York: Negro Universities Press, 1969), 150.
42. Cassidy and Le Page, *Dictionary,* 249.
43. George Eaton Simpson, "Jamaica Revivalist Cults," *Social and Economic Studies,* vol. 5., no. 4, (December 1956): i-iv, 321-442, v-vii, qt. 424.
44. Frederic G. Cassidy, *Jamaica Talk: Three Hundred Years of the English Language in Jamaica* (1961; Kingston: University of the West Indies Press, 2007), 262.
45. Douglas Kennedy, *English Folk-Dancing: Today and Yesterday* (London: G. Bell, 1964), 44, 46.
46. Ibid., 47.
47. Quotation could not be located.
48. Edward Long, *The History of Jamaica or, General Survey of the Antient and Modern State of That Island...,* Vol. II (London: T. Lowndes, 1774), 425.
49. *Lady Nugent's Journal* (Institute of Jamaica, 1966), 48.
50. Alexander Barclay, *A Practical View of the Present State of Slavery in the West Indies...,* (London: Smith Elder and Co., 1827), 13, cited in Patterson, *Sociology of Slavery,* 241.
51. I. M. Belisario, *Sketches of Character, In Illustration of the Habits, Occupation, and Costume of the Negro Population in the Island of Jamaica* [no. 2] (Kingston: Published by the artist, Printed by J. R. De Cordova, 1838), n.p., reprinted in *Art and Emancipation in Jamaica: Isaac Mendes Belisario and His Works,* Tim Barringer, Gillian Forrester, Barbaro Martinez-Ruiz (New Haven: Yale University Press, 2007), 227.
52. Cassidy and Le Page, *Dictionary,* 250.

53. Patterson, *Sociology of Slavery*, 240.
54. Matthew [Monk] Gregory Lewis, *Journal of a West India Proprietor, Kept During the Residence of the Island of Jamaica* (London: John Murray, 1834), 51, cited in Cassidy and Le Page, *Dictionary*, 249 [C & LP does not cite the full text, but Wynter does].
55. Cassidy, *Jamaica Talk*, 257.
56. Philip D. Curtin, *Two Jamaicas: The Role of Ideas in a Tropical Colony, 1830-1865* (1955; New York: Greenwood Press, 1968), 27.
57. Exact language can also be found in *The New Act of Assembly of the Island of Jamaica, ...Commonly Called, The New Consolidated Act* (London: B. White and Son, et al., 1789), 7.
58. Beckwith, *Black Roadways*, 154.
59. Belisario, op. cit.
60. Martha Warren Beckwith, *Christmas Mummings in Jamaica* (Poughkeepsie, NY: Vassar College Folk-Lore Foundation, 1923), 2.
61. Monti, *African Masks*, 62.
62. Beckwith, *Black Roadways*, 151.
63. All quotations above Beckwith, ibid.
64. Long, *History of Jamaica*, vol. II, 416, cited in Cassidy and Le Page, *Dictionary*, 313.
65. Beckwith, *Black Roadways*, 144.
66. Thomas Banbury, *Jamaica Superstitions, Or the Obeah Book...* (Kingston, Jamaica: M. DeSouza, 1894), 35-36, cited in Cassidy and Le Page, *Dictionary*, 383.
67. Patterson, *Sociology of Slavery*, 187.
68. Long, *History of Jamaica*, Vol. II, 417, cited in Cassidy and Le Page, *Dictionary*, 314.
69. Beckwith, *Christmas Mummings*, 46.
70. Sloane, *A Voyage*, vol. I, xliv
71. Cynric R. Williams, *A Tour Through the Island of Jamaica, From the Western End to the Eastern End, in the Year 1823* (London: Hunt and Clark, 1826), 25.
72. Long, *History of Jamaica*, Vol. II., 424, cited in Cassidy and Le Page, *Dictionary*, 249.
73. *Lady Nugent's Journal*, 25 December 1801, page 28, cited in ibid.
74. Lewis, *Journal*, 56 cited in Cassidy and Le Page, *Dictionary*, 249.
75. Chambre cited in ibid., xx.
76. Ibid.
77. H. Carrington Bolton, "Gombay: A Festal Right of Bermudian Negroes", *Journal of American Folkore*, Vol. 3, No. 10 (July-September 1890), 223, cited in Beckwith, *Christmas Mummings*, 6. In this instance, "Gumbay" is spelled with an "o" as in "Gombay," although the other spelling is quite common.
78. Sachs, *World History of the Dance*, 55.
79. Sachs, Ibid.
80. Cassidy, *Jamaica Talk*, 260.
81. Cassidy and Le Page, *Dictionary*, 402.
82. Cassidy, *Jamaica Talk*, 261.
83. Reginald M. Murray, "Quadrille Invitation", *Kingston Daily Gleaner* (August 6, 1961): 20. [Poem name not as noted by Wynter].

290 WE MUST LEARN TO SIT DOWN TOGETHER AND TALK ABOUT A LITTLE CULTURE

84. Belisario, *Sketches of Character,* No. 1, 210.
85. Beckwith, *Christmas Mummings,* 2.
86. J. Stewart, *A View of the Past and Present State of the Island of Jamaica; With Remarks on the Moral and Physical Condition of the Slaves, and on the Abolition of Slavery in the Colonies* (Edinburg: Oliver and Boyd, Tweeddale-House, 1823), 270-271.
87. Patterson, *Sociology of Slavery,* 236.
88. Ibid. Patterson is quoting from *Marly, or the Life of a Planter in Jamaica,* 46.
89. Ibid., from *Marley,* 46, 47.
90. *Lady Nugent's Journal,* 7 August 1801, 14.
91. Patterson, *Sociology of Slavery,* 235-236.
92. Cassidy, *Jamaica Talk,* 261.
93. Both epigraphs in ibid., 226, 404.
94. Source not located.
94. Quoted in Cassidy, *Jamaica Talk,* 272.
96. Long, *History of Jamaica,* vol. II, 424.
97. Jahn, *Muntu,* 88.
98. Jahn, *Muntu,* 83.
99. Cassidy, *Jamaica Talk,* 272.
100. In *The Artist in West Indian Society: A Symposium,* ed. Errol Hill (Port of Spain: UWI Department of Extra-Mural Studies, nd. c. 1963).
101. Edward Seaga, "Revival Cults in Jamaica: Notes Toward a Sociology of Religion", *Jamaica Journal,* Vol. 3, No. 2 (June 1969): 3-13, qt. a 5.
102. Earl Leaf, *Isles of Rhythm* (New York: A.S. Barnes, 1948), 70.
103. Redfield, *Peasant Society and Culture,* 71-72.
104. Donald William Hogg, "Jamaican Religions: A Study in Variations" (PhD Dissertation, Yale University, 1964), 142.
105. Source not located, but for an account of the healer Mother Rita from the Blake Pen balmyard, see Leonard Barrett, "The Portrait of a Jamaican Healer: African Medical Lore in the Caribbean", *Caribbean Quarterly,* vol. 9, no. 3 (September 1973): 6-19.
106. Source not located.
107. Seaga, "Revival Cults in Jamaica", 7
108. Ibid.
107. Cassidy and Le Page, *Dictionary,* 150.

· NOVEL AND HISTORY, PLOT AND PLANTATION

First let us define our terms. What, in our context, is the novel? What, in our context, is history? What *is* our context? George Beckford, a Jamaican economist writes:

> In America, the *locus* of the plantation system is the Caribbean. Indeed, this region is generally regarded as *the* classic plantation area. So much so that social anthropologists have described the region as a culture sphere, labelled Plantation America.[1]

The Caribbean area is the classic plantation area since many of its units were "planted" with people, not in order to form societies, but to carry on plantations whose aim was to produce single crops for the market. That is to say, the plantation-societies of the Caribbean came into being as adjuncts to the market system; their peoples came into being as an adjunct to the product, to the single crop commodity – the sugar cane – which they produced. As Eric Williams has shown, our societies were both cause and effect of the emergence of the market economy; an emergence which marked a change of such world historical magnitude, that we are all, without exception still "enchanted", imprisoned, deformed and schizophrenic in its bewitched reality.

Now, the novel form itself, according to Goldmann, came into being with the extension and dominance of the market economy, and "appears to us to be in effect, the transposition on the literary plane, of the daily life within an individualist society, born of production for the market."[2] The novel form and our societies are twin children of the same parents. No wonder Miguel Ángel Asturias, a Plantation novelist of a Plantation Republic, Guatemala, wrote in unbelieving despair, after the C.I.A.-backed overthrow of the legally elected Government of Árbenz: "These things that happen? ...It's best to call them fiction!"[3] History, then, these things that happen, is, in the plantation context, itself fiction; a fiction written, dominated, controlled by forces external to itself. It is clear then, that it is only when the society, or elements of the society rise up in rebellion against its external authors and manipulators that our prolonged fiction becomes temporary fact. The novel *New Day* shows not one, but two of these historical collisions and links them, suggesting in fiction their factual connection.

The epic form, Lukács remarks, knows nothing of questions. The hero is essentially at one with the values of his world. With the novel form, the rupture of the hero and the now inauthentic values of his world begins. The novel form is in essence a question mark.[4]

In *New Day*, the second, and younger hero, the hero whom we can term the "positive hero" as distinct from Davie, the earlier and "problematic hero" asks his great uncle, the narrator, a question which is crucial to the novel and to our discussion.

> Tell me Uncle John. You have spoken of the old things, but you have never given me an opinion. We have been taught in our history classes that Gordon and Bogle were devils, while Eyre was a saint who only did what he did because it was necessary. You knew both Gordon and Bogle. Were they as bad as they were painted?[5]

The old man's answer is evasive and ambivalent. It is part and parcel of the evasive ambivalence of the "ideology" of gradualism which was the ideology of the more idealistic middle-class movement summed up in the People's National Party, a party which emerged after the upheavals of the Jamaican people in 1938. In fact, it is clear that Garth himself is a thinly disguised portrait of Norman Washington Manley. On the negative side, one could dismiss this movement, as Ken Post does,[6] by calling it merely the "middle-class backlash" against the threatened takeover by varied and manifold popular forces. But in the context of plantation societies like ours, the usual terms cannot be applied without examination.

To evaluate the old man's answer, we must examine the basic significance of the question. The question he is asked is one of historical fact. Yet, from the way Garth asks the question we see that the history taught in the schools is a history based around a Manichean myth. Bogle and Gordon are devils. Eyre is a saint. This was the version of history taught by the forces that upheld the plantation. And the forces that upheld the plantation were the forces of the market. These forces, the forces of the *emporium* (*emporio*) (to borrow Asturias's pun) are the forces of the *imperio* – the Empire. The emporialist forces and the imperialist forces are one.

Bogle, Gordon and Eyre are personalities, figures caught in a clash and conflict that are not even primarily of their making. For they are caught in a collision and a clash that was inherent and inbuilt, and still is, between the plantation system, a system, owned and dominated by external forces, and what we shall call the plot system, the indigenous, autochthonous system. Miguel Ángel Asturias defines this clash as the struggle between, "...the indigenous peasant who accepts that corn should be sown only as food, and the *creole* who sows it as a business, burning down forests of precious trees, impoverishing the earth in order to enrich himself".[7]

Basically then this is a struggle between the indigenous man still involved in a world of what Marx terms *use-value*, where a product is made in response to a human need; and the market economy world with its structure of *exchange-value* where the product is made in response to its profitability in the market. In the world of use-value, human needs dominate the product. In the world of exchange-value, the product, the thing made, dominates, manipulates human need.

Now, as Goldmann argues, the novel form is, "among all literary forms, the most immediately and directly linked to the economic structures in the narrow sense of the term, to the structure of exchange and production for the market."[8] But because the writer, the artist, is by the very nature of his craft linked to the structure of use-value statements, the impulse of creation thus being directed by human needs, he remained as a hangover in the new form of societies. The novel form reflects his critical and oppositional stance to a process of alienation which had begun to fragment the very human community, without which the writer has neither purpose, nor source material, nor view of the world, nor audience. The novel form, a product of the market economy, its exchange structure – its individual here set free to realise his individuality by the "liberal" values of individualism, linked to the very existence of the market system – nevertheless, instead of expressing the values of the market society, develops and expands as a form of resistance to this very market society. In effect, the novel form and the novel is the critique of the very historical process which has brought it to such heights of fulfilment.

V.S. Naipaul's *A House for Mr. Biswas*, whilst it celebrates the talent of its author, and awards him a recognised place among the elite world, is nevertheless a profound indictment of a deprived world in which, to realise his being, Biswas must alienate himself from an impossible community, distorted by phantasmagoric circumstance, to shelter in a jerry-built house and a Prefect car. The individual, dreamt of in the liberal market economy as being now totally sovereign and free, is shipwrecked by the later developments of this structure which prohibits his fulfilment and leaves him huddled in a house, escaping from civilisation; a Robinson Crusoe clinging to his island for survival through escape from the outside world. His victory, like ours, is pyrrhic.

The "problematic hero" is the corollary of the problematic novel. This problematic hero is exemplified in Davie and, to some extent, in his father. For like Okonkwo in Chinua Achebe's *Things Fall Apart*, old father Campbell, clinging to his belief in God's order and in the inevitability of British justice, is shot down by British soldiers, defending the market economy, i.e. the plantation, against the challenge of the peasant farmers and the agro-proletarian workers. To make the world safe for the market economy, families are broken up, as in Ngugi Wa Thiong'o's, *Weep Not Child*, and indeed, in *New Day*. Hundreds are shot down. The techniques of terror which will be brought to perfection under Hitler and Stalin against Europeans, in Europe itself, are perfected in the *emporium-imperium*, plantation units. Vic Reid in *New Day* describes the actual historical fact of Colonel Hobbs, a gentleman, who grew roses up at the barracks at Newcastle, getting nine "rebels" to hang each other in a chapel at Fonthill, ordering thirteen others to dig a trench, and then having the soldiers shoot them into the mass grave. Hobbs had a problem of finding enough quicklime to sanitarily dispose of the bodies. He had another problem too. Afraid of being mocked for his natural inclination to clemency for the rebels, he felt he had to match and outdo in terror his fellow officers. He committed suicide afterwards. In Ngugi Wa Thiong'o's *Weep Not Child*, the hero confronts and is tortured by the English settler-farmer who grows pyrethrum for the market.

The reaction of the planters in 1865 to the death of a handful of the manager colon-creole class who are killed by Bogle and his followers is one of outrage, not only at the thought of bloodshed but at the threat to the plantation, which was to them the very core and seat of the structure of their "civilised" values. It is not accidental that H. G. de Lisser, a colon-creole writer who dealt with 1865 in a novel called *Revenge* sees the battle between the plantation forces and Bogle's forces as a battle between light and darkness. Bogle's followers watch anxiously for a sign from heaven, after a Cecil B. DeMille-type ritual ceremony. Joyce, the English plantation heroine, watches anxiously too, as she observes

> a great mass of black clouds... moving slowly across the sky ...It seemed as though the inky mass were gaining inch by inch on the shining space [i.e. lit up by the moon] ... were menacing it with an inevitable doom of obliteration; it was like a huge formless monster advancing slowly but with pitiless tread towards a thing of beauty which it had doomed to extinction...[9]

The symbolism is quite clear. This passage illustrates what Ramchand, paraphrasing from Fanon, has called "the terrified consciousness" of the Whites.[10] But I am trying to shift from the ground of race, which is but one factor in the equation, to the ground Asturias defines. Bogle's followers are men who predominantly sow for food, secondarily for the market. Thus, use-value determines their structure of values. Joyce belongs to the plantation system, the exchange structure; and "the thing of beauty" whose extinction she fears is the complex of values by which she lives; values which have their positive aspect; for example the hero shows a sense of responsibility, thoughtfulness; but values, too, which bolster their dominant and exploitative position.

Bogle's followers, according to de Lisser, cheer wildly when the black clouds cover the moon. It is a sign that they will be helped by God to purge wickedness from the land; and the white creole hero's mother is in no doubt that it is her race, class and their structure of values that are to be purged out of the land. In both De Lisser's novel and in Vic Reid's, the basic confrontation is between the plantation and the plot and the structure of values which each represents. I suggest that the conflict and clash that has taken place between two defined groups in this conference[11], between those who defend the "autonomy" of the "civilised", highly educated artist and those who defend the claims of the community and the folk, has little to do with racial division and everything to do with those who, like Joyce, defend the values of the plantation and those who, like Bogle, represent the values of the plot. Perhaps most typical of all is the "silent majority", ambivalent like *New Day's* narrator-hero between the two. For if the history of Caribbean society is that of a dual relation between plantation and plot, the two poles which originate in a single historical process, the ambivalence between the two has been, and is, the distinguishing characteristic of the Caribbean response. This ambivalence is at once the root cause of our alienation; and the possibility of our salvation.

To explain briefly the plantation-plot dichotomy we are compelled to make generalisations.

1. Before the unique Western experience which began with the discovery of the New World, all societies of mankind existed in what Senghor describes as dual oscillatory process in which Man adapts to Nature, and adapts Nature to his own needs.

2. But with the discovery of the New World and its vast exploitable lands, that process which has been termed the "reduction of Man to Labour and of Nature to Land" had its large-scale beginning. From this moment on, Western Man saw himself as "the lord and possessor of Nature".[12] The one-way transformation of Nature began. Since man is a part of Nature, a process of dehumanisation and alienation was set in train. In old societies with traditional values based on the old relation, resistance could be put up to the dominance of the new dehumanising system. In new societies like ours, created for the market, there seemed at first to be no possibility of such a tradition.

3. But from early, the planters gave the slaves plots of land on which to grow food to feed themselves in order to maximise profits. We suggest that this plot system was, like the novel form in literature terms, the focus of resistance to the market system and market values.

4. For African peasants transplanted to the plot all the structure of values that had been created by traditional societies of Africa; the land remained the Earth – and the Earth was a goddess; man used the land to feed himself and to offer first fruits to the Earth; his funeral was the mystical reunion with the earth. Because of this traditional concept, the social order remained primary. Around the growing of yam, of food for survival, he created on the plot a folk culture – the basis of a social order – in three hundred years.

This culture recreated traditional values – use values. This folk culture became a source of cultural guerilla resistance to the plantation system.

But since he worked on the plantation and was in fact the labour, land and capital, he was ambivalent between the two. After the abolition of slavery, the slave-turned-peasant grew crops both to feed himself, and to sell on the market. The plantation, dependent on mass-labour, was determined to use their ownership of the land to compel him back to work, and to his role in the structure of exchange-value. The plantation was the superstructure of civilisation; and the plot was the roots of culture.[13] But there was a rupture between them, the superstructure was not related to its base, did not respond to the needs of the base, but rather to the demands of external shareholders and the metropolitan market. The plantation was run by the manager class, the colon class. This class and the labouring indigenous class faced each other across barricades that are inbuilt in the very system which created them. That is why the clash in 1865 and the clash in 1938 and the future clashes are unavoidable unless the system itself is transformed.

In 1865, in the historical records, the rebels as they killed Charles Price, a black building contractor, shouted back to his claim that he was black: "You are black but you have a white heart!"[14] Several white doctors were allowed to escape, unhurt. There is, as Barrington Moore points out, a logical and rational basis to peasant resistance to the market economy.[15] "A white heart" aptly describes the man whom Miguel Ángel Asturias calls "the man who sows for profit",[16] the man involved in a structure of exchange value – which is all of us. Our place in the confrontation is largely determined by whether we accept or reject this structure.

Our appreciation and revaluation of the folk is not, therefore, the heroic folkish mythology of a Hitler. For we accept folk culture as a point outside the system where the traditional values can give us a focus of criticism against the impossible reality in which we are enmeshed. But there is no question of going back to a society, a folk pattern, whose structure has already been undermined by the pervasive market economy. Robert Serumaga shows this in *Return to the Shadows*. Joe, running away from yet another army takeover, goes home to his mother, to tie himself back to the umbilical cord. But his mother has been raped, and his young cousins raped and murdered by soldiers who are the representatives of the large central force which monopoly capitalism, with or without state intervention, must, by the logic of its existence, have at its disposal, to crush any dissent from its totalitarian power.[17] The plantation system which, under the liberal free-trade rhetoric, the rhetoric which freed the slaves, compensated the masters and set the slaves free in a world dominated by market relations, to fend naked for themselves, was the first sketch of monopoly capitalism. George William Gordon, we suggest, wheeling and dealing, buying land, speculating, owning a newspaper, acting as a produce dealer, speaking vehemently in the House of Assembly, claiming the rights of Magna Carta as a freeborn son of Jamaica, embodied the liberal rhetoric and took it seriously. When he became a threat to the emporio/imperio dominance he was hanged by the *reality* of a totalitarian monopoly system. The outcry in England was made by Liberal elements who could, in England, enjoy the freedom offered by liberal free-trade politics. But Carlyle saw clearly that plantations were made for lazy Negroes to learn the gospel of work under the spur of the whip. No one dissented when Crown Colony Government was imposed, and the Assembly discarded. The Assembly, like Gordon, was a piece of liberal rhetoric which the brute reality of the system could no longer afford. Bogle and his followers were taught a lesson – in the same way as Indian peasants rioting in Bengal in the 1860s against having to grow indigo as a commercial crop for the English had to be taught a lesson. The world had to be kept safe for the market economy.

History, to help in this task, had to be distorted. The myth of history was used by the plantation to keep its power secure. It was necessary that Gordon and Bogle should be painted "black"; and since "remembrance of things past can give rise to dangerous insights" much of the history was suppressed. As the old man in *New Day* complains:

> They do no know what we have seen, for no place has been found in their English history books for the fire that burnt us in 'Sixty Five.[18]

He tells his grandnephew Garth some of it; and this consciousness of the past and of his grandfather Davie's role in it, causes Garth to see himself as the new dedicated elite leader of the masses. But his historical apprehension will be different from theirs. For he still asks "Were they as bad as they were painted?"[19] The history he has been taught is the history of the plantation, the official history of the superstructure; the only history which has been written.

But the plot, too, has its own history. A secretive history expressed in folk songs "War down a Mona and the Queen never know, War O War O War O", and the old Anglo-Indian General Jackson hunting down the rebels in a tragicomic folksong:

> Oh General Jackson
> Oh General Jackson, you kill all the black men dem.[20]

In the Kumina ceremony, Bogle appears through an initiate as an ancestor-god. When asked in 1965 about Bogle, Morant Bay people answered about Bogle and Gordon:

> Is Justice they were seeking! Justice for the people.[21]

Again as Moore points out, there is a profound peasant sense of justice which is separate from the abstract concept of the law of the plantation. The law of the plantation is based on the rights of property. The justice of the peasant is based on the needs of the people who form the community. There is hardly an aspect in which there is not this dichotomy of attitudes. No aspect in which the attitudes and values of the dominant "colon-creole plantation structure" is not used in an essentially exploitative relation to the indigenous plot values.

The clashes of 1865 and 1938 are episodes in a historical continuum. It is significant that de Lisser sees 1865 as an isolated episode told through the personal relations of three white characters – the hero, the heroine, and the villain who joins with the black "against his race and class" in order to win Joyce, but who dies protecting her from an "unmentionable horror" in the end. The real conflict is banished and suppressed even though de Lisser senses the continuing unease in his society and writes his book as warning to the dark clouds *not* to cover the moon.

Reid on the other hand, caught up in the release of 1938 and the growth of national feeling, wrote his novel to restore the written past to a people who had only the oral past; and to the middle class who thought, as Naipaul did, that nothing was created in the West Indies and therefore there was no history. Reid wanted to prophesy the future by placing his then present in the context of an almost epic past. In the first part of his book when he deals with the problematic hero Davie who fails (he goes off to the Morant Cays and creates a community, which is broken up once his son establishes wage scales to respond to the market business of shipping bananas). But Davie died before that, having lost Lucille Dubois, his wife, through his new obsession. His quest then turns out to be in vain and finally inauthentic, as with all the great novels. He dies in a hurricane, imprisoned under the weight of a tree.

The second part of the book with its "positive" hero fails because Garth is made to bear the weight of an expectation that can never be realised. Whilst the first part of the book parallels and patterns the structure of its society, and reflects its failure to satisfy human needs, the second part fails by ignoring the fact that changes in the superstructure of the plantation – a new Constitution, even Independence – were changes which left the basic system untouched, and which only prolonged the inevitable and inbuilt confrontation between the plantation and the plot: between the city, which is the commercial expression of the plantation, and its marginal masses, disrupted from the plot; this is the conflict and the clash that we have seen reflected here in this conference, on different levels of awareness, between those who justify and defend the system; and those who challenge it.

Endnotes

1. George L. Beckford, "The Economics of Agricultural Resource Use and Development," *Social and Economic Studies*, vol. 18, no. 4 (December 1969): 325.
2. Lucien Goldmann, *Pour une sociologie du roman* (Paris: Éditions Gallimard, 1964), 24.
3. Miguel Ángel Asturias, *Week-end en Guatemala* (Buenos Aires: Editorial Goyanarte, 1956), title page.
4. George Lukács, *The Theory of the Novel: A Historio-Philosophical Essay on the*

Forms of Great Epic Literature, trans. by Anna Bostock (1920; Cambridge, MA: MIT Press, 1977), 66.

5. V. S. Reid, *New Day* (1949; Chatham, NJ: Chatham Bookseller/Alfred Knopf, 1972), 277.

6. Ken Post's account of the 1938 worker rebellion and the middle class response is in *Arise Ye Starvelings: The Jamaican Labour Rebellion of 1938 and its Aftermath* (The Hague: Martinus Nijhoff, 1978).

7. The specific quotation could not be located but the same sentiment expressed can be found in Asturias, *Hombres de Maíz* (Buenos Aires: Editorial Losada, 1949), 13.

8. Goldmann, *Pour une sociologie,* 189.

9. H. G. de Lisser, *Revenge: A Tale of Old Jamaica* (Kingston: The Gleaner, 1919)

10. The phrase comes from chapter xiii of Kenneth Ramchand's *The West Indian Novel and Its Background* (London: Faber, 1970), 223-236.

11. The conference referred to in this essay was the Association of Commonwealth Literature and Language Studies (ACLALS) conference of 1971 at the Mona (Jamaica) campus of the University of the West Indies. At this conference, described from a participant point of view by Kamau Brathwaite in *LX: The Love Axe/l* (forthcoming), there were major clashes between political and aesthetic radicals and the "old guard" and defenders of the Creole "all o' we is one" settlement that was profoundly suspicious of the attempts to restore submerged African "folk" elements to visibility.

12. Léopold Sédar Senghor, "Le problème de la culture" in *Liberte I: Négritude et Humanismse* (Paris: Éditions du Seuil, 1964), 93.

13. The Custos Baron van Ketelhodt, one of the principal figures of 1865, defended the needs of sugar against beet, by claiming that the sugar estate was the centre of civilisation in the island.

14. The exact wording of Wynter's quote could not be located, but Gad Heuman's *The Killing Time: The Morant Bay Rebellion in Jamaica* (Knoxville: University of Tennessee Press, 1994), 9, has the quote as: "...he has got a black skin and a white heart."

15. Barrington Moore, *Social Origins of Dictatorship and Democracy: Lord and Peasant in the Making of the Modern* World (Boston: Beacon Press, 1966).

16. Miguel Àngel Asturias, *Hombres de máz* (Buenos Aires: Editorial Losada, 1949), 13.

17. Robert Serumaga, *Return to the Shadows* (London: Heinemann, 1969).

18. Reid, *New Day,* 262.

19. Ibid., 277.

20. "Oh, General Jackson" in *Jamaican Song and Story: Annancy Stories, Digging Songs, Ring Tunes and Dancing Tunes*, Walter Jekyll, collected and ed. (1907; New York: Dover Publications, Inc., 1966), 233.

21. The source of this quotation could not be located.

JAMAICA'S NATIONAL HEROES

Preface

In August 1969, the Prime Minister, Mr. Shearer, appointed his Advisory Committee for the purpose of the Order of National Hero. The Committee consisted of:

The Hon. Roy McNeil, Minister of Home Affairs – Chairman; Senator the Hon. Hector Wynter; Minister of State – Ministry of Youth & Community Development; Senator Ken Hill; Mr. F. A. Glasspole, M.P.; Miss Sylvia Wynter, Novelist; Mr. Frank Hill, Chairman – Jamaica National Trust Commission; Mr. Clinton Black, Archivist.

The Committee recommended unanimously that Sir William Alexander Bustamante and Norman Washington Manley be proclaimed as National Heroes of Jamaica.

At the Committee's request, Miss Wynter prepared the Argument to support this recommendation under three main headings:

- The concept of the National Hero in the context of Jamaica.

- The historic roles of Sir Alexander Bustamante and Norman Washington Manley within the context of Gordon, Bogle and Garvey.

- Their transformation of pre-1938 society by ideas, words, deeds, and their creation of institutions which laid the bases for our nation.

The Argument formed the report of the Advisory Committee to the Prime Minister and is now published for public information

Frank Hill Chairman,
Jamaica National Trust Commission

FOREWORD

The present would be meaningless without a proper understanding of the events and the personages who shaped our past, especially those five outstanding Jamaicans we now honour as National Heroes.

It is not enough for Jamaicans to pay lip service to the idea of a National Hero. I feel that we owe it to ourselves and to our children to learn their histories, to understand the social conditions of the times in which they functioned, to understand their motivations and their courage in helping to secure for us many of the freedoms we now take for granted. Only through this understanding can we fully appreciate their work and pay genuine tribute to these outstanding Jamaicans.

For this reason, I commend this volume most highly to everyone; it places the activities of each of our National Heroes in historic perspective, linking the work of all five into a sustained unity. By presenting this volume during National Heroes Week, the Jamaica National Trust Commission is once again holding up to us a mirror of our past, to help us to forge a national identity in the present.

H. L. Shearer
Prime Minister

(1)

THE CONCEPT OF THE NATIONAL HERO

...the spilling of Englishmen's blood three centuries ago... was not done for the love of Jamaica, but for acquisition through conquest, which greed all nations possessed in those days, inclusive of England.

William Alexander Bustamante, May, 1936.

...the vast majority of our people were political zeros, with no voice, no right and no share in the affairs of the country. Born to obey its laws and to suffer its hardships, and for the rest, to pass silently and unnoticed to their graves.

Norman Washington Manley, November, 1944.

The trajectory of Jamaican history can be defined as the struggle of the majority of our people to transform ourselves from being the object of the history of other nations, into the agent and creative subject of our own. The national heroes of Jamaica – those already honoured, and those still to be so, are all defined by the fact that at some time in their lives, they made the choice to dedicate themselves to this transformation. At some time in their lives they refused to continue to accept their colonial status as a part of other people's history. With this refusal they began the process of creating their own. It has often been argued that it is paradoxical that ex-colonial nations like Jamaica, in asserting our independence, should borrow from our former imperial masters both the very concept of the nation as well as the symbols of national flag, anthem, national hero. We contend that the paradox is only seeming. The concept and the symbols translated into our historical experience, take on meanings and implications that are in sharp opposition to those used in the imperial context.

The nation-state first emerged in Europe out of the breakdown of the pre-international order of medieval Christendom.[1] In that first period the nation-state was identified with its ruler or sovereign. It was the duty of the ruler to extend his possessions at the expense of that of his rivals. The discovery of the New World sharpened their rivalry. Columbus had claimed the New World for Spain and the Spanish sovereigns who had backed his expedition. But the Portuguese had reached the Guinea Coast of Africa in the mid-fifteenth century. A papal bull had authorised them to reduce to servitude all infidel peoples in order to Christianise them.[2] The Portuguese began to exploit the slave trade, selling Africans to work on the vast estates in the south of Spain and in Portugal itself. When Columbus returned with his news, the Portuguese claimed that the New World came within the former Papal authorisation. Spain said no. The Pope mediated. He drew a line on the map – a meridian line 100 leagues to the west of the Azores, or the Cape Verde Island. This line gave Portugal exclusive rights in Guinea and Brazil. To Spain it gave the rest of the Americas. But the other nation-states refused to accept this division. Like

Francis I of France they claimed that the sun shone for them as well as for others; and that there was no clause in Adam's will that excluded them from a share in the world.

Jamaica, in its modern context, began as a part of the world to be shared out. Spain tried to make the Caribbean a closed sea, forbidding all other nations to trade or have traffic with or settle in the Indies. But she could not enforce her prohibition. The New World was up for grabs. It became an outlaw frontier territory in which contraband smugglers, pirates, buccaneers, privateers, gentlemen-adventurers attacked and captured Spanish ships, laden with treasure, exploited, in turn, from the Indians, as well as with produce. They burnt and looted towns, extorting money and treasure with ferocity, and with a disregard of any moral or legal considerations. They did this when their own nations were at war with Spain; and equally, when they were not.

Yet in Europe, the concept of international law, of the correct dealing between nation-states, was being codified and accepted by the rulers. War between them was to be conducted according to certain rules. Since the essence of the New World experience was its very lack of law or rule, Spain and the other nations came to accept that, even when the nation states were at peace in Europe, that peace – as it was phrased in a Franco-Spanish Treaty of 1559, "should not hold good south of the Tropic of Cancer and west of the Meridian of the Azores". Beyond these two lines, the ships of nations, at peace in Europe, might attack each other and take their fair prize as in open war.

"No peace beyond the line" became a catchphrase. Jamaica, like the rest of the Indies, was a lesser territory without the law. There, the ordinarily binding law of nations did not apply. Cromwell sent his expedition to capture Hispaniola when he was at peace with and negotiating with Spain. They were beaten off at Hispaniola and took Spanish-Jamaica as a consolation prize. Cromwell expected that the "No peace beyond the Line" theory would apply and that the Spaniards would acquiesce in their loss. But the strategic situation of Jamaica made her "an armed fist"… "in the belly of Spanish commerce".[3] War broke out. Cromwell's war manifesto, written by the poet Milton, declared that England was determined not to be shut out from the commerce "in so opulent a part of the world".[4] What Cromwell took, he held. With that illegal capture, the settlement of modern Jamaica began.

English commerce needed products with which to trade. Sugar soon became the main export product. Sugar needed an intensive labour supply. This labour was found in Africans, captured or traded for in Africa. There was at first nothing "racial" about it. Sugar needed labour power. Under the Spaniards all over the New World and in Jamaica, the Indians had died off from the brutality of forced labour, and the breakup of their cultural pattern, from epidemics against which they had no immunity; from resistance to the Spaniards. Indentured labour from Europe was also tried. But African labour won out, not least because the slave-trade itself was a source of capital. And sugar needed capital as well as labour.

The slave was reckoned and sold in units of labour power. The horrors of the Middle Passage and the slave system tend to obscure the fact that, like the later factory owners of the Industrial Revolution, what the planters needed most of all was an available and disposable supply of labour power. At that time in history, slavery provided, or seemed to provide, the best answer. The brutality of slavery was a brutality designed to ensure that the African was reduced from manhood to being a labour machine. As has been pointed out, even the method of sale was one of the techniques employed to reduce a man to a commodity. Here the labour of a man was a commodity in its most naked form. The slave was sold in the New World as a *"pieza"*. A pieza-piece was the equivalent, for example, of a "count" bunch of bananas – a count bunch of bananas is a stem of nine hands or more and this is the norm. A stem of six hands for example would count as a quarter bunch. The amount of stems of bananas is therefore more than the amount of bunches.

So with the African, the "pieza" was the norm. The norm was a man who represented the largest possible amount of labour power. He had to be above average height, without physical defect, with good teeth, and between thirty to thirty-five, the years in which he had most labour to give.[5] Others who did not attain these qualifications had to be added together to make up a *pieza*. Three boys or girls between eight and fifteen would make up two pieces. Between four and eight years old, two boys or girls made up one. Between thirty-five to forty, when physical powers were waning, two made up one. Over forty they were sold as "refuse" at cut-rate prices. These were the "unskilled" slaves, the raw labour power. After they had been trained in the special skills required for sugar making, their skills would increase their value on the market in exactly the same way as the technically trained man today earns a far higher category of pay than the unskilled. But under slavery, the worker did not own his skill or his labour power. His skill and his labour power was him. His being was involved with his commodity. He did not own the property of his labour. His property was him, and this property belonged either to the merchant who traded in this line of goods; or to the planter who bought him.

There was no cruelty for cruelty's sake in this. It seemed, as injustice always seems, a supremely rational way of exploiting the vast unused lands of the New World in the most efficient way possible – with slave labour. As Aristotle, living in Greece in a society based on slave labour, had done before, so European thinkers now rationalised the system. Aristotle had claimed that some men are naturally inferior and deserve to be enslaved and treated as "living tools". But Aristotle did not differentiate by race. Circumstances now made it easy for a mythology to be built upon the inherent inferiority of the black man. Once he accepted this inferiority he would the more easily accept his lot as a supplier of labour. To reverse a later phrase of Bustamante, capital was determined to bend the power of labour to its will.

Jamaica, captured by Cromwell, without formal declaration of war as it was laid down in the law of nations, began its passage from bondage to freedom at a time when its future nationhood could only be conceived by its total negation; when the majority of its people began their sojourn in their new land as commodities. As such they were the negation of the men who comprise a nation. They were, in Manley's phrase, *zeros*. The aim of our history has been, is and will be, the almost improbable and impossible task of the negation of that negation.

(II)

THE HISTORIC ROLES OF BUSTAMANTE AND MANLEY WITHIN THE CONTEXT OF GORDON, BOGLE, GARVEY

... there are certain officers working with that Company (The West Indies Sugar Co. Ltd.) who belong to the old school of overseers who believe that they can treat the people today as they did in days gone...

William Alexander Bustamente, October 4, 1938.

... there was a solid block of people in Jamaica whose aim and intention was that the new constitution should be taken away, so that they will be restored the old and ancient privilege of the backstair and the Cocktail Party.

Norman Washington Manley, November, 1944.

The tradition of the revolt of labour began early in Jamaica, when in the early sixteenth century, the Arawak Indians were shared out to the Spanish settlers and put to forced labour to dig for mythical gold, and to plant and build etc. Many of the caciques and their tribes resisted and were killed, hunted down with dogs. Many committed suicide by drinking bitter cassava water. Many fled to the interior of the mountains and hid themselves there. By these means, to use a modern term, they withdrew their labour, and went on permanent strike. The African was even more intractable than the Indian. As early as 1502, after a few had been sent to Hispaniola, the Spanish Governor begged that no more should be sent as they ran away and encouraged the Indians to join them. But their labour was vital; it was their labour that would be exploited to build the New World. More and more were sent, and all over Latin America the tradition of the cimarrones – the Maroons – sprang up. Revolts, and escape to the mountains, or to inaccessible coastal or jungle areas were a constant feature of life. The slave was determined to deny, to negate his status as merchandise. With every revolt, every escape, he was claiming that his labour power was his property and not his master's, and he as a man had the choice to dispose of it as he wished. Until emancipation, the basic issue at stake was a man's right to his own labour, and therefore within the value-system of the society, to his rights as a man.

The last great slave revolt in Jamaica, in 1831, bears this out forcibly. It was led by a literate domestic slave and Baptist deacon, Daddy Sam Sharpe, who, after the failure of the revolt and his capture, told a missionary that part of his plan had been mass passive resistance. When the cane reaping was due to start after Christmas, the slaves had planned to sit down and refuse to work until their masters paid them wages. Afraid that the masters would have killed some, to terrorise the others into working, they had organised a military regiment of some 150 men with fifty guns. Passive resistance would have been backed up by armed force against the planters' usual resort to violence. A historian puts it accurately when she says:

> The movement he [i.e. Sam Sharpe] organised did not aim to establish a new world, but to make specific and limited changes in Jamaican society: the slaves were to establish their right to sell their labour for wages.[6]

The constant revolts in the Caribbean, added to the great humanitarian pressure against slavery in England, were additional factors that led to Emancipation. But the new economic concepts of Free Trade with its corollary "free labour" – sugar was now being cultivated in the East Indies more cheaply with "free labour" paid mere subsistence wages than in the West Indies with slave labour – played the main part in bringing about the abolition of slavery. And so in 1838 the first part of the struggle had been won – the struggle for the right of man to own his labour. Some three hundred thousand men, women and children, who according to the legal definition of a seventeenth century Attorney General of England had been "accepted merchandise", were now people. As people they now had the property of their labour to sell. The planters would now have to buy. The very concept of bargaining meant that the old relationship would be reversed. But the legal fiat of emancipation had not changed the world-view of the employer-class – the owners, attorneys, overseers. They wanted to keep labour subordinate to their purpose "as in the old days". As W.K. Marshall explains it, in order to keep their labour supply, they tried many methods to keep the slave close to his former servile status. For example, they evolved a system of tenancy, by which the ex-slave, in order to continue to live in the estate hut in which he had lived, and to till the estate plot of land from which he had fed himself, was forced to work long hours on the sugar estate. The wages they paid were low, the rents for the huts high, and the free worker was insecure in tenure.

One factor came into play as a bargaining counter between employer and worker – the existence of large areas of unused and available land. The exodus of many of the ex-slaves from the estates after emancipation and their settling down as cultivators on small plots of lands, especially in the hilly interior, was the greatest withdrawal of labour the planters had witnessed until then. The fact that cultivation was one of the few skills that the majority of the ex-slaves possessed meant that the cultivation was successful, and the free peasantry of Jamaica was established, at once providing an alternative, however rudimentary, to the sugar estate. The creation of a peasantry and the withdrawal of labour was, as the planters saw it, a direct threat to their export crop – sugar.

In the twenty-seven years between emancipation and the riot of 1865, the planters used every means to frustrate the growing peasantry in order to keep their labour supply. They did this through the planter-magistrates who dealt out rough planter-justice, and through the House of Assembly which for so long had represented only their interests. But the House of Assembly, which had once spoken only with the planter's voice, was now beginning to resound with a voice speaking on behalf of the ex-slave.

TWO TRADITIONS OF REVOLT – GEORGE WILLIAM GORDON AND PAUL BOGLE

That voice was the voice of one of our national heroes – George William Gordon. He had been voted into the House to represent the parish of St. Thomas in the East by ex-slaves turned peasant farmers, men like Paul Bogle, one of his chief supporters. One of the more significant aspects of Emancipation had been the fact that former merchandise had also become full citizens, and those few who could meet the property qualifications were free to vote for, or to put themselves up for election to the Jamaica House of Assembly, and so control, to some extent, a part of their own destiny. In George William Gordon and Paul Bogle, the labour tradition of revolt joined and fused together with the Parliamentary tradition of revolt – a tradition which paradoxically had been started and maintained by the planter class, but a tradition to which the majority of the population now threatened to become heirs to.

Jamaica had been captured by the forces of Cromwell, a Parliamentarian who executed his King. Even after the Restoration of King Charles, many of the men who rose to wealth and power in Jamaica – men like Samuel Long and William Beeston – were ex-Parliament men. Long before the French Revolution established this fact, they had begun to contend with the Crown in England, that the interests of the nation are not to be identified with the ruler, but with the people – the people, meaning, the men of property. The elected House of Assembly established in 1664 was their forum. In this forum they fought the Governor and representatives of the Crown to make sure that their economic interests and not the Crown's should remain paramount. For example, they fought with the Crown for a free trade in slaves from Africa against the interests of the monopoly, the Royal African Company, in which the King and almost all the aristocracy of England had shares. In this struggle, as we can see, the majority of the people of Jamaica were not only political zeros – but property and pawns.

To defend their economic rights, the planters laid claim to their rights as Englishmen. They argued that the law had accorded to all Englishmen born in Jamaica all the laws and statutes of the Kingdom of England; that all English "liberties, privileges, immunities", had always been in force, and that they belonged "unto all his Majesty's liege people within this Island as their birthright." They voted then time after time for the right to spend their taxes as they wished and for the "freedom of Englishmen" to control their internal affairs without being subject to other "liege people" at home.[7] When the French and the American Revolutions established the identity of the nation with the men of property – the Jacobins who had suggested that "people" should mean the workers and the common people, and that there should be universal manhood suffrage, had been defeated – the planters were strengthened in their claim. And since the revolutionary Rights of Man also protected the rights of man to his property, some slave-owners could even appeal to this as an argument to defend their right to their slaves against the insistence on Abolition on the part of the Imperial Parliament. Paradoxical as it may seem, the abolition of slavery was at one and the same time a blow for freedom *and* the triumph of the economic interests of Great Britain who now wanted free trade and cheap sugar, against the economic interests of the planters who wanted to keep the slaves, their easy profits, and their protected market.

The planters lost this time, but they had had many a victory before. The House of Assembly had prevented full colonial status and had given the handful of planters a say in the running of Jamaica – naturally to the disadvantage of the majority. But in 1830, after a long struggle both in Jamaica and in England, "the coloured and black people of free condition" were also given the vote and were declared to be "entitled to have and enjoy all the rights, privileges, immunities etc." as if they had "descended from white ancestors". All the rights that the planter class had struggled for now belonged to free men – black or mulatto – as long as they had a certain amount of property. In 1838 with Emancipation, these rights now passed to any of the majority of the people of Jamaica who had the amount of property that could entitle them to vote. But the majority did not now claim these rights as Englishmen. The rights of Englishmen had undergone a sea-change and had been translated into a new reality. They would now claim, as George William Gordon claimed in the House of Assembly in November 1863:

> I stand here tonight as one of the sons of Free Jamaica. I claim all the ancient privileges and rights granted to us by Magna Carta and the Bill of Rights.[8]

The consciousness of being Jamaican, rather than a commodity, or Englishmen overseas, began to transform itself into reality.

But it was to be a painful transformation attended with agony. The Jamaican planter, now without a protected market in Great Britain, tied hand and foot to the merchants in Jamaica and in England who held mortgages on his estate, exposed to the competition of slave-grown sugar from the virgin lands of places like Cuba or of cheap-wages sugar from the East Indies, became desperate in his attempt to ensure a cheap labour supply. He imported indentured labour from India at the public expense, raising already high taxes to do so. More than that, he began by all available means to ensure that the

Jamaican majority should not be provided easily with land for rent. As for the landless who worked on the still numerous sugar estates in parishes like St. Thomas in the East, he cut and reduced wages wherever possible. The demonstration led by Paul Bogle on the 11th of October, 1865 was based mainly on problems of land, wages, and the harsh justice dealt out by the planter-magistrates designed to keep labour in check. But it was also a political demonstration. For Bogle, a small settler cultivating land at Stony Gut, was a freeholder and a voter – and so were many other of his followers. In fact they were known as George William Gordon's Party in St. Thomas-in-the-East.

The ties of Gordon with the small settlers all over the island were religious – Gordon had become baptised as a Native Baptist although he had been confirmed an Anglican, and was a lay preacher at his tabernacle in Kingston, and there he had ordained Bogle as a deacon – but they were also economic. Gordon had become a produce-dealer with his counting house on Port Royal Street. He bought up old sugar estates, rented out land to the small settlers, advanced them money to grow crops like coffee and then sold and exported their produce. He was therefore involved with that peasant activity which deprived the sugar estates of labour, or rather of subsistence wage labour. The peasant alternative threatened the whole mono-cultural export crop plantation economy itself. As W.K. Marshall points out:

> The peasants were producing cash crops as well as food. It was the availability of much peasant-produced food which might have cancelled out the advantages of large-scale production for export markets by introducing important elements of self-sufficiency into the economy.[9]

Politically Gordon was organising and mobilising the people all over the island. He wanted, and worked for, an extension of the franchise, knowing that the House of Assembly, if it were to represent the interests of the majority, would have to be elected on a far wider basis of voters. His enemies claimed that he gave cattle to his supporters, so that by paying taxes on this livestock they could be eligible to vote; it was claimed that he paid the taxes himself. And in 1865 he complained to the Colonial Office in a letter that,

> The House of Assembly, as at present constituted, by reason of the restrictions of the Election Law (which has been amended to a very limited extent) cannot be said to be a fair representation of popular rights...[10]

Gordon was, then, an advocate of mass and popular democracy. He was an opponent of the sugar estates. Once the franchise was extended, the people would have the power to pass laws making land available, laws which would promote diversified agriculture and strike a blow at sugar. What Gordon and Bogle threatened and represented was nothing less than a social, economic and political revolution.

The planters' retort to this threat was nothing less than the famous letter from the Colonial Office which has come to be called *The Queen's Advice*. The

Queen's Advice is a classic, and early example of a strike-breaking manifesto. A group of people in St. Ann, perhaps encouraged by Gordon, had sent a letter to the Queen through the Colonial Office, in which they complained that the planters would not rent them land, that they were starving; they asked the Queen to rent them the Crown lands so that they could grow crops for themselves. Since the interests of Great Britain were linked to sugar and the interests of the dominant economic section of England, the Colonial Office did not hesitate to take Eyre's and the planters' advice and drafted a letter in which they, in so many words, told the people to give up schemes of working the land for themselves – instead they should accept that it was their lot and duty to work for the planters "steadily and continuously" at the times when their labour was wanted, and for so long as it was wanted. And, it was implied, at whatever wages the planters wanted.

Gordon's fiery answer to *The Queen's Advice* saw the letter for what it was – a declaration of war on the part of the planters. At meetings up and down Jamaica, and in St. Thomas-in-the-East, he brought up the problem of the already low wages that the planters were paying. The problem of labour was, then, foremost in the agitation, as well as the problem of land, the problem of the high taxation put on by the House of Assembly where Gordon constituted a one-man opposition, the problem of the high cost of living, the lack of social welfare and education for the people – and the problem of political victimisation in St. Thomas-in-the-East. Several years before, Gordon's followers, led by Bogle, had voted in Gordon as a member of the Vestry which ran the local government of the parish. The Custos and the planters, on the technicality that Gordon was now a Baptist and no longer an Anglican, ejected him and refused to let him take his seat. Gordon took the case to Court, but the juries, intimidated, found against him. This rankled in the hearts of the St. Thomas voters. As Bogle wrote to Gordon, his heart burnt when he thought of the persecution he had suffered. In 1865, the economic and political and social grievances exploded. The suppression was brutal. Eyre was out to teach a lesson and he taught it. The planter class voted to abolish the Assembly rather than to extend their rights to the majority. The Colonial Office, who had long planned to do this, acted swiftly. Gordon and Bogle and countless others were hanged. The Assembly was abolished.

What had also been crushed was the first attempt at a labour movement in Jamaica. One of the plans of Bogle and his followers was to drill "fleets of men" to send to the sugar estates on payday, to see that the workers were paid their proper wages. What had also been crushed was the attempt at mass democracy through the parliamentary tradition, by which the majority of the people in Jamaica could have promoted their social and economic interests. Crown Colony Government was instituted in 1866 by Sir John Peter Grant. Reforms were effected, but in the end Crown Colony Government became what Norman Washington Manley would later describe it as: a system in which the rich and affluent and the employer class had obtained influence through "the backstairs and the cocktail party", whilst the majority of the people would function as "political zeros". It was a system, too, in which Capital could bend labour to its will, and the overseers and officers on the sugar estates, the employers in the towns, could, in the words of Bustamante, "treat the people today as they did in the days gone by."

THE FORERUNNER — MARCUS MOSIAH GARVEY

During the Crown Colony period from 1866 until the key year of 1938, the majority of the Jamaican people underwent what was, perhaps, the most damaging years, psychologically, of their existence. When one is a slave one maintains at least a vestige of self respect; one is a slave because of superior force. During Crown Colony rule, the very structure of the society and the value system which it created caused the majority of Jamaicans to come to accept that whilst they were free men, they were conditionally free. And that they were conditionally free not only because they were poor, but because they were black. The majority of Jamaicans came to accept, too, that they were poor because they were inherently inferior, and they were inherently inferior because they were black. Such acceptance was bound to make them a more tractable and docile labour force. Crown Colony rule, however, extended certain benefits like free elementary schooling and rudimentary medical services to the black majority. The medical service reduced the high mortality rate, and the growing birthrate, endemic to extreme poverty, provided a larger and larger pool of the unemployed and of reserve labour. Work came to be seen not as a man's right but as a few bones flung to hungry dogs, who had to be careful that they did not lose them. The elementary schooling was designed to provide literate artisans, but not intended to allow them to rise above their stations. Yet it was this elementary school system that educated Marcus Mosiah Garvey, who was born in August 1887 in St. Ann's Bay. He attended school there until he was 14, then left to take a job in a printery. William Alexander Bustamante was three-years old when Garvey was born. Manley was eight when Garvey left school. He was to be the forerunner of both. In a social, cultural, political and economic sense, Marcus Mosiah Garvey was the forerunner of the movement of 1938.

In 1884, the year Bustamante was born, pressure from vocal elements in Jamaican society led to the modification of "pure" Crown Colony Government. Nine elected members were added to the Legislative Council, elected on a very limited franchise, limited to those with a certain amount of property. In 1895, the nine were increased to 14, one to represent each parish, but they represented only 38,376 people out of a population that was well over 600,000. Even when the agitation of an educated Jamaican Negro, Robert Love, led to the election of black and coloured members from 1906 onwards, so that in the 1920s the white element was outnumbered, the fact remained that through the limited franchise, the elected members were not really representative of the masses of the people of the country. A few outstanding ones like J.A.G. Smith and others would fight to represent the people's interests. But the majority "did not consider themselves agents of the Negro masses".[11] Bustamante was later to call them "the Black Royal Family".

They were trapped by the fact that the Crown Colony system gave them the illusion of power without its substance – they could delay legislation but they could neither prevent, nor implement it – the Governor and his officials having the final, absolute say. They were also believers in the ideology of nineteenth-century middle-class nationalism. As E.H. Carr puts it, in this ideology, the man without property had no stake in the country, and was not a member of the nation; the "worker, in this sense had no fatherland".[12] The worker in Jamaica, therefore, first sought a fatherland in heaven through the messianic movement of Bedward in August Town. The large pool of unemployed urban and rural labourers who were pouring into the city believed fervently in the escape to this fatherland, even after Bedward was judged insane and sent to the Asylum.

Marcus Mosiah Garvey, faced with the total displacedness of the black worker and the black masses in the United States and Jamaica, gave to the world the concept of Africa, free from colonial rule, as the fatherland of the dispossessed black masses of the New World. He founded the mass organisation of Negroes in the United States – the Universal Negro Improvement Association, in which he stressed self-help and self-reliance. Through his writings, speeches, associations and various schemes, he tried to get the black masses, the Negro worker, who had been almost reduced to non-human status and transformed literally and figuratively into a "living tool" to recover his self-confidence as a man. The message was simple. He wanted all men, and most of all black men, to understand that:

> Negroes are human beings... They have feelings, souls, passions, ambitions, desires, just as other men.[13]

The dream of a return to Africa, and a Universal Association of black men failed. American justice sent Garvey to jail and deported him, as Jamaican justice sent Bedward to the asylum. Garvey's dream threatened the European colonies in Africa, and much else. He was sent back to Jamaica and there, from 1928 to 1935, he was to play a part on his native scene that would leave, in the words of a recent historian, "a lasting though hidden mark on the national spirit." Once returned home, his struggle began to take on a two-sided aspect. The Sixth Convention of his U.N.I.A. was held in Jamaica in 1929; the fantastic impact of the sheer organisational skill, the pride of self that came to the Negro masses, the dream of the return to Africa took deep roots. But on the other hand, Garvey at once also began to play a part on the Jamaican scene. That part was directed towards the betterment of the Jamaican masses in Jamaica. As Gordon Lewis puts it,

He openly challenged the reigning false standards of racial values. Equally, he was the pioneer of organised political life, for he demonstrated, in Kingston, as in Harlem, that the Negro could be organised, and that he was eager... to support sincere Negro leadership.[14]

In 1929, Garvey launched his People's Political Party, and his election manifesto initiated the expectation of "coherent party programmes". Some planks of this manifesto were:

1. To secure representation in the Imperial Parliament for a larger modicum of self-government for Jamaica.
2. Protection of Native Labour.
3. A minimum wage for the labouring and working classes etc.
5. Land Reform.
8. A Jamaica University and Polytechnic[15]

In 1930, in order to implement part of his party programme, he founded a trade union: The Workers and Labourers Association. In 1935, he was forced out of Jamaica by "continuous harassment" from the forces of inertia and wealth, determined that there was to be no change in the social fabric. In his immediate goals, Garvey had failed, and he went to London where he died, still dreaming of a return to Jamaica. But his stay in his native land had helped to sow the seeds of 1938. Two men would emerge to give reality to the most important planks of his manifesto: plank one that called for self-government, plank two that called for the protection of "Native Labour". Both of these men, each with his particular obsession, would help in the attaining of that fatherland which Garvey had dreamt of in Africa; and at the same time had worked to achieve in Jamaica. The paradox of Garvey's life and career was to be that, stirred up by his words and deeds, even by his defeat, the masses of Jamaica were now prepared to take the next large leap. They would no longer wait for a better life in Heaven, or in Africa. They wanted Garvey's programme put into action and they wanted it here and now. In the local circumstances of '38, had Garvey been in Jamaica, might he not have agreed with Bustamante that, "We in Jamaica have one Africa. That is Jamaica"?

To borrow the later words of Manley "this little country was now our all". The majority of the Jamaican people wanted a reckoning. The time had come for them to begin to claim as their own the country which they had built with their sweat and blood.

The historic roles of William Alexander Bustamante and Norman Washington Manley cannot be grasped except they are seen as the culmination of a long line of protest and revolt, a culmination which would end once and for all an unjust and oppressive colonial society and initiate a nation – and a nation born on an impatient premise of freedom, equality and justice – now.

THEIR TRANSFORMATION OF THE OLD JAMAICA, THEIR CREATION OF THE BASES FOR THE NEW.

"The fight has just begun for more pay. We are going to organise the entire Jamaica Labour into one Union."

William Alexander Bustamante, May, 1938.

"The time has come, here and now, when we should all march forward to this goal of self-government. The cause is a righteous one... it is God's work in this land."

Norman Washington Manley, 1942.

The hero is as old as human memory. To all peoples, at all times, the hero has symbolised their particular ideal of behaviour. And yet the hero cannot be accused of perfection. His weaknesses are often as pronounced as his virtues. Like Achilles he may have courage and be a great warrior, but he is also arrogant and selfish. Like Ulysses, and like Anansi, he survives through a kind of cunning which is none too scrupulous. What then distinguishes the hero? The Greeks had a word for it. They called this quality of the hero his *arete*. The *arete* – the essential quality – of a knife for example is its cutting edge, not its carved handle; that of a horse is its speed, not its flowing mane. This essential quality of the hero differs from society to society, from age to age. Yet one thing remains the same. It is a quality of energy, expressed in choice. Among oppressed people, this conscious decision to choose between alternatives, and to choose the improbable one of standing up to the strong, is the *arete*, the essential quality of the hero. It is of the essence of the colonial situation that the colonised should accept his status as given, as one of pragmatic fact. Any revolt on the part of the colonised immediately makes actual the possibility of an alternative condition. That is why, even when the revolt fails, the legend of the attempt always remains. Gordon, Bogle, Garvey, all made a choice between freedom and success, or death and failure. It was the choice itself which mattered. Having made a choice the hero defies the fatalism which is inherent in the relation between the oppressed and the oppressor.

We contend that in the Jamaica of 1938, the choice which Bustamante made – to build an island-wide Union, and that which Manley later made – to achieve self-government for Jamaica, was a choice which was, in the context of the time and circumstance, a *revolution* against the given facts; the facts which had been established and were upheld by the economic and political regime of Great Britain. At the time, when each man decided on his particular obsession, there was no way to tell that political colonialism was on its way out, that what they flung down as a daring new challenge would, within a generation, become a reality; that economic colonialism, even more powerful and long-lasting, would begin its tortuous and longer retreat as its nature came to be recognised and its power to be challenged. To attempt to establish a union in the Jamaica of 1938 was not only to challenge the Jamaican employers. Jamaica was a political colony of Great Britain and, through powerful companies like the West Indies Sugar Company, and the United Fruit Company, was also an economic colony of Great Britain and of the United States. The *raison d'être* of these companies operating at all in these underdeveloped areas was built on the basic tenets of available supplies of cheap labour. The principle of trade unionism in Jamaica, therefore, meant the negation of the tenet of cheap labour.

Cheap labour had been assured by imperial policies which were carried out because of political dominance over the area. The principle of self-government also cut across this basic tenet of cheap labour. Labour, having a vote and a voice in its own affairs, organised in trade unions would no longer offer a disposable labour force. The conflict of three hundred years was locked in this decisive struggle. The main protagonists of that struggle, on the side of the majority of the masses of Jamaica, were Bustamante and Manley.

William Alexander Bustamante was born in 1884, the year in which, in England, agricultural labourers and miners got the vote for the first time. In that year, the relatively small number of "men of property" of Jamaica were allowed to elect nine members to the Legislative Council. In 1895, two years after Manley's birth, the nine elected members were increased to 14, one for each parish. But trade unionism, or the rights of workers was unheard of, even in the years of the last Liberal Government in England, when, between 1905-1915, measures were passed which ended the long trade union struggle in England for institutional rights, giving the trade unions immunity from any damages caused during strikes; and instituting such measures as Old Age Pensions, Workmen's Compensation, Unemployment and Health Insurance. But what was the norm in the Mother Country would have been considered subversive in the colony. There, it was taken for granted that the social structure was immutable and unchangeable. O.W. Phelps describes this situation well:

> Long before the disturbances of 1938, the pattern of exploitation was solidly set in the social and economic structure of the island. Absentee landlords and a tiny minority of resident whites owned and controlled the great majority of the natural resources of value: land, power sites, business locations, wharfage, etc. and with them the accompanying facilities – crops, animals, buildings, transport facilities. Supporting the whites in philosophy and interest was a limited middle-class of higher clerks, technicians, sub-professionals and tradespeople, composed mainly of the coloured (Negro-Caucasian) population with the addition of certain other non-African groups – Chinese, Syrians etc. – engaged primarily in trade. Beyond these was the great underlying proletariat of African descent – mainly agricultural, propertyless, destitute, semi-literate, and insecure, separated from both their coloured and white neighbours... by opportunities in education and in business, and restrained by law, force and custom from organisation for protest or revolt.[16]

Yet Phelps, in this brilliant summary has left out one class – the class from which both Bustamante and Manley were in part to spring – the small farmer and peasant class, the original class which had established itself on the land after Emancipation, and the class which, with the advent of the American capital influx in the 1870s, and the beginning of the banana production as big business, had begun to provide the alternative to sugar, which had been so long resisted. The peasant farmer with his few acres of land set a pattern which began to include middle farmers, such as Bustamante's family (by marriage) and Manley's grandfather, Alexander Shearer, a pen-keeper and farmer.[17] Little analytical work has been done on what is best described as a social strata, rather than a class. Their relationship with workers and smaller peasant families was often entirely feudal. Just as these families were usually a fusion of white and black, English and African, so they were a fusion – or symbiosis – of the decayed sugar estate and the rising peasantry. Bustamante and Manley would have known what the poverty of the peasant can be. On the other hand they would have grown up in an atmosphere where poverty was relieved by close bonds, by what Manley in a fine phrase was to call "the infinite charity of the poor to the poor". This early influence was incalculable. It meant that neither man could ever quite accept what the majority of the well-off managed to do.

Like Garvey, Bustamante, because of poverty, did not have much schooling. Manley made it through scholarships and was assimilated into the central tradition of British values, through the Rhodes Scholarship to Oxford. But arriving in Britain during the first World War, a war fought between European nations primarily for economic advantage and rivalry for colonies, brought him face to face with realities. Bustamante, in his odyssey in search of a living and a role in the world – taking in Spain, Latin America, the United States – lived in himself the experience of many Jamaicans (as had Garvey) who in order to find freedom from the rigid social structure of Jamaica, and to fulfil their abilities, had to emigrate. Manley came back and began to practise at the Bar in 1922. With his legal brilliance, he was soon absorbed into the system. With the kind of success he gained, with the general acceptance he met with among the upper echelons, the obvious thing was for him to have become an honorary Englishman, fulfilling himself as the undoubted leading "legal luminary" of the Caribbean. The events of 1938, and the influence of Bustamante – because it is clear that one of the most important factors in the development of Jamaica from 1938 on was to depend on the way these two men, whether through cooperation or rivalry, influenced one another – led Manley to make a radical choice – to change the nature of his role in society, to transform himself from being a company lawyer – he held a watching brief for the West Indies Sugar Company in the inquiry after the Frome riots – into being a barrister for the Company workers; from being the lawyer primarily of the employer class, to becoming the advocate for the unemployed; from being the defender of the legally protected interests of the haves to the defender of the have-nots who lived their lives on the margin of the law. It was a choice few men at the time would have made. Few men make it now. He made it in full awareness. As he himself later expressed it:

> "All my life I have carried responsibilities on my shoulders. I have spent my life on many cases and now I turn my back for good and all on that life and take into my hands the case of the people of Jamaica, before the Bar of History, against poverty and need – the case of my country for a better life and freedom in our land..."[18]

Even before 1938, he had begun to respond to the national needs of the country. What has been termed the "banana war" between the powerful and rapidly expanding monopoly of the United Fruit Company and its rivals had ended with the almost complete triumph of the American monopoly. But with help from the British Government – The United Fruit had swallowed up and tended to swallow up all the British companies who tried to break into the banana business – a co-operative of banana growers, the Jamaica Banana Producers Association had tried to stand up to the powerful pressures of United Fruit, in an attempt to get decent prices for growers etc. In 1936, Manley appeared as the lawyer for the Banana Producers Association before a Colonial Office commission dealing with the banana industry. His advocacy was such that he made the United Fruit Company decide to temper their tactics with a generous gesture. Samuel Zemurray, then operating Manager and later President of the United Fruit Company, offered to set up a fund to be contributed to by all the banana exporting companies as a gift to the island, "for the promotion of schemes of civilisation value, in the development of the agricultural peasantry in Jamaica".[19]

Manley, as the lawyer for the Banana Producers Association, was asked to set up and administer the organisation. Jamaica Welfare Limited was the answer and the beginning of the concept of organised social welfare in the island. The scheme was begun in 1937, and started up a programme of community organisation, a Better Village Plan, a Cottage Industries Pro-gramme, the establishment of a Junior Centre for reading, drawing, and other activities for children in Kingston etc. Jamaica Welfare did a splendid job, but in the conditions of the time this job was a drop in the bucket. Social welfare by itself, as Manley would come to realise, was in the classic tradition of all imperial concessions, whether political or economic – too little and too late. The eruption of William Alexander Bustamante on the scene through a long series of letters to the press from 1935 on; and labour unrest spreading throughout the Caribbean, including Jamaica, in two waves 1934-35, and 1937-38, was to impel Manley from the concept of social welfare and patch-work reform, to the wider concept of self-government and total reorganisation – to the concept of the creation of an independent nation. Each of these men had his obsession. Each began to obsess the other with something of his obsession. Bustamante set out to found a union, and in order to strengthen his union, founded a political party. Manley set out to found a political party and to strengthen his party founded a union. Between them they created a two-party – two-union system, unique in the world of the developing countries, unique in its potential to either to fulfil the dreams of social and economic equality inherent in the upheaval and actions of 1938; or to deny this fulfilment and therefore prepare the ground for another explosion that might not, this time, find the kind of leadership able to channel the frustrated rage of a people into creative institutions, since the institutions created out of the 1938 upheaval would have denied the passion and dedication of their founders.

> "... we and they are building, not just unions, but fortifications to protect the rights of the workers of Jamaica."
> William Alexander Bustamante, October 4, 1938.

If the word "charisma" had not existed, the eruption of William Alexander Bustamante on the Jamaican scene in the 1930s would have caused some political scientist or other to have invented it. "Charisma" in its original meaning is the gift that God makes to man, freely, outside compulsion – like the gift of grace. In its political meaning, the word is complex. First used by the great German sociologist, Weber, as a tool of political analysis, the word has since become enmeshed in an intricate academic web of interpretation. In the life and times of William Alexander Bustamante we see the word "charisma" made flesh. For the charismatic leader is always a Messianic leader, a Saviour – he embodies the role of chance in history, the incalculable. The charismatic leader pits himself against impossible odds – and persuades others that he can win. In persuading others he persuades himself. This is most clearly seen in the long letters which Bustamante wrote to the *Daily Gleaner* from 1935 to 1938, letters which actually helped to create the situation of '38. In those long letters, William Alexander Bustamante, by persuading others that conditions were intolerable and had be changed, came to persuade himself. He had returned home in 1934, not sure whether he would stay or not.

At first it seemed to him that he would not. His lack of formal schooling, his wanderings up and down in a wider world, made him look at the tight imitation-British society, with its hierarchy of money, colour, status, education, with the eyes of an outsider, a marginal man. Although he had brought back some capital – he first set himself up as a beekeeper, then later began to make loans to the low income groups who had no security to offer, from a Duke Street office – and therefore with his "high colour" could have claimed a place for himself in Jamaica's narrow, exclusive society, he saw that it was a society without generosity – a society in which, because his experience had been outside the British sphere of influence, he would have to "prove" his respectability. Under normal circumstances, he would have got out of Jamaica and returned, as Garvey had done, to a wider world. But the social and economic conditions of post-depression Jamaica were appalling. As a moneylender to the have-nots and the poorer echelons of the haves, he heard tale after tale of misery and woe. As with

George William Gordon, his way of living brought him into contact with the people and with the unbelievable deprivations that they suffered. He had returned home as a man of fifty, the time of life when most men put their feet up and prepare for death, but as with Manley, for Bustamante the moment of decision had come. But it did not come all at once.

His letters to the *Daily Gleaner* roamed at first over the wide range of his interests. The note they struck was a new note. Each stand on each issue was his own – and never quite predictable. Whilst taking a passionate stand on an issue, he always kept his passion under control, and if an argument developed, he knew how to veer and tack. The early letters show no interest whatsoever in his entering politics, nor indeed forming a union. They ranged over issues such as the Anti-Watermeter protest, in which he defended the rights of the consumers; in another letter he corrected the facts about the life and death of a former President of Cuba; in another he argued to save the Victoria Market from being demolished; in still others, he argued about the proposed site for the Tuberculosis Sanatorium, about Tourism and hotel charges, about the police force, about corruption in the Kingston and St. Andrew Corporation; he defended the Republican Government of Spain, defended the Scotsman who was Fire Brigade Chief, defended a bandsman who was refused reinstatement and re-employment.

From the beginning, however, in all his letters, there were references to the high cost of living, high taxes, low wages. Gradually their range of interest began to narrow down to directly economic and political issues. He said in one letter that what Jamaica needed was plain-speaking. He spoke plainly, never hiding behind a *nom-de-plume*. But he spoke flexibly and never one-sidedly. Because of this, he was able to use the letter column of the *Daily Gleaner*, itself one of the main props of the system, as the forum for the social revolution against the system that was to erupt in 1938.

From as early as 1936 his letters show his distress at the high rate of unemployment, at the lack of protection for Jamaican labour. Foreign musicians came to work in Jamaica, foreigners got jobs in the police force – the few jobs there were – whilst, as he put it, there was "No work in sight for the middle-class, labour going from door to door knocking in vain for work."

In January 1937, in a letter comparing life in Jamaica and in other countries where he had lived, he maintained that "wages paid in Jamaica are a disgrace and a calamity" and that the cost of "living in Jamaica is the highest of all living in comparison to wages paid in other countries". When he defended the Republican Government of Spain against the charges of Communism levelled at them by a society who saw any move towards social and economic justice for the masses as subversion, he still supported the Republican Government's stand for a more equal distribution of income, for the buying up of unused lands from the three percent of the excessively rich and distributing it to the poor; and above all he defended the Spanish Government's passing of minimum wage laws, workman's compensation, and other such laws to protect the masses. Already amongst the rich and the middle classes rumour had it that Bustamante was a Communist. Not much later, a *Gleaner* columnist, Meddler II, was to write that "pests" like him who were "stirring up the workers" should be "ruthlessly exterminated". The threat was very real. The governing class in a colony, because they lack the ultimate responsibility for events – they can depend in the last resort on Imperial forces – are always more nakedly brutal.

Yet it was not until September 1937 that Bustamante, in a letter to the *Gleaner*, announced that he had now become the special adviser and treasurer to a trade union, and was now "organising labour". His letters from here on deal with the problems of labour. In 1937-1938 the problems of labour were the most vital and urgent questions of the colony. The question had everything to do with freedom or slavery. If a man in a "free-market economy" was not free to bargain for the rates at which he was to sell his labour, then he was not free. And Bustamante believed, with conviction, in a free-market economy. He believed in its corollary – as he had seen it in the States and in Latin American countries like Cuba – a free trade union movement. In one letter he spoke of the "beauty of unionism". In another he asked:

> "Why should man in this civilised world not be allowed to exercise his right in a constitutional manner under the laws of this island which permits every man and woman to organise in a union or society?"

Like Gordon, Bustamante would come upon one hard cold fact. Jamaica was a colony. The rights that were enshrined in the laws of the island were colonial laws – and where they were not colonial were colonially interpreted... The Mother Country needed her colonies as pools of cheap labour for English investment capital – and as a market for her exports – nothing more. To organise a union in Jamaica was to come face to face with the colonial condition; and either accept this condition, run away from it, reject it with sterile protests, or set out to transform it. With the crisis of 1938, Bustamante stopped asking questions and set out to find the answer. In his letters he had challenged the old society with his words. The year 1938 saw him set out to change it with words and actions. His forum became not only the *Gleaner* column, but the street corner in Kingston, the open air meeting in St. Thomas at Serge Island, at Frome, at Port Antonio, all over the island, up and down. The name Bustamante had become a household word – by the few uttered with a curse, by the many with a new, and almost fearful, hope.

THE CRISIS OF 1938 — HOW IT CAME ABOUT

The crisis had been building up for a long time – ever since the end of the First World War in fact. In the last year of the war and in 1919 there had been a series of spontaneous strikes and riots in Kingston where the unemployed had kept drifting in until they formed a large body of placeless nomadic city-dwellers.

The Crown Colony Government, designed to hold society static, could not cope with the growing pool of the unemployed except by offering the occasional relief works on roads etc. But that was not much. The postwar wave of disturbances led to the passing of the Trade Union Law in 1919 by the Legislative Council. This legalised trade unionism in the colony, and workers were free to organise "95 years after their brethren in England, and 77 years after (those)... in the United States".[19] But omitted from the Law were two important points – Unions could still be held liable for suits for damages arising from strikes and peaceful picketing was not legalised – deficiencies the Moyne Commission was later to point that out.

But the few attempts at setting up unions did not become effective, even after 1924, when a few strikes in Kingston turned into riots. The labour situation was like a running sore, erupting every now and then, then quiescent until the next rash of riots. One Thousand Nine Hundred and Thirty-eight, the 100th year after Emancipation, when men became free to own their labour as their property, was to change all that.

1937 had been a sort of prelude. Workers at Gray's Inn Sugar Estate in St. Mary refused to work. They said the pay was too small. It was. The Jamaican economy, largely tied to overseas trade, had been hit by the depression of the late 'twenties and early 'thirties. The cost of living was high. Work was scarce. Protest meant losing one's job and another jobless taking one's place. But as frustration built up, it began to reach explosion point. The people had no say in their destiny.

The electorate was no more than one-sixth of the total male population. The qualification to vote was ten shillings per year in direct taxation. The majority of labourers earned as little as one shilling and threepence a day, about the same as they had earned in 1865.

Whilst some workers refused to work at Gray's Inn, the police protected others who harvested the crop. The law implemented strikebreaking as *The Queen's Advice* had promoted it in 1865.[20] But that was as far as the parallel went. Kingston, restless with the unemployed, caught fire. Marches of the jobless began in April. Railwaymen came off the job in June. Ex-Servicemen marching for work clashed with the police. Boatmen and stevedores in the banana trade of the United Fruit Company and others stopped work. Shop assistants protested against their sweated labour and low rates of pay. The employees at the Mental Hospital were dissatisfied. Incidents of violence occurred. The pot of discontent was boiling over and the next year the lid flew off.

The troubles began in January 1938 at the Serge Island Sugar Estate in St. Thomas. Labourers paid tenpence halfpenny a ton for cutting cane asked for more. Police cleared them out. They continued to demonstrate demanding two shillings a ton. Clashes took place. By January 7, thirty-four workers and one policeman had been injured, and sixty workers arrested. The old order was breaking down. The Police Force, used at that time by the Colonial Government as a force of repression, could cope only by the sort of measures that would stir up more explosions.

It was at this moment that Bustamante took charge. He spoke to the workers, supported their demands, tried to persuade them to accept one shilling a day instead of the two they had asked for. In that single action he established two points. One, that the employer had better begin to bargain with labour; two, that labour could channel the threat of violence into a creative programme, rather than indulge in violence merely as a relief from pent-up tension.[21]

But the employers would take a long time to learn their lesson. To teach them that lesson was Bustamante's declared intention. In April, when the pattern was repeated at Frome Estate, the arrogant attitude of the estate officials in charge, led to a riot. Estate guards and police reinforcements were called. The workers rushed the police who fired into the crowd. One woman and three men were killed, nine wounded, and eighty-nine imprisoned. The Frome riot kindled the entire island, but the flashpoint came in Kingston. Spontaneous marches, demonstrations, strikes – waterfront workers asking for one shilling instead of 4d per hour, the unemployed marching on the Kingston and St. Andrew Corporation in search of work, crowds invading the power station and the sewerage pumping station – became the order of the day. The old order seemed to have collapsed. This was when Bustamante made the absolute choice. He began to take charge, to lead the marches, to organise the meetings, to fire defiance and challenges at the old order in a way that kept the crowds roaring in a fervour of emotional release. This cemented once and for all a bond between leader and followers that was stronger than any other bond that bound the majority of the masses to the Government of the colony, from whom they now withdrew the dumb and passive allegiance that they had been intimidated by fear, habit and custom into giving for so long and for so little.

When, on May the 23rd 1938 the Inspector of Police ordered a crowd of Bustamante's followers to move, and in a symbolic and spontaneous gesture they refused to do so, the Inspector ordered his men to fire. Bustamante stepped forward, bared his chest and told them to shoot him but to leave the defenceless alone. He took a calculated risk with death. Life, the only possession of the poor, is doubly precious to them. At that moment the crowd sensed that he was challenging the enemy, standing up to them as man to man, triumphing over them, because he would come to terms with death if necessary. The police, too, sensed that if they had shot him, they would have been torn to pieces by the crowd. It is one of these moments in time when a Rubicon is crossed by all. From then on, in a sense, the rest is history.

"We came for the purpose of bringing to the people of this country the benefit of organised political life – for the purpose of putting an end to the conditions under which the vast majority of our people were political zeros…"
Norman Washington Manley, November, 1944.

Bustamante had gone to Frome on hearing of the disturbances, but the management, unlike that of Gray's Inn, had refused to negotiate. He knew then that he would have to break the back of the resistance of the employer class. Amid the spontaneous firing of shops, breaking of shop-windows, with bus and train services halted, Bustamante took over the streets of Kingston, giving purpose to the eruption and an aim. On May 24, he was denied permission to hold a meeting but he held it anyway. In the afternoon he and St. William Grant, a former Garveyite, were arrested and sent to jail for inciting people to unlawful assembly. Governor Edward Denham declared a state of emergency.

This was where Manley's co-operation with Bustamante began. Manley, too, had rushed to Kingston from the country on hearing of the riots and the troubles. Now, as the situation erupted even further with Bustamante in jail, barmaids and match factory workers striking for higher pay, dockworkers on strike swearing not to return to work until Bustamante was released, Manley went to Denham and pointed out the dangers, urging that Bustamante and Grant should be released. Denham refused. Bustamante had also been booked on a charge of sedition – a grave charge. J.A.G. Smith, K.C., a member of the Legislative Council, and one of the few elected members who represented the masses, argued for Bustamante's release on a writ of habeas corpus. The writ was argued twice. At the second hearing Manley gave evidence in support of the two labour leaders. They were freed.

As soon as he was released, Bustamante, together with Manley, went to the wharves where the striking workers were assembled. He began union organising, this time forming the Union that was to bear his name. He formed several unions, embracing all categories of workers. He went up and down the country, and back to Port Antonio, where, for instance, the year before, when organising for the Jamaica Workers and Tradesmen's Union under the Presidency of A.G.S. Coombs, representatives of the United Fruit Company had broken up his meeting. This time there was no stopping him. Tirelessly, up and down the country he went, accompanied by Miss Gladys Longbridge, his private secretary and assistant, who later became his wife. Soon he gathered all the unions which he had formed under one large umbrella; he was determined to organise Jamaica labour into one Union.

But organising was not enough. He had to keep up his position of strength, to fight battle after battle with the employer-class who were determined not to give up their power and privilege. Declaring that he was not against Capital, but only determined that Capital should share its profits more evenly with the workers, Bustamante also vowed that he would "bend Capitalistic power in Jamaica". But the employer class was now backed up by a "strong" Governor, Sir Arthur Richards.[22] In February 1939, Bustamante, fighting to establish an island-wide union, clashed with his former ally, A.G.S. Coombs, who was strong in Montego Bay. Here Bustamante made one of his few mistakes. By calling a general strike in February to prove his strength against Coombs, Bustamante played into Richards's hands. The Governor declared a state of emergency. The regulations were repressive and were designed to break Bustamante and the Union.

Manley and Bustamante worked closely together here. Manley intervened, saw the Governor, and negotiated a compromise. A trade union advisory body would be set up which would represent even the smallest trade union; even the largest union would not have more that five representatives. The Bustamante Industrial Trade Union and all the unions would accept the authority of this body. The Trades Union Council was launched at a mass meeting at Kingston Race Course, once the Governor had accepted the proposal. Bustamante supported the Trade Union Council, but after a time he withdrew from it, at the same time tacitly withdrawing from the political party which Manley had formed in 1938, which he had joined, and even paid his dues. Whenever the interests of his Union (BITU) were threatened, Bustamante was on the alert. Nothing was going to stand in the way of that. His withdrawal from the Trade Union Council marked the split between the two leaders, which was inevitable given their different values, emphases, and their different obsessions.

For, in 1938, whilst Bustamante was organising his union, Manley was busy, up and down the country, inviting groups to Kingston for a huge meeting in September at the Ward Theatre for the launching of his People's National Party. There, Manley made the first of his major political declarations that were to inspire his Party – following in the way that Bustamante had inspired his Union following with his letters, speeches and actions. Manley's approach was always more conscious and planned — reflecting his training in ideas along Fabian Socialist lines. Bustamante shared far more of the United States experience, and the Spanish-cum-Latin American approach which stamped and marked him, not only by his change of name, but by his personalist approach to trade unionism and politics. But the personalist approach is also the approach of the masses, especially in developing countries. Bustamante had the common touch – Manley appealed at first more to the middle and lower middle classes. And these latter classes had also been stirred by the events of 1938. They responded to the ideas of nationalism which Manley set out before them as he said:

> "I totally disagree with the proposition that the political life of the country is something to forget and to allow to lie unawakened. I am a Jamaican who takes the view that politics is essential to the vitality of this country. I take the view that no amount of benevolent administration will ever produce a people with a national spirit unless they possess a political organisation in which they share and which marches with the destiny of the people."[23]

And he asked for "two obvious reforms" – the right to vote for all and an increase in the number of elected members.

BUSTAMANTE, MANLEY, RICHARDS
AND THE WAR YEARS

The Second World War broke out in September 1939. The effects of the war soon began to be felt. Ships of the banana trade were diverted to wartime purpose. Wharf-workers, longshoremen were without work. To force wharfowners to create more work Bustamante called out his dock workers. Non-union labour broke the strike. Bustamante declared that he would call a general strike. Richards had him arrested and placed in Preventive Custody at Up-Park Camp for an alleged violation of the Defence of the Realm Act during war time. He was arrested on September 8, 1940 and was not released until February 8, 1942. During that time, Manley consulted with Bustamante and he and N.N. Nethersole acted as advisers to the Union. The Bustamante Industrial Trade Union called a strike on the sugar estates in St. Thomas and won, signing an agreement for increased wages with the Sugar Manufacturers' Association. They continued organisational work, and Union membership increased.

With Bustamante in prison, Manley pressed on with the political aims which were his chief obsession, one of these aims being the achievement of a socialist system of government. The Moyne Report which was issued as a result of the Commission of Inquiry held after the 1938 riots made proposals for constitutional reform. The Inquiry had been useful in many ways. Bustamante had represented labour and had come out for representative government. But his principal concern had been with the workers and trade unionism; and it was during the enquiry that it came out that trade union law in Jamaica did not give legality to peaceful picketing – nor cover the trade unions against damages. The amendment to change this was passed in 1938, as were a Minimum Wage Law and a Workmen's Compensation Law, among other measures. But there had been a division among the members of the Commission as far as constitutional development was concerned and these proposals did not go far enough.

This was Manley's bailiwick. His legal training enabled him to take the lead, together with his party followers, in demanding changes and alterations which would move Jamaica towards the goal of self-government. These changes were sent to the Colonial Office and the final proposals of the New Constitution bore the stamp of his suggestions.

Manley was now to find his finest hour in his clash with Richards. Tribute has not really been paid to the "strong" governors of the former Colonial Empire who by the measures of repression that they took to stifle the national trade union and political movements, helped to seal the alliance of the people with their new leaders. The self-government campaign launched by Manley and the People's National Party in 1942 channelled the rising tide of nationalism, but brought strong opposition from Richards. The self-government campaign had begun with meetings up and down the country. A mass meeting was planned at Edelweiss Park in Kingston. On the eve of the launching of the campaign, left-wing organisers of the People's National Party were put in detention by the Governor. Bustamante had twice got the accolade of jail. Now some members of the People's National Party also received it. There would be no looking back after that. Just after this, Richards announced that the greatest military display Jamaica had ever seen would take place shortly – right around the island. This was the challenge to Manley, as 1938 had been the challenge to Bustamante.

Manley, in the face of Richards's threats, launched the self-government movement at Edelweiss Park. He had cast aside his former intellectual aloofness and had begun to take on something of the Messianic fervour of his cousin and rival, Bustamante. He, too, was acquiring his own kind of charisma. The goal of self-government, he told the rapt crowd at the Park, was "God's work in this land". In February, 1942 when Bustamante had been released, he had at once taken back control over his Union. The split between Manley and his cousin was now complete. Bustamante feared that his union, his creation, would become an instrument of the People's National Party. (Manley, in turn, would not have allowed Bustamante to control the People's National Party, his creation and obsession.) But Manley also realised that his party needed a union if it was to maintain mass support. The Trade Union Congress became the Party's union, organised by People's National Party's organisers such as N.N. Nethersole, Florizel Glasspole, Ken and Frank Hill, Richard Hart, Arthur Henry and others. They soon clashed with Richards. As they organised subordinate workers of the Government into Unions, Richards attempted to outlaw these union organisations. Manley brought mandamus proceedings to force recognition of the unions. Richards's action was judged to be "improper" and a usurpation of the functions of the Labour Adviser, whose office had been set up as a result of the 1938 troubles. Still, the unions were denied access to the courts to test the question.

By February 1943, the goal of self-government began to be achieved. A new Constitution for a five-year experimental period with a Two-Chamber system of Government – one wholly elected – and adult universal suffrage, was won from the British Government. This new Constitution was to come into effect in 1944 and was to establish for the first time a fully elected House of Representatives based on universal adult suffrage. As the *Gleaner* commented, this achievement owed much to Manley and his party who with –

> "...their campaign for self-government have certainly played an impressive part in this awakening (i.e. of political consciousness) and the present proposals can be said to flow in a measure from their representations both here and in Britain where they have influenced friends and spokesmen."

These friends were the members of the British Labour Party, men like Attlee, Creech-Jones and Sir Stafford Cripps and the English Labour Movement against colonialism. In the fiery days of 1938, Bustamante had cabled and written them, and had received support against British imperialism. He had given also a warm welcome to Sir Walter Citrine, the British trade unionist, who had been one of the members of the Commission of Enquiry, and who had been helpful with advice and influence.

But Bustamante had become wary of the People's National Party and its move for self-government. He saw it as one more attempt of the "brown men" – that is, the middle class, to capture and control his mass movement. But once he saw that political changes were inevitable, he too sent in comments on the proposals for the new constitution. In the first election of 1944, his hastily formed Jamaica Labour Party, based on the mass solidarity of his union branches, quietly and without fanfare, defeated both the People's National Party and the Jamaica Democratic Party, the flung-together last-resistance party of the employer and the planter class – the class which even after the elections kept hoping that the Jamaica Labour Party would so fail in their attempt at governing that the constitution would be taken away and they, in the lucid phrase of Manley, could return to "the old and ancient privilege of the backstairs and the cocktail party". Bustamante had put up as candidates many of the organising secretaries of his union branches, men from the humblest stratum of society. As they took their places in the House, the social revolution, which had hovered on the horizon in 1865, had at last come about.

BUSTAMANTE, MANLEY AND THEIR POLITICAL LEADERSHIP

Without experience in governing, with a country accustomed for so long to the idea of British leadership, with a middle class and an upper class ready to defect to the former colonial status at any moment, against all the forces of tradition, the Jamaica Labour Party set about the business of running a country and running it with only a limited amount of power. And the People's National Party set about learning to be an opposition, and also limited in its learning by the fact that the British Governor still held the whip hand. Fortunately, the Governor had been changed from the "strong man" to Sir John Huggins, then later to the Fabian socialist, Hugh Foot, who was dedicated to the idea of self-government for the colonies.

But the main tasks belonged to Bustamante and to Manley. The latter, though losing his seat, directed party policy from outside the House. The legal constitutional approach of Manley set the measured pace of progress, and influenced Bustamante, whose ability to learn from his opponents and his friends, added to his quick adaptability, confounded the wishful Jeremiahs. Manley, too, learnt. For Bustamante's strength was his awareness that his mass following came from his trade union – and always with him the trade union would take precedence over the party. This was the lesson the People's

National Party learnt from Bustamante, at first through the Trade Union Congress, then later through the National Workers Union, as they widened their mass support. The Jamaica Labour Party gradually came to take interest in party organisation, like the People's National Party, although it always kept the charismatic personal stamp of Bustamante's leadership.

In 1944 and again 1949 Bustamante took his party into power and office. During his first term he chafed against the limited power given to him, making angry speeches in the House against the whole concept of "Ministers in embryo". The People's National Party, too, kept pressing for constitutional advances. These followed, perhaps too slowly, but at any rate surely. In 1955, the People's National Party under Manley took over the reins of office. Bustamante, in his second period, had become Chief Minister and seven of his party members had been given full ministerial responsibility. In 1957, under Manley, the Executive Council was replaced by a responsible Cabinet, and the Governor ceased to be the Chairman and even a member of that body. In 1959, internal self-government was achieved; Manley was named Premier; all ex-officio members were removed from the Cabinet, and for the first time a Jamaican minister was given responsibility for the police and internal security. That year the People's National Party won a second term in office.

Federation of the British Caribbean Islands was, to Manley, a fundamental cornerstone of modernisation and rationalisation of the economy. At first Bustamante had co-operated, and the initial talks had been held when he was in power. Federation was established formally in 1958. But Federation was to be Manley's Achilles heel. Because, as in other developing countries, one lesson of the modernisation programme had still to be learnt. And this was that because of capital possessed by the employer classes, and skills by the middle classes, modernisation schemes tend to benefit these classes far more than the masses; and, in spite of great improvements in the general welfare, the gap between the haves and the have-nots therefore tends to widen. Federation as one of the concepts of this modernisation programme was obviously of more advantage to the upper and middle classes. With his instinct for the feeling of the Jamaican masses as distinct from that of the middle sector, Bustamante swung back into the fight. He galvanised the masses with his old magic, and his growing suspicions of the Federal venture. At first, in 1958, he fought in the Federal elections and won the majority of seats. The People's National Party came back to win the island elections of 1959. But suddenly, in the middle of a campaign to fill a Federal vacancy in St. Thomas, Bustamante withdrew from the fight. The Jamaica Labour Party, he declared, would now press for secession from the Federation and for Independence for Jamaica on its own and by itself.

Manley's flair for skilful negotiation had got the other territories to accede to Jamaica's demands for a "weak" central Government and for a form of proportional representation for Jamaica's large population. He had decided to remain in Jamaica rather than to run for Federal elections in 1958 and lead the Federation as Prime Minister, sensing that without his presence, Bustamante, by attacking the Federation, could undermine his party at home. He may have sensed too, from early, that the structure of the Federation could not really bear the weight of its expectations. In 1961, he allowed Jamaica to choose its destiny, and called a referendum on the question of whether Jamaica should remain in the Federation or not. In this, Bustamante won, by a large majority. But in calling the referendum, Manley established the principle of universal suffrage and universal adult decisions – even if this meant that his rival would take Jamaica into independence.

After a bipartisan committee of the Jamaican Parliament had settled the outlines of the Independence Constitution in Jamaica, Manley and Bustamante conducted the final negotiations with the British Government in London. Following that, Manley called an election in April, 1962. Bustamante led his party to victory. When the island became an independent country on August 6, 1962, William Alexander Bustamante, now Sir William Alexander Bustamante – he had accepted a knighthood from the Queen in 1955 – became the first Prime Minister of an Independent Jamaica. It had been a long road since 1938. And, even as Prime Minister of an Independent Jamaica, Bustamante remained President of the Bustamante Industrial Trade Union which, together with the National Workers Union, were now the mammoth unions of the country. When in 1967 illness compelled him to retire, Donald Sangster, who had been both union official and party member, and who had acted for him as Prime Minister for some two years, succeeded Bustamante as Head of the Government. But Sangster died a few weeks after taking office. After Sangster's death, Bustamante's chief lieutenant in the Union, Hugh Lawson Shearer, who had also taken part in political life, became Prime Minister. Once more, the union and party leadership was cemented.

At Norman Manley's retirement in 1969, his son, Michael Manley, a leading trade union official of the National Workers Union, who had also taken part in political life, was chosen by the Party to succeed his father. Once again the union and party leadership was cemented. Unlike other developing countries, the middle sector in Jamaica had not inherited the mantle of the upper classes entirely. Because of the unions cum parties, the Jamaican masses had institutions through which they would now work to spread and implement that total transformation of the society which their two great leaders had initiated. We honour them at a time when our society, too, stands at a crossroads similar to that of 1938. Both leaders realised this.

The generation of young men and women that emerged from the changes made in the fabric of society by Bustamante and Manley have now come of age. They take for granted the cultural changes initiated by both men – the conscious awakening of artistic endeavour by Manley and his wife, the great surge of writing and painting out of 1938 – the awakening by Bustamante of the people to the consciousness of their own strength and power through their participation in union and Jamaica Labour Party branches. It is impossible to overestimate the social and psychological impact that the two men had, by the quality of their own lives. Manley's trained intelligence did away with the fallacy that black and coloured men were in any way unequal in "brains"; and the quality of his family life and his total sense of responsibility had its impact on his followers. Bustamante's generosity, physical courage, audacious initiative, and determination to *lead* at all times, his respect for and protective attitude towards women of all classes, his ability to hold together all classes of society and to be himself with all; and his sense of humour, quickness of wit, helped to cement the meaning of being a Jamaican. Both men made mistakes, both men would, perhaps, now find it difficult to come to terms with this new Jamaica that has emerged from the work of their hands and minds. Cold rational analysis will point out this and that point where they failed, where they seemed to turn their backs on progress. But then progress is an abstraction, the abstraction that this new generation and its leaders must rake into a reality.

What we honour in these two men is this; that under the stress of violent circumstance in 1938 they both came out into public life, took hold, channelled, changed and transformed a colonial society into a nation. From 1938 - 1962, they did more for the people of this country than colonial rule had done in three hundred years of history. What they set out to do, they did and did well. They helped to initiate in Jamaica that worldwide movement that Arnold Toynbee has described as:

> ... the greatest and most significant thing that is happening in the world today... a movement on foot for giving the benefits of civilisation to that huge majority of the human race that has paid for civilisation, without sharing its benefits during the first five thousand years of civilisation's existence.[24]

Their mission has been accomplished.

The memory that they have left us is of those great moments in which they proved that stability does not lie in the sterile defence of the status quo, but rather in the capacity to initiate, to control and challenge change, and change in the direction of the future, a future whose categorical imperative is equality – economic, social, political and cultural equality. Toynbee goes on to say that:

> this awakening of hope and purpose in the hearts and minds of the hitherto depressed three fourths of the world's population, will, I feel certain, stand out in retrospect as the epoch-making event of our age.[25]

It is safe to say then that when future generations come to weigh and balance the historic roles of William Alexander Bustamante and Norman Washington Manley, they will still declare, as we do today, that their epoch-making achievement was the "awakening of hope and purpose in the hitherto depressed three-fourths of Jamaica's population". It is their achievement that now challenges us. Can we direct that purpose, fulfil that hope? In proclaiming them as national heroes, we honour their achievement, and pose the challenge that their achievement holds out to us.

Long may the lives of these five National Heroes continue to be a source of inspiration to all Jamaica.

Endnotes

The original publication had no endnotes, but only a handful of unnumbered asterisked footnotes. These are identified (SW). Some inaccuracies of dating have been corrected.

1. See E.H. Carr's analysis of the changing concept of the nation in *Nationalism and After* (London: Papermac, Macmillan, 1968).
2. The Papal Bull being referred to is *Romanus Pontifex* (1454), which granted the Portuguese rights of sovereignty to "newly discovered" lands in Africa south of Cape Bojador. The Papal Bull, *Inter Caetera* (1493) granted the rights of sovereignty to the Spanish in the Americas. The *Treaty of Tordesillas* (1494) moved the line 370 leagues west, which made Brazil a Portuguese colony and kept the Spanish out of Africa.
3. Source of this quotation could not be located.
4. John Milton, *A Manifesto of the Lord Protector of the Commonwealth of England, Scotland, Ireland, & c.,* 2nd ed. (1655; London: A. Millar, 1738), 27.
5. One authority claims, however, that the vintage years of an outputter of labour was twenty-five to thirty-five (SW).
6. See Mary Reckord, "The Slave Rebellion of 1831", *Past and Present*, No. 40 (July 1968), 123. (Reprinted in *Jamaica Journal*, Vol. 3. No. 2, 1969).
7. Agnes M. Winston, *The Constitutional Development of Jamaica, 1660-1729* (Manchester: Manchester University Press, 1929), 33.
8. Whilst the source of Gordon's speech cannot be located, Ansell Hart's *The Life of George William Gordon* (Kingston: Institute of Jamaica, nd [c. 1970], 56-60, gives selections from Gordon's speeches in the Assembly in this month.
9. Woodville K. Marshall, "II: Aspects of Rural Development in the West Indies: Notes on Peasant Development Since 1838", *Social and Economic Studies*, vol. 17 no. 3 (September 1968) 252-263, qte at 260.
10. Quoted in Ansell Hart, *The Life of George William Gordon*, 84.
11. This quotation cannot be located, but it summarises what James Carnegie's *Some Aspects of Jamaica's Politics 1918-1938* (Kingston, Institute of Jamaica, 1973) 63-95 has to say.
12. The edition of Karl Marx and Friedrich Engels's, *The Communist Manifesto* (1848) from which this quotation comes has not been located. The Penguin edition (Harmondworth: Penguin, 1967) uses the Samuel Moore translation of 1888 which gives "The working men have no country", 102.
13. Marcus Garvey, "An Appeal to the Soul of America", in *The Philosophy and Opinions of Marcus Garvey*, Part II ([1925] London: Frank Cass, 1967), 2.
14. Gordon K. Lewis, *The Growth of the Modern West Indies* (New York: Monthly Review Press, 1968), 177.
15. A. Jacques Garvey, *Garvey and Garveyism*, Kingston, Jamaica, 1963, 196. Garvey

returned to Jamaica in 1927; his objective 'economic freedom within twenty four months.' In 1934 he established a Permanent Development Commission towards this end. He launched two newspapers and lectured to spread these ideas. In 1935 Garvey lamented 'there was no national objective'. In 1938 the 'national objective' became a reality. See J.A. Carnegie: *Some Aspects of Jamaica's Politics 1918-1938.* (SW)

16. O. W. Phelps, "Rise of the Labour Movement in Jamaica," *Social and Economic Studies,* vol. 9, No. 4 (December 1960), 417-468, qt. at 417.
17. Bustamante and Manley shared a common grandmother (SW).
18. In *Manley and the New Jamaica: Selected Speeches & Writings 1938-1968*, ed. Rex Nettleford (London: Longman Caribbean, 1971), 193-195,
19. On the banana schemes see *Manley and the New Jamaica*, cviii-cxi.
20. Phelps, "Rise of the Labour Movement in Jamaica," 420.
21. "At first the workers refused to accept Bustamante's suggestion. When 33 were injured, 60 arrested and some jailed, the strike was settled as Bustamante had suggested" (SW).
22. "Later to be Lord Milverton" (SW).
23. Nettleford ed., *Manley and the New Jamaica*, 12.
24. Arnold J. Toynbee, *The Economy of the Western Hemisphere* (London: Oxford University Press, 1962), 12.
25. Arnold J. Toynbee, *America and the World Revolution: And other Lectures* (London: Oxford University Press, 1962), 40.

ONE LOVE – RHETORIC OR REALITY?
– ASPECTS OF AFRO-JAMAICANISM

One Love, by Audvil King, Althea Helps, Pam Wint and Frank Hasfal. Introduction by Andrew Salkey. London: Bogle-L'Ouverture Publications, 1971, 82 pp., $2.20.

One Love is the title of a collection of articles and poems. It is published by Bogle-L'Ouverture Publications, a West Indian publishing company, set up in London, run primarily by expatriate West Indians. As a publishing company it has answered a need – the need of an outlet for the new wave of consciously experienced black feeling which, emanating from the black struggle in the United States, has touched on deep responsive chords in the Caribbean islands and, especially, the English-speaking Caribbean. The populist-nationalist wave of the 1930s, which gave rise to the independence movement of the later thirties and early forties, had owed much of its power to the underground influence of the Garveyite movement, a movement which functioned both on the international level – from the U.S.A. – and on the national level. Deported from the United States on a technicality designed to crush his movement, Garvey had at once tried to enter the local colonial politics of his homeland. But the limitation of the franchise to a small handful of property-holders, with the unpropertied black masses having no say in the elections, foredoomed these efforts to failure. Yet the impact of Garvey's organisational skill and revindication of the humanity of the black, was to leave, as Gordon Lewis points out, "a lasting, though hidden, mark upon the national spirit".[1]

The Garvey movement in its turn had been nourished on a constant underground stream of African cultural survival, which Price Mars of Haiti had been the first to define in his seminal book – *Ainsi Parle L'Oncle* published in 1928. This book had sparked the "Negritude" movement launched from the French-speaking Caribbean. Price Mars showed how the African religions, beliefs, myths, had been retained from Africa through the oral traditions; how these, transplanted to Haiti, had helped to "humanise" the landscape, to convert the Nature of Haiti into the cultural ecology of the black man – African now metamorphosed into Haitian. The African survivals, reinvented in a new setting, created a cultural *matrix*, which demonstrably Haitian, now borrowed from other cultures – the French – other religions – Roman Catholicism in the case of Haiti, but borrowed selectively, borrowing that which fitted in with its own categorical imperatives. This religious and cultural matrix, sprung out of a people's response to that dehumanisation which would convert them into merchandise; out of resistance to European culture which defined them as the opposite of light, purity, grace, spirit; the dark side of the soul, the symbol of sin, went underground in order to survive, René Depestre and others refer to this underground existence as a "marronage", i.e., the retreat into the fastnesses, the turning of the back on the process of historical change introduced by the European masters. There is a tendency therefore to stress the *negative* side of this black culture of resistance; to argue that this black cultural stream, like the Maroons, retreated into a cultural and political cul-de-sac in order to survive.

But Roger Bastide has shown in his book *Les Amériques Noires* (1967) that there were two streams of African survivals in the New World – the stream which retreated and preserved itself with minor changes in the Maroon areas; and the stream which, in a great syncretic process, re-established itself as the cultural subsoil of the peasant relation to the new land; which reinvented religion, folk songs, folklore, folk beliefs, peopled innumerable "duppy plants" with the spirits of ancestors, with old and new gods. It was this stream which fed the roots of culture. Out of this stream, for example, there came the spirituals, the urban blues and the still more urban jazz. This stream has been at once a "black" stream and a "native" stream. From here comes its complexity. It was Léopold Sédar Senghor who pointed out that when in the twenties the United States wanted some art, some culture, to call her own, she turned to the people. Now the people were the blacks. The problem of the blacks in the United States springs from their dual relation: a political minority of the U.S.A., yet the neo-natives of the U.S.A. As the neo-natives their history belongs to what [Miguel de] Unamuno has defined as the "intrahistory" of a people – the secret underground current of people's lives, myths and dreams which lives outside the time continuum of dates and surface deeds; the current of pervasive *continuities*. Leroi Jones (now Imamu Amiri Baraka) has defined this zone as "the frontier zone". And he writes that black musicians of the U.S.A. have outdistanced black novelists in creativity, precisely because the black musicians feed on a creative tradition, carried on by the "lower classes of black society"; those who "preserved their fundamental identity as blacks". And we would add here, reinvented their identity as the neo-natives of the New World. That preservation and reinvention both took place in what Jones/Baraka calls:

> that frontier zone in that No Man's Land where the beauty and logic of black music was born. That is for the black the only manner in which he can put forward his personal vision of his country, taking off from that No Man's Land, sheltered great currents of that black region, which is almost totally invisible to the White Man, but which is such an essential part of them that it stains everything with a threatening grey...[2]

The revindication of blackness, which is in a sense the revindication of the *native*, the revindication of the humanness of Man, has taken place in the Caribbean each time that vast movements of social upheaval have put the articulate section of the population in touch with this "frontier zone"; however intuitively, however sketchily; however inadequately. Voodooism, the Haitian Revolution, the Messianic Movements of the religious prophets, Garvey's secular Messianic movement, Afro-Cubanism, Afro-Antillanism, Negritude, Jamaican Rastafarianism, and now the Black Power Movement in the United States and in the Caribbean, all well up from an Antaeus-like relation with the springs of "native" and "black" feeling that are fed by an underground cultural dynamic; a dynamic which had remained in opposition to the colonial and neo-colonial superstructure of the society; has remained as an alternative way of apprehending reality. For as Lamine Diakhaté has pointed out:

> ...among all peoples there exists a precious cultural deposit which escapes the alienating enterprise of the colonisers. That cultural deposit is maintained permanently by the community. It consists of gestures, customs, reflexes, a way of thought, a way of apprehending reality. Indeed it deals with a more than formal unity, a dialectical unity...[3]

One Love gains its significance, less from its intrinsic merit, than from its being one of the first texts of an emergent, but as yet confused, conscious apprehension of a movement that we might label *Afro-Jamaicanism*. The bulk of material in the collection is written by Audvil King, who also edits and selects the material. Indeed the other bits and pieces are thrown in rather to plump out Mr. King's efforts than for much intrinsic merit. The most important revealing aspects of the collection are the letter-essay and poems of King; and the introduction to the collection by Andrew Salkey.

All the contributors to *One Love* are born in the forties; except one, born even later, in the fifties. They belong then to a "new wave" of Jamaican writing, as distinct from the first "national" wave of writers who erupted out of the 1938 upheavals that provided the catalyst for the birth of national consciousness. The great names of this movement, in the literary aspect, were Roger Mais and Vic Reid. Mais's best novels, *The Hills were Joyful Together* and *Brother Man*, explored the marginal world and lives of the pool of unemployed and semi-employed who had been disrupted from the land, due to the progressive erosion of the minifundia in the country areas; this, in turn, due to the high birth rate, and the increasing mouths to be fed off the same subsistence area; this, in turn, due to the monopoly of land-use by foreign-owned and local estates dedicated to cash crops for export, all subject to the ups and downs of the market, the low prices given for the tropical export monocrop, and the increasing competition from other areas where mechanisation and other innovations increased production at lower costs.

The exodus into the towns, and the creation of the slums which became a way of life – the way of life of the marginal man – was itself the result of the colonial economic relation of the Caribbean to the metropolitan countries. As

Gunder Frank has demonstrated, the syndrome of underdevelopment was most entrenched in areas like the Caribbean where the relation with the metropolitan countries had been longest, and where the cycle of development, undertaken for the advantage of the imperial "mother" country, in a gold rush atmosphere, had inevitably been followed by periods of slump, in which the island economies functioned as ghost-town economies. The people, the human resource displaced and disrupted by the cycle of goldrush-ghost town, flocked into the cities that had never been really cities, but rather depots, points of embarkation to despatch exports and receive imports. The marginal man, disrupted from the land and its patterns, lived in the unstable flimsy world of the yards and the "barracks". These yards and barracks became central to our literature. Earlier novels from Trinidad like C.L.R. James's *Minty Alley*; and his short story "Triumph" deal with this marginal life of the yard. Roger Mais's two powerful novels continued this exploration, insisting on the liberation of this marginal man as the categorical imperative of an "authentic" nationalism. But it was "inauthentic" nationalism that followed upon the '38 upheaval, and the gradual granting of political independence which began in 1944 and was not formally concluded until 1962.

Even before 1962, the active neo-colonial era was initiated, to a greater or lesser extent, by two alternate governments. Following the "enlightened" economists of that era, they aimed at all the apparatus of "modernisation" – the drive to set up local industries, the invitation to foreign capital to invest; the stimulation of the so-called "progressive" sector of the extortionate merchant classes by featherbedding their façade-screwdriver-industries in high-priced protected markets. The corollary to this was the neglect of agriculture, the so-called traditional sector, and thus the encouragement of the "traditional" poor to get poorer. A fast growth rate, with a rate of distribution of income whose inequality was extreme, led to a growing gap in income, and increased the economic power of the wealthy at the expense of the political power of the poor. The intervention of foreign corporations in all areas of industry meant that both before and after independence, a substantial part of growth-benefits accrued to foreign interests. In a supposedly expanding economy the rate of unemployment and underemployment grew; the increased costs of foodstuffs and necessities all lead to a heightened consciousness of the growing separation in the society between the have-gots and the have-nots, the powerful and the powerless. Since the black majority remained the powerless have-nots, and entered an increasing dispossession, the imported slogan of "black power" fused with its imperative necessity. The demand for an end to black alienation swept one government out of power under the cry of justice for the have-nots, in 1962; and another in 1972, under the slogan of "Power for the People" – a slogan whose meaning had been reinforced by the intense feeling of powerlessness, to which Reggae songs, beating out on the electronic media, exploding out of the Afro-Christian cult music, and the Rastafarian politico-religious movement, gave popular expression. For what these songs have been daily recording is the growing feeling of alienation of the Jamaican masses from the so-called developing process in the underdeveloped world. Increasingly, it is seen that the masses suffer from, and are the sacrificial victims of, the Rostow take-off-stage development process by which the underdeveloped countries are supposed to "catch up" with the developed areas. What, of course, happens is that the so-called entrepreneur classes "accumulate" their capital for development by extortion via high prices from the middle and working classes. The middle classes in particular, commanding skills, are able to demand salaries that are equivalent to those paid by the developing countries; the labour aristocracy of the working classes, like the bauxite workers, and the workers protected by strong unions, manage to get in on the act. It is this cross section that begins to catch up in their life style with the developing countries. This catching up is done at the expense of the rest of the masses, the rural employed, semi-employed and unemployed; the vast masses of unskilled and underemployed and unemployed in the towns.

The growing black consciousness is, at one and the same time, a racial and an economic and social consciousness. Hence the complexity of this consciousness. In a country like Jamaica where the majority of the population is black, yet the majority of economic power is owned by a handful of whites, (mainly agents of foreign corporations – for the most part Jews, Syrians, and honorary whites such as the Chinese and members of the mulatto class, and the occasional black man of wealth); where the education system is geared only to the indoctrination of "western culture" (so the more widespread education initiated exists as a process of mass alienation); where the radio and television carry mass "white entertainment" and "white" symbols from the U.S.A.; where the essential concept, dating from slavery, of white at the top, black at the bottom and in between the mulatto class and the "black-but-educated" Creole class still pertains, then Aimé Césaire's recent statement that the black struggle goes beyond the usual Marxist definition – since the black is at once a member of the proletariat, and a member of the only race whose humanity has been questioned – has total validity. If we go further to examine the vanguard revolutionary class in the Caribbean as the marginal class – the agro-proletariat, the semi-proletariat, the fringe proletariat who scuffles and hustles for occasional employment, outside the aegis of the trade union system and the Capital and Labour accord, then the taking on of consciousness by this class is of vital importance.

This class in the Caribbean is both rural and urban. With the establishment of the islands as plantations, the plantation unit became, in embryo, the modern total company town. As has been pointed out, the plantation, with its vast numbers of slaves "mechanised" in long rows to dig cane holes, for example, and with its factory for the boiling of sugar after the grinding of the cane etc., was the nearest thing to a modern industrial set-up that existed at that time. The slave lived both in a rural and an urban context on the plantation. After the abolition of slavery, the great masses of the agro-proletariat who clustered near the estates became seasonal workers – augmented by the minifundia of family subsistence-farming – working as casual labour on the estates during croptime. This provided, in so-called rural areas a marginal "barrack yard" social cluster, which was later transferred and extended to the principal towns. The rebellion or riot of 1865, which Vic Reid explores in his novel *New Day*, was carried out by these vast masses of agro-proletariat who worked on the sugar estates of St. Thomas, as well as by small settlers like Paul Bogle, whose sons also worked on the estates seasonally. Part peasant revolt, it was equally part-proletarian revolution. Both Vic Reid and Roger Mais, who spearheaded this first wave of Jamaican writing, touched on the endemic confrontation between the official reality allied to the superstructure of the plantation and the unofficial, yet majority reality of the marginal and excluded classes.

Andrew Salkey is a later and more minor figure of this first wave. His first novel, *A Quality of Violence* (1959) attempted to continue the revindication of the use of the Jamaican Creole speech, an amalgam of West African structural forms with a primarily English vocabulary, which exists in a dynamic continuum with more African forms at one end, and more standard English forms at the other. Reid and Mais in their novels had sought to bring the masses into focus as the principal actors on the Jamaican historical stage, by using the "dialect" Jamaican speech as part of the reality of the people excluded until then from status and recognition. But Salkey's lesser talent, plus his middle-class ignorance of the true significance of Jamaican cult religions, and the mechanics of these cult religions, *trapped* him into a fraudulence which has been endemic to the whole New World attempt to revindicate the despised "native". Salkey's novel and his inartistic use of the dialect places him among those lesser members of the old wave, who in seeking to revalue, committed a new degradation. A kind of Cecil B. De Mille cult, complete with flagellation and a Hollywood Voodoo dance called the Giant X, designed to "whip" drought out of the land, goes hand in hand with an equally inauthentic use of language.

This literary "blackism" – as contrasted with the exploration of a neo-autochthonous blackness – involves a middle-class exploitation of cult religions and folklore, which has become widespread in the cultural life of the neo-colonial Caribbean. In the dance, Rex Nettleford, director of the National Dance Theatre Company has carried this manipulation to its height, reducing the power of the cult religion to a prettified exoticism, which smacks of instant folk-art served to suit a bland middle-class palate. This kind of dance (accompanied by the same type of folk singing, combined with Nettleford's own interpretation of the cultural and political reality of *blackness,* as noted in his books whose blurblike effect springs from the glib journalese which distinguishes the style and content not only of Nettleford, but of the class he represents – the new brown and black professional classes hesitantly come to power) is the replica of Salkey's *Quality of Violence*. Both represent a cultural middle-class movement, the cultural compromise of an agent-bourgeoisie – as contrasted with the indigenous bourgeoisie of the metropolitan countries

– and parallel to a similar trend in Latin America "Indianismo", which the Peruvian novelist, Vargas Lhosa, condemns in Peruvian creole writing:

> Peruvian novelists discovered the Indian four centuries after the Spanish conquistadores, and their treatment of him was no less criminal than that of Pizarro.[4]

Since that novel, however, Mr. Salkey, living in exile in London, has written several novels which are more authentic because they are closer to his own experience – the middle-class West Indian, making it abroad, in the limited world open to spades. Recently he has gained distinction as an imaginative journalist, his *Havana Diary*, touching among other things upon the ambivalent and difficult problem of blackness in the context of a conventional Marxist interpretation of the Cuban revolution. His introduction to the collection of pieces that make up *One Love* tends then to waver between the inauthenticity of his earlier exploration of black consciousness, and the new and more valid insights, gained from his London experience and his Cuban safari. He also constitutes an interesting bridge, of parallels and contrasts between the old wave of Afro-Jamaican consciousness and the new.

The consciousness of the "old wave" of writers was formed in a colonial matrix. The experience of going away to the mother country to further one's education, the movement away, for however short or long a period, was an essential part of the experience of the old wave. The movement away was not only physical but psychic. Vic Reid, who has rarely left Jamaica, was none the less involved in that inner emigration, that Daedalus-Icarus leap out of the old patterns of the colonial emigration into a new consciousness, which all writers caught up in the catalyst of the 1938 populist-national upheaval experienced. Hence the title of his novel *New Day*. The movement away was bolstered up by the clear-cut goal of a return to an independent Jamaica, with its own flag and anthem. The economic confidence trick that political independence would embody was not yet even envisaged. The movement away was a voyage of discovery, exhilarating in its certainty of a point of return.

The younger generation of new-wave writers were born and grew up in a world in which the gradual "stages" to independence were being "achieved" and the quest for the Grail had almost been accomplished. They write now in a world in which the Grail marks our independent spot on the world's map, and, looking, they see that not only is the Grail cracked, but that it is made of plastic manufactured in Manchester or Miami. The certainty is gone. The name of the game is changed. The stage was only a stage. Alienation in a neo-colonial situation, in a world dominated by a handful of metropolitan mega-corporations, increases. It is our only truly national growth product, yet a growth product that links us in Jamaica to the equally neo-colonialised Third World, to vast sections of the youth, and some sections of the workers and middle classes of the developed world themselves.

They are born into a world in which for the first time the humanity of Mankind as a whole is questioned. And since the black man was the first and only race to have his humanity questioned, he lives and moves in the vanguard of that frontier area of experience, As Jack Corzani, exploring the concepts of Negritude and Antillaneity, wrote:

> The West Indies has symbolized the breeding ground par *excellence* of the resistance against the cultural oppression of the West, and because of this were the first spokesman of what was later called the Third World. [5]

The new wave is born to a struggle at once national and international. Although, unlike the old wave, they remain physically present in their own islands, the intensive alienation which they experience as the mega-corporations spread out their industrial tentacles, introducing a technology designed not to improve the quality of life, but to maximise profits, this generation suffers a psychic uprooting, an inner exile and disruption which is edged with despair, since the certainty of a point of return to national independence as the solution has been removed for them. For it is that national political independence (of which the old wave dreamed) that has paradoxically served to modernise the old colonial structure enough to prepare and make it ready for the new industrial corporate imperialism. It is the intensity of this experience of alienation that links the new wave of writers to the earlier Caribbean Movements of Negritude – the literary counterpart of the politico-social movement of Garveyism, itself national and international – and even to the earlier mode of writing that took place in the Spanish-speaking Caribbean, and was spearheaded by poets like the Cuban Emilio Ballagas, the Puerto Rican, Palés Matos, and the *mestizo* Cuban Nicolás Guillén. That both Ballagas and Palés Matos are "white", points up the insistence of Wilfred Cartey that the literary and cultural revindication of the humanity of the black lies at the core of, and is *essential* to, the solution of an urgent and fundamental problem with which all modern literature and art grapples: the reconstruction of man's humanity in a world of increasing and rapid dehumanisation.[6] For the death of man in a world dominated by things, a death prophesied, is now in the full sweep of its realisation.

Lorca, Yeats, Eliot, Pound, experiencing a waste land of alienation, on which the culture of which they were the bearers was becoming increasingly marginalised, turned to marginal men, symbolic of their own psychic condition. Lorca's unforgettable clashes between the Civil Guards, blackbooted, cloaked, spurred, their gun a part of their metallic being, and the gypsies, trapped in their festival of images and their carnival of dream and moon, show the confrontation between the official reality and the marginal man, nonexistent in the official definition; to be hunted down, exterminated, the last of the natives. What Lorca captures is the unofficial opposed alternative "human" self, whose humanity survives, precisely *because* of their exclusion from the inhuman reality. Cartey shows how the writers in the mode of literary Afro-Antilleanism, brought the black out of the mass, in which he was presumed to exist "without common traditions and common interests in spiritual and other matters" and therefore to exist without *a self*. They were the forerunners of Negritude and the first revindication of the black being carried through by poets like Césaire. It was a self, Cartey suggests, that had to be revealed, glimpsed, illumined by *poetry*. History, the political and economic sciences, ethnology, and sociology played their part, but it was in poetry, in literature, that the self of the black, till then presumed to exist in an absence of self which made him nonexistent, first "was" in terms of the written word. Poetry was the literary clearing in the forest where he first had his fictional being. This suggests an important fact which Cartey pinpoints:

> This suggests that the task of making him known has required the imagination – a faculty far different from fictional ability – as a form of cognition, a form of knowledge.[7]

It is a lack of imagination, in Salkey's introduction, that makes it difficult for him to grasp the significance of both the importance and the failure of the volume of essays and poetry which he introduces. Not that the correct thing, the valid thing, is not put forward, but it is put forward without its imaginative context. Without its context the valid thing negates itself. Salkey begins his introduction with an awareness of what other Caribbean writers have defined as the existence of the black in the spotlight of the EYE OF THE OTHER. He mirrors his existence, borrowing his self-definitions from the reflected image which he sees in the EYE OF THE OTHER. Rex Nettleford aptly entitles his book of essays about race and identity as *Mirror, Mirror: Identity, Race and Protest in Jamaica* (1970). His title is taken from the children's fairy story rhyme:

> Mirror, mirror, on the wall
> Who is the fairest of us all?[8]

It is part of the paradox that Nettleford's non-conclusions are themselves tailored to meet the Procrustean bed of the Other's latest confidence trick – that black and white see themselves together, like the lion with the lamb, through a glass, multiracially.[9] It is the measure of *One Love's* grasp that it does not play about with these weary clichés. Indeed, in his introduction, Salkey does not try to obscure the confrontation between the self and the other. Indeed, he argues that writing in the Caribbean has until now been addressed to the EAR AND EYE OF THE OTHER:

> For most of us in the Caribbean, writing has usually meant saying something of importance to somebody other than ourselves, to the outsider, in fact, and putting it in the language and needs most appropriate to the standards and needs of that external audience and not to those of our own.[10]

But it is part of the complexity of our problem, a complexity that only Fanon has so far grappled with, that we the New World blacks, the first total colonials of capitalism, have internalised the "standards and needs" of the external audience. Fanon writes:

> The collective unconscious is not dependent on cerebral heredity; it is the result of what I shall call the unreflected imposition of a culture. Hence there is no reason to be surprised when an Antillean, exposed to a waking-dream therapy, relives the same fantasies as a European. It is because the Antillean partakes of the same collective unconscious as the European... It is normal for the Antillean to be anti-Negro. Through the collective unconscious the Antillean has taken over all the archetypes belonging to the European... ...in the works of Anatole France, Balzac, Bazin, or any of the rest of 'our' novelists, there is never a word about an ethereal, yet ever present black woman or about a dark Apollo with sparking eyes... But I too am guilty, here I am talking of Apollo! There is no help for it; I am a white man. For unconsciously I distrust what is black in me, that is, the whole of my being..."[11]

In the context of this kind of analysis, Salkey's strictures that hitherto, writing has helped to alienate us from ourselves, that writing has been the writing of examinations designed to climb the ladder of colonial success into a professional status or a member of the commercial class, whilst correct, brushes only the surface of the iceberg. To explore these insights in a Fanon-like context is to realise that the EDUCATION SYSTEM has been and still is the chief agent of indoctrination by which the colonised black internalises the standards of the coloniser OTHER. As a child, Fanon tells us, his mother, obviously middle class and educated,

> ...sings me French songs in which there is never a word about Negroes. When I disobey, when I make too much noise, I am told to 'stop acting like a nigger'... Somewhat later I read white books and little by little I take into myself the prejudices, the myths, the folklore that have come to me from Europe...

In this process of cultural imposition, Fanon points out,

> ...without thinking, the Negro selects himself as an object capable of carrying the burden of original sin. The white man chooses the black man for this function, and the black man who is white also chooses the black man. The black Antillean is the slave of this cultural imposition. After having been the slave of the white man, he enslaves himself. The Negro is in every sense of the word the victim of white civilisation.[12]

Writing in the Caribbean then has either reflected the values of "white", values which reduced the Black self to a non-self, assimilated to ugliness, sin, darkness, immorality; or has been in the fundamental sense of the word, *revolutionary*. Like Fanon, for example.

It is here that the term "cultural revolution" leaves the world of jargon and cliché to take on tragic meaning. For when the educated black Antillean wakes up to the fact of his white collective unconscious, his interior colonialism, it is then that a tragic and internecine conflict is joined. It is the paradox, too, that usually it is the more imaginative Antillean who, steeped in Western thought, is able to use areas of Western thought and imaginative inquiry and to turn these against the fraudulent white mythology. But the black will extend the implications even further than the European thinker has done. Whilst there is still a quality of abstraction in European denunciations of the great European betrayal of humanity, the black *suffers* in his person, in his psyche this betrayal; he is at once its symbol and its concrete victim. When the black, educated and alienated, takes up his pen to explore his condition, he is the sacrificial victim who, refusing his place on the altar, springs up and takes the knife, setting in motion the destruction of the entire apparatus and paraphernalia of his domination. It is because it is committed, however ineptly at times, to this task, that *One Love* merits our attention.

It is in this context, too, that the Essay-Letter of Audvil King remains the most relevant of the prose pieces that make up *One Love*, in spite of occasional areas of purple prose which always herald the areas of mystification that have accreted around the taking on of black consciousness. The actual "Letter to a Friend" is prefaced by a short piece entitled "One Word". In this preface, King defines his audience:

> Here's what we have: a face-to-face talk with ourselves... coming off from the pages to you.[13]

Salkey pinpoints the fact that this piece of "committed writing" breaks out of the writing of the past which, he writes, has never been for *all* of us. And this is, of course, in the past we did have committed writing, written usually through the newspapers for all of us. One thinks of Roger Mais's violent assault on Churchill's statement that the sun would never set on the British Empire, entitled "Now we Know", the newspaper piece which earned Mais a jail sentence for sedition. But, as we pointed out before, that was essentially part of the political movement – it was in his novels that Mais began the more imaginative cultural revolution. King's essay seeks to carry on this cultural revolution, exploring it at today's new stage of intensity. For it is important to note that in a largely black country any exploration of the aroused black consciousness is still taboo, whether in the main conservative *Daily Gleaner*, or in *Public Opinion*, the weekly that once suffered with Mais for its publication of the anti-imperial piece. The fear of blackness haunts the society. Under the cover of the multiracial myth, the ruling and middle classes of the society seek to perpetuate the status quo in which the majority black members are an economic, social and cultural minority.

Attempts have been made to start weekly newspapers, like *Abeng*, magazines like *Tussle, Bongo Man, Black Man Speaks, Harambee*. But harassed, for lack of funds, full-time staff, widespread circulation, they have all too often taken on a sectarian aspect, and become strident with sectarian shrillness, attempting quick political results with insufficient analysis, attempting, in fact, to "cash in" on blackness, to manipulate it, rather than to relate the black struggle to its firm political and economic basis in the context of a worldwide monopoly-capitalist domination. One of the greatest temptations of the black movement, one into which it is tempted by the neo-imperialist, is to lose itself in a revindication of the "black mystique", obscuring the basic relations of the denial of black humanity to the rise and extension of the capitalist system; and therefore linking the revindication of black humanity to the destruction of the worldwide capitalist system. Indeed, we can define this movement which separates the revindication of the black mystique from its political and economic base to a political, literary and intellectual movement that we have already labelled as *"blackism"*. What makes this collection of essays valuable is that, unconstricted by the length of a newspaper piece, Audvil King can explore the concrete relation of the nonexistence, material and spiritual, of the black marginal man and woman in Kingston, Jamaica, to its real source and origin.

Salkey, in exploring the reasons for our self-loathing as a people, has brought up the question of cultural underdevelopment, only to pass it by lightly, not seeing it as the root cause which imprisons us in certain inevitable attitudes, but rather in a fundamentalist manner ascribing it to our personal sin, that is "our loss of faith in our own ample social resources". Yet this loss of faith is an attitude inevitable in the structure of underdevelopment. King puts his finger on this when, in his prefatory piece, "One Word", he attempts to establish the identity that binds black people, and suggests a similarity of experience in which "outside agencies are, most times, more influential on our behaviour, conditions of living, and enjoyment of life, than we ourselves are."[14]

King however goes off into the unfortunate rhetoric of phrases like "individuals acting in terms of their peopleness", and "from the reactions which are ours, when we really look, see, feel, to the actions we initiate from the Universal Ground of the Self in which we all partake"; to "and then we'll discover our individual inner-self as well as our people-self."[15]

The rhetoric is unfortunate because it obscures the importance of what he is saying – that black people all over world live in colonial situations, in a psychic relation of underdevelopment to a neo-imperial economic and cultural system, and therefore, through that imposed exploitative relation, suffer a pseudomorphoses, where their so-called rate of growth only directs the economy and cultural dynamic into extending areas of alienation; that this common experience creates a common ground of feeling and response; that this feeling and response can lead to local action, which can nevertheless be concerted. And that what Audvil King is therefore setting out to do is to discuss "our experience among ourselves, in the light of how we feel and react".[16]

The rhetoric that King gets trapped in, in this most valid attempt to explore areas of direct personal reaction, which can break through political jargon, comes from perhaps the most important and difficult problem that faces the Caribbean writer – that is, the use of language. Fanon deals with this problem in the entire gamut of its tormented complexity. It is a problem that is peculiarly the New World Black Man's; the problem that separates him from the rest of the Third World; that intensifies his experience of alienation.

The disruption across the Middle Passage was a disruption for each individual tribal man, from his tribal language, and therefore – to borrow Heidegger's definition – his disruption from that "clearing in the forest where man has his Being".[17] The experience of exile was linguistic, from the moment the tribal African arrived at the "factories" on the coast and entered the world of the "pidgin" languages, a *utilitarian* amalgam of varied European and African language words. His communication with other Africans, black like him, had to take place within this pidgin, or some form of a quick lingua franca established between them. The clearing in the forest shifted; became unstable. On the ships, at the port of embarkation, perhaps the same pidgin continued. But on arrival at the plantations, the dominant language of the master, the language of command, imposed itself on the former patterns. Language became the area of the plantation where he negated his Being. His response was at once to assimilate this language to his own structure of thought, of imagination; to subvert this clearing, to reinvent it, recreating its essence through the trauma of his new existence. The creation of dialect and Creole forms of the European masters' languages was an original act of self-preservation and rebellion as important as the innumerable slave revolts; and not any the weaker because it was a reaction and resistance of the Unconscious; since it was this very Unconscious that the master's cultural mythology, implicit in his language, sought to subvert, and in subverting persuade the slave of his own nonexistence.

As Fanon points out, "To speak a language is to take on a world, a culture."[18] Equally to retain a language is to retain a world, a culture. But the dual response of the Caribbean black, reflected his contradictory position *vis-à-vis* European languages and Western civilisation. In the extent to which he spoke the language of the European masters, assimilating vocabulary and sound patterns to pervasive tribal structures, usually from some variant of the West African grouping of languages, the slave began to create a cultural matrix, which marked out a new clearing in the forest for the constantly reinvented new Being. The Jamaican Creole differed, therefore, from both Standard English and Standard Twi, for example, as the new Being of the Black differed from the alien English Being; and the now distant African Being. The slave now transformed his own language into the crucible for the transformation of the master's language; and appropriated that language to become a part of his new and reinvented being. It was not now then, the use or non-use of the master's language that proclaimed his preservation of self, but whether he assimilated to that language mechanically, or whether he entered into a relation with this language – a relation in which, negating the totality of both the master's language and his former African language, he created a new synthesis springing out of his new experience.

The revolutionary Caribbean writer – and for the black to write at all in the context of the Caribbean was a revolutionary act, since to write is to affirm existence out of nonexistence – at once turned to the Caribbean Creole to revindicate its use in the context of the written word; and even when using Standard English, to filter that English through the crucible of the oral Creole sounds, speech patterns, directness, concreteness. For the black to write at all implied that a man who existed in an oral speech structure was now transferring oral patterns into written language. Now, oral language implies face-to-face speech. The abstraction of written speech, where the words on paper confront the reader, is replaced by one man talking to another – with all the intimacies of relation and rancour that this implies.

In his introduction, Salkey places great emphasis on the use of the Jamaican dialect and what he terms the demotic of the Rastafarian brethren. In the litany of accusations that he makes against Caribbean society, the rejection of the use of dialect takes first place:

> Trap or record the 'shame-making' dialect in written form, and it makes certain segments of our Caribbean societies uneasy. The true images of ourselves are the first to be rejected by us. It's very nearly our native Golden Rule.[19]

Yet what are the true images of ourselves? In recording the shock of some Jamaicans when Vic Reid's *New Day*, which used a form of Jamaican Creole, was published in America in 1949, Salkey writes down, in dialect, what one shocked commentator said. And here we come upon the paradox. The use of the Jamaican dialect as a medium of language, as indeed, the use of all language, calls for a process of selectivity in which the highly conscious and elaborate language used in writing is made to seem natural, realistic. This is Mr. Salkey's bugbear. The moment he touches the dialect his artistic skill lapses, and the use of dialect which he employs, in order to justify the use of dialect, is highly fraudulent. The image of ourselves, far from being reflected, is distorted in the trick mirror of second-rate writing. To use language is not to copy language but to reinvent it. The paradox remains. It is V. S. Naipaul, who in his essays rejects everything black, popular and Caribbean, who, in his fiction, succeeds in using the Trinidadian Creole speech with a delicacy and an artistic accuracy that provides this true image that Salkey calls for.

The rejection of Salkey's novel and his use of dialect was more complex than Mr. Salkey imagines. On the one hand he is right. Novels written in dialect were to be rejected because dialect was "bad" English; standard English was "good" English. And "good" English, its acquisition, was one of the Holy Grails to be used in the black's psychic journey from darkness into light; from nonexistence to humanity. The education system was an alphabetic River of Jordan, in which "bad English" was to be washed white. For the educated to use his education to deliberately write in "bad English" was to threaten a lapse back, a fall from the grace of full humanity. If bad English was to be "overcome", the peasant, the black peasant who had been responsible for its continuation, was to be ignored. The urban contempt for the peasant pictured him as even blacker, more African – the Bongo-man, the quashie man. Bastide has pointed out the contempt with which even the urban revolutionary or black-nationalist blacks ignore the peasant cultures, the repository of that crucible of African-descended cultures. So it was logical that Salkey's father should decry, "the fact that the novel was almost wholly written in rural dialect, and structured on a representation of peasant reality."[20]

But the failure was also Salkey's. For his novel is finally neither written in the one, nor structured on a representation of the other. Both the dialect and the peasant reality as portrayed by Salkey, with its emphasis on the "irrational" cultists, who flagellate themselves to get water for the land, is a cliché, a stereotype, one more variant of the other's fabrication, a variation in the pattern drawn by,

> the white man, who had woven me out of a thousand details, anecdotes, stories...[21]

This inauthenticity of language is carried over whenever Salkey moves out of the standard English into a kind of black American, with it Afro jargon: "Things are bad very bad, on the self-esteem front in our own backyard".[22] A complex language is reduced to a one-dimensional language, already devalued by the ubiquitous disc jockeys and the ad-boys, all up to the modish minute. The chic, the with-it, the boutique world of fashion, the ad-sphere, all reduce black liberation to the latest fashion. Salkey, however, is convincing when he leaves the affected artifice of dialect and Right-On jargon and writes in that form of English which takes on its authenticity from its impulse to commu- nicate rather than to posture. Fanon quotes Leiris on those educated black poets who by the nature of their circumstance would now find it an artifice "to resort to a mode of speech that they virtually never use now except as something learned."[23] Salkey's long exile from Jamaica makes this axiomatic in his case. He acquires authority when he writes in the form of English which only sets out to convey what he wants to say. It is in this language that Salkey discusses Audvil King's use of language in his Essay-Letter:

> And there's evidence of a new style in Audvil King's work. He has discovered a personal knack in writing down his statements of concern and love for all our societies in the Caribbean. He has freed himself, and hopes to free his readers or rather those of us who will attempt to appreciate the liberating force of his inventive way of chatting to us, on the printed page. It is the most impressive literary approximation to the actual patterns of speech we use in talking to one another: in our natural mixture of the easy oral vernacular style and the less easy formal one, a quick fusion of the two which results, for example, in the following description of the condition of the young unmarried women Sufferers in West Kingston: 'Something else I have noticed, too, is that plenty of these women, with nuff pickney, acquire them by a process of calculated risk.'[24]

The key words in the above quote are *Sufferers* and *nuff pickney*. The *nuff pickney* belongs to the dialect, the standard creole dialect. The word *Sufferer* is a word of recent origin, springing out of the ten year experience of independence, an experience, inevitably, of intensified frustrations. For the rising expectations are inbuilt and endemic to the kind of economic planning, which, whilst vastly expanding the opportunities of the society, have reserved the larger share of these opportunities for the upper and middle classes, and a select portion of the working classes. An occasional sprinkle of opportunity falls on the populace as a whole – enough to remind them of the extent of their dispossession from the real areas of growth. The unbridled advertising campaigns of the consumer capitalist superstructure, plus inflation, the increased cost of foodstuffs and the heightened feeling of powerlessness to affect a society whose increase of power has fallen mainly to the wealthy and middle classes, have all helped to intensify the consciousness of being "black" and therefore "suffering the system".

Applied by those who suffer the system to themselves, the word is most precise. Used, as it is now used, as an "in word", part of the Afro-modish demotic that comes out of the immediate utilisation and manipulation of the response-language of the people to new phases of experience, it takes part in a general trivialisation of experience and meaning – which is implicit in the one dimensionalism of Language and experience that Marcuse analyses. The Jamaican Creole, too, or areas of it, also suffers this trivialisation. For the dialect is now used in advertisements, in order to increase sales and maximise profits. With the widespread acceptance of this general ethos and goal, the use of the dialect no longer meets with that same disdain as heretofore. It is not only the rise of black consciousness, of the "new black Majority of our people in the Caribbean" that now accepts the use of the dialect, but also the new consumer consciousness, programmed by the admen, to accept that anything goes as long as it sells; that a selective banal use of the dialect expresses the 'Natural you' who drinks Red Stripe Beer, or makes it modish with Appleton Rum.

The writer, wanting to explore the areas of new black feeling, is threatened by an instant devaluation of language, by a process that all over the world not only disrupts vast peasant majorities into urban slums, but at the same debases his traditional speech patterns. The inventiveness with which new language responses to new kinds of existence are created is itself exploited by the Ad-sphere when it creates its linguistic universe of non-sense, where Being in general is threatened with non-Existence. By contrast, Eldridge Cleaver, brought off in *Soul on Ice* a tour de force in which the spoken black language erupted onto the page.

Audvil King moves in his letter-essay between standard English, Afro-modish demotic, cant cult phrases, dialect turns of speech. What keeps it together and gives it authority, in several parts, is the felt and genuine quality of what he wants to say. It is significant that Salkey should single out for praise the one sentence where Audvil King is trapped by the gulf of separation that exists in our society between the consciousness of the educated and the marginal man. Thus Audvil King in his letter to a friend, discussing the plight of the unmarried woman with many children from different fathers, who react to their economic situation by having more children for more men – depending on the fact that, for a time at least, they will get some help and support from the latest father – sees this response as a logical and rational one in the context of her economic circumstance. But writing his letter to his middle-class girl friend, to whom he tries to explain the realities and necessity of the black struggle, he still sees the majority class in the context of the old planters *these people*. When, in the midst of a standard English sentence, which displays, unconsciously, his command of the standard English, he mixes in "plenty of these people with nuff pickney" he is using the dialect not as a means of communication, but as a means of displaying his withitness with "these people". That which he uses consciously to bridge a distance only marks the distance – like the Martiniquan students returning from France, who, Fanon tells us, deliberately use the Creole to their gathered friends and relatives to show that they have not changed, are not putting on airs. They use the Creole to assure that a stereotype of themselves still exists, rather than for communication. They use it, therefore, as the whites use pidgin-language in talking to the blacks. By using pidgin the White paternally condescends to show the black that be understands the simpler processes of his mind.

Here, instead of confronting standard English and the Creole in a dialectical relation, Audvil King drops in two or three expressions from the dialect, taking them out of context, simplifying, creating a fabricated demotic, the kind made popular in the Stella Column in the *Star* newspaper, the chatter, the trivial gossip that replaces communication between human beings. Like the admen, the television boys, the gossip columnists, King here reduces the dialect, the popular "now" speech to a form of pidgin. The Sufferer is reduced to a cliché – a powerful enough cliché as the recent election propaganda showed – but a cliché nevertheless. Indeed the entire air of inauthenticity that pervaded the election campaign sprang from the central cliché of the marginal men as *Sufferers* in Egypt land, waiting for a Joshua to lead them to Zion. The real expression of the people, taken from them, manipulated, is then sold back as a cliché; and they buy this stereotype of themselves. Of course, when they wake up to the confidence trick, that will be another matter altogether. For the abuse of language and meaning has occurred on both sides of the political spectrum. On both sides, the ad-men who trade in all shades of the half-lie determined the non-issues on which the campaign was run. But under the advertising instant-demotic the symbol contains its pristine power – and the full value will be demanded, one day, by the masses.

For this pidgin, essentially manipulatory use of language, instead of liberating the people whose liberation is intended, reduces them simplistically to Sufferer-victims, alienates them from their role as self-liberators, traps them in sporadic outbursts of violence interspersed with long stretches of passive waiting for the new Moses to lead them out of Egypt. As Fanon puts it:

> To make him talk pidgin is to fasten him to the effigy of him, to snare him, to imprison him, the eternal victim of an essence of an *appearance* for which he is not responsible.[25]

Yet in sharp contrast, still on the same point, King uses the standard English and the Creole for purposes of communicating meaning. He writes:

> Questioned as to why they pursue the folly of child after child, with different men, none of whom remains, they many times give the reply, 'Then me no a'fe try, sah?'[26]

Both the Standard English and the dialect are used for different purposes. King, as the welfare worker, observing, asking a question, uses the language of description. The woman's answer could have been phrased in no other language but the dialect. Her short phrase expresses her awareness of the Sisyphean aspect of her method of survival, her acceptance of its inevitability in the context of the circumstances of her existence. As a writer, King acknowledges the gulf that exists between the two different logics, springing out of two cultures, two languages, two ways of apprehending realities. All they have in common is their race. All that binds them is the consciousness of black dispossession, a more abstract feeling on his part; a more concrete one in hers. The question that he asks is a non-question in her world; it does not exist in the complex of her reasons for living, for "motherhood" is not a simple function, one other function among many, as it is for the women in his world – the woman to whom he writes his letter, for example.

In the world of the marginal culture, motherhood is for the women their destiny – a means of trying to survive. It is through becoming the mother of a child, making a man become the "baby father" that relationships are established at all. Marriage in the Western sense does not exist in her world – even the old "faithful concubinage" which belongs to the world of stable peasant relationships have tended to disappear in the world of total flux and instability. The temporary quality of each relationship is taken for granted. What is often forgotten is that during the temporary stay of the male, he takes on some economic responsibility for the entire brood; then he goes off and strikes up a relationship with another "baby mother". The link between them, the hub of the relation, is the bearing of the child. Yet every other child that she has decreases her viability on the baby-bearing market. As King reports, one woman explains the circular inevitability of child after child in this manner:

> 'When 'im (the man) come pan top o'me in the night, me cawn tell 'im no, else 'im no gone like the res'a them. An which man woulda come tek me now wid six pickney? Ow I woulda manage fe feed them pickney deh!'[27]

The seeking after each temporary relation on the woman's part is matched by the same on the part of the male. This male has often been accused of irresponsibility by middle-class critics and sociologists. Rex Nettleford in his *Mirror, Mirror* with certain fascist overtones – approved by his publishers who place the extract prominently on the cover of his book – writes:

> It may be that the black man will have to stop littering the countryside with illegitimate children, dull the memory of his proverbial castration by slavery and face the responsibility of fathering a family unit as a base from which to build his social and economic security.[28]

The book, a propaganda piece in defence of the status quo, has been highly popular in Jamaica. It offers the rationale that the middle and upper classes *want* to hear. The irresponsible social and economic system, which condemns a large majority of its people to a condition of semi-employment, underemployment, casual employment, or unemployment, forces them to construct a fabric of relations which reflect the instability and temporary quality of their economic base. The family unit, which Nettleford sees as the ideal, needs the material foundation of regular employment in a secure world on which to base itself. Once this material base exists, then the responses of responsibility, the "fathering" of children in an economic and psychological sense becomes possible. Indeed the heavy paternalism of the father in the lower-middle class, the middle class and the upper-middle class where the economic base makes the family unit viable, is exaggerated by the feeling that lack of "fathering" is the hallmark of the casual classes; the stigma of the lower orders.

The irresponsibility of the social system is placed on the marginal man; the victim of the system is made to bear the stigma of irresponsibility. Yet this response is no more than his logical response to a condition of casual, or semi-employment. His temporary material base is matched by his temporary relationships. The need for human relationship, his desire to have children, shown in his insistence that his women *prove* the validity of this relationship by having a child for him, can only be reflected in a pattern, a social pattern which corresponds to the casual and unstable economic base of his material situation. As King points out, the women, asked about the fathers of their respective children answered: "'Im run 'wey" and "Me couldn tell when las' mi see 'im".[29]

That is to say, both sides accept and are clear-eyed about the temporary nature of the relationship; the material base does not allow, or afford, "fathering", "responsibility", a "family unit". The mother, with the possibility of domestic work, or day work far more within her reach, with the possibility of another man as temporary wage-earner, is far better placed, from a material point of view, to accept the responsibility of the children. Motherhood becomes her profession, one of her means of survival – and her woman's burden. The high birth rate is therefore an inbuilt part of the economic status quo, which opens such a great gap between the new privileged professional class, to which Mr. Nettleford belongs, and the marginal classes, whose numerous members – in that revealing word of Nettleford's – "litter" the countryside. Like so much garbage.

The ambivalence to birth control on the part of the women of the marginal classes (which King shows in the talk with the woman who has had nine children and would prefer if "them couldn' plan something fe offa people little job"[30]) shows their awareness of the fact that birth control is one more panacea, one more adjustment to enable an unjust system which condemns a large majority to the nonexistence of casual or no work, to continue to function. It shows her awareness, too, that a high birth rate is itself the natural fruit of a system which, whilst holding up the family unit as the ideal, is programmed to function by withholding from an exploited marginal majority the material economic base that alone makes the family unit, and all its cultural superstructure, viable. But the family unit of the haves, with its emphasis on paternal responsibility, exists through its exploitation of the have-nots, with its pattern of temporary responsibility on the part of the fathers and total responsibility on the part of the mothers.

It is here that we agree with Salkey's statement which singles out the central importance of King's essay:

> But even more than that, 'Letter to a Friend', is about the necessary unitary relationship between our men and women, on the one hand, and the ideological demands of the new social and political changes, on the other.[31]

For King has used this man-woman relation, in all its distortion and tragic conflict, as his point of departure from which to make us equally experience his own tormented reactions to the brutalisation which the system inflicts on its victims, reaching into the deepest levels of their personal relationships. The language of the preface to the letter is still modish Afro-jargon:

> …like destructive, where it is obnoxious weeds we're dealing with; like whatever we look into ourselves and see… that it doesn't fit and yet is forced on us.[32]

Therefore, it tends to obscure the reality of what King is saying: i.e. that we "suffer" the system, are forced onto its procrustean bed of personal relationships, images, style, fashion:

> …for instance, the 'thought' that you have 'bad' hair and can seem to have 'good' hair from a Wig or Hot Comb. From the time you accept that 'thought,' then you must buy the Wig or the Heat, and that's not choice; that's bowing to pressure you don't even see.[33]

Once King begins his letter to Ann, the language, apart from occasional posturing, already discussed, settles down to find its own expression, an expression dominated by the urgency, and the political quality of what King has to say.

His letter to Ann comes out of his own present and future wished-for relation with her. He takes upon himself the responsibility of exploring the barriers to this relationship; and through exploring these barriers explores their relation as a black man and woman to the world of reality in the latter part of the twentieth century. They stand in the relations of victims, cultural, psychological, material, political to the agents of a world system. As Fanon defines it:

> The Negro problem does not resolve itself into the problem of Negroes living among white men but rather of Negroes, exploited, enslaved, despised by a colonialist capitalist society that is only accidentally white.[34]

But the fact of this whiteness of the masters of the colonialist capitalist society has terrible consequences for the black victims of the system. They internalise the white collective unconscious and seek to exile themselves from themselves. The society that needs them as victims, that makes this inferiority complex inevitable,

> derives its stability from the perpetuation of this complex in a society that proclaims the superiority of one race...[35]

The superiority of the white race becomes bound in with the stability of the society that victimises King and Ann and makes their personal relationship problematic and difficult, from the pressure of alien objective circumstance over which they have no control. Ann, born with the tight-curled hair of a black woman, looks in her mirror and sees projected the image of the straight hair of the white women, an image that is projected into her from fairy stories, novels, films, advertisements. Straight hair, like "good" English, is the Grail which can convert her to humanity, as it is defined by the dominant section of the system. She straightens her hair, like all the others of her group. Then comes the black revolt, and the instinctive turn to the Afro – where the hair is cut and shaped and not straightened. The Afro becomes part fad, part mode, part fashion. In some cases, it is the gesture of rebellion that replaces the rebellion. In others it is a sign that the wearer has awakened to the realisation that:

> The environment, society are responsible for your delusion. Once that has been said, the rest will follow of itself, and what that is we know. The end of the world.[36]

King addresses himself to Ann, to show how the delusion of straight hair is caused by the society, the system, of which she is a cultural victim. Above all, he wants her to become aware that her reluctance to wear an Afro is part of her reluctance to adopt a symbol of personal revolt that would entail her commitment to the destruction of the system, the society that has tricked her into this negation of herself. He wants her to see, too, how the irrationality and irresponsibility of the system which damages her psychologically leads to a more brutal oppression, to a direct exploitation of the marginal masses of her fellow-blacks, and, too, to see her own exploitative relationship to these marginal masses.

"The Letter", and its wide range of argument, hangs around the central problem:

> Remember, when I suggested you stop using the Hot Comb?[37]

All its wider implications, that she, as a 'nice' middle-class girl, is somewhat apprehensive of, because the wearing of the Afro involves her in the *Weltanschauung* of the Rastafarian sect, a sect whose cultural life-style, or rather its trimmings, has invaded black and brown middle-class society. The Afro fashion-revolution movement from the U.S.A. has coincided, too, with this older semi-secular, semi-religious movement. The Rastafarian movement began somewhere in the early thirties, sparked off by Garveyism and by the worldwide shock which black men all over the world experienced with the invasion of Ethiopia and the dispossession of Haile Selassie. The projection of his image in innumerable newspapers and magazines, plus the psychic certainty that in him the fate of all black colonials were tied and linked, plus the kingly paraphernalia of power – however temporarily powerless – and the biblical prophecies and references which seemed to identify the feeling of exile of black men in a white world with his black exile, led to an urban and at times semi-rural movement adopting Haile Selassie as the Black God and defined Jamaica as a place of exile and Ethiopia as the promised Zion.

The complete rejection of the established order was symbolised in a communal life style: the preference to be self-employed and refuse to work for others; the non-cutting of locks and hair – in the case of the Nyabinghi, a special sect, taken to more rigorous lengths. The tight curled black hair, until then, as far as men were concerned, close cut and shaved, as an evasion, was now flaunted as a symbol of benign favour. Marijuana became the herb of wisdom, ritually smoked in order to lead to the perception of God. Sprung up in a time of anxiety and alienation, the Rastafarian movement spread rapidly during the decade of political independence when economic planning, competently carried out within the prescribed developmental patterns, increased the growth rate, but intensified the economic and social stresses.

Like other messianic movements in Africa, the Rastafarian sect have become symbolic of the protest by the masses against a system designed mainly for the upper classes and the elite. In conditions of rapid urbanisation and industrialisation, with old values swept away and no new ones to take its place; with widespread and increasing economic disparity and unemployment matched by the disillusion and alienation of black and brown middle-class children, turned off by the symbols of white power and eager to assert a new black identity, the Rastafarian movement has offered a life style, a demotic, which expresses a rejection of official reality. The Afro hairstyle copied from the United States and the black revolt there was augmented in Jamaica by the adoption of the long locks of the Rastafarian.

The sect began to spread, began to take part in the explosion of popular music which, borrowing from former cult religious music, fulfilling itself in new forms like Ska and Reggae, used versions of Biblical themes of alienation or exile:

> By the rivers of Babylon
> Where we sat down
> And there we wept when we remember Zion
> For the wicked carried us away in captivity
> Required of us a song.
> How shall we sing the Lord's song
> In a strange land.[38]

The persecution that the Rastafarians encounter from the police (who as the guardians of the official reality – a reality which accepts that blackness is to be toned down, controlled – resent the brethren), makes them martyrs and true sufferers. From this marginal sect there has exploded an outburst of music, painting, and the writing of poems with the emphasis being put on the assertion of the person. The Pronoun *I* used both in the nominative and the accusative ease, claims the full right of identity of the individual backed by his faith. The phrase "I Man" was manipulated by some politicians in the recent elections when much of the Rastafarian rhetoric, especially the original Rastafarian greeting of "Peace and Love" was appropriated.[39] But the important thing is that the Rastafarians try to live *their* revolt rather than to suffer the system.

The adoption of the hair, the uncombed, shaggy long hair of the Rastafarians by the young unemployed and the middle-class rebels at once falls into two patterns: into the general pattern where:

> Shaggy hair as a form of protest against resented social forms is a current symbol in our own day.[40]

The other pattern is where the black man, in combat with his own prescribed whitened image, revolts by seeking to find and display his own true image, rebelling against the cultural imposition of the official society. By using the problem of hairstyle as the centre of his argument, King, therefore, explores all the complexities of the reactions of the varied members of his circle – the black nurse working in England, home for a holiday, wearing a wig, a straight-haired wig to a party at the university, where of course the cult of the Rastafarian is assiduously practised by the rebellious students. King records her description:

> She continued, 'A party', she said. 'Somewhere up Mona. Cultural-like. But when we reached, I couldn't see anything but people with hair and beard, all over the place. Some shouting "Burn!" And the woman, them? Just the same. "Down wid Babylon! and all that.'[41]

She was all for Black Power in its English and American forms, but found it difficult to accept it in its essentially lower-class Rastafarian form. And, to be fair, although King blames her,

...she had left Jamaica too long now to believe that a party 'up Mona' could be swinging it Black on a Rasta basis.[42]

One rather understands her scepticism about that "Rasta Business" as practised by the Jamaican black and brown middle class. Working as a minority black in England, her blackness has to be really laid down on the line. She therefore suspects the enormous potentialities of middle-class fraudulence where the Rasta gesture and rhetoric can replace any revolutionary reality, in a society where black is in the majority, yet the economic structure places white, brown and middle-class black in a position of exploitation *vis-à-vis* their supposed black brothers. As the recent elections showed, the Rasta rhetoric of Peace and Love swept a Government into power, solidly supported by the merchant and middle classes on the one hand, and by the masses on the other. The shout of power did not define power for whom.

It is in describing the genuinely powerless and the delusions that accompany this powerlessness that King breaks out of the limitations of middle-class black power, Rasta Power, – just always too much *à la mode*, too boutique fashioned. He takes issue with Ann's Puritan-capitalist imposed ethic of hard work, her belief that hard work would transform the marginal man, like everybody else, into a success story. He explores with accuracy the world of the marginal man in which the formidable limitations to enterprise, and the stifling of potential, make hard work seem like a bad joke; whilst at the same time the marginal man is stimulated by the same "glamourous norms" as those that stimulate the haves, who *can* achieve them. He shows this man, crucified in a world whose values he cannot share, not having the material base, frustrated, trapped, ready to explode. He shows the woman contemptuous of her unsuccessful man who is always failing, in a Tantalus situation, wreaking his frustration in fits of anger, in aggressive displays of bad manners. Perhaps his most poignant story is that of the comments heard on a bus when a Chinese driver, having knocked over a black woman, stops and helps her up. The women then argue that if it was a black man he would never have done that:

'Is true; our colour noh good y' know!' [...]
'Me neva see a black man...' [...]
'Them noh good, yah!'[43]

King wants to shout at them that they are all black; doesn't; gets off the bus before his usual stop; recalls that:

this exhibition of deep-rooted racial self-contempt was by women.

and that

the fact that it was Black Women, who voiced themselves, with such unprovoked bitterness, against Black Man...

springs from the Black Woman's burdened position. He concludes this incident:

Which all leads me to think that this release of bitterness, I witnessed, is as much, maybe more, a result of continuing social conditions, as a result of that deep-rooted mixture of fear and racial self-contempt.[44]

Another episode in which he hails a young girl in the poorer section of Kingston, a black girl with a child on her lap, as "African Mother" leads to the girl's shouted affirmation that "Black is the Beauty" with a

blaze of self-appreciation which had been held down too long, to be released in any temperate way.[45]

And, in spite of a few statements here and there, where an earnest fundamentalism – "...I must now do my part in keeping *that* Move on the constructive, upward line Destiny has set it..."[46] (one thinks of Fanon's warning, "there is no Negro Mission; there is no white burden") – mars the main thrust, the letter-essay succeeds because, in demanding as Fanon puts it "human behavior from the other",[47] King is basing his claim for a revolution in the socio-economic and cultural establishment on a universalist basis, whilst at the same time that universal claim is based on the concrete experience of a black man and black woman seeking a human relationship with themselves – with and for the marginal masses of their society – a human relationship which can only be achieved by the negation of an inhuman and irresponsible system. King ends his letter:

So, if after going through this, you decide on wearing your hair natural, we both know it is in full appreciation of what that implies for you socially. More, we will be clear on its implications as far as our relationship is concerned, and *that* clarity, *that* seeing, is, after all, the whole purpose of this...[48]

If, as Fanon points out, an "authentic love" can only be attained when one has "purged oneself of that feeling of inferiority, or that Adlerian exaltation, that overcompensation, which seems to be the indices of the black *Weltanschauung*",[49] the letter-essay of King does give this sense of a purging. That is why, finally, a critique of King's letter goes beyond the considerations of whether or not he has found a new style. Nor are the "literary" merits of the piece, or the non-merits, essential. The letter is not directed towards this kind of approbation; it does not seek to achieve "high culture". Rather it starts to chop away the underbrush, to make that new clearing in the forest of a liberated black and human experience of Being. Fanon argues that:

It is my belief that a true culture cannot come to life under present conditions. It will be time enough to talk of a black genius when the man has regained his rightful place.[50]

The letter-essay has this as its purpose – and goes a long way on the way.

The other pieces, like Althea Helps, "Woman: Out of One Many" ("A Revival of Spirit") and Pam Wint's "Woman Move", are brave attempts to help in a similar task. The latter deals with the life of Harriet Tubman, "the black

Moses of our Race" and others, and does not escape the journalese fate of all propaganda exhortatory material. The information it carries about outstanding black women to a people, a readership ignorant of the heroism of the black survival struggle in the New World, is valuable; and excuses somewhat the declamatory jargon:

> Many women leave their footprints behind, in history, expecting us to fertilise the crops they have planted; so, girls, do it now: MOVE![51]

Essentially a pep talk, it remains unpretentious. Althea Helps' piece, however, enters a rather blood-and-soil mystification area. The intention – to revalue the African family unit and the African past – is praiseworthy; even more, the attempt to show the Western-capitalist family unit – so much for Nettleford's ideal – as being merely relative. She realises, too, the perversion of human relationships in the present system, but seems to cast the blame on the women caught in the system, and falls into the trap of calling for a "moral Revolution" on the woman's part, marginalising the need for the material and economic revolution. A kind of black Moral Rearmament is then urged; the New World woman is accused of condoning divorce, "irresponsible motherhood and further irresponsible rearing of children…" She does admit, however, that the woman's vision is blinded by the "moral weakness" and "corruption that surrounds her".[52]

Miss Helps repeats the cultural void theory, which is so widespread; under slavery, everything was lost, consciousness and all – all was a void, a black void. She writes:

> The moral consciousness that was disrupted was never, understandably, replaced; and so, the distortion produced by slavery led to an unwholesome ethic which was continued in practise and conduct after slavery.[53]

Here, the complexity of the reinserted cultural web and the moral imperatives which black women followed in this country, living lives of bowing-the-head, and bending-the-knee heroism to bring up their children and nurture their survival, is too easily dismissed. Miss Helps confuses the prevalent "culture of poverty" disintegration born from neo-colonial industrialisation with the entire 300 years of history. Earnest and enthusiastic, Miss Helps terribly simplifies.

Frank Hasfal's piece about Sojourner Truth is competent, straightforward, and well told. He quotes Sojourner Truth's prophecy:

> 'The Black People are going to be a great and Noble People. Do you think that they've been robbed and trodden over, all the days of their life, for nothing?'[54]

The second part of the collection consists of Audvil King's poetry. The image of the Black Mother, for King, plays a parallel role to that of the Black and Mulatto as Woman for the Afro-Antillean poets who antedated Negritude. The Black Mother is finally an abstract symbol – the queen, the Beauty –

whom the poet leads "from deeps of shame" to "Selfness". The Black mother is a "spacious womb", the hair on her head, "the flag of your pride".[55] But in the letter-essay Mr. King had done all of this on a far higher level of intensity; here the same subjects are trivialised – too obviously propagandistic without the fire, the urge, the flair of valid propaganda. The dialect poem "The Big Wash" uses dialect uneasily, postured; the jargon phrases "Black Awareness", "Black Emergence" stick out like lumps in a coir-stuffed mattress. The poem "Civilisation" altogether fails.

Only in the last, a prose poem, "The Awakening" do we feel the spark that illuminated the letter, blazing here and there. It is subtitled: "A Journey into Rastafarian Experience", its obvious inspiration in Césaire's famous *Return to my Native Land*, e.g.:

> ...when with pieces of compressed cardboard, bamboo, an old soft wood carton box, or barrel, in a single day, shacks rose over mama and papa, and pickney, still wet with dung...[56]

responds to King's awakening, decades after, to the same reality in Jamaica that Césaire returned to in Martinique. He uses standard English infused with urgency, as he portrays the marginal No Man's land behind the Black-White frontier – the No Man's Land of Non-Existence out of which the belief of the Rastafari in a Black King reinvented an essence for their existence:

> ...RASTAFARI, at last an identity! RASTAFARI, for the first time a Black King and Saviour for the throne of each Black Heart... Rebirth! Rebirth!... Sincere throats, armed with the Prophets and prophecies, attacked the streets... Africa! Africa for all! Hope reborn and spirits renewed declared the path of salvation: Africa! Africa for the Black Man! Africa for the African!... A black King for the black man crowned!"[57]

Here King describes the Rastafarians exalted awaiting of the actual visit of Haile Selassie, where the alienated centuries found home at last. The visit of Selassie did have a psychological effect on the entire society; there, clearly demonstrated in a king, was all the paraphernalia of power and authority that the West had made synonymous with humanity, and that the blacks now had to claim as the first stage of their dialectic.

The poem uses all the symbols of the Rastas, the Akete Drums, taken over from the Maroons, the herbs, explained as "the bifocal for the spirit" which "gathered spirits in a reasoned, disciplined wrath, such as hungry depressed people never before know..."[58] the "red dance", the drum's rhapsodic heart shout; the experience of the return to "a Place native in ways I could not at first tell..."; the experience of the longing for home, "...the Lance, ...the Spear, Damn the oppressor!"[59] Yet King is aware that this experience is called racist by the white racists:

> They call this racist, this experience, which, for you, lies waiting wherever ancestral tones sing their most recent hymn; this racist, which speaks the same to every Race, which tells a man the language, colour and rhythm, of *his* people.[60]

And yet, what King, one of the alienated fringe middle class, has undergone is a "cultural" experience, a return to traditional patterns, but traditional patterns constantly reinvented, drawing in from new sources in a direct response to experience. It is here at the core of the marginal culture that the full potentiality of an authentic being remains. That is why the Rastafarian music and their painting are "native" in a sense that defies logical analysis. The "Place native in so many ways" was not really Africa, but King's native land, in which his nativity still had to be realised. The Africa that the Rastafarians dreamt of was a possibility of fulfilment. The oppressor was the worldwide socio-economic system that made such a fulfilment impossible. The awakening of King is an awakening to a potentiality.

And yet, and yet! Borges, the Argentinian writer has said that there are no camels to be found in the Koran. The Rastafarian symbols, taken over by the mass ad-world, carry the seed of their own trivialisation. King's urgency towards the end of the prose poem trembles, falls into banality:

> The Baton of unlawful law and the deafness of Black souls have dimmed the Churchical sounds. Yet, Ossie's gay, festive beat I full appreciate; it's the child of countless, of mine, for when from some jukebox, gully-side or captured lot moves the pulsing dance of the Ke-Te rhythm, then, also, in me stirs the African Lance.[61]

King's lance becomes the over-ostentatious camel of, finally, a transient Koran.[62] In the end it is Jamaican poet Tony McNeill – not included in the collection – who says it, who fuses the Rastafarian – as Lorca did with his gipsy facing the Civil Guards, his gipsy of dream and moon – with his imaginative reality. McNeill's St. Ras faces the traffic lights, the automatic Civil Guards of an automatic system programmed to trap him, to hunt him down, to negate him, to wipe him out. But so total is its negation of his dream that there can be no evasion. Awakened from his dream, back, it will be either him or the end of the world; the fall of the traffic light civilisation.

> Every stance seemed crooked. He had
> not learned to fall in with the straight
> queued, capitalistic, for work.
> He was uneasy in traffic.
>
> One step from that intersection
> could, maybe, start peace. But he dread-
> fully missed, could never proceed
> with the rest when the white signal
>
> flashed safe journey. Bruised, elbowed in
> his spirit stopped at each crossing,
> seeking the lights for the one sign
> indicated to take him across

to the true island of Ras.
But outside his city of dreams
was no right-of-passage, it seemed.
Still-anchored by faith, he idled

inside his hurt harbour and even
his innocent queen posed red
before his poised inchoate bed.
Now exiled, more, or less,

he retracts his turgid divinity,
returns to harsh temporal streets
whose uncertain crossings reflect
his true country. Both doubt and light. [63]

There are no camels.

Endnotes

1. Gordon K. Lewis, *The Growth of the Modern West Indies* (London: McGibbon and Kee, 1968), 177.
2. Leroi Jones, "The Myth of Negro Literature, in *Home: Social Essays* (New York: William Morrow, 1966), 114.
3. Lamine Diakhate, "Processus d'acculturation in Afrique Noire et ses rapports avec La Négritude," *Présence Africaine*, (Fourth Quarter, 1965), 68-81.
4. Mario Vargas Llosa, "José María Arguedas y el indio", *Casa de Las Americas*, vol. 4, no. 26 (October-November 1964), 139 [139-147].
5. Jack Corzani, "Guadeloupe et Martinique: la difficile voie de la Négritude et de l'Antillanite", *Présence Africaine*, no. 76, (1970), 16 [16-42].
6. Wilfred Cartey, "Three Antillan Poets: Emilio Ballagas, Luis Palés Matos and Nicholás Guillén" (Ph.D. dissertation, Columbia University, 1965), 201.
7. Ibid. 202.
8. Rex Nettleford, *Mirror; Mirror: Identity, Race and Protest in Jamaica* (Kingston: Collins Sangster, Jamaica Ltd., 1970).
9. The problem of the "true image" in the Jamaican context is fraught with ambivalence. In the Introduction, Salkey attacks a Jamaican Prime Minister who insisted that he did not want, in a projected picture book of Jamaica "pictures of barefoot boys leading donkey carts or country women with baskets on their heads". *One Love*, 6. Yet, in his attack, Salkey meets the politicians' simplification with one that is equally misleading. The politician, convinced that modernisation is all, wants to show the changes that have taken place under his regime. Planes, cars, trucks and buses, the supermarkets that are taking over from the vendors (higglers) are to him the only things worth showing. He wants to blot out anything that seems a reflection on his own ability to modernise Jamaica completely.
    But it is equally a fact that journalists etc. have still remained with a Louise

Bennett-market woman cliché picture of all Jamaica studded with market women and donkeys.

The cheerful "mammy"-type market woman hides the reality of the fact that the majority of higglers go to market overnight jammed-packed on a truck or a bus, sleeping all night on a piece of crocus bag spread on the concrete of the market, getting soaked at night, with rain. Nothing picturesque about that. Both sides in effect, Prime Minister and Salkey, are trapped in simplified stereotypes. Indeed the whole syndrome of middle-class folkism needs exploring. The dialect poems of Louise Bennett – and her Pantomime roles – have frozen this version of the folk as part of the "cultural establishment". Through its lack of development and change, it has become an acceptable middle-class "populist" version of the living language. Indeed, Miss Bennett's daily involvement in radio and television dialect-advertising, and "talks" have helped to hasten the trivialisation of the dialect. Salkey's long absence makes him unaware of these changes, and he fights a battle for the acceptance of the dialect when the dialect is being "accepted" but on a one-dimensional basis- to its detriment.

10. *One Love*, 5.
11. Frantz Fanon, *Black Skin, White Masks*. Trans. C.L. Markman, (1952; New York: Grove Press, 1967), 191.
12. Ibid., 192-193.
13. *One Love*, 13.
14. Ibid.
15. Ibid., 14
16. Ibid.
17. Although not an exact quote, this idea can be found in Martin Heidegger, "The Origin of the Work of Art", (1935-36) in *Off the Beaten Track*, trans. *Holzweg*, by Julian Young and Kenneth Haynes (Cambridge: Cambridge University Press, 2002), 30.
18. Fanon, *Black Skin, White Masks*, 38.
19. *One Love*, 6.
20. Ibid.
21. Fanon, *Black Skins, White Masks*, 111.
22. *One Love*, 7.
23. Fanon, *Black Skins, White Masks*, 40
24. *One Love*, 8.
25. Fanon, *Black Skin, White Masks*, 35.
26. *One Love*, 29.
27. Ibid.
28. Nettleford, *Mirror, Mirror*.
29. *One Love*, 28.
30. Ibid., 27.
31. Ibid., 8.
32. Ibid., 14-15.
33. Ibid., 15.
34. Fanon, *Black Skin, White Masks*, 202.
35. Ibid., 100.

36. Ibid., 216.

37. *One Love*, 15.

38. "By the Rivers of Babylon" written and recorded by members of The Melodians in 1970 and appeared in the 1972 classic film, *The Harder They Come.*

39. (SW) Indeed the whole manipulation of the Rastafarian rhetoric and black power consciousness in the recent elections (February, 1972) by the winning party deserves close study. For the winning party was backed heavily by the merchant class and some of the foreign-corporation groups, with money etc. These had been alienated from the previous big business/populist government by the latter's efforts to collect reasonable taxes; and a dubious and problematic Jamaicanisation of some foreign businesses. Yet the winning party successfully used the popular symbols of exploding black consciousness – the leader was pictured in underground pamphlets as one of a triumvirate of Haile Selassie, Claudius Henry, the black Moses, and Michael Manley as the young Joshua, The opposing party's attempt to smear this as a blasphemy brought forth loud protests from the official Church, many of whom – angered by the previous government's refusal to stop the National Lottery – declared in full-page ads that Mr. Manley was a good Christian; perhaps the most open intervention by the Church in any election so far.

But the fact remains that all the effective symbols used in the elections were the symbols of the Rastafarians who claim that Haile Selassie is the Black God. The Biblical rhetoric of the Rastafarians was used in pamphlets which declared that the leader Joshua, "tarried not to come to the help of his perishing Brothers and Sisters?" On the political platform, the "rod of correction" given to the Leader by Haile Selassie became the most burning issue of the campaign – had the leader dropped the rod when he ran away as the opposing party had claimed? or had he kept it at all times in his possession? At a public meeting the Leader had the rod unwrapped and handed to him by his mother and a friend – the lie had been disproved! The Leader declared that he was the biggest "science man" of all – a science man is dealer in magic and witchcraft. Party members carried rods; middle-class candidates wore woollen Rastafarian caps, but these made up in boutiques – not home grown like the real thing; party followers wore love beads, a symbol taken from cult religions, and modish Afro wear; a prominent Jewish merchant and industrialist, whose family owns a great part of the economy of Jamaica, called his black audience "Brothers and Sisters". As violence erupted all over the country, in brief yet effective outbursts the Rastafarian greeting "Peace and Love" was plastered on election hoardings – used in the Ad-men slogans by which the campaign was waged on both sides. The opposing side tried a plane, writing in sign language, lit up by lights. But they just could not compete with the bandwagon that went about the country playing specially composed reggaes; and the compelling cry of Power! The adjective "Black" was carefully avoided. (See *The Sunday Gleaner*, 2, February 1972.)

40. Mary Douglas, *Natural Symbols, Explorations in Cosmology* (London: Barrie and Rockliff, 1970), p. 72.

41. *One Love*, 17.

42. Ibid., 38.

43. Ibid., 38.
44. Ibid., 39.
45. Ibid., 40.
46. Fanon, *Black Skin, White Masks*, 228.
47. Ibid., 229.
48. *One Love*, 41.
49. Fanon, *Black Skin, White Masks*, 42.
50. Ibid., 187.
51. *One Love*, 53.
52. Ibid., 46.
53. Ibid.
54. Ibid., 64.
55. Ibid., 68.
56. Ibid., 75.
57. Ibid., 76.
58. Ibid., 77.
59. Ibid., 79.
60. Ibid.
61. Ibid., 81.
62. Yet the insistent use of these symbols respond to another cultural imperative. Ruth Katz in an article, "Mannerism and Cultural Change: An Ethnomusicological Example", *Current Anthropology*, vol. 11, nos. 4-5 (October-December 1970): 465-475, points out that in any process of trying to hold on to a culture, or reinstate that which has passed, which has been lost, especially at a time when the people of a culture are experiencing pressures to change, a certain mannerism of style develops in the expression of the threatened culture. There is a tendency to emphasise not so much the entire aspects of the culture, but its bold stereotypes – for example, since Western thinkers see the ornateness of the melodic line as a stereotyped feature of Oriental music, young Oriental groups, grown away from that music, and wanting to return to their now threatened identity, tend to over stress the ornateness of the melodic line. This very kind of over-adherence to emphasised and selected traits tends in itself to initiate a process of change, and leads to the repetition of "di maniera" symbols – such as, in this case, King's drum and Spear, herbs and Lance. As Katz argues: "The central proposition of the theory is that the apparent resistance to acceptance of majority group culture may be expressed in 'manneristic' terms, i.e., in terms of the exaggeration and embellishment of those elements of traditional culture by means of which the majority identifies the minority and the minority comes to identify itself". Ibid., 469.
63. See Anthony McNeill, "Saint Ras", *Savacou*, vol. 1, nos. 3, 4 (March 1971): 155. Republished in *Wheel and Come Again: An Anthology of Reggae Poetry*, Kwame Dawes, ed. (Leeds: Peepal Tree Press, 1998), 135.

CREOLE CRITICISM – A CRITIQUE

Critique is concerned with the truth content of a work...
                                                    Walter Benjamin[1]

...'stylistic criteria' are being advanced to give an impression of objectivity
while the author pursues a more subjective hypothesis and one that has
little to do with literary criticism.
                                        Ramchand in *Caribbean Quarterly*[2]

The central distortion of Dr. Ramchand's criticism is a reflection of the
ambivalent Creole eye with which he views his society, its literature and
himself. The Creole eye is part the eye of the native, part the eye of the
stranger. It is deceptively lucid. A confusion of self-image haunts its most
illuminating discoveries. It looks out upon the world with a myopic brilliance.
It pins the facts down in a precise analytical stare. But the searchlight of
its gaze is directed by a grid of misconceptions prepackaged in the cornflakes
of a colonial education; patterned by a ready mix Western-Liberal
Weltanschauung. The Creole eye is thereby the eye of the evader. The mirrors
of its criticism are trick ones. Nothing is ever what it seems. Dr. Ramchand's
comment on the German scholar Janheinz Jahn, the comment quoted
above, can with precision be applied to his own critical method. This
aptness is even more acute when he speaks of Jahn's "peculiar circularity".

  For when he calls that autochthonous English critic, Dr. Leavis, into
the balance, in order to use him as a stalking horse against Gordon Rohlehr's
critical essay on Naipaul – one of the essays included in the collection
The Islands in Between[3] – he reduces Leavis to the narrow dimension of
his own neurosis. Yet, if one applies the formula of close textual analysis
to Ramchand's criticism, one can find no better description of his critical
circularity, than Leavis's assessment of an essay by T.S. Eliot. This essay,
Leavis wrote, is

> ...notable for its ambiguities, its logical inconsequences, its pseudo-precisions,
> its fallaciousness and the aplomb of its equivocations and specious cogency.
> ...Its technique in general for generating awed confusion help to explain
> why it should not have been found easy to deal with... [4]

I have not found Ramchand's criticism easy to deal with. Leavis, faced
with Eliot's stance of 'impersonality' as critic, is suspicious,

...because it suggests not the true expression of an exploring consciousness, but the playing of an already calculated part...[5]

I have had to come to terms with a more complex mimicry; with Dr. Ramchand's imitation of an impersonal and objective critical stance. The role that Dr. Ramchand plays is at second-hand. I must try to seize hold of a reality of which the borrowed mimic gest is but a multiple mask; must grapple with subtle indirections, camouflage, with an apparent impartiality expressed in "above the battle" clichés, with radical-liberal posturing, false universalism, texts misinterpreted with such sleight of hand that the texts confirm the prejudices of Dr. Ramchand; with the misuse of quotations to fit them onto the Procrustean bed of his central obsession. What is this obsession?

Under the mask of "concern for criticism" – the title of his article in *Caribbean Quarterly* – under his preoccupation with "stylistic criteria", Dr. Ramchand wages quite another battle. His mission is to negate, destroy, diminish, disguise the African centrality in the cultural dynamic of the Caribbean peoples; to obscure the cultural, social and political consequences that spring from any recognition of such a centrality.

In his *Caribbean Quarterly* article, Ramchand has this to say about Gordon Rohlehr's "ambitious" [sic] essay on Naipaul:

> Rohlehr precludes any real discovery of his author through the critical performance itself by beginning with a conviction: 'Naipaul is a Trinidad East Indian who has not come to terms with the Negro-Creole world in Trinidad, or with the greyness of English life or with life in India itself where he went in search of its roots.'[6]

Dr. Ramchand rejects this statement on the grounds of "stylistic criteria":

> Because Rohlehr does not work towards this sweeping pronouncement, and does not seek to convince us by the methods of literary criticism, the reader who does not already agree with the judgement of Naipaul the man, finds the essay as a whole difficult to accept.[7]

The above exemplifies Ramchand's critical method; his multiple masks. Rohlehr's article is the best in the collection of essays *The Islands In Between*. He has in general an acute critical intelligence. His high opinion of Naipaul's talent is not in any way negated by his critic's desire to explain the naked neurosis displayed by Naipaul in *The Middle Passage*. To explain this neurosis, the critic must pinpoint the problem of being a minority in a majority culture to which one is doubly marginal as man and as a writer. To explain this neurosis in the specific Trinidadian context is to explore the resentful consciousness of a Naipaul – or a Ramchand – growing up to find himself despised by a brown and Creole middle class, who, as successful mimics of Western culture, looked down on East Indians as "coolies" who lacked "culture". However, once the latecomers, the East

Indian immigrants, began to enter the educational system, to take their place in the Creole class, they not only claimed their full share in Western "culture", but also pointed to the "high" culture of India to give them one more point in the game of one-upmanship between themselves and the blacks. Yet the real counter in the game, was, and is, the ability to "acquire" Western "culture". The high culture of India was comparable to Western culture; the Indian nose and hair were "Aryan". Africa, in the Creole consciousness, black, brown, white, East Indian, Chinese, remained vague; a place which Western culture designated as a land of savages; the heart of darkness. The rise of the new-Negritude/Black Power Movement in the Sixties has begun to change the name of the game. The revaluation of Africa, of the African connection, the search for African ancestral roots, real and imagined, the attempt to forge an Afrocentric myth to counterbalance the Eurocentric reality are new factors which change the ground rules of the game. The formerly privileged players are disconcerted. The Jack threatens to devalue the King. And the Jack in the Caribbean is mainly black. As "culture" has been used as a weapon against him, so many of his Black Power advocates are prepared to use "culture" as a weapon against others. In claiming his black identity, Jack can seem to refute the claim of minority groups or, at least to ignore the claim – to theirs. Yet there are two aspects to Jack and his black quest for identity. One aspect of this quest is imitative – the mere negation of "white power", the claim to have this power take on a black face. The status quo of privilege and injustice is not to be changed; only the masters. This quest is the quest of "blackism". It is no less sick than its white counterpart. In the final analysis both are allied against the other aspect of Jack's quest: the quest of nativity. This creative aspect of Jack's quest is at once particular and universal. It asserts that the dynamic agent of the cultural matrix which provides that grid of communication that patterns the national identity of the Caribbean people – black, brown, white, East Indian, Syrian, Chinese – is to a great extent, a legacy from Africa. It is the African heritage which has been the crucible of the cultural deposits of the immigrant peoples, transforming borrowed elements of this culture into something indigenously Caribbean.

Yet, this assertion, imperfectly formulated, can also seem to exclude. It is in reaction to this feeling of exclusion that Dr. Ramchand assaults and batters the concept of a central African element in culture. Whenever he touches on things African and the African connection, one is startled by a rancorous animosity, all the more distasteful, because, unlike Naipaul's, it lacks the courage of its conviction. This animosity calls for our attention. Unlike Naipaul, Ramchand does not reject the West Indies. It is his attempt, as a Trinidadian Indian to claim his full place in the Caribbean context that informs his rancour. Where his confusion comes about is in his concept of what this place should be; of how this context should be defined in the past and the present; of the directions in which these definitions should transform the future. His resistance to the African connection is political rather than a merely compartmentalised critical one. His political position is one of "creolism" – that is, the Liberal ideology translated into a neo-colonial structure. Creolism is essentially the politics of rhetoric. It is the politics of those who want the appearance of change without its painful reality. Rhetoric is the weapon with which it obscures areas of conflict; and creates a verbal consensus which seeks to dam up new directions in the dry river bed of Creole custom.

In his Book, *The West Indian Novel and its Background*, Dr. Ramchand uses a quotation from Wilson Harris, at head of a chapter, labelled "The Aborigines". Harris writes, Ramchand quotes:

> 'It's all so blasted silly and complicated. After all I've earned a right here as well, I'm as native as they, aint I? A little better educated, maybe, whatever the hell that means.'[8]

This is the real question that informs Dr. Ramchand's criticism. What Dr. Ramchand asks repeatedly under many "critical guises" and "literary pretexts" is:

"I'm as native as they, aint I?"

This question, and the resentful consciousness which it implies, is the organising principle of Ramchand's criticism. It determines his approach to criticism which in turn determines the arrangement of his material. It determines the selectivity of his exploration of the background to the West Indian novel; his choice and evaluation of books and authors; above all, his interpretation of the works of West Indian writers. I make no apology then for criticising his criticism in a wide context. Hereon:

> ...a real literary interest is an interest in man, society and civilisation, and its boundaries cannot be drawn; the adjective is not a circumscribing one.[9]

II
THE APPROACH TO CRITICISM

Given the central preoccupation, Dr. Ramchand's arrangement of his material is both logical and necessary. The book, *The West Indian Novel and Its Background* is divided into three parts. In his introduction, Ramchand implies that Part I is to deal with the "objective" background to the West Indian novel. He posits the thesis that in this part:

> ...although a distinctive body of fiction has emerged from the West Indies in the twentieth century, life in the islands is still what it has been for over three hundred years – a life without fiction.[10]

Arranged under this fictionless background are five chapters headed:

(a) Popular Education in the West Indies in the Nineteenth Century
(b) The Whites and Cultural Absenteeism
(c) The Coloureds and Class Interest
(d) New Bearings
(e) The Drift Towards the Audience

This Part, as Dr. Ramchand tells it,

> ...takes in general a deterministic view of the effect of social factors upon the growth of a literature.[11]

Part II, labelled Approaches carries the main burden of the argument of the book. It is well over half its length. The Chapters in this part are headed:

(a) The Language of the Master
(b) The Negro
(c) Aborigines
(d) The Commonwealth Approach
(e) The Achievement of Roger Mais
(f) The World of *A House for Mr. Biswas*
(g) Novels of Childhood
(h) Terrified Consciousness

This part, Dr. Ramchand says, is to "deal with the background of Language, Race and Empire". This is a tall order. It is not made any easier by the fact that the powerful conditioning factors of Empire with its conditioning attitudes to Race and language, is not to be dealt with in the more "objective" Part I, but in Part II. In this Part II, as Ramchand informs us, "the emphasis is different". This part "drives towards a view of the autonomy of art". This concept of the autonomy of the work of art is central to Creole Criticism. Art for Art's sake; criticism for criticism's sake, politics for "politics" sake, are all fallout clichés of the metropolitan liberal ethos. And the phrase "the autonomy of the work of art" is the rhetoric which disguises the cliché. Yet, as we shall see, there is an underlying method in Dr. Ramchand's arrangement.

Part III of the book is headed "Precursor". Here Ramchand restores the neglected Claude McKay to his more central place in Caribbean literature. This is the most successful part of the book; the part in which the critical function takes precedence over the neurotic obsession; even if the latter does not entirely disappear. But in this part Ramchand at least reminds us of the critical capacity he displayed in his editorship of the West Indian Anthology.[12] Indeed, at one's first reading of Part III, one might be tempted to agree with Rex Nettleford when he writes:

> The future may well be with Samuel Selvon who writes with the soul of a Trinidadian, or Kenneth Ramchand, the creolised East Indian, who can write passionately, and with scholarly integrity of the work of the black Jamaican poet Claude McKay.[13]

On a second reading, one bites on the worm in the wood. Nothing is ever quite what it appears on the surface of Ramchand's criticism. The useful and valuable restoration of Mckay is there, and not to be denied. But even with Mckay, one sees that in the Ramchandian obsession, an author is there to be operated on not only for the "autonomy" of his own purpose; but as a weapon of attack, through disparaging comparison, against those authors whom the critic has set out to negate. It is only with Mckay however that the second becomes subsidiary.

In the very act of proclaiming the "autonomy" of the work of art, Dr. Ramchand allows his authors little. West Indian literature, through the filter of his interpretation, is reduced to a "Ramchandian Theory about Society". It is in the rare moment that Ramchand goes about the true business of the critic that he reveals to his readers how literature "operates on us". All too often, scalpel in hand, Dr. Ramchand is busy "operating" on West Indian Literature in order to reduce it to the cut and finish of his own psychic necessities. This private utilitarian view of West Indian literature is extended to a more banal plane. West Indian writing gets the final accolade. In his preface, Ramchand assures us that even after his discussion of individual authors,

> there is enough relevant and interesting material left to justify the establishment of a School of Caribbean Studies at the University of the West Indies.[14]

Writers at one stroke have become the folk. They exist only as raw material to be quarried by critics; as worker bees to provide texts for the supremely important academic exercise.

This glorification of criticism at the expense of the creative impulse is a persistent thread in Ramchand's book and article. We begin to suspect that Ramchand's rancour is directed not only against the "African" centrality, the indigenist apologia, but even more at these as the source of creativity; that Dr. Ramchand's resentful consciousness is directed against the act of writing itself. Nowhere are we persuaded that Ramchand enjoys the reading of literature. Yet, once literature is used as an instrument, it loses its magic. Susan Sontag describes this loss of magic as "literary pollution":

> Ours is one of those times in which the project of interpretation is above all, reactionary and suffocating, in the same way as gases from cars and heavy industry pollute the urban atmosphere, in the same manner, today's effusion of interpretations of art, poison our sensibilities. Ours is a culture whose now classic dilemma is the hypertrophy of the intellect at the expense of energy and sensual capacity; interpretation is the vengeance of the intellect against art. It is the vengeance, even more, of the intellect against the world.[15]

It is in this context that we must see Ramchand's refutation – in his *Caribbean Quarterly* article – of a previous statement that I made about the implications of the writers' exile from the Caribbean. I had argued that one of the effects of this exile was that whilst the critics functioned at the University, using the "products" of the writers, the writers were cut away from the living tradition of the reality of their own societies. And that their societies suffered from this decapitation, from this historical disjuncture of the literary and the popular tradition. Dr. Ramchand replies to this obvious fact with an assault on those who are not respectfully mindful of the critic's priestlike role. With the dramatic question,

Who cares about literary criticism in or for the West Indies?[16]

as the opening shot, Ramchand goes on to accuse me of writing with "contempt and unawareness of its [criticism's] potential"; of underestimating "the gravity of the situation, and the responsibility it imposes upon literary criticism in these islands."[17]

Having accepted the writers' exile as a given fact – the status quo of the society's structure that arranges this exile is not open to question – Dr. Ramchand goes on to assert that it is critics who must play the writers' role in the society. Yet, he argues, critics do not displace the creator. At the University critics are employed to function as pedagogues. It had been my assumption that the teaching of literature at an University implied an involvement, with one's students, in the critical activity. Indeed, that the more learned articles of criticism one wrote, the more one climbed the ladder of promotion. That in fact the critic-cum-pedagogue has never had it so good. Yet, Dr. Ramchand views himself as critic as a martyred man with a mission:

> I doubt very much whether our creative writers could survive long in the conditions that the critic has to put up with in our society. By his teachings and by the fanatical practise of his craft, however, the critic at the University can help spread the belief that literature matters; primarily, in the sense described by Dr. Leavis's 'What is Wrong with Criticism'; and only secondarily in the senses to which the sociopolitical commentators like Mr. Moore and sometimes Miss Wynter herself have too often reduced it.[18]

Ramchand here shows no awareness of the fact which constitutes the difference. The fact that Leavis functions as a critic in a metropolitan society in which his English writers are firmly rooted. Ignoring the difference, he adopts the Leavisian role. And betrays the craggy, if limited, originality of that Messiah by borrowing his scheme for redemption for a society whose sins are hardly washable in the blood of an English Lamb; or for that matter, an English solution. Striking a Leavis stance, Ramchand absurdly declaims, by implication, that it is his mission to labour:

> ...successfully to create a consciousness throughout their society that literature matters as literature and not as something else; and that literary criticism is a craft calling for maturity, intelligence, and sensitivity to the organisation of words on a page.[19]

The critic's organisation of words on a page is all that matters. The organisation of society which encourages the hypertrophy of the critical activity at the expense of creativity, would of course be dismissed as "sociopolitical analysis!"

Again Dr. Ramchand merely reflects a worldwide trend in the long dying of literature and its attendant, literary criticism. In an essay, "The Language Animal", George Steiner writes:

> Literary criticism and literary history are minor arts. We suffer at present from a spurious inflation of criticism into some kind of autonomous role...
>
> A plain view of the dependent, secondary nature of literary criticism, literary and historical comment is more than a necessary honesty. It may, in fact, open the way for a legitimate future for criticism and rescue it from some of its current megalomania and trivia.[20]

III
BACKGROUND OF THE VOID

In the background of the liberated slave was a cultural void.
Ramchand, *The West Indian Novel...*[20]

The two key chapters of Dr. Ramchand's book, one headed "The Negro", the other "The Aborigines", counterpoint one another. The rest of Parts One and Two, only reinforce, brick by brick, hint by hint, the insinuated conclusions of these two chapters. It is here that we get most clues as to Ramchand's handling of a theme central to the Caribbean novel: the theme of the black man in the twentieth century. It is a theme impossible to ignore. But the Creole eye sees it through a peripheral focus; marginalises it, and this so subtly that the casual reader will finish the book accepting at its face value, one of the ingenious masks of Dr. Ramchand – that of a Fanon-disciple, Third World radical.

The distorting focus carefully arranges that "The Negro", unlike the Whites and the Coloureds is not the subject of a chapter in Part One; is not examined as an "objective" factor. The conclusion that is therefore drawn is that, due to the failure of the Whites and the Coloureds to "create" literature, the life lived in the Caribbean was, and still is to some extent, a life lived "without fiction". Because of this lack of a "cultured class" to set the tone, to provide models, there was "in the background of the liberated slave, a cultural void". That is to say, the failure of the two minority classes is seen as the cause of the blacks' cultural deprivation.

This focus on the majority class, which presents them as passive objects, is first noted in Part One, where the blacks appear only as the objects of a process known as "Popular Education in the Nineteenth Century". The deficiencies of the colonial system of elementary and secondary education are insisted upon. So deficient was and is this system of education that the "darkness" of yesterday is still here today. The "underprivileged masses" are still unable to read enough to constitute a "reading public" for the novels; whose "imagined worlds" might have "released their smothered capacities".[22]

The "civilising agent" of education, according to Dr. Ramchand, failed ultimately, because of "administrative incompetence, unimaginativeness, lack of purpose and conflicting interests within a social and economic depression". The planters wanted labour for their estates, not educated citizens. The teachers tried their best. But as one inspector complained, the influence of the home life of their students undid all the schools' "civilisation", The failure of "civilisation", i.e. the education system, meant, according to Dr. Ramchand, that:

> some of those who had parroted their way through the Reading test had lapsed easily back into their untutored states.[23]

Education having failed to accomplish its civilising mission – the new Liberal manifest destiny that replaces the former Christianising mission – the poor objects, fallen from grace, lapsed back into a void. Those who did not had to face the fact that:

> The unrelieved factualness of approach to reading books prevented both pupils and teachers from even the suspicion of the pleasures and possibilities of the imagination.[24]

Education having failed them, they dwelt in an outer darkness, either as "discontented recruits to the teaching profession", or as "self-important clerks" with office jobs "holding on jealously to their limited privilege"; or as "the depressed and inarticulate masses". The void was deep and wide. Only a "handful of minor poets" wrote, and "their poetry reveals the alienation of the insecure and embryonic black middle classes from the uneducated and illiterate groups to which they or their parents had belonged."[25]

The void was wide and deep. The underprivileged lived "a life without fiction" the fault of the "deficiencies of popular education." That the Whites and Coloureds also lived this life without fiction was due to an "absence of nationalism".[26] All was lack, deprivation, absence. The problem with the underprivileged was that "they just aint got no culture". The trouble with the others was they just didn't feel national enough. That the problems were interrelated does not occur to Dr. Ramchand, since he suffers from his education in the same way that the Whites and the Creole Class in the nineteenth century suffered from theirs. The great myth of a colonial education in the Caribbean was, and is, that the people – the blacks – were a "tabula rasa"; that they dwelt in the darkness of a cultural void.

This concept of the cultural void is central to the Creole world view, to Dr. Ramchand's criticism. The role that the culture of the people plays in the creation of any literature; and, in particular, of Caribbean literature, remains a side issue for Dr. Ramchand, where it is not entirely negated. Yet it is his prophet, Dr. Leavis, who, in a penetrating essay, attacked this very concept of the void which Dr. Ramchand posits. Dr. Leavis traces, in an essay, "Literature and Society", the process by which, in a still unified seventeenth century-English culture, the popular culture, "a rich traditional culture", could, as in Bunyan's great classic, "merge with literary culture at the level of great literature". He shows how this fusion between the popular and the literary culture was later disrupted due to the economic process which lead to the Industrial Revolution. What had come to an end was:

> ... the old organic relations between literary culture and the sources of vitality in the general life. By Wordsworth's death, the Industrial Revolution had done its work, and the traditional culture of the people was no longer there, except vestigially.[27]

But this popular culture which has been destroyed in England, was transported to the New World; and Cecil Sharp went to the remote valleys of the Southern Appalachians to discover what had been lost. He brought back not only a "fabulous haul" of folk songs but something more – a new concept of culture. Dr. Leavis puts it in this way:

> More than that, he discovered that the tradition of song and dance (and a reminder is in place at this point of the singing and dancing with which the pilgrims punctuate their progress in the second part of Bunyan's Calvinistic allegory) had persisted so vigorously because the whole context to which folk song and folk dance belong was there, too; he discovered in fact, a civilisation or 'way of life' ...that was truly an art of social living. [28]

In Sharp's description of the people who had preserved and extended this 'culture', we read that the majority were illiterate. Yet, Sharp argues:

> That the illiterate may nevertheless reach a high level of culture will surprise only those who imagine that education and cultivation are convertible terms.[29]

It is clear that in spite of the absence of a "cultured class" as Dr. Ramchand defines it, these mountaineers did not live in "a cultural void". They shared in "the supreme value of an inherited tradition".[30]

The same economic process – the Industrial Revolution – which disrupted the "organic" culture of England, earlier created our societies as plantation societies. The folk culture of England, transported to Jamaica, was to be largely exiled by the plantation system, which disrupted the earlier small farmers of England and Scotland. But, as we shall show later, the African folk culture was able to reroot itself in Jamaica and to become "the sap" of the living indigenous tradition from which the writers would create their novels. That this folk culture is not "objectively" examined as a living and pervasive cultural dynamic of the society, that in fact Dr. Ramchand assumes that without education, in the Western sense, there was a void, is a misconception and a distortion so fundamental that the entire concept of the "background" of the West Indian novel has been betrayed. That is not to say that here and there – and later on through the subjective approach of certain selected novels – Dr. Ramchand does not discuss this tradition, but either it is tacked on as afterthought – as in the chapter on language – or it is recognised only to be determinedly denied.

Dr. Ramchand here follows the tradition of Caribbean criticism. As Dr. Edward Brathwaite complained in 1967:

> Our folk tradition, however, and the urbanised products of this tradition ... has been ... largely ignored; and where it has been examined, the examination has been usually cursory, uncritical, sometimes patronising. The assumption has been that these are debased forms; hybrid forms; formless peripheral forms.[31]

Dr. Ramchand is not unaware of Brathwaite's observation. Indeed Brathwaite figures among those critics who get a slyly severe treatment from Dr. Ramchand. We begin to be confirmed in our opinion that the refusal to analyse the "folk" background of the West Indian novel as an objective factor is part of that escape which is endemic to Dr. Ramchand's view of Caribbean reality – the evasion of Africa.

With this evasion, Dr. Ramchand misses the fact that the West Indian novel, like West Indian nationalism, was born out of a process in which the Creole blacks and Browns, (and a White, here and there) who had hitherto despised and ignored the folk culture, turned back to that folk culture, back to the people or at least to the idea of the people. It was at that moment when a new literary tradition – until then an imitative Western tradition – in technicolour – turned back to an indigenous popular culture recognised as such, to function, however gropingly and ignorantly, as the literary tradition, that the beginnings of a national feeling and a national literature exploded. Dr. Ramchand quotes George Lamming's significant declaration, yet avoids its implication. Lamming wrote:

> Unlike the previous governments and departments of educators, unlike the businessman importing commodities, the West Indian novelist did not look out across the sea to another source. He looked in and down at what had traditionally been ignored. For the first time the West Indian peasant becomes other than a cheap source of labour. He became through the novelist's eye a living existence, living in silence and joy and fear, involved in riot and carnival. It is the West Indian novel that has restored the West Indian peasant to his true and original personality.[32]

Lamming looked down, away from the mono-crop export complex and its imported and imitative superstructure of culture to the only living tradition in the Caribbean – that of the peasants. They were now for the writer not a source of labour, but of culture, of a way of life, of an art of social living – battered, tormented, assaulted, dispossessed, ignored, despised, but alive – the culture of the peasant, of the landless marginal man; of the indigenous man. For it was only by drawing from, by feeding from him, that a truly national literature could begin. As long as the literate class turned its back on the source of its vitality, there was no writing. Writing began when the "High Tradition" emerging from the popular tradition turned its gaze back; and that complex interaction which is at the base of all creative national cultures began. The turning back of the novelist to the popular tradition was the movement of return, the long passage back from the exile of alienation. The future of Caribbean literature, and of the Caribbean people, whose psychic journey it structurally parallels, will depend on that disputed and almost impossible passage.

If the West Indian novelist restored the West Indian peasant to "his true and original personality" via the written word, it was the West Indian peasant, tenaciously preserving, stubbornly re-inventing that personality through the re-invention of its culture against impossible odds, that made the West Indian novel possible.

The cultural void concept for Dr. Ramchand is more than a critical oversight. It is a psychic necessity. If the cultural void of the liberated slave is broadly accepted, it means that the African origin of his folk culture can be trivialised. The attack on the "African connection" reaches its climax in Part II, in the two chapters we have cited; but it began long before. Indeed we shall see that the final betrayal of criticism by Dr. Ramchand takes place with the choice not only of his authors, but of their particular works. Those who are condemned by Dr. Ramchand are condemned more for dealing with the themes that he wants to avoid, or negate, than for the fact that their novels are bad. Those to whom he extends salvation, both books and authors, are those which can seem to confirm his preconceptions. Dr. Ramchand uses, manipulates and exploits West Indian literature in order to sustain his own staged scenery view of it; and his own role. It is this that we consider unforgivable.

In the Introduction, with that subtle sleight of hand which distinguishes his method, he chooses some authors to praise in order to condemn others; themes to exalt and themes to denigrate; and always underlying is the threatening theme of Africa and its connection with the Caribbean. The pervasive African-descended cultural dynamic which offended Naipaul was dismissed boldly. "Nothing", said Naipaul, "had been created in the West Indies".[33] The West Indies had no history. A new myth of the Caribbean past has been built; not by the colonisers this time; but by their Creole inheritors. Dr. Ramchand repeats the myth, but insinuatingly; among the ills of society to which West Indian novelists apply themselves are, he tells us:

a) the lack of a history to be proud of
b) the absence of settled or traditional values

The void is rephrased. As we shall see later, Ramchand also paraphrases Naipaul as far as (b) is concerned. This is an extension of the abyss. Having no culture, the folk can have no values; nor can the society. For, where could they have got them from? Western education betrayed them.

Writers like Lamming, in Dr. Ramchand's interpretation of Lamming's explanation of how writing began, came and took them out of a void. As Orlando Patterson, the Jamaican writer, once said:

The writer in the West Indies is like God. He creates out of a void.[34]

As Naipaul, quoted by Ramchand early in his introduction, has it: "Living in a borrowed culture, the West Indian, more than most, needs writers to tell him who he is and where he stands".[35] It is Naipaul who consciously lives most in the borrowed culture. The part of him with which he writes is fed by the culture of that very folk whom he affects to despise; now that, like most of us, he has made the one generation passage away.

For Dr. Ramchand, it is only with the writer that the black man comes into the centre of the picture. The fact that the black man, the folk, the people, took the centre of the stage and initiated a national movement which made the writer possible, remains largely unnoticed. Dr. Ramchand sees only the problem of the writer faced with this void:

...the challenge of articulating the hitherto obscure person has affected characterisation in other ways.[36]

It is far more than "characterisation" that is affected. Now that the peasant masses, the majority of the world's people, are erupting into the centre of the stage, the writers who come from these masses – mainly all Caribbean writers and critics – are faced with the problem of whether they can use the novel form at all. For the novel form is the literary form of the European bourgeoisie and its colonial extension. The novel was born with the bourgeoisie and structured its rise as it now structures its fall. In using the novel form, the writer who must formulate in a written context the articulate but largely oral dreams and aspirations and new dispossession of the peasant, uprooted from the land, flung into the urban "yards", is face-to-face with a complex of problems in which the concept of characterisation taken by itself has become inadequate. As we shall see, the problem of formulating in a written language the articulate spoken and oral language is the problem. As Heidegger points out, "language is the clearing in the forest in which man has his being". But it is in the question of language that Dr. Ramchand is most confronted with the African presence; we shall see how he disposes of it.

Dr. Ramchand is never clumsy. His confrontation is never head on. In the introduction he chooses for praise Michael Anthony, a black Trinidadian writer of considerable merit. Here the Woolworth Glass Bead Game begins. The praise of Anthony is to be selective: Dr. Ramchand, all objective stance, proclaims Anthony the "good guy" as opposed to nameless villains:

> Some writers seek ancestral inspiration in 'African traits' or an African personality. Others, notably Michael Anthony (Trinidad b. 1932) ignore such imaginary but unimaginative props.[37]

The game has been marked. We crawl, crabways, on. Without being conscious of having been indoctrinated, we are comfortably aware that "African traits" in a West Indian writer involves a fanciful unimaginative exercise, in which one dreams to find African ancestors in the Caribbean bush. A quick and low-keyed flicking of the knife. Out, in… As if it had never been. The impression is made. But no scars. How cleverly done!

If Michael Anthony is for Dr. Ramchand a gifted acolyte, it is Wilson Harris who is the high priest of that Manichean literary cult whose principle of evil is the search for imaginary and unimaginative African traits. It is Dr. Ramchand who has created the cult; it is he who assigns roles and interprets the Sphinx-like pronouncements of Harris to suit the particular ritual. The ritual takes place against the void-like backdrop that Dr. Ramchand describes as,

> the formlessness of West Indian society and the existential position of the individual in it.[38]

In such a society, the West Indian lacks, once again, "character", the kind of character we get in English novels. Lacking this character, one would have thought that since he existed, he had something also to put in his place. But no such luck. What he has is not a positive but a negative – an "instability" of character. Michael Anthony, Dr. Ramchand assures us, displays "fidelity" to the "open consciousness" of his "youthful characters"; he shows their instability, and all of this, "adds up to a genuine exploratory attitude to the person".[39]

On reading this, one may be tempted to reach for a Jamaican expletive. Anthony's novel deals with adolescents and the youthful, and he shows the formlessness of their characters narrowing and being channelled into shape and pattern by the forces of their Trinidadian society. All this is very well and sensitively done, and Anthony has no quality of mystification that deserves his being involved in cult terms like "open consciousness" and the "person". Dr. Ramchand willy-nilly inflicts his literary mania on his helpless authors. Wilson Harris lends himself to this interpretation; or rather to the possibility of misinterpretation. His complex groping towards a new approach in the writing of the novel lends itself, like Mark Antony's Roman ears, to a cunning and one-dimensional interpretation.

The negativity of this West Indian non-character, Dr. Ramchand argues, is itself a positive; if not in real life, then in literature. Out of the void, the black void, the magic wand of literature can bring universal salvation. Wilson Harris, Dr. Ramchand assures us:

> sees the obscurity of the broken individual in the West Indies as the starting point for a creative inquiry into the question, 'What is man?'[40]

"Obscurity" and "broken individual" are by now cult words. These are parallel terms to the concept of the void. One remembers Lamming's angry decision to write *In The Castle of My Skin*, a West Indian classic, primarily to prove to Walcott that the black man of the Caribbean did not live amongst "the swine". He was not interested in finding out "What is Man?" Perhaps if the cockroach survives the bomb and takes over what is left, he will be able to do that. But this "false universality", the liberal ideal that denies the liberal reality, is a part of the Creole complex – a worked-out humanist vein borrowed at second-hand to "help weave the veil".

The more urgent question for Caribbean man, a man at the crossroads of almost all the world's cultures, is not to find a new identity, but to formulate, articulate that which he was, is, and is in the process of becoming. The very articulation of what is at once posits the choice of what can be. Novels of the search for identity tend to be engaged novels, novels rejecting even more than they accept. In search for new possibilities in the future they engage with reality; usually on behalf of the majority who are economically and culturally exploited by the minority. The search for a revaluation of the African roots is, therefore, connected with "engaged" writing, which can be good or bad writing. But in Dr. Ramchand's criterion, this kind of writing is always a dangerous invitation to heresy; a temptation all the more threatening in the wilderness of the void:

> In an area of deprivation, longing and rootlessness where so many people are inarticulate, the novelist may find himself tempted into passionate documentaries, or criticised for not adopting prescribed stances.[41]

The key word is "tempted". The Creole cult has its literary orthodoxy of form; but it is an esoteric orthodoxy, on guard against the vulgarity of "prescribed stances".

Who "prescribes the stances" we are not told, although Lamming is here sorrowfully accused of sharing in the banned prescription. For Lamming had accused Hearne of not "being identified with the land at a peasant level"[42] among other things. Now this fear of identification is the prescribed stance for excellence of Creole society. Lamming's and others' attempt to break away from this prescription was the revolution. The defence of Hearne which Dr. Ramchand puts up against this charge does Hearne an injustice. For he writes about the Creole society in which he has his being; and in those novels where he is aware of the unreality and tension inherent in his position in this aspect of the society, his choice of theme is justified. But Dr. Ramchand defends only to attack. Hearne's least valid novel – *Land of the Living* – is praised by Dr. Ramchand. This technically accomplished novel, whose truth content is almost nil, is useful to Dr. Ramchand because it appeals to his own Creole sentimentality; above all because he can interpret its theme to peddle that fraudulent multiracialism which is the greatest barrier to the negation of racism.

In *Land of the Living*, Ramchand tells us, Hearne celebrates "love as a positive" and "distressed Negro, displaced Jew, and disorientated female are seen as equal subjects for love's reclaiming and responsible clasp".[43]

To be fair to Hearne, nowhere does he degenerate into this kind of soap opera. All his novelist's skill, however, fails to persuade that in the Jamaica of today or yesterday a Jew, a white Jamaican upper-class woman, and a Ras Tafari cult leader are equal in anything – except a common alienation in a world in which love itself is alienated. At a higher creative level, Hearne's novel, like Dr. Ramchand's criticism, fails because of the failure of its truth content; its Creole evasion of black reality.

With Naipaul, Ramchand shows his potentiality as a critic when there are no black axes to grind. But even Naipaul must take second place to Harris. Indeed, Naipaul does not lend himself to cultism. His black repulsion is too openly expressed; his prose too explicit for misinterpretation. Harris, however, is the escape. For Harris's technical and philosophical approach to the problem of writing in the novel form in a society where its structural underpinnings do not exist can be narrowed down to the Procrustean bed of Dr. Ramchand's preoccupations. Harris's "technique" of the novel allows Dr. Ramchand not only to evade the black centrality, but to justify this evasion in the guise of a literary theory. The escape can be intellectually rationalised, even if it means a pollution of Harris's meaning. Naipaul is compared, impartially but unfavourably:

> And whereas Naipaul's relentless accumulation of realistic particulars from the social scene persuades us and the character that that society has an 'inevitable existence', Harris's fiction suggests a particular society only to deny its overpowering and absolute reality.[44]

When Naipaul tells us of the black woman who, wanting to buy flesh-coloured stockings, but being given black ones by the East Indian sales girl, flounces out angrily, while the girl remains amused, bewildered, we are offered no possibility of escape. In one telling and cruel moment Naipaul has revealed a society's intimate and psychological alienation; its interpersonal cruelty, its smouldering resentment; its ignorant innocent indifference; the potentiality of a blind whirlwind in which both the black and the East Indian pawn will be caught in a confrontation they didn't really make; for which they are not finally responsible. These are the kind of confrontations that Dr. Ramchand is at pains to evade.

The difficulty of Harris's prose helps. We are told, helpless to dissent, that *The Far Journey of Oudin* is a "witty analogy of slave history".[45] The wit escapes us; and, trapped in our intimate relation to this slave history, we can neither catch the joke, appreciate the wit nor understand the analogy. Nor can we even glimpse the possibility of another view of a "conventionally deprived character", which Harris is supposed to offer us, according to Ramchand, since the society in which we exist standardises, stereotypes us all; depersonalises not only our possible selves, aborting their fulfilment, but deforms our "real" ones, derealising us. Dr. Ramchand's view of Wilson Harris's novels offers us, on a cheapback tinsel tray, a shoddy justification, wrapped in rhetoric, of our daily and common mutilation. Oudin, analogue, we suspect, of that slave, whose witty history we are to puzzle out, may be a slave apparently. But let him take heart. As Dr. Ramchand tells it:

> Two versions of Oudin's life take shape; there is the socially realistic figure who suffers as a slave in an oppressive social order, and who dies having covenanted even his unborn child to the grasping Ram; and there is the godlike inheritor of the Kingdom who fulfils destiny by abducting the virgin Beti, a bride and prize, coveted by Ram.[46]

Let Ram grasp on. His grasping may deform the "real" Oudin, but the "ideal" Oudin escapes him. The virgin and the kingdom.

That Dr. Ramchand banalises Harris's intention is clear. Harris is too serious a writer, to be so nakedly involved in this ancient liberal escape hatch, even where the failure of his intention can make it appear so. For Harris tries to achieve in his Guyanese novels what the Cuban Alejo Carpentier manages to do in his novels. Carpentier contrasts the "rational" world of the European experience in the New World with the "magical realism" or "lo real maravilloso" of the world of the Indians and the Blacks; explores two different kinds of reality stemming from two different kinds of cultures. In his novel *The Kingdom of this World*, for example, Carpentier shows a black slave who coexists in the world of his master at the same time as he lives the full fiction of the imaginative world, peopled by metamorphosing heroes and demons of his African-descended Haitian culture. But then this slave is an illiterate, according to Dr. Ramchand, a man living a life "without fiction!" According to Alejo Carpentier, the slave in his world of "magical realism" apprehends the world differently. And he shows this apprehension as being perfectly "logical" within the structure of his beliefs. Harris's failure stems from his inability to portray "the logic" of this other world, by his refusal to anchor this world firmly in its own reality. All his verbal fireworks are not enough to disguise an essential vacuum.

Dr. Ramchand on the other hand is determined to deny this rich imaginative other world, so long as its source is Africa; determined not to make it exist at all. In the two key chapters he uses literary criticism to achieve

382 WE MUST LEARN TO SIT DOWN TOGETHER AND TALK ABOUT A LITTLE CULTURE

his wish fulfilment. With delicate strokes he cuts the Caribbean's navel string with Africa, burying it under a non-question about a non-issue.

CACTUS VILLAGE – AFRICAN SURVIVAL OR ANALOGOUS THEORY?

W.G. Ogilvie who wrote *Cactus Village*,[47] prefaces his novel, Dr. Ramchand tells us, with an attack on those "Negraryans" who wish the world to believe that all their ancestors come from Western Europe and "who dread any backward glance at our national beginnings". It is Africa then that W.G. Ogilvie refers to. The black ARYANS, anxious to avoid Africa, therefore avoid what W.G. Ogilvie sees as their "national beginnings". Dr. Ramchand uses this book to pose a non-question about the possibility of an African survival. Having posed a non-question, he gives a non-answer. But his main purpose, the rejection of the African connection, has been achieved; and in an ostensibly liberal manner of "frank and free discussion". Let us examine the manner in which Dr. Ramchand discusses the question of African survivals in West Indian Fiction: (Secular).

In *Cactus Village*, (1950) Dr. Ramchand argues,

> there appears to be evidence for those who argue that the system of exchange labour is an African survival, and for those who take the view that the system evolves in different parts of the world in response to analogous conditions.[48]

What Dr. Ramchand is really posing here are sociological theories about the extent of the African heritage in the Caribbean; and this in spite of his attack on his introduction on those misguided, second-rate overseas critics who do this:

> As the better metropolitan critics show little interest in the literature of underdeveloped countries, it is always possible that in the hands of their colleagues, novels might become primary evidence for theories about societies.[49]

Not of course, that he blames overmuch these inferior overseas critics; after all they are foreigners and lack the native eye. Therefore their

> ...difficulties might well lie not so much in judging these works parochial as in becoming too engrossed in the raw material to apply critical standards.[50]

We are supposed to register here that non-West Indian critics either consider West Indian novels parochial; and/or, swept away by the raw material, they go overboard. If they manage to struggle to the shore, their critical faculties go beachcombing, drunk on the Skokian[51] of Caribbean prose.

Even here, they are more sinned against than sinning. More in sorrow than in anger, Dr. Ramchand deplores the fact that these overseas victims were led into temptation by a certain kind of West Indian commentator with "...a tendency... to value novels according to their immediate social or political relevance". Both overseas and West Indian critics having been disposed of, that leaves us of course only with Dr. Ramchand, agonising, in a critical Garden of Gethsemane, between "a disproportionate valuation of content as against form" and "an aestheticism that denied social function altogether."[52] This Messiah-like role allows Dr. Ramchand to break the rules he makes for others. The novel *Cactus Village* is used by Dr. Ramchand to propagate his theory about society.

This is done with the usual indirection. He quotes Ogilvie:

> Hezekiah was slim but wiry and strong. He was determined that none of these men who had given him a free day's labour should do more than he. His axe rang out with the best of them. His blows were measured and slower than some of those of his companions, but he was very accurate. He very seldom made a foul cut. As time went on the others noticed that his voice called most frequently when a tree was about to fall.
>
> During this time the women were not idle. As the cutlass men cleared the bush, the women followed with long hooked sticks behind them ... All worked hard, but all were cheerful.[53]

Dr. Ramchand also quotes Ogilvie's explanation in which the author explains the "established custom", among "the Jamaican peasantry". According to this custom when a man had to start a new cultivation and clear the land, "he would call on his friends to give him a day's work". He did not pay them but provided food and drink. In return he would give the same help when called upon. Ogilvie concludes:

> Still if a man were not very popular he would get only a few people to attend his 'match' and those who came would not labour very hard.[54]

From these two passages Dr. Ramchand draws the comforting conclusions that

a) Ogilvie abstains from claiming that there is an African element
b) Even if it were an African cultural survival "Ogilvie was not sophisticated enough to be aware of it"
c) His seeming to celebrate this form of peasant life as peculiarly Jamaican tends to imply at least an unconscious leaning towards the "analogous conditions" theory

Dr. Ramchand then sums up:

> The ambiguous case in *Cactus Village* is not of literary significance in itself, but it does help to demonstrate how elusive African cultural survivals in the West Indies may be, or at any rate how little scope there is for the West Indian novelist who wishes to evoke Africa in these terms.[55]

We have gone a long way round with Dr. Ramchand to come to what was after all, his predetermined conscious leaning to the theory of "analogous conditions" whose main importance as theory is that it negates the African connection.

For the non-question posed about the non-issue does not give the true force of Dr. Ramchand's evasion except we see it in the wider and more obsessive context of Dr. Ramchand's book as a whole. Indeed the chapter on "The Negro" starts off with the attack on Janheinz Jahn, which Dr. Ramchand later repeats in his article – "Concern for Criticism" rephrasing the same rancour against this German scholar who has dared to put forward the concept of a Neo-African literature and a Neo-African culture in which the Caribbean is included. In his attack on Jahn, and on the West Indian Brathwaite, Dr. Ramchand is at his most dismissive; it is here we see the centrality of his obsession. Under the guise of inept criticism on the part of Jahn, Dr. Ramchand attacks what he says is Jahn's idea "of a single traditional African culture". Ethnologists, Dr. Ramchand assures us, have stressed, "that there was a plurality of primitive cultures in Africa".[56]

Faced with the fact that Jahn is himself aware of the ambiguity of all approaches to the past; of the constant reinventing of the past which underlies any people's concept of themselves, Dr. Ramchand denigrates Jahn for arguing that the "concept of a single traditional African culture" is, "if not objective, a conception which as it appears in the light of neo-African culture is the only true one, since it is the one which from now on will truly determine the future of Africa."[57] Jahn sees that the "cultural bias" necessary to colonialism sets in motion a dialectical process,

> For several centuries Africa has had to suffer under the conception of the African past formed by Europe...
> But the present and future on the other hand will be determined by the conception that African intelligence forms of the African past.[58]

This complex process Dr. Ramchand fails to understand, even though it is a process formulated with more awareness of its ambiguities by Fanon, whom Dr. Ramchand also selectively quarries, negating his meaning in order to defend Ramchand's own theories. Dr. Ramchand manages to evade his mentor Fanon when Fanon argues, as does Jahn:

> Colonialism did not dream of wasting its time in denying the existence of one national culture after another. Therefore the reply of the colonised people will be straight away continental in its breadth ... The unconditional affirmation of African culture has succeeded the unconditional affirmation of a European culture.[59]

Fanon does not attempt to deny or negate the dangers of this affirmation, but he sees it in its dialectical context as a "historical necessity". What he warns against is that if a mere stage in a process is taken as the solution, then the attempt to replace a national culture with an African culture will lead black men to "racialise" their claim to a denied manhood; and this will "tend to lead them up a blind alley".

Dr. Ramchand quotes this warning, without any awareness of its tormented complexity. In the same way that he dismisses Jahn, without accepting the fact that the Neo-African theory, the unified approach, is a parallel reaction of elements of an original cultural pattern faced with the same dehumanising process of colonialism. The myth by which colonialism denied the humanity of the colonised needs first a counter-myth, in which the colonised claim their places as men; this is the universal ecumenical myth by which we can approach nearer to ourselves. For as Fanon insists, a culture can only be national – not racial, not universal.

But the supra-national response to a supra-national colonialism is a stage in the journey, a perilous but necessary stage. It is this stage that Dr. Ramchand wants to avoid, and with one blind leap, reach for the "unity of man", that false universality which Fanon condemned as the opposite danger to the "blind alley".

Dr. Ramchand accuses Jahn of betraying the work of anthropologists who have proved,

> without recourse to myth, that far from being a land of savages from time immemorial, and long before the European incursions, Africa had been the scene of a number of advanced civilisations.[60]

Which of course is not the point at all. We are grateful of course that Africa has been rescued from the void. But as Fanon points out,

> ... you do not show proof of your nation from its culture but... you substantiate its existence in the fight which the people wage against the forces of occupation.[61]

The "fact" of the past, opposed to the lies of the past is not the important fact; it is the creative myth of the past inherent in the cultural dynamic by which a people transform the colonial reality into genuine nationhood. It is this creative myth which lies at the heart of all cultures. We, as Caribbean persons, are concerned with four myths – in the most universal, the myth with which the peoples of the world can free themselves from a long history of exploitation by different minorities; the myth by which they can begin to write what Brecht called the "history of the ruled class"[62] as well as the ruling class; secondly we are concerned in the myth with which the majority Third World peoples must transform itself from the marginal into the mainstream future of the world; thirdly, the myth by which people who inhabit African or African-descended cultures must redeem the notions of themselves as the dregs of humanity because "they aint got no culture"; fourthly and more precisely, the myth by which the native peoples of the Caribbean can actualise their nativity, economically, socially, culturally, and so create a nation out of a country that as yet only has certain national manifestations.

There is no contradiction between these four. They are the synchronic and necessary patterns of our liberation; and none of the chickens come before the egg.

Neo-African culture and Neo-African literature is the witness to our involvement in the third aspect of our human liberation. Dr. Ramchand interprets Jahn:

> According to this interpretation Neo-African culture arises out of the assimilation by the 'traditional African culture' of European influences.[63]

Since Dr. Ramchand's mission is the denial of the existence of this "traditional African culture" in the Caribbean, he then goes on to state:

> But my purpose is not to examine the correctness or the possible relevance of Jahn's views for the future of Africa itself. My concern is with how the West Indies and West Indian literature became involved in the neo-African theory.[64]

Dr. Ramchand accuses Brathwaite of being influenced by the "Neo-African theory" in his article, "Jazz and the West Indian Novel". The reading of this article will show that there is no question of influence; Brathwaite comes to parallel conclusions on his own. He shows in this article, as Leavis does with Bunyan, the way in which an oral culture influences and creates the language of literary culture, pervading it with the stylistic elements of an oral culture. This process, as with Bunyan, is clearly seen in the *Brother Man* of Roger Mais. Dr. Ramchand's total and arrogant incomprehension of this book leads not only the distasteful comment aimed at Brathwaite who is said to climax his attempt to find in the West Indies some mode of New World Negro cultural expression based on an African inheritance, no matter how unconsciously, with a discussion of *Brother Man* [sic]. His later analysis of *Brother Man* is ludicrous; and painful to read.[65]

It is not only Brathwaite and Jahn who get this kind of treatment. Any critic who has studied Caribbean literature as part of a wider African complex, is at once dismissed. In the Introduction, Dr. Ramchand dismissed as "heavy handed" the approaches which include "West Indian writing" as part of a wider unit, especially those who "take notice of some basic features – the centrality of the Negro, the aftermath of slavery and colonialism, and the use of English in a community drawn from different parts of the world."[66]

In his Chapter – The Language of the Master – he therefore dismisses, a book – *Terranglia: The Case of English as World Literature.*[67] Among, the varied reasons of its dismissal, Dr. Ramchand sandwiches his main purposes. Since English is a first language in the West Indies and Australia, while in Pakistan and Nigeria it is a learned and second language, Dr. Ramchand argues there can be little useful comparison between them. The West Indies and Australia, it is implied, have more similar problems in the use of English than the West Indies and Nigeria. For, he goes on to argue, African writers "are able to draw upon resources in their social situation which do not exist for writers whose only language is English."[68]

The language problems of Nigeria, with its numerous African languages, bear no relation to Caribbean problems. They bear no relation to Caribbean problems, because:

> For the modern West Indian writer there is no possibility of a choice between English and another language. English is his native tongue and he uses it as a matter of course.[69]

At one stroke the artistic problem which the West Indian writer faces of forging a new language from written English and, for example, spoken Jamaican, an African-influenced Creole, is negated. When the problem is discussed by Dr. Ramchand it will be discussed under the abstract formulation of the gap between the language of the narrator and the language of his character. That the language of his characters is heavily African influenced is a consideration which is excluded from Dr. Ramchand's eye-view.

It is not only the language approach which comes in for dismissal, but also the Commonwealth Approach. The point of this short chapter approached with Dr. Ramchand's "circularity" shows that the chapter should have been headed "the Black Approach". But a spade is never called a spade. After delicate play as to differences between the white and black Commonwealth, and a judicious quoting of Fanon about the "dramatic problem" of decolonisation, Dr. Ramchand comes to the meat of the matter:

> Once a broad distinction is made, however, we have to give up the notion of a Black Commonwealth, too. There is little sense of tradition or social convention in the West Indies, for example, no equivalent to the tribal world and traditional life which the Nigerian Chinua Achebe draws upon in *Things Fall Apart*... commentators on West Indian Literature are only too aware of this particular distinction.[70]

The commentator subsumed under the plural is, of course, Naipaul, for whom the entire Caribbean area is disintegration, void; for whom Africa does not exist in the Caribbean, since nothing exists.

Yet this chapter, apparently inconsequential, innocuous under the old lady's tea party Commonwealth Approach label, is important. For it shows what we have contended, that Dr. Ramchand's attitude to the negation of Africa is a political attitude by which he evades the present Caribbean reality with its endemic catastrophic conflict and confrontation. Dr. Ramchand goes on to argue about "the idea of the Commonwealth as a way of approaching literature."

"In the first place", he objects, "it forces us to concentrate on political and social issues to a degree that invests these with a disproportionate influence upon our attempts to offer critical opinions on what are, above all, works of imaginative literature."[71]

It is, of course, clear that it is not the Commonwealth idea that forces to such a task, but the imperatives of a critique of literature in which the truth contents of the works of art are as important as their subject matter – "the imaginative" process of literature. But for Dr. Ramchand, literature must not be a means to explore a society's consciousness but a means to evade – a space craft taking off into the blue, existing in a free fall. What shocks him, he complains, is the consolidation of a "tendency to oversimplify the relationship between literature ('local literature') and the society ('local situation') from which it takes stimulus". This kind of criticism, Dr. Ramchand implies, can "stir up trouble". Or as he, with usual sleight of hand, phrases it:

> These misdirections are particularly harmful in the West Indies where the death marks of slavery are still to be seen in the economic condition of the masses, and in race and colour tensions only on a more subtle scale than in pre-Emancipation society.[72]

Dr. Ramchand hints at his distress that:

> So many West Indian writers make these the inspiration and the substance of their fictions that in the first critical book on Caribbean writing in general we read...[73]

Dr. Ramchand then goes on to quote from Gabriel Coulthard's pioneering *Race and Colour in Caribbean Literature* in which he discusses the problem of race, colour and culture in the entire Caribbean and the relation between the black man and the white world. Coulthard's book and this problem is waved away without further comment since

> In an earlier part of the book [i.e. *The West Indian Novel* etc.] a racial aspect of this boring socio-literary phenomenon was examined in detail and in a head-on way.[74]

In the novels of individual authors, Dr. Ramchand says, "avoiding the more obvious race and colour and social protest themes, it is proposed to work by indirection." Dr. Ramchand of course, never works by any other method. Faced with the pyramids, he avoids the pyramids – and creates fanciful and evasive patterns from the shadows that they cast.

This "boring" socio-literary phenomenon is, under the affectation, not "boring" at all. Indeed, even where Dr. Ramchand claims to have tackled the racial aspect head on, it is clear that the confrontation has been muffled. For what Dr. Ramchand poses with non-questions about "African cultural survivals", in the Chapter headed "The Negro", is not a racial, but a cultural problem which, in the colonised and neo-colonised Caribbean, has assumed racial aspects. In fact it becomes impossible not to suspect that Dr Ramchand's own determined negation of the African connection is not itself tinged with a certain racist cultural contempt. So that when Dr. Ramchand, attacking Jahn, argues:

> Behind the peculiar circularity with which Jahn protects himself is the *assumption* of African cultural survivals in the Caribbean...[75]

It is difficult not to paraphrase, that behind the peculiar circularity with which Dr. Ramchand protects himself is the assumption of the non-existence of African cultural survivals in the Caribbean; and therefore of the non-implications of the existence of such survivals.

Indeed, the indirect focus through which Dr. Ramchand views these survivals gives us a clue. Dr. Ramchand tells us that:

> How the African cultures in the West Indies were modified physically and psychologically by the slave experience and the new geographical environment has already been demonstrated by historian-sociologists.[76]

In a note, he tells us to see especially Orlando Patterson – *The Sociology of Slavery*. But there is no discussion of what Patterson actually says, because at no point in Ramchand's book is there to be an objective examination of the African influence and element in the Caribbean. In fact, in his introduction to the historian-sociologists, Dr. Ramchand interprets them as all agreeing that it is not the African origin, but the modification of slavery, a European economic system – and geography that really matter. The cultural baggage that the slaves carried is skilfully avoided, and the modifications that this cultural baggage would itself make on the system of slavery and the environment is ignored, in order to be sidetracked.

Cleverly, Dr. Ramchand chooses his focus: "The treatment of African cultural survivals (secular and religious) by West Indian novelists consolidates such objective findings, and helps us to understand the range of attitudes to Africa and the Africans in fiction from the West Indies."[77] We are here at once faced with a misconception of magnitude. The basic difference between contemporary Western culture and all other precapitalist cultures, including the African, is that the secular is not distinct from the religious; the practice or skill or organisation is not separate from the worldview. As we shall see later, this is where Dr. Ramchand's quotation from *Cactus Village* is subversive of his own interpretation. But for now, let us see what Dr. Ramchand has to say about an African survival that he calls "Obeah and Cult Practices in West Indian Fiction":

> ... the frequent occurrence in novels of obeah and cult practices has sometimes been held as evidence of survivals in the religious field. Few West Indian novelists see these practices as anything more, in fact, than the incoherent remains of African religions and magic; and in all cases, obeah and cult manifestations are associated with socially depressed characters. It is possible, indeed, to be critical of the writers for having reproduced the social reality only too exactly, and without enough invention or imagination.[78]

Here's the rub. One of the most powerful springs of creativity in the background of the Caribbean novel is to be seen only through the novels; without any attempt to relate the fictional version to the reality.

Yet, in the social and political and educational context of the Caribbean, the West Indian novelist, however well meaning, approaches Caribbean cult religions through a web of misconceptions foisted on him by a Christian-Western education. Even in his most anguished attempt to break through to the reality, his education had bred in him a pervasive curtain of prejudice through which he may glimpse the power of the cult religions, but only rarely understand the rationale. The rationale, highly logical, is not imagined to exist in Western scholarship, until the advent of anthropologists. Their most powerful achievement was the breakthrough of Western intellectual arrogance which had assumed that "primitive people" can't think. It was only through turning to the ethnologists and the anthropologists, through the universal ecumenical highways of the revaluation of what Lévi-Strauss calls "savage thought", that we, as novelists, are becoming able to "approach ever more nearly to ourselves". The approach is through the intellect; the intellect in its true role as a releasing agent. Now one approaches with new eyes that which the insufficient intellect had condemned. As Lévi-Strauss concludes:

> We have had to wait until the middle of this century for the crossing of long separated paths, that which arrives at the physical world by the detour of communication, and that which, as we have recently come to know, arrives at the world of communication by the detour of the physical. The entire process of human knowledge thus assumes the character of a closed system. And we therefore remain faithful to the inspiration of the savage mind when we recognise that the scientific spirit, in its most modern form will, by an encounter it alone could have foreseen, have contributed to legitimise the principles of savage thought and to re-establish it in its rightful place.[79]

In dealing with Caribbean cult religions there is not one West Indian novelist who has not, through ignorance of the logic and rationale of these cults, failed in the truth content of our work; in the technical requirements that such truth content should call for. The total failure of my one and only novel, the betrayal which it constitutes of the imaginative reality of the Caribbean people, was never more forcibly brought home to me than by Dr. Ramchand's assertion that "few West Indian novelists see these practices as anything more than the incoherent remains of African religions and magic." It is impossible to deny that by one's own inadequate knowledge of the truth, and lack of the novelist's craft, one should have placed the kind of cultural ammunition in Dr. Ramchand's hand by which, basing himself only on our novels – rather than on supplementary works of ethnologists and anthropologists – he is able to reduce the imaginative experience of the majority of the Caribbean peoples to "incoherence".

The incoherence of course, is in the eye of the beholder. We groped for coherence and failed. Dr. Ramchand looks for evidence of the incoherence which he requires; our failure provides him with the evidence. By avoiding the objective findings that are more than available in studies of Caribbean African-based religions, he is able to use his novelists, to manipulate them into making his kind of statement. Where the truth content of our novels can, in spite of the technical failure, threaten his preconception of incoherence, Dr. Ramchand misinterprets. Two other possible "African cultural survivals" are discussed. The first is the "problem" of the concubinage pattern rather than western marriage in which, as we shall show later, the real issue is avoided; in the second the example is taken from my novel, *The Hills of Hebron*.

Dr. Ramchand uses an ineptly handled part of the novel, a particularly inept part that is, in order to extend his concept of the slave experience making a tabula rasa of the African legacy. He argues:

> If African economic and social organisations were changed beyond easy
> recognition in the slave context, traditional arts and crafts were virtually wiped
> out. In this connection it is useful to look at the only instance in West Indian
> fiction where an author allows a connection to be made between an element
> of West Indian secular life, and the African heritage.[80]

Dr. Ramchand tells us that Obadiah, "the central character... is possessed of an instinctive skill at wood carving". He quotes to reinforce this, and then points out that towards the end of the book,

> Miss Wynter introduces a second wood carving episode.[81]

He makes the point that the first time Obadiah had carved unconsciously; the second time, consciously, carving a doll for his child. He takes the doll down to the town and sells it in order to obtain food. The man who buys the doll realises that it has been carved from a legend, a belief. At least all this is made plain in the quotation that Dr. Ramchand uses. The man is able to recognise this, he is an anthropologist who has worked in Africa. My inept use of this symbol in the novel does not, however, justify Dr. Ramchand's non-discussion as to whether or not a woodcarving skill had survived or not as "the instinctive expression of an obscure heritage preserved in the African personality." And, according to Dr. Ramchand, whether this is so or not, "Miss Wynter is careful not to show her hand".[82]

I wasn't dealing with this question at all. What I wanted to show was the similarity and persistence of a world-view, which in Africa and Jamaica still saw art as the expression of a concept of reality, embodied in certain beliefs, in a way of seeing the world. This survived, not passed on in any blood and soil mystification, but in the rationale of a culture, which transplanted, had taken root conditioned by its new reality, yet preserving certain basic concepts from the old, discarding trivia. This is the connection. This is what explains the powerful originality of the paintings and carvings of Kapo today. With the works of Kapo the connection is there. Kapo, like Obadiah, is a cultist. Only my writer's inadequacy could have made his fictional counterpart seem "contrived" – and Dr. Ramchand's desire to negate the connection.

The same distortion of focus is carried over into the discussion of concubinage patterns in the Caribbean, patterns that, as Ramchand shows, are central to the novels. This he discusses as "another possible African influence"; and points to its pervasiveness among "Negro characters belonging to the socially depressed class". He puts forward the view of Curtin, that concubinage is "one example of the adaptation of African cultures to Jamaican life". But only to deny this view. Using a quotation from *Lady Nugent's Journal*, Dr. Ramchand argues:

> It is possible to argue... that the conditions of slavery were by themselves enough to establish concubinage among West Indian Negroes, especially in view of the examples set by the masters and lamented by Lady Nugent.[83]

The masters, of course, for good or ill, had to set the pattern. Passive objects, the slaves brought nothing, for good or ill. Instead of adapting their former traditions to new conditions, as the masters certainly did with theirs, we are to imagine a tabula rasa, which receives patterns, but does not create. The essence of humanity, the universal quality which makes man, is denied. Theirs is only a void.

Yet, as can be seen from the quotation from *Lady Nugent's Journal*, the question of marriage or non-marriage from the masters' viewpoint depended largely on which system would make "the generative belly" – to borrow a phrase from Gilberto Freyre – generate more. Men and women were mated in the context of economic patterns. The promiscuousness of the masters paid off. Some of their own progeny made valuable slaves. The majority grew up to constitute the manager-agent Creole Class which served as a buffer between themselves and black revolt.

Far from setting a pattern for the slaves, the masters were prepared to accept those patterns which made it easier for the reproduction of more units of labour power. They were concerned primarily with economic results. This is not to say that their humanity did not, now and then, get in the way and muddle up the matter. But by and large there was always a rationalisation ready. Lady Nugent, for example, argues for Christian marriage, by citing the case of married slaves who "have fourteen grown up children, all healthy field negroes".[84] Marriage, she writes, would produce enough slaves in the island to make the slave trade unnecessary. Marriage was both Christian and productive of labour power. Morality was profitable. Lady Nugent wrote out of the economic concept of Christianity which her capitalist culture had bred in her. The slaves, victims of this culture, alien to its concepts, came to see Christian marriage as a *rite de passage* to the world of the whites. But this crossing over was reserved for the few. The majority opposed to the Christian capitalist concept of marriage adapted patterns of concubinage which responded more to the reality of their condition, but above all was an adaptation conditioned by the alternative cultural focus from which they viewed the world. And as we saw in *Cactus*

CREOLE CRITICISM: A CRITIQUE

Village this alternative cultural focus was part and parcel of an alternative economic tradition. It was this culture and this tradition which had become indigenous.

Dr. Ramchand's quotation from *Cactus Village* betrayed his intention. It negated both his and Naipaul's contention that no social convention, no traditional values exist in the Caribbean. For Ogilvie describes in *Cactus Village* a way of life whose values are in direct opposition to the dominant Creole values of the official society. In the community of Cactus Village we find the unofficial Jamaica. Here, the relation with the land is a peasant and not a capitalist one. The Russian economist, Chayanov, has explored the economic differences between these two relations. Ogilvie's *Cactus Village* shows that the differences are not only economic ones, but a difference of cultural values. In *Cactus Village*, in its world view, the economic motive is not primary; rather it is embedded in a web of social relations. Capitalist values – production for production's sake, accumulation, the profit motive, the individualist ethic – are lacking; they are alien.

In the quotation from *Cactus Village*, Hezekiah does not conceive of labour as a commodity to be sold for wages. Chayanov sees this as the main difference between the peasant relation and the capitalist relation. The peasant – not the kulak class or middle peasant – who works his land without paid labour establishes a relation in which the category of wages, vital to the capitalist relation, does not appear. This relation cannot therefore be conceived or analysed in capitalist terms at all. In the peasant relation the profit motive of capitalism, and the attendant concept of accumulation, is replaced by what Chayanov labels as the "labour-consumer balance".[85] The needs of the peasant and his family determine the amount of labour put into the land. To obtain the use of this land he will pay uneconomic rental; or if he is buying would pay far more than the man who, thinking in rational capitalist terms, calculating profit and loss, would ever be able to afford to pay.

The same balance of needs and labour extends out to the community. The concept of exchange labour practised in Cactus Village springs from this central concept. Labour is socially useful, it is not economically profitable. Hezekiah is therefore not concerned with getting as much labour as he can out of the others. In a capitalist relation, this would be necessary. In a peasant-community relation, Hezekiah works himself harder than the others. His social usefulness is his test of manhood. The others come to work for him; to exchange "labour". They work hard in proportion to his "popularity", and his popularity will consist in the generosity with which he offers food and drink; in his willingness to work shoulder to shoulder with the others.

Hezekiah realises himself through his performance within the framework of social values. Not only does he not exploit the labour power of the others, in order to accumulate capital at their expense; but whatever he had saved goes in food and drink for the others. By respecting these obligations, fulfilling them, Hezekiah gets the exchange labour of his friends. If he refuses to accept these values, he will have to clear his land himself; or hire labour to do it. He would enter, then, an alternative pattern of values: the capitalist relation. From the precapitalist world of use-value he would enter the capitalist world of exchange value; he would begin to take a place in the dominant Creole structure.

Yet, even as Ogilvie wrote *Cactus Village* the world of Cactus village was already marginal. Since then, increasingly, the mass-communication media has extended the dominant values of supra-national monopoly capitalism through newspaper, radio, television. Consumer-oriented advertising develops needs that cannot be satisfied in the labour-consumer equilibrium of Cactus Village. The exodus from the village, before a trickle, becomes a flood. The villagers erupt into the cities. The "yards" now become central to Caribbean fiction. In the "yards" there is a tension between the old values of a community existence and the need to discard the old value system if one is to get ahead, to divest oneself of humanity. The yards become the focal points in which there is a tormented clash between cooperation and competitiveness. C.L.R. James's 'Triumph', Mais's *The Hills were Joyful Together* and *Brother Man* explore this urban alienation, this new dispossession. In the cities, the new marginal masses, emigrants from the decaying villages, try to hold their shanty world together with new shifts and guises as the world of the village with its stable values begins to fall apart.

They carry from the village to the city their Afro-Christian cult religions. They transmute them into new forms to accompany their psychic trespass. Folksongs are transformed into urban jazz, calypso, ska, reggae. These songs spring from the tension of a new exile; the same sense of exile out of which the novelists write. The songs, like their cult religions, are expressions of an a-capitalist sense of values, an a-capitalist cultural dynamic. In the purely capitalist plantation societies of the Caribbean, how did this alternative cultural dynamic arise? In the beginning, the transported models were as much English as African. According to an early seventeenth-century account, English settlers, many of them ex-soldiers, settled down side by side with the Maroons in the same peasant relation to the land. The English and Scots folklore component of Jamaica began its fusion with African folklore then. But the plantation system gradually forced the English settlers off the land. It was mainly the African peasant tradition which remained to transform itself, that was able to create a web of inherited and reinvented beliefs, with which they fashioned "surrogate autochthonous" values. How did this come about?

Endnotes

1. Walter Benjamin "Goethe's Elective Affinities (1924-1925)" in *Walter Benjamin: Selected Writings, Volume 1, 1913-1926,* Marcus Bullock and Michael W. Jennings, eds. (Cambridge, MA: Belknap/Harvard University Press, 1996), 297

2. Kenneth Ramchand, "Concern for Criticism", *Caribbean Quarterly,* vol. 16, no. 2 (June 1970): 53 [51-60].

3. Gordon Rohlehr, "The Ironic Approach: The Novels of V.S. Naipaul", *The Islands In Between: Essays on West Indian Literature,* Louis James ed. (London: Oxford University Press, 1968).

4. F.R. Leavis, "T.S. Eliot's Stature as a Critic: A Revaluation", Commentary, vol. 26, no., 5 (November 1958): 400 [399-410].

5. A paraphrase of Leavis by the writer of the Review Article 'The Critic As Man' in *Times Literary Supplement,* no. 3, 431 (November 30, 1967) 1121.

6. Ramchand "Concern for Criticism", 58-59.

7. Ibid., 59.

8. *The West Indian Novel and Its Background* (London: Faber & Faber, 1970), 164

9. F. R. Leavis, *The Common Pursuit* (London: Penguin Books, 1952), 200.

10. *The West Indian Novel,* 13.

11. Ibid., 14.

12. Kenneth Ramchand, *West Indian Narrative: An Introductory Anthology* (London: Nelson, 1966).

13. Rex M. Nettleford, *Mirror, Mirror, Identity, Race and Protest in Jamaica* (Kingston: Wm Collins and Sangster, 1970), 190.

14. Ramchand, *The West Indian Novel,* p. xi.

15. Susan Sontag, *Against Interpretation and Other Essays* (New York: Farrar, Strauss and Giroux, 1966), 7.

16. Ramchand, "Concern for Criticism", 55.

17. Ibid., 56.

18. Ibid., 59-60.

19. Ibid., 56.

20. George Steiner, "The Language Animal", *Encounter,* vol. 33, no. 2 (August 1969): 19 [7-24].

21. *The West Indian Novel,* 38.

22. Ibid., 12.

23. Ibid., 19, 23.

24. Ibid., 24.

25. Ibid., 30, 31.

26. Ibid., 31.

27. F. R. Leavis, "Literature and Society", *The Common Pursuit,* 192.

28. Ibid., 190.

29. Cecil Sharp, quoted by Leavis, ibid., 191.

30. Ibid., 191

31. Kamau Brathwaite in "Jazz And the West Indian Novel", *BIM,* vols. 44-46 (1967-1968); reprinted in *Roots* (Ann Arbor: University of Michigan Press, 1993), 73.

32. *The Pleasures of Exile* (London: Michael Joseph, 1960), 38-9, quoted by Ramchand in *The West Indian Novel*, 4.
33. V. S. Naipaul, *The Middle Passage: Impression of Five Societies – British, French and Dutch – in the West Indies and South America* (1962; London: Andre Deutsch, 1974), 29.
34. At a meeting of the New World Group in 1969.
35. Naipaul, *The Middle Passage*,68, quoted by Ramchand in *The West Indian Novel*, 4.
36. Ramchand, *The West Indian Novel*, 5.
37. Ibid.
38. Ibid.
39. Ibid.
40. Ibid.
41. Ibid., 6
42. Lamming, *The Pleasures of Exile*, 45-46.
43. Ramchand, *The West Indian Novel*, 6.
44. Ibid., 9.
45. Ibid. A certain susceptibility of the imagination, of the ear, leads Dr. Ramchand to imitate some of the more unfortunate aspects of the prose style of his approved authors. This sentence reads like Harris at his worst. On p. 12, in speaking of Harris's *The Waiting Room*, we get two sentences of an unsurpassable mystified illiteracy. They are:
"Such a distribution of strengths and weaknesses between animate and inanimate objects in the room allows for a relayed digestion of the whole catastrophe while offering mutual protection from its annihilating powers." And again: "...Harris's exploration of this condition in the person has gone so far that the personal relationship – violent rape, irresponsible lover, involuntarily responsive mistress learning to digest catastrophe – absorbs the burden of an equally rapacious imperial relationship." Ibid., 12.
46. Ibid.
47. *Cactus Village* (Kingston: Pioneer Press, 1953).
48. Ibid., 118.
49. Ibid., 13
50. Ibid.
51. A South African term for a "native" drink made in the shanty towns of Johannesburg from methyl alcohol, calcium carbide, treacle, tobacco and so on. Janheinz Jahn writes in *Muntu*, that the Boers' police prescription of African beer, led to this substitute, the "legitimate offspring of African slums and European moral principles". Janheinz Jahn goes on to attack Malinowski who saw the revival of African traditions as "an unhealthy and sophisticated" nationalism, a product of psychological retreat before European pressure, "modern-mythmaking" a drug, that is "Skokian". See *Muntu: An Outline of Neo-African Culture* (1958; London: Faber and Faber, 1961), 14.
52. Ramchand, *The West Indian Novel*, 14
53. *Cactus Village*, 8, quoted in *The West Indian Novel*, 118.
54. *Cactus Village*, 9, quoted in *The West Indian Novel*, 119.
55. Ibid., 119.
56. Jahn, *Muntu*, 17-18, quoted by Ramchand in *The West Indian Novel*, 117.

57. Ibid., 117.
58. Ibid., 117, quoting *Muntu*, 17-18.
59. Fanon, *The Wretched of the Earth*, trans. by Constance Farrington (New York: Grove Press, 1966), 171-172.
60. Ramchand, *The West Indian Novel*, 117.
61. Fanon, *The Wretched of the Earth*, 179.
62. Bertolt Brecht, "Das Manifest" in *Bertolt Brecht: Gesammelte Werke*; vol 10 (Frankfurt am Main: Surkamp Verlag, 1967), 912.
63. Ramchand, *The West Indian Novel*, 117.
64. Ibid., 117.
65. Ibid., 116, 125-126, 182-185. Had Ramchand been not so concerned to negate the general theory of a Neo-African approach; and more concerned to actually examine Brathwaite's application of his jazz theory to the sound patterns of *Brother Man*, a case could be made out for the need of a closer, more precise exploration of the way in which the spoken language infiltrates and sounds through the prose of *Brother Man*. Brathwaite can be faulted for a lack of precision, but his general theory about the "community" expressed in terms parallelling jazz improvisation, and the contrast with the novel of the Faustian individual experience, the positing of an alternative indigenous cultural tradition, cannot be refuted. It is this indigenous alternative cultural tradition that Ramchand is at pains to deny.
66. Ramchand, *The West Indian Novel*, 14.
67. Joseph Jones, *Terranglia: The Case for English as a World Literature* (New York: Twayne Publishers, 1965).
68. *The West Indian Novel*, 81.
69. Ibid., 82.
70. Ibid., 177.
71. Ibid.
72. Ibid., 178.
73. Ibid.
74. Ibid.
75. Ibid., 118.
76. Ibid.
77. Ibid., 123.
78. Ibid.
79. Claude Lévi-Strauss, *The Savage Mind* (Chicago, Illinois: University of Chicago Press, 1966), 269.
80. Ramchand, *The West Indian Novel*, 121.
81. Ibid.
82. Ibid., 123.
83. Ibid., 120.
84. 8 April 1802, *Lady Nugent's Journal of Her Residence in Jamaica from 1801 to 1805,* Philip Wright, ed. (1966; Kingston: University of the West Indies Press, 2002), 86.
85. Alexander Chayanov, Peasant Farm Organization, trans. by R.E.F. Smith in *The Theory of Political Economy*, Daniel Thorner, Basile H. Kerblay, R.E.F. Smith, eds. (Homewood, Il: American Economic Association, 1966).

AFTERWORD TO HIGHLIFE FOR CALIBAN
(by Lemuel Johnson, published Ardis Publishers, USA, 1973)

Lemuel Johnson writes out of the African/Creole experience of Freetown, Sierra Leone. The name is "portuguese marked in stones" independent out of England into a third world fed out of a first world. That's how and where the trouble starts

Put your money

on zero
I would bow low, down
from the waist down
and so tranquilize the heart, ease
the warm desire
to eat human flesh
the corners of my lips raised
on zero

on perhaps this or that tedious day
inheritance is everything
bones a mere rattle[1]

The white man wove me out of a thousand anecdotes (Fanon).[2] It is not the consciousness of man that determines his social being, but his social being that determines his consciousness (Marx).[3] Do not call us *negro*. To call us *negro* is to call us *slave*. Call us *prieto* (the Congolese to a Spanish Capuchin missionary in the seventeenth century).[4] But that was in another country. Another time, another place. Africa, integral then, dictated its definitions. The words were words that came in the ships of Christians – *negro/prieto*. But there was danger to them. Wanton, malicious, they were the bridge that Eshu built with his penis. The Christian ships came to trade. They traded gold and slaves. *Oro* was their word for the yellow metal. *Negro* was their word for slave. The Congolese accepted their word, and attached to it a social fact they knew, a social being defined by his role.

Somewhere the penis bridge began to break. The Congolese sensed the treacherous word close in a net that bound together biological black skin, cultural black being, with the social being of slave. The bridge broke. The black entered the Western architecture of signs, conjoined as fact and fiction, black slave.

The metamorphosis through the Middle Passage, conjoined master and slave in the enterprise of the Indies. Hawkins, thief, merchant, mariner, sailed to Africa in a seaworthy ship; and got black slaves partly by the sword, partly by trade; he sailed to that other point of the triangle, islands and a continent gotten by storm, with his prey; and there threatened to cut the throat of the Spanish colonists if they did not trade. To traffic in men would call down God's vengeance, Queen Elizabeth had first said. But she profited largely; knighted bold enterprisers right and left. From Virgin Queen the line extends to the "Captain want jig jig" in Freetown, Sierra Leone, recorded by Graham Greene. From here, then, Johnson writes.

Freetown, Sierra Leone, is a part of the continent of Africa. Yet, in part, it is also a Creole island, like an island in the Caribbean. The Creole experience is born out of the condition of exile; out of a Middle Passage of body and mind. But if the Caribbean islands were settled as plantations in which the forced labour of the slave was to produce that initial capital that would enable Europe to "take off" into the dynamic paradise of capitalist development, Freetown was to be their exact opposite. For Freetown was to be a monument to that great act of British/European philanthropy – by which the English, having enslaved the Africans for centuries, had accumulated enough wealth from their labour and sale to afford an exquisite frisson of conscience.

The 1772 judgment of Lord Mansfield in the Somerset case that a black, landed on the soil of Britain was free, was no longer "accepted merchandise" as defined by an earlier English Attorney General, created a group of liberated slaves in England. Freetown was settled by these liberated slaves. Other slaves set free by the British Navy, (recaptured by them from other European nations intent on getting their share of the black loot) were also landed in Freetown. Their Middle Passage was one of departure and return. As Lemuel Johnson explains it elsewhere:

> The city and its people were to be symbols of Christian enlightenment over the inhumanity of the past. The inhabitants were returned "exiled sons of Africa." They had originally come from tribes up and down the Slave Coast.
>
> *The Devil, the Gargoyle and the Buffoon*[5]

The Cross of Christ was made of wood. The Cross of the Freetown Christian was an arrangement of genes: black skin, lips, eyes that existed to negate, perversely, the white skin of Christ. They took up their Cross and walked. They endured their passion – "their hell in small places" – and proceeded to sweat in thick English flannels, to answer in Latin, to endure the incongruity of their passions, and to re-enact the Crucifixion not as tragedy but as farce.

"Seek ye first the political Kingdom…"[6] Nkrumah, as prophet, had thought that that was all there was to it. But the political kingdom was his only on hire, lease, so to speak. When he wouldn't vacate the real owners pulled the strings

– and had him locked out of state and life. And for this and that reason there will be the devil to pay "out of a ragged root". The alchemist and a most magical company put money on zero

> but imagine now,
> out of an inclination to
> worry the wound, imagine a
> most magical company of young men
> with no addresses[7]

From here, this country, time and place, Lemuel Johnson weaves his skein of words. The gods are in exile. In his seven poems to His Excellency, the poet weaves his verbal skein through a labyrinth of disparate images, patterning a political motif, a pattern sketched out of the dust of the new kingdom. He has confessed to an obsession to transfer to the politics of the second coming Balzac's indignation: "When at night one sees the beautiful stars here, one just wants to unbutton one's fly and piss on the heads of all the royal houses."[8] And so the ceremonies of Fort Thornton. For purposes of trade, Africa was at first a coast. The coast was dotted with forts. In many of the forts, there was a "factory". Prime Men, Stout Men, Lean Men not sick with the pox were bartered for pieces of cloth, basins, rum, guns, old sheets, beads. The Factory Fort looked out to sea against the other Christian slave-dealing nations. It swivelled around to keep order among the raw material for trade, "a fortress of white stones on a small hill".

Not only a fort, it was a way of life: the very model of the cultural ecology of a white skin; the fairy castle in the imposed enchanted landscape. The Wizard, the Governor himself, castled in white uniform and sun helmet and white feathers, brushed the sky and awed the sun. Here, incarnate, was the accumulated power of a superior juju. All-embracing, a fate that witchdoctors could no longer turn aside; the gods themselves feared so blue an eye. This god commanded the sky.

His spirit moves in Fort Thornton, where he once lived

> an englishman, plumed.   in white flannels
>
> who lived in large houses
> needing more air.
> the tropics being, as they are, the tropics.[9]

The new Head of State, Caliban in fancy dress, inherits his fort, and his tropics, and his eye. The fort itself was an Ark, its denizens limited. Fearing the flood by fire "we unthatched our houses/in time for rainstorms".[10]

And there are new ceremonies in Fort Thornton after the Second Coming: the Wa-Benzi elite, mannered a la Modigliani, conscious of masks that Picasso, having extracted lines, forms. The wood-locked secret terror, called up and suspended, is made respectable, acceptable, charted points of intellectual chatter up and down flowing stairs: "stationed just so along woodwork and cornice."[11]

Out in the streets the storm beats on the Messianic hope. Nationalism, that magnificent song (Fanon)[12] became mute with the going up of the flag and the military tattoo ushering in the new rulers. The people suck their sorrow, act out the "perverse comedy" in "His Excellency: II". They pick their teeth with the sliver of bone left over from The Hope. Disillusion, clear like water:

> this man. *ecce homo.* for love
> of whom some took kerosene lamps
> to the water's edge. the dark edge of water.
> and there learned
>
> the sea teaches nothing but water[13]

and the violence against one another, not for an explicit cause but for that simulacrum of action with which briefcase nationalists assure themselves their power exists

> so we picked burning kerosene, broke
> skulls with one another,
> vagrant calendars in which we saw marks,

The end of the journey to the expectation is a return to the same chains:

> the shapes of our skulls are now no different
> than they were, yesterday. the day before yesterday?[14]

In "His Excellency: III" the people attempt to propitiate with traditional bundles of tied red cloth the twisting turns of unpredictable gods; since no man chooses to live in hell.

But the gospels and actions taken by power (even in the first act) gloss the return of hell with words like clouds of dust. Democracy shuffles the cards; takes an absurd delight in forms; its style is all there is to it. The two-party state as definition could not quite fit the Procrustean bed of the neo-colonial whose circumference (their centre being outside themselves – London, New York, Washington, Paris, Moscow) needed another name. The Eunuch Scholars, homegrown and foreign, spoke about the One Party State. The Party was His Excellency, the State was His Excellency. His Excellency should live in State.

Osagyefo this, Osagyefo that, (Armah, *The Beautiful Ones Are Not Yet Born*). And the people? Must make do with statistics; tighten their belts. They are there to be regulated by the State; they are by reason of the State. The flag, the anthem, the clapping after names of the powerful are the substances of their soul. They are statistics for the nation's sake:

> …waiting to forgive
> rulers their odd invasions into the body
> politic our mouths dance
> in shreds in our faces.[15]

But the working out of a little nastiness, the hells in small places, extend in infinite circles; there really are no circles outside this hell. Inferno is multinational. In "His Excellency: IV", the Kreen Akrore tribe of Indians hide in rain forests, lurk in fear from the invasion of patient anthropologists, coming with new Christian ships, now secular; not for the sake of their souls, but for science. For the extension of Prospero's magic arts. The Kreen Akrore know enough to fear these men, with power like fireworks in their hands. The anthropologists, wanting to publish another book, to look once more on that which survived, molding its own forms, wait and wait, ready to barter *pacotille* for a way of life.

> and so they wait, these men,
> in supplications of glass bead and axe.[16]

The Pope pronounces *pacem in terris*, long and short words in Latin; a violin in Bucharest, a contact lens luxury-pampered dog killed by car in Spain, where Lorca was killed by the "patriotic" forces to preserve nations that were no longer nations – the design that continues the coincidence of untidy passions in time. The design negates itself, disintegrates, reveals the purposeless Fate we are helpless to avert.

In "His Excellency: V", we have terror, in everyday dress, or dandified at the end of a stick; with a casually elegant holiday in Prague where Power rides in on the gun turrets of Russian tanks. And a student, to protest, provides the local colour for the tourist (hara-kiri with petrol and a match):

> the ambitious burning of flesh in a public square.[17]

For the poet, a smaller fate. No suicide, since even that has become domestic. Rather than the lamentations of Jeremiah, the picking away at the corner of things; the poet, like poetry, at odds with strange emperors. In spite of *pacem in terris*, in correct Latin, the peace remained like incense, only sanctifying the genuflexion of the sword. In "His Excellency: VII", France, an ancient Christian kingdom, centre of Western culture, narcissistic at the sight of its own intellect, echoing to hear the sound of its own language, suffers too that strange disease; sings the Marsellaise; chants a forgotten phrase of a hymn, and erects heroes like ikons. And the nation implies European glory, European destiny; and who dared to hint Marshal Pétain did not incarnate the nation rather than the geographically-minded De Gaulle who had finally said Algeria was not biologically French?

These modern grave snatchers, taking Pétain out of a "traitor's grave" – who defines whom? – bury him anew in a Pharoah's tomb of mummified memory. The cinema shows "Wild Strawberries" and coffins with bodies tumble on to the street; fact and fiction conjoined in an apocalypse at noon. We have lost ourselves – our biographies grown to rags – and surrendered these rags to the coffins of our leaders. The proper burial becomes as important as for Antigone. She feared to displease the gods. We fear to lose that rag of a self we have left.

Yet their First World reburial of fallen leader and fallen self is backed by an expanding growth rate; a standard of living safe behind atomic tests.

Our Excellency, caught in the contradiction between the global expectation and the hunger rising on the horizon, has domesticated obscenity; burial and reburial in the name of the State:

> I speak now of death, ours
> stumbling as we do upon the white bone of power.

The labyrinth of white bones encloses a landscape, imposed like a Picasso painting. There is no escape. No breakout. Only the delicate placing of the thread to chart the way that we have come; to explore, like the monk embellishing his text with blue and gold flowers, the corners and angles that spell out new names for hell

> devotions before Mass
> yield us tentative loaves broken
> in vichy water or water at Lourdes...[18]

The post-Independence, neo-colonial agony deprived us of His Excellency as Imperial Devil; and placed instead His Excellency as the Caliban Messiah, who, in the wilderness of jail, agreed to gamble with the devil.

The geographic range of metaphors, Brazil, Bucharest, Prague, a dog run over by car in Spain, a violin in Rumania, the Pope conjuring up peace, encyclically, in Latin, juxtaposes the hells. The cards are dealt out in an absurd political universe designed by Ionesco.

> we creep among mangrove shrouded creeks
> a supplication of latin things about our necks.[19]

Yet – in "Equilibrist" – the protocol for His Excellency must be observed. Legitimacy must not be questioned; a place for everything; everything in its place:

> an itch in the right
> places...
> [...]
> broken meat back in our bones[20]

★   ★   ★

Lemuel Johnson in this first group of poems gives us Caliban Agonistes, blinded by the white bone of instant power, tossed to him when he had once snapped and growled. But the bone had been shaped into dice. The dice were loaded; the obscenity of the neo-colonial experience, worked out in the terrible centuries of Haiti and Latin-America, has spread out like a blood-red stain: Christophe of Haiti, whose fact and alienated French Court, complete with dancing master, could not be outdone by Césaire's fiction; then the peculiar terror of an Estrada Cabrera of Guatemala, of a Trujillo, of Duvalier;

a particular "underdeveloped terror". As if fear is the only product indigenously produced.

It is the neocolonial event that finally divests Caliban of that which had kept him whole – a dream of revenge against Prospero. But how shall he now revenge himself upon himself? The poet, like the poetry, marks the terror-laden pilgrimage on the *via purgativa*. Cheated of expectation, stripped, we take up our bed, and complaining, begin to crawl.

In Part II, the momentous meeting between Europe and Africa is reduced to its real fact – barter. The poet prefaces "High-life for traders" with Orwell:

> *Under the spreading chestnut tree*
> *I sold you and you sold me*[21]

Out of this barter came Freetown. The land was bought for guns, cloth, rum, glass beads. A history of unequal exchange. And the Creole language formed and fashioned itself out of this barter. Freetown – free trade in cunt priced to suit each dick is fixed by Graham Greene (and others) in its incongruous landscape: the new desert for Western man's wrestling with fine shades of Anglo-Catholic ethics; whilst sellers at the port cry their wares

> Captain want jig jig, my sister pretty girl
> schoolteacher, captain want jig jig[22]

The reductionism of language, the reductionism of a relation; stereotypes confronting one another: exchange value for casual use. Africa, the psychological brother of Europe, its instant pornography. A labyrinth of presuppositions, lurid imaginings, invest Caliban with the Manichean opposite of Europe's conceptual universe.

This second sequence of poems represents, as Johnson himself explains it, percussive attempts to drum out, drum in, drum together a variety of contradictory experiences which shaped persons of my generation in our exposure to Western culture – Roman Catholicism, Anglican High Church and classical, latinate grammar schools, modelled after Eton and Harrow in England. In one of his best poems – "Juju" – we see a verbal landscape, closing down like shutters of ivory filigree on the Freetown port/Fort. The verbal landscape becomes real in a metamorphosis of ecology:

> the bone dust of sicilian mountains
> growing green with bees and honey and vergil[23]

The title of the poem "Juju", dislocated from its cultural architecture of meaning, becomes a *thing* in the Western definition. Juju, meaning a charm dispensed, sold by witchdoctors for either protective or malignant purposes, is separated by a broken bridge from its cosmogony, its theology, its rationale. No longer the expression of the power of man, symbolised in his gods, to confront and master his reality, it is now a charm left over from the days of power. Its meaning misted, a defensive amulet with which to *suffer* an imposed and alien universe.

Prospero's culture then, is his potent counter Juju. And the European teachers are the witchdoctors of this defence against a too clamorous Freetown reality. For what was then (and is) being fashioned is the black "humanist" class: new converts to Europe's secular religion of Reason and *humanitas*. Fragments of Greek and Latin, of the iron lays of Beowulf and the sanctified, long-vanished rude vigour of "the Gauls our ancestors". And time – time marked in notches of real enough events in real enough countries; distant, yet close to the inner flesh; close, because conjured up, kept in motion with a juggler's art that imposed consciousness and landscape and affirmed a reality that existed on the pages of *the book*. The true reality of "ideal forms". I read, therefore I am. These pages create me – memories, nostalgia. My life measured out by

> ...an ivory man
> whose hammer marked the terms
> at michaelmas
> at trinity
> at epiphany but he too believed
>
> in stones an
> ivory man of gray ashes...[24]

Witchdoctor, he passed on to me an amulet, a Juju, like a do-it-yourself kit with which to forge cards of identity: signs, symbols, language, bits of quotes, fragments of allusive references, clusters of association, sounds and the structuring of sounds with which to fabricate a biography.

"Juju" juxtaposes existence and consciousness; ambivalent as to which is which. Consciousness imposed through "words/in their especial candour"; existence, treacherous, like a dangerous poem at odds with strange emperors. And so the dialectic of an existent consciousness and an unconscious, evaded existence:

> ...madame northway, conjugating
> love of St. Augustine out of the iron
> heat of the equator over our heads,
> non amabat, did not love; but then
> loving to love, sed amans amare, seeking
> querens amare to love beyond our windows...[25]

African St. Augustine; some argue that he was not only North African but black too. But his cultural world was as far removed as the jewelled blackness of Sheba ceremonious, on a state visit to Solomon, is removed from the Freetown students who met her in the Bible. St. Augustine, seeking to love, did not seek to exorcise the unreality of a black skin or black gods; he sought rather to bridge the black Manichean gap that yawned in his soul. The problematic was different. Here, in "Juju", straining against experience, the poet is conjured into seeking St. Augustine's tortured seeking to love – while his is another kind of torment:

> the smell of black buttocks rubbing raw
> faeces on the barks of trees. seeing that
> paper was scarce among us. and rags were
> needed to keep inquisitions of a too
> curious nature from our bones
> blackened with lust of St. Augustine
> and Carthage burning[26]

The ambivalence is realised in the metaphors of comparison. The "witchdoctor": the marvel of that little white english woman, her face a febrile imposition, a charm to be used

> against the reign of the beast
> rising out of our empty harbors –
> her teeth, small-white
>
> so she flicked out conjugations of love
> and drove us mad.[27]

In the simulacrum, Eton/Harrow, love, the love of God, intellectualised. Down in the ports, Eros for sale.

For in a sense, the law of price was the law of empire (a delicate shuffling of letters to shape *emporio* into *imperio*). And the law too of the superstructure of illusions:

> ...the alphabets of empires met
> outside. in the dry seasons of our windows:
> the tambourines of Byzantium
> moist skulls under stone in rome...

obscuring the context:

> ...papers
> round as rosetta stones. and heavier.
> between our windows and ourselves.[28]

But the Caliban who revolts uses language to curse. The word is in revolt, the word of Prospero turned against the part of him, his consciousness, that had betrayed him whilst he slept. Caliban hating the creature made of him; yet half-seduced by such Miranda strains.

From imitation he awakes to exorcism, though liberation is only half-imagined, barely glimpsed. "Figures in Wood" is a kind of "summary introduction". Implicit here is Ulysses with his ships – the "patron Saint", ancestral spirit of the West. The ships of Christians descending on the Congolese are here the British Navy which used West African ports during the war. Ulysses, Johnson explains, still comes and still leaves the ports of the One-Eyed in some disarray:

> falling out of the sky foreskins
> peeled back[29]

The poet, using the word in revolt, reverses the images, shuffles the protagonists; the "villains" are brought full centre. The objects of the Western Enterprise become the subjects. Johnson writes:

> In a sense, the protagonists of these poems are those like Cyclops, Lazarus ("exorcism"), Shylock ("Shylock, after"), Caliban ("calypso for caliban"), Ophelia ("ophelia at elsinore") – these characters who prowl the fringes of the 'positive humanism' of the imported culture. Perhaps they are more significant to the history and psychology of thirdworlders.[30]

The black cannibals, the mindless hordes, the foils for Tarzan and Jane ("A.T.&P. Ltd.") revolt against the crowd scenes, against the script, factual and verbal. Somewhere in that first encounter, in the trading, the main outlines of the text had been fixed. Caliban revolts against the barter of roles. In the exchange he had lost. How much was still not clear; not even the extent of the occasional gain:

> we bartered. unclear
> what we won or lost...
>
> ....
> Call us Ishmael, (if you wish) or Barabbas
> or Cain...
>
> the ports lie now in slack water
> our fingers scrape the sides of empty bowls
> and go back to our lips.[31]

In this part, Johnson uses a sequence of long poems in short, tightly rhythmic lines with frequent monosyllabic percussions that provide both hesitation and propulsion for a mixture of sometimes lurching, sometimes dancing outbursts. The basic rhythms, Johnson says, of these acts of exorcism, are derived from the compulsive drumming of African (or sometimes Caribbean "Vèvè" and "Calypso for caliban") rhythms. So the highlife, the calypso are specifically mentioned. But other beats consciously followed are voodoo drumbeats ("Vèvè) and the more energetic form of the high life, *goombay*, which survives in creole society in Sierra Leone. An acrobatic, semi-burlesque, flagrantly erotic gymnastic of the buttocks, the *goombay* survives in the West Indies too.

The title of the poem "Vèvè" is taken from the ritual marks in white made on the floor at the start of voodoo worship. Voodoo was the syncretistic religion, embracing aspects of other tribal religions as well as Roman Catholicism, which provided ideology for the rebellion of the slaves. A religion which began as subterranean and subversive, it still patterns the life and the imagination of the vast majority of Haitians. It is also an affirmation of the gods' migration across the Middle Passage; their rerooting in the new world. The Vèvè marks out the parameters of the ceremony in which the gods, old and new, are summoned to interact in the life of the living.

The poem deals with the invocation for the gate to be lifted so the gods can enter. The worshipper enclosed in the steps of the ritual is, like Camus's Sisyphus, whom one must imagine (for Camus's sanity?) to be happy. *"Il faut imaginer que Sisyphe est heureux"*. But Sisyphus's point of sanity and Camus's may not coincide, and the worshipper is seen, like Othello, a wheeling stranger of everywhere. The cosmogony of voodoo is used again in "Covenant". *Baron Samedi*, one of the powerful god-figures, creator of zombies, is invoked; and a few lines are patterned like the Vèvè, the complex intricate world of meaning, reduced to the schematic lines of the Haitian "primitive" painters:

> pick/clear/geometries of repose
> opalescent hieroglyphs
> of bones...[32]

The poem, "Witchdoctors", like "Juju", seizes on a word whose bridge to its original meaning has been broken. The poet, son of an organist who played on pedal organs ("with their ineffable quality of hand-barrel-monkey parody and anachronistic sanctity. I breathed, ate, smelled that sound Sunday after Sunday after Sunday"), the poet comes into conflict when he enters the imaginative world of the witchdoctors. Reduced from the prophets who could interpret the symbols of a fixed universe of metaphor, when that universe fell apart they had to take up fragments – jujus – and convert themselves to technicians:

> disbelieving in the accidental
> we came warily enough.
> with raffia brooms
> this other one
> with bamboo whistles, power
> against witchcraft; for
> ease of strange sicknesses
> goatskin pouches.[33]

Then came the ships. The witchdoctors come down, skulls distended, to meet our fates. To others, the ships may have seemed accidental, a casual event. But they came warily, reading the signs:

> ...walls that leaned in
> frantic eagerness
> towards the atlantic[34]

Their doom was in the "gray man", a lover of laterites, a believer in stones. The creative phase of the neolithic slowly retreats before this gray "vague man...maddened with granite".

In "A dance of pilgrims" the paradox of Freetown, paradox of the poet's biography – of his organ-playing father, a provincial priestly petty bourgeoisie

– is well caught, evoked in the first few lines:

> my father, wheezing esthete,
> before he died...
> ... played
> on pedal organs:
> small-gaited pilgrimages,
> peregrinations that
> faded at odd crossroads...[35]

The modulation of sound that should have echoed in the corners of some gray English provincial town, musty in summer, a decent Hallelujah for Spring, muted in winter, wheezes out here in some arklike transient church against the sound of rain and the silence of drought:

> the two-toned dry
> visitation or wet
> of nature is our inheritance[36]

For the Prodigal in his "canticle", the exile begins in the landscapes: "dutch castles/and/stones/marked in/portuguese". Chronicle, monument and slave trade. The ritual ceremony, the bringing forth of a new child to be presented, *ku omo jade*, is now ambivalent among alien signs. The lions that had seemed formed from the rocks, and caused the Portuguese to give it a name (the Sierra of lions), are seen to be charlatan lions. There is in reality no return; no fatted calf; nor can the "succulent/ passages of/fine women redress the rage/and riot of substance." There is only the awakening to the knowing of himself, native now only to exile:

> and I come to
> myself
> drumming
> a canticle of dry
> sticks
>
> travelling.[37]

"Calypso for Caliban", which is central to the title, begins with the awakening to the reality of his inheritance. The island now returned to him is a chain of leached bones. Prospero has joined the ancestral gods – Papa Prospero, Papa Legba. But he introduces into the licensed ritual disorder that is a part of the Voodoo ceremony, a dualism that moves in the coordinates of medieval bestiary: the Beast is to be born white. The dialect of the Calypso form takes on the wasteland of the western sexual psyche; the "vaginas" are "derelict"; and the Immaculate Conception satirised, negated:

> him goin to kiss the whores
> in she certain parts...[38]

The calypso form, the Creole dialect, its assumptions free from the sexual angst of Prospero's kingdom, play with the "beast" role assigned to Caliban. But Caliban, poet, educated and therefore "partaking of the same collective unconscious as the European" (Fanon) can afford no such ironic distance. The geography of his imagination has been charted from Homer's Ulysses to Eliot's "what seas what shores what grey rocks and what islands."[39] He has identified with the pilots of these psychic journeys from Homer to Tarzan ("A.T. & P. Ltd."). It is the world of Voodoo and Calypso to which he is alien; to which he must make a conscious return. His unconscious, patterned by the menace of our education, negates the fact of his being black, of being Caliban. Polyphemus blinded:

> the stake
> in the center
> of my head...
> [...]
> believing
> nothing but
> the black
> water (once my
> eye)
> [...]
> but they go
> the sun visible
> and
> Penelope waiting[40]
>   "Exorcism"

To negate the negation, the poet can only choose its anti-symbols, defined by itself. Making these anti-symbols his, accepting their fact and fiction. It is a complicated psychic manoeuvre. He pays for this schizophrenic conscious-ness – only through Ulysses can he reach Cyclops; only through Prospero reach Caliban – with new areas of pain explored, grayer rocks, more sunless seas, more Circeian islands. Through the Virgin Mary, in "Calypso for Caliban", he sees the beast. The Beast is himself.

> ah! Virgin Mary
> keep the carnival of Lent
> the feast of ashes
> in the dance
> of the open thigh
> the flexed knee while
>
> black beasts
> prowl
> the pastures of my brain[41]

Through Miranda he sees his own face in the mirror:

> derelict
> I prowl
> these quays

dissatisfied with my face
prospero
against the face
of your daughter...[42]

I grow dissatisfied
with this and that corner of my face.[43]

In "Highlife for Traders" the Creole dialect and the Creole form exist in a
precarious mockery of itself. The items traded are pitiful in their precision.
The irony lies in the enormity of their historical significance. In the *Autobiography
of a Runaway Slave*, the old Cuban, Montejo, tells us that it was the African's
love of the colour scarlet that had trapped them into slavery. When the sea
peddlers waved scarlet handkerchiefs in the hot and oleous air, we ran down
to the Christian slave traders' ships, bartered our future for a piece of scarlet
cloth:

item: 2 bags lead
balls
10 yards of
scarlet
scarlet
cloth
item: for a stout man

item: for a lean man
not sick
with pox[44]

And the barter continues. The new leaders, "their excellencies," make
the same unequal exchange. They root like hogs among the luxuries of
power, the nation-state becoming consumer product:

the politics of the second coming.
thinking
it was chop-
ful[45]

The people in Achebe's *Man of the People* pointed out that since the colonisers
enriched themselves, had eaten, why not the new leaders? Let them all eat as
long as they ate within limits; didn't eat enough for the owner to see. But once
there had been an owner – in a context that forced the tribal gods to enforce
limits on those who would tend to eat too greedily, that is, to chop. Now that
context had gone and with it the gods. Some eat gold protein, others starve on
starch. The feasting of the greedy is noisy and ostentatious – even flamboyantly
indelicate. Hence the Creole is the precise instrument of communication:

"I chop
you chop
we all chop"
and oga

> palaver finish
> in the kingdom[46]

"Exorcism" and "Shylock, after" move within the parameters that are the poet's strength – and so avoid the tendency in the occasional poem towards verbal indulgence: a too verbal agony. The poet has told of his schooling and what he refers to as the seductive Latin phrases of our exposure to Roman Catholicism. "Exorcism" is dedicated to his teacher (English?). The poem is formal, a space marked out by cadences and a sense of procession, penitential. He exorcises the place built for them, storied, by strangers, narrow as a calvinist's ark. Yet, when there is a death in the house, in this same place, all mirrors and pictures are turned to the wall. This gesture is part of the ritual of African religions, which survived the seas into the Caribbean; and back to Sierra Leone. The spirit of the deceased, due to be released through ritual into the clear status of ancestor, must see no reflection of himself that could trick him to stay, trap him in the dimension of the present.

So many fragments in "Exorcism" – from "what seas, what shores, what grey rocks, what islands", arklike surviving of floods! The poet creates his essence from such rags of memory: Titian-eyed ladies, madrigals, Chaucer, candid in language, announcing Spring; then the Cyclops blinded in his cave, like a great yawn in the earth, impotent, hearing Ulysses just out of reach.

> the ships
> too far
> the rocks
> too heavy[47]

And then Lazarus, resentful of exile from death, of being the proof of Jesus's miracle, cursed with life

> set upon
> by wishes
> not my own[48]

Called by the *magister* Jesus, Lazarus must respond, take up his life like an alien bed, on new and alien terms. Once more reduced to apprenticeship; to be moulded by the master's skill. (Some West African schools are so "gentlemanly latinate" – as Johnson tells us – that roll calls are done in Latin):

> *Salve Magister* greetings, master
> *Salvete pueri* greetings, boys[49]

And so, in the poem, Lazarus answers *adsum*, I am here.

Lazarus comes reluctantly out of the dark back into the painful light of Jesus. Shylock, assaulted in the ghetto of his Jewish being, is dragged into an alien universe, the scapegoat for its self condemnation; to find himself cramped against the night, condemned, against his will baptised, aroused to Christian life, his true self being able to survive only by the direst cunning:

in nomine
by name the jew
sed semper
the jew
golem in yellow
gold pax
tecum[50]

Caliban/poet goes on his travels. There are no further seas for him. His journey is psychic, testing this fabricated self, as Quixote his helmet, through his responses to the world that had sent out its myth to make him. Thus, there is a group of poems in which the responses to places are more immediate, "less enchanted into mythology". They record, some more piercing than others, the bruise on the heart that these responses bring.

The cities are haunted by sickness; the interior walled with the disgust of the flesh, women in particular. The city receives the viaticum, the sacrament of the eucharist given to those in mortal danger

here, in the center, the acid
perfumes of badly douched women who

sit cross-legged at cocktails...
these things leave a bruise in the heart.[51]

Outside, the cold cracks like a whip/wild geese feint paths over the edge of the sky/and fly south. Even further removed, on the journey back, from the plane

the continent surprises: brown earth
edging the smooth tips of the southern atlantic.[52]

Then there are the varied textured encounters, through the European Grand Tour, taking in places and women – finding carnal closeness, that is distant:

a syntax of yellow barricades
hangs between your speech and mine[53]

And the Tour takes in the coincidences of "hell in small places": soviet jews in soviet prisons ("Viaticum"); soviet jews cheated in Israel's heaven where eggs didn't lie about the streets as believed ("San Rafael"). Pan becomes another guise for Caliban through whom conception would come again to Bethlehem but "for no real purpose". Then varied responses to women, real and imagined, exorcising the ghost of Miranda; but here is no brave world; more preferable, Cleopatra's mummy, fabled with reality ("coronation"). In Venice, romantic with gondolas, the Venetian gentlemen sing no serenades under the moon. Rather they are busy...

...wondering how well you (blonde of hair) and I did it.[54]

Venice, locus of Othello – fishbones, screams of urgent cats, water that sucks at the rotting stones of hotels ("Venice"). The poet and the Grand Tour respond to, circle Caliban's priapic image: the ultimate phallus; yet though "the waters are warm/ between the corners of your blue white legs/there are bones in my private parts..."[55]

"Letter to my tailor" narrows down to the bonehard, enclosed predicament of the self, taken to walking with care. The world is mined

> the human mind, it's true, survives
> all but its own hanging.
> lately I have taken to walking
> with my elbows close to my body[56]

Twelve stitches inside the mouth, should keep the word in place and elbows keep the rebellion of brittle bones polite.

Part Five moves into a different mood – the poet responding to the poetic ecology of Northern Nigeria. Lemuel Johnson was born there, of Sierra Leonian parents, and it lives in imagination as "a sometimes perplexing configuration in my childhood memories of sand, river confluences, camels, the Koran and parched, walled cities." These poems open a mood of fan-like delicacy. The landscape is not the verbal, literary landscape of earlier poems. Here the poet recreates an ecology that is not strained through the tension of a conflictual situation. Water flows through these poems, crystal water on which float precise bamboo-ribbed sails, the water of the rite of ablution, of purification with which the al-Mukhlit poem opens. But this is no psychic purgation, rather a translucent age-old pattern, too patterned for the torment or terror of the Christian psyche.

These poems, technically too, have the clarity of water: "having shaved the insides of/our nostrils and ears, sit down/ to food   for which/there exists no botanical names." There is contrast between an opalescent relation of river and architecture:

> the upper reaches
> of the river curve away
> from long-jointed minarets
> the scales of fresh water fish are in our clean nostrils

and the stagnant damming up of poverty, traditional, unhallowed. "Djenne smells like a drowned lake/there are dead fishes among the roots of bamboo trees/the red eyes of hungry lepers search among broken pots".[57]

Here in a backwater where there are no deltas, no commercial activity of profit to the West (as in the South), Time and Nature are repetitive, in fixed monotony like prayer chants:

> in december the harmattan blows cold sand
> our grey fingers keep warm inside the grey bellies of fish
> there are small scales floating to the deltas
> on the thin red entrails of the dead.[58]

Here the question of black and white is absent. Black skin is one more feature of life and its ecology. And black skin, gray with cold, and accustomed hunger, writes a hieroglyph enclosed in its own meaning. The tone of this poem is continued in "split fences". Prospero's economic system is distant. It may have helped to reinforce the cycle of waiting, the limited hope but its effects are silent. Prospero is absent. His culture is ineffectual against these minarets of consciousness, this universe summoned into being by the muezzin's call. Prospero's arrogance, laughable in the face of a Nature, of an earth that turns the wrong way, where rivers wash the veins out of dry mountains. Here Prospero's linear time has no meaning and seems as alien as his progress. Here numbers, squares recur in a kind of dry and rigid mathematics. The limits are known, fixed. There is the calm of bitter certitude.

> our expectations are modest:
> we search the verses of the dead son of Abdullah bin Abdul Muttalib
>
> we pick at sores, they heal.
> there is silence between our teeth.[59]

The task, the pattern, like the river washing the veins from the mountains, reweaves itself, the same texture, the same skein.

But there are intrusions, insidious. In the poem "Immigrants", the child wheels "hoops of discarded british bicycles". The technological fact is an accepted excrescence of a nature which has become poverty-stricken; an extended shanty town of discarded hoops, tins, tires. Here flies mate on the dried spit; there is the smell of burning flesh/half-finished faces. Man survives only by gestures of defence plucked, like rags, from the old patterns

> we ululate and keep dogs away from those we burn.
> there is no wind.[60]

But in this shantytown space of huddled, temporary Nature, there are areas still of silent water for "ablution". There is stillness, opening like a fan: the ceased flick of washerwomen's paddles.

> I will tether the canoe to a river willow
> the river is full
> crested cranes fly banking against the moon
> shadows remain on the paddles of washerwomen.[61]

The sound patterns of the poem emerge from a new ecology; the literary landscape and the sound of the Sicilian bees buzzing in Vergilian landscape exist only as absence. Here we have an old landscape, new storied; named and existent; a landscape of sound and silence.

★　　★　　★

One returns in Part VI to a harsher response. No childhood memories here smelling of faeces, or shimmering with sunlit sails; but the confrontation, the response to the new imperial center: the emporium that has done away with the Vergilian myth of Empire. Not now to *regere imperio populos*, to teach black boys to scan Vergil, struggle with *querens amare* of St. Augustine amidst tin roofs and temporary structures. Rather to educate them to become consumers; to integrate their souls with Coca Cola and Cadillacs.

The poet makes a *rite de passage* from Vergil, St. Augustine, the conjugation of love and bark-raw buttocks, to a new reality, one out to:

> ...wreck the delicate
> phrases of our british tutelage

The visa is the initiation seal into *Playboy* models of men. The black, obsessed with his own reality, cuts out his cardboard outline in sharp clothes:

> narrow lapels and narrow-brimmed hats
> slanted
> dangling in dance like empty clothes
> on meat hooks

The hysteria rises, held on a tight rein, once one comes to terms with the absurd fantasy of trapped skyscrapers, dealing with it by small defences; learning the way its technology works; behaving correctly, as if nothing:

> down in the hotel's toilet
> my children and I urinate with ease
> for ten cents against white porcelain
> We get enough paper
> to keep pissdrops from the flaps of our trousers
> from my daughter's knickers[62]

In Freetown, there had never been enough. Now here, where toilet paper is a multi-million dollar industry, there is infinite choice, so many colours, so many patterns. The small breasts of his wife are untaxed. So far, so good. Then the break-up begins; the surrealist nightmare cannot be held at bay by the ritual of small actions. Hell is domestic here:

> ...my color falls apart in my hands
> [...]
> in new york city I
> await flight patterns hanging
> in new york city by
> fingertips to my skin.[63]

But Caliban can dress himself in Prospero's hair. Here fabricated, ready-made men are for sale. In "shopping list", he can buy, by mail:

> ...new hair
> that is smoothslick gold
> like fish streaking for deep waters
> at the edge of the mediterranean[64]

The hair divides. Matthew, the little boy, wants to play neighbours with my children; he stares through the glass but his hair is the wrong colour. Colour, between the eyes outside the glass, and the eyes inside, is taut, like a high tension wire. The tower of Babel – of tongues; and multi-coloured hair.

Tension strains, twists in on itself, agony without release in "Feb 14th & the bed of the king of france." Violence, not now like cherry pie, but casual, anonymous, like a mass production line; fragments of images leaning on paper-littered streets; and fungoid men against walls, high on life and screams of jangled wires. Violence seeps around the angles and corners of the streets:

> the shards of broken heads
> tonight are jazzily   easily
> cacophonous tonight   three
> black men/
>   under stress/
>   have
>
> been shot, in proportion, by
> three policemen,
>   under stress
> [...]
> and impolite bullets under stress
> in the ears of undertakers[65]

Through this and the following poems the poet works out and over to the far side of despair. The poems become patterned, integral again in "Children's choice". Experience can have form; no longer need broken images be huddled together, like a pack of cards crazily dealt out by the joker, dealing himself first and last of all. Death enters in "Children's choice" and reasserts old significances in the neon wilderness:

> may you keep to yourself
> even the delicate cartilage of your nose
> against the work of maggots
> and the weight of stones[66]

The protocol of death, in the next poem, exorcises the terror of unshriven exit, in a world of reverence. Death is no longer the affirmation of one's existence (once invested by the gods); it is now deserted by them, reduced to its biological negation:

> Old women limp beyond me
> coughing up their livers in small pieces
> on frozen plains
>
> the deranged underwears of changing
> old men   change   merely to plug
> the leakages of private griefs
>
> let them.
> [...]
>
> I die keeping the cancers away
> from the rattling of my voice[67]

In the last poem, we return to the wrestling with literary "angels". Johnson has explained:

I suspect I'm interested in Judas, Ophelia, Shylock for the same reasons, thirdworlders all of them; outsiders, but not heroic ones like Manfred or Childe Harold, rather, confused, impotent, schizophrenic – which, I suppose, is the way I see my problems with Prospero's apparently inexplicable prosperity in the light of our (my?) inexplicable dispossession. (Also Quasimodo's.)

"Quasimodo's bolero" moves within the fields of force of drum and bell; Quasimodo twice-disinherited, as deformed outsider; as black companion to bell and gargoyles, crucified on a belfry of signs; in an iron lay that defined its heroes: and denied its villains with:

> ...the fat of metal
> that shivers in shocks of ecstasy
> through the open spaces
> of my rags[68]

The bell's resonance, the beat of its tongue against iron and bronze and the gargoyle desperation of Quasimodo/Caliban ringing in salvation for another – to affirm the negation of himself! Quasimodo, now questioning his fief to the Western world, grown cynical; sour like Caliban, strips off melodramatic evasion of sentiment:

> my sometime six-inch penis leaks
> stale water below me   my legs
> and the bottoms of my feet fly
> over flagstones   there are black fields
> below   black with faeces   with
> the stale faeces...[69]

The bells are a magnificat of terror and anguish, haunted by the cough of drums. Caliban's Bethlehem has come round at last under a doom-laden star. The shepherds watch Mannix on T.V. The Wise Men have gone about their petroleum and gold investments in Africa. Judas/Caliban/Shylock/Polyphemus/ Lazarus/Quasimodo is set free from the white shadow of the Cross. The countryside invades the cities of the earth. Cyclops in iron ships bear upon Ithaca. Caliban hammers out magic towers of mythology, to imprison Sicilian mountains, green with bees, honey and Vergil. He imposes his landscape now, existential, like the horn of Armstrong, mocking his own pretence of lyric cadences for an agony as dry as bone, causal as water, matter of fact.

Out of this agony-as-farce, Caliban announces his Annunciation with brazen images, upon the world:

> my back swells with the noise of breaking wind
> and the urgency of bronze and iron
> copper and iron   giving birth
> to a dance of concave bones.[70]

Endnotes

1. Lemuel A. Johnson, *Highlife for Caliban* (Ann Arbor, MI: Ardis Publishers, 1973), 30.
2. Frantz Fanon, *Black Skin, White Masks,* trans. *Peau Noire, Masques Blancs* by Charles Lam Markmann (1952; New York: Grove Press, 1967), 111.
3. Karl Marx, *A Contribution to the Critique of Political Economy,* trans. N. I. Stone (1859; Chicago: Charles H. Kerr, 1904), 11-12.
4. Antonio de Teruel, *Narrative Description of …the Kingdom of the Congo* (1663-1664), Ms. 3533: 3574, National Library, Madrid, Spain.
5. Lemuel A. Johnson, *The Devil, the Gargoyle and the Buffoon: The Negro as Metaphor in Western Literature* (Port Washington, NY: Kennikat Press, 1971), 7-8.
6. Ama Biney, *The Political and Social Thought of Kwame Nkrumah* (New York: Palgrave Macmillan, 2011), 79.
7. Johnson, *Highlife,* 29.
8. Honoré de Balzac, "Letter to Victor Ratier" (21 July 1830), Correspondence, Tome I (1809-Juin 1832), Roger Pierrot, ed. (Paris: Éditiones Garnier Frères, 1960), 463.
9. Johnson, *Highlife,* 19.
10. Ibid., 20.
11. Ibid., 19.
12. Fanon, "The Pitfalls of National Consciousness," in *The Wretched of the Earth,* trans. by Constance Farrington (New York: Grove Press, 1966), 161.
13. Johnson, *Highlife,* 21.
14. Ibid., 21-22.
15. Ibid., 24.
16. Ibid., 25.
17. Ibid., 27.
18. Ibid., 28.
19. Ibid., 26.
20. Ibid., 15.
21. Ibid., 39.
22. Johnson, *The Devil, the Gargoyle and the Buffoon*, 6.
23. *Highlife*, 60.
24. Ibid., 57.
25. Ibid., 59.
26. Ibid., 59.
27. Ibid., 59.
28. Ibid., 60.
29. Ibid., 37
30. Not located.
31. Ibid., 38.
32. Ibid., 56.
33. Ibid., 58.
34. Ibid., 57.
35. Ibid., 57.
36. Ibid., 45.

37. Ibid., 46.
38. Ibid., 48, 52
39. Ibid., 34.
40. T.S. Eliot, "Marina" in *Collected Poems, 1909-1962* (New York: Harcourt, Brace and World, 1963), 105.
41. Ibid., 62, 63, 64.
42. Ibid., 34.
43. Ibid., 35.
44. Ibid., 36.
45. Ibid., 41.
46. Ibid., 42.
47. Ibid., 43.
48. Ibid., 64.
49. Ibid., 65.
50. Ibid., 126.
51. Ibid., 70.
52. Ibid., 75.
53. Ibid., 76.
54. Ibid., 78.
55. Ibid., 75-79, 88.
56. Ibid., 85.
57. Ibid., 93.
58. Ibid., 108.
59. Ibid.
60. Ibid., 109.
61. Ibid., 111.
62. Ibid., 112.
63. Ibid., 113-114.
64. Ibid., 114.
65. Ibid., 115.
66. Ibid., 117-118.
67. Ibid., 119.
68. Ibid., 120-121.
69. Ibid., 122-123.
70. Ibid., 123.

ETHNO OR SOCIOPOETICS

This talk, although based on certain initial assumptions, has also developed as a response to certain ideas thrown out in the course of this conference. But time, in the Western sense of the Western world in which we live, is short – and now that I write up the talk as a paper, space is limited. I shall therefore develop the *context* of my argument as a set of bold propositions, anchored by specific references in the notes of the written paper.

The main argument of my talk hinges on the assertion that *Ethnopoetics* can only have validity if it is explored in a context of *Sociopoetics* where the *socio* firmly places the *ethnos* in its concrete historical particularity. Already in this conference, George Quasha has seen the need to give us in his paper – "The Age of the Open Secret" – a definition of the term *Ethnopoetics*. He tells us:

> At root 'Ethnopoetics' has to do with the essentially 'local' incidence of 'poesis' or acts of 'making'. The word *Ethno* derives from Indo-European *seu* which the American Heritage dictionary lists as 'people', 'our people', we 'ourselves', 'of our kind' – and it lives on in the word 'self' and in the reflexive pronouns of French and Spanish. So Ethnopoetics is rooted in 'self-poetics', 'our kind' of poetics, which by an inevitable extension of *poesis* becomes that activity which has gradually become conscious of itself since the Romantics – Self-making. What does 'ethno' do? That question translates as: What does any local band of people living together do in their poetry? Answer: They say themselves. They say who they are. They speak their name in what they do. (How many names of peoples mean simply, the People?) They heal themselves and keep themselves whole. They know who they are.[1]

But who are "we"? We who are gathered here can be labelled as people who come from the First World, people who come from the Third World. Although these terms have been much abused, they serve an *operative* function; they serve to define a *relation* – a *relation* between a *We* and an *Other*. This takes us to the second, dialectical meaning of *ethno,* the meaning which is most pervasive, since it is a meaning based on a concrete reality.

In a recent article in *Commentary,* titled "Plural Establishment", the writer points out that: "The very history of 'ethnic' should be cautionary. New Testament *hoi ethnikoi* and Septuagint and New Testament *ta ethne* render Hebrew (*ha-*) *goyim* as Gentiles, pagans".[2] He goes on to quote Paul writing to the Christians in Rome that he would like to have a successful mission among them as he had had *en tois loipois ethnesin*... "among the rest of the Gentiles... "[3]

The point here is that the term *ethnos* refers to an *other* – the Gentiles as distinct from a "we", in this case, the Jews. The further point here is that Paul, in turning to the *ethnos,* is breaking out of the confines called Christianity, which was to dislodge both monotheistic Judaism and polytheistic Roman paganism, and to institute itself as the central *ethnos* against which the rest of the world would be, in religious terms, *the other.* The point of my paper will be to develop a parallel here – to argue that the validity of this conference will depend on the extent to which we *make* the term *Ethnopoetics* come to concretely mean an activity – in a different time, a different place, and in different terms – similar to Paul's as far as the revolutionary breaking out of an orthodoxy is concerned. We will have the later, negative aspect of Christianity to remind us that the replacement of one orthodoxy by another is not the point. And we will also have the positive side, the stress on Christianity as a universal religion as distinct from the particular "we" of Judaism, to remind us that that is what we too are about. It is here that I agree with Quasha's point that: "It [Ethnopoetics] stands for an event in our readiness to think about certain problems not necessarily called up by literary history or Western Cultural history as we are used to viewing it."[4]

In fact it is here that I would like to make a central point. The exclusion of these "certain problems" from Western literary history and Western cultural history *is not* an accident. Rather it is central to what I shall develop as the thesis of Western secular *ethnocentrism* in which the *West* became the *we* to the *ethnos* of all other peoples, who all became *The Other.* How did this come about?

Pre-sixteenth-century Europe defined itself essentially as Christian. It therefore took over the We/Other of Judaism, carrying on the meaning of *ethnos* used in the New Testament, where the *goyim* of Hebrew was translated as Gentile, but converting itself from the Other – Gentile converted to Christian – to the *we,* and therefore increasingly using the term *ethnos* for the Other: the Heathen, the non-Christian.

So, for example, in the seventeenth century, speaking of pagan religions, a writer comments: "The Ethnics do still repute all great trees to be divine".[5] Earlier in the same century another writer speaks of "a kind of mule, that's half Ethnic, and half a Christian."[6]

In 'the eighteenth century, the meaning of the pagan non-Christian classical world persisted and a writer can speak of "fabulous ethnicity" with its "feigned Venus" and its "idolatries".[7]

In the nineteenth century the opposition Christian/heathen takes on a division between universal "truth" and sectarian heresy. One writer comments: "Heresies are at best *ethnic;* truth is essentially *catholic.* "[8] Carlyle, also writing in the nineteenth century, saw *truth* as the status quo, and wrote dismissively of "a mind... occupied... with mere Ethnicism, radicalism, and revolutionary tumult."[9]

Ethnic, then, had come to take on connotations of meaning that we shall develop in this paper – connotations of *heresy* as opposed to *orthodoxy*, *revolution* as opposed to the *status quo*. It is my contention that if *Ethnopoetics* is to exist as that "act of magic" of which Quasha speaks, then it can only do so in the context of its essential contemporary historical connotation – i.e., as the focal point of our *poetical/political* assumption of *Otherness*, an assumption at once heretical and revolutionary which alone can negate the *we/they* dichotomy and restore to *ethnos* its original integral meaning: of *we*.[10] If Ethnopoetics is our *self-making* – as Quasha argues, then it is, imperatively, first of all, a negating of the present *dominant self*, structured by the contemporary social forces, a *self*, a *we* that exists only through the negation of an *Other*. What do we mean by this? Let us establish our context.

The really fundamental split between the *we* and the OTHER, between Western and non-Western cultures, began in the sixteenth century when the world-market economy was first established, and a world economic system, global in reach, became a reality. A recent book by Immanuel Wallerstein explores this development. He writes:

> In the late fifteenth and early sixteenth century, there came into existence what we may call a European world-economy. It was not an empire, yet it was as spacious as the grand Empire and shared some features with it. But *it was different and new*. It was a kind of social system the world had not really known before and which is the distinctive feature of the modern world system. It is an economic but not a political entity, unlike empires, city states, and the emerging nation-states. It is a world system not because it encompasses the world, but because it is larger than any juridically defined political unit. And it is a 'world-*economy*' because the basic linkage between the parts of the system is economic, although that was reinforced to some extent by cultural links and eventually, as we shall see, by political arrangements and even confederal structures. 'An Empire by contrast is a political unit.'[11]

Western civilisation, as we experience it today, is the *expression* of that new social system: an economic world system. I suggest that what took place then – i.e., in the sixteenth century – was a *mutation* rather than a simple evolutionary process; a discontinuity that called for a detotalisation and a retotalisation of, to borrow Nathaniel Tarn's terms, the *European-Western "heraldic vision"*.

I suggest also that the X factor of this *mutation* was the discovery of the New World; that is, the discovery of vast areas of land which in becoming the *frontier* of what was then still primarily a *Christian* civilisation, transformed that group of people and of states into what we today call the *West*, i.e., that group of states and people that Immanuel Wallerstein defines as the *core-states*. The West became the *We*, and the people of the *Periphery-states* became the *Other*. But the point is that neither the *We* nor the *Other* now existed as autonomous entities.

Both *We* and *Other* were now bound in a *concrete* relation, a hierarchical global relation. It was in the context of this relation that the *Christian* civilisation of the West was metamorphosed into *Western* civilisation and all other entities into the Non-West. It is this distinction that it loosely called today First/Third World. Immanuel Wallerstein shows that concreteness of this relation in its initial state. He writes:

> What was it about the social structure of the sixteenth century world-economy that accounts for a social transformation of a different kind, one that could scarcely be called homeostasis?... It must be that the world economy was organised differently from earlier empires, and in such a way that there existed social pressures of a different kind...
>
> We have already outlined what we consider to be the pressures of Europe to expand. Expansion involves its own imperative. The ability to expand successfully is a function both of the ability to maintain relative social solidarity at home (in turn a function of the mechanisms of the distribution of reward) and the arrangements that can be made to use *cheap labour far away* (it being all the more important that it be cheap the further it is away, because of transport costs).[12]

The *cheap labour far away* was to become the concrete *Other* of the West, the ultimate polarity in a series of hierarchical polarities. Wallerstein explains:

> Expansion also involves unequal development and therefore differential rewards, and unequal development in a multilayered format of layers within layers, each one polarised in terms of a bimodal distribution of rewards. Thus concretely in the sixteenth century, there was *the differential of the core of the European world economy versus its peripheral areas,* within the European core between states, within states between regions and strata, within regions between city and country, and ultimately, within more local units.
>
> The solidarity of the system was based ultimately on this unequal development, since *the multilayered complexity provided the possibility of multilayered identification...*[13]

This multilayered identification would take, in the global system, both the form of *class* and the form of *race*. In the form of *class* the basic struggle would be internal – which class should define and determine the distribution of reward inside the unit; in the form of *race* – even *within* the confines of a unit (cf. the Blacks/Indians inside the USA) – the struggle was imperatively *global;* i.e., these groups would have to challenge the imposed rights of a few units – the West – to monopolise the lion's share of the world/the earth's natural resources in land and labour. Wallerstein explores this global structure:

> Such a system of multi-layers of social status and social reward is roughly correlated with a complex system of distribution of productive tasks; crudely, those who breed manpower sustain those who grow food who sustain those who grow other raw materials who sustain those involved in industrial production, and of course, as industrialism progresses, this hierarchy of productive services gets more complex as this late complex is ever further reified.
>
> The world economy at this time had various kind of workers. There were

slaves who worked on sugar plantations and in easy kinds of mining operation...
'serfs' who worked on large domains where grain was cultivated and wood
harvested... 'tenant' farmers on various kinds of cash crop operations... and
wage labourers in some agricultural production. There was a new class of
'yeomen' farmers... a small layer of intermediate personnel... and a thin layer
of ruling classes... both the existing nobility and the patrician bourgeoisie...
the Christian clergy and the State bureaucracy.[14]

The *we* of the West would be defined by this ruling class in the context of
the new capitalist world system and the relation of this *we*, both internally to
the ruled *classes* and externally – and internally – to the ruled *races*, were an
intrinsic part of the mechanism/system of capitalism. As Wallerstein shows:

A moment's thought will reveal that these occupational categories were
not randomly distributed either geographically or ethnically within the
burgeoning world economy. After some false starts, the picture rapidly evolved
of a slave class of African origins located in the Western Hemisphere, a
'serf class' divided in two segments; a major one in Eastern Europe and a
smaller one of American Indians in the Western Hemisphere. The peasants
of Western and Southern Europe were for the most part 'tenants'. The wage
workers were almost all principally from Northwest Europe. The intermediate
classes were pan-European in origin (plus mestizos and mulattoes) – the
ruling classes were also pan-European...[15]

In the global system, *labour* itself constituted a multilayered system. As
Wallerstein goes on to ask and answer:

Why different modes of organizing labour – slavery, 'feudalism' wage labour,
self-employment – at the same point in time within the world-economy?
... And why were these modes concentrated in different zones of the world-
economy – slavery and 'feudalism' in the periphery, wage labour and self-
employment in the core, and as we shall *see,* sharecropping in the
semi-periphery? Because the *modes of labour control* greatly affect the political
system... and the possibilities for an indigenous bourgeoisie to thrive. *The
world economy was based precisely on the assumption that there were in fact these
three zones and that they did in fact have different modes of labour control. Were this
not so, it would not have been possible to assure the kind of flow of the surplus which
enabled the capitalist system to come into existence.*[16]

It was the core zone, the zone which used wage labour and self-employment
as its mode of labour control which increasingly defined the relation, definitions
based on the extent to which that zone became enriched by the exploitation of
its own labour, and of the even *more devalued* labour of the semi-periphery and
the periphery. The core zones would be bearers of Western "civilisation", the
agents and the main benefactors of the world economy. But this core zone itself
was now what it was, by nature of a *relation;* to what it *conceptualised* as a negation
– the NON-WEST, i.e., *The Other.*[17]

The conceptualisation which began with the new relation involved changes
of considerable magnitude; involved detotalisation of the prevalent and

previous world picture; and the retotalisation of another. The bold speculative departures in Western thought that were taken responded to the enormous change in *consciousness* that the discovery and impact of the New World had upon the Old. It was in Europe – i.e. the core-zone – that the world, responding to its new frontier, was first made really new.[18]

It was the concrete, material, essentially *economic* impact of the New World upon the Old, that would essentially transform that Old World from one civilisation amongst others – the Christian, to *The One*, the West, to which all other civilisation were *Other*. What was at work in the sixteenth and seventeenth centuries in Europe was a total transformation of the social and economic bases of the society, and in consequence, of its *Christian* world picture – or, to borrow the term, developed by Nathaniel Tarn during the conference, the Christian *"heraldic vision"*.[19] It is in the context of this transformation of the heraldic vision that John Donne wrote: "The new philosophy calls all in doubt,/the elements of fire are quite put out".[20]

Here we see the detotalisation picture at work. The "new philosophy" dissolves the former world picture and its very act of constituting a new one. In Descartes' *Discourse on Method* we see the retotalisation picture at work. We sense his excitement when he writes:

> For they have made me see that it is possible to reach a kind of knowledge which will be of the utmost use to men, and that in place of that speculative philosophy which is taught in the schools, we can achieve a practical one by means of which, by ascertaining the force and action of fire, water, the air, the heavenly bodies, and the skies, of all the physical things that surround us, as distinctly as we know the various trades of our artisans, we can apply them in the same way to all the uses for which they are fit, and thus make ourselves as it were, the lords and masters of nature.[21]

The *Nature* that man was to be totally the lords and possessors of could never have been merely the *Nature* of the Old World. Nature was there the repository of Christian Natural Law, the *Other* to *Man* which guaranteed humanness. The concept of Nature was now transformed by the vast presence of an *alien* frontier Nature; and this alien Nature was, for the West, totally *land*, unhallowed by traditions, customs, myths. The conquistadores dreamt to grab gold, but the bait held out to the colonists from Spain, and later from all Europe, was *land*.[22]

Whilst much has been written about the way in which the *European* working class was forced off the land in Europe to be made into the landless proletariat, very little attention is paid to the fact that it was a parallel movement to the manner in which large sections of the middling and the poorer classes in Europe, became *landed* in the New World; and of how this new and dizzy social mobility would strengthen and extend the power of the bourgeoisie, until then cabined, cribbed and confined by the trammels of an aristocratic feudal Europe with power still based on birth and lineage. That is to say, the fact that it was the new world that made possible the rise to total power of the western bourgeoisie, until then merely an element of European life, is disregarded, as is the fact that the *essential determining factor* of the much-debated western transition "from feudalism to capitalism was the discovery and existence of the vast new lands of the new world", and that it was these lands that served as the catalyst for that total "commercialisation of land and labour" that is the central dynamic of capitalism.

Nature in the New World became mere land, to be exploited. The *change in the relation to Nature* was a change, hitherto unknown, in its new *qualitative* phase in human experience, in the very *concept of culture*. Léopold Sédar Senghor has pointed out that *culture* is the *expression* of the relationship between Man and his natural environment. It is in effect "the result of a double effort of the integration of Man with Nature and Nature with Man". That is to say, Man adapts himself to Nature, at the same time as he adapts Nature to his own exigencies. From this contradictory, dual process, springs his social and economic structure, his art, and his philosophy. This balance lay at the heart of all traditional cultures until the discovery of the New World and the concomitant expansion and mutation of Western civilisation. From here on, Senghor writes, "an economic and instrumental civilization could make us believe that one part of the process, the transformation of Nature by Man, is the very essence of Culture."[23]

The passage I have quoted from Descartes could be called the manifesto of this new and revolutionary break in thought, attitudes, and consciousness that we have termed a mutation; not so much a transition[24] as a rupture, a *discontinuity* caused by the introduction of a new factor which acted as a catalyst for change in the context of the New World and its large-scale exploitation by the West that initiated Man's revolutionary new relation of Nature. And the new relation to Nature was a new relation to Other Men. This new relation to Nature and other men, metamorphosed Western man and his sense of *self*.

Before, European man had conceptualised himself *religiously*. On the Chain of Being he stood between the angels, on the one hand, and the animals, on the other.[25] The angels represent the ideal of purity to which he could aspire; the animals the non-ideal, which marked the limits of what he could not be; what he should strive against being. It was this concept which Pico della Mirandola still expressed in humanist terms, when he exulted in the fact that man alone, on the Chain of Being, had no fixed place, but could make himself what he wanted to be – as high as the angel; as low as the beast. With the post-New World mutation rupture, European man would now define himself *secularly* in relation to other men. In response to a new concrete relation, he detotalised his former world picture – i.e., one thinks of the aesthetically satisfying world picture of the still Christian Elisabethan world as developed by Tillyard, with its ordered hierarchy, in which the social order was guaranteed by the natural order which it was supposed to parallel; with the Pope, the king, the nobles, the people imaging the stable pattern of the universe; with the earth at the centre and all planets revolving round in ordered and stately harmony.[26] Then he retotalised another.

For the first time in human history a small group of peoples now had at their disposal the rest of the peoples and the resources of the earth, due to an initial technological superiority which was to grow by leaps and bounds as wealth accrued from the frontier territories that the West, uniquely in human history, had suddenly acquired. It is at this conjuncture that with the shifts in the bases and areas of power and the change in relations of power, the former heraldic vision – no longer serving – disintegrated like Humpty Dumpty. And when the pieces were put back again, they formed a mutant whole.

In the new retotalisation European man was transformed from Christian man to Western man; the other peoples of the earth were transformed into *negroes* and natives. The "negro" was to be a particular form of the generic "*natives*". The European socio-cosmic vision of the world in which the social order paralleled the *natural* order was not discarded, but retained, transformed to serve the purposes now not of Christian theology, but of secular ideology.[27] If the sun was now recognised as being the centre of the natural universe, the West, its countries and its people, paralleled this centre here on earth. In a form of bricolage, the elements of the old heraldic vision were not so much discarded as rearranged. Non-western man, non-western lands now provided a *periphery,* by which Western man and lands could dialectically become the *centre.* The domestication of Western lands and peoples could be more *easily* carried out in a context in which all that was non-West became the *adynaton*[28] of all that was the West. The non-West territory became the frontier/ jungle/ Nature "red in tooth and claw". Non-Western man became the "noble savage" or the savage monster. Indeed the very definitions of the term "natural" (cf. the call during the conference for a phenomenology of the "natural") would change in order to legitimise the insertion of Western man, paralleling the sun at the centre of the physical order, at the centre of the new – now global – world picture. In other words, the new definitions of the "natural" institutionalised Western man as the *norm of man*; and non-Western Man as the *Other*, the not-quite, the non-men who guaranteed the Being of the Norm by his own non-being. In creating themselves as the norm of men, the Western bourgeoisie *created* the idea of the Primitive, the idea of the savage, of the "despised heathen", of the "*ethnos*": they created the idea of their own negation.[29]

The idea of the savage black, writes Césaire, was a European invention. Roy Harvey Pearce points out that in the U.S.A. the settlers created the idea of the *savages* as the further limit of what they could not allow themselves to be, what they should not be. The "savage" was not a fact but a negative concept of Western man; he existed as a sign.[30] As western man "pacified" New World nature, eliminated the "savage", penned them up in reservations, he did the same with whole areas of his Being. Indeed it would be difficult to explain the extraordinary nature of his ferocity if we did not see that it was, first of all, a ferocity also wrought, in psychic terms, upon himself. Western man – as defined by the bourgeoisie – retained those areas of Being whose *mode of knowing* could sustain the narrative conceptualisation (the heraldic vision) of his new world picture, but eliminated, penned up on reservations – those areas of *cognition* which were, by their mode of knowing, *heretical* to the conceptualised orthodoxy that was required. The mode of cognition that was penned up was a mode which Western man (all of us, since it is no longer a racial but a cultural term) remains aware of only through poetry – and poetry as the generic term for art.[31]

Hence, it would seem to me to be the point of this conference: the exploration of this *alternative mode of cognition* ideologically suppressed in ourselves, yet still a living force amidst large majorities of the third world peoples. In this common exploration there can then be no concept of a liberal mission to save "primitive poetics" for "primitive peoples". The salvaging of ourselves, the reclamation of vast areas of our being, is dialectically related to the destruction of those conditions which block the free development of the human potentialities of the majority peoples of the third world.

For the expansion of the Western self, the auto-creation in the sixteenth century was only made possible by the damming up of the potentiality of non-Western man, by the negation of *his* Being. Once the idea of the Christian medieval ethnos of the West had broken down, it was replaced by another universal, the secular ideology of the bourgeoisie, the concept of *Humanism*. This was the new conceptualisation of the new *ethnos* of Western man, as compared to his former Christian *ethnicity*. It would be part of the ideology of humanism that whilst it saw itself as a universal, it was universal only in the context of a Western-dominated world. To quote Orwell, and to paraphrase: *All men were equal but Western man was more equal than others.*

The new *ethnos* of the West was created by the bourgeoisie, as a secular *ethnos,* based on their need to attack the privilege of birth bound by biological limits, based on the blood of the monarcho-feudal aristocracy. Humanism became the secular theology/ideology of the bourgeoisie's *universal* of universal freedom. But the dialectical achievement of the concept of universal freedom was limited by its necessary negation – the fact that universal freedom was defined by a class in the interests of a class – of the Western bourgeoisie who also created the modern concept and reality of the West. If internally the European working classes were the *Other* to the Western Bourgeoisie, externally, the non-Western masses were the *Other* to a temporarily allied bourgeoisie-working class Western man.

That is, the presence of the *Other* made possible the existence of an internal *We* which bound all classes of the Western world in a *temporary* relation. But it is a *We* that is no longer, as was the Christian *We*, autonomous. The Western self existed, and could only exist as defined and posited, with the non-self of the non-Western world. The *We* of the West could only be defined by the Negation that the *Other* constituted.

The Mayan prophetic book, *The Chilam Balam of Chumayel*, brings out this dialectic with pathos and precision. In former times, before Columbus and the discovery, life was lived as a near Utopia at least in memory. Then,

> There was wisdom in them. There was no sin. There was a sacred sense of devotion in them. Then, there was not disease, no pain in the bones, no fever, no small pox, no burning in the chest, no pains in the stomach, no withering away. Then they walked with their bodies straight. But when the foreigner came, all changed. They taught fear and came and withered the flowers. So their flower should live, they hurt and sucked our flowers – to castrate the sun, that is what the foreigners came to do.[32]

But it is important to realise that this reinvention of the Western self was determined by a *concrete* relation. What is usually referred to as Western "racism", in which this *racism* is taken as an absolute and mystified, is the term used both to define and to avoid a concrete class relation between the West and the rest of the world. *Racism* was the *form* through which, in the context of the world market economy, the class structure as relationship between core and periphery peoples expressed itself. Indeed *racism* was the indispensable ideology of the forms or modes of labour control that were imperative to the capitalist exploitation of the periphery peoples.

In the context of this statement, what I shall label the *Sepúlveda syndrome* takes on a central significance. Ginés de Sepúlveda was a sixteenth-century Spanish theologian who argued that the Spaniards had a right to enslave the Indians because the latter were culturally inferior:

> Now compare those gifts of prudence, sharpness of wit, magnanimity, temperance, humanity and religion (of the Spaniards) with those of those little men (homuncili) in whom you will hardly find a trace of humanity. They have no culture, no system of writing (nor do they) preserve monuments of their history; they have the vaguest obscure memory of facts recorded in certain pictures, they lack written laws and have barbarous institutions and customs.[33]

The quotation is paradigmatic of the posture of European civilisation as it defined itself in a relation of negation to oral-precapitalist cultures. Above all it shows the *instrumental* use of European culture as a weapon of domination. European culture was posited as a gold standard of value, its "possession" acting as a definition of manhood, of humanity. As I wrote before:

> Culture and humanity resided in writing. Without writing there was a void. The oral culture of the indigenous civilisation was a non-culture, was barbarous. By a process of repetition, "humanity" came to be synonymous with being European; with the "possession" of European culture. To be non-European was to be non-human. The myth of the cultural void of the non-West – The Other – was to be central to the ideology which the West would use in its rise to world domination.[34]

In a world in which there were, in the Western world view, two kinds of men – men and the little men (*homunculi*), culture and non-culture, the former Chain of Being of the West underwent a new retotalisation. Where Italian humanist Pico della Mirandola's man had stood between the angels above and animals below, striving to reach the one, striving to avoid lapsing into the latter, a new arrangement, *secularly,* put Western man in the place of the angels, whilst below him is non-Western man – not quite man, not quite animal – able to attain the status of manhood only if he *imitated* as closely as he could the gold standard of manhood, the normative model of man, Western man. In an abstraction which alienated him also from the reality of himself, Western man was translated from a *fact* into a signifier, signifying the *normative model of man.* It is this abstraction that lives and moves at the core of the ideology/ conceptualisation of *humanism.*

It is our intention in this paper to suggest that the black experience in the New World has been paradigmatic of the non-Western experience of the native peoples; and that the black experience constituted an existence which daily criticised the abstract consciousness of humanism; that the popular oral culture, which the black created in response to an initial negation of this humanness, constitutes, as culture, the *heresy of humanism;* and that is why black popular culture – spirituals, blues, jazz, reggae, Afro-Cuban music – and its manifold variants have constituted an underground cultural experience as subversive of the status quo Western culture as was Christianity in the catacombs of the Roman Empire. For it was in this culture that the blacks reinvented themselves as a *We* that needed no *Other* to constitute their Being; that laid down the cultural parameters of a concretely universal *ethnos.*

How did this happen? In the Sepúlveda definition we see that Western man alone has the *property* of manhood, of humanness. What was the purpose of this conceptualisation? What was this a conceptualisation for?

To answer this question, we must look at the context in which Sepúlveda made his definition. As I wrote before:

…what I shalt label as the Sepúlveda syndrome – the mythology of the inferiority of the non-white, and specifically and more totally of the black, the devaluation of his humanity, the elaborate construction of a world view in which Africa became the negation of all humanity – the heart of darkness – serves, as it had served in the New World with the Indians, a specific *material* purpose. The full implications of the Sepúlveda statement became clear when we realise that he had been hired by the Spanish colonists of Santo Domingo to defend what they claimed to be their rights *as Spaniards* to the unfettered utilisation of the labour power of the Indians, through the perpetuation and continuance of the *encomienda* system, a particular form of relations of production by which Indians were assigned as a labour force to individual Spanish colonists, their labour power being exchanged for the doubtful value of the allegedly Christianising influence on them of the Christian colonists who commanded their labour. The rip-off came in the unequal exchange.[35]

Sepúlveda defended the *rights* of the colonists against Las Casas, who pointed out the dehumanisation of the Indians that the *encomienda* system entailed, and the evil of this system in the light of Christian doctrine.

It was in the context of this ideal doctrine – all men had souls and were sons of God – that Sepúlveda brought forward the thesis that some men were more equal than others. The signs of the more-than-equal were their possession of a "culture"; of the less-than-equal, their lack of "culture". With no other race on earth as with the black would this "cultureless thesis" be more elaborately constructed, more vulgarised, more commonly accepted. The European slave trade out of Africa, in the context of nascent Western humanism, and the plantation system in the New World in the light of a nascent bourgeois rationality, made imperative the construction of such a powerful *ideology*. The stereotype of the black as Sambo, the nigger minstrel, was a cornerstone in this architecture of defamation.

T.W. Adorno has shown the imperative necessity for men to fabricate ideologies like this:

> The system in which the sovereign mind imagined itself transfigured, has its primal history in the pre-mental, the animal life of the species. Predators get hungry, but pouncing on their prey is often difficult and dangerous; additional impulses may be needed for the beast to dare it. Their impulses and the unpleasantness of hunger fuse into rage at the victim, a rage whose expression in turn serves the end of frightening and paralysing the victim. In the advance to humanity this is rationalised by projection. The "rational animal" with an appetite for his opponent is already fortunate enough to have a superego and must find a reason. The more completely his actions follow the law of self-preservation, the less can he admit the primacy of that law to himself and others; if he did, his laboriously attained status of a *zoon politikon* would lose all credibility.
>
> The animal to be devoured must be evil. Idealism... gives unconscious sway to the ideology that the not-I, *l'autrui* and finally all that reminds us of nature is inferior, so the unity of self-preserving thought may devour it without misgivings. This justifies the principle of the thought as much as it increases the appetite. The system is the belly turned mind and rage is the mark of each and every idealism.[36]

The Not-I of the Western idealist philosophy of humanism with its concomitant, the later rights of man, was, most ultimately, the non-white sub-man assimilated to Nature, and the most ultimately non-white was the black. The systematic devaluation of the black as human went hand-in-hand with the systematic exploitation of his labour power.

The non-white labour that was to be exploited has to be perceived as evil. In the context of idealistic humanism, their less than human status had to be rationally justified. In the context of emergent capitalism, the naked form of slavery under which the labour power of the plantation slave or the *encomienda* Indian was exploited, the Sepúlveda syndrome – like the later more scientific Darwinian-derived theories – served a specific purpose – i.e., it rationalised emergent capitalism's need for relatively more devalued labour power.

The cultural racism implicit in the Sepúlveda syndrome cannot be described as an autonomous response of the superstructure, a psychological response inherently embedded in the European psyche. Rather, this cultural racism constituted a central part of the complex ideological apparatus by which *Western capitalism* would fulfil its imperative of extracting surplus value from non-white labour. Cultural racism is therefore organic to – and not anomalous to – Western capitalism, and *ipso facto* to Western civilisation.

In other words, the perception of the Indian, black, native as inherently inferior plays a central role in the actual concrete determination of the value of "inferior" men, and of their "inferior" labour power. The devaluation of their cultures, which implies the devaluation of their humanity, far from being a merely *cultural* (i.e., superstructural) phenomenon, was rooted in a material base, in the economic infrastructure. It was the "belly" which saw the black as Sambo/brute beast; and the "natives" as *homunculi* and lesser breeds.

We note then that the negation of the "humanity"/manhood of the Indian was the justification by Sepúlveda of the devaluation of the price of his labour power, but that this devaluation was dialectically implied with the over-valuation of Western man's. The spread of the world market system would increasingly correlate the "Value of Being" of the "self", with the relative market value of each man's labour power. Out of this came the axiom that Western man had a right to the over-valuation of Being, whilst primitive man was condemned to devaluation.

We note, too, that the new world picture, the heraldic vision, far from being innocent, is more than self interested – in other words, it is ideological. Indeed, it is imperatively ideological since it must *conceal-oversee* the truth of a relation. For *humanism as* concept becomes operative now, not because Angels/Animals are the Other but because of the existence of those defined and forced to accept their definition as *Subhuman*.

In the emergent world economic system, a market system which increasingly made of a man's labour, a man's *being,* a commodity, humanism functioned as the *creative ideology* of the Western bourgeoisie. To forget or to oversee the brilliant achievements of this caste/class, spurred on by this ideology in its creative ascendant phase, is to oversee the complexity of the task before us. To refuse to see its dialectical opposite, the extent to which this ideology demanded as its obverse side the degradation of all non-Western peoples – the elimination, negation, freezing of all other cultures seen as heretical to the totalitarian Western orthodoxy, is to take an ideological position which makes impossible the aim of this conference as postulated by Quasha – that of self-making. To reinvent the concrete self it is necessary to first *recognise* abstraction of the self which, imposed on us, we have inherited.

To oversee the above dialectic is to oversee the extent to which the concept of *humanism*, which was the postulated ideal of the economic process which reduced the labour power of man to a commodity and his Being to a market value, had to remain an *abstraction,* an ideology, a creed, helping the faithful to accept that they were still men despite a system which increasingly reduced them to ciphers. In this context the real concrete self was increasingly alienated from the postulated *ideal* self. It would seem to me that the purpose of the conference is not so much to recover the "primal state", to recover the "Natural" – for even these terms are ideological – but rather to begin to validate, to define and to work for the concretely human that is posited, negated in the abstract web of humanist ideology, and to do this in the context of the concrete relations of productions which made this ideology both necessary and possible.

It is because poetry is the inventor/guarantor of the concretely human, i.e., of the "natural", that this conference takes on its significance. For underlying many of the activities of the past few days, has been the pervasive feeling that we have come here on a quest for the "primitive", yet if we discard the dross that has accreted to such a quest over the centuries, we still find that the quest of the primitive is a metonymy (a misnomer) for the quest of *human being* now reified into a commodity.

Western man is the first human being in the history of the world to totally inhabit a commodity-culture. Humanism has ended in its negation. Men have become the objects they have created. Western man creates his Being as a thing. The "natural" chain of Being has been replaced by a market, a historical-Chain of Being.[37] Because of this the difference between Western and non-Western cultures is not the difference between civilised and primitive. That is an ideological reading. *The difference is that between the first commodity-culture in the history of human existence and all other cultures. A mutation has occurred.* All other cultures, including the pre-sixteenth-century Western one, existed as the agent and product of the process by which man invented himself as *human.* Commodity-culture, on the other hand, is the agent and product of the process by which objects invent man as another object labelled *human.* Man's power to name objects is turned against him. Objects name him. Freedom is a Cadillac.[38]

Poetry is the agent and product by which man names the world, and calling it into being invents his *human* as opposed to his "natural" being.

For to *name* the world is to *conceptualise* the world; and to conceptualise the world is an expression of an active relation. A poem is itself *and* sign of man's creative relation to his world; in humanising this world through the conceptual/naming process (neither comes before the other like the chicken and the egg) he invents and reinvents himself as human.

In a world named by objects, poetry dies except insofar as it laments its own loss, reconciled to obsolescence. And after, what? The quest for the primitive is once again a misnomer; the quest for the primitive that we have come here for today *is a quest for the continuing possibility of poetry itself.* The continued possibility of poetry is itself the continued possibility of humanness. To quote Heidegger, in reply to Hölderlin's "…what are poets for in a destitute time?"

> It is a necessary part of the poet's nature that, before he can be truly a poet in such an age, the time's destitution must have made the whole being and vocation of the poet a poetic question for him. Hence 'poets in a destitute time' must especially gather in poetry, the nature of poetry. Where that happens we may assume poets to exist who are on the way to the destiny of the world's age.[39]

The poet names the world. When it is destitute he names its destitution. But poetry itself becomes destitute except that its naming is an accusation. And to accuse one must first understand the why of destitution. I suggest that the destitution – psychic destitution unique to our times – began in the sixteenth century with the initial relation between the Western Self and its Other. I take the Robinson Crusoe-Friday relation in a paradigm of that relation. Here we see the *naming* process at work, the social naming of relation between the powerful and the powerless. By calling the Indian *Friday*, Crusoe negates his former name, the meaning of his former culture, its architecture of significance. With the past, the cultural world of Friday wiped out, he is reduced to his role as Crusoe's servant. The relation changes, metamorphoses Friday. But we must note that it also changes, metamorphoses Crusoe.[40]

Before he had the power to name things, now he has the power to *name other men*. This power, new to Columbus, is pyrrhic. Once called into existence it will play out its total possibilities. For it is an OBJECT, Crusoe's gun, which gives him this power *to name other men*. The object has inserted itself. Friday, seeing the ease with which the gun has wiped out his at once fellow/and enemy Indians, assimilates the gun as Object to a Natural force, and therefore to a God. He prays to the Gun, pleading that it does not harm him. Crusoe is now the agent of the power of the gun, and as such is master.

It is not Crusoe but the gun that sustains Friday's definition as servant: Crusoe's definition as master. The gun makes Crusoe as MAN, since he owns it, and Friday a Native, since he is without it. Men are masters; natives are servants. The gun, the object, assigns roles and definitions in the heraldic vision.

In his excellent study *The Prison House Of Language* Fredric Jameson discusses the problem of naming. He writes:

> Saussure's definition of the sign runs as follows: The linguistic *sign* unifies, not a thing and a name, but a concept and an acoustic image, 'latter terms being then replaced by a new set, the signifié and the signifiant,' the signified and the signifier. The point is made further that the sign is wholly arbitrary, that its meaning rests entirely on social contentions and acceptance and that it has no 'natural' fitness in and of itself.[41]

Here we see that the social convention accepted by both Friday and Crusoe, of the latter's power to name, is *historical,* not natural, and is based on the power of the gun.[42] For the power that Crusoe has to name Friday is part of the power that he has to force him into the role of servant. Without the gun there would have been two men. With the gun, there is a master on the one hand, servant on he other.

Jameson shows that after Saussurian linguistics what became clear was that "what distinguishes human beings is no longer that relatively specialised skill or endowment which is the power to speak, but rather the more *general power to create signs*."[43] The general power to create signs becomes Crusoe's power and his alone, just as in our contemporary society it is the production process that increasingly creates signs, and not the societal processes as a whole.

It is poetry, the poem, that continues, with increasing difficulty, the general human power to create signs. For the poem constitutes each time that it happens – since a poem is an "event" rather than an object – a field force which reinterprets and reinvents anew the meaning of the sign – that is, the poem creates anew the sign. Each poem reinvents the nature of the sign as *not* arbitrary, but depends on the "openness" of the sign to be able to reinvent it. The market reality produced by the production process reifies the sign into a finite category. It is through its imperative to dereify the market-created signs that poetry finds itself poetically/politically on the opposite side of the barricades, the rebel side of the battle lines.

To name, to create a sign, is to conceptualise, to draw into a universe of meaning. Friday, for example, was drawn into Crusoe's universe of meaning and dispossessed from his. To Crusoe he signifies the day on which he was met: a time and date measurement. The imposed name suits the imposed role of servant.

Friday as a sign is arbitrary in Friday's original universe, meaningful in Crusoe's. The gun, the object, is central to this decision, this differentiation of meaning and non-meaning.

On the other hand, Friday recognises that the gun is the real power, that Crusoe is the mediator. But Crusoe cannot ideologically afford to recognise this. His assumption is that his victory over the Indians is due to his God who has created him as superior *ethnos* to the Other – as a chosen people. He is the Norm. He is *Man*. The Indian is the savage. When converted to civilisation, he is almost a Man, a servant. Crusoe's mastery over the Other is, as Crusoe sees it, *inherent* in his Being; in his truly uniquely human essence.

The myth of Crusoe is central to what we shall call the Western myth – the myth of its own Immaculate Conception. The myth is discussed under the neutral-seeming rubric of the transition from feudalism to capitalism. What is at issue there is to prove that the West became a capitalist developed civilisation because of its inherent virtue and foresight, its wise – virgin – prudence.[44] Always overlooked is the true explanation of its rise to world power, the X factor of its relation to the New World Other; of its exploitation of Friday's labour, and Friday's lands; of his dispossession of Friday from human being.

The oversight of the Friday relation allows for a smooth evolution from Western feudalism to Western capitalism, with the Western subject-feudal lords, bourgeoisie, proletariat, always centrally subject. To conceal a relation the label *First/Third World* with its sleight of hand then becomes the political/ ideological parallel to civilised/primitive. Implicitly, a conference named *Ethnopoetics* is at once assumed to constitute the binary opposition *Poetics* (Western/ real/true poetics) – *Ethnopoetics*– The Other Poetics.[45]

In attempting to negate the ideological meaning that is inherent in such a name, despite of our conscious intentions, we must first recognise that these binary oppositions of a Western-dominated structure, expressed in a Western-dominated language, are ideological; i.e., that they mystify and hide the fact that the First World is only First to the extent that the Third World is Third and vice versa; that the ideological meaning of Ethnopoetics and the real meaning that we try to give it, can only be defined in the overall context of the relation between First/Third World – i.e., in its sociopoetic context.

It is in this context alone that we can see that the so-called "primitive" is only "primitive" to the extent that the capitalist Law of Unequal Development called for the stagnation of all other cultures, for the blocking of their dynamic. It is in this context that we note that the magnificent tribal poetry of the American Indians – the poetry of an oral culture, and as such open to change, to reinvention – by and large remains fixed, codified. This fixed quality testifies to the fact that this culture and its bearers have been penned up, coralled on *reservations* while their ecology, the world of their cultural imagination, was drained away. This tribal poetry is the past poetry of a people who have been metamorphosed from an autonomous *ethnos* into a *Reservation Native,* part of a binary opposition constituted by *Native/Western man.*

That "folklife" which we study as "primitive", beautiful as it is, remains "natural" only because it has been unnaturally (historically) frozen in its development. The real cultural changes that take place only take place in those areas where, as with the nineteenth-century Ghost-Dance and the Peyote cult of the American Indians, elements of the culture formed a matrix, drew in stranger elements and used this new entity as part of their rebellion against this blocking of their existence, of its creative dynamic; created a new cultural form as an accusation against cultural destitution, and as the dynamic of revolt.

So, if we turn to the powerful past tribal poetry of the American Indian to study it, appropriate it, outside of this perspective, this conference would only sustain and extend that ideology which, in order to be, it is committed to fight against. If we approach it from this perspective, we release the potential transformative effect of this conference by approaching the *Cultures of the Other* in order to construct an alternative process of making ourselves human; and to free the Western concept of humanism from its tribal aspect of *We* and the *Other*, transforming its abstract universal premise into the concretely human global, the concretely WE.

Endnotes

1. Quoted from an earlier draft of Quasha's "The Age of the Open Secret." The final version appears in the second and third paragraphs of the paper, 65. (Eds.)
2. Milton Himmelfarb, "Plural Establishment", *Commentary,* vol. 58, no. 6 (December 1974), 72.
3. Ibid.
4. Quasha, as above. (Eds.)
5. All examples were originally taken from the *Compact Edition of the Oxford English Dictionary* and have been reprinted in "Ethnic, ethnical, ethnicity, ethique: Entries from the Oxford English Dictionary", in *Theories of Ethnicity: A Classical Reader*, Werner Sallers, ed. (New York: New York University Press, 1996), 3-12. This particular example is from 1644 (Evelyn).
6. Ibid., 1625 (Ben Jonson).
7. Ibid., 4, 1772 (Nugent).
8. Ibid., 3, 1875 (Lightfoot).
9. Ibid., 4, 1851 (Carlyle).
10. In an interesting article, Fernández Retamar of Cuba argues that revolutionary Latin Americans must assume the identity of Caliban as against the identity of Prospero or Ariel. "Caliban: Notes Towards a Discussion of Culture in our America", *Massachusetts Review,* vol. 15, nos. 1-2 (Winter-Spring, 1974), 7-72.
11. Immanuel Wallerstein, *The Modern World System I: Capitalist Agriculture and the Origins of the European World Economy in the Sixteenth Century* (New York: Academic Press, 1974), 15. Emphasis added.
12. Wallerstein, *The Modern World System I*, 85.
13. Nathaniel Tarn, "The Heraldic Vision: A Cognitive Model for Comparative Ethics", presented at *Ethnopoetics: A First International Symposium,* University of Wisconsin-Milwaukee, April 10-12, 1975.
14. Wallerstein, *The Modern World System*, 86. Emphasis added.
15. Ibid.
16. Ibid., 87.
17. Ibid. Emphasis added.
18. A recent book by Chinweizu, *The West and the Rest of Us: White Predators, Black Slavers and the African Elite* (New York: Random House, 1975), explores this relation in its concrete results.
19. In his book *The Old World and the New, 1492-1650* (Cambridge: Cambridge University Press, 1970), 8, J. H. Elliot has called attention to the extensive nature of this impact, which until now has been ideologically minimised, when not altogether evaded: " 'It is a striking fact' wrote the Parisian lawyer, Étienne Pasquier, in the early 1560s, 'that our classical authors had no knowledge of all this America, which we call New Lands.' With these words he caught something of the importance of America for the Europe of his day. Here was a totally new phenomenon, quite outside the range of Europe's accumulated experience and in its normal expectation. Europeans knew something, however vaguely and inaccurately, about Africa and Asia. But about America and its inhabitants they knew nothing... The very fact of America's existence, and

of its gradual revelation as an entity in its own right, rather than as an extension of Asia, *constituted a challenge to a whole body of traditional assumptions, beliefs and attitudes."* Elliot goes on to quote contemporary sixteenth century comments on "the magnitude and significance of the events which were unfolding before their eyes". Among the comments that he quotes are those of Juan Luis Vives who writes "truly, the globe has been opened up to the human race..." (9) and of Gomara's that, "The greatest event since the creation of the world (excluding the incarnation and death of Him who created it) is the discovery of the Indies." Ibid., 10.

20. Nathaniel Tarn, "The Heraldic Vision: Some Cognitive Modes for Ethnopoetics", *Alcheringa,* vol. 2, no. 2 (September 1976), 23-41.

21. See John Donne, *John Donne: The Anniversaries,* ed. Frank Manley (Baltimore: The Johns Hopkins Press, 1963), 73.

22. Descartes, *Discourse on Method,* trans. Arthur Wollaston (London: Penguin Classics, 1960), 84.

23. In 1513, two decades after the discovery, King Ferdinand of Spain drew up a law which would be central to the colonisation of the new frontier: "It is our will that houses, lots, lands, caballerias and peonies be or may be distributed to all those who go to colonise new lands according to the will of the Governor..." This law was put into effect soon after. As two contemporary writers explain it: "The landowner ship pattern began early after the arrival of the Spanish. Lands were distributed among the infantry in lots called *peonies,* and among the cavalry, *caballerias,* so that they could support themselves. Those in higher positions in the governing force of colonial society received *encomiendas* as well. The latter constituted a certain number of indigenous villages, whose inhabitants could be taxed and who could also be used as a work force in the town and in the fields. Their village lands were not taken from them as such, but they were required to pay such exorbitant taxes, and to render so much labour, that they slowly lost possession of their lands, and soon became actual slaves." Thomas and Marjorie Melville, *Guatemala – Another Vietnam?* (N.Y.: Penguin Books, 1971), 32.

24. Léopold Sédar Senghor, "Le problème de la culture" in *Liberte I: Négritude et Humanisme* (Paris: Éditions du Seuil, 1964), 93-94.

25. Western cultural nationalism, the ideology of Western economic dominance has always insisted on what we shall term, the *Immaculate Conception of the West.* Within this context, scholastic disputes about the "transition" in Europe from feudalism to capitalism, have all had as their point of departure the underlying implication that it was some "unique" Holy Ghost of the West that set in motion the immense processes of transformation that we refer to as a *mutation.* The *oversight* of the X factor has been ideologically deliberate. Immanuel Wallerstein comes nearest to my position when in a complex argument he points out: "There was only one historical moment when men successfully transformed a redistributive world-system (in this case based upon a feudal mode of production) into a capitalist world economy. This was in Europe (*defined as including Iberian America* [italics mine]) between 1450 and 1640. There were no doubt other attempts throughout history. One might perhaps classify the developments in the Mediterranean basin between 1150 and 1300

as such an attempt. And there were others in other regions of the world. *But for various reasons all the prior attempts failed."* It is not so much why they failed as why the other succeeded. Wallerstein goes on to say: " …The moment cannot be located in a day, a month, a year, even a decade. It involved, as we say, a *'transition.'* But transitions contain *'points of no return'* where *qualitative* shifts occur. If one wanted to date this for the modern world-system, one could suggest that 1557 is the symbolic date, the point of no return in the wake of this transition which went on for two centuries." See Wallerstein, "From Feudalism to Capitalism: Transition or Transitions?", *Social Forces*, vol 55, no. 2 (December 1976): 276 [273-283].

26. See E.M. Tillyard, *The Elizabethan World Picture* (New York: Macmillan, 1944), 84.
27. Ibid., 82. Tillyard quotes a passage from Shakespeare's *Troilus and Cressida* (I, iii, 85-86), which makes this point: "The heavens themselves, the planets, and this centre,/ Observe degree, priority, and place".
28. Hence the biologisation of the Negro; i.e., not his historical social fact of being a *slave,* but his biological fact of being black was used as the factor which destined him to the lower rank on the scale of *being* below Man (white).
29. Ernst Robert Curtius, *European Literature and the Latin Middle Ages* (Princeton: Princeton University Press, 1953), 96.
30. Retamar, "Caliban", 13, points out that the noble savage and the savage monster were: "simply options in the ideological arsenal of a vigorous, emerging bourgeoisie. The notion of an Edenic creature comprehends, in more contemporary terms, a working hypothesis for the bourgeois left, and as such offers an ideal model of the perfect society free from the constrictions of that feudal world against which the bourgeoise was in fact struggling… As for the vision of the cannibal, it corresponds… to the right wing of that same bourgeoisie. It belongs to the ideological arsenal of politicians of action, those who perform the dirty work, in whose fruits, the charming dreamers of Utopia will equally share."
31. Roy H. Pearce, *Savagism and Civilization* (Baltimore: Johns Hopkins University Press, 1967).
32. Heidegger, "Poetically Man Dwells", in *Poetry Language and Thought* (New York: Harper & Row, 1971), 218. "Poetry is what first brings man onto the earth, making him belong to it, and thus brings him into dwelling."
33. See G.R. Coulthard, *Dos Casos de Literatura No – Enajenada en la época colonial: Los Libros de Chilam Balam y Guamán Poma de Ayala* (Merida, Yucatana: University of Yucatan, 1972), 11.
34. G.R. Coulthard, "Parallelisms and Divergencies between 'Negritude' and 'Indigenismo', *Caribbean Studies,* vol. 8, no. 1 (April 1968), 32. [31-55].
35. Wynter, "The Sepúlveda Syndrome and the Myth of the Cultural Void" in "Black Metamorphosis: Natives in a New World", 10, unpublished manuscript.
36. T.W. Adorno, *Negative Dialectics*, trans. E.B. Ashton (New York: Seabury Press, 1973), 22-23.
37. The being of modern man is more and more defined and graded according to his consumption patterns. Cf. Jean Baudrillard, *Pour une critique de l'économie politique du signe* (Paris: Gallimard, 1972), 38-39.

On peut penser que les objets, de par leur présence matérielle ont d'abord pour fonction de durer, d'inscrire le statut social "en dur". Ceci était vrai de la société traditionnelle, où le décor héréditaire témoignait de l'accomplissement social et à la limite de l'éternité sociale d'une situation acquise... Cette fonction d'inertie des objets, résultant en un statut durable, parfois héréditaire, est aujourd'hui combattue par celle d'avoir à signifier le changement social. A mesure qu'on s'élève dans l'échelle sociale, les objets se multiplient, se diversifient, se renouvellent. Très vite d'ailleurs, leur circulation accélérée sous le signe de la mode en vient à signifier, à donner à voir une mobilité sociale qui n'existe pas réellement. C'est déjà le sens de certains mécanismes de substitution; on change de voiture faute de pouvoir changer d'appartement. Il est plus clair encore que le renouvellement accéléré des objets compense souvent une aspiration déçue à un progrès social et culturel.

38. For U.S. Blacks, blocked in so many ways from full participation in the society, the Cadillac became a substitute for freedom. They changed their car as a mechanism of substitution for being unable to change their human status.

39. Heidegger, "What Are Poets For?" in *Poetry, Language, Thought*, 94.

40. Rarely have the effects of colonialism on the coloniser been studied. Yet the consequences must have been and still must be enormous.

41. F. Jameson, *The Prison House of Language: A Critical Account of Structuralism and Russian Formalism.* (Princeton: Princeton University Press, 1972), 30.

42. The technological power too (i.e., spells, charms) that Prospero is able to exercise over Caliban.

43. Jameson, *The Prison House of Language,* 31.

44. Marx speaks of the bourgeoisie's conviction that it owes *its* accumulation of capital to its own thrift and prudence:

Thus primitive accumulation plays in political economy about the same part as original sin in theology. Adam bit the apple and hereupon sin fell on the human race. Its origin is supposed to be explained when it is told as an anecdote of the past. In times long gone there were two sort of people; one, the diligent, intelligent and above all frugal elite; the other, lazy rascals spending their substance, and more, in riotous living. The legend of theological original sin tells us certainly how man came to be condemned to eat his bread from the sweat of his brow, but the history of economic original sin reveals to us that there are people to whom this is by no means essential. Never mind! Thus it came to pass that the former sort accumulated wealth, and the latter sort had at last nothing to sell except their own skins. And from this original sin dates the poverty of the great majority that, despite all its labour, has up to now nothing to sell but itself, and the wealth of the few that increases constantly although they have long ceased to work. Such insipid childishness is everyday preached to us in defence of property. Karl Marx, *Capital*, vol. I, chapter XXVI (London: J.M. Dent & Sons, 1930), 713-714.

It is the same kind of insipid childishness that we get in the comment by the reviewer of Wallerstein's book. Keith Thomas, "Jumbo History", *New York Review of Books* (April 17, 1975): 28

"Many economic historians will go on thinking that the real origins of capitalism were internal to Western Europe itself; and many students of underdevelopment will persist in doubting whether the vagaries of Latin American development, can all be attributed to Western exploitation."

The original virtue of the West is the cause of its own Immaculate Conception; the original sin of Latin America is the cause of its Immaculate Underdevelopment!

45. Indeed, the use of the concept of binary opposition in thought can itself be ideological as Anthony Wilden points out in *System and Structure: Essays in Communication and Exchange* (London: Tavistock Publications, 1972). In the Surrealist-related movements of Afro-Cubanism, Harlem Renaissance, the then *problems* of Western culture created an adynaton of the Other – the primitive – i.e., the black, the Indian, as concept to go in search of. Alejo Carpentier who had been involved in that exercise recanted in his novel *The Lost Steps* (*Los Pasos Perdidos* (Mexico: Compania Geneval de Ediciones, 1967), arguing that artists of his generation had gone in the search for the primitive, not realising that the artifacts, etc. of other cultures never had a primitive function for their creators, but were part of an ordered, articulated whole. It was the Crusoe/ Friday thing all over again, and remains a real danger for a conference and movement like this. Caribbean Négritude on the other hand, with Price Mars, whose research into Voodoo and Haitian folk culture attempted to come to terms with the different rationale – as Lévi-Strauss would later comprehensively do – of the Other culture in all its complexity; and the levels of irony of Césaire's famous poem *Return to My Native Land* – a finally *political* poem – come from the fact that in creating the concept of Négritude, he was contesting an implicit Western assumption of *Blanchitude* (the term is Jacques Leenhardt's) that created characteristics of its own negation in the *Negro*; so that Negritude took as much issue with this implicit concept of the *negro* as it did with the assumptions of *blanchitude*. The term itself with its abstract *-tude* took cognisance of the existence of the *black as abstract sign* rather than as *hombre de carne y hueso*.

It is here that the real danger – and the real promise of this conference – can lie. Ethnopoetics seen simply as the poetics of the Other, i.e. that which is Not the West, is transformed into the noble savage concept of *noble savage/ corrupt civilisation* binary opposition which is itself part of the set which includes as its reversal civilised man/uncivilised not-quite man. Ethno-poetics placed in its social and historical context then constitutes a contradiction. To the poetics of the dominant strata – the West – it opposes the potentially creative poetics of a non-divided society of the future, a poetics developed by the most negated of those who suffer from the Western-imposed division *men/ natives*. That is to say, a "binary opposition" which is not intrinsic to human thought (Leach) but which represents a real material split between the West and the rest of us, can only be overcome by concrete political action, to negate division. Wilden shows the cultural function of binary opposition, the way in which this is reduced to a biological explanation, and concludes "No matter what Leach intends, what he says is that all human thought, all human relationship, and all human experience are founded, in the last analysis, on opposition – which is precisely what the social ideology of the survival of the fittest also say." Wilden, *System and Structure*, 424. Wilden's book is of great importance to the thesis we are exploring. Beginning from Derrida's attack on the ideological use of binary opposition, Wilden develops Derrida's concept of the inextricable link between writing and *oral* speech, ibid., 398: "Thus it is possible for Derrida to insist that writing, in the widest sense of the trace, the-gram, or the-graph, is the logical prerequisite for speech." He then goes on: "In the cool civilisation (he uses this term to avoid the ideological use of the term "primitive" or "archaic") without writing as such, the past of the society – its memory, its set of instructions, its sacred text, is literally embodied in every domicile, in every person or group marked by a kinship term or by a taboo, in every person or group who exemplifies a ritual or who recalls a myth." One begins to understand here the function of the dance, the drum, in the black oral tradition. In religious ceremonies in the Caribbean each particular god is codified by his own rhythm which summons him to the ceremony. Rhythm, music, in the black oral tradition in the New World, embodies and will embody the writing of that society. But this "writing" is concrete, not abstract. It is learnt *only through* living. Wilden writes: "Except in so far as the group plan of the village and/or various cultural objects and implements provide a minimal objective memory for the survival of the organisation of the society from generation to generation, the significant distinctions in such a society have to be maintained, reconstructed, represented, and in essence *RE-INVENTED IN THE VERY FLESH OF EACH GENERATION.* Every living member of the system is both a message in the code and a message which maintains the code, a message which retains and remembers a part of the code." Ibid., 407. This is very relevant to my later development of the counter-poetics of the Blues and Jazz. Blues and Jazz reinvent in the context of the system of Black music, are a form of communication, communicating areas of information/feeling suppressed in the larger society.

That is to say, that we do not posit the black oral tradition (or Ethnopoetics) as the negation of what is, of the Western *literate* tradition, Western poetics. That is what was done in the primitivist movements of the Twenties. The *Other* was still seen as existing only to the extent that it revitalised Western Culture. The rationalism of the West was binarily opposed by Bergsonian intuition; and the non-West peoples were fitted on to the procrustean bed of negation. Hence Senghor's fatuous Reason is European; intuition *negro!*

Hence the Jazz Age and the vogue of the Negro. Learning our lesson, we must be careful that we do not make a later version of the same mistakes where we seek in *oral* poetics for binary opposite qualities to *revitalise* Western poetics. Rather than binary opposition what we seek in other poetics are the areas which Western poetics by its imperative of conceptualising itself in a concrete historical situation of dominance over all others, *had to eliminate.* T. W. Adorno, *Negative Dialectics.,* 8-9:

> The matters of true philosophical interest at this point in history are those in which Hegel, agreeing with tradition, expressed his

disinterest. They are *non-conceptuality, individuality,* and *particularity* – things which ever since Plato used to be dismissed as transitory and insignificant, and which Hegel labelled *lazy Existenz.* Philosophy's theme would consist of the qualities it downgrades as contingent, as a *quantité négligeable.* A matter of urgency to the concept would be what it fails to cover, what its abstractionist mechanism eliminates, what is not already a case of the concept.

Bergson and Husserl, carriers of philosophical modernism, both have innervated this idea but withdrawn from it to traditional metaphysics. Bergson, in a tour de force, created another type of cognition for non-conceptuality's sake... The hater of the rigid general concept established a cult of irrational immediacy, of sovereign freedom in the midst of unfreedom. He drafted his two cognitive modes in as dualistic an opposition to that of the Cartesian and Kantian doctrines as he thought had ever been; the casual mechanical mode, as pragmatistic knowledge, was no more affected by the intuitive one than the bourgeois establishment was by the relaxed *unself-consciousness* of those who owe their privileges to that establishment... The celebrated intuitions themselves seem rather abstract in Bergson's philosophy... Every cognition, including Bergson's own, needs the rationality he scorns, and needs it precisely at the moment of concretion.

It should be the purpose of this conference to *recover* from Other cultures the mode of rationality which does not eliminate *intuition,* but dialectically contains it. Lévi-Strauss's *The Savage Mind* (Chicago: University of Chicago Press, 1970), has been epoch-making in this regard. It was only by the most developed use of Western scientific procedure he argues that the West could grasp the mode in which 'savage' thought thought itself." Adorno, *Negative Dialectics,* 9:

> He (Bergson) did not mind that the thing he groped for, if it is not to remain a mirage, is visible solely with the equipment of cognition, by reflection upon its own means, and that it grows arbitrary in a procedure unrelated, from the start, to that of cognition.

THE EYE OF THE OTHER: IMAGES OF THE BLACK IN SPANISH LITERATURE

In his book on the Jewish Question, Sartre points out the tragic imperative of the Jew in Western civilisation, to constantly question himself and confront "that phantom person, unknown and familiar, ungraspable and yet near, that person that haunts him, and that is no other than himself as he is seen by the Other".[1] Both in his literary work and in his philosophic thought, Sartre distinguishes three modes of Being: Being-in-Itself, Being-for-Itself, and Being-for-the-Other. The first, Being-in-Itself, is the external world. The second, Being-for-Itself, is human consciousness. The third mode of Being is the being that each man has for other men. At the beginning of an acquaintance, each sees the other as a mere Being-in-Itself, as a natural phenomenon. It is through his look, his gaze, that the Other reveals himself as a Being-for-Himself.

Sartre is here basing himself on and extending the doctrine of Hegel which postulates that our self-consciousness exists only for another person. Self-consciousness is, finally, recognition on the part of the Other. Each is an object for the Other, the Other who looks and judges; each needs to obtain the recognition of his Being from the Other. The Other is the mediator between me and myself.

Hegel argued that self-consciousness is real only to the extent that it recognises its echo in another person. Sartre develops this further, arguing that if we exist for others we exist by and through their look. The look of the Other not only reveals to me that I am an Object for him, but also that the Other is a Subject.

For the eye is not only a physiological organ which looks at me; it is the other person as consciousness. Thus, the look of the Other includes all classes of judgments and valuations. To be seen by the Other means to apprehend oneself as an unknown object of unforeseen configurations. The fact of being seen changes me into a person defenceless before a liberty that is not my liberty. On being seen by other persons we are slaves. Looking at other persons we are masters.

In the novel *Invisible Man*, Ralph Ellison makes this Eye of the Other the central problematic of his work. The narrator begins his story:

> I am an invisible man... The invisibility to which I refer occurs because of
> a peculiar disposition of the eyes of those with whom I come in contact...

A matter of the construction of their inner eyes, those eyes with which they look through physical eyes upon reality.[2]

To explore certain basic aspects of the black in Spanish literature, it is necessary to view the black in the context of the "inner eye", the eye with which seventeenth-century Christian Catholic Imperial Spain looked through its physical eye upon the reality of the black Other. Even more important for this exploration is the theory of Pierre Macherey, in his book dealing with the concept of literary production, in which he develops the argument that any writer, in setting out to write a play, poem or novel, is faced with pre-existent conventions, devices, and formulae, within the limits of which, or perhaps more precisely *with* which, as his given means of *production*, he must produce his work from the raw materials of his historical experience, his given historical *situation*.[3]

Let us look quickly at the key facts of this historical situation. In the mid-fifteenth century, Europe – Portugal, to be exact – discovered Africa, and discovered her as, above all else, a source of slaves, of labour power to work on the latifundia – the large estates recaptured from the Moors, who, in 1492, after some eight centuries, had finally been driven from the Iberian Peninsula. The need of the Iberian latifundia for labour power was to determine the increasingly widespread presence of the black on the Peninsula. The black was, therefore, to be incorporated into Western civilisation, its fact and fiction, through the institution of the latifundia.

But in the mid-fifteenth century, the economic motive was still subordinate to the societal whole, at least symbolically, and the black presence was defined and categorised not in economic but in religious terms. As early as 1551, Antão Gonçalves and Nuno Tristão, both of the retinue of the Portuguese Prince Henry, the Navigator, returned from Africa with the first load of black captives. The prince was pleased at this lucrative "trade" and the chronicler who relates these "bold exploits" piously adds "that although their bodies were placed in subjection the fact was of small importance compared with the eternal freedom of their soul".[4]

The ideology by which the Christian nations of Spain and Portugal would at once pose and resolve the problem of the black as slave and the black as Christian subject was paradoxical. Indeed, the justification for enslaving not only blacks from Africa but Indians from the recently discovered New World, a justification couched in terms of exchange by which the "native" gave his material labour power in exchange for his spiritual freedom, would be central to the debate which later raged, among whose main protagonists were Las Casas and Sepúlveda. Other theologians both supported and rejected this rationalisation; one, in particular, reasoned from the tenets of Natural Law that there was nothing in the Law of Christ which stated that "the liberty of the soul must be paid for by the servitude of the body".[5]

But the ideology which provided the rationalisation won out, as the material bases – the extension of the latifundia, the discovery of the New

World, the decimation of the Indians following their widespread enslavement, the replacement of Indians by black slaves – increasingly dictated its
imperatives. In the seventeenth century, the ideology would not be altogether racial; indeed, its tenets were still partly religious, and it was a logical
extension of the practice of both Mohammedans and Christians (as well as
of Africans) of keeping prisoners captured in war as slaves. The paradox of
the situation in the seventeenth century was, however, that just as the
slavery of Western man began to disappear from Europe, it expanded in the
Iberian Peninsula and in the New World as the black was enslaved. What
has been referred to as the dialectic of freedom and unfreedom had begun.[6]

After the establishment of the slave trade by the Portuguese, the
dominant fact of black existence in Spain and Portugal was his existence not
as a black, but as a *slave*. A Spanish Capuchin missionary, Antonio de
Teruel, pointed out in a narrative that he wrote of his mission to the Congo
in the seventeenth century that the Congolese

> do not wish to be called blacks, but swarthy. Only slaves are called blacks.
> And so, as far as they are concerned, it is the same thing to say black as
> to say slave.[7]

They were all "naturally" black, they warned; they were not all "naturally"
slaves. But the warning went unheeded. Through the institution of the
latifundium in the Iberian Peninsula, and the plantation in the New World,
the black entered the Western architecture of signs conjoined as fact and
fiction – black slave. He was black (*negro*) because he was naturally a slave
(*esclavo*); he was a slave (*esclavo*) because he was naturally black (*negro*). To
be a Negro was to be a slave.

Literary images of the black predated the Portuguese discovery of Africa
in the fifteenth century. These images responded to the reality of an earlier
and established black presence. This presence was related to a reality
contrary to that created by the Portuguese African slave trade. The earlier
black presence was related to the Arab conquest of Spain in the eighth
century and the assertion of the Mohammedan faith, rule and culture on
the Peninsula.

The Mohammedan religion expanded with missionary impetus throughout northwest Africa and into the Iberian Peninsula, as the Moors, including many pure blacks, enlarged their empire. In her valuable article on the
portrayal of blacks in a Spanish medieval manuscript, Miriam DeCosta
shows that the actual historical reality of black Moors appears both in the
illuminations and the text of the thirteenth-century *Cantigas*.[8] The black
Moor is portrayed as the opposed term to the Christian religious metaphor.
Like the other Moors, he is cast in the dread role of infidel, invader and
defiler of Christian altars. The Moor, "black as pitch", was not only the
opposed religion; his colour was the opposite of "white", symbol of
Christianity. It is important to note two important aspects of this relation,
this symbolic structure. As the writer points out, the black Moor was not

"denigrated (or feared as the case may be) because of his colour, but because of his religion". Also, the relation of the black Moor, symbolically, to the Devil was a relation which sprang from a reality in which the Mohammedan was the dominant power. The "black as devil" concept sprang from an impulse which, as Lemuel Johnson points out, is similar to the twentieth-century Black Muslim definition of the dominant Westerner as a "white devil".[9] The use of symbols, in myth, religion, legend, literature has powerful consequences.

In literature, the topos by which the prevailing reality is criticised by turning its structure of symbols upside down is known as *adynaton*. This topos was traced and studied in early Western literature by Ernst R. Curtius. Indeed, Macherey's more modern insistence on the only partial autonomy of literary forms, on the fact that literary devices are never "neutral" but weighted with former accretions of significances, was prefigured by the patient reconstructions of Curtius in his book on *European Literature and the Latin Middle Ages*, even though Macherey was to put this method of investigation to somewhat different uses. Curtius, in his illuminating chapter "The World Upside Down", writes:

> The frame of the antique *adynaton* serves both as censure of the times and denunciation of the times. Out of stringing together *impossibilia* grows a topos: 'the world upside down'.[10]

The dominance of Islam in Spain was, for the Spanish Christians, the "world upside down". In Christian symbolic terms, the black Moor became the "god upside down", assimilated to the Being whose presence indicates the absence of an implicitly white Christ/God – the Devil. This play-paradox between the white Sacrament and the black skin of the Negro would later become a central literary device.

In analysing the *Cantigas*, DeCosta underscores the counter-missionary aspect of thirteenth-century Christianity. Such is the power of the Virgin Mary that she is able to rescue a black Moor from the Devil, and to convert him to Christianity. Thus, the power of Christianity is exalted by its capacity to convert its opposite (in terms of colour) to its own faith, to its own white/Christian identity. But the opposition is essentially one between Mohammedanism and Christianity. While in the *Cantigas* the image of the Moor and the black are interchangeable, the myth of Prester John, which was pervasive in the Peninsula, saw the black legendary figure as constituting a third, and separate, figure. The original legend had located Prester John in Asia, but the legend itself was one of many exotic Western myths.

Henri Baudet, in his book *Paradise on Earth: Some Thoughts on European Images of Non-European Man*, points out that Europe, originally an outpost of Asia, was a "classic invasion area open to all manner of migrations and expansion movements sweeping in from the east".[11] It was only with the Greeks, who took to the sea, that Europe developed a consciousness distinguishing Europe from Asia, the West from the East, the European from the non-European. This consciousness, which structured the inner eye with which Europe would look through its physical eyes upon the reality of the Others, was further developed by the stream of invasions and threats of invasions from the East which marked the history of Europe until well after the Renaissance. This "semi-permanent state of siege, of attack and counterattack" helped to create the "defensive mentality" with which Europe responded to the "recurrent threat of an Asiatic tidal wave that would engulf the entire continent".[11] The Mohammedan invasion of the Iberian Peninsula was part of this general movement.

Baudet goes on to point out that the Greeks shaped the European spirit by a dual opposition/orientation towards Asia – much as the "Third World" today shapes its own consciousness by a dual opposition/orientation towards Europe – and this led to a paradoxical process of hostility/inclination, rejection/ reabsorption towards the people of the outside world. This dualism was apparent in the myths and fantasies of the Greeks, who imagined archetypal peoples at the four quarters of a great inhabited land mass. They created the monster stereotype, a race of non-European monstrous people, dog-headed men with eyes in their chests. Ethiopia, which figured in these early myths, was, according to the Greeks, a land of "remote" peoples who became either objects of a Golden Age dream (i.e., Noble Savages) or threatening monsters projected by the undergrowth of the European imagination. But the Christians changed the classical image of Ethiopia (land of the Ethiopian Eunuch) to the archetype of the Christian convert. Finally, the memory of the Ethiopian Eunuch (the potential convert) came to be assimilated to the legend of Prester John; and it is this legend which functioned as a device that would be central to literature, especially to the pastoral. For it is clear that the Ethiopia of Prester John is the imagined antecedent of the *locus amoenus*, the pleasant spot, which alludes to and contradicts the real world by that which it selects, and that which it eliminates. What is eliminated in the legend of Prester John is robbery, poverty, sin, death, and the contradiction between the Christian faith, which denies the world, and the Christian State, whose raison d'être is power in the world. What was retained was saintliness, charity, hospitality, abundance, rejuvenation and the marvellous. The retention and the elimination delineated the features of a pastoral "Golden Age". Prester John, to the hard-pressed Christian world facing the real power of the Mohammedans, became a dream of Christian power, a projection of power by the relatively powerless.

In the situation of a locked and equal struggle between two variants (Christianity and Mohammedanism) of a religious truth, a third, an outsider, is imagined by one side; he is an outsider who validates the truth of the Christian side in the imagination and whose imaginary reality helps to structure the Christian's conviction of his own truth. The Christians' creation of the legend of Prester John, and Lope de Vega's creation of the Mohammedan black Prince Antiobo, who converts to Christianity and fights the Mohammedans, respond to the same impulse. The inner eye that imagined Prester John, and the inner eye of pre-Lope Iberian writers who created changing variants of the black figure in response to changing situations, would themselves set up a process of creation which would help to structure the eye of later writers. The images of the black in Hispano-European literature, although related to the stereotypes of the *esclavo* in real life, respond also to a more complex and, at times, separate process. Baudet puts this well:

> Two relations, separated but indivisible, are always apparent in the European consciousness. One is in the realm of political life in its broadest sense, in the atmosphere of... concrete relations with concrete non-European countries... The other relationship has reigned in the minds of men. Its domain is that of the imagination, of all sorts of images of non-Western peoples and worlds, which have flourished in our culture – images derived not from observation, experience, and perceptible reality but from psychological urge.[12]

The image of the black in Hispanic literature responds to the second relationship; yet, at the same time, it mediates between the second and the first; its projection of the imagined relationship is always related to the "real" relationship, and – except when, as "bad" literature, it is reduced to ideology and, as such, only reflects the myth – it at once embodies the myth and is critical of it.

If, in religious metaphor, the image of the Black Moor Devil in the *Cantigas* is opposed to the Christian Prester John of the legend, in social terms, in medieval literature, the images of the black varied from king to slave. The reality of the *prieto* was not yet reduced to esclavo, and indeed it would be only with the expansion of the capitalist mode of production that this reduction would be made. One aspect of the medieval portrayal of the black, whether as king or as slave, is the idea of the black as a marginal man, an outsider. In the mid-twelfth-century *Auto de los Reyes Magos*, King Baltasar is not described as black or Moorish, specifically. Howard Jason describes him as such, most likely bearing in mind the traditional development of medieval Christian drama based on the feast of the Epiphany and the dramatic *Officium Stellae*.[13]

Karl Young, in his study of the drama of the medieval church, points out that a description of the Magi, most likely dating from the twelfth century, describes the first king as *senex, canus*; the second as *rubicundus*; and the third, Baltasar, as *fuscus* (i.e., "dark").[14] The tradition of the *fuscus* Moorish king was in the literary tradition which developed with medieval church drama. Young shows that the tradition of the three kings was intended to prove that the Christ child was king of all the earth, of all peoples. If we assume that Baltasar, in the Spanish twelfth-century *Auto de los Reyes Magos*, responds to this tradition, then his implicit delineation as Black-Moor is seen as the extreme form of the heathen-sage, whose science must see itself superseded, yet realised, in the Child-King of the Christians. For in the *Auto*, King Baltasar is in a sense the most sceptical and the "most scientific" in a play in which doubt exists in dialectic with affirmation.

The scepticism of the black king links this image with that of the negro in one of the stories of *El Conde Lucanor* written by Don Juan Manuel in the first half of the fourteenth century. In this story, a king was deceived by three men who told him they could weave a cloth of such virtue that only legitimate sons could see the fabric. When the duped king rode naked through the streets, his pretentious subjects marvelled over his fine "robe", until

> a Negro who looked after the King's horse and *who had nothing to lose*, came to the King and told him: 'Your majesty, it doesn't matter to me whether people think me the son of that father that I say I am or the son of another; therefore, I can tell you this – either I am blind, or you are naked.'[15]

The black, who tended horses, had no possessions and, therefore, no need to worry about his lineage, since preoccupation with lineage was linked to the possession of goods, which could be inherited. He is, therefore, the perfect example of what Sartre defines as the "contingent man", the marginal man, who can be truly revolutionary because he is outside of the prevailing social structure and its concomitant ideology.

The black sees the truth because he is in an existential situation where, to borrow an Althusserian formulation, he has no need to *over see* the truth.[16] His factual existence makes it possible for him to negate the prevailing consciousness, to demystify one variant of the dominant ideology. The *negro* is the outsider, the "lump" in the social structure. The black as *sceptical* heathen Magus/King, and the black as sceptical marginal outsider (the second even more distinctively so) are the literary devices by which the writer – who exists in a dual relation to the official reality of his society (i.e., a part of it, yet marginal to it) – poses the ideology of his society as problematic. Juan Manuel's story can very well be seen as the exemplification in art of the critical comment that Althusser goes on to make:

> What art makes us *see*, and therefore gives to us… is the *ideology* from which it is born, in which it bathes, and from which it detaches itself as art, and to which it *alludes*…[16]

Baltasar questions the "science" of the revealed truth, although he finally accepts it; the *negro* contests the ideology by which the others sustain a reality in which they all have a stake. The Eye of the Other, of each, conspires in the collective fiction. The Eye of the Other, which is literature, reflects and contests the fiction. In the story, it is the black's eye which functions as the literary Eye of the Other. Thus, the legendary Prester John and the black existentially sceptical outsider emerged as literary formulae with which post-medieval Iberian literature would structure the image of the black.

With the introduction of the Portuguese slave trade in the fifteenth century, the image of the black in literature, responding to the new reality, alternated around the axis of king/slave. The image of Prester John as a powerful king fades as the reality of Ethiopia, itself relatively powerless in technological, warlike terms, dislodged the myth. The slave/king axis the post-medieval black image was first projected in Portuguese literature. Here, the black appeared in the farcical/satirical mode; that is, he was portrayed as a comic type in the low style of literature which dealt with the rustic.

By the mid-sixteenth century, the black-as-slave was a pervasive presence on the Iberian Peninsula. There are references to the Negro presence in the fifteenth-century *Cancioneiro Geral* by Garcia de Resende (c. 1470-1536), and in these presentations of the black, certain constants are already structured. One of these constants is language, the stage language, or *negroide*, which was put into the mouth of the black. In a poem by Fernam da Silveyra, written before 1485, the black appears as the King of Sierra Leone. Although a king, his language is *negroide*, a fabrication which draws on an already established linguistic stage convention. According to Frida Weber de Kurlat, this idiomatic deformation of Spanish "is deeply engrained in the medieval secular tradition that utilised the mixture of languages, primarily Latin and the vernacular language, for satiric or comic purposes…"[17]

This identification of the Negro through his use of a deformed Castilian Spanish was primary in the development of the stage Negro. This linguistic stereotype in literature was to parallel the factual stereotype of the black, even though the literary usage would carry positive elements foreign to the real stereotype. The kind of "sambo" language which defined the stage black referred to a characteristic peculiar to the black-as-slave – his use of a language, Spanish, which he learned only through the oral process and which he picked up without any formal instruction and transformed, accordingly, to his own linguistic emphases. In the factual stereotype, the black's version of Spanish was seen as evidence of an incapacity, an inability to grasp language – language seen ethnocentrically as Western language.

Stage *negroide* presents the black not only as comic, but also as uneducated. When Antiobo, the hero of the second half of *El negro del mejor amo*, is portrayed as a prince who speaks perfect Castilian, his speech is a sure sign that he is the exemplary black. Speaking of the Negro in the Caribbean, Fanon notes that, "he will be proportionately whiter – that is, he will come closer to being a real human being – in direct ratio to his mastery of the French language."[18] From the beginning, the comic Negro becomes, according to Johnson, "negatively decorative and as slightly obscene as a Gargoyle". In his valuable book on the black as metaphor in Western literature, Johnson picks out as significant in the Hispanic context the use of the stage negro linguistic convention, and compared this with the absence, in English literature, of a Negro voice. Othello, for example, does not speak in an "identifiable Negro English". This caricatured Negro voice, Johnson argues, "allows for several levels of parody… the visible physiognomical oddity, the quality of song, and the precariously dislocated Spanish in which the voice sings."[19] As we shall show, *negroide* is used for two effects: one, comic caricature, the other lyric. As with later Afro-Antillian poetry, the dialectic of lyricism/caricature fuses the reduction to the one element or the other. The lyric elements contest the caricatured elements and vice versa.

It must not be forgotten that the black presence was assimilated to the strong current of *lo popular* which was central to Hispanic literature. It was out of this tradition that Luis de Góngora, perhaps Spain's greatest poet, whose poetry achieves a superb fusion of *lo popular* and *lo culto*, wrote poems about blacks in which the caricature element is negated by the lyric intention. In one of Góngora's *letrillas*, "En la Fiesta del Santísimo Sacramento", two black women, Juana and Clara, speak. The poem is balanced between caricature and lyricism. But the truth of the situation, the black girl constituting in her person the symbol that negates the white symbolic purity of the metaphor of the Sacrament, imposes itself. The figurative language of the poem, its black/white antithesis, responds to the lyrical despair of Clara (note the name), who, in rejecting the colour black as the anti-symbol of the Sacrament, rejects herself. The tone is playful; the intention is not.[20]

The actual desire of black slaves, the dream which negates their real situation, fuses with that "promesse de bonheur" which is the imperative of all art. The caricature aspects of *negroide* are contested and redeemed by authentic lyricism, in which reality and its transposition in literature demands the use of *negroide*, not as a cultural cosmetic but as an artistic imperative. For blacks to voice their imperative of human freedom, from their actual existential situation, a literary voice has to be found for their real voice. This real voice is redeemed of its caricature elements and is transfigured.

The constant of a stereotyped language was soon matched by the established constant of the *negra* as metaphor of unbridled licentiousness and sex. Cervantes, in his account of the development of Golden Age theatre in Spain, wrote that in the time of Lope de Rueda:

> The plays were dialogues like eclogues between two or three shepherds and a shepherdess; [these plays] were pepped up and enlivened with two short pieces about a Negress, or a rogue, or a fool, or a Biscayan...[21]

Lope de Rueda uses his *negra* type to satirise the most deeply rooted obsession of Spanish society – its obsession with noble lineage. The noble lineage/honour/ *limpieza de sangre* axis was central to sixteenth- and seventeenth-century Spain. These constituted the social passion of the upwardly mobile. However, in these plays the black slave, who can have no ancestry to speak of – who is not self-aware, as was the negro in Juan Manuel's story – shares in the mania, the persistent obsession of the society, and reveals its ridiculous aspect. The comic eye of Rueda distances itself from the obsessive ideology of the time, the myth by which all Spaniards shared in the collective fiction that noble birth or pure Christian birth were the norms on which human society was built.

Another constant of the black image is the Black-as-Eunuch. Indeed, the black as sexual monster, the bad nigger, is one side of the dialectic; the black as Eunuch, or Uncle Tom, is the other. In Cervantes's exemplary novel, *El Celoso Extremeño*, the servant/slave Luis is physically a eunuch. In the portrayal of Luis, one of the constants of the black type also appears – the black's love of music. Cervantes uses this stereotype for the purpose of art. He makes Luis's relation to music central to his story. An old man, having married a very young wife, puts his eunuch slave to guard the only entrance to the house. The suitor suborns Luis with music, playing the guitar and promising to teach the Negro certain songs. In this way the young man gains entrance to the house. Cervantes had observed a real fact – the black's adherence to dance and music – and used it for artistic rather than caricature effect.[22]

The affinity of blacks for music and dance was noted by an early chronicler, who pointed out that in Seville

> Blacks were treated with great kindness, since the time of King Henry the Third, who allowed them to congregate for their dances and celebrations on holidays, so that they would be more amenable to work and would better tolerate their captivity.[23]

The same chronicler narrates how the blacks organised into *cofradías*; they took full part in the Corpus and other religious processions and customs. The fact that a *popular* religion like Iberian Catholic Christianity existed made possible the transculturation. Dance and song were transplanted; the exiled gods took up their new place behind the masks of the saints. African dance, called by one anthropologist "the liturgical technique of the body" and "one of the typically African means of sustaining a dialogue with the gods",[24] metamorphosed the gods.

The stereotype of the dancing/singing minstrel *oversaw* an important truth: the black transplanted the dance because it was a central part of the oral/ritual structure of his religious world. As time passed, and Africa and his origin became remote, the world of this symbolic universe deserted him, this universe which had defined his former being. Fragments, powerful ones, remained. But the black, like Caliban, was now exiled from his structure of meaning. Dance became disjointed from religion. But it existed as collective art, as non-alienated physical "labour", the *adynaton*, the world-upside-down of his daily reality of forced labour. The former universe as metaphor fell apart; the fragments remained, obsessive by their very disjointedness. The eye of the writer saw these fragments and used them either for art, as in Cervantes's story, or as the caricatured stereotype of ideology and the stock-characters of inferior literature.

Endnotes

Extract from *The Eye of the Other: Essays on the Black as Fictional "Other" in the Literature of Spain and Latin America*.

1.   Jean Paul Sartre, *Réflexions sur la question jüive* (Paris: Gallimard, 1946), 101.
2.   Ralph Ellison, *Invisible Man* (New York: Random House, 1952), 3.
3.   Pierre Macherey, *Pour une théorie de la production littéraire* (Paris: Maspero, 1966), 15.

4. Raymond Sayers, *The Negro in Brazilian Literature* (New York: Hispanic Institute in the United States), 15. The reference is to Azurara, the fifteenth-century chronicler of the Conquest of Guinea.

5. Bartolomé de Albornoz, "De la esclavitud", in Bibioteca Autures Españoles, vol. 65, *Obras Escogidas de Filosofos*, Adolfo de Castro ed. (Madrid: Edicionas Atlas, 1953), 233.

6. Joel Kovel, *White Racism: A Psychohistory* (New York: Pantheon Books, 1970), 15.

7. Padre Antonio de Teruel, *Descripción narrative de la misión serafica de los capuchinos, y sus progresos en el Reyno de Congo, 1663-1664*, Ms. 3533, Biblioteca Nacional, Madrid.

8. Miriam DeCosta, "The Portrayal of Blacks in a Spanish Medieval Manuscript", *Negro History Bulletin*, 37 (1974), 193-196.

9. Lemuel Johnson, *The Devil, the Gargoyle and the Buffoon: The Negro as Metaphor in Western Literature* (Port Washington, N.Y.: Kennikat Press, 1971), 176.

10. Ernst Robert Curtius, *European Literature and the Latin Middle Ages* (1953; Princeton: Princeton University Press, 1967), 96.

11. Ernest Henri Philippe Baudet, *Paradise on Earth: Some Thoughts on European Images of Non-European Man* (Westport, CT: Greenwood Press, 1965), 3-4.

12. Ibid., 6.

13. Howard M. Jason, "The Negro in Spanish Literature to the End of he Siglo de Oro", *CLA Journal*, IX, no. 2 (December, 1965), 121-131.

14. Karl Young, *The Drama of the Medieval Church*, vol. 2 (Oxford: Clarendon Press, 1962), 31. Descriptions from the twelfth-century *Collectanea et Flores* of Pseudo Beda.

15. Don Juan Manuel, *El Conde Lucanor*, Enrique Moreno Baez, ed. (Valencia: Editorial Castalia, 1962), 129.

16. Louis Althusser, *Lenin and Philosophy and Other Essays* (New York Monthly Review Press, 1971), 203.

17. Ibid.,, 222.

18. Frida Weber de Kurlat, "El tipo del negro en el teatro de Lope de Vega: tradición y creation", *Actas del Segundo de la Asociation Congreso Internacional de Hispanistas*, Instituto Español de la Universidad de Nijmega (Nijmega, Netherlands: Janssen Brothers, Ltd., for the Spanish Institute for the University of Nijmega, 1967), 695.

19. Frantz Fanon, *Black Skins White Masks*, trans. Charles Markham (New York: Grove Press, 1967), 18.

20. Lemuel Johnson, *The Devil, the Gargoyle*, 16, 69.

21. Luis de Góngora, "En la Fiesta del Santísimo Sacramento", in *Mapa de la Poesía Negra Americana*, Emilio Ballagas, ed. (Buernos Aires: Editorial Pleamar, 1946), 282-283.

22. Miguel de Cervantes Saavedra, *Comedias y Entremeses*, Tomo 1, Rodolfo Schevill y Adolfo Bonilla, eds. (Madrid: Imprenta de Bernardo Bernardo Rodríguez, 1915), 6.

23. Cervantes, "El Zeloso Extremeño" in *Novelas Exemplares*, Tomo II (Madrid: Gráficas Reunidas, 1923), 172-259.

24. Diego Ortiz de Zúñiga, *Anales ecclesiásticos y seculares de la muy noble y muy Leal Ciudad de Sevilla*, Lib. XII (1474), 374.

"WE KNOW WHERE WE'RE FROM"
THE POLITICS OF BLACK CULTURE FROM MYAL TO MARLEY

In the *historical* sense the U.S. was the setting in which the *political* implications of Black Cultures *should* have been worked out.

Harold Cruse, "The Amilcar Cabral Politico-Cultural Model"[1]

The slave-ships carried on board not only men, women and children but also their gods, beliefs and traditional folklore.

Roger Bastide, *African Civilisations in the New World*[2]

PART ONE

It was the baggage unlisted in the slave ships' logs that was to constitute the "radical difference" of the black presence in the New World. In Africa this baggage – gods, beliefs, folklore – had constituted a cultural signifying system, articulated *tribally*. With the Middle Passage diaspora this *cultural signifying system* (articulated tribally) was to be *metamorphosed*, *syncretised* and *rearticulated*. Like the syncretic religious systems that had sprung up, as the end of Classical Antiquity approached, the reconstituted syncretic system of the black Americas was to provide a cultural counter-world to the pervasive dominant world of Western rationality, whether in its Liberal-democratic *cum* capitalist or orthodox Marxist/neo-Marxist statist forms.

I therefore intend to argue in this paper that the sustained ideological conflict between the latter and the many variants of black "cultural nationalism" – a conflict to which Professor Macdonald refers in his pioneering and valuable paper, and of which the latest "clash" between the Democratic Socialist Prime Minister Manley of Jamaica and the Rastafarian reggae singer Bob Marley is an example – is logical at a deep structure level.

I make a distinction between the *surface level* and the *deep structure level* for two reasons. At the surface level, Marxist theory and praxis, as institutionalised by the Communist Party after the widespread social upheavals of the Russian Revolution of 1917, and black nationalism as an overt and increasingly universalised political force, mutually, for a while at least in the twenties, sustained and supported each other. The mass constituency on which black nationalism could always count – at least in times of crisis – provided a recruiting base for Marxist organisers bedevilled by the fact that they remained a sectarian movement in the larger complex of the normatively White and middle class American (i.e. USA) reality.

On the other hand, Marxist theory which defined "blacks" as an oppressed section of the "proletariat" gave a more "material" and thereby ostensibly more rational underpinning to black nationalism. Hence, for a while the varied comings and goings between black nationalist and Communist groupings in the twenties which Harold Cruse has documented.[3]

However at this level of mutual support, there was also a struggle for power. This struggle was waged between different branches of the newly skilled black classes for control of the burgeoning black movement. The more skilled and incorporated into the dominant structure blacks were, the more they tended to think and operate in the rational mode of Western Marxism. The exposé that Cruse makes of the paper that W.A. Domingo, a black Jamaican, submitted to a Communist group (Whites, largely) warning of the menace and threat that Negroes presented to the radical movement in the United States, is a prime example of this kind of Marxist "rationality". The reported hesitation of Huey Newton of the Black Panthers to join in the anti-Bakke coalition[4] on the grounds that Affirmative Action should not use the category of *race* but should base itself only on economic categories, is another.[5]

Against these "rational" blacks were the lumpen-skilled, the newly skilled, whose schooling was minimal and paper qualifications nonexistent. Because of their lack of formal Western schooling they were able – and Garvey would be, of course, the outstanding member of this group – to *move in the counter world of the popular cultural signifying system*. They were therefore able, Garvey in particular, to create a global black mass following who were *symbolically* articulated and organised.

It was precisely because of this *symbolic mode of articulation/organisation* that Garveyism, after the defeat of Garvey himself, was able to go underground, spreading out in secret subterranean currents all over the black diaspora, including a then colonised Black Africa itself. There, in the underground, it hooked into the central cultural traditions that had come into existence in the post-1492 world of the Caribbean and the Americas, both rooting and reinventing themselves in myriad new forms, in the wake of the first slave ships reaching *terra firma*, together with the landing, in chains, of those who had survived the ordeals of the Middle Passage. Garveyism itself had sprung from the cultural seeds of this tradition, as it had evolved over several centuries in the island of Jamaica. It is the "politics" of this tradition – from Myal to Marley – that we shall look at later in this paper. And this tradition, we hope to argue, is itself related to the powerful symbolic counterworld that was reinvented in response to the forced exodus, of the Middle Passage subjects-as-slaves, from Africa, this followed by their enforced diaspora, from the first decades of the sixteenth century onwards in the *slave labour* plantation archipelago, one that was to be instituted as the ultimate periphery of the Western World system, itself, the first such in human history.[6]

Garveyism itself was later to provide, in the above context, the cultural seedbed for later forms of black revolt including those that took apparently, the most "rational forms", e.g. independence movements in the then still colonised Caribbean territories, as well as in Black Africa. But in the United States, the antagonism between the Garveyite black nationalists and the Marxist Leninist Blacks was especially fierce and bitter. Harold Cruse has well documented this clash in his landmark book, *The Crisis of the Negro Intellectual*. Much of the polemical power of the book comes from Cruse's own rejection of the orthodox Marxist formulations of the Thirties and of *its vanguard bearers at the time, the primarily Jewish intellectual class*. Much of the critical power of the book, too, comes from the fact that Cruse's own Marxist formation gave him the methodological tools – Marx's great contribution – to critique Marxism itself as a system.

On the other hand, if the distorted biases of the book reveal the lack of a fully elaborated theoretical basis which could underpin Cruse's proposed project of cultural revolution, many of its insights and strengths come from Cruse's own secular modern version of the black nationalist tradition. Since it is this tradition with its own varying emphasis on *cultural revolution* which has faced American Marxism with concrete questions for which theoretically it had no adequate responses – forcing it either to quest beyond its orthodox limits, as in the theoretically creative case of C.L.R. James, or to hold to sectarian positions, repeating formulaic incantations in order to dismiss as mere petit-bourgeois ideology, the position from which this tradition spoke, yet of which the latter was to be only one aspect.

Cruse discusses in his book the Twenties clash between Garveyism with its mass organisation, undoubted fervour, and *Back to Africa* Program, and the Black Marxist Leninists with their implicit Program of Forward to the Dictatorship of the Proletariat. The conflict expressed itself in two significant slogans – Class First or Race First.

It is these slogans which together emphasise the aspect that I want to primarily explore in this paper, that of cultural identity and self/definition/perception. At this point, I therefore want to risk giving the concept of culture that will inform this paper. Culture is for me, *primarily, the societal machinery with which a particular society or group symbolically codes its co-identifying sense of self, with reference to which, it then acts both individually and collectively upon the world.*

The French psychoanalyst Jacques Lacan has pointed out, the links between self-definition/perception and action, as links carried out through what he calls "the Symbolic function".

> The Symbolic function presents itself as a double movement within the subject; man makes an object of his action, but only in order to restore to this action in due time its place as a grounding. In this equivocation, operating at every instinct, lies the whole process of a function in which action and knowledge alternate.[7]

He goes on to give two examples of this, the second of which, the historical example most concerns us here:

Phase One, the man who works at the level of production in our society considers himself to rank among the proletariat, phase two, in the name of belonging to it, he joins in a general strike.[8]

Orthodox Marxist theory defined and defines the identity of the black masses as belonging to the identity of the "proletariat" – a universal, international class defined by its relationship of non-ownership to the means of production, and by the wage labour form in which the wealth that it produces is expropriated by the capitalist owners of these means – the bourgeoisie. On the basis of this definition the program of action is clear. The revolutionary task of the proletariat, black and white, is to unite and fight, expropriate the expropriators, nationalise/socialise the means of production, dissolve the system of power based on the category of ownership, and install the dictatorship of the proletariat, presumably both black and white.

Cultural nationalists, on the other hand, defined themselves and perceived themselves as primarily black or Negro. This self perception is founded on the concrete fact that for a very long time, even when they were exploited along with their fellow white proletariat at the work place, they were relatively more exploited. Indeed, for a long time the white proletariat took an active part in seeing that the black proletariat were relatively more exploited than themselves.[9] Even more centrally, in his overall life situation the black proletariat experience even greater exploitation, social cultural and economic – inferior schools, housing, health care, segregation, back of the bus transportation, etc. In this *life* situation the white proletariat, exploited in the workplace, nevertheless joined and joins the ranks of the bourgeoisie, like them taking whiteness as his valued property – even lynched the black to keep him in his black place.

Thus for the cultural nationalists it was not the primacy of the mode of production nor of the black's relation of non-ownership to the mode of production that exploited him materially in his workplace, materially and psychically in his life situation. Rather it was/is the societal production and reproduction of its own hierarchical social relations, ones enacting of its own co-identifying "sense of self" in whose terms, the black was/is exploited both materially and *symbolically* as the Negative Other who grounds the general post-Civil War, post-abolition/Reconstruction American perception of itself as a "white" nation. Negated in his total life situation as black – his negation also as proletariat was only a part of his overall negation – the black nationalist saw his slogan as *Race First* and its programme one as defined by George Lamming's fictional Trumper in his novel, *In the Castle of My Skin*. A black Barbadian who had immigrated to the United States as a guest farm worker, Trumper tries, on his return home to the Caribbean island of Barbados, itself then still a colony of the British empire, to explain to his boyhood friend G., what being black in America – as distinct from being a black colonial subject of the British island of Barbados – meant. Trumper explains,

> Sometimes here (in Barbados) the whites talk 'bout the Negro people. It ain't so in the States… There they simply say the Negroes… an' sometimes this nigger or that nigger an' so on… 'Tis a tremendous difference… One single word makes a tremendous difference, that's why you can never be too sure what a word will do. I'm a nigger or a Negro an all o' us put together is niggers or Negroes. There ain't no *man* an' there ain't no *people*. Just "nigger" an' "Negro." An' little as that seem 'tis a tremendous difference. It makes a tremendous difference not to the whites but to the blacks. 'Tis the blacks who get affected by leavin' out that word *man* or *people*. That's how we learn the race. 'Tis is what a word can do. Now there ain't a black man in all America who won't get up and say I'm a negro an' I'm proud of it… I'm going to fight for the rights o' the Negro and I'll die fighting. That's what any black man in the States will say. *He ain't got time to think 'bout the rights o' Man or People or whatever you choose to call it. It's the rights of the Negro 'cause we have gone on usin' the word the others use for us, an' now we are a different kind o' creature, but we got to see first an' foremost 'bout the rights o' the Negro 'cause it's like any kind o' creature to see 'bout itself first. If the rights of man and the rights o' the Negro was the same said thing, 'twould be different, but they ain't 'cause we're a different kind o' creature. That's what a simple little word can do, and 'tis what you goin' to learn sooner or later.*[10]

It is this difference, *Negro* or *Man*, *Negro* and/or *Proletariat*, a difference of *relative position* within the social "whole", and therefore of the resultant self-definition or program for action, that Professor Macdonald also points to, in his account of the clash between the black Trinidadian activist George Padmore and the Comintern in 1934. Padmore was a communist and occupied a high position in the Comintern. As editor of the *Negro Worker*, he played the role of agitator/propagandist against the imperial powers, continuing the Leninist strategy of preparing the "colonial reserves" for action should the imperial Liberal democracies attempt to again attack the Soviet Union.

But by 1934 the growing power of Hitler and the threat of the Nazi menace, defined a more powerful enemy from the point of view of the Soviet Union's survival. Padmore who was in Morocco working with the Moroccan liberation movement, was ordered to stop all agitation in the French colonies. This was the price that the Russians had to pay in return for a mutual defence pact with France. From the point of view of the Soviet Union it was an entirely legitimate decision, and Padmore recognised it as such. In addition there was no doubt that the defeat of the Soviet Union would itself entail the delay if not defeat of the then hoped-for global socialist revolution.[11]

But Padmore, as Macdonald puts it, "marched to the cadences of a different drummer". His primary aim was "black liberation and emancipation from colonial rule". Like Tito before Titoism and Mao before Maoism, he put his own referent population's interest first and continued publishing his paper. The infighting was rough. His funds were cut off and he was expelled from the

Party, stigmatised as a petty-bourgeois nationalist deviationist.[12]

What we must note here, however, is that Padmore's choice was not a simple either/or. For long periods the program and goal of the proponents of the dictatorship of the proletariat reinforced and continues to reinforce the program and goal of black liberation and emancipation from colonial rule. The cases of Guinea-Bissau, of Angola, Mozambique, of South Africa/Azania make that clear.

This mutual reinforcement is based on the fact that Western Europe's post-medieval economic system, to which we now give the name of capitalism, had been initiated as a world-systemic one, in its then founding mercantilist form, on the basis of the also post-medieval political-statal order of the Absolute Monarchy of Western Europe's then first world empire, that of Spain. It was under the political aegis of empire, therefore, that the model that was to be defining, in Immanuel Wallerstein's terms, of the mercantilist capitalist economic system as a world-system, that is, a three-tiered interacting model, based on three different modes of labour control – i.e. wage labour in the core areas of the world-system, serf/neo-serf labour in the semi-periphery, and forced slave labour in the periphery – was to be first enacted.[13] While if in its then post-1492 social matrix New World form, this model had been instituted as that, firstly of the "core" tier of the European settler-archipelago defined by European indentured or wage labour, secondly that of the militarily con-quered Caribbean indigenous peoples in their neo-serf (or *encomienda*) labour archipelago, and ultimately, that of the transshipped enslaved Black Africans' plantation slave labour archipelago, it would be the model's imperative of maintaining the *relative* relation of degrees of non-coercion and coercion, and/or of inclusion/exclusion, that would be transferred to all areas of the eco-nomic world system. This in the wake not only of the West's further ongoing imperial expansion, and conquest of non-Western peoples, but also to all areas of both Western and Eastern Europe itself, as Wallerstein documents. What would therefore be imperative to the functioning of this model, was that of its being able to ensure, in varying forms, the almost total disposability of the three forms of labour indispensable to its functioning. This as a total dispos-ability whose iconic example, had been that of the semi-periphery indigenous peoples, firstly of the Caribbean, then of the Americas, the majority of whom, torn, after conquest, from their once multiple, auto-centred "senses of the self" and/or respective cultural signifying systems, and instead, now generi-cally classified/homogenised as "Indians" by their conquerors, had to submit to their newly imposed roles. Secondly, that of the periphery's enslaved peoples of Africa. All of whom, finding themselves enslaved, whether through conquest or through the slave trade, had also found themselves torn (even if originally slaves in Africa), from what had been their also then multiple auto-centred senses of the self (including the quite different, and multiple, mean-ings of what it was to be a slave[14]), and, instead, all now generically classified/homogenised by their slave traders and slave-owners as "Negroes".

And although in the case of Catholic, later Counter-Reformation imperial Spain, their imperialising enterprise had been backed by the Papacy, on the basis of the understanding that the latter's Absolute Monarchy would support and facilitate the Catholic Church's Christian evangelising mission, a struggle was to be waged by several outstanding Catholic missionaries, in the sacred name of their religion, against the Spanish settlers' attempt to reduce the indigenous peoples to the status of mere *encomienda* labour – a reduction that was clearly *unjust*, within the terms of Catholicism's Christian theology – with the later imperialising military expansions both of France and England into the Caribbean and the Americas, a transformation, as was to occur, if more totally so in the case of the Reformation/Protestant latter. In that, increasingly, all religious considerations vis-à-vis Indians and Negroes and their dehumanising treatment were to be swept aside. While if the successful Haitian slave revolution, itself followed by the Protestant religious movement for the abolition of Negro slavery in both England and the United States, was to lead to the slaves' freedom, their new institutionalised post-slavery role as a secondary form of low wage, lowly skilled *native* labour, was to coincide with the then new Free Trade economic system, of a now, in its bourgeois configuration, therefore, as such, a fully realised capitalism. Whose goal was now the accelerated industrial development of the productive forces, a goal that would lead it to define itself on the basis of a new realpolitik conception of human freedom. Freedom, that is, as one from all traditional ties and their related "senses of the self" which could hinder this homogenising dynamic.

Consequently, given that its expansion was now dependent on the global scope made possible by the West's continuous imperial and neo-imperial expansion, it was now to continue to transfer to all areas of the world-system, the almost total rationalisation of the use of labour power that had been initially implemented in the new-serf *encomienda*, and slave plantation archipelagoes, of the Caribbean and the Americas; thereby coming to reduce all workers-as-workers, to a *common condition of economic powerlessness*. It was to be, therefore, this shared and therefore common experience of ultimate powerlessness that would lead the normal proletariat (i.e. the "core" working class of Western Europe and Great Britain, together with those of the latter's settler extensions in the U.S., Canada, Australia, and New Zealand), to its self-perception as such. While in the case of the U.S., it was to be on the basis of this *commonality*, that the proletarian goal – *Where we are going* – and the black goal reinforce and support each other.

But the commonality is one side of the dialectic. Differentiation is the other. Capitalism's logic, especially in its now fully realised post-nineteenth century form, not only needed a global division of labour, it also needed a globally relative *hierarchisation* of labour. While given that the extraction of surplus-value on a global scale needs the mechanism of relatively unequal levels of development, this necessarily calls for the institution, in the West and its colonies for the institution and stable reproduction of societal systems, in the logic of whose core/semi-*periphery/periphery* differentiated functioning, the proletariat itself, became relatively more or less exploited, materially and psychically.

Colonialism – in its nineteenth-century form, like Jim Crow legislation in the United States after the end of Negro slavery – was the post-slavery form of the imposition of this hierarchisation of, in Marxian terms, the social relations of production. It therefore ensured that the productive system of the colonial countries played the part necessary to the smooth functioning of the "whole" (i.e. world-systemic) economic system, thereby enabling the *whole* to respond to the hegemonic ruling class needs of the bourgeoisie: of, at first, the needs, therefore in Wallerstein's terms, the *core* countries. While since the proletariat of these countries were *nationally* coded, with respect to the "symbolic function" of their "sense of self," they had come to perceive themselves, once they had been politically enfranchised, as being in bourgeois specific terms, primarily *national* subjects, in a relation of opposition to other nations, and their respective proletariats. This as a self-perception, which empowered them to be able to share, however unequally, in the proceeds from the relatively greater exploitation of the periphery's, post-slavery "native labour" proletariat, at the same time as they themselves continue to be exploited materially and symbolically by their own respective capital accumulating bourgeoisies.[15]

In the colonies and their respective "Mother" countries, the contradiction was expressed as between the politically enfranchised, normative workers at the centre, and the colonised, politically disenfranchised, or "cheap" low wage, lowly skilled native labour in the periphery. The difference was expressed not only materially in the relative difference/size of the historical basket of goods that each obtained in return for the expenditure of their labour power. It was also expressed at the level of the psyche, in the pre-ascribed degrees of relative self-valuation, self-perception, self-worth as human beings, that each category was allowed to have, as the condition of the stable reproduction of the overall world system. And where orthodox Marxism was to see the former as *the* site of political struggle, *given that as an emancipatory theory, it had been developed from the perspective* of the core, from the perspective of the periphery of the ex-slave archipelago of the post-1492 Caribbean and the Americas on the other hand, both aspects of the overall struggle are necessarily inextricably linked, with this linkage coming to be expressed in the variant forms of "cultural nationalisms".

Thus in the case of George Lamming's character Trumper, his awakening to this new form of struggle, when leaving his British island colony of Barbados – as a colony in which the polar differentiation of the overall hierarchy of the order is enacted between, on the one hand, the English colonisers who, self-classified as "English", staff the imperial bureaucratic/military administration, together with the "Creole" descendants of the original English settlers and slave-owners (and who, although a minority had continued to exercise financial-economic as well as cultural-educational hegemony) and, on the other, their colonised "native subjects", the "Negro people"; with this thereby enabling the empirically actualised racial hierarchy to be enacted and to be experienced by both sides *only implicitly* – he arrives in the United States. There he experienced a different reality, one in which "there ain't no man an' there ain't no people. Just nigger an' Negro."[16]

For in the United States, that major region of the ex-slave archipelago, where "core" and "periphery" were to be sited in the same politically inde-pendent ex-settler nation-state, the hierarchical status differentiation, had overtly enacted itself in the polar categories of *White/Black, Man/Negro*, at both the intra-worker class level as well as at all others. This given that, in the wake both of the abolition of slavery and the failed attempt at Reconstruction, the social structures of the nation as well as of its overall cultural signification system – in the terms of whose "inner eyes", as the narrator of Ralph Ellison's *Invisible Man* points out, "we look with our physical eyes upon reality"[17] – had come to depend, for their dynamic articulation, one now incorporating of both the post-Civil War North and South, and stable reproduction, upon a single a priori. That of the invisibility of the *negro* as *man* (indeed as *woman*); in both cases, therefore, with no claim, as members of the same population, to the "rights o' Man", rights then exclusive to the White (i.e. European, if optimally, middle class) U.S. population. Hence the logic of Lamming's Trumper's variant of the Black cultural nationalist struggle as one based on his claim to the "rights o' the Negro" as a "different sort o' creature"; the same logic therefore as that shown by Ralph Ellison by his portrayal of Ras – in his novel, *Invisible Man* – as the fictional depiction of the real-life Marcus Garvey's own, once powerful and globally widespread variant of the same claim, of its countering "sense of self."[18]

However, in both the Caribbean and the United States, a mutation was to occur. This is that, in the wake respectively of, in the first case, the anti-colonial struggles – which erupted in the British Caribbean colonies in the late Thirties, as struggles that were to be themselves initiated, both by the "native"/labour uprisings which took place on the sugar plantation estates, as well as by the marginal "casual" labour in the cities – had led to these colonies gaining of political independence, together with their institutionalisation, in primarily bourgeois or middle-class terms as new nations on the basis of a now "*national*" (rather than "*native*") "sense of self". While in the case of the second, in the wake of the anti-segregation, Black Civil Rights movement for, *inter alia*, their political enfranchisement, as a population, the success of both struggles were to have parallel outcomes. Seeing that in the latter case, if the outcome was to be the assimilating incorporation of the former peripheral middle class of the Black population into the "core" normative structures of white U.S. middle-class society, in its case as well as of the Caribbean's now ex-colonies, a far-reaching paradox was to emerge. This was that a substantial majority of their respective post-slavery, lowly skilled "native labour" and/or "negro labour" workforce were to find themselves, after several centuries, in a no-way-out situation. One in which what had once been their respective post-slavery "native" or "negro" labour, seasonal or semi-jobless subordinate status, as a status to which, before the anti-colonial and Civil Rights struggles they had had to become, however, despairingly, accustomed – indeed the latter as the then situation, out of, and in response to which, the Rastafarian movement, in its original form, and partly modelling itself on the earlier Garvey movement, had arisen in Jamaica – had taken a different turn. A turn which, in the case of the now post-colonial ex-British Caribbean colonies, the very processes of modernising economic development initiated by the new national governments, and in that of the second, the very nature of the incorporation of the Black population, hegemonically, of its middle classes, into a now consumer-driven and, as in the case of the first, increasingly automated, full-fledgedly techno-industrial economic system, had set afoot a new form of intra-worker status differentiation.

One no longer, in the case of the first, as it had earlier been, between the workers of the "core" countries, and those of the periphery of the world system, and in the case of the second, between the "core" white workers of the nation, and the then largely segregated periphery "negro" workers, but now instead, and increasingly so, more sharply between the internal sectors both of the post-colonial nations and the post-Civil Rights U.S. population. In both cases therefore, between what was to become the minority modernised elite of highly and/or technologically skilled, workers, now fully integrated into the normative status of the "core" labour cadres, on the one hand, and on the other, the remainder mass sector of the largely lowly-unskilled "native"/"negro" *cum* casual labour, school dropout category. All of whom had now come to find themselves redundant in the context both of their national, as well as of the overall world-systemic labour market, in an increasingly automated "workplace". Relegated, thereby, to their criminalised, impoverished "inner city ghettoes", together with the latter's prison extensions, as a permanent underclass mired in techno-industrially "expendable" as so much human "waste product". It was in this post-colonial context, that in the Caribbean, the Rastafarian movement, as its message came to be globally iconised in the Reggae singer Bob Marley, as well as in many others, would initiate a new form of the struggle. One in which the struggle with respect to the "symbolic function" – as now, in their case, the imperatively uncompromising struggle against their new ultimate negations as so much techno-industrial "refuse" – this by the logic of our present macro-economic system in its now planetarily extended, consumer-driven, and, increasingly *technologically automated* phase – not only remains, inextricably linked to Marxism's ongoing dedicated struggle, with respect to the, so to speak, material function", i.e., that is, its relentless struggle against the above's specific mode of material provisioning which the terms of that "function" now world-systemically dictates. But, in addition, because in Bob Marley and the Rastafarians unique *periphery/underside cum liminally deviant* case, *the* imperative, is necessarily that of the recoding of the "symbolic function", in now *humanly* revalorising terms, hegemonically so linked.

PART TWO

What liberates is the knowledge of who we were, what we became; where we were, whereunto we have been thrown; whereto we speed, wherefrom we are redeemed; what birth is and what rebirth.

Hans Jonas, *The Gnostic Religion: The Message of the Alien God and the Beginnings of Christianity*[19]

During the election campaign last December Michael Manley's campaign slogan was "We know where we're going." Shortly afterwards, Marley wrote "Exodus" and the Rastafarian brethren believe the song was the appropriate reply to Manley's assertion. "Open your eyes and look within," Marley wrote. "Are you satisfied with the life you're living? We know where we're going. We know where we're from. We're leaving Babylon into our father's land."

Jon Bradshaw, "The Reggae Way to Salvation"[21]

I have been referring to the conflict between orthodox Marxism and different varieties of cultural nationalism. Let me define the first term. By the term "orthodox Marxism", I mean Marxist thought as it has been officially institutionalised to legitimate and justify, *inter alia*, the post-colonial rise of a newly ascendant class – the highly educated, highly skilled, bureaucratic-technocratic bourgeoisie whose raison d'être lies in State control, and therefore, political hegemony over, if to varying degrees, the economic system. However, the model of orthodoxy, the Soviet Union, had itself undergone a widespread social upheaval in which the traditional hierarchies had been transformed by the actions of the people themselves – an-archically (from below). As a result, the material conditions for a large sector of the broad masses had been almost miraculously improved by the rationalisation, based on the nationalisation of the economic system, of the apparatus of redistribution now controlled by the Party-State; and therefore by the fact that the moral justification of the new techno-bureaucratic power structure rested on its implicit contract to deliver the material goods to the masses.

In the case of the anti-colonial struggles, which had taken place in the then British imperial Caribbean colonies, however, the overwhelming reality of our then colonised situation, had led to the multifaceted nature of the "native"/casual labour uprisings and overall social upheavals, coming to be channelled externally by the majority of each colony's respective Western-educated elites towards the hegemonic goal of mass enfranchisement and political independence as new nation-states. With the result that when variants of orthodox Marxism's model began to be adopted by some political leaders – this in urgent response to the fact that after political independence, they had come to find themselves/ourselves economically reclassified, and as such reinstituted in the structural hierarchies of the Western world economic system of Free Market capitalism, as "underdeveloped" Third World nations – these variant models were being adopted in countries where no popular social revolution, conceptualised and fought for as such, had taken place internally, as it had done in the Soviet Union. As a result, such forms, together with their doctrines, were to be implemented in the ex-colonial countries by leaders whose goal was to initiate such revolution from above – *hierarchically* – through bureaucratic electoral coups. This has been the recent case with the Caribbean island of Jamaica from which both Manley and Marley come. Manley has called his diluted variety of orthodox Marxism – *Democratic Socialism*. To the "democratic socialism" of Manley based on his interpretation of the "bible" of orthodox Marxism, Marley opposes Rastafarianism, based, if only partly so, on the Rastafarian "version" or interpretation of the Judeo-Christian Bible.

What is Rastafarianism? It is one of the latest variants of Ethiopianism, a movement which Professor St. Clair Drake analyses in a recent monograph. He points out the significance of *Ethiopia* for blacks all over the diaspora. In 1896, St. Clair Drake writes, the warriors of, "an indisputably black ruler [of Ethiopia], ...shattered an Italian invading army in these mountains and sent waves of pride coursing throughout the black world... Menelik II vindicated The Race by defeating a white nation on the battlefield."[21] In 1930, the descendant of Menelik, Haile Selassie was crowned King of Ethiopia, his coronation portrait disseminated by newspapers all over the world. His photograph was to play a central role in the *imaginative architecture* of Ras Tafarianism.

In the world of the 1930s, the effects of the 1929 depression were beginning to be felt. None felt them more than the shantytown dwellers, the large marginal masses disrupted from the rural areas into the towns, masses who were now redundant to the productive processes of capital, masses who were economically and socially powerless. Even more, in the dominant symbolic order of the Western world system, Blacks occupied a place at the *very bottom of that unequal valuation of social being which was centrally logical to the rational processes* of its economic system of capitalism. To these largely lowly and/or unskilled black masses of the world systemic periphery, negated as *the sons of no one*, and identified as such by the mark of their black skins, the visible evidence of the power and majesty of Haile Selassie was overwhelming. Together with Ethiopia, Haile Selassie with his titles and royal lineage, King of Kings, Elect of God, conquering Lion of Judah, Power of the Holy Trinity, 225th Emperor on the throne of the 3,000 years line of Solomon and the Queen of Sheba – came to constitute the central cultural unit, in that reinvention of the self with which blacks in the diaspora would continue their subversion of the dominant system which had negated them. Haile Selassie became the Symbolic Father in a counter Symbolic order.

St. Clair Drake, in his monograph also touched on the Rastafarian phenomenon out of which Marley comes:

> The name of Ethiopia still has the power to move black men. Thousands of Ras Tafarians in the slums of Jamaica have separated themselves among from their fellows and dream of the day when *their* God King, *Ras Tafari*, Haile Selassie will send his ships to take them home.[22]

I shall use Jon Bradshaw's account of the Ras Tafarian cult in the *New York Times* article to give a brief idea of the movement today. Bradshaw writes:

> For nearly 50 years the Rastafarians have been feared and persecuted in Jamaica. They have been accused of being rabble-rousers, layabouts or dealers in the lucrative ganja trade. But what began as a small, rural religious cult has now become a *popular movement*. By some estimates, there may be some 20,000 Rastas in Jamaica and nearly as many among the 400,000 Jamaicans in New York City.[23]

Bradshaw goes on to say that the Rastafarian movement was started by Marcus Garvey. This was not *factually* so. But Garvey's movement – The Universal Negro Improvement Association founded in the Twenties is recognised by Rastafarians as the precursor to their movement. And his "Back to Africa" slogan was the precursor matrix of the Rastafarian's constitution of Zion, in the wake of their movement's founding in the early Thirties after the appearance of the photograph of Haile Selassie. Hailed as the *living God* Jah – as opposed to the dead God, Jesus – he became the integrating sacred icon for the three men who started the movement with three groups, thereby initiating the *decentralised* structure of Rastafarianism.

The most famous of the three Rastafarian founders was Leonard Howell who paid the price of several years in prison for his refusal to pay "King George's taxes" – Jamaica was then still a British colony. At his trial Howell explained to the judge the reasons for his refusal. Howell argued that he was not King George's subject, as he was the subject of another King, he and his Rastafarian brethren. Hence he told the brethren not to pay taxes on the grounds of *who* they were and he said, "I told them that our King had come to redeem them home to our Motherland, Africa."[24]

Years before the nationalist movement spearheaded by the middle class would begin in Jamaica, therefore, Howell was here rejecting the political identity coded for him in the cosmos of the British Empire as a "native" subject. To the actual and symbolic elements that articulated the "British Subject" he counterposed a counter-signifying system in which his King and *Africa*, his Motherland, are legitimated as the one as his 'true' God/King, the latter as his "true" symbolic home, and Jamaica – the British colony – delegitimated as "exile in Babylon". While this latter would be central to the overall versions of cultural Pan-Africanism initiated and sustained by the black popular masses of the post-Middle Passage Caribbean and the Americas.

It is at this point that I would like to make an explicit parallel with the great Gnostic heresies that helped structure the spiritual and imaginative revolutions, including centrally that of Christianity, which were to transform the psychic structures of large masses of people and hasten the end of Classical antiquity and its long dominant symbolic order.

As Hans Jonas explains:

At the beginning of the Christian era and progressively throughout the two following centuries, the eastern Mediterranean was in profound spiritual ferment. The genesis of Christianity *itself and the response to its message* are evidence of this ferment but they do not stand alone... In the thought of the manifold *gnostic* sects which soon began to spring up everywhere in the wake of the Christian expansion, the spiritual crisis of the age found its boldest expression and, as it were, its extremist representation.[25]

Jonas goes on to point out that the Gnostic religion, like other religions of its time, was a religion of salvation. And one of the central points of comparison for us is his analysis of the word "gnosis" itself:

The *name* "Gnosticism", which has come to serve as collective heading for a manifoldness of sectarian doctrines appearing within and around Christianity during its critical first centuries, is derived from *gnosis*, the Greek word for "knowledge". The emphasis on knowledge as the means for the attainment of salvation, or even as the form of salvation itself, and the claim to the possession of this knowledge in one's own articulate doctrine are common features of the numerous sects in which the gnostic movement historically expressed itself.[26]

Jonas then goes on to point out how very different the Gnostic type of knowledge was from the idea of *rational theory* in the terms of which Greek philosophy had developed the concept. As he explains:

The ultimate "object" of gnosis is God: its event in the soul transforms the knower himself by making him a partaker in the divine existence (which means more than assimilating him to the divine existence). Thus... the "knowledge" is not only an instrument of salvation but itself the very form in which the goal of salvation, i.e. ultimate perfection is possessed... here [in this form of knowledge] the subject is "transformed"... by the union with a reality that in truth is itself the supreme subject in the situation and strictly speaking never an object at all.[27]

Howell, "knowing" this reality of the Rastafarian God, is transformed as subject, not only politically but far more symbolically. Foucault has pointed out, in this context, the relation between the individual psyche and the overall social/cultural structure. He argues that ethnology and psychology, "have only one point in common, but it is an essential and inevitable one: the one in which... they interact at right angles; for the signifying 'chain' by which the individual is constituted is perpendicular to the formal system on the basis of which the significations of a culture are constituted..."[28]

What I want us to note here, is the way in which the *rejection* of the dominant formal system and its significations is central to the mechanism of self-transformation – i.e., to the transformation of the signifying chain by which the self is constituted. What we see here at work is a counter-signification of the self/formal system in which elements of the opposed self/formal system still enter, but as elements that are now delegitimated. In being a Rastafarian, the subject of *His King*, Howell is no longer *King George's subject*. His new identity is constituted by his brotherhood in a group, now constituted as counter-world. The parallels with Garveyism and the Black Muslims of the U.S. are clear.

The counter-world therefore invents and structures its own symbolic order as a counter to that of the dominant society. The new symbolic order is based, therefore, on the acceptance of certain tenets. Bradshaw summarises these:

> Today, Rastafarians differ among themselves on specific dogma, but generally they believe they are black Hebrews exiled in *Babylon*, the true Israelites, that Haile Selassie is the direct descendant of Solomon and Sheba and that God is *black*. Most white men, they believe have been worshipping a *dead god* and have attempted to teach the blacks to do likewise. They believe that the Bible was distorted by King James 1ˢᵗ, the *black race sinned and was punished by god with slavery and conquest. They see Ethiopia as Zion, the Western World as Babylon*. They believe that one day they will be repatriated to Zion and that Armageddon is now. They preach peace, love and reconciliation among the races, but also warn of imminent dread judgment on the downpressors.[29]

As King George's subject is counterposed by the Rastafarian identity, so is Babylon by Zion. While as Hanns-Albert Steger has seminally pointed out, the Gnostic syncretic systems and New World black syncretic systems like vodou, are both systems related to, and arising in opposition to economic systems based on slavery. As he writes,

> ...in both cases it was precisely the slaves who – carrying with them their original religiosity, shatter, or at least begin to question the solid traditional culture of their masters.[30]

He goes on to point out that the concept of the *Kosmos*, the universe, was for the Greeks of the classical epoch, equal in meaning to the plenitude of existence, and was therefore a positively and highly valued element. The cosmos, he argues, was for the classical age a reflection of the *polis*, the original political system now translated into much larger structures. For the Gnostics, this view was turned upside down. As Steger writes:

> ...*cosmos* comes to be negative, disdained. It is a universe punished oppressed and dominated by transcosmic powers whom it has rebelled against and whom it has betrayed.[31]

The cosmos has become Babylon. The program then is clear – withdrawal and separation from Babylon, from this cosmos created by inferior powers, which is like a vast prison. But for the Gnostics, man, whilst his body and soul are created by the lower powers, has still within him a spark of the divine spirit which has fallen from the beyond into the cosmos. The lower powers have created the cosmos (Babylon), to keep the spirit captive here. Jonas puts it, "The goal of Gnostic man's striving is the release of the 'inner man' from the bonds of the world (Babylon) and his return to his native land (Zion)".[33] But it is ignorance that entraps him here, ignorance of his origins (*We know where we are from*, sings Marley). In order for him to escape, "...it is necessary that he knows about the transmundane God and about himself, that is, about his divine origin as well as his present situation, and accordingly also about the nature of the world which determines this situation."[33]

The words of the Marley song quoted by Bradshaw and the famous Gnostic formula coincide. Both "know" of their glorious origins in the Beyond, in Zion; of why they were fallen, of how they have been reborn. Having been reborn they acknowledge their *true self* – as the SONS OF JAH – know what their programme is. We know where we are going/We know where we are from/ who we were, what we became, whereto we speed, wherefrom we are redeemed. The "knowledge" prescribes the behaviour. As Bradshaw summarises, "They don't vote, tend to be vegetarians, abhor alcohol, and wear their hair in long uncombed plaits called dreadlocks or natty dread; the hair is never cut since it is part of the spirit and should neither be combed out nor cut off."[34]

Like the Gnostics, the Rastafarians achieve an unyoking from the dominant world and its symbolic order. The *counter-symbolic order that they create goes far beyond a simple inversion of terms. Rather there is a displacement, a change of signs.* The long uncombed locks become a sign of the symbolic pact they make with their God. It is this symbolic pact that guarantees their new identity. The basic distinction of this identity is shifted from the binary opposition of black/white. Rather it is between the *heathens* and the Sons of Jah – i.e., those who have awoken from their ignorance, who have come to realise that their life on this earth in Babylon is a life of exile, that they are strange – "just passing through", says Marley – that as the Gnostics phrased it, they are aliens here. Their true origin, their true identity – where they are from – is different. Hence their goal – the *where* they are going, is logically different.

Black hair, black skin is revalued as a sign, not an index.[35] One can have a black skin and be an "heathen." One can have a "white skin" and have a "black" heart; i.e., awaken to a knowledge of self as the Sons of Jah, and as such cease to perceive the self as "white."[36]

A new symbolic order and semantic field displaces the hierarchy of the dominant world systemic bourgeois order in which "whiteness" – like "noble blood" for the feudal nobles – has come to constitute a mass-privileged self perception. It is this antithetical privilege/disprivilege of self perception for which, if in religious terms, the Protestants in Belfast – vis-à-vis the Catholics – and the Catholics in South Boston (white) – vis-à-vis the blacks – fight. For which whites lynched blacks. For which Bakke supporters claim legal justification. The obdurate Fascist policies of the white Rhodesians and the white South Africans – inevitably in the long run, self-destructive from a purely material point of view – are driven by the imperative of protecting this privilege, the surplus value of the self which constitutes their very being.

It is this privileged self perception, in its racialised form, this pathology of *whiteness* as the alleged bio-evolutionarily selected/eugenic attribute of the bourgeois norm of being human, to which Marley addresses himself when, as Bradshaw writes:

Marley breaks into 'War', a speech of Haile Selassie's he set to music. It is like an invocation. 'Until the philosophy which holds one race superior and another inferior is finally and permanently discredited and abandoned, everywhere is war...,' he chants ... 'Until the colour of a man's skin is of no more significance than the color of his eyes, there will be war, everywhere war,' he sings and all those clean and fresh-faced kids who wouldn't know the difference between an Ingram M-10 and a machete scream and throw their fists in the air.[37]

But Marley's weapon is his song. Like the Gnostic creed, his song begins the widespread subversion of the signifying chain that constitutes our now hegemonically institutionalised normative respective psyches – white and black – functional to the dominant order.

To understand the power of symbolic subversion that is at work here in the Ras Tafarian doctrine – and behind this doctrine, in the range of the constituted counter-cultures of the Black Americas – we must understand the role that the white/black division plays in the Symbolic Order of Western civilisation. As Baudrillard points out:

No other culture besides ours has produced the systematic distinction of Black and White. And this distinction applies not as an afterthought but as a structural element which is reproduced even more dynamically today under the appearances of a flattering liberalism. And the objectification of the Black as such *is not that of exploited labour power, but an objectification by the code*.[38]

It is this objectification by the code specific to the matrix of the cultural signifying system of a then imperially expanding Western Europe that the seventeenth-century Congolese protested against when they told a Spanish Capuchin missionary, "Do not call us *Negros*, Negros are slaves. Call us *prietos* (Black)".[40] The semantic field related to the Congolese social order made a distinction between a black slave (Negro) and being black (*prieto*). In their social order, a slave had a social status and clearly defined roles. *He was not conceptualised as labour power for a mode of production,* because as Baudrillard also points out, the concept *mode of production*, did not exist in societies like those, for whom the Western paradigm of *production* would have been meaningless.[40]

Being black, for the then autocentric Congolese, therefore, one could be a slave, but one could also be, because freeborn, a king, an artist, a priest, a warrior, a hunter. One was not circumscribed to one social role – that of being a Negro/a slave, i.e., labour-power. However, in the Western semantic field and its corresponding social order, the word "Negro" was to be initiated at the beginning of Western modernity as the brand name for labour power in its *pure commodity* (i.e. *slave*) *form*. When Marley, therefore, entitles his contemporary song "Exodus", the power of the symbol comes not only from its biblical association of Exodus with exile, but also from the specific historical event, the actual referent that haunts the New World Black imagination at the deepest levels. This Exodus was the empirical event of the forced Middle Passage

Exodus, i.e., the West's purchase, transportation, and sale of innumerable interchangeable units of labour power from Africa, in order to provide the labour force for the first New World mass production units of the plantation system, based on *negro* (man)/*negra* (woman) slave labour.

The slaves were bought and sold as *piezas* – pieces, in a long-established rational quantified system which took the norm of productive labour power a man of about twenty-five, of certain height, good teeth, etc., as a standard of measurement with which to calculate profit and loss, with respect to their largely manual labour, productive value. Two or three teenagers would make up one *pieza*, several old slaves – above forty who were seen as "refuse" once their productive capacity had lessened with age – also made up one. *What I want to note here is that the* pieza/negro *was, at the beginning of modernity, the first and most total example of the reduction of the creative possibilities of the human men, women, and children to one single possibility – man/woman/children as producers. It is this reduction of the human Being from the totality of our possibilities that has come to define the now fully realised form of capitalist rationality;* while this form of rationality is itself only possible within the terms of the overall paradigm of production.

As Baudrillard argues, it was the bourgeois development of productivity itself that enabled the concept of production "to appear as man's movement and generic end".[42] In other words, the "*Negro/Negra*" whether labelled a *Mina negro* and/or *negra* and shipped from the Portuguese factory at Elmina, exactly like a Sears product, at the very origin of our present world-system, or labelled today as a discardable "waste product", or as the now expendable shantytown, inner-city ghetto or *favela* "refuse", is the expression of a historical trajectory, itself one only enactable in the hegemonic context of the central paradigm of production, of whose conceptualisation/institution the mechanised intensive labour, from sun-up to sundown, of the original *Mina negro/negra* would have laid the basis. Baudrillard continues:

> In other words, the system of political economy does not produce only the individual as labour power that is sold and exchanged: it produces *the very conception of labour power as the fundamental human potential.* More deeply than the fiction of the individual freely selling his labour power in the market, the system is rooted in the identification of the individual with his labour power and with *his act of transforming nature according to human ends.* In work, man is not only quantitatively exploited as a productive force by the system of capitalist political economy *but is also metaphysically overdetermined as a producer* by the code of political economy. In the last instance the system rationalises its power here. And in this Marxism assists the power of capital. It convinces men that they are alienated by the sale of their labour power, thus that they are censoring *the much more radical hypothesis that they might be alienated as labour power,* as the *'inalienable' power of creating value by their labour.*[42]

What Baudrillard develops here is the concept that the worker, white or black, who accepts his definition/identity as "proletariat" is at once circumscribed in his role as *only producer.* The *identity* as *producer* then prescribes the program, *the to where we are going* – *and* this goal is to produce. Even when fighting for his/her rights, the proletariat and/or Negro/Negra legitimated the context and the code by which s/he is defined as proletariat/Negro/Negra. The Marxian priority of the liberation of the productive forces, therefore, replaces that of the self-liberation of man into his royal human status. The "new man" of Marxism is to appear *after* the development of the productive forces – the "where we are going" therefore – replaces what would be, alternatively, in Baudrillard's terms, human self-liberation from their/our alienated self-conception as being merely labour power for the "productive forces" of the economic system. This given that in the context of the latter's now hegemonic superordinate telos, the promised "new Man" is to appear only *after* the fully realised development of the productive forces; thereby, as both function and effect of the latter's realisation, rather than of his own.

Yet it is precisely their royal human status to which the Rastafarians lay claim when they define themselves as the Sons of Jah; when their symbolic exodus is set in motion out of Babylon – out of the paradigm of production – into their "father's land". While they are able to arrive at this far more radical subversion by the very nature of their concrete *non-place*, as an ostensibly "waste-product" or "human refuse" in the increasingly globalised system of production. Nevertheless, for orthodox Marxists, Rastafarianism is merely the ideology of the *lumpen* proletariat, this as a category whose only function is the negative one of serving as the "reserve army of labour" whose availability for occasional employment, enables the capitalist employer to put a cap on the wages of the "normal" proletariat.[43] So that, for Western and westernised Marxists, the label *lumpen* can be used to dismiss the phenomenon of the total *qualitative* exploitation of millions of marginal masses whose labour is now, increasingly, no longer needed, as the productive force shift to capital intensive technology based on a knowledge economy; and permanent, semi-permanent unemployment becomes institutionalised, massively so, in the New World systemic periphery of the post-colonial Third world nations.

In spite of the above, however, orthodox Marxism still clings to the purely *quantitative* model of exploiting – i.e. the *amount* of surplus value extracted from the wage labourer. It refuses to see that the quantitative exploitation of labour power can have been only accomplished on the basis of a concomitantly *qualitative* change in the social relations of society – and thereby in the self-perception of the members of that society; as the change would have then been able to induce the worker, the peasant, etc., to come to accept himself as members of the "proletariat", as it had earlier induced the *prieto* to see himself as *negro*, i.e., as productive units whose aim is only to produce. However, a fundamental difference needs to be recognised here. Which is that whilst the core workers, to use Immanuel Wallerstein's world-systemic theory, whose labour power was primarily extracted through the wage-labour form, if in varying modalities, including that of indentured labour in the Euro-settler

Caribbean and the Americas – were controlled ideologically in their enclosed self-perception, the plantation periphery workers whose labour power, from the sixteenth-century origin of that system, was primarily to be extracted by physical force, had to be *seasoned*. The African had *first to be broken into the acceptance of his identity as a born-to-be-a-slave*, *Negro*, i.e., as productive labour and nothing but productive labour.

Frederick Douglass's account of his breaking in by a professional "nigger-breaker" – the very Christian Mr. Covey, should therefore be taken as the concrete example of the ideological seasoning process by which all members of the *"negro/negra"* proletariat would be brought to accept their reduction from any possibility of *"prieto/prieta"* status, i.e. born as a Black human being, with all its possibilities, to being *"negro/negra"* (being born *to be* a slave, male and female because born Black). In this account, Douglass shows how the then society, in order to institutionalise the need for the slave's second sense of self, had kept the slave from learning to read. Yet it was to be his learning to read, Douglass further shows, that started his self-liberation from accepting himself as a *slave-by-nature*. He then shows how, before he *physically* dominated Mr. Covey, in their almost-to-the-death-struggle in which he had been prepared to die, he had led a brutish, weary, exhausted existence, with all his faculties deadened. In other words, he had been *seasoned*, into being born to be a slave until he initiated with prepared-to-die rebellious force his *counter-seasoning* of the self.[44]

In this context, it can be said that Douglass and the other innumerable *piezas* of the plantation archipelago did not only serve the purpose of providing surplus-value through their super-exploited labour-power. Instead, the paradigm of production needed *Negros* and *Negras* not only to work with, but ideologically to symbolise with; needed the category *Negro/Negra* not only as empirical facts but as a symbolic cultural unit – that is, as the embodiment of *symbolic death*[45] to Mr. Covey's self-conception, in both individual and group terms, as the incarnation of symbolic *life*, i.e. as *by nature* free men and women, *because* born White. Baudrillard, in discussing the coding of Black/White in Western culture in the same context, points out that:

> One can easily verify that it is sustained by a whole arsenal of significations *irreducible to economic and political determinations.* [...] In this doctrinaire confusion there is a mystification of Marxist thought which, by *circumscribing the economy as the fundamental determination,* allows mental, sexual and cultural structures to operate efficaciously.[46]

PART THREE

From the "acceptable merchandise"/"almost another species" imposed sense of self of the Slave Plantation Cosmos to "Expendable Refuse" in that of the Contemporary Techno-Industrial Cosmos, their Respective "Arsenals of Significations": Marley, Manley, and the Symbolic Function

The functioning of the post-1492, *Negro/Negra* slave Plantation order or cosmos validates Baudrillard's thesis. For while that order depended for its stable reproduction, as a structure of domination, on the repressive forces of the state in the last instance, this repressive force was aided in the daily run of things by the "mental, sexual, and cultural structures", new variants of which are still active in the stable reproduction of today's world. While Edward Long, an English settler and planter-historian of late eighteenth-century Jamaica, a man of the Enlightenment, an admirer of Voltaire, whom he quotes in his three-volume history of the island, provides a perfect example of the constitution and elaboration of the "mental, sexual, and cultural structures", of the "arsenal of significations", which, as generated from the West's post-medieval macro-trope of *Natural Reason*, legitimated the overall cosmos of the order by conceptually and empirically coding/institutionalising the *Negro* and *Negra* slave as embodiment of the extreme *symbolic death*/negative Irrational *Other* to the then norm of English/European free men and women; optimally this *symbolic life* norm of being human as incarnated in an English settler/slave-owning planter-historian like Long himself.[47]

In the logic of the Western plantation system, from its post-1492 initial institution of the Caribbean and the Americas, *Negros* and *Negras* had therefore been defined/institutionalised as "accepted merchandise" (i.e. *piezas*). However, a legal structure, unique to the plantation's functioning as such an order, had come to provide – within the logic of the latter's overall order-instituting "arsenal of significations" – *freedom* for any admixture of white/black "blood", which gave origin to someone who was fifteen-sixteenths *white*; in effect, who was *only* one-sixteenth *black*. A hierarchy, that is, of *being human,* extended between the two poles of the ostensibly naturally born *free-white*, on the one hand, and *unfree Negro* on the other, had therefore been constructed as the basis of the formal system, perpendicular with which the *signifying* chain of the individual was constituted.[48] The different categories of individual mixtures were then given names ranging from Sambo, at the bottom, to Octoroon, etc., at the top. Thereby with the members of each group being socialised to perceive her/himself, as having a relative privilege of the Self (i.e. of being human), in relation to the grade below him, even though, he himself were relatively underprivileged with respect to the grade above. Seeing that the constant criterion of being human here, would come to be measured by the degrees of what the planter-historian-slaveowner, Edward Long, identified as "the pride of amended blood"[49], i.e. of redemptive white "blood".

Body features, hair, lips, skin, became the *signs* of devalued or valued being, each group with respect to their ratios of whiteness, and inverted ratios of blackness. The *pure White* [Long's term], even when, as the indentured labourer, worked half to death and reduced to an interchangeable unit of labour power, usually for a period of some seven years, was nevertheless still socialised to see/experience normatively himself as "human" to the extent that he was "white" and thereby juridically, of free status. He could see himself thus – and oversee the harsh effects of his real indentured, semi-servile condition – to the extent that he could compare himself relatively with the Negative Other, who, reduced as a population (men, women, and children), to being atomised units of labour power, concealed from him the reality of his own empirical condition also, of his systemically inferiorised subordination. As a result, because that Negative Other was the *symbolic death* of the Negro, as embodied in its population, the white worker, identifying with the normative prototype of the symbolic Pure White, had logically manned the frontier to keep the actual concrete Negro Other in his place. Given that the value of *pure White* was a value only realisable on condition that the cultural (i.e. the Symbolic Order's) signifying system which legitimated "Whiteness" as a normative attribute, attesting to its bearer's belonging to the category of *symbolic life* was not threatened by a displacement and inversion of signs – i.e. by the movement of the Black population out of its empirical slave status place; thereby also, out of its signifying *symbolic death* place and function.

Edward Long, develops in this context a part secular-rational, because *natural* and part Christian-Deist myth of origin vis-à-vis the respective origins of the categories of both Black and White. Because both categories had their origin in Nature and its Divine Fabricator, both had had their places assigned to them in the Natural Order and therefore, by analogy, the political order, or cosmos, of the Plantation. As he wrote in his *The History of Jamaica*:

> We observe the like gradations of the intellectual faculty from the first rudiments received in the monkey kind, to the more advanced stages in the apes, in the oran-outang, *that type of Man and the Guiney Negro*; and ascending from the varieties of this class to the lighter casts, until we mark *its utmost limit of perfections in the pure White*. Let us not then doubt, but that every member of creation is wisely fitted and adapted to the certain uses and confined within the certain bounds *to which it was ordained* by the Divine Fabricator. The measure of the several orders and varieties of these Blacks may be as complete as that of any other race of mortals; filling up that space or degree, beyond which they are not destined to pass; and discriminating them from the rest of men *not in kind but in species*.[50]

The above, therefore, as the "rational" expression of the formal system, the Chain of Being of the Symbolic Order, whose "arsenal of significations" instituting and inducing of the "mental, sexual, and cultural structures" had enabled the stable functioning of the slave plantation's order, then still hegemonically mercantilist agricultural paradigm of production; as one which, now in *new* post-slavery forms, still encodes the relative self-perception of varying groups within the terms of the paradigm of production, in its also now new post-slavery, i.e., capitalist/techno-industrial variants.

It is, therefore, from this cosmos and its ostensibly extra-humanly predestined and preordained order – that is, in Long's terms, by both Nature and its Divine Fabricator – that the syncretic Afro-religious cults were to withdraw;

as also, will the millenarian one of contemporary Rastafarianism, from what has become, as the successor to the slave plantation's cosmos, the now post-colonial but no less ostensibly extrahumanly determined globalised contemporary techno-industrial order. This given that the opposing counter-traditions, from Myal to Marley, are ones in whose logic the "mental, sexual, and cultural structures" in the terms of whose "arsenal of significations", their referent populations, must law-likely be institutionalised as not-quite-human, is *totally delegitimated*. Thereby, with the hegemonic reality and history of these respective Babylons, all of which successively gave rise to varying forms of the absolute negation of being fully human as it had to do with the Black population, whether as slaves, as "native labour" or now as unemployable "waste product" labour, are now being seen by the Rastafarians as illusions in which only "heathens" can believe. As Steger points out,

> Gnosis and voodoo [and Rastafarianism] are permanent revolutions against the history lived and suffered here and now in this world represented by a domination which does not matter now since they have been metaphysically revealed to be false.[51]

Seeing that, in the analogical case of the millenarian movement of Rastafarianism, the Rastafarian too now knows where he is from; his different origin, predetermines for him, a different destiny from the destiny predestined for him in the cosmos of our contemporary technologically globalised order. Thus Jah guarantees his identity not as *pieza* – interchangeable productive unit – or as *lumpen* – structurally unemployable, and therefore expendable, because of no "economic value" – but as the son of the most High, the son of Jah. This sonship guarantees that man will eat bread not by the sweat of his brow but by his sonship. Thus, the provision of his material needs is no longer the end, but rather a means, a secondary activity which enables man to realise himself, to partake in divinity, here and now. *It is therefore this radicality of a desire which refuses all limits* that is the central revolutionary impulse of Rastafarianism. Thus, if as Bradshaw writes:

> The Rastas say I-in-I, for *we* and tend to shift 'I' to the front of all important words, such as *'I-tal'* for *natural* and *'I-nointed'* for *anointed*, one of Marley's songs calls on his people to *Inite thyself and Imanity*.[52]

The insistence here is on the I, the now royally valued self, negates the long history of being interchangeable [i.e. *pieza*] disposable units. It is an assertion of selfhood in circumstances designed to negate any possibility of such self-assertion.[53]

I would like to refer here to the "clash" between Marley and Manley. To put it, briefly, in context. After 1962 and the granting of political independence to Jamaica by Britain, the successive two-party national Governments, whether of one party or the other, had continued the modernisation plans that had been prescribed for the economy, under the mantra of "development" by either English- or British-educated West Indian liberal economic theorists. The paradoxical but logical result was the "growth" of an economy which widened the dispossession of the broad masses, whilst it benefited the category of the middle classes, as a hegemonically secular, Western-educated minority. In the context of the increased material and psychic stresses brought about by the above separation of the interests of the middle classes from those of the increasingly jobless shantytown masses, the Rastafarian movement, formerly restricted to a cult, began to have a widespread impact on the larger society. This, at the same time, as the parallel Black Power movement that had erupted in another part of the ex-slave archipelago of the post-1492 Americas, the U.S., would come to fuse both musically and conceptually, with the Rastafarian's millenarian symbolism which now exploded in a rich creativity of artistic and musical expression, including the ska and reggae forms. This expression took its point of departure from the long tradition of popular music born out of underground, Afro-New World cult religions which had structured a coun-ter-symbolic order. As, therefore, the society as a whole began to break out of the definitions of the dominant system, and a revolution in consciousness began to take place, the Rastafarian symbols emerged from marginality to find widespread acceptance as the articulation of popular discontent. In this context, the Rastafarian uncombed locks became the symbol of an oppressed identity to the officially prescribed, and normatively bourgeois identities of the dominant order. It became the symbol of a transformation of self-perception in the context of the great disillusionment that had followed in the wake of political independence, as popular forces, and middle-class youth, groped towards the demand for revolutionary change in the increasingly unequal socio-economic order. It was a social order in which, in spite of the new national flag and anthem attesting to our national/political independence, at the level of the globally controlled economic system, some thirty percent of the population was unemployed, a large percentage underemployed and both imprisoned in a shantytown/ghetto-like existence – the Trench Town of Marley's songs.

It was on the basis of this groundswell of discontent that Michael Manley, son and heir of a former Prime Minister, one of the leaders who had steered the island to political independence in the wake of the anti-colonial struggle, came to power. Bradshaw tells us that "Bob Marley had supported Michael Manley during the 1972 campaign but had since become disenchanted."[54] For in the 1972 political campaign, Manley had co-opted not only the formerly apolitical Rastafarians like Marley, but the entire architecture of their symbol-ism. Supported by a coalition of wealthy merchants, industrialists, large sections of the middle classes as well as the discontented and rebellious popular forces, Manley won an overwhelming victory at the polls. While his electoral campaign was based largely on the *rational manipulation of the symbolic signifying system expropriated from the Rastafarian Movement*.

The branch firm of a large United States advertising agency mounted a campaign in the press, on radio and on television in which Manley was evoked as a secular Messiah in religious terminology. The popular forces were defined as *sufferers*. As *sufferers* they were helpless, needing a Saviour to redeem them from their conditioned fate. Manley adopted the biblical name of Joshua. In photographs distributed throughout the country he was portrayed in a kind of Holy Trinity between Haile Selassie, on the one hand, and another influential cult leader, on the other. Both in the photograph and in the campaign he displayed a rod supposedly handed down to him by Haile Selassie. With his rod Joshua was to smite and defeat his opponent, the leader of the governing party, who was portrayed as Pharoah, although blacker and of a far lower social origin than Manley. The ten years of Pharoah's party's rule was portrayed as "exile". The clear implication was that the Messiah had come to redeem his people, to take them "home". The slogan, "Power to the People", was interspersed with the Rastafarian salutation of "Peace and Love". *Love* became a campaign slogan as violence rocked the country. It was an unprecedentedly brilliant piece of political manipulation. Joined to the force and power of the genuine popular discontent it was unbeatable. Reggae musicians composed songs "hailing the man"[55] and Manley swept into power on a wave of a song.

The widespread symbolic manipulation used both in the 1972 and in the later 1976 campaign had a purpose. Manley and the group of skilled technocrats who surrounded him were not interested only in winning an election – they wanted a large scale victory which would serve as the basis for an electoral bureaucratic coup, in which they could, by legally changing the constitution, initiate a revolution from above.

An electoral coup, a bureaucratic revolution, is the very opposite of a popular revolutionary movement. In the latter the masses move – *anarchically*, from below – out of the place assigned to them in the dominant social order. By the very *act* of they themselves moving out of their assigned place, they transform the social relations of the dominant social order. By their action the barriers and constraints of the former symbolic coding which negatively structured their self-perception are swept away. They explode into creative energy. In the absence of such a self-initiated movement by the people themselves what occurs, however, is a simulation of revolution by the bureaucratic bourgeoisie, whether of the right or the left, or the in-between of Democratic *Socialism*. In this simulation very little creative change is possible.

By 1976, there was even more widespread popular discontent and disillusionment. The reggae songs became increasingly critical of the new ruling class, that of the skilled technocratic bourgeoisie. Material conditions, bad enough in 1972, had worsened in the context of the world recession, inflated oil prices, and contradictory policies. Hunger, increased joblessness, food shortages, and increasing political and criminal violence undermined the society. The exodus of the wealthy with their money was followed by that of the skilled middle, and lower-middle classes with their skills. Even, also, to the U.S.A. the hub of the exploding popular music industry, by that of some of the Rastafarian reggae singers themselves. The financial and social deterioration of the country began to erode confidence. In the face of this, the rational manipulation of the symbolic function and the strategic use of violence – on both sides, Government and opposition – was to become central to the 1976 campaign. As Bradshaw puts it, hundreds were killed and Jamaica became "a black Belfast".[56] It was therefore in this climate that Marley – who was scheduled to sing at a concert for the people of Jamaica under Government auspices, was shot up along with some of his fellow musicians. No one died. The shooting seemed designed *not* to kill.

Several versions of the shooting went the rounds. One, the first, was flashed all over the world by the news media. In this version Marley was said to have planned to sing at a concert in support of Manley. The clear implication was that the opposition had shot him. The political symbolic *mileage* had therefore accrued, in the first place, to the Government Party. So the other Party's version of the story was that the Government itself had staged the coup to win political sympathy and Rastafarian votes. Neither version was ever definitively proved.

Marley pointed out that the men who shot him were never caught. Were it the Prime Minister who had been shot, he further argued, they would have been caught. His fellow Rastafarians were certain that the incident was due to *politricks,* while Marley himself felt that it might also have been due to that, or to the jealousy of fellow musicians. The point here is that whether it was the opposition or a staged coup by members of the Government themselves, it was clear that in the Politricks of Babylon, the Rastafarians were, once again, what the black man or woman, the Black population, had always been, in the dominant order of the post-1492 slave/ex-slave archipelago, a pawn in the context of the hegemonic interest of other peoples' projects, their "where we are going" telos.

The song "Exodus" was therefore Marley's declaration of a second withdrawal, this time one not only from Babylon, but from all the varieties of its politics.

Manley's campaign speeches had blamed Jamaica's severely worsened conditions on global-economic factors, on the I.M.F., the machinations of the capitalist clique, of the Opposition, of the sinister CIA, on every other factor but his own policies. And while the global-economic factors as world-systemic ones, were as they continue to be indeed determinant in the long run, Marley, in his *New York Times* interview, blames, however, the Government and its, so to speak, short run policies.

> De Government is tramplin' over de people's sweat and tears. Comin' down hard, hard. We're oppressed, so we sing oppressed songs and some time people find themselves guilty. And dey can't stand the terrible weight of it. *But Babylon don' want peace, Babylon want power.*[57]

Manley had ended his opening 1976 campaign speech with the words:

> We know where we are going. We are creating a new man. We have begun the building of socialist man. We are working towards the day when there will be no more masters and more servants, but only one together in the Lord.[58]

In his song "Exodus", Marley replies to Manley. Over against the "new Socialist Man" that is to be built "one day" by the Manley leadership and his new order, Marley legitimates man as he is now, in the flesh, the son of Jah, not waiting for heaven – "We're tired of your ism-skism game, to die and go to heaven in Jesus name",[59] as another song has it – nor indeed for Manley's secular apocalypse in which in order for man to deserve happiness, rather than effecting his own self-liberation, he must be built anew. With the consequence that it is in that space-time of waiting for the apocalyptic day that the new leadership tends to install itself as the new masters. Rather, the Rastafarians "know" they have been guaranteed Paradise and Zion – *now* in the Kingdom of Jah man shall reign. Not the leadership of the Party. With "Exodus", Marley recaptures the expropriated popular revolt. Himself from the popular shanty-masses, Marley becomes the articulator of the popular revolt articulating itself by itself for itself.

The clash between Manley's definition of man as the "new Socialist man," and Marley's as already the "sons of Jah", is one based on the fact that Manley's definition and program for Action – the Where We're Going – still operates within the Western-bourgeois paradigm of production; a paradigm which whether in its matrix Liberal capitalist or Marxist, neo-Marxist forms, autonomises the economic sphere of the overall social order by making either the expansion, or the restructuring of the economic system, the determinant and primary goal of revolution. The autonomisation of the economic is, therefore, central to the ideology of the intellectual bureaucratic *cum* technocratic skilled class of the bourgeoisie (as distinct from the latter's capital-owning accumulating elites), since it presupposes that the transformation of private property into nationalised State property – the empirical basis of this class's power – is the *end* of the revolution, the basis therefore as it conceives it, of our human emancipation.

Over against this materialist conception, it is instead, a revolution in the Symbolic Order as prescribed by our present world systemic cultural signifying system, and which then underlies and prescribes the socio-economic hierarchies of its structures of power, that the Rastafarian millenarian self-redefinition/ program articulates. It is in this sense that the deep structure clash between Orthodox Marxisms and the revolutionary aspects – as distinct from its conjoined reactionary possibilities – of the counter culture of the Black Americas can be defined as the difference between a partial economic revolution and a total cultural (i.e. at once social and cultural), revolution. And here, Jean Baudrillard, writing out of the perspectives of the cultural revolution of May 1968 in France, puts this new telos well:

...the cultural revolution is no longer tied to the economic political revolution. It cuts through the economic-political as a partial revolutionary discourse, and, in a certain rationalizing and mystifying way. A revolution that aims at the totality of life and social relations will be made also and primarily *against the autonomization of the economic*, of which the last "('revolutionary' and 'materialist')" avatar is the autonomisation of the mode of production under the form of a determinant instance. Because today the system has no better strategy than that of the dialectic of political economy, the cultural revolution must make itself *against the economic-political revolution.*[60]

It was therefore from the periphery-perspective of the Western world system, that Harold Cruse had insisted, long before this, on the fact that a total cultural revolution (one implicit in the politics of Black culture) that is, and can be, the only viable revolution in the complex American (U.S.) system. While, long too before it would find its intellectual formulation, the "politics" of the Black counter culture, not merely in Cruse's U.S., but more comprehensively, across the range of the slave/ex-slave archipelagos of the Caribbean and of the Americas, had been engaged in this cultural revolution. The former *pieza* could call for no less. This, given as Aimé Césaire said when he resigned from the Communist Party, the black had been doubly negated, both as "proletariat" and, as well, as the only population whose humanity had been totally negated, empirically, symbolically, thereby conceptually.[61]

It is here, therefore, that the particular struggle of the black culture of the Americas – the counter-culture of the *piezas* – takes on universal dimensions. For the rationality of the paradigm of material production – of which the *piezas* on the plantation archipelago were to be the first mass victims – has extended itself globally. The forces of production have therefore been developed over the past some five hundred years, as never before in human history. Yet never before have such large masses of people experienced themselves as being both *materially* and *psychically dispossessed*. While if it is *for* the materially dispossessed masses that Marley's message articulates an imperative revolution in our present world system structures of social relations, as structures whose everyday reproduction calls for severely unequal levels of the redistribution of wealth, on the one hand, and of poverty on the other, law-likely leads to a contemporary situation, a situation in which as Marley sings, "Them belly full but we hungry."[62] Nevertheless, the Rastafarians' material dispossession, urgent as it is, is for them, the result of a larger dispossession, one from full human status, from being free, therefore, to control the symbolic function, to thereby invent/code/invest one's sense of self with meanings that are not prefabricated and imposed by our present world-system's ostensibly universally applicable and determinant paradigm of material (i.e. economic) production.

Hence the fact that it is in the context of sterile aridity of the overwhelming reality to which the latter has led, that even the materially affluent, or, at least, well-fed consumers – as, for example in the case of the youth of the developed world, the psychic dispossession of those who feel themselves helpless pawns

– *piezas* – in an order whose very productive rationality can leave no room for their human fulfilment/self-realisation, that the radicality of Marley's demand – to love life and live that's all – joins forces with the conjoined demand for bread, fulfilment, and self-realisation rising up from the shantytowns, the inner city ghettoes, the *favelas*; from all the lumpen, in fact and spirit.

For this is a new form of the original *piezas* Middle Passage experience which links us all now, therefore, on the basis of a shared commonality of experience in which we all now find ourselves the new nameless, experience ourselves as the undifferentiated statistics of interchangeable producer-consumer units – here to increase the sale of Coca Cola or of Geritol, or alternatively, how to figure in the master plan of a techno-bureaucrat. This given that as the power of the Free-Market economic (U.S.A.) and the politico-statal (Soviet Union) processes of decision-making are processes concentrated in fewer and fewer hands, a large majority of mankind begin to experience ourselves as merely consumers; as, therefore, the very negation of the *I*, as *piezas* cast adrift – without any anchor in a realised sense of self – in the contemporary world of Western and Westernised, therefore hegemonically secular, techno-industrial modernity.

St. Clair Drake has analysed the process by which in the context of the original Middle Passage, the individual/tribal African slave was to be, on arrival in the New World expropriated of the former cultural signifying system whose symbolic coding had formerly constituted him, even where a slave, as a "human" rather than as not a merely "biological" being. As he writes:

> …whatever the fate of an African was to be after he had become part of plantation society in the initial stages of enslavement, all shared a common experience. At home in Africa, Kofi not only had a name that was of symbolic significance to him, but also had an unambiguous group identity, and was respected as an individual. To make a plantation-mass slave of Kofi, he had first of all to be transformed from a tribesman into "a worthless nigger," "a heathen black."[63]

It is therefore against this process of *reduction to nigger*, thereby, to ultimate non-human status, that we must attempt *to grasp the revolutionary significance of that counter-invention of the self* – which I see as the *central and universally applicable strategy of the "politics of black culture"*.

Already, on board the slaveship the *piezas* had begun to translate the former age group tie of traditional African societies into another symbolic relation – and *man* becomes *human*, Lacan points out, the moment he enters into a symbolic relation.[64] They, therefore, called themselves *shipmates* – "we who went through the experience of the Middle Passage together". Then, once landed on the earth of the New World, they transformed the place from which they had come – Guinea, Africa – into a symbolic entity. Africa became the parallel of the Gnostic's Beyond – *The True Origin*. The place, the antithesis of Dante's *Inferno* in which they now find themselves, from *where they were from*. The here and now was exile. The dream of the return became central. A seventeenth-century account of black slaves in Jamaica attests to this dream. Describing what he calls "their death lamentations and funerals", the Rev. John Taylor tells us, "When these slaves die they make a great adoo at their burial... carry the corpse to the grave in a mournful manner..." At the grave they placed the corpse in the grave and with it "casadar bread, rosted fowles, sugar, rum, tobacco and with fier to light his pipe withall..."[65]

This is done, as the slaves explained to Taylor; "In order to sustaine him in his journey beyound those plesant hills in their own countrey, whither they say he is now goeing to live at rest." After they had placed the food in the grave, Taylor writes, "they fill up the grave and eat and drinck thereon, singing in their own language verey dolefully, desiering the dead corpse (by ciseing the ground), to acquaint their father, mother, husbands and other relations of their present condition and slavary, as he passeth thro' their countrey towards the plesant mountains, which message they bellow out to the dead corps in a doleful tone."[66]

Here began the spirituals, the blues, the culture of exile, the aesthetic/ symbolic rearticulation of the self, ever against its *pieza* negation by the logic of the slave plantation order. This self, through the ritual observance, now "knew where it was from", and knew that it had a destiny other than that of being a mere producer of surplus value; since *its* destiny, the where it was going, was quite other than the destiny allowed it in the plantation slave labour archipelago's master plan. Thus Taylor tells us that the slaves he spoke to were quite certain of the soul's "redemption after death which they say is beyond the Pleasant Mountains of their own country where, after death, such which lived well shall go to and there in the full enjoyment of all things shall be eternally happy."[67]

From Taylor, too, we learn how the former symbolic relationships of tribal African cultures were transmuted into a new role, articulated into a culture whose central purpose was both the symbolic subversion of, and the concrete rebellion against, the dominant social order. The reinvention of the self, and with it the control of Lacan's symbolic function, was articulated in the ritual of the funeral. The ritual itself transshipped the *macro-symbol of the Earth* as the base, at once material and symbolic – one that had been instituting of traditional African communities – as a counter-community to that of the slave-plantation system.

As Taylor tells us:

These Negroas have a great veneration for the Earth, by which they sweare and bind themselves to punctuall obedience and performance... and if you bind 'em to secresie by cising of ye earth, then all the tortures that can be inflicted on them shall never make them confess or discover it, which is the reason they allways die so obstinat in their rebellion, without tears or conffesing their dissignes or confederats, for if they ciss the earth 'tis to them a solemn and certaine oath by which they swear.[68]

The symbolic pact, an oath sworn to not by slaves but by men initiated into a symbolic relationship, is coded by a symbolic order alien to that of the plantation. The oath bound each man not only to each other, but to the whole world of their ancestors; and behind them to the gods who guaranteed their counter-identity, their non-*pieza* condition. And this identity was also legitimated by the *existence* of Guinea, as one's true, because an empirical origin, now ritually converted into what would become in the course of time, a trans-tribal symbolic origin.

Taylor tells us of four rebellions that took place in the latter part of the seventeenth century in Jamaica. After the rebels were crushed, they "were all putt to death; *some were burnt, some roasted, others torn to pieces with doggs, and others cutt in peice alive*, and their head and quarters plac't on poles to be a terror to others…" But the power of the oath sworn was such that, "nevertheless for all this torture, they remained soe obstinate that whilst they were burning, rosting etc., they continued singing and laughing, not one of 'em once been seen to shed a teare or desier mercy, …and by noe tortur would they ever confes ye designe or who was concerned therein. And soe their torment seem'd in vaine."[69]

C.L.R. James has pointed out the central role that the religion of vodou and the oath sworn at the vodou rituals played in the successful revolution in Haiti.[70] Writing in the eighteenth century, Edward Long warned of the dangerous thrust of the Myal cult – the Jamaican equivalent of vodou – and described, if not fully recognising it as such, the ritual ceremony in which the "initiate", after having died to his old self (as slave), is reconstituted as a "new" man.[71] This "new man" not only believed himself invulnerable to the white man's bullets, i.e., to his power, but as Taylor, and later, Long shows, were prepared to die in collective defence of this new self. For like vodou, Myal was the reinvented syncretic, somewhat Afro-Christian, system of beliefs, in which the Creole slaves, distant now from Africa, reinterpreted the rituals, reinvented the traditional gods in new forms. But in vodou as in early (i.e. still hegemonically African-centred) Myal, Africa, Guinea, the place left behind was invoked in ritual through the techniques of religious ecstasy which breached the iron walls of exile, transmuted the Beyond into the *now* of the ritual itself.

Later Africa, Guinea, the place left behind, would become Heaven, as elements of Christian symbolism were drawn into the old framework, in the context of the rise of varying forms of a syncretic Afro-Christianity. But this Heaven was freighted with all the old symbolic power. Herein lies the force and passion of the spirituals. Singing of the sweet chariot coming to take them home, the slaves claimed their true origin, as a population, denoted the present order as a vale of tears, delegitimated its principalities and powers.

While if in the rituals it was the techniques of possession which breached the iron walls of the prison of their everyday slave plantation existence, black music, from the spirituals to the blues to jazz and all its variants, and now to Marley and Reggae, secularised the formerly spiritual religious ecstasy, displaced it into an aesthetic space, where it made the ultimate revolutionary demand, *the demand for happiness/fulfilment now*. One that we know is possible, since it is "known" – partaken of during the aesthetic experiencing of the song. As Marley sings, exile itself is made absent:

> Move, move, move, movement of Jah people
> Jah come to break down downpression, rule equality
> wipe away transgression
> and set the captive free
> Exodus, movement of Jah people
> Exodus, movement of Jah people...[72]

To all who partake in the song – and Bradshaw's description of a Marley concert with the shouted responses of the audience, denotes the intensity of shared communication between the singer and his co-partakers – the world outside the song, the so-called objective reality is delegitimated as that of Babylon, the non-real world, the world of Babylon's capitalistic illusions that must be burnt. It is not they, the poor, the materially and psychically dispossessed – nor, indeed, their, although well-fed, no less psychically dispossessed audience, by their reduction to being mere consumers – who are "wrong", but Babylon. Everything will be alright once they who are made to feel themselves "wrong", "see the light". The keyword is *see*. One sees the light. One does not, as in Orthodox Christianity, "hear the word" which must be obeyed.[73] Rather in the heresies of the popular black cultures of the Americas one sees, and one participates in Godhood. For the walls of iron which imprison men, are not only external walls. They are the far more imprisoning walls of the structured psyche that the audience brings with them from their Babylonian lives. This given that the very structure of the unconscious articulated on the basis of the formal system – one from the mid-nineteenth century onwards, legitimating of the Western and Westernised upper bourgeoisies, as the ruling stratum – is necessarily so instituted and legitimated only by means of what Baudrillard genially identified as [that of the formal system's] "arsenal of significations", its correlated "mental, sexual, and cultural structures". With both, in turn, thereby serving to induce the normative individual and collective behaviours, indispensable to the dynamic enactment and stable reproduction of our present, hegemonically secular, world-systemic order. An "arsenal of signification" therefore, in whose now techno-industrial automated terms, the innumerable variants of the global archipelago of Marley's shantytown jobless, must law-likely be both materially and psychically dispossessed.

Hence the Rastafarian recoding of the formal system's concept of *oppression* as that of their existentially lived phenomenological concept of "downpression"; with this "downpression", if in their case only at the level of their psychic dispossession, being no less experienced by the usually job-holding, therefore well-fed, reasonably affluent members of his audience; yet who, in their everyday lives, must also find themselves being on the one hand, made into interchangeable units or cogs in the now corporate system of economic production, and on the other hand, but no less so as an also interchangeable functional unit of that system, since socialised to be the docile consumers, whose ever increasing "wants", as induced by the ad industry, is now centrally indispensable to the latter's functioning.

It is therefore precisely the "walls of iron" of the present "mental, sexual, and cultural structures", ones determinant of our normative psyches, and thereby of the usual run of our behaviours, that the pulsating rhythms the Rastafarian reggae songs, together with the taut direct words/sentences of the oral Jamaican Afro-English in which the songs are composed – i.e. as for example, Marley's "Dem (them) belly full/but we hungry/The pot a fire (in the fire)/but the food no nough (not enough) – together function to powerfully subvert. To bring crashing down, at the level of the psyche, individual and collective, all such walls. Thereby, untuning, unstringing the respective interacting dynamics of their institutionally imposed structures, and together with them our present normally, existentially experienced hegemonic quantified sense of time as labour time. Time, that is, linearly, rigidly channelled towards the productive purely material (i.e. economic) finality, of our present techno-industrial order of things.

Pamela O'Gorman describes the sharply opposed sense of time of the reggae song. It has, she writes,

> no beginning, no middle and no end. The peremptory up-beat of the traps, which seldom varies from song to song, is less an introduction than the articulation of a flow that never seems to have stopped. There is no climax, there is no end. The music merely fades out into the continuum of which it seems to be an unending part. Like the Blues, which shares with it these same characteristics, it lies outside the post-Renaissance sense of time and in this it is essential non-European.[74]

The subversion of our present hegemonic socially conditioned psychic structure, therefore occurs through the mechanism of the music which makes present the experience of a concept of freedom, *anarchic* in its true sense – that is, freedom *for* the realisation of selfhood, the negation of serving an imposed end, the end of the dominant order of Babylon, the return to the "father's land", the return from *negro* to *prieto*, to the now autonomously created sense of the self, *its* determinant recoding of the symbolic function.

The principle of the aesthetic structuring of the music itself, is therefore symbolic of a "free" structuring of a human psyche which can be concomitant with freedom from the *downpression* both of the dominant system, and of its unconscious. So that, as the techniques of ecstasy of religions like vodou and Myal had opened the path to a parallel experience of freedom which one *knows* because one *partakes* in it – so the aesthetic experience makes known a freedom articulated by a popular tradition, which transcends and goes beyond the telos of the liberation of the productive forces, a telos conceptualised *as* freedom within both the Liberal democratic capitalist and the Marxian-statist paradigms of production.

The "politics" of black culture has as its function the symbolic subversion, therefore the deconstruction of the signifying chain with which the "old" individual, beginning in its case with the nameless *pieza*, is constituted. To do this and to deconstruct and subvert the cultural signifying system of the dominant order, was/is one and the same dialectical process. Seeing that, the deconstruction of the assigned "self" in its assigned "place" begins when, in the structure of the unconscious, the symbols of the dominant order are subverted: control of the code is undermined. At the moment when the dominant order is counter-coded as Babylon, with all of the power and force of its Biblical reference, not only verbally but also aesthetically, musically negated, as the place of exile from which the new Exodus must begin, the listeners, black and white alike – now black and white *only* in the difference of skin, no longer in terms of the binary opposition of the symbolic order which sustains these categories – is made to vanish. All now feel their psychic *downpression*, their alien "namelessness" in the aridity and barrenness of empirical reality, as one determined by the telos of productive finality, disappears. The latter's symbolic Father, together with the bourgeois psyche to which He gives rise, is dethroned.

Over against the dethroned Father, his negated symbolic order, a new order which is a non-order asserts itself. It is a non-order because the new Symbolic Father has no power in this world. He is a symbol of nonpower which is nevertheless, not powerless. *Against* the downpressor, he is powerful beyond compare. He is powerful symbolically, musically, aesthetically.

For the sons of Jah are co-terminous with the Father. As brothers they participate with him in both fatherhood and sonhood, negating a power relation between them, or, even its possibility. While the song lasts therefore, all structures of power, all time is absent, made not to exist. In the aesthetic space created, the partakers experience *Zion. When it ends the memory remains constituting a radical desire for the realisation in real life of this happiness.* Until the desire is fulfilled in this world, therefore, the movement of Exodus exists as the radical negation of anything less.

The concept of God, Horkheimer writes,

> was for a long time the place where the idea was kept alive that there are *other norms besides those to which nature and society give expression in their operation.* Dissatisfaction with earthly destiny is the strongest motive for acceptance of a transcendental being. If justice resides with God, then it is not to be found in the same measure in the world.[75]

The power of the Rastafarians' critique of our this-worldly destiny lies in the fact that it is symbolic, that it inhabits its own space outside the trammels of the "real" world. So that, if as Horkheimer points out that "The more Christianity brought God's rule into harmony with events in the world, the more the meaning of religion became perverted",[76] nevertheless, when the actual Ethiopian Emperor Haile Selassie was overthrown by a coup, killed, and his place taken by a Marxist regime, Marley and the other Rastafarians refused to take cognisance of it, in order to adjust their self-liberating faith to a mere "event in the world", the world of Babylon. Assailed on all sides, they had their responses ready. As Marley tells it: "Many people, dey scoffers, many people say to me: 'Backside, your god dead! How he can dead? How can God die, mon?'"[77] For what the Rastafarians, through Marley here take on, is our present deep-seated materialist superstition, its secular belief in the impossibility of any referent for humans but a supposedly non-symbolic, and thereby, ostensibly "objective" one. As Umberto Eco writes:

> What, then, is the meaning of a term? From the semiotic point of view it can only be a cultural unit... Recognition of the presence of these cultural units... involves understanding language as a social phenomenon. If I declare /That there are two natures in Christ, the human and the divine, and one Person/ a logician or scientist might observe to me that this string of sign-vehicles has neither extension (condition of truth) or referent (concrete object to which it refers) – and it could be defined as lacking meaning and therefore as a pseudo statement. *But they will never succeed in explaining why whole groups of people have fought for centuries over a statement of this kind or its denial.* Evidently this happened because the expression contained precise contents which existed as cultural units within a civilisation.
>
> Seeing that once such units have been brought into imaginative existence, they become the support for connotative development and *opened up a whole range of semantic reactions that directly affected behaviour.*[78]

Jah lives for Marley and his audience because the imperative conditions for his *signification* – and therefore his existence – exists. He exists as the demand for justice of the systemically made jobless marginal millions reduced to *subhuman* status materially; and for those other millions reduced to another form of subhuman status, the secular denial of any symbolic significance to their existence. Jah lives as the unwavering accusation against the rational cosmos not only of the once seemingly extrahumanly determined (i.e. by Edward Long's Nature and its Divine Fabricator) obligatory order of the slave plantation system, but also against that (the rational cosmos) of our *present* – no less extrahumanly, because, ostensibly, bio-evolutionarily determined no less obligatorily by the order of our present world-systemic capitalist economic order/ordering of things. This whether in its original Liberal democratic Free Market private ownership matrix form or in its later Marxian Party-State ownership contestatory variant. It is therefore against both that, for I-man, that Jah lives as the unwavering assurance that although now predetermined to be, according to the logic of the first, members of the expendable underclass of the shantytown, inner-city ghettos, each with their prison extensions, there can be no doubt as to the triumphant reality of their imaginatively reinvented – outside the terms of the formal system – and performatively enacted, new sense of self as the sons of someone, the Most High.

And with that assurance Jah also lives as the certified prophetic prediction that in the kingdom of Jah, I-man shall reign, None will reign in his name. Pass it on! Pass on the good news! That is what the reggae songs do. They are the prophecy of Jah made flesh in words and music and rhythm, thereby concretely weighted with millenarian hope. This at the same time as they structure states of feeling which, ineluctably – *as the Gnostic heresies had done in the context of the rise of Christianity* in the then *still hegemonically pagan Roman empire* – push toward an analogical transformative mutation of contemporary Babylon's real surrounding world. Yet, there is a paradox here. One central both to the Gnostic heresies as well as those which have fuelled the politics of the counter dynamics of the black Americas. This is that *the power of the black religious counterculture of Rastafarianism in its now, with Marley, hegemonic musically aesthetic doctrinal form, lies precisely in its symbolic negativity, thus its politics is a politics that can never be realised except in that symbolic world – ZION – in which with all structures of power having been overturned, not only the* "autonomisation of the economic sphere" *but also the ostensibly autonomous, separate concept of politics – necessarily politricks – will have been made obsolescent and meaningless.*

Thus the fact, that the strength of its "politics" lies in the total critique it is able to make of all the secular Jerusalems, of all the secular Messiahs. *Seeing that the cultural seedbed from which it arises is one which is objectively revolutionary, only from the liminally deviant **point of view**, of a specific transhistorical category;* of one for which, revolution can only mean the bringing to an immediate end, of their institutionalised material and psychic dispossession, as such a category. One that the shantytowns of the Rastafarians, like that of their *pieza*-as-negro slave and "*native* labour" ancestors before them, have now been institutionally made to reembody; if now in transumptively new contemporary, post-colonial terms.

This liminally deviant category was first identified as a universally applicable one by the anthropologist Asmarom Legesse, as one that is systematically made to function in all human societies as "the conceptual 'antithesis'" to the "structured community" to which it both belongs, and not belongs at one and the same time. Seeing that, as Legesse further notes, it is only "by reference to this category" that the "structured community" both "defines and understands itself". It is therefore here that we can grasp the reality of what Legesse also emphasises as the "injustice inherent in structure".[79] In that, as he shows, it is only through the mediation of the negative mirroring provided by the liminally deviant category or person, that the community can be structured (by, in Baudrillard's terms, its "arsenal of significations") to phenomenologically experience themselves as an inter-altruistic-kin-recognising, collectivity.

With this, thereby imperatively calling, in all cases, for that *insider/outsider* category to be securely institutionalised in its pre-ascribed role, as the negative antithesis whose represented *abnormal* and/or pathological *difference* is then made to invertedly generate the specific mode of *similarity* or of *sameness*, defining of that community's now co-identifying shared "sense of self", as all being *equally* the "normal" subjects of their specific societal order, and with their members, therefore, all now being able – this whatever the sharp caste/class inequalities of the divisions between them, with respect to inequalities of power, wealth, social status, educational and/or skills-acquisition opportunities, etc. – to both experience and performatively enact themselves as collectively being of/belonging to *the same kind*.

Consequently given the Rastafarians' existentially lived experience as the liminally deviant or pariah category, one now indispensable to the functioning both of our contemporary world-systemic, economically, techno-industrial societal order as well as those of the latter's magma of nation-state sub-units, the religio-aesthetic doctrinal force of their millenarian counter-politics can be seen to lie in the latter's projection of, and demand for, a world freed from all pre-ascribed "structures of or powers"; and with that an end being put to their institutionalised dispossession as such a category, both to adapt one of Marx's most incisive formulations, in its specific Rastafarian case, as a "particular wrong", as well as in all such other transsocietal, transhistorical, indeed trans-Western cases, also as a "general wrong" hitherto indispensable to the instituting of all our human societies.

In this context, therefore, given the far-reaching implications of the projected emancipatory telos of the Rastafarians' millenarian counter-politics, this entails a correlatedly strong injunction. One which prescribes that as the Rastafarian protagonists of this millenarian counter-politics, their members must at all times, be *not only prepared to refuse, to negate any* new structures of power that a this-worldly Messiah may seek to institute ostensibly in their name, but also, to turn their backs on all those – some including their own members – who would seek to make their counter-politics into a function of this world's *politricks*. Since once this millenarian counter-politics allows itself to be co-opted into that of this world, as Duvalier of Haiti did with vodou, and Manley (if only briefly) with elements of Rastafarianism, it becomes destructively dystopian. Given that, by subverting its true function, it deserts the symbolic mode in which it articulates *its* emancipatory telos, for the rational world in which such a telos is necessarily betrayed.

With the song "Exodus", Marley, therefore, does not only challenge Manley's alternative Democratic-socialist emancipatory telos, *its* "where we are going". In doing so, he returns the Rastafarian movement to its true, prophetically redemptive, role: this given the liminally deviant nature of its part/not-part, insider/outsider ultimate, underside status, one indispensable to the instituting of our now post-colonial world-systemic order.[79]

It is therefore from the contemporary periphery-form of this part/not-part, insider/outsider perspective, that Bob Marley and the Rastafarians articulate their critique, directed now primarily against the capitalistic Babylonian illusions of the Liberal democratic, capital accumulating, privately propertied upper bourgeois elite, but also against the no less bourgeois "power illusions of the New Class of the skilled/technocratic/bureaucratic bourgeoisie[80] – whether Democratic socialist or orthodoxly Marxist. For, in both cases, this critique, verbal/music, ethical/aesthetic is based on the insistence that I-man, as the Son of Jah, has an *inherited* right – not one that he has to "earn" – to being not only able to secure the material conditions of his existence, but also and above all, to be able to realise himself spiritually/creatively here on earth.[81] But that even when the first "right" has been met, the priority of the realisation of the second over the first, for the Rastafarians, should never in any way be reversed, as indeed it must be within the terms of our present paradigm of production in its Old Class/New Class but in both cases, hegemonically economistic, therefore bourgeois, terms. Will not permit them, above all, given their self-ascribed sonship status to Jah, to replace His/their emancipatory telos with that of the latter's materially redemptive telos. Not as long as they continue to perceive their imaginatively reinvented sense of self, as the only such self coterminous with Jah, His reigning in His kingdom.

Marley and the counter-culture of the ex-slave archipelago of the Black Americas, as disseminated globally – if paradoxically so, by the productive finality and "reasons of profitability" of the bourgeoisie's now globalised *Western and Westernised* Free Market capitalist economic system – by its reggae songs, do not talk *about* the revolution in the psyche, in the counter-symbolic order which recodes *Imanity* in its new fully human status. Rather it is this new self-perception, together with the new states of feeling to which the songs give rise, that will make inevitable the transformation of our present material order; of the now seemingly unchallengeable objective reality of its autonomised economic system and its paradigm of production, whether enacted in its Free Market, capitalist, or Party-Statist forms.

For already in that rhythmic-musical, verbal-aesthetic space in which the songs exist, and the revolution in the symbolic order, and in the psyche, is immanently enacted, Jah *is*. And I-man – no longer the paradigm of production's logically expendable techno-industrial "refuse" – in his royal sonship status, *lives*.

Paper presented at the joint meeting of the African Studies Association and the Latin American Studies Association, Houston, TX, November, 1977.

The African and Afro-American Studies Program
Stanford University
Stanford, CA
October, 1977

Endnotes

1. *Black World*, vol. 24, no. 12 (October 1975), 23, emphasis in original.
2. *African Civilizations in the New World* (New York: Harper Torchbook, 1971), 23.
3. Harold Cruse, *The Crisis of the Negro Intellectual: From Its Origins to the Present* (New York: Quill, 1967).
4. The case, *Regents of the University of California v. Bakke* (1978), was one in which the consideration of race in college admissions was upheld, but the use of quotas as was used in the University of California, Davis School of Medicine was struck down.
5. The point about the reported "hesitation" – the Panthers *did* join the coalition – is that it would represent the Orthodox Party Line, a theoretical line whose "autonomisation of the economic" (Baudrillard) is largely responsible for its failure to come to grips, theoretically and practically, with the black experience in the United States. See for the above concept, Jean Baudrillard, *The Mirror of Production*. Trans. Mark Poster (St. Louis: Telos Press, 1975).
6. See Immanuel Wallerstein, *The Modern World-System: Capitalist Agriculture and the Origins of the European World-Economy in the Sixteenth Century* (New York: Academic Press, 1974).
7. Jacques Lacan, *The Language of the Self: The Function of Language in Psychoanalysis*, trans. Anthony Wilden (New York: Dell, 1968), 48.
8. Ibid., 48.
9. In his autobiographical novel, *Black Boy: A Record of* Childhood and Youth (1937; New York: Harper and Brothers, 1945), 64, Richard Wright recounts the following incident. Hired by a Yankee employer while still in the South, he is supposed to be instructed by two Southern *white* employees in the "mechanics of grinding and polishing lenses". He does the odd jobs about the place, but as the weeks pass, the two white men make no attempt to teach him. He asks one of the men, Reynolds, to tell him about the work. The following dialogue ensues:

    > "What are you trying to do, get smart nigger? He asked me.
    > "No sir," I said.

    Wright was baffled. He decided to try the other worker, Pease, instead, reminding him that "the boss said that I was to be given a chance to learn the trade." The following dialogue ensued:

    > "Nigger, you think you're white, don't you?"
    > "No sir."
    > "You're acting almighty like it," he said. Pease shook his fist in my face.
    > "This is white man's work around here," he said.

10. George Lamming, *In the Castle of My Skin* (1953; New York: Collier Books, 1970), 334. Emphasis added.
11. See R.J. Macdonald, "Building Jerusalem: The Construction of a Black Utopian Ideology, 1934-1939". (Paper presented at African Studies Association Conference, Houston, TX, November 1977).
12. I am indebted to Professor St. Clair Drake of the Stanford African and Afro-American Studies Program for further information with regard to the inside story

of the Padmore/Comintern clash, as well as to his lucid account of the complexity of the choice that Padmore faced.

13. In his pathbreaking study, *The Modern World-System: Capitalist Agriculture and the Origins of the European World-Economy in the Sixteenth Century*, Vol. 1 (New York: Academic Press, 1974), Immanuel Wallerstein, although giving a hegemonically economistic interpretation of the origin and reality of the Western world system, nevertheless devotes a chapter to the *political* aspect of the origin of this world-system. He begins this chapter – titled, "The Absolute Monarchy and Statism" – with the following question: "It is evident that the rise of the Absolute Monarchy in Western Europe is coordinate with the emergence of a European world economy. But is it cause or consequence?" See ibid., 93.

14. For this fundamental difference one which serves to relativise the West's conception – whether in terms of the Christian-religious or in those of post-medieval, secular-humanism of slaves, see Suzanne Miers and Igor Kopytoff, *Slavery in Africa: Historical and Anthropological Perspectives* (Madison: University of Wisconsin Press, 1977).

15. Christian Palloix in his book, *The Internationalization of Capital* (Paris: Maspero, 1975), discusses the self-expansion of capital. Margaret Bald and David Levy translated a part of Palloix's book, which was published as an article in the *Review of Radical Political Economics*, vol. 9, no. 2 (Summer 1977). In his introduction to Palloix, Robert Cohen writes:

Palloix's critique is rooted in the realisation that the self-expansion of capital can no longer be entirely accomplished within one capitalist formation, since commodities or rather "commodity groups" are only produced at a world level. Thus in today's economy there is a new mode of accumulation of capital, but also by:
1) an international differentiation of the working class through deskilling, differentiation of the labour process, and the differentiation of the production and the reproduction of the values of labour power...

In an unpublished monograph written in 1973, I had pointed out that the Caribbean plantations were the site where forced slave labour was differentiated from "normative" labour in the coloniser countries; and that this relative differentiation was itself necessary to the process of capitalism. It was, of course, Rosa Luxemburg's original and great insight that capitalism was *imperatively* from the beginning, a world system, even where it itself, was to be, *as a system*, a later form of the mercantilist – i.e. directed by the Absolute state, of which before the rise of the bourgeoisie to ruling class status, in the nineteenth century, capitalism itself, had functioned only as a powerful element in terms of the former. The "unit fallacy" dear to Western Marxists, i.e., the inherent development of capitalism in the West, its Immaculate Conception, is ideological. In the same way that the Western bourgeoisie saw their capital, as capital accumulated by their own thrift, so Western Marxists want to claim that the wealth accumulated in the West is the unique product of the Western Proletariat; and is therefore the legitimate inheritance of the West's socialist heirs. The unit fallacy is widespread. In 1974, however, Immanuel Wallerstein called this fallacy in question with the publication of his seminal study, *The Modern World System*; a pathbreaking and definitive study, even where his purely economic interpretation is open to question.

16. Lamming, *In the Castle of My Skin*, 333-334.

17. Ralph Ellison, *Invisible Man* (New York: Random House, 1952), 3.

18. Lamming, *In the Castle of My Skin*, 334

19. Hans Jonas, *The Gnostic Religion: The Message of the Alien God and the Beginnings of Christianity* (Boston: Beacon Press, 1963), 45.

20. Jon Bradshaw, "The Reggae Way to 'Salvation'", *The New York Times Magazine* (August 1977), 30.

21. St. Clair Drake, *The Redemption of Africa and Black Religion*. (Chicago: Third World Press and Atlanta, GA: Institute of the Black World, 1970), 9.

22. Ibid., 10.

23. Bradshaw, "The Reggae Way to 'Salvation'", 28.

24. Ken Post, *Arise Ye Starvelings: The Jamaica Labour Rebellion and its Aftermath* (The Hague: Martinus Nijhoff, 1978), 166.

25. Hans Jonas, *The Gnostic Religion*, 31.

26. Ibid., 32

27. Ibid., 35.

28. Michel Foucault, *The Order of Things: An Archaeology of the Human Sciences* (New York: Random House, 1973), 380.

29. Bradshaw, "The Reggae Way to 'Salvation'", 28.

30. Hanns-Albert Steger, *El trasfondo revolucionario del sincretismo criollo, aspectos sociales de la transformación clandestina de la religión en Afro-América, colonial y post-colonial* (Cuernavaca, Mexico: CIDOC, 1972), 11.

31. Ibid., 18.

32. Jonas, 44.

33. Jonas, 44.

34. Bradshaw, "The Reggae Way to 'Salvation'", 28.

35. Roland Barthes, in *S/Z: An Essay*. Trans. Richard Miller (New York: Hill and Wang, 1974), 39, makes a distinction between the index and the sign. As he writes:
    "In the past…money 'revealed'; it was an index, it furnished a fact, a cause, it had a nature; today it 'represents'…it is an equivalent, an exchange, a representation: a sign."

36. Bradshaw, "The Reggae Way to 'Salvation'", 28.

37. Ibid., 25.

38. Jean Baudrillard, *The Mirror of Production*, trans M. Poster (New York: Telos Press, 1975), 136. Emphasis added.

39. P. Antonio de Teruel: *Descripción narrativa de la mission seráfica de los capuchinos y sus Progresos en el Reyno de Congo*. (1663-4). Unpublished manuscript in the Biblioteca Nacional, Madrid, Spain. (MS 3533, 3574).

40. As Baudrillard writes:
    "It is not tautological that the concept of history is historical and that the concept of dialectic is dialectical, and that the concept of production is itself produced… Rather, this simply indicates the explosive, mortal, present form of critical concepts. As soon as they are constituted as universal they cease to be analytical and the religion of meaning begins… There is neither a mode of production nor production in primitive societies… These concepts analyse only our own societies, which are ruled by political economy" (*Mirror of Production*, 48-49. Emphasis added.

41. Ibid., 30-31.
42. Ibid., 31. Emphasis added.
43. Ken Post, "The Bible as Ideology: Ethiopianism in Jamaica, 1930-1938", in *African Perspectives: Papers in history, politics, and economics of Africa, Presented to Thomas Hodgkin* (Cambridge: Cambridge University Press, 1970), 185-207.
   After finally predicting the demise of Ethiopianism with the rise of labour union movements and political party activity, Post concludes:
   "From this point on, Ethiopianism was effectively restricted to its more extreme, Rastafarian form, as the ideological expression of the lumpen-proletariat, or at least Jamaica's equivalent, the unemployed and semi-employed inhabitants of the slums of West Kingston and other towns". Ibid., 206.
44. Frederick Douglass, *Narrative of the Life of Frederick Douglass, An American Slave* (NY: Signet, New American Library, 1968), 66-86.
45. Peter Winch, "Understanding a Primitive Society", *American Philosophical Quarterly*, vol. 1, no. 4 (October 1964): 307-24.
46. Baudrillaud, *The Mirror of Production*, 138.
47. Edward Long, *The History of Jamaica or, General Survey of the Antient and Modern State of That Island...*, Vol. II (London: T. Lowndes, 1774).
48. Foucault, *The Order of Things*, 380.
49. Long, *History of Jamaica*, 332.
50. Ibid., 324-355. Emphasis added.
51. Steger, *El trasfondo*, 42.
52. Bradshaw, "The Reggae Way to Salvation", 28. Emphasis added.
53. Ibid.
54. For instance, Junior Byles with songs "Joshua Desire" and "Pharoah Hiding".
55. Bradshaw, "The Reggae Way to Salvation", 28.
56. Ibid., 26.
57. See Michael Manley, *Jamaica: Not for Sale*, with a supp. by C.L.R. James. (San Francisco: Editorial Consultants, Inc., 1977), 24.
58. Bob Marley and the Wailers, "Get Up, Stand Up", *Burnin'*.
59. Bob Marley, "Exodus", *Exodus* (London: Island Records, 1977).
60. Baudrillard, *The Mirror of Production*, 151.
61. Aimé Césaire, *Lettre à Maurice Thorez* (Paris: *Présence Africaine*,1957).
62. Bob Marley and the Wailers, "Them Belly Full (But We Hungry)", *Natty Dread*, 1971 and *Live!* Tuff Gong/Island, 1975.
   Them belly full but we hungry.
   A hungry mob is a angry mob.
   A rain a-fall but the dirt it tough;
   A pot a-cook but the food no 'nough.
   You're gonna dance to Jah music, dance.
   We're gonna dance to Jah music, dance.
   Forget your troubles and dance.
   Forget your sorrow and dance.
   Forget your sickness and dance.
   Forget your weakness and dance.
   Cost of living get so high,
   Rich and poor, they start a cry.

> Now the weak must get strong.
> They say, "Oh, what a tribulation."
> [...]
> A angry mob is a angry mob.
> A rain a-fall but the dirt it tough;
> A pot a-cook but the food no 'nough...

63. St. Clair Drake, op cit.

64. Lacan, *The Language of Self*, 48.

65. Taylor, John. (MS.) Multum in parvo or parvum in multo (Taylor's second part of the "historie of his life and travels in America. Containing a full geographical description of the Island of Jamaica..."). Quarto vol. 236 written pages. Sylvia Wynter consulted the original manuscript, which has since been published as *Jamaica in 1687: The Taylor Manuscript at the National Library of Jamaica*, ed. David Buisseret (Kingston: University of the West Indies Press, Mill Press and National Library, 2008), 272.

66. Ibid., 272

67. Ibid., 272

68. Ibid., 272

69. Ibid., 275, 278. Emphasis added.

70. C.L.R. James, *The Black Jacobins* (1938; New York: Vintage, 1963).

71. "The most sensible among them [the Creole slaves, born in the island and therefore already 'seasoned' as distinct from the "imported African" who in the eighteenth century as distinct from the early nineteenth, led most of the rebellions] fear the supernatural powers of the African *obeah-man,* or pretended conjurers; often ascribing those mortal effects to magic, which are only the operations of some poisonous juice or preparation dexterously administered by these villains...

    "Nor long since, some of these execrable wretches in Jamaica introduced what they called the *Myal dance*, and, established a kind of society, *into which they invited all they could*. The lure hung out, was that every Negroe, *initiated into* the Myal society, would be invulnerable by the white man; and although they might in appearance, be slain, the *obeah-man* could...restore the body to life", Long, *History of Jamaica*, vol. II, 416. Emphasis added.

72. Bob Marley and the Wailers, "Exodus." *Exodus*. Tuff Gong/Island, 1977.

73. Hanns-Albert Steger, *El trasfondo*, 36.

74. Pamela O'Gorman, "An Approach to the Study of Popular Music", *Jamaica Journal: A Quarterly of the Institute of Jamaica*, vol. 6. no. 4 (December 1972), 51.

75. Max Horkheimer, *Critical Theory*, trans. Matthew O'Connell (New York, 1972), 129.

76. Ibid.

77. Bradshaw, "The Reggae Way", 28.

78. Umberto Eco, *A Theory of Semiotics* (Bloomington: Indiana University Press, 1976), 67-68. Emphasis added.

79. Asmarom Legesse, *Gada: Three Approaches to the Study of African Society* (New York: Free Press, 1973), 115.

80. As Asmarom Legesse concludes, it is only this liminal category (whether person or group) who, by implication, in attempting to step out of its preassigned role in

the "obligatory order" of all human societies, is able "to *remind us that we need not forever remain prisoners of our prescriptions*". In Baudrillard's related terms, our "arsenal of significations," together with "the mental, sexual, and cultural structures" whose iron walls. Such arsenals function to stably institute/reproduce. Seeing that in so doing, this category is able to "generate *conscious* change, by exposing *all the injustices inherent in structure*." Legesse, 271.

81. The counter-doctrinal imperative of these rights as inherited ones, common to all, is put forward by Marley in his 1974 song "So Jah Seh." *Natty Dread.* Tuff Gong/Island, 1974:

> So jah seh,
> Not one of my seeds,
> Shall sit in the sidewalk
> And beg bread [...]
> Inite oneself and love Imanity
> [...]
> Ye are the sheep of my pasture
> So verily, thou shall be very well
> [...]
> And down here in the ghetto
> And down here we suffer
> I and I a hang on in there
> And I and I, I nah leggo [...]
> I'm going to prepare a place
> That where I am thou shall abide
> So jah seh

HISTORY, IDEOLOGY, AND THE REINVENTION OF THE PAST IN ACHEBE'S *THINGS FALL APART* AND LAYE'S *THE DARK CHILD*

Several interrelated problems will be explored in this paper. These are: the problem that confronts the Black writer and, in particular, the African writer, in his fictional reinvention of the past; the problem of the Western conceptualisation of the history of African peoples as "prehistory" or as nonhistory; the problem of ideology and its relation to fiction; and, lastly, the problem of the "normative" illusion in criticism, the illusion that all works of fiction should be evaluated in relation to an implicit absolute model.[1]

These problems shall be explored primarily with respect to Camara Laye's *The Dark Child* and secondarily to Chinua Achebe's *Things Fall Apart*. By and large Achebe's *Things Fall Apart* has met with an unmixed critical reception, one deservedly so, of acclaim. Camara Laye's The *Dark Child,* equally a classic, has, however, been caught in a more critical crossfire.[2]

Jeanette Macaulay has discussed the contradiction between critical recognition for *The Dark Child* and the sharp criticism from some sections of the new African elite who, she argues, began "to study this work in the light of their political and social background, interpretation of life or world view".[3] That is to say, much critical African response was based on the ideological presuppositions of anticolonialism, presuppositions whose validity and limitations are only now beginning to be examined. The main presupposition that concerns us here is that of an overtly political anticolonial stance as a normative prerequisite for the African novel. Thus, the main charge against *The Dark Child* was that it did not deal with "the problems created by the French system of colonisation".[4]

In the vanguard of this attack, as Macaulay points out, was the writer Mongo Beti, who unfavourably compared *The Dark Child* to Richard Wright's *Black Boy*. Beti puts the comparison sharply: "Wright disdains the slightest pandering to the public taste. He poses the problems, however crude. Laye, on the other hand, is stubbornly satisfied with the anodyne, facile and picturesque and also the most lucrative. Does this Guinean, a fellow African who was, as he would have us believe, a highly intelligent boy, never see any but the tranquil, beautiful eternal Africa? Is it possible that Laye was not even once witness to the smallest trial of the colonial administration?"[5]

Macaulay perceptively sees the central problem. Beti has chosen to dictate what an author should write.[6] Pierre Macherey analyses this critical approach as it is related to the normative illusion in criticism. In normative criticism, he argues, the novel is subordinated to a principle of legality, an aesthetic legality that has a juridical rather than a theoretical status. The principle of legality seeks to control the writer, restraining him by rules. It constitutes a value judgment which ceaselessly corrects the novel, writing on its margin "could do better".[7]

The Dark Child has suffered not only from normative judgment, but from the fact that even those who praise the novel – we shall later refer to Gerald Moore's assessment of the novel – critically misread it from their own particular bias. No other criticism has been more damaging than the assertion that his work is not fiction but, rather, romanticised autobiography. The writer Phillipe Thoby Marcelin, who introduces the English translation of The Dark Child, repeats what is by now a critical cliché. The Dark Child, he argues, is "properly speaking... not a novel... It is an autobiographical story".[8]

This paper seeks to show that the confusion as to genre arises from a lack of differentiation between story and plot. The Russian formalists make a valuable distinction between the two. The story merely recounts what happened. All autobiography is based on the story. It is the transformation of story into plot that defines the genre of fiction. And the plot itself is the rearrangement of the story, its transposition into a fictional system. It is this transposition that enables the particular experience (the story) to take on universal dimensions. It is the transposition by Laye of his autobiographical story into the plotted fictional system that results in the very fine novel The Dark Child.

In this context it is worthwhile to discuss Achebe's critique of Laye's The Dark Child, referring it to his own classic novel Things Fall Apart. Achebe's critique of The Dark Child is posed in a perceptive discussion of the problem faced by the African writer in his reinvention of the precolonial past, a problem which also poses questions about the relationship of the writer's ideology to his writing of fiction. Implicit also in his discussion is the problem posed explicitly in Things Fall Apart, the question of the writing and conceptualisation of the history of the African past. Achebe writes:

> The question is, how does a writer re-create this past? Quite clearly, there is a strong temptation to idealise it – to extol its good points and pretend that the bad never existed... This is where the writer's integrity comes in. Will he be strong enough to overcome the temptation to select only those facts which flatter him? ...We cannot pretend that our past was one long technicolour idyll. We have to admit that like other people's pasts, ours had its good as well as its bad sides.[9]

The problem is well posed. The temptation for all Third World writers to select only those facts which flatter is a temptation itself postulated by that prior reinvention of the past which Western imperialism used both as ideological justification for conquest and as the motive force of its own actions in the present. The pervasive cultural nationalism of the West, vis-à-vis other peoples whom it has subjugated, invites as its negation an inversion of its own presuppositions. The past has been reinvented as ideology by the West, to sustain the West's consciousness of itself as Subject, a consciousness which needed the negation of the Other, the non-West. This presents the Third World writer with the temptation to fabricate a counter-ideology.

Such has often been the first step in the movement of political revolt by dominated peoples against Western political and cultural imperialism. The Western myth of origin – its history began with the Greeks, representing a continuity with the very origins of human intellectual thought – was politically contested by a counter-reinvention of their past by the non-Western dominated peoples. The concept of the dream of Africa, of Aztlán for the Chicanos, became a mythical construct, which takes on, at the right conjuncture – as in the Sixties – a material and revolutionary force. It is in this context, too, that the seeming illogic of the Black Muslims' myth of origin can be apprehended as a supremely logical exercise. It functions as a coherent conceptualisation for a large number of the Black popular masses only because it negates and therefore contests, point by point, the parallel myth of origin held by white Americans. Moreover, the myth is bolstered and sustained by the power arrangements of concrete reality. Thus the ideology of the Black Muslims answers the ideology of the dominant society. That is, it counters the web of implicit beliefs and commonly shared assumptions which constitute and perpetuate the fabric of society, producing and reproducing its existing social relations. The achieved novel, Laye's or Achebe's, does not answer ideology. Rather, they construct a functional truth which lays bare the untruth of ideology.

A central assumption of the West is that native peoples, particularly Blacks, are historyless. Even where they had some kind of history it was a prehistory as distinct from a "true" history, that of the West's. Black people were therefore outside history. The myth of the historyless people, of lesser breeds outside the law, authenticate the West's image of itself as a people appointed by History to a historical mission, a mission which was ordained by the nature of its origins as a civilisation.

To this the Black Muslims respond with a myth of history in which Original Black Man was the first man to inhabit the earth; in which slavery, terrible as it was, was only part of God's plan; and in which, as E.U. Essien-Udom summarises:

> Redemption of the Black Nation will come after the final judgment. 'The New World' will come into being here on earth. The chosen, namely the righteous blacks who hitherto have been oppressed by the Caucasian race, will inherit power over the whole earth. This will be the culmination of history, and the Black Nation will surpass in glory all previous regimes. It will have no successors and black men will rule forever under the benign guidance of Allah. In this 'New World' there will be eternal peace and happiness.[10]

Here we see the power of the Black mythology, a power which resides in the way it counters the lived ideological negation experienced by Black peoples. But the source of its power was the source of its necessary limitation. In inverting the Western myth of dominance, it negated the oppressor within the context and the code defined by him.

Here we rejoin Achebe. The work of fiction, the work of art, is not ideology. The temptation to flatter one's self, and to selectively use the past in order to do so, is, to use Lukács's formulation, an ethical problem which is also the aesthetic problem of the novel. The novel which falls back on ideology is an inferior one whose aesthetic formulation is unable to institute the principle of veracity which each achieved novel creates, for itself, in constituting itself as form. In becoming ideological, the novel ceases to be a work of art; rather, it is now a work which has a special relationship to ideology. Louis Althusser defines this relationship when he writes:

> *I do not rank real art among the ideologies*, although art does have a quite particular and specific relationship with ideology.... I believe that the peculiarity of art is to 'make us see' (*nous donner à voir*), 'make us perceive', 'make us believe' something which *alludes* to reality. ...Balzac and Solzhenitsyn give a 'view' of the ideology to which their work alludes and with which it is constantly fed, a view which presupposes a *retreat, an internal distantiation* from the very ideology from which their works emerged. They make us 'perceive' (but not know) in some sense from the outside, by an internal distance, the very ideology in which they are held.[11]

We can observe the truth of Althusser's definition in Achebe's first and classic novel, *Things Fall Apart.* The novel which reaches its climax with the suicide of the hero, ends with this comment:

> The Commissioner went away taking three or four of the soldiers with him. In the many years in which he had toiled to bring civilisation to different parts of Africa he had learned a number of things. One of them was that a District Commissioner must never attend to such undignified details as cutting a hanged man from a tree. Such attention would give the natives a poor opinion of him. In the book which he planned to write he would stress that point. As he walked back to he court he thought about that book. Every day brought him some new material. The story of this man who had killed a messenger and hanged himself would make interesting reading. He had already chosen the title of the book, after much thought: *The Pacification of the Primitive Tribes of the Lower Niger.*[12]

The word pacification and the word primitive – with all the connotations of Noble Savage, Savage Monster, "close" to Nature, with all the connotations of the "natural" that constitutes "white" mythology – gives us the clue as to the relationship of Achebe's novel to the implicit Western ideology which is involved in the writing of history itself. Rather than formulating a counter-ideology trapped in the context and the code defined by the Other, the novel contests the abstraction of the ideological terms. The term "primitive tribe" is an abstract construct which functionally enables the physical and cultural genocide of peoples to be subsumed under the "neutral" technical term of "pacification". What the novel does is to present us with the concrete experience of "pacification" by creating fictional characters who enable us to see through the abstract construct, the ideological stereotype. By doing this, it gives a view of the ideology to which it alludes, through establishing an internal distanciation from the "very ideology in which they are held".

Behind that ideology, which constitutes Western history vis-à-vis the non-Western world, Achebe gives us, through the means which he uses to contest that historical ideology, an experience of the bundle of events behind the mythology of the historical fact. In addition, he calls the abstract historical categories into question, the same categories which Western historical thought uses itself.

What is presented in his novel is not a historyless people, nor a people whose history is an inverted reflection of "white" history, but a people whose lived and theoretical concept of history was different from the one which the colonisers – represented by the commissioner and the Christian missionaries – brought with them and imposed under shadows of guns, churches, schools, trading posts, courts of justice, and colonial bureaucracy. They created a new lived experience which was formed by a new relationship to history.

In *Things Fall Apart*, the tragedy of Achebe's hero, Okonkwo, is that he who sought legendary fame in another context and in another world view, stumbles into a new world where, in order to validate the old values and the traditional ethic, he must negate them. That is, after killing the court messenger, he must commit suicide to escape the even greater shame (the negation of fame) that would occur were he to be arrested and humiliated in a world of aliens with their alien concept of justice. Yet, in killing himself, he desecrates the most sacred taboos of the world view which sustained his old world; in seeking to validate the values of the old world, he finds himself in a double bind where the only action open to him is one which will, at the same time, make him a stranger. He may not be buried by his clansmen, and he thereby is deprived of his role after death as an ancestor. But he knew, the moment after his action when he stood alone – no one moved to support him – that the things which bound them together had fallen apart.

His death after that was, to use a phrase, history. At that moment for the first time in his life, he stood isolated and alone, exiled in life. His death by suicide, and his consequent exclusion from the past, present and future of the tribe were only ratifications of his exile, of the terror of bitter rupture. He was ripped from the past and from those traditions which had constituted him – and Umuofia – as the centre of their own universe. He and Umuofia are now forever decentred, deterritorialised. The forms of the past would continue but its essence, the relationship to a material reality which gave it meaning, was now, irrevocably, gone. To keep faith with the past that was, he dies, sacrilegiously, with it.

It is the dialectic of exile, of rupture, that is defined here as the Middle Passage experience, an experience which is central to the poetics of the literature of the

Black diaspora. The term itself, the Middle Passage, was the historical designation for the passage from Africa to the New World in the triangle trade, the slave trade initiated by the West. Millions of transported tribal Africans represented the first mass labour force that the emergent global economic system of capitalism was to expropriate not only from its means of production, but from that superstructure of traditions, cultures and myths of origin which coded the former concepts of self, the former perception of being.

New World Black slaves were, therefore, the first form of that super-exploited variant of labour – native labour – which the non-West would provide for the production process dominated by the West. This process, as it spread out over all the world, disrupted native peoples from their former cultural being, not in one definitive rupture but in a series of ruptures. Increasingly all former social orders, all men, became adjuncts to the productive process. Thus the slaves, freed in the American South after the Civil War, were disrupted to the cities, to the ghettoes, just as today all over the world the native peoples pour into their ghetto variants: shantytown, barricades, favelas, etc. They, too, now undergo this Middle Passage experience of exile from the past, of disruption from traditional cultures.

Exile is now the native condition. Thus the theme of exile, as well as the unrealisable dream of the return to the native land, haunts Third World poetry and fiction. Its historical time is constituted by a before and after the fall. The expulsion from the Golden Age, from Eden, eternally recurs; and the past is commemorated only through the mourning rites that lament its loss.

It is within this context that I would like to look at the classic African novel, *The Dark Child* by Camara Laye, a great book of exile and the Middle Passage experience.

In the context of his previous remarks, Achebe made the following reference to the work:

> That is why, in spite of my admiration for Camara Laye, as a writer I still say that I find *The Dark Child* a little too sweet. I admit that recollections of one's childhood tend naturally to be spread over with an aura of innocence and beauty; and I realise that Camara Laye wrote his book when he was feeling particularly lonely and homesick in France. But I maintain that any serious African writer who wants to plead the cause of the past must not only be God's advocate, he must also do duty for the devil.[13]

Achebe's critique of Laye's novel comes from a serious misreading, a misreading related to the critical normative illusion. Unconsciously, Achebe seems to have the model of his own achieved novel, *Things Fall Apart,* in mind. In his own work it obviously was his conscious intention to recreate a past in which he would do duty for the devil also. It was a past in which Okonkwo, a driven, impatient man, ambitious for titles and honours, spurred on to negate his father's failure, and thereby alienating his son, acts as the prototypical Greek hero with the tragic flaw and hastens his own downfall. In fact, by his own actions he helps to bring it about.

But in the means which he uses to tell his story, in the figurations, the embodyings, the figuring forth which he uses, Achebe goes beyond his original intention. He reconstructs a society in whose cultural coordinates Okonkwo moves. This is a society whose world view and material organisation provide the conditions of possibility for both his achievements and his defeats. It is a world, in fact, in which Okonkwo lives and moves as a subject amongst other subjects, all of whom are the inheritors of the fabric of significations which they collectively extend and perpetuate through ritual. In this world Okonkwo walks protected by the rules, sanctified by the ancestors. Even when he commits his first sacrilege, the traditional system has its own rules, rules which constitute his being, and through accepting them, he confirms his being, however objectively hard the punishment may seem. That the "bad side" is there, as well as the "good side", Achebe all the more shows Okonkwo as a man validating the basic concepts of his society, even to the extent of embodying its contradictions. Indeed, what Achebe does is to show us not an underdeveloped culture – underdevelopment only begins when the colonial relationship starts – but an entire and integral culture. Drawing the "bad side" only makes the portrayal more complete.

Between the original intention, to show the bad as well as the good side, and the achieved result, a new intention has interposed itself: the intention to negate the implicit Western assumption of the cultureless Blacks, of a culture that was not a culture at all. The novel therefore constitutes as its absence the ideological thesis of Western imperialism which presented itself as the universal culture, the chosen culture, and denied to other peoples – especially the Africans – any culture or history at all. The fictional constitution of an integral culture, with its own values, history and concept of history, a constitution using the novel form, i.e., in the very terms of the civilisation and culture which denies it culture and history, is therefore part of the dialectic central to Third World poetics. Over and against the ideological thesis of the cultural void in which the native peoples lived, Achebe creates a society with its own aesthetic and its own contradictory system of ethics. The infringement of the code of ethics by Okonkwo all the more convincingly recreates the ethic as a lived concrete reality, i.e., as a constitutive part of the culture in which Okonkwo moves and has being. It is to the extent that he is fashioned by his culture that, when the alien civilisation comes upon him, he finds himself in a world in which, suddenly, he walks unprotected by the rules, unsanctified by the gods, groping in a darkness come at noon. For it is the unforeseen coming of this new world, the industrial culture of contemporary man, that converts the minor flaw of Okonkwo into the tragic flaw of personal and collective catastrophe.

Okonkwo finds himself dead in a life, now unstructured by custom, no longer autochthonous or autocentric. He finds himself unable to accept or to come to terms with a life, which, through no fault of his own, has now become, in Laye's phrase, "the temporary highways of exile".[14]

The theme of the Middle Passage of experience is also central to Laye's novel; it is this theme which gives the work its classic grandeur. What Achebe sees as "sweet" responds to what some sixteenth- and seventeenth-European theorists called aesthetic delight, a delight whose tragedy cannot be reduced to the safety of an ethical poetic justice where no moral flaw in any individual agent precipitates suffering. It is one in which world-historical forces (conceived of as fate in earlier times) sweep up individual men, individual groups, and lead them ineluctably from the known and native state to a state of change. It moves men from familiar paths marked by familiar trees, skies, clouds, and earth to unknown and barren highways of exile.[15]

The progress of disruption from the known to the unknown imparts a tragic tension to Camara Laye's novel, making it a classic of Third World and twentieth-century fiction. The progress of disruption constitutes the plot, to borrow the formalist's distinction, as it is marked by two thematic objects: the narrator's mother's hut at the beginning of the story and the map of the Paris Metro at the end. In his criticism of the *The Dark Child*, Achebe, in order to dismiss the novel, recounts it only at the story level, that is, as a chronological sequence of events. Laye as a writer, lonely in Paris, looks back and recalls his childhood. Commonplace enough. A story of Laye's life would relate the same sequence. It is the plot, the narrative structuring, the selection and combination of events and motifs, the analogical world of correspondences, in other words, the means which Laye uses to tell his story, which transform the story into a work of fiction. And in this transformation a mutation occurs. It is the mutation which constitutes Laye's particular progress from a native culture into the contemporary world, as the universal disruption of modern man from the still stable patterned world of childhood, still structured by rules, sanctified by gods (adults), into the emptiness and loss of modern life. It is another passage from Combray to the present, from nativity to exile. Its paradox lies in the fact that it is only the recognition and experience of present exile that makes possible the boon of memory with which the writer recalls the past only on the condition that, like Orpheus, he must accept the past as forever behind him, forever recalled only in song.

Thus to sing the Blues, Laye must pay his dues. Sartre defines this paradox in his introduction to the anthology of Black poetry, *Black Orpheus:* "In choosing to see that which he is, he has split himself in two, he no longer coincides with himself. And reciprocally, it was because he was already exiled from himself that there was the duty to declare himself. He begins thus by exile; the exile of his body offers a striking example of the exile of his heart."[16]

Laye's conscious intention may well have been, as Achebe puts it, to recall, in his Parisian loneliness, the comforting warm world of his childhood. But as Macherey points out, the means which the writer uses to construct and to express what he wants can very often structure quite another fictional reality from the one which he intentionally started.[17] I propose to argue that at the deep structural level, at the heart of *The Dark Child,* there is a central parallelism; that this central parallelism consists of an initiation into the known which is at the same time an initiation into the unknown; and that the theme of this parallelism is the theme of the exile of the heart.

The dual parallelism is constituted by the boy growing up into adolescence, his rite of passage into adulthood, and his growing away into the colonial world, i.e., his rite of passage from his traditional world into modern and contemporary civilisation. The first rite of passage is fully prescribed, patterned by an ancient culture, its rituals prepared and planned to test the young boy, in order to prepare him for the challenges of the adult world; for the challenges of a world whose lineaments are fixed, whose traditional ordeals have been recurrently met and overcome; a world which has passed down its traditional accumulated lore, a lore structured in the "writing" which is its ritual forms.

Anthony Wilden has developed Jacques Derrida's concept of the inextricable link between oral speech and forms of writing as the "logical prerequisite for speech". And he goes on to point out that in societies without writing in the Western sense: "the past of the society – its memory, its set of instructions, its sacred text, is literally embodied, in every domicile, in every person or group marked by a kinship term or by a taboo, in every person, or group who exemplifies a ritual or recalls a myth."[18]

The known *rite de passage,* the known initiation, is then a reinvention in the flesh; it is ritual and meta-ritual. Here we note the paradox that Laye's novel is really one form of writing about another form of writing. Further, the second form of writing cannot constitute itself except out of the absence of that other form of writing of which it speaks, of its own exile from that other form. Hence, the novel whose content commemoratively recalls the past is that form which witnesses its irrevocable loss.

The novel recalls the known traditional rite of passage as present, explicit and central; indeed, it recalls it in loving, concrete detail. But there is a second rite of passage, one unpatterned, not even seen to exist as such, yet powerful in the absence of its explicit presence. This second rite of passage is overlooked by both the critics who attack Laye and by those who insist on his "innocence". Gerald Moore, in his critique of the novel, writes that:

> Camara Laye [was] born only three years before David Diop...[yet he] inhabits an entirely different world. In Diop's writing the menace and cruelty of Europe are never absent, oppression seems to enclose his writing on every side, making his talent spring like a tiger. In Laye's work the colonial world hardly obtrudes at all. The Kouroussa of his first book, *The Dark Child,* might be a town in an independent country, so marginal is the presence of the colonial power.[19]

The presence of the colonial power, made explicit in Achebe's *Things Fall Apart,* is itself but a form of the far greater confrontation between a culture sprung from the neolithic revolution and a new culture based on the industrial revolution. Superseded by the technological superiority of the latter culture, the former finds itself undergoing a mutation. The culture of production based on the industrial revolution is the first culture in the history of man in which the social order – and the values which accompany the hegemony of the social order – finds itself transformed into an adjunct to the economic goal, the economic order. The great transformation which began in the West in the sixteenth century was to become, ineluctably, a cultural mutation on a global scale. It is this experience of the painful process of cultural transformation that the novels of Achebe and Laye evoke and portray.

When Gerald Moore points to the marginality of the colonial presence, he puts his finger on one of the powerful means by which the writer evokes the confrontation between the old culture and the new. Both in *Things Fall Apart* and in *The Dark Child,* the power of the new culture, in its colonial form, comes from the very marginality of its first appearance, the insidiousness of its penetration.

In its very marginality, the coming of the colonial world constitutes fate. Fate lurks, unsuspected, until it reveals the results of its obscure workings. It is that marginal world which patterns the second, invisible rite of initiation, a rite whose power will not only initiate the boy into a new unknown, unforeseen world, but will forever put barriers between himself and the lost traditional culture of his childhood.

From the beginning, the novel structures this central parallelism. The family compound in which the boy lives is near the railway. Both the railway and the compound function as thematic objects. The former is the symbol of separation and the latter, the native land. The railway is the antithesis of the family compound. Marginal at first to the story, the railway represents the forces of disintegration.

Inside the compound the father's workshop employs a mode of technology in which human energy is still central. Quite simply, the apprentices blow the bellows. In the railway, the source of energy is different. Its more complex construction is powered by steam. The railway represents more than distance in physical space; it is distance in technology. Moreover, it represents a different relationship with nature. In the traditional relationship, man both adapts himself to nature and adapts nature to his purpose. With technology, man conquers nature, utilising it for his purpose and separating himself from nature by increasingly abstract operations.

Through a small detail, snakes attracted by the hot oil on the railway lines, the natural and the symbolic worlds are juxtaposed. The railway is aesthetically perceived as a piece of Western technology imposed on a traditional society where man and nature still interact, where distances between villages were measured by foot and limited by the physical abilities of the human body. Now the railway, its reach and energy endless, link the traditional villages to the city, the market emporium of the colonial system. The market links the city and the villages to the colonial centres across the seas. The still stable world of

Kouroussa is subversively being decentred by forces which are almost invisible: forces of the market-centred economic organisation of modern society.

It is in this context that the father's workshop and the school antithetically parallel one another. Juxtaposed are two different modes of education corresponding to two different world views.[20] In his father's workshop, the apprentice learns by imitation, as does the boy. The acquisition of skills is only a part of the education and training necessary to live one's life creatively in and through the social order. In the Western school the acquisition of skills becomes an end in itself; it reflects a world view in which production is the goal and labour power is a commodity. Skilled and literate labour are more highly valued as machines replace human sources of energy. The workshop trains for life as it is lived in the prevailing social order. The school trains for production for the market order of society. Since the market calls for the conquest of nature in order to transform nature into a source of commodities, to make nature itself a commodity, the skills taught are all related to rational enquiry into the processes of nature. Different goals create different systems. The father's workshop and the school are, therefore, the thematic objects which fictionally portray what Pierre Erny describes as "different anthropologies, different ways of perceiving human reality".[21]

The central contrast between the two world views, and the Middle Passage from the one to the other, is fictionally portrayed through the use of two rhetorical devices, parallelism and antithesis. The father's compound represents fixed stability to the extent that the railway fictionally suggests movement away, change; the father's workshop represents the stable traditional world view to the extent that the school represents the intrusion of a new world view whose very principle is change. The parallels are more implicit, to be found at the deep structure level: the boy growing up in his father's compound, parallels the boy growing away, by means of the school and the railway, from the father's compound and the world which it encloses.

Here we note the complex focus initiated by the narrative structure of the book. It is the grown man, the grown-away man, who tells the story both of the "I-growing-up" (the compound); and of the "I-growing-away" (school/railway/plane). The story unfolds as if from the window of the train/plane while he looks at the vanishing world of his childhood. It is the irrevocable act of vanishing that negates the novel as a mere apologia for the past. For it is not that there were not harshnesses and cruelties in that world too. But that world had also been the privileged kingdom of Laye's childhood world; and that world had vanished as absolutely as his childhood. In memory, therefore, the time of the vanished world is regained as the time of all childhoods, of all Combrays. Here the particular theme of Paradise Lost joins a universal theme of loss.

This is not to say that in the novel Laye does not note the drawbacks of the traditional systems of the old world. But he sees them as a child experiences them, primarily through adults' reactions and words.[22] For example, in his evocation of the process of the smelting of gold in his father's workshop, opposed to the lyrical description of the praise singer drunk with the joy of creation, of the magnificent dangerous dance of the *Bouga,* is his mother's critical comment that the smelting of gold is ruining his father's eyes. Here we note a relative drawback of the traditional system. In the rational Western system, a system in which production is directed towards the abstract aim of production, the unlimited nature of the abstract goal carries as its corollary the imperative of maximum efficiency. In such a context, since good eyesight is imperative to the production process, some kind of visor would have been invented which could have protected the now valuable vision because of its role in the overall process. What we note here is that the main goal-seeking activity of the society determines the kind of problems posed and the kind of solutions found. Each society pays its dues. Ruined eyes and lack of rapid productive development are part of the price for the stability of the social order in Laye's traditional world. Similarly, we pay our price: psychological destruction, loneliness like a disease, in exchange for the rapid development of the productive process.

Hence the parallelism-antithesis of certain objects: on the one hand, there is the forge, the hammer, the ram's horn with magical substance, the snake, traditional lore, apprentices, competition only along prescribed lines, competition used only to promote group cohesion; on the other hand, the railways, steam, rational inquiry, the school system, teachers, competitive individual assertion, the bullying by the older, stronger boys.

The trajectory of the novel lies in the trespass, the rite of separation, from one world to the unpatterned, unforeseen initiation into the other. His mother's hut is one pole of his life passage within the traditional patterns, within the compound, within the society of which the compound forms an integral part. Childhood and growing up within this structured pattern is a passage from his mother's hut (before he is circumcised) away from his mother's hut (after he is circumcised). Pierre Erny points out that the traditional *rite de passage* is part of the process which educates the child in social relationships, in his relationship with the others.

In the movement from his mother's hut to his own there is a movement of withdrawal, of rupture, at one stage, only to effect a movement of return, of reintegration into another stage. But in the parallel process which moves from his family compound through the withdrawal into the school, there is no movement of return, of reintegration. Rather it is a movement which separates the child, now transformed into an atomised individual, and sends him on his quest into the unknown, i.e., into that world which the thematic object, the map of the Paris metro, embodies.

It is in this context that the novel's evocation of the traditional initiation rite is weighted with a poignancy and pathos. As the boy lives it, the writer, for the last time evoking this past, knows too that it is part of that past, the past of the traditional world, which, like himself, has stumbled into exile and severed its continuity with itself. It is a past which, like him, no longer "coincides with itself".

Lévi-Strauss and Sartre debate over the concept, postulated by Sartre, that societies like that of Laye's world at Kouroussa were, prior to colonialism, societies without history. In Sartre's formulation, although societies like Laye's suffered scarcity – scarcity is the category which Sartre constitutes as the ontological genesis-cause of history – these societies would have to wait for the coming of Western colonialism to endow them with "true" history as distinct from prehistory. In other words, societies like Laye's were rude prefigurations of the true "Annunciation of the Coming of the West". As Sartre writes: "In effect, we see that they begin to interiorise our history, for they have passively suffered the colonial enterprise as a historical event. But it is not their reaction to their scarcity which historialises them."[23]

Briefly, it should be noted that scarcity as a category is only conceivable within the horizon of thought constituted by capitalism; and that, as Lévi-Strauss argues, Sartre historically imposes the normative Western capitalist concept of history on another and different concept/material reality of history. He has placed one historical code on a different historical code.

For what Sartre calls our history is essentially the form of history related to the culture of production based on the global-market system. It is through the relationship with the non-West created by the market that the mutation, defined as the transition from feudalism to capitalism in Europe, took place.

The X factor of the European mutation was the discovery and appropriation by the West of the vast frontier lands of the New World, lands which then needed a mass labour force. It was this combination of external land and external labour force that constituted the conditions of possibility for the global-market system of capitalism.

It was in Europe that the first impact of change caused the world to be made really new for the first time; it was in the New World that the world was made really underdeveloped – as distinct from undeveloped – for the first time. The recorded resistance of the Indians – and the Blacks – to their extermination, subjugation and reduction to the sole role of producer shows that their modern history, as distinct from their traditional history, was a history which began with an experience of rupture from the past, of a discontinuity, an experience of exile – a Middle Passage travail. The doom that had come upon them as integral cultures was a doom postulated by the new market system, a system of which the Western bourgeoisie were the bearers and beneficiaries.

But in the West, although more imperceptibly, the disintegrative forces of the new market system were at work. There, too, a rupture, a Middle Passage, a discontinuity, took place. It was out of the experience of discontinuity, of rupture, that the novel form was born.

It was this form that expressed man as no longer native to experience, as man in search of a being and of a world in which he could be once more humanly at ease. In Europe, as well, traditional cultures based on a stable social order were swept away. From Cervantes's *Don Quixote* onwards, the novel form chronicles man in quest of a meaningful role now that all the old meanings are gone. Man searches for a meaningful identity now that all codes that formerly constituted his identity are being progressively decoded.

The modern history of Laye's narrator begins by and through a rupture with a different network of meaning. It is a different history, one which the Western mind conceives of as "prehistory". It is this concept which the fiction of the novel, through recreating the traditional world at the moment of the boy's rupture from this world, is able to make us perceive as ideology. The fiction of the novel negates the abstract construct of the implicit Western historical discourse – Kouroussa as a prehistorical society – by its concrete evocation of another mode, not an earlier or prior one of lived experience, but another mode of history.

The category of scarcity as used by Sartre springs from the ideology of Social Darwinism. Scarcity was the natural condition which allegedly gave birth to real history. Scarcity, Sartre argues, only founds the possibility of human history; there must be other factors in order for true history to be actualised. And these, he implies, include the existential choice which each society makes about itself. Societies, he goes on to argue, that are without history and are therefore based on repetition and recurrence are societies which have established a mode of production in which a certain decision has been made about the nature of the human being: Man is stunted and deformed, living to work from dawn to night with rudimentary techniques on an ungrateful and threatening land.

Sartre conceptualises a traditional society like Laye's Tindican where the hoe is still the "rudimentary" technical means of production, as a nasty, brutish, short state condemned to repetition and the void of history. Lévi-Strauss takes Sartre to task:

> And indeed what can one make of peoples 'without history', when one has defined man in terms of dialectic and dialectic in terms of history? Sometimes Sartre seems tempted to distinguish two dialectics: the 'true' one which is supposed to be that of historical societies, and a repetitive, short-term dialectic, which he grants so-called primitive societies whilst at the same time placing it very near biology... Alternatively Sartre resigns himself by putting a 'stunted and deformed' humanity on man's side, but not without implying that its place in humanity does not belong to it in its own right and is a function only of its adoption by historical humanity: either because it has begun to internalize the latter's history in the colonial context, or because, thanks to anthropology itself, historical humanity has given the blessing of meaning to an original humanity which was without it. [24]

Yet the tragedy of exile for the boy in Laye's novel is precisely his rupture from a system of signification, from a total and interrelated world of meanings. Later, writing in Paris, he will question whether any fragment of those past meanings exist. "But, at the moment of writing this, does any part of the rite still survive? The secret... Do we still have secrets?"[25] And already, even as a boy, standing with the others, yet apart, in the fields at Tindican, realising that he no longer had a place in his father's forge or in the Tindican fields, he had been assailed by a new question: "But where was my life?"[26]

The symbol of the hoe, the tool given to all the other members of his age group, no longer binds him to them. The exercise book and pen, given him at the same initiation rite, mark his new class separation from them. As his labour becomes mental, their labour becomes manual. In addition, as he develops his intellectual and technical skills, he will move into a world which now uses the tractor, while the hoe remains the means of production in Tindican. Yet the world of the hoe will be invisibly related to the tractor world of France through the marketing processes of unequal exchange.

The city, his uncle who is an accountant in a firm, and the railways are thematic objects which mark a new relationship. In this relationship Kouroussa and Tindican will become the exploited hinterland of that other world to which the boy journeys alone.[27]

Thus the journey of the boy also parallels the incorporation of the former autocentric worlds of Kouroussa and Tindican into a new relationship, a new global history unified by the capitalist mode of production, by its different concept of time and history. The boy and his society move from one concept of time to another. In the traditional world, time was event-oriented; calendars were not numerical, but phenomenological, calendars in which events or phenomena which constitute time "are reckoned or considered in their relation with one another and as they take place... For the people concerned, time is meaningful at the point of the event and not at the mathematical moment."[28]

There is no conceptualised objective external time. Time is a series of events reckoned through the social processes which constitute individual and collective life, stabilising the social order. In this world view, the past is not considered as the binary opposite of the present. Rather the past, Zamani, is conceived of in relation to the present, Sasa, a present that is always actual.[29] The central dimension is the present, Sasa. The memory of events, ritualised, constitutes a present time extended by the past. The concept of the future is negligible, the concept of progress unthinkable.

Events as they occur are translated backwards from the Sasa dimension, where they actualise themselves, to the Zamani dimension, the dimension coded in myth which legitimatised the present. It is in the Zamani dimension that the ancestors, as those who knew them physically die off and their memory fades, come into their own as luminous spirits, the ideal model of being for the society.

Lévi-Strauss suggests that the distinction between peoples without history and people with history could be more accurately described as the difference between societies seeking, "by the institutions they give themselves, to annul the possible effects of historical factors on their equilibrium and continuity in quasi-automatic fashion"; and societies which, on the other hand, "resolutely internalise the historical process, making it the moving power of their development."[30]

The conceptualisation of past and present, the concept of history in Laye's society, would therefore respond to the first principle of coding change within continuity. Since its goal is equilibrium, the maintaining of the social order, concepts of time and history are devices which ensure this continuity and domesticate change. Thus, societies born out of the original Neolithic revolution elaborated, as a concomitant of the social order, a concept of history which was coded as paralleling the return of the seasons of the year, seasons to which agricultural patterns were bound. In this conceptualisation, the natural seasons were therefore taken as the model on which the time of the society was constituted. The natural forces provided not only the material conditions of production – rain, sun, etc. –but also the signifiers – sewing time, planting time, harvest time. Above all, it provided the cyclical model, the eternal cyclical return of the seasons that the social order demanded.

The series of rituals are the forms of writing which code the concept of time and of history. Myths, too, were as much a form of writing as a content, perhaps more so. It was not mythical history but history coded in the form of myth that responded to the Neolithic time. Like all histories, the history of Laye's society, coded in the form of myth, was, to borrow Lévi-Strauss's phrase, "history – for", i.e., history with an ideological purpose.

In the initiation rite, central to the social birth of the age group as adult members of the clan, is their internalisation of the clan's ideological concept of history, of time, of the past. The before and after of the initiation rite, dated/ marked by the thematic objects of the narrator's mother's hut before the ceremony and of his own hut after the ceremony, are the codings of the abstract conceptualisation in which the past is seen as eternally present, that is, as an extension of the present. The rite conceptualises the ancestors as reincarnating themselves in the newborn, the past as never past since it eternally recurs. Its coding, myth, ritual must therefore be cyclical. What is seen as "repetitious" is conceptually logical. It is not that objective time necessarily repeats itself, but that objective time needs to be reinterpreted in Laye's society as cyclical. It is not that the society imitates nature, but that it uses natural signifiers to constitute its ideology.[31]

The social birth of the boy into the group is structured in order that he will perceive it as the metaphor of all change: change in continuity. His mother's hut does not disappear when he enters his own hut. It is his relationship to her hut which has changed. But the change, because of the rites which domesticate it, is not perceived by him as a natural biological change; the *rite de passage,* by formalising this change, by using natural change only as the signifier of cultural change, of social change, helps to withstand the contingency of death, of natural change. And the mourning rites themselves transform death into a passage to another form of life: life as an ancestor.

The rite which commemorates the ancestors is an act of remembering, which is itself both a concept and a form of history. It is this continuity of the past into the present, through the central metaphor of the ancestors who interact with the living, that basically stabilises time. The ancestors act as guarantors of the present, as the embodiment of the ideal model which the present must validate in order to be. The ideal model conceives of a past as timeless, as outside time.[32]

Over and against the conceptualisation of change only within continuity and its related concept of time and history, the modern world substitutes the principle of change as the motive force of its concept of history. Both time and history are conceptualisations themselves produced by different historical processes. To the extent that the second concept of history would take itself as absolute, as not itself produced by a historical process, it saw itself as the "true history", the "real" history, and therefore conceptualised all other history as its negation, its prehistory.

Colonialism was for societies like Laye's the harbinger of a process of change so total that it can no longer be contained by the old conceptualisations. For Laye's narrator there is no code from the ancient world which can domesticate the passage from his mother's hut to the Paris metro. And in the new world, there are no rites to domesticate change. Change is seen as natural; the naturalness of change becomes the licensed orthodoxy. The fact of rupture must be met head on.[33]

Both the modern history of the Third World and its modern fiction begins with this discontinuity, this experience of a rite of passage from traditional history to a history which is lived as exile. Such is the central significance of the thematic object of the map to the Paris metro that the narrator feels in his pocket as Marie, the girl he loves, leaves him at Dakar; and, for the first time in his life, he is on his own in an uncharted world, a world no longer structured by familiar landmarks. It is another world with another concept of being, time, history. What he experiences now is the passage from a history whose coding domesticated change, integrating it within the principle of continuity, to another whose coding internalises change as the principle of its continuity.

It is in this sense that the rite of passage for the boy from one history to the other is a rite of separation, a rite felt in the flesh. And the brunt of the pain of separation is felt not so much by the boy as by his mother. For this changed concept of time, of history, and of separation – in the traditional rites she felt the pain of his separation after his initiation when he became an adult, but that pain was domesticated by custom – comes subversively upon the boy's mother. He leaves her hut now, not only for his own, but for another, unsuspected era, another, undreamt of world. Thus the full weight of the mother's agony begins when the boy gets a scholarship to study in France. She had been prepared for the traditional rupture, but not for this.

The scene in which the blow falls is moving. She pounds the pestle in the mortar, keeping at bay the news. For it is her very being which will rupture.

That being, that self, has been fashioned in a system in which she had continuity, contiguity, with her children. To be a mother was to have been a lifelong role. After physical death, her life was to have continued as an ancestor, in the memory of her children; and after their death, it was to have been commemorated by her clan, the clan with which she would have interacted from the other world of the past, the other world that extended this one, the present. Life and death had been not discontinuities but stages in an extended process. Now that process is brought full stop. The mirror of herself, her son in his traditional role, now reflects her no longer. She is undermined.

Somehow she suspects that this rupture has been imposed by an alien system where family ties, like all else, are subordinated to the imperative of the productive process. Have they no mothers, these people? They want everything. Now they take away her son to their land. His separation from her imposes, for the first time, the burden of a *new* type of isolation on her. She cries: "You won't leave me alone, will you? Tell me you won't leave me alone?" The father, however, has sensed that the separation would be inevitable: "Each one follows his own destiny, my son."[34]

Once individual destiny had been only thinkable within the framework of the collective experience. Now the collective destiny will be one of separation. Each now has his own destiny. A separate destiny. The compound is emptied of the occupant of one hut. Soon the others will go. The group gives way to the individual.

The narrator promises his father that he will return. But the "I" that will return will be an "I" that will have entered a crucible of conversion and traversed a Middle Passage of experience. That "I", the "I" of "before" will never really return. The Middle Passage now constitutes the phenomenological event that numerically dates a fixed before and after, a now no longer linked to the past, a now always oriented to the future. It is a now buoyed up on the wheels of the train, the wings of the plane, a now ceaselessly questioning, but never coinciding with itself.

For this new now, alienated in the future, Laye uses the thematic objects of wheels, wheels which concretely institutionalise only one continuity, the continuity of change. Thus, when the mother cries, " 'Oh I had a son once but now I have none,' " the narrator reflects:

> She must have guessed that this was a matter where there were wheels within wheels. They had taken me from the school in Kouroussa to Conakry and finally to France. All the time she had been talking and fighting against them, she must have been watching the wheels going round and round: first this wheel, then that, and then a third and greater wheel, then still more, many more, and perhaps, which no one could see. And how could they be stopped? We could only watch them turning and turning, the wheels of destiny turning and turning. My destiny was to go away from home.[35]

The wheels of the railway give way to the wheels of the plane. The narrator notes: "the earth, the land of Guinea, began to drop rapidly away ..."[36] Like Icarus and Daedalus, he has stepped out of the old patterned dance, the old patterned ritual, out of the security of ancient custom, where time stretched backward from the present to infinity, an infinity that guaranteed the present, to another now, a now which he would live as "the temporary highways of exile". He is embarked. After Marie leaves at Dakar he feels in his pocket and finds the map of the Paris metro.

The earth of Guinea, the traditional earth, is left behind. He enters the labyrinth of exile. The now of Guinea lives only in memory; a now becomes a past, the "before" to the "after" that will be his new life whose physical co-ordinates will be marked by the map to the Paris metro, but which bears no guidelines for the heart. It is the life of the Paris metro, of the auto-assembly plant. And that past, his childhood past, unlike the traditional past, is not a stable given, hallowed in ritual, coded in myths, rites and legends. That past lives only in memory, a memory no longer collective, but frail, fragmented, dispersed.

In that now which is the after – after the Fall – Laye turns to the novel form to reconstitute the past, consciously as a reference point for that absence of which the map to the Paris metro speaks only by negation. In exile, to reinvent himself as human in the geometric aridity of a technological wasteland, alone he recalls that idyllic time before the Fall.

And his time regained is a time forever lost.

Endnotes

1. Pierre Macherey, *Pour une théorie de la production littéraire* (Paris: Maspero, 1974), 26-27.
2. Jeanette Macaulay, "The Idea of Assimilation: Mongo Beti and Camara Laye" in *Protest and Conflict in African Literature,* Cosmo Pieterse and Donald Munro, eds. (London: Heinemann, 1969), 82.
3. Ibid.
4. Ibid.
5. Ibid., 83.
6. Ibid.
7. Macherey, *Pour une théorie de la production littéraire,* 27.
8. See his introduction to Camara Laye's *The Dark Child: The Autobiography of an African Boy* (New York: Farrar, Strauss and Giroux, 1975), 7.
9. Chinua Achebe, "The Rise of the Writer in a New Nation", in *African Writers on African Writing,* G.D. Killam, ed. (Evanston: Northwestern University Press, 1973), 9.
10. E.U. Essien-Udom, *Black Nationalism: The Search for an Identity* (Chicago: University of Chicago Press, 1962), 157.
11. "Ideology and Ideological State Apparatuses", *Lenin and Philosophy and Other Essays* (New York: Monthly Review Press, 1971), 221-222.
12. Chinua Achebe, *Things Fall Apart* (New York: Fawcett, 1959), 191.

13. Achebe, "The Rise of the Writer", 9.
14. Camara Laye, *The Dark Child,* trans. James Kirkup and Ernest Jones (New York: Farrar, Strauss and Giroux), 178.
15. See particularly the Spanish sixteenth-century theorist, Alonso López Pinciano, in his *Philosophia Antigua Póetica* (Madrid: Thomas Iunti, 1596/1953), 111, especially where he develops the distinction between *tragedia mortata* – in which poetic justice constitutes the *deleyte,* and the *tragedia patetica* in which the delight is of a different order; the one, *ethical* delight; the other, *aesthetic.*
16. Jean-Paul Sartre, *Black Orpheus,* trans. S. W. Allen (Paris: Presence Africaine, 1963.), 18.
17. Macherey, *Pour une théorie,* 58.
18. "Order from Disorder: Noise, Trace and Event in Evolution and History" in *System and Structure: Essays in Communication and Exchange* (London: Tavistock Publications, 1972). 407.
19. Gerald Moore, *Seven African Writers* (London: Oxford University Press, 1966), 25.
20. Pierre Erny, *Childhood and the Cosmos: The Sociology of the African Child* (New York: New Perspectives, 1973).
21. Ibid., 225.
22. See the comment by the boy on a form of dishonesty prevalent in the traditional society, *The Dark Child,* 45.
23. Jean-Paul Sartre formulates this thesis in *Critique de la raison dialectique, Tome 1: Théorie des ensembles pratiques* (Paris: Librairie Gallimard, 1960), 203 (footnote).
24. Claude Lévi-Strauss, *The Savage Mind* (Chicago: University of Chicago Press. 1966), 248-249. Lévi-Strauss argues against Sartre in the chapter "History and Dialectic", 245-267.
    After presenting this paper at the MLA in 1975, I received a copy of Jean Baudrillard's *Le Miroir de production,* (translated by Mark Poster as *The Mirror of Production*) and published by Telos Press, 1975. Baudrillard's comments on history and scarcity parallel my own. He develops these comments in a sustained critique of the mode of production as conceptualised by both bourgeois and Marxist thinkers. In my longer version of this paper, I have discussed some of Baudrillard's concepts in the context of *The Dark Child.* I will quote here his relevant comments on history and on the Sartreian concept of scarcity. His view on history: "The proposition that a concept is not merely an interpretative hypothesis but a translation of universal movement depends upon pure metaphysics. Marxist concepts do not escape this lapse. Thus, to be logical, the concept of history must itself be regarded as historical, turn back upon itself, and only illuminate the context that produced it by abolishing itself. Instead, in Marxism, history is transhistoricised, it redoubles on itself and is thus universal." p. 47. And, on scarcity: "Marxism has not disencumbered itself of the moral philosophy of the Enlightenment. It has rejected its naive and sentimental side... but it holds on to its religion: the moralising phantasm of a nature to be conquered. By secularising it in the economic concept of scarcity, Marxism keeps the idea of necessity without transforming it... What is not recognised here... is that in this symbolic exchange primitive man *does not gauge himself in relation to nature.* He is not aware of Necessity, a Law that takes effect only with the objectification of nature. The Law takes its definitive form in capitalistic political economy; moreover, it is only the philosophical expression of Scarcity. Scarcity, which itself arises in the market economy, is not a given dimension of

the economy. Rather, it is what *produces and reproduces* economic exchange. In that regard it is different from primitive exchange which knows nothing of this 'Law of Nature' that pretends to be the ontological dimension of man. Hence, it is an extremely serious problem that Marxist thought retains these key concepts which depend on the metaphysics of the market economy in general and on modern capitalist ideology in particular." pp. 58-59.

25. Laye, *Dark Child*, 109.

26. Ibid., 60.

27. In his later novel, *A Dream of Africa*, the narrator returns to find that his father's craft has been marginalised by the cheap trinkets imported by the Lebanese and Kouroussa impoverished. Camara Laye, trans. James Kirkup (London: Collins, 1968).

28. John S. Mbiti, *African Religions and Philosophy* (New York, Praeger, 1969), 24.

29. Ibid., 29.

30. Lévi-Strauss, "Time Regained" in *The Savage Mind,* 233-234.

31. As Lévi-Strauss writes: "They [Marx and Freud] have taught us that man has that meaning only on condition that he views himself as meaningful. So far I agree with Sartre. But it must be added that *this meaning is never the right one*. Superstructures are *faulty acts* which have 'made it' socially. Ibid., 253-254. The meanings have 'made it', that is that have become accepted and acceptable, relates to conditions of signification, if not to truth conditions, in the prevailing social structure.

32. It is in this context that one can understand the vehemence of the sixteenth-century debate in Europe between those scholars who defended the legitimacy of historical truth and those who defended the universality – the higher logical typing – of poetic truth as exemplified in the genre of the epic. The epic, and poetry in general, was seen as providing universal timeless models of the past for the present to imitate, whilst history was seen as dealing only with contingent, time bound, and therefore inferior facts.

   Yet the processes of change initiated by the modern world would begin to invert this argument. Soon historical, empirical truth would be conceptualised as absolute. It was out of this clash and conflict between poetic (timeless) truth and historical (contingent) truth that the novel form – as the resolution of the contradiction – was born.

33. Laye, *Dark Child*, 185.

34. Ibid., 182.

35. Ibid., 185-186.

36. Ibid., 187.

A version of this paper was presented at the Modern Language Association's Seminar on Third World Literature on December 26, 1975.

A UTOPIA FROM THE SEMI-PERIPHERY: SPAIN, MODERNISATION, AND THE ENLIGHTENMENT

Stelio Cro, ed. *Descripción de la Sinapia, Península en la Tierra Austral: A Classical Utopia of Spain* (Hamilton, Ont.: McMaster University, 1975), LVII + 146 + 72 pp., $7.50.

This edition of a hitherto unpublished Spanish manuscript makes an original contribution to utopian scholarship. The manuscript, together with another – a treatise on education almost certainly by the same anonymous author – was found by Professor Cro in the archive of an eighteenth-century lawyer and political bureaucrat, the Count of Campomanes (1723-1802); Professor Cro has published the second ms. as an appendix to the edition. Both manuscripts are undated. There is no doubt however, as Professor Cro argues in his lucid and well-researched introduction, that *Sinapia* is an eighteenth-century utopia of the Spanish Enlightenment.[1] It had long been believed that Spain produced no systematic literary utopia.[2] We share Professor Cro's excitement at his find.

There is an additional factor: *Sinapia* may well constitute, up to this point, the only literary utopia written from the perspective of what has been described as the semi-peripheral areas of the modern world system. It therefore raises some useful questions as to the relationship between utopias and what a contemporary scholar has called "the tidal wave of modernisation."[3]

Professor Cro relates the writing of More's *Utopia* to the widespread transformation of European life, concepts, and attitudes subsequent to the Spanish discovery and conquest of the New World, to the change and disruption that initiated the modern era. Central to this transformation was the development of the first global economic system. This world system, as described by Immanuel Wallerstein,[4] incorporated three areas, each defined by a different dominant mode of labour control – the core by free wage labour, the semi-periphery by serf labour, the plantation system of the periphery by forced slave labour. The world market which linked these areas produced through the mechanism of trade – equal exchange between unequally valued labour – the relatively unequal levels of development of the three areas. The mechanism of trade served as a conduit for the accumulation by the core areas of a disproportionate share of the social wealth that was now produced globally. This access of social wealth was one of the factors that enabled a "spontaneous" dynamism of growth which transformed the core areas into today's developed First World. The other areas had instead to find ways and means of grappling with the correlative cycle of underdevelopment.

This may explain the perceptive observation by Professor Cro that, although *Sinapia* is heavily influenced by other previous utopias, the manuscript reveals "...a line of political thought original to its creator... the perfect state is a Christian state based on science and technology" (p. XIII).[5] If, as Professor Cro conjectures, the author of *Sinapia* was a *feijoista,* this would further suggest that a contributing cause of the political originality of the manuscript is to be found in the nature of Spain's semi-peripheral relation to European countries such as France, Holland, England.

Benito Jerónimo Feijóo y Montenegro (1676-1764) was both a priest and an academic, one of the elite minority group, who like Campomanes – in whose archive both manuscripts were found – represented the Enlightenment in Spain. Professor Cro quotes the excellent Spanish historian, Vicens Vives, who argues that with the inauguration of the Bourbon monarchy in 1700, a European conception of life came to modify and substitute the Spanish mentality moulded by the Counter-Reformation. But as with all semi-peripheral areas – Russia with its Slavophile and Narodnik movements is a case in point – there is always a strong ambivalence towards the wave of modernisation emanating from the core.

Both Feijóo and the author of *Sinapia* express an ambivalent attitude to the European conception. Both, like all the elites of underdeveloped areas, share the dream of "catching up with the core"; and both aspired – as did the other *ilustrados (i.e.,* members of the "enlightened" elite) of the time – to a "utopian city from which the remnant of medieval barbarism would disappear, fused in the crucible of a superior culture moulded by progress and tolerance."

However, Feijóo belonged to the Church-cum-academic bureaucracy, partaking of the scholastic tradition which had fused intellectual and religious orthodoxy with national orthodoxy. Most probably this is also true for the author of *Sinapia,* who, as Professor Cro speculates, might well have been a priest. Like Feijóo, he was clearly receptive to the new intellectual stimuli that came from abroad, but he also shared in this group's identification of the national with the Christian-Catholic that had marked Spain's brief, if dazzling, imperial hegemony.

In the sixteenth century, Spain had been the first core country of the emerging world system. Her domination of Europe under Charles V, her conquest and expropriation of the New World, seemed to provide empirical evidence for the national belief that she was a country destined by God for providential mission, i.e., to realise a Christian utopia on earth. Professor Cro refers to the "remarkable utopian flavour" that marks the sixteenth-century chronicles and reports of travellers to the Indies. More "fiction than history," the narrative impulse of these chronicles was "the search for happy land, the quest for a perfect society in America" (XI).

For with the discovery of the New World a transposition was made by the European imagination. The former ideal world remote in time, related to a "lost Christian paradise" and/or "the Golden age of the ancients," was transposed to a "world remote in space".[6] The New World reality was incorporated into the topos of an *adynaton* – which "serves both as the censure of the times and the denunciation of the times... the world upsidedown".[7] In Peter Martyr's *Decades, e.g.,* the factual lineaments of the New World are drawn into the stock literary representations of the pastoral *locus amoenus,* and of the innocent neo-Horation *aldea* (village, countryside) as contrasted to the corrupt court/city/civilisation. Through these devices the New World is portrayed as a fusion of the Garden of Eden and the Golden Age, a figuration that was central to the religious enthusiasm, to the reason-as-nature paradigm of Christian humanism. The mechanism of world reduction[8] common to utopias works through a series of exclusions or eliminations. Thus Martyr's Christian-humanist portrait of the New World utopia – the "goulden worlde of which oulde wryters speake so much" – ritually excludes "pestiferous money" and the legal state apparatus: "where men lyved simply and innocently with inforcement of lawes, contente only to satisfy nature..."[9]

The paradox was to be that, although there was an early attempt to model two cities in New Spain on the model of More's *Utopia* (V-VI), the actual Spanish New World societies were in fact organised by the Church and State bureaucratic apparatus whose minutely regulated laws – the famous laws of the Indies – negated the humanist dream of a stateless paradise. And in Spain itself, this same apparatus, by representing the Christian humanism of Erasmian thought as religious heresy, censored out this revitalising current of thought. The movement of Christian rationalisation – a secularisation of theology and a theologisation of the secular – that had been central to the ongoing cultural transformation in the core countries of Europe was thereby postponed. Indeed, through its imposition of religious orthodoxy as national orthodoxy – heresy came to constitute Un-Spanish Activities – the Church/State apparatus stifled the rise of the incipient Spanish commercial and industrial bourgeoisie. Spanish capitalism was thus thwarted and the wealth transferred from the Indies to Spain was siphoned off, through the mechanism of unequal exchange, in trade to the new core countries: Holland, France, England. During the seventeenth century, Spain was displaced to the semi-periphery. In the eighteenth century, she would have to cope with the fall from grandeur, the retreat from "manifest destiny" – with the new phenomenon of underdevelopment.

The underdeveloped semi-periphery is always out of date. If the eighteenth-century European Enlightenment was marked by a wave of dechristianisation which followed on the earlier stage of Christian rationalisation, *Sinapia* may be called the utopian manifesto of the eighteenth-century Spanish attempt at a form of Christian rationalisation. This mode of rationalisation might be called – and the paradox is instructive – the Spanish Christian Enlightenment.

The utopian imagination in the semi-periphery must confront the empirical existence of superior models of social transformation in the core countries, models which constrain its projections, preventing it from postulating an autonomous and wholly other system. Because of this, the referential sub-text of the utopian discourse of *Sinapia* – *i.e.*, the social reality from which it takes its departure and which it constitutes through negation/inversion[10] – relates at the same time to eighteenth-century Spain, to the core countries, and to the *relation* between them. The utopian "development" plan of *Sinapia* projects a model which can set the terms of a new relation, and which – as with the Russian's Narodnikis and the Spanish *ilustrados* – can incorporate selected aspects of the core model by and through traditional institutions. Feijóo and the author of *Sinapia,* members of the Church bureaucracy and of the intellectual scholastic tradition, would seek to use institutions of the Church in order to create a national form of the European "universal" Enlightenment.

The theoretical problems which Feijóo deals with in his essays, as well as the possible solutions, are both posed and resolved by the narrative machinery of *Sinapia.* The ideological contradiction facing the Spanish *ilustrados* determines both the structure of the text and the structure of the proposed social order.

Feijóo had posed the central problem in the context of addressing what is today a widespread Third World dilemma – the problem of the literary and other "backwardness of our nation". In pushing for educational reform, he argued that Spain should not be held back by fear of religious heresy from taking advantage of the scientific knowledge offered them in foreign books. Feijóo's argument was that theology and philosophy each had their own sphere, that the former as revealed knowledge was superior to the latter which was the result of mere human knowledge. Spain was well supplied with trained theologians who could discern what was opposed to Christian Faith and what was not.

The Holy Tribunal of the Inquisition was always on guard to defend religious doctrine by removing, in Feijóo's words, any "poison" that might accompany the "liquor" of the new learning.[11] The new climate of thought was to be filtered through the selective framework of bureaucratised Christian orthodoxy.

Sinapia, in giving narrative representability to this solution, both resembles and differs from the utopian structures of the French Enlightenment. This relationship of parallelism and divergence can most usefully be envisaged in terms of Mannheim's and Deleuze/Guattari's analyses of utopia. Mannheim's distinction between ideology as the legitimation of the ruling group and utopia as the manifesto of a social group aspiring to hegemony is reinforced by

Deleuze and Guattari's analysis of the role played by utopias in the legitimation and delegitimation of desire. They argue that utopias function not "as ideal models but as group fantasies, as agents of the real productivity of desire, making it possible to disinvest the current social field, to de-institutionalise it..."[12]

Like contemporary French utopias, *Sinapia* disinvests the social field of the aristocracy, delegitimates its accompanying climate of thought. Professor Cro points to the difference between Plato's *Republic* and *Sinapia* (XVII-XVIII). The former legitimates the rule of a military aristocracy, the latter delegitimates the representational categories of the still powerful landed aristocracy. By limiting war and preferring peace, even if gained through bribery and stratagem, *Sinapia* displaces the military code with the work-ethic. It replaces the aristocratic code of honour with the bourgeois utilitarian ethic; the prodigality and conspicuous luxury consumption of the aristocracy with the sober moderation of the middle class. The speculative imagination here acts as "a general solvent"[13] of the system of representation of the aristocracy.

In this, *Sinapia* is at one with the European Enlightenment, sharing in its "social equalitarianism and rationalism" (XXVIII). This is borne out by the internal evidence of the utopian stock figures in the text. The figures of the Persian prince Sinap and the prelate Codabend, and in particular that of Siang, the Chinese philosopher, are all borrowed from the French Enlightenment. And it is the wave of dechristianisation in Europe, Baudet suggests, that may have been responsible for the enthusiasm "for China and other lands that swept across Europe in the eighteenth century". The real historical figure of Confucius – the philosopher who was not a religious founder – was central to the European representation of the Chinese "who honour everything, their parents and the ancestors." This mixture of reverence for tradition allied to a secular morality coming out of a higher culture provides the ideological legitimation for the figures of one of the founders of *Sinapia,* the Chinese Siang. The other two founders, the Persian prince and prelate also come out of the eighteenth-century literary stock in which – together with the Noble Savages – "Turks, Persians and other Non-Westerners were installed alongside the Chinese."[14]

However, if *Sinapia* borrows figures from the European Enlightenment, it uses them in a specific manner. The narration in which the Chinese philosopher Siang is converted by the Persian Christians signifies a reconciliation between Christian orthodoxy (the Persians) and the natural sciences (Siang). In addition, by re-transposing the imagined ideal world back in time – the Persian Christians represent an earlier mode of Christianity, that of the third and fourth centuries – and combining this with the European Enlightenment's use of cultures of a higher order, *Sinapia* turns its back on both the prelapsarian Golden-Age-type utopia of the Christian Humanists and on the Rousseauist perfect state of nature with its emphasis on the *individual*.

In the European conception, the theme of economic freedom "defined as social equality based on the division of labour and private property"[15] was linked to the representation of man's individual origin in a state of nature. The concept of the originally free and unbound individual with his natural right to private property was to be the mythological charter of the commercial and industrial bourgeoisie on their rise to hegemony. The feudal rights of the nobility to their large landed estates was delegitimated along with the concept of rights based on birth. In the state of Nature there is a reversal of all ranks. Merit is what now counts in the competitive free-for-all.

Sinapia also joins in this delegitimation of the property rights of the nobility. But it postulates as its ideal imagined world the earlier Church structure with its emphasis on the Christian *community,* where all property is held as collective state property. Thus in *Sinapia,* with its ritual exclusion of private property, money, and markets, capitalism is put off limits. If the "natural state" conception led in France to the idea of remaking the world anew on the model of its imaginary origins, the remaking of the social order in *Sinapia* means a conservative return to earlier political structures, which are paradoxically able to incorporate the natural sciences represented as the pagan tradition of thought of "higher cultures". The state of Nature is in it implicitly delegitimated; thus, the "noble savage" American Indian and Black can play no ideal role in *Sinapia.* Rather they are subjected to the "civilising" influences of the superior Christian and Chinese cultures. The ideal Incas, the model for Campanella's *City of the Sun,* become in *Sinapia* Peruvian Chinchas whose "rusticity" has to be civilised, just as the Malay's "ferocity" has to be "domesticated" (6).

It is the Black, however, who is most displaced from the natural state ideal of "noble savage", to the lowest rank in the pecking order of races and cultures. Blacks are represented as simple and docile, as *negrillos* called Zambales. They were cleared out of the geographical space by the Malays who drove them into the adjoining country of the Galos. Later, in the context of Christian universality, the Blacks are represented as one of the races involved in the mixture which has produced the Sinapian. Here, their "race" is designated by the literary term of Ethiopian. They are assimilated by the use of this term to a legendary medieval utopian figure – the priest-king of Ethiopia, Prester John.

When Europeans were themselves semiperipheral to the then hegemonic Mohammedan power, Prester John had played a powerful role in the European imagination as the black image of Christian power who would one day deliver them from the Moors.[16] His imagined kingdom – a magical utopia with a pool which rejuvenated men, and a magic table which cured drunkenness – was also the ideal model of a Christian state in which a Priest King combined religious and temporal power. This original model of a priest king becomes, in the utopia of *Sinapia,* the model of the ideal state patterned on a church hierarchy. The magical model of Prester John is transformed into the rationalised model, in which the Christian community is converted into a paternal social machine. Geographically *Sinapia* is divided into units – family dwellings; several such units constitute a *barrio,* several of which constitute a *villa* (town), several of which constitute a city, several of which constitute a metropolis, several of which constitute a province, nine of which constitute *Sinapia.* Socially and politically, each unit is ruled by a Father, each Father with prescribed degrees of power to punish their family members and the two slaves allotted to them. Slaves, private and public, are made slaves as a punishment for their crimes, but the power to decide on limited or perpetual slavery is confined to the top Fathers and to the Prince who functions as chief magistrate. Thus the fathers of the family are punishable by the fathers of the *barrio,* who in turn, are punishable by the fathers of the *villa,* and so forth. The prince, with the Senate's approval, alone has the right to punish by death, life-slavery, or exile. *Sinapia* thus exemplifies the carceral complex, designed to identify deviance and the social norm of orthodoxy.[17]

Exile is retained as the punishment for heresy. Heretics are given a chance to recant; if they do not, they must be totally excluded from the Kingdom. For *Sinapia* is, above all, a social and ideological autarchy, that mode of utopia central to all forms of the bourgeois – i.e., both non-aristocratic and non-popular – imagination. As Roland Barthes points out, the sites of utopia are always rigidly enclosed so that they can constitute a social autarchy. The inhabitants of these bourgeois modes of utopia are always shut in so as to "form a total society, endowed with an economy, a morality, a language and a time articulated into schedules, labours, and celebrations. Here, as elsewhere, the enclosure permits the system, i.e., the imagination."[18]

Sinapia is represented as completely enclosed from the rest of the world; it is well protected by armed forces against any outside intrusion. Trade is strictly regulated and only carried out by a few selected bureaucrats; exit and entrance visas are strictly supervised. And if *Sinapia* rigidly excludes Christian religious enthusiasm, a new kind of rational enthusiasm for totalitarian supervision and control pervades the text. The real stroke of imaginative brilliance in the work is to be found in the meticulous arrangements for a form of censorship which will enable the incorporation of the novelties of the natural sciences without any danger of deviationist heresy.

Merchants of Enlightenment – *mercaderes de luz,* much as in Bacon's *New Atlantis* – are dispatched to purchase, with no expense spared, the "new technology": books and models for "the advancement of the sciences and the arts" (58). When brought back, all material must first be decontaminated, distilled by a highly ingenious form of censorship. A group of censors – gatherers, miners, distillers, improvers – select out the material that can be utilised, and even improve upon the models and scientific paradigms. Whatever is considered ideologically dangerous to the Christian-bureaucratic mode of organisation, to its static perfection – for *Sinapia* is a classical utopia

– is filtered out, the "poison" removed (to repeat Feijóo's metaphor) as the "liquor" is distilled.

Sinapians are therefore locked within a totalitarian representation of reality. *Equal* material distribution is used as the legitimation for *unequal* access to the means of information and communication. The desire disinvested from the social field of the landed aristocracy is reinvested not into the private property bourgeoisie but into the social field of the technocratic/bureaucratic bourgeoisie whose representational categories legitimate an intellectual and imaginative autarchy. In fact, the utopian mode of *Sinapia* seems to prefigure the dystopian realisation in our time of the representational autarchy – with its managed reality and managed fantasy – imposed by the bureaucratic/corporate elite of the First, Second, and Third World through the mass-media.

Indeed, correlative to this, *Sinapia* can also teach us something about modern science fiction. Our century has seen the beginning of the end of the Eurocentric cultural autarchy with the historical emergence of former utopian fictional Others – the Chinese, the Persians, the Blacks, the Mohammedans – from exoticism. In the context of this historical movement another transposition has been made from terrestrial to extraterrestrial time/space, and fictional Others. If we see science fiction as the updated pseudo-utopian mode of the global (and increasingly dominant) technocratic bourgeoisie, as the expression of its group fantasy, then one of science fiction's more troubling aspects – a neo-fascist elitism that reminds one of *Sinapia's,* based as it is on the projection of "higher cultures" – becomes theoretically explicable. From Clarke's *2001: A Space Odyssey* to *Star Wars,* science fiction – like *Sinapia* – ritually excludes or marginalises the "Lesser breeds without the law", outside of technological rationality – what Ursula Le Guin has called the social, sexual, and racial aliens.[19] Such SF excludes, in fact, the popular forces who today embody the millenarian heresy of utopian longing,[20] and who are on our world scene the only alternative to the new, non-propertied technocratic bureaucracy.

Endnotes

1. The ms. dating has led to an ongoing critical dispute between Professor Cro and Professor Miguel Avilés Fernández, who has also published an edition of *Sinapia: Una Utopía Española del siglo de las luces* (Madrid: Ed. Nacional, 1976). Cro in his later work *A Forerunner of the Enlightenment in Spain* (Hamilton, Ont.: McMaster Univ., 1976) argues on the basis of a newly discovered reference for a 1682 date, which would imply that the author is a forerunner rather than contemporary or follower of the *feijoista* current. Against this, Avilés Fernández argues from internal evidence that *Sinapia* is a product of the Enlightenment and was most probably written by the Count of Campomanes in the last third of the 18th century. I agree that this work belongs to an 18th-century discourse, even though I would place it in the earlier part of that century, so that I am reluctant to attribute it to Campomanes. For a balanced

discussion of the opposing viewpoints see Francisco López Estrada, "Más noticias sobre la Sinapia o utopia española," *Moreana*, No. 14 (1977), 23-33.

2. Monroe Z. Hafter, in "Toward a History of Spanish Imaginary Voyages", *Eighteenth-Century Studies*, vol. 8, no. 3 (Spring 1975): 265-82 discusses a "full-length Spanish imaginary voyage written in the Enlightenment" which pretends to be the true account of a philosopher who voyages in an unknown civilisation, *Selenopolis* (Madrid, 1804). Hafter argues that although no study of imaginary voyages lists so much as a single original Spanish text, nevertheless this account, while it "stands out for its developed portrait of the ideal lunar society of Selenopolis ... forms part of a trajectory to which interest is astronomy, distant travel, and social satire contributed over a period of many years" (266). The parallels between *Sinapia* and *Selenopolis* are clear – the problem of incorporating the natural sciences and the need to rationalise society. But the basic difference is that Selenopolis is an open society (encouraging trade, internal and external) which marginalises religion, while Sinapia is a closed theocratic society. The narrative device of the *voyage* to a land which is projected as existing – Selenopolis – leads to somewhat different conclusions than does the projection of a utopia – a nowhere – whose existence is figuratively located in the geography of the narrative itself. But *Sinapia* does belong to a wave of speculative thought, typical of underdeveloped countries, ceaselessly seeking to correct a "backwardness" whose causes are as much external – in the system of relations – as they are internal; a history of thought therefore marked by a Sisyphean futility. Hafter discusses the history and extension of this wave, expressed both in book form and in journalistic literature.

3. Ernest Gellner, *Thought and Change* (Chicago: University of Chicago Press, 1964), 166.

4. Immanuel Wallerstein, *The Modern World-System: Capitalist Agriculture and the Origin of the European World-Economy in the Sixteenth Century* (New York: Academic Press, 1974), 86-87.

5. Jaime Vicens Vives, *Manual de historia económica de España* (Barcelona: Editorial Vicens-Vives, 1969), 431; my translation of the original Spanish quoted by Professor Cro (XIX).

6. Henri Baudet, *Paradise on Earth: Some Thoughts On European Images of Non-European Man* (New Haven: Yale University Press, 1965), 32; and J.H. Elliott, *The Old World and the New, 1492-1650* (Cambridge: Cambridge University Press, 1970), 25.

7. Ernst Curtius, *European Literature and the Latin Middle Ages* (New York: Princeton UP, 1953), 96.

8. Fredric Jameson, "World Reduction in Le Guin: The Emergence of Utopian Narrative", *Science-Fiction Studies* vol. 2, no. 3 (Nov. 1975), 221-230.

9. Peter Martyr, *Decades,* trans. Richard Eden (1555) in *The First Three English Books on America,* ed. Edward Arber (Birmingham, 1885), 71; quoted by J.H. Elliot, 26.

10. See Fredric Jameson, "Of Islands and Trenches: Naturalization and the Production of Utopian Discourse", *Diacritics*, vol. 7, no. 2 (June 1977): 9.

11. Padre Feijóo, *Cartas eruditas y curiosas, etc. 1742-1760;* see the letter, "Causas del atraso que se padece en España en orden a las ciencas naturales" in the

anthology *Spanish Literature 1700-1900*, Beatrice P. Patt and Martin Nozick eds. (New York: Dodd, Mead, 1965), 7-16.

12. Karl Mannheim, *Ideology and Utopia* (New York: Viking Press, 1940), 38; and G. Deleuze and F. Guattari, *Anti-Oedipus: Capitalism and Schizophrenia* (New York, 1977), 30-31.

13. Jakob Burckhardt, *Reflections on History* (New York: Pantheon Books Inc., 1943), 110; quoted by Baudet, *Paradise on Earth*, 72.

14. Ibid., 43 and 45.

15. Ibid., 59.

16. See Ibid., 15-20; also Robert Silverberg, *The Realm of Prester John* (Garden City, New York: Doubleday, 1972).

17. See Michael Foucault, *Discipline and Punish: The Birth of the Prison* (New York: Pantheon, 1977), 30.

18. Roland Barthes, *Sade/Fourier/Loyola* (New York: Hill and Wang, 1976), 17.

19. Ursula Le Guin, "American SF and the Other", *Science-Fiction Studies,* vol. 2, no. 3 (Nov. 1975), 208-210.

20. The emergence, in the periphery areas of the world system, of political/religious cults like Jamaican Rastafarianism – the Reggae singer Bob Marley expresses in his hit song "Exodus" the inversion/negation of the social order through its delegitimation as Babylon compared to the projected true home of Zion – are the contemporary expressions of popular movements of insubordination. The parallels with the Gnostics who delegitimated the classical *kosmos* at the end of antiquity, thus ushering in the new figurative space which Christianity was to inhabit, are clear.

IN QUEST OF MATTHEW BONDMAN: SOME CULTURAL NOTES ON THE JAMESIAN JOURNEY

I. What Do Men Live By? From the National to the Popular-Aesthetic Question

He, [Garfield Sobers the West Indian batsman], does not need the half-volley of a fast or a fast-medium bowler to be able to drive. From a very high backlift he watches the ball that is barely over the good length, takes it on the rise and sends it shooting between mid-on and mid-off... The West Indian crowd has a favourite phrase for that stroke: Not a man move. – C.L.R. James, "Garfield Sobers"[1]

In the fine points of Marxist thought, confronting the work ethic is an aesthetic of non-work or play... This realm beyond political economy called play, non-work or non-alienated labour... remains an *esthetic*, in the extremely Kantian sense, with all the bourgeois ideological connotations which that implies. Although Marx's thought settled accounts with bourgeois morality, *it remains defenseless before its esthetic, whose ambiguity is more subtle but whose complicity with the general system of political economy is just as profound* [emphasis added]. – Baudrillard, *The Mirror of Production*[2]

It took England to reveal to me the hidden aspects of Constantine's personality... (He) was the same man on the cricket field as he was in our private and public life. The *difference* was that there, or rather in the Lancashire League, he was able to *give his powers full play*. – *Beyond a Boundary*[3]

We are still in the flower garden of the gay, the spontaneous, tropical West Indians. We need some astringent spray. – *Beyond a Boundary*[4]

In the autosociographical system of *Beyond a Boundary*, C.L.R. James places his act of separation from Trotskyism within a *larger question*, which is the structuring motif of the book. In posing the fundamental Tolstoyan question "*What do men live by?*" the system of *Beyond a Boundary* displaces at one thrust the bourgeois "mirror of the natural" and its related "mirror of production".[5]

The presuppositions of both "mirrors", i.e. of man as a "natural being", of man as identified by the *labour* with which he produces his "*material life*", his means of *physical subsistence*,[6] represses the awareness that these definitions are cultural representations. That, like the feudal definition of man as a *spiritual* being, they are *context-bound* and *historical,* and become a "mythology" when they are spread over the expanse of human life; made into a teleology.

Beyond a Boundary relativises and de-absolutises the "material representation" of man's identity when it asks the question central to the *cultural life* of man: *What do men live by?* The answer to this question moves the Jamesian poeisis beyond the national, the class question, into the contemporary dimensions of the popular question. James writes, chronicling another stage on his journey:

> Fiction-writing drained out of me and was replaced by politics. I became a Marxist, a Trotskyist... In 1938, a lecture tour took me to the United States and I stayed there for fifteen years. The war came. It did not bring Soviets and proletarian power. Instead the bureaucratic totalitarian monster grew stronger and spread. As early as 1941, I had begun to question the premises of Trotskyism. It took a decade of incessant labour and collaboration to break with it and reorganise my Marxist ideas to cope with the postwar world. That was a matter of doctrine, of history, of economics and politics.
>
> ...In my private mind, however, I was increasingly aware of large areas of human existence that my history and my politics did not seem to cover. What did men live by? What did they want? What did history show they had wanted?
>
> ...A glance at the world showed that when the common people were not at work, one thing they wanted was organised sports and games. They wanted them greedily, passionately.[7]

The pattern of *Beyond a Boundary,* working out the logic of its own motifs, uncovers "large areas of human existence", as James points out, that his "history, economics, politics" had left unaccounted for. Here it reveals that a separation, a gap appeared between the mode of popular desire, i.e., what the masses wanted to "live" by and what the "ruling elements" wanted them to live by. In other words, what is at issue here is a struggle between two modes of desire: that of the bourgeoisie and that of the popular forces – the bourgeoisie for whom sports were "mere entertainment", for whom play served as "recuperation" from the *real work* of *labour,* rather than as an *alternative life-activity in its own right,* for whom the aesthetic was a luxury or even in the case of bourgeois *aesthetes,* for whom the "fine arts" – split off from the popular arts – were the high culture used to cultivate individual sensibilities to mark off the differential value of bourgeois concerns, to be guarded from the *hoi polloi,* as the sacred animal in the sacred pool (in Lévi-Strauss's term) that canonised the middle-class mode of desire as a desire for the "higher things" whilst stigmatising all non middle-class desire as crass.

James first analyses the reflex stigmatisation of the masses' desire for sports, by a middle-class eye's view:

> They wanted them greedily, passionately. So much so, that the politicians who devoted themselves to the improvement of the condition of the people, the disciples of culture, the aesthetes, all deplored the expenditure of so much time, energy, attention and money on sports and games instead of on the higher things. Well, presumably it could not be helped. It had always been so and was likely to continue for a long time.[8]

He then reverses the stigmatisation, revealing the "mythology" of the middle-class eye's view.

> But that was quite untrue. Organised games had been part and parcel of the civilisation of Ancient Greece. With the decline of that civilisation they disappeared from Europe for some 1,500 years. People ran and jumped and kicked balls about and competed with one another; they went to see the knights jousting. But games and sports, organised as the Greeks had organised them, there were none.[9]

And, although James does not mention this, the intervening ages were not to miss organised games, because the great festival-complex common to pagan traditional societies (the dominant element in the imperatively popular cultures of Africa), incorporated by the Catholic church, had provided the macro-institution of Carnival. That institution, as Mikhail Bakhtin points out, had functioned in pre-capitalist Europe, as it functioned in traditional Africa, as it functions in the Afro-Euro-derived Trinidadian, New Orleans and Brazilian Carnivals, to provide the great "dramatic spectacle" that the Greek games, and its successor, Greek tragic drama, as James notes, had provided – the same dramatic spectacle of which organised sports were to be the contemporary modality of industrial society.

> Carnival is not a spectacle seen by the people; they live in it, and everyone participates because its very ideal embraces all the people. ...During carnival time life is subject only to its own laws, that is, the laws of its own freedom. It has a universal spirit; it is a special condition of the entire world, of the world's revival and renewal in which all take part.[10]

Thus the grace and style of Bondman's batting, the innovative genius of W. G. Grace, the "ferocious" wit and inventiveness of a Mighty Sparrow, all derive finally from the same source – the overwhelming vitality of the exclusive nature of the popular arts – popular in the sense of being both the "common people" and the "whole body of the people".

With the rise of the bourgeoisie, Bakhtin points out, *Carnival,* the dramatic spectacle of the whole body of the people, disappeared from Europe. The categories of *blood* and *birth* had enabled the aristocracy to mingle with the peasantry, at least during the Carnival period. The bourgeoisie, like the Jamesian clan, had no such *permanent* and "inherent" mode of status-differentiation. The "class-body" had to be kept from "physical" contact if it were to signify – and thereby realise – its "differential value". Both the categories of the bourgeois code of knowledge, and as Bakhtin points out in his study of Rabelais, the canons of bourgeois aesthetics were to reflect this setting apart. The "fine arts" separated themselves off from the "popular arts", establishing a categorisation into higher and lower. The aesthetics was the politics. The new mode of social relations in which an absolute breach occurred between the two groupings was reflected and constituted by the aesthetics of the bourgeoisie, an aesthetic which now redefined the mode of coexistence in what was now not the polis of the whole body of the people, but the polis of the bourgeoisie in which the popular forces, transformed in the bourgeoisie's definition, into the mass, came to serve the same signifying role of the "Negroes", i.e., as the symbolic inversion of the bourgeoisie, the memento of all that they were not.

The categorising of art into higher and lower reveals that the bourgeois aesthetics replicates *within* the structure of its own aesthetic system, the same bimodal Head/Body, Reason/Instinct categories that subtend both the categories of bourgeois thought; and of its global polis.

The separation of the class-body, representationally constituted itself in the languages of the arts, of their critical canons, as Bakhtin points out:

> The Renaissance saw the body in quite a different light than the Middle Ages, in a different... *relation to the exterior nonbodily world*. As conceived by these canons, the body was first of all a strictly completed, finished product. Furthermore, it was isolated, alone, fenced off from all other bodies... The accent was placed on the completed, self-sufficient individuality of the given body. Corporal acts were shown only when the borderlines dividing the body from the outline world were sharply defined. ...The individual body was presented apart from the ancestral body of the people.
>
> Such was the fundamental tendencies of the classical canons... [F]rom the point of view of these canons the body of grotesque realism was hideous and formless. It did not fit the framework of the "aesthetics of the beautiful" as conceived by the Renaissance.[11]

The popular forces desired "organised sports and games" because they, unlike the middle classes, had no other institutional framework which could provide in modern contemporary terms what Carnival and rural life had originally provided before their disruption into industrial civilisation; into the stresses and trauma of the factory-system and industrial colonisation. Organised sports provided what Carnival and the rural ethos had provided in another form. As James reveals, the act of watching is a participatory act. When the West Indian crowd shouts "Not a man move!" as they do after a stroke by Sobers so escapes the trap both of bowler and of the set field that neither bowler nor fieldsman could react fast enough, the game is no longer a spectacle, seen by the people. Rather, as in Carnival, they live in it, and everyone participates because its very idea embraces *all* the people. Like Carnival too, the game is "subject only to its own laws", which are the laws of freedom.[12]

Thus if for the bourgeoisie the condition of the realisation of its powers is an imperatively individual and class-restricted realisation (brilliant in its own way yet incapable, as in the great ages of transition – i.e., of a Rabelais, a Cervantes, a Shakespeare, a Chaplin – of drawing on the multiple resources of a cross-fertilisation of aesthetics for the popular imperative), then the realisation of its powers, the aesthetics of its participatory art, depends precisely on its ability to enact and incorporate and give image to the "whole body of the people".

The people wanted organised sports because these sports and games were institutions that they helped to found and continue, institutions that they had helped to found as surely as their working class struggles led to the formation of trade unions, as their struggles for the right to vote – to control the conditions of their life-activities – had also led to the founding of modern mass-political parties and to the grounding of the concept of democracy – however much, when wearing bourgeois masks on their popular skins, they would be led to negate their own imperative.

Cricket as a national sport, with universal elements, as James chronicles it, was to be a reorganisation of the contributions of the different elements in the social order, under the hegemony of the middle classes. In other words, cricket was to be a fusion of three different aesthetic canons, three different imperatives:

> The world-wide renaissance of organised games and sports as an integral part of modern civilisation was on its way. Of this renaissance, the elevation of cricket and football to the place that they soon held in English life was a part, historically speaking, the most important part; the system as finally adopted was not an invention but a discovery, or rather a rediscovery.... Cricket and football provided a meeting place for the moral outlook of the dissenting middle classes and the athletic instincts of the aristocracy. Finally, cricket was one of the most complete products of that previous age to which a man like Dickens always looked back with such nostalgia. It had been formed by rural and artisan Englishmen who had aimed at nothing but the creation of an activity which would disinterestedly express their native artistic instincts. If it could so rapidly be elevated to the status of a moral discipline it was because it had been born and grew in an atmosphere and in circumstances untainted by any serious corruption. The only word that I know for this is culture. ...The proof of its validity is its success, first of all at home and then almost as rapidly abroad, in the most diverse places and among peoples living lives which were poles removed from that whence it originally came. This signifies, as so often in any deeply national movement, that it contained elements of universality that went beyond the bounds of the originating nation.[13]

Cricket, then, was very much the invention and creation of the "whole body of the people," even where it was to be expressed in a middle-class form.[14] The middle class was to contribute, as James points out, the least, yet due to their gift for rationalisation and organisation, they were to appropriate the game and convert it into a national institution.[15]

Yet, if the struggle was not as obviously political as in Trinidad, the middle classes, as they prepared themselves for class hegemony, had to face the new pressures of the popular masses, whose organisations had emerged precisely out of the collective struggle they waged in cooperation with the middle classes for popular democracy in England.

As James notes, the organisation of modern sports and games was co-temporal with the modern popular forms of trade union and political struggle. The "intervention" and input of the popular forces into the creation of the national game of cricket – into the aesthetic production of the more-than-bread by-which-men-live – went *pari passu* with trade union struggles for a *higher living standard.* Here the Marxian doctrine which revealed the labour contribution to the national product played a powerful role. But the praxis had been initiated before Marx. And the struggles of the working classes at a cultural and epistemological level were struggles which stopped the automatic functioning of the accumulative dynamic, a dynamic kept in motion by the global differential structure of social relations, by the bourgeois cultural control of the mode of identity and desire, by its diffusion of bourgeois masks, its equation of identity-value with accumulated value.[16]

If, as Castoriadis points out, it was the working class struggles that fuelled the dynamic expansion of capitalism – since the higher wage packets led to the rapid development of internal markets, and to the wider social provision of technological skills, thereby compelling higher levels of development – its input into the national game of cricket was no less decisive.[17] In other words, the conjunction that hit James was not fortuitous, and the conjunction is itself crucial to the doctrine of his book.

The co-evolution of new popular forms of social organisation, i.e., trade union organisations, political parties, international organisation, organisational forms of struggle for popular democracy with the rise of the desire for organised sports, all within the decade 1860-1870,[18] provide the basis for the Jamesian reflection on the complexity of human needs, for his implicit affirmation that the "realisation of one's powers" at both the individual and the group level is the most urgent imperative of all. Thus the conjunction of the institution of organisational forms for the struggle for popular democracy – in multiple forms, the trade unions, political parties, the Communist International, etc. – was a conjunction that hit James only because, unlike Trotsky, he had moved outside the mono-conceptual labour frame to the wider frame of a popular theoretics.

For if, as James argues, the "conjunction had hit me as it would have hit few of the students of the international organisation to which I belonged",[19] this was because James had already *moved outside the categories in which they were still embedded.* For if within the labour conceptual frame, whose logical goal is the development of the productive forces, *the development of production is the means of realising one's labour-value,* the value through which one expresses one's human potential, then Trotsky was quite right to say that "sports" deflected the worker from politics – "labour" politics.

With popular politics, it was a different matter. In the ecumenicism of the politics of the latter, labour, and labour geared to a specific end, the realisations of men's powers both singly and collectively, was only one of the possible means for Man's self-realisation of his powers.

Which leads us to Matthew Bondman and the popular imperative versus both the public school and labour code. Bondman lived next door in Tunapuna to James, the child. "His eyes were fierce, his language was violent and his voice was loud"; he refused to take a job but "with a bat in his hand [he] was all grace and style". The contradiction seemed inexplicable. "The contrast between Matthew's pitiable existence as an individual and the attitude people had towards him", James recalls, "filled my growing mind and has occupied me to this day."[20]

Matthew Bondman played cricket but moved entirely outside the public school code. For him a straight bat was literal, not figurative. And it "isn't cricket" was meaningless in its moral/ethical sense.

Indeed he would not even stand to benefit from the normal workings of the code. One might theoretically widen the code to struggle with the problems that Matthew Bondman, who would not work, presented for the implicit morality system of the labour code – but the class-body of James's schoolmates would refuse Matthew charity on the grounds that poor chaps ought to be deserving. Matthew was certainly not.

Nor was he in any sense of the term a member of the *deserving proletariat*. In the great utility-code of the productivist ethos of bourgeois classarchy, he was, in the words of James's aunts, *"Good for nothing except to play cricket."*[21] Bondman, like contemporary ghetto Blacks as defined by J. B. Fuqua, an adviser to ex-President Carter, was precisely *depreciated machinery*.[22]

Matthew Bondman, then, like the ghetto Blacks today, like the good-for-nothing macho Benoit of *Minty Alley,* like his Becky-Sharp-type heroine, Maisie, who refuses to work for pittance-wages and finally escapes to America, and who, like Bondman, breaks every prohibition of the bourgeois code in order to realise her powers, to take her womanhood upon account, cannot be revindicated in the name of their *labour-value* (or needless to say, of their capital-value). Yet, Matthew Bondman, like the Blacks of the ghetto-prison-system-shanty-towns archipelagos of the modern world system, had not always been useless.

In fact in the earliest phase of the historical process of bourgeois accumulation, Matthew Bondman and his ilk had been amongst the skilled slave specialists who had actually run the plantation, then the most highly organised and efficient mode of accumulation in existence, until it was displaced by the new mode of accumulation, the factory-system of production.

At that time, Bondman was the value core of the world that the bourgeoisie modelled in their own image.[23] He was both capital value and skilled labour-value, as James pointed out in a talk in Montreal in 1966 – "The making of the Caribbean peoples".[24] In other words, Matthew, coerced, yet trained in necessary skills, had been subordinated to the "time" of the great positivity of the development of the productive forces. He had truly done his bit to set in train *"their"* liberation.

And the paradox was that since he was central to the process, he was allowed to realise those skilled and specialist powers that the accumulative telos needed to realise its objective rationale. Those powers not needed for the telos of accumulation, therefore not historically viable, were pushed aside, excluded. To realise his own powers, to give them full play, the Bondsmen had to live in an alternative cosmology, an underground culture which they reconstituted for themselves. In addition, it meant that the total blockage of the realisation of their powers, the prevention of their living of their own radical historicity, their subordination, to the historicity of the productive forces, would therefore impel the Bondmens of the world (*Les damnés de la terre*, as Fanon defines them) to demand, *to desire as that by which alone they can live,* not the liberation of the productive forces (Liberalism and Marxism-Leninism) but the "liberation of Man".

For the autonomy of a Bondman had been totally subordinated to *the autonomy of the accumulative telos.* When the logic of its own process needed him as a specialist, he was made one. As a sharecropper breaking his back, he became one. As a native agro-proletariat, he accepted his one shilling per week and withstood his lot. When it needed him as labour reserve to the "real" proletariat, he left the rural area for the town. He reserved his labour.

As the Cybernetic Revolution began to displace the Industrial Revolution and it became clear that his reserve labour was in reserve in perpetuity – machines were the skilled specialists now – Bondman would have to come to terms with the fact that he had become *"refuse"* (the term given to the slave too old and worn-out to contribute labour). He could hustle a day's work here and there, sweep a yard or two, live from hand to mouth. Jump Jim Crow. Or he could drop out.

Matthew dropped out. His "abominable life" was the end result of a historical process which had built a world that had no place in it where Bondman could realise his powers; establish his identity; enact his radical historicity. Above all, where Matthew could live according to the popular-aesthetic code that surfaced only when he batted. The perceptiveness of James in *Beyond a Boundary* is to have counterposed Bondman batting at the beginning of the book with the problematic of a cricket now trapped by the barbarism of a rationalised code, one which had led not only to the perversion of "body-line" cricket, but had also compelled cricket greats like Sir Donald Bradman of Australia, one of the greatest batsmen of all times, to bring to a close the Golden Age of Cricket, subordinating the aesthetic code of the game to the technicised rationality of the "national" competitive code.

For *"it isn't cricket"* had functioned only partially as a moral code. It had functioned too as an *aesthetic code. It was by this code alone that a Bondman could even contemplate batting.* The great Bradman, responding to the technological rationality of his time with its imperative of efficiency and utility, could – as he tells us in his autobiography – afford to bat like that only once in a lifetime. All his life Bradman had batted a "defensive" game designed to win matches – except for one glorious inning when he cut loose.

James quotes the incident, for it is crucial to the aesthetic imperative of his own "doctrine":

> Yet what are his sentiments after he has made the hundredth run of the
> hundredth century? He felt it incumbent upon him, he says, to give the

crowd... some reward... *He therefore proceeded to hit 71 runs in 45 minutes. This, he adds, is the way he would always wish to have batted if circumstances had permitted him.*[25]

James, startled by this admission of Bradman, uses it as the point from which *Beyond a Boundary* can reflect on the question – What had happened to the game that W. G. Grace had built, that Arnold had transformed into a part of the educational system, transforming it into a vision of life? What, too, had happened to the "art and practic part of cricket?"

The times had changed. The ruthlessness of body-line cricket, the technicised efficiency of a Bradman's batting, were merely the logical development of that crisis of bourgeois *rationalism,* a philosophy and master-conception which, creative in its springtime,[26] had now become destructive in its decline, focusing only on one end, losing the balance between the *aesthetic* and the technical, the physical and the mental that had calibrated the great cricket of the Golden Age, its fusion of mind and body, its flow of motion and "mechanics of judgment". The fusion that had marked a W. G. Grace, that defined the grace and style of a Bondman batting in the *only* way he could bat; a *Bradman,* in that Carnival moment when he made 71 runs in forty-five minutes – and said to hell with the utility code! With the bourgeois mode of rationality!

Here the juxtaposition in the structure of *Beyond a Boundary* – of a Bondman and a Bradman, the latter subordinated to the code of technological rationality, the former immersed in the imperatives of the popular underground counterculture of Trinidad, a culture derived from Africa, yet toughened, suffered a sea-change, transformed from a normative culture of traditional African societies to a culture of liminality.[27] Liminality, with respect to the global polis of bourgeois classarchy, reveals a culture clash, a clash of *Reasons;* a clash between the rationalism of the bourgeoisie and a new popular reason. This latter reason is the reason of the culture of that Afro-American archipelago which gave rise to the calypsos of Sparrow; to the jazz popular culture, the first universal musical culture; to the Rastafarian reggae – a culture in which the reason of accumulation of the bourgeois polis had been contested and held at bay by a counter-reason – the reason of the social that had defined the imperatively popular cultures of African traditional societies.[28]

What we note here is a fundamental clash of telos between a society coordinated symbiotically by the imperative of *redistribution,* the imperative of the *social,* and another coordinated by the imperative of *accumulation* and *expansion,* i.e., the reason of the productive forces. As Rodney himself comments:

> The above is a beautiful set-piece of the moral terminology of capitalist accumulation – the 'assiduous' and the 'industrious' who will inherit the earth, while those who do not share grace are the ones who were 'lazy'. It pointedly illustrates the difference between the African and European cultures. ... Even within the empires of Ghana, Mali and Songhai, the explosiveness of class contradictions was lacking, as Diop stresses in his *Nations Nègres et Culture.* In the states of Ashante and Dahomey, whose growth was

contemporaneous with European mercantilism, there was no concept of the 'market' in the sense of supply and demand, and the social redistribution of goods made accumulation impossible.[29]

It is this dialectic and tension between the technological rationality of the bourgeois master-conception in its decline and consummation, i.e., the complete mechanisation of men,[30] of thought (theoretics), of feeling (aesthetics) – and the counter-reason of the underground popular-aesthetic imperative that gave rise to the West Indian cricketers. In very much the same way, as James tells it, another great age of transition, the age of Hazlitt's England,[31] had given rise to W. G. Grace, the innovative genius – and founder of modern cricket.

Thus, that technological rationality which had discarded a Bondman as "refuse", which had dictated the technical reason that held the full powers of Bradman in check during his normal batting lifetime, found its sovereignty overturned by the autonomy of the aesthetic imperative which ruled the playing of the West Indian Cricketers in their triumphant tour of Australia with Frank Worrell – the first *Black* player ever selected as Captain.

With the governing categories of the bourgeois polis reversed socially, aesthetically, the West Indian cricketers kept the theoretics of its technological rationality in the rightful place – as the mere secondary means to a Jamesian defined and popular end, the realisation by the genus Homo of the free-play of faculties.

Thus the climax of *Beyond a Boundary* is the climax too of the Jamesian quest to assert the autonomy and radical historicity of men over the historical process; over the time of the productive forces and the mode of social relations which the sovereignty of the latter necessarily entails. For if, as James quotes in *Beyond a Boundary,* a poetic work must be defined as a verbal function whose aesthetic function is its dominant, then the value-system implicit in the contrast between the batting of a Bondman and the everyday batting of a Bradman, between the everyday efficient batting of a Bradman dictated by the overriding criteria of utility of winning, and the glorious innings when Bradman *batted to reward the crowd and to purely realise his own powers,* suggest that in cricket too, as in all organised sports, *there is a criterion of evaluative judgment that responds to the aesthetic imperative of all art.* For in that crowning innings, Bradman's batting rewarded the crowd – and the Australian crowds, James notes, are at once proud of Bradman and ambivalent towards his mode of batting – by making the aesthetic function, hitherto secondary to the technological code, the *dominant.* This was/is the apex moment of *Beyond a Boundary,* too, the moment when the West Indian cricketing team under at last the captaincy of a Black and professional, which means to say of non-middle-class or of marginal middle-class origins, returned cricket to the Golden Age of W. G. Grace, the *genus Britannicus* of a fine batsman who founded the game; and in doing so, fused the aesthetic imperative of a Bondman with the technical imperative of a Bradman, but reversing the order of priority – yet won the game. They were displacing then the rational hegemony of the bourgeoisie with its implicit categorisation[32] into the Head/Body, Reason/Instinct *social imaginaire* with a liminal reversal, that is, not of the specific categories as in Marxism-Leninism, (i.e., Labourism), or in *Black* nationalism (which represents *Black* as a biological rather than as a socio-historical category), but of the mode of categorisation, the system itself.

It is this transformation of hierarchical categories into a continuum, this transformation of the bourgeois *social imaginaire* which defines the aesthetic imperative of the great popular arts – the arts of the whole body of the people: the arts of the Greek games, its tragic drama; of the great African festival complex; of modern organised sports. It was the affirmation in action of the popular *social imaginaire* – of the Bondman aesthetic – that drew a quarter of a million people of Melbourne, Australia, out in the streets to pay tribute to and say goodbye to the West Indian cricketers who had rewarded the crowd with the kind of playing in which the "aesthetic function" was the dominant. With stroke after stroke hitting ball after ball *beyond the boundary*, strokes after which, as the West Indian crowd would say: *Not a man move!*

James's prose as he tells it enacts the "flow of motion" of bat and ball and fieldsmen in the rhythms of his prose:

> ...Frank Worrell and his team in Australia had added a new dimension to cricket history... The West Indies team in Australia, on the field and off, was playing above what it knew of itself... What they discovered in themselves must have been a revelation to few more than to the players themselves. ... This [was] not 'playing brighter cricket for the sake of the spectators who pay', that absurd nostrum for improving cricket... No, it was simply the return to the batting of the Golden Age... The first innings of Sobers at Brisbane was the most beautiful batting I have ever seen. Never was such ease and certainty of stroke, such early seeing of the ball, such late and leisured play, such command by the batsman not only of the bowling but of himself. He seemed to be expressing a personal vision... Yet my greatest moment was the speech-making after the last Test... Frank Worrell ...was crowned with the olive... If I say he won the prize it is because the crowd gave it to him. They laughed and cheered him continuously... I caught a glimpse of what brought a quarter of a million inhabitants of Melbourne into the streets to tell the West Indian cricketers goodbye, a gesture spontaneous and in cricket without precedent, one people speaking to another.[33]

Or as James would say, insisting on the fusion of man and nature, on the continuum rather than hierarchy of mind and body, insisting with the elegance of a Worrell driving through the covers:

> We have had enough of the flower-garden of the gay, the spontaneous West Indians. We need some astringent spray.[34]

Never was there such ease and certainty of phrase. Such late and leisurely play!

II. The Jamesian Ethics/Aesthetics

The bushmen's motive was perhaps religious, Hambledon's entertainment. One form was fixed, the other had to be constantly recreated. The contrasts can be multiplied. That will not affect the underlying identity. Each fed the need to satisfy the visual artistic sense. The emphasis on style in cricket proves that without a shadow of doubt; whether the impulse was literature and the artistic quality the result, or vice-versa, does not matter. If the Hambledon form was infinitely more complicated it rose out of a more complicated society, the result of a long historical development. Satisfying the same needs as bushmen and Hambledon, the industrial age took over cricket and made it into what it has become. The whole tortured history of modern Spain explains why it is in the cruelty of the bull-ring that they seek the perfect flow of motion. That flow, however, men since they have been men have always sought and always will. It is an unspeakable impertinence to arrogate the term "fine art" to one small section of this quest and declare it to be culture. Luckily, the people refuse to be bothered. This does not alter the gross falsification of history and the perversion of values which is the result.

Beyond a Boundary[35]

The tools chosen by Castoriadis were those of orthodox Marxism. Yet the implicit logic of his political approach contained in germinal form an essential element of his later critique of Marx, which bears mention here. The working class will continue to revolt against its immediate conditions, showing its willingness to struggle now for a better life. Yet so long as that better life is imagined in Russian tonalities, the political translation of this can only be the Communist Party... Implicit in the suggestion is *that it is the stunting of the creative imagination of individuals, due to the existence of a socially legitimated collective representation* – an *imaginaire social*, as Castoriadis refers to it later – which must be analysed. The imaginary social representations are, in effect, a material force in their own right.

Dick Howard, *The Marxian Legacy*[36]

Ah! *Vanitas Vanitatum!* Which of us is happy in this world? Which of us has his desire? or, having, it is satisfied? – Come children, let us shut up the box and the puppets, for our play is played out.

WilliamThackeray, *Vanity Fair*[37]

Put baldly, the second central question of *Beyond a Boundary* might seem remote from the Jamesian clash with Trotsky; from the Negro Question; from the Bondman contradiction and the popular question; from the decline of orthodox Marxism as a viable alternative projection of the futural and a new hope for our times, from the Sixth Pan-African Congress and the stagnation of Pan-Africanism, for the debate of the Third World, for the growing totalitarianism of both Wests, i.e., the U.S.A. and the Soviet Union, a tendency foretold by James.

Yet they are all of a piece. The aesthetic question that James raises when he asks and answers *What is Art?* is all of a piece and cut out of the same cloth as all other aspects of the Jamesian quest.

The chapter, *What is Art?* delegitimates bourgeois mythology in its aesthetic form and deconstructs a central aspect of the ruling *social imaginaire*. It critiques both the theoretical canons of a Trotsky, for whom productive labour is necessarily hegemonic, and the aesthetic canons of the Liberal art critic, Berenson. James first takes issue, however, with the distinguished cricket commentator Neville Cardus, who had often defended cricket's right to be called an art. Yet, James points out, it is the same Cardus who nevertheless stigmatises cricket's audience. "Nothing fine" in music or in anything else, Cardus wrote, can be understood or truly felt by the crowd. Given this initial presupposition, it is logical that whilst Cardus often introduced music into his writing on cricket, he never introduced cricket into his writing on music. As James comments:

> Cardus is a victim of that categorisation and specialisation, that division of the human personality, which is the greatest curse of our time. Cricket has suffered, but not only cricket.[38]

James then breaches this categorisation with a deliberate flinging down of the critical gauntlet.

> I have made great great claims for cricket... [Cricket] is an art, not a bastard or a poor relation but a full member of the community... and we have to compare it with other arts.[39]

And in his brilliant analysis of cricket as "a dramatic spectacle... [which] belongs with the theatre, ballet, opera and the dance",[40] he not only takes issue with the aestheticians, but like Bakhtin, he liberates the critical imagination from the closeted confines of the *aesthetic* as a separate realm from the realm of the real, and from the value categories of fine arts and non-fine arts.

> Cricket is first and foremost a dramatic spectacle. It belongs with the theatre, ballet, opera and the dance.
>
> In a superficial sense all games are dramatic. Two men boxing or running a race can exhibit skill, courage, endurance and sharp changes of fortune, can evoke hope and fear. They can even harrow the soul with laughter and tears, pity and terror. The state of the city, the nation or the world can invest a sporting event with dramatic intensity such as is reached in few theatres. When the democrat Joe Louis fought the Nazi Schmeling the bout became a focus of approaching world conflict...
>
> These possibilities cricket shares with other games in a greater or lesser degree. Its quality as drama is more specific. It is so organised that at all times it is compelled to reproduce the central action which characterises all good drama from the days of the Greeks to our own: two individuals are pitted against each other in a conflict that is strictly personal but no less strictly representative of a social group. One individual batsman faces one individual bowler. But each represents his side. The personal achievement may be of the utmost competence or brilliance. Its ultimate value is whether it assists the side to victory or staves off defeat. This has nothing to do with morals. It is the organisational structure on which the whole spectacle is built. The dramatist, the novelist, the choreographer, must strive to make

his individual character symbolical of a larger whole. He may or may not succeed... The batsman facing the ball does not merely represent his side.... *For that moment, to all intents and purposes, he is his side.* This fundamental relation of the One and the Many, Individual and Social, Individual and Universal, leader and followers, representative and ranks, the part and the whole is structurally imposed on the players of cricket. What other sports, games and arts have to aim at, the players are given to start with, they cannot depart from it. Thus the game is founded upon a dramatic, a human relation which is universally recognised as the most objectively pervasive and psychologically stimulating in life and therefore in that artificial representation of it which is drama.[41]

The aesthetics is the politics. James is not negating the fine arts. He is taking them out of the box in which bourgeois critical canons, responding to a socio-ideological code rather than to a purely critical conceptual imperative, have confined them.

And in this displacement of imperative the fine arts too, like cricket closeted from the reality of their times, face the same aridity, the same death. James points out that in defining the arts according to bourgeois prescriptions, the aestheticians have scorned to take notice of popular sports and games to their own detriment.

> The aridity and confusion of which they mournfully complain will continue until they include organised games *and the people who watch them* as an integral part of their data.[42]

James engaging with the art critic Berenson refutes the latter's decision to deny the criterion of art to wrestling matches because (as Berenson argues) of the game's "confusion and fatigue of actuality". Thus, Berenson maintains, only the artist manages to extract the "significance of movements", as in the rendering of tactile values only the artist can embody the corporal significance of objects. Against Berenson's emphasis on the solitary artist as mediator and on the painting as the only medium of art, James argues:

> I submit... that without the intervention of any artist the spectator at cricket extracts the significance of movement and of tactile value. He experiences the heightened sense of capacity... [The] significant form... is permanent present. It is known, expected, recognised enjoyed by tens of thousands of spectators. Cricketers call it style...
>
> What is to be emphasised is that whereas in the fine arts the image of tactile values and movement, however... magnificent, is permanent, fixed, in cricket the spectator sees the image constantly re-created, and whether he is a cultivated spectator or not, has standards which he carries with him always. He can re-create them at will. He can go to see a game hoping and expecting to see the image re-created or even extended... The image can be a single stroke, made on a certain day, which has been seen and never forgotten. There are some of these the writer has carried in his consciousness for over forty years, some in fact longer, as is described in the first pages of the book.[43]

Here James notes a significant fact about Berenson's art criticism – the fact that whilst praising paintings like Pollaiuolo's "Hercules Strangling Antaeus" as well as Michelangelo's drawings as the ultimate yet reached in the presentation of tactile values and sense of movement, never once does Berenson analyse the fact that is for James of central importance, "the enormous role that *elemental physical action plays in the visual arts throughout the century.*"[44]

The omission is not accidental. The separation of the physical and the mental is maintained even for a "physical" art such as painting. The abduction system of the Head/Body division rules in *aesthetics* too.

The wrestling match or the game of cricket could not be regarded by Berenson as being among the "fine arts". The bodies always in tense dynamic movement, the coordination is never static, finished, completed. Its aesthetic is itself dynamic.

> Cricket, in fact any ball game, to the visual image adds the sense of physical co-ordination, of harmonious action, of timing. The visual image of a diving fieldsman is a frame for his rhythmic contact with the flying ball. Here two art forms meet.[45]

But James's greatest breach with bourgeois aesthetics is his refusal to see it as "play", as the Marcusean-defined rest from labour and recuperation for labour. Rather, the art of cricket or of any sports is seen as a creative activity in its own right and one intimately linked to human existence as is labour. In other words, the aesthetic ceases to be merely a residual social activity; it becomes centrally meaningful.

In this part of his book James expresses the summa of his poesis – a summa that expresses what Gregory Bateson calls the *aesthetics of being alive.*[46]

In Chapter 16: "What is Art?", the first in Part Six, the "Art and Practic Part", James formulates an aesthetics that moves outside the bourgeois aesthetic code. He calls in question the ruling *social imaginaire, i.e.,* the *socially legitimated collective representations* which "value" the value-systems which control the mode of desire through the mechanism of its representation of the optative identity, of the optative canons of thought and feeling.

It is here that we grasp the dimensions of the Jamesian heresy. The critique in *Beyond a Boundary,* rather than merely an attack on *capitalism* as the economic expression of bourgeois society, goes beyond the absolute of the economic.

As James writes, summing up his credo:

> After a thorough study of bullfighting in Spain, Ernest Haas, the famous photographer, … his conclusion is: 'The bull fight is pure art. The spectacle is all motion… the perfection of motion, is what people want to see. They come hoping that this bull-fight will produce the perfect flow of motion.' Another name for the *perfect flow of motion is style, or, if you will, significant form.*
>
> Let us examine this motion, or, as Mr. Berenson calls it, movement. Where the motive or directing force rests with the single human being, an immense variety of physical motion is embraced within four categories.

[...]

The batsman propels a missile with a tool. The bowler does the same unaided... He may bowl a slow curve or fast or medium, or he may at his pleasure use each in turn. There have been many bowlers whose method of delivery has seemed to spectators the perfection of form, irrespective of the fate which befell the balls bowled. Here, far more than in batting, the repetition conveys the realisation of movement despite the actuality. Confusion is excluded by the very structure of the game.

As for the fieldsmen, there is no limit whatever to their possibilities of running, diving, leaping, falling forward, backwards, sideways, with all their energies concentrated on a specific objective, the whole completely realisable by the alert spectator. The spontaneous outburst of thousands at a fierce hook or a dazzling slip-catch, the ripple of recognition at a long-awaited leg-glance, are as genuine and deeply felt expressions of artistic emotion as any I know.

You will have noted that the four works of art chosen by Mr. Berenson to illustrate movement all deal with some physical action of the athletic kind. Mr. Berenson calls the physical process of response mystical...

I believe that the examination of the stroke, the brilliant piece of fielding, will take us through mysticism to far more fundamental considerations, than mere life-enhancing. We respond to physical action or vivid representation of it, dead or alive, because we are made that way. For unknown centuries survival for us, like all other animals, depended upon competent and effective physical activity. This played its part in developing the brain. The particular nature which became ours did not rest satisfied with this. If it had it could never have become human. The use of the hand, the extension of its powers by the tool, the propulsion of a missile at some objective and the accompanying refinements of the mechanics of judgment, these marked us off from the animals. Language may have come at the same time... Sputnik can be seen as no more than a missile made and projected through tools by the developed hand.

Similarly the eye for the line which is today one of the marks of ultimate aesthetic refinements is not new. It is old. The artists of the caves of Altamira had it. So did the bushmen. They had it to such a degree that they could reproduce it or, rather, represent it with unsurpassed force. Admitting this, Mr. Berenson confines the qualities of this primitive art to animal energy and an exasperated vitality. That, even if true, is totally subordinate to the fact that among these primitive peoples the sense of form existed to the degree that it could be consciously and repeatedly reproduced. It is not a gift of high civilisation, the last achievement of noble minds. It is exactly the opposite. The use of sculpture and design among primitive people indicates that the significance of form is a common possession. Children have it. There is no need to adduce further evidence for the presupposition that the faculty or faculties by which we recognise significant form in elemental physical action is native to us, a part of the process by which we have become and remain human. It is neither more nor less mystical than any other of our faculties of apprehension. ... The impression I get is that the line was an integral part of co-ordinated physical activity, functional perhaps, but highly refined in that upon it food or immediate self-preservation might depend.

Innate faculty though it might be, the progress of civilisation can leave it unused, suppress its use, can remove us from the circumstances in which it is associated with animal energy. Developing civilisation can surround us with circumstances and conditions in which our original faculties are debased or refined, made more simple or more complicated. They may seem to disappear altogether. They remain part of our human endowment. The basic motions of cricket represent physical action which has been the basis not only of primitive but of civilised life for countless centuries. In work and in play they were the motions by which men lived and without which they would perish. The Industrial Revolution transformed our existence. Our fundamental characteristics as human beings it did not and could not alter. The bushmen reproduced in one medium not merely animals but the line, the curve, the movement. It supplied in the form they needed a vision of the life they lived.[47]

The aesthetic is not less "material" than the *economic*. The expropriation of the means of aesthetic perception, of the mechanics of critical judgment are no less and perhaps far more terrible with respect to its consequences than the expropriation of the means of production. The means of providing for material existence are vital, but so too are the means of enacting, exercising, developing the innate faculty – *the eye for line and for significant form,* an eye physical in earlier circumstances where the natural environment was the dominant challenge, now conceptual and aesthetic in a situation where man's greatest obstacle to the realisation of his powers, to the free play and development of his faculties, is now the socio-cultural environment.

This socio-environment is never natural; nor is it arbitrary. Nor are the attitudes and responses – of approval, recognition, or aversion, rejection, in other words, of intersubjective valuation – ever purely subjective. Rather these subjective attitudes are responses in line with the value-systems of the hegemonic *social imaginaire*.

And it was this *imaginaire* that persuaded the masses that their desire for organised sports had nothing to do with their *material* needs, that aesthetic needs were for eggheads. That the satisfaction of a "visual artistic sense" could only be fed in art galleries. That aesthetic appreciation was something from which they were excluded.

Like the man speaking prose without knowing it, so the West Indian cricket audience shouting "Not a man move!", the bullfighting crowd shouting "Olé!" and "the spontaneous outburst of thousands... the ripple of recognition" at a moment when the player plays above himself, outside himself, is engaged, as *Beyond a Boundary* reveals, in "genuine and deeply felt expressions of artistic emotions". For it is this above all that people live by. Deprive them of it. Or sell the game by faking it, by massifying it. Reduce the aesthetic to the mechanically orchestrated in thought and feeling – as in Hitler's Germany, Stalin's Soviet Union, Jonestown, and now increasingly in the United States, and in many areas of the Third World – and all that is human of Man will be gone. The "stunted" creative imagination will call for gas ovens. And the burning has already begun.

Endnotes

1. "Garfield Sobers" in *Cricket, the Great All-Rounders: Studies of Ten of the Finest All-Rounders of Cricket History,* John Arlott, ed. (London: Pelham Books, 1969), 157.

2. Jean Baudrillard, *The Mirror of Production,* trans. Mark Poster (St. Louis: Telos Press, 1975), 39.

3. *Beyond a Boundary,* (1963; London: Hutchinson, 1969), 130.

4. Ibid., 131.

5. Marx shattered the fiction of *homo economicus,* the myth which sums up the whole process of naturalisation of the system of exchange value, the market and surplus value and its forms. But he did so in the name of labour power's emergence in action, of men's own power to give rise to value by his labour *(pro-ducere).* Isn't this a ...similar naturalisation – a model bound to *code* all human (life) ...in terms of value ... and production? Through this mirror of production, the human species comes to consciousness in the imaginary, ...finalised by a sort of ideal ... productivist ego... in the identity that a man dons with his own eyes when he can think of himself only as something to produce, to transform, or bring about as value." Baudrillard, *The Mirror of Production,* 18, 19, 20.

6. "The definition of labour power as the source of 'concrete' social wealth is the complete expression of the abstract manipulation of labour power: the truth of capital culminates in this 'evidence' of man as producer of value." For [Marx] ... "men begin to distinguish themselves from animals as soon as they begin to *produce* their means of subsistence... But is man's existence an end for which he must find the means?... Is he labour power (by which he separates himself as means from himself as his own end)?" *The Mirror of Production*, 25, 22.

7. *Beyond a Boundary,* 149,150.

8. Ibid., 150

9. Ibid.

10. Mikhail Bakhtin, Rabelais *and His World,* tr. Helen Iswolsky (Cambridge, MA.: MIT Press, 1968), 7.

11. Ibid., 29.

12. Ibid., 7.

13. *Beyond a Boundary,* 164.

14. Ibid., 158. "In all essentials the modern game was formed and shaped between 1778, when Hazlitt was born, and 1830, when he died. It was created by the yeoman farmer, the gamekeeper, the potter, the tinker, the Nottingham coal-miner, the Yorkshire factory hand. These artisans made it, men of hand and eye. Rich and idle young noblemen and some substantial city people contributed money, organisation and prestige. Between them, by 1837 they had evolved a highly complicated game with all the typical characteristics of a genuinely national art form, founded on elements long present in the nation, profoundly popular in origin, yet attracting to it disinterested elements of the leisured and educated classes." Ibid.,,, 164.

15. Ibid., 159.

16. The "white masks" worn by Blacks (Fanon) are not so much *white* as "normative masks", i.e., the set of desires, aspirations, in the identity package which it then codes as Norm. In attaining to this normative middle-class identity, the individual acts according to the grammar of action coded in the identity package. In realising his "individuality" as prescribed, the "unit" acts so as to constitute and verify middle-class reality as the really real. The middle-class co-optation of the identity and desires of the popular forces is even more powerful because more invisible. Nazism, the rise of the moral majority, and Jonestown reveals this contradiction, i.e., the power of middle-class pseudo-populism to coerce the popular forces through their control of the social imaginaire. James's reading of *Moby Dick* reveals the hold of Ahab on the others prefiguring Hitler, Stalin, Jim Jones. Who next? Others by compelling a reversal of the accumulative telos; compelling some measure of redistribution at the popular levels.

17. Cornelius Castoriadis, *L'Institution imaginaire de la société* (Paris: Seuil, 1975).

18. "... after this long absence they seemed all to have returned within about a decade of each other, in frantic haste... Golf was known to be ancient. The first annual tournament of the Open Championship was held only in 1860. The Football Association was founded only in 1863. It was in 1866 that the first athletic championship was held in England. The first English cricket team left for Australia in 1862 and a county championship worthy of the name was organised only in 1873. In the United States the first all-professional baseball team was organised in 1869. ...[L]awn tennis was actually invented and played for the first time in Wales in 1873 and was carried next year to the United States. ... The public flocked to these sports and games. All of a sudden, everyone wanted organised sports and games.

    But in that very decade this same public was occupied with other organisations of a very different type. Disraeli's Reform Bill, introducing popular democracy in England, was passed in 1865. In the same year the slave states were defeated in the American Civil War, to be followed immediately by the first modern organisation of American labour. In 1864, Karl Marx and Frederick Engels founded the First Communist International and within a few years Europe for the first time since the Crusades, saw an international organisation composing millions of people. In 1871 in France Napoleon III was overthrown and the Paris Commune was established. It failed, and popular democracy... seemed doomed. ... In only four years it had returned and the Third Republic was founded. So that this same public that wanted sports and games so eagerly wanted popular democracy too. Perhaps they were not exactly the same people in each case. Even so, both groups were stirred at the same time." *Beyond a Boundary*, 150-151.

19. Ibid., 151.

20. Ibid., 14.

21. Ibid., 15

22. Fuqua created quite a stir when he stated that Blacks are the "least capable of producing in our society. You park a certain percentage of them – like antiquated machinery (which you depreciate) – and you support them through welfare... which we're doing." See Joel Dreyfuss, "The New Racism", *Black Enterprise,* vol. 8, no. 6 (January 1978): 41 and "White Complacency Masks

a New, Subtle Form of Racism", *Berkeley Barb*, vol. 27, no. 3, Issue 649 (January 20-26, 1978): 4.

23. "Concerning the treatment of slaves, I may mention as a good compilation, that of Charles Comte, *Traité de la législation,* Third Edition, Brussell, 1837. Those who want to learn *what the bourgeois makes of himself and his world,* whenever he can, *without restraint, model the world after his own image,* should study this matter in detail." Karl Marx, *Capital: A Critique of Political Economy,* Vol. 1 (Chicago: Charles Kerr, 1909), 824.

24. James quoted from an excellent work of Richard Pares to prove his point. Pares noted *inter alia* that: "in all the inventories which are to be found among the West Indian archives it is very usual for the mill, the cauldron, the still and the buildings to count for more than one-sixth of the total capital; in most plantations one-tenth would be nearer the mark. By far the greatest capital items were the value of the slaves and the acreage planted in canes by their previous labour.

"Yet, when we look closely, we find that the industrial capital required was much larger than a sixth of the total value. With the mill, the boiling house and the still went an army of specialists – almost all of them slaves, but none the less specialists for that.

"They were not only numerous but, because of their skill, they had a high value. If we add their cost to that of the instruments and machinery which they used, we find that the industrial capital of the plantations, without which it could not be a plantation at all, was probably not much less than half its total capital." James, "The Making of the Caribbean People" in *Spheres of Influence: Selected Writings* (Westport, CT: Lawrence Hill, 1980), 178-179.

25. *Beyond a Boundary,* 187. Emphasis added.

26. In *State Capitalism and World Revolution,* James defines this crisis. As always where he analyses the crisis in terms only of the division of labour in production, I suggest that his literary and fictional system and the underground heresy of his theoretics widen this analysis to the *global social division* imperative *to the telos of accumulation, and based* on the *social imaginaire* of the Reason/Instinct, Head/Body division. The division of labour is then seen as a subset, as the division *white* captain, *Black* team; or *white* quarterback, *Black* footballers. As James wrote:

"The crisis of production today [the crisis then of the global social order] is the crisis of the antagonism between manual and intellectual labour. The problem of modern philosophy from Descartes in the sixteenth century to Stalinism in 1950 is the problem of the division of labour between the intellectuals and the workers. In the springtime of capitalism this rationalistic division of labour was the basis of a common attempt of individual men associated *in a natural environment to achieve control over nature.* Today this division of labour is the *control in social production* of the administrative elite *over the masses.* Rationalism has reached its end in the complete divorce and absolute disharmony between manual and intellectual labour, between the socialised proletariat and the monster of centralised capital." James with Raya Dunayevskaya and Grace Lee, *State Capitalism and World Revolution* (Chicago: Charles Kerr, 1986), 114, 115.

27. "The structural analysis [of Borana society, Ethiopia] demonstrated that structures

resting upon cognitive discrimination can be as orderly as the grammar governing language. We cannot assume that this is the only kind of order in human society. In the analyses of instability we saw the kinds of regularities that are not based on *native conceptual schemes*... There are rather events, processes, and trends that exist in spite of structure... [Yet] ... there is a third domain that is both anti-structural and anti-empirical. This is the domain of creativity, ecstatic religion, prophetism." This is where Turner's classic *The Ritual Process* "has finally established liminality and multi-vocality as the third major area of anthropological analysis... He [Turner] has extended the interpretative power of the concept of liminality [and] has established that the topsy-turvy world of transitional and marginal groups, dominated as it is by a rich multi-vocal symbolic medium, is nothing less than the third facet of human society... It is a domain *in which the categoric distinctions* that normally segmentalise the social field are temporarily held in abeyance, allowing the human community to experience the bonds of total empathy. These inordinately fragile liminal societies exist only for very brief periods of history, and in the very process of dying, they give rise to new forms of social structure or *revitalised versions of the old order.* Liminality is the repository of the creative potential underlying human society". Asmarom Legesse, *Gada: Three Approaches to the Study of African Society* (New York: Free Press, 1973), 248-249. Emphasis added.

28. Walter Rodney was the first to underscore this clash of ratio between the accumulative telos of the bourgeoisie and that of African traditional societies at the beginning of the Atlantic Slave Trade:

"What is most fundamental is an attempt to evaluate the African contribution to the solution of the problems posed by man's existence in society; and hence the stress placed in this paper on matter pertaining to social relations: codes of hospitality, processes of the law, public order and social and religious tolerance. In each of those areas of human social activity, African norms and practices were given a high value by Europeans themselves. They often reflected that the hospitality they saw in an African village was lacking in their communities; that the security of goods stood in marked contrast to brigandage and depredations in Europe...

"... On the other hand, African norms were frustrating to capitalists. For instance, the whites resented the polite formulae of African greetings since they were lengthy and could delay business for a whole day. One European denounced African hospitality in the following terms: 'The law of hospitality is obstructive of industry. If there is provision in the country, a man who wants it has only to find out who has got any, and he must have his share. If he enters any man's house during his repast, and gives him the usual salutation, the man must invite him to partake. Thus, whatever abundance a man may get by assiduity, will be shared by the lazy; and thus they seldom calculate for more than necessaries. But the laws of hospitality are not restrained to diet. A common man cannot quietly enjoy a spare shirt or a pair of trousers. Those who are too lazy to plant or hunt are also too lazy to trade." Walter Rodney, *Groundings With My Brothers* (London: Bogle L'Ouverture Publications, 1969), 56, 57.

29. Ibid., 57.

30. "When we reach state-capitalism, one-party state, cold war, hydrogen bomb, it is obvious that we have reached ultimates. We are now at the stage where all universal questions are matters of concrete specific urgency for society in general *as* well as for every individual. As we wrote in *The Invading Socialist Society*:

'It is precisely the character of our age and the maturity of humanity that obliterates the opposition between theory and practice, between the intellectual occupations of the 'educated' and the 'masses'.'"

'All previous distinctions, politics and economics, war and peace, agitation and propaganda, party and mass, the individual and society, national, civil and imperialist war, single country and one world, immediate needs and ultimate solution – all these it is impossible to keep separate any longer. Total planning is inseparable from permanent crisis, the world struggle for the minds of men from the world tendency to the complete mechanisation of men." *State Capitalism and World Revolution* (1950; Detroit: Charles Kerr, 1986), 113.

31. "Hazlitt's strength and comprehensiveness were the final culmination of one age fertilised by the new. In prose, in poetry, in criticism, in painting, his age was more creative than the country had been for two centuries before and would be for a century after. This was the age that among its other creations produced the game of cricket." *Beyond a Boundary*, 158.

32. James: "The revolutionary bourgeoisie which established its powers against feudalism could only develop a philosophy of history and of society in which, on the one hand, it spoke for the progress of all society, and on the other, for itself as the leaders of society. This philosophy can be summed up in one word: *rationalism*. Rationalism is the philosophy of bourgeois political economy. It is materialist and not idealist in so far as it combats superstition, seeks to expand the productive forces and increases the sum total of goods. But there is no such thing as a classless materialism. Rationalism conceives this expansion as a division of labour between the passive masses and the active elite. Thereby it reinstates idealism. Because it does not and cannot doubt that harmonious progress is inevitable by this path, the essence of rationalism is uncritical or vulgar materialism, and uncritical or vulgar idealism." *State and World Revolution*, 115. Emphasis added.

33. *Beyond a Boundary*, 251-252.

34. Ibid., 131.

35. Ibid., 204-205.

36. Dick Howard, *The Marxian Legacy* (New York: Urizen, 1977), 265.

37. William Thackeray, *Vanity Fair: A Novel Without a Hero* (London: Bradbury and Evans, 1848), 624.

38. *Beyond a Boundary*, 191-192.

39. Ibid., 191.

40. Television reproducing the movements of footballers, baseball players, basketball in slow motion, reveals not only that sports are modalities of dance, but also why all theoretical dance, classical ballet and modern, have become the vestiges of a museum-performance, irrelevant.

41. *Beyond a Boundary*, 192. Emphasis added.

42. Ibid.

43. Ibid., 198.
44. Ibid., 201.
45. Ibid., 203.
46. "Today, we pump a little natural history into children along with a little 'art' so that they will forget their animal and ecological nature and the aesthetics of being alive and will grow up to be good businessmen." Gregory Bateson, *Mind and Nature: A Necessary Unity* (New York: E.P. Dutton, 1979), 142.
47. *Beyond a Boundary*, 201-204. Emphasis added.

NEW SEVILLE
AND THE CONVERSION EXPERIENCE OF
BARTOLOMÉ DE LAS CASAS

PART ONE

The priest Casas having at the time no knowledge of the unjust methods which the Portuguese used to obtain slaves, advised that permission should be given for the import of slaves into the islands, an advice which, once he became informed about these methods, he would not have given for the world...[1]

The remedy which he proposed to import Black slaves in order to liberate the Indians was not a good one, even though he thought the Black slaves, at the time to have been enslaved with a just title; and it is not at all certain that his ignorance at the time or even the purity of his motive will sufficiently absolve him when he finds himself before the Divine Judge.[2]

Las Casas, History of the Indies.

Clearly one cannot prove in a short time or with a few words to infidels that to sacrifice men to God is contrary to nature. Consequently neither anthropophagy nor human sacrifice constitutes just cause for making war on certain kingdoms... For the rest, to sacrifice innocents for the salvation of the Commonwealth is not opposed to natural reason, is not something abominable and contrary to nature, but is an error that has its origin in natural reason itself.

Las Casas's reply to Ginés de Sepúlveda on the occasion of the 1550-51 debate at Valladolid, Spain, as to whether or not the new world Indians were equally "men" (Las Casas) or "slaves-by-nature" (Sepúlveda).[3]

In June, 1514, a certain Pedro de la Rentería who was on a business trip to Jamaica stayed for a while at the Franciscan monastery in New Seville.[4] Whilst there, he underwent a conversion experience. This experience took place almost at the same time as a conversion experience undergone by his partner on their jointly owned estate near the recently settled town of Espíritu Santo, Cuba.

Pedro de la Rentería remains a somewhat obscure figure. What we know of him we know from his partner's account of their parallel experiences. And there was to be no one, after Columbus himself, who was to be more historically significant in the new era of human affairs that opened with

Columbus's first arrival in the Caribbean in 1492, than de la Rentería's partner, Bartolomé de Las Casas.

Nor was there to be an event of more crucial significance to this era of history that had opened, than the conversion experience of Las Casas which, like St. Paul's vision on the road to Damascus, shifted Las Casas's way of seeing out of the normative reference frame and uniform perception of his fellow Spanish settlers. This religio-conceptual leap led to the transformation of Las Casas from an *encomendero* – i.e. an owner of an allotted number of Arawaks incorporated as a labour force (an *encomienda*) under a traditional Spanish system which, however, took on new and harsher aspects in the frontier context of the new world – to the most determined antagonist of the entire system of Indian forced labour, whether in the form of the *encomienda* or in the form of outright Indian slave-labour.

Two consequences of this transformation were to be of special significance to contemporary Jamaica. The first was that as a result of his conversion-inspired mission to secure the abolition of all forms of Indian forced labour, Las Casas was to propose the importation of a limited quantity of African slaves both to recompense the settlers for their Indian labour supply, and as an incentive to Spanish peasant migration. This limited scheme proposed to the Emperor Charles V and his royal bureaucracy was the initial occasion for the subsequent sale by the Crown in 1518 of a licence to one of the Flemish courtiers at the court of the half-Burgundian King of Spain, one Gouvenot – who later sold it to some Genoese merchants – to import 4,000 slaves from West Africa into the Caribbean islands and the mainland. This *asiento* was to be the charter, at one and the same time, of the transatlantic slave trade, and, at a terrible human cost, of the African presence as a constitutive unit of the post-Columbian civilisation of the Caribbean and the Americas.

Once he was informed of the unjust methods used in the enslavement of the Africans, Las Casas, who had worked on the assumption that he was submitting men and women who had been justly enslaved according to the moral-legal system of Latin Christianity, for Indian men and women whom he knew from personal experience to be unjustly enslaved within the context of these same moral-legal doctrines, was to bitterly repent of his original proposal.[5]

The second consequence of his conversion experience was to lead to a daring conceptual leap made by Las Casas. This was during the course of his theoretical dispute with the theologian-humanist scholar and official royal historian, Ginés de Sepúlveda in the context of the formal debate held at Valladolid, Spain, before a conclave of theologians, jurists, scholars, royal bureaucrats and councillors in 1550-51.

Sepúlveda in order to provide a legitimatising basis for the Spanish conquest of the Indies, to represent it as "just" and "holy" and to derive the *encomienda* system as therefore just and lawful, used a Neo-Aristotelian formulation to argue that the Indians were "slaves-by-nature"; that there is a difference of "natural capacity" between peoples, and that this differential gave those of a higher "natural capacity" (the more perfect) the right to rule and govern those of a lower "natural capacity" (the less perfect).

Las Casas, in the course of countering Sepúlveda's thesis of a predetermined *natural* difference of rational capacity between peoples, and the servile-by-nature Neo-Aristotelian formulation of his antagonist, made a conceptual leap to propose – almost heretically, given the context of his time – that the human sacrifices made by peoples like the Aztecs and their ritual eating of human flesh was not, as his antagonist Sepúlveda took it to be, evidence and proof of a *lack* of natural reason but rather that it was an *error* of natural reason.

In other words the practice of human sacrifice for the Aztecs did not constitute a *mode of irrationality* but rather a *form of rationality*, an error made by natural reason itself. And in this form of natural reason, practices seen as vices by the Spaniards "in truth were not thought of as vices by the Indians but virtues answering to a life view much closer to natural reason than that of the Spaniards".[6]

Within the frame of this reason, assuming their false gods to be the true God, those Indians who sacrificed humans to their gods offered as they did so, "what seemed most valuable to them", "sacrificing innocents for the good of the Commonwealth", only because it seemed to them supremely rational to do so.[7]

With this formulation Las Casas anticipated by some four and a half centuries what anthropologists, post-Einstein, and post-Lévi-Strauss, are only now beginning to make us see, in the reference frame of an ongoing Copernican and decentring revolution, as the *relativity of all human systems of perception including our own*; as the reality, not of a single absolute reason, but of culturally determined modes of reason, as the reality of the cultural-historical relativity of our own.

There are two paradoxical implications here. The first lies in the fact that as the terms of Las Casas's repentance with respect to his first proposal reveals, in proposing the importation of African slaves as a means of ensuring the abolition of the *encomienda* system and the Indian slave trade, he too had been trapped by an "error" of natural reason, i.e. not only by the fact that he had not known of the unjust methods and therefore of the unjust titles by which the Africans were enslaved both by the Portuguese and their "African" partners[8] but also by the logic of a specific mode of cultural reason, that of the fifteenth and sixteenth century Catholic Christianity. For, as J.F. Maxwell points out, it was not to be until 1965, that the common teaching of the Catholic Church handed down by its "fallible ordinary *magisterium*" (a teaching which had approved of the institution of slavery, on condition that the slaves were held by specifically defined "just titles") for some 1400 years, was finally to be corrected by the second Vatican Council.[9]

The second paradox lies in the fact that it was by his daring, if necessarily limited given the time and circumstances, and religio-monarchical frame of his thought, implication of the existence of *culturally relative forms of rationality*, that Las Casas not only laid the basis for the theoretical delegitimisation of all forms of inter-human domination and subordination, but also laid the conceptual basis, some four and a half centuries before it was to become an empirically urgent necessity, for that "higher-order of synthesis" now vital to the survival of the post-atomic human subject.

> Indeed mankind is already unified in a material sense. *It is this very fact that renders higher orders of synthesis necessary if mankind is to survive.* The race has always existed, but its unity was in earlier times mostly a dream, a distant image. Now, almost suddenly, mankind has become an intercommunicating and interdependent whole in which every part is vulnerable to destruction by other parts. For the first time our planet is living a single history. The material unity which already and irrevocably exists must be reinforced by legal, moral and spiritual unity, which sadly – despite all of our good intentions – still does not exist.[10]

We shall attempt in this article to glance at the background and implications of both paradoxes. To do so it will be necessary to look briefly at the *before* and *after* of the conversion experience; the before of Las Casas's life in Española and Cuba, the conversion experience itself, and the *after* which was to climax in the formal Valladolid dispute against his humanist/theologian antagonist, Ginés de Sepúlveda.

Bartholomew (Bartolomé) de Las Casas was born in Seville, Spain in 1474. When he was 20 years old, his father, one Pedro de Las Casas, and a merchant, sailed with Columbus on the second voyage of settlement, the expedition with which Spain was to lay the basis for the emergence of what Gerhard Hirschfeld calls the "single history" that all mankind is living today. (It is often forgotten that this basis was first laid by Spain, even more forgotten that it was in four Caribbean Islands, i.e. Española (today's Santo Domingo and Haiti), Puerto Rico, Jamaica and Cuba.)

When Las Casas's father returned to Seville in 1495 he brought back an Arawak whom he had enslaved – and gave him to his son as his personal attendant. Neither father nor son saw anything wrong with this, in the climate of belief and practice in which a non-racial and non-credal slavery (i.e. slaves were both white/European, black/African, Berber and Arab, Christian, Pagan and Muslim) essentially domestic and artisan, was traditional and widespread.

When Las Casas's father returned to Española to settle there, Bartolomé soon joined him, sailing in the retinue of the newly appointed governor of the Indies, Nicolás de Ovando.

From the time of his arrival in 1502 until the time of his conversion in June 1514, Las Casas, even though he was to be ordained as a priest in 1510 and was always to treat the Arawak peoples more considerately than most, behaved more or less like any other Spanish settler, even as a "conquistador". From the scanty indications that we have of his early life in Hispaniola, i.e. that he took part in the pacification campaign on the east end of the island, as well as "in several Indian hunting expeditions", that although he does not seem to have "engaged in gold mining at this period", he owned food production estates and had allotted to him numbers of Arawaks within the *encomienda*, serf-labour that had been set up to secure a steady labour supply; that he supervised the Indians in the growing of cassava and the making of cassava bread, and that he made considerable sums of money from this,[11] Las Casas fully shared in what might be called the "land/gold/and hidalgo complex", of the average conquistador/poblador; in the psychic complex that underlay the expansionist drive of the first world empire, that of Catholic-Christian Spain.

Spain's year for destiny had been 1492. After eight centuries of having been occupied and invaded by the expanding forces of Islam, the Spanish Christian troops laid siege to, and finally conquered, the last outpost of the Islamic faith in Spain – the city and province of Granada.

The contract that the Spanish sovereigns signed with Columbus was signed in the town of Santa Fé from where the siege of Granada was being directed. Spain's conquest and her expansion into the new world following on Columbus's windfall find at once shifted both the balance of power and the dynamic of expansion decisively away from Islam to the Latin-Christian European peoples and their dazzling rise to world domination spearheaded by Spain.

The latter's expulsion of all Jews who refused Christian conversion in the high year of 1492 was an act related to her growing sense of national destiny, as well as to the rise of a new system of centralised monarchy based on the unifying cement of a single faith – the Christian.

With her capture of Granada in 1492, Spain now gave the descendants of the former Islamic invaders the same ultimatum that she had given her Jews – convert or leave. Many converted, both Jews and Muslims, and were to become known as the "New Christians" or *conversos*. Purity of faith, *limpieza de fé*, became linked with purity of old Spanish Christian blood, i.e. *limpieza de sangre*, and both were increasingly linked to loyalty to the rising new monarchical state. To be a *morisco* (a converted Muslim) or a *marrano* (a converted Jew) was to be suspected, before the fact, of un-Spanish activities.

The concept of *limpieza de sangre*, cleanliness of blood, was a centralising concept deployed by the monarchical revolution to cut across the rigid caste hierarchy of the feudal nobility. All Christians of genetically Spanish birth, of whatever rank, were now incorporable as "we" and the *limpios* (of clean descent and faith), as opposed to the non-*limpios* i.e. the Spaniards of Jewish or Moorish descent. For the monarchical revolution did not abolish the feudal status-prestige system of *nobleza de sangre* (nobility of blood) but rather drew it into a new symbolic machinery of monarchical rationalism, one in which the *hidalgo* complex (the aspiration to noble status, and to the title of Don), and the *limpieza* complex (the aspiration to "clean" status, to being the Spanish Christian socio-symbolic norm) cross cut, balanced and reinforced each other in a dynamic equilibrium.

J.H. Elliott in his perceptive book on imperial Spain, points out that the concept of *limpieza* was used as a class weapon by a new stratum, i.e. the sons of lowly born peasants and artisans who through "natural" ability and education were able to aspire to the higher levels of the Church and state bureaucracy. Finding their way to these posts blocked by powerful members of the aristocracy who reserved them for their own highly-born caste, the new *letrado* class (the lettered class, the literati, consisting of jurists, theologians, scholars) pushed the introduction of new statutes which reserved these higher posts, especially those in the Church, for those who could prove their "purity of blood" during several generations.[12]

In medieval Spain there had been considerable intermingling between the aristocracy and powerful members of the Jewish community, many of whom controlled the higher reaches of finance and of the learned professions. In addition, in 1492, many Jews had accepted conversion rather than endure expulsion, and they now formed a powerful stratum, officially Christian, able to rival the Spanish *letrado* class in learning and to outrank them, backed as they were by highly-placed aristocratic connections.

With the rise of a theocratic monarchical state, the new *letrado* class, making social use of the theological stigma placed on Jews as a people who had "rejected" Christ and refused "His Word", had constructed a concept of orthodoxy in which the heresy of this original act of rejection was represented as being carried in the blood, generating in all their non-*limpio* descendants a "natural inclination" to heresy.

Men risen from lowly origins, from the villages, where there had been no intermarriage, were therefore represented as bearers of the socio-theological orthodoxy of *limpieza de sangre/limpieza de fé*, as the nobility – including the powerful *converso* Jews – were the bearers of the socio-symbolic orthodoxy of *hidalguía* and noble blood. Each group, the nobility and new *letrado* class, vied to play off their orthodoxies against each other.

Recent scholarship has raised the possibility that Las Casas was of *converso*, New Christian Jewish descent, i.e. a *marrano*. Las Casas himself was to insist that he was of "good old stock", i.e. an old Christian. He could genuinely have believed this. Once converted, families went to great lengths to "pass", to repress all traces of their Jewish or Moorish origins, since these origins barred many avenues to preferment in church and state. Indeed, new Christians, whether of Jewish or Moorish descent were officially banned from entering the New World even though their *de facto* widespread clandestine and unofficial presence is now being documented by scholarly research (several documents, for example, indicate the presence of both *marranos* and *moriscos* in New Seville).

But even had he known it, Las Casas would never have admitted to it. The lesser evil, he insisted in another context, was always to be preferred to a greater. Superb strategist that he was, he would have known that the struggle that he fought to abolish the *encomienda* would have been lost even before the start had he admitted to such a "taint". Nevertheless, his struggle for a universally applicable, rather than for a "nationalist", Christianity, might have not been unconnected to the creative ambivalence of his own origins.

Both complexes, that of *limpieza de sangre* and that of *nobleza de sangre*, can only be understood in the context of the centuries-long crusade waged to reconquer Spanish territory from the Moors. This crusade, called the Reconquest was essentially a long "anti-colonial" struggle against the religious imperialism of Islam. For in a wave of expansion, after the death of their prophet Mohammed, the followers of Islam had entered Spain in AD 711, advancing into Europe as far as Tours until stopped by Charles Martel (AD 732) in a battle which saved Christendom.

Christian Spain, however, from the eighth century onwards, was corralled in, and confined to, the small northern-enclaves, whilst Islam occupied the rest of Spain, developing a dazzling civilisation which reached its high point in a tenth century apogee of commercial development and learning. This civilisation was based on the coexistence of the three Semitic-derived monotheistic faiths: Judaism, Christianity and Mohammedanism, with the latter of course, hegemonic, but relatively tolerant.

Although an interracial faith, Islam was primarily borne by the Arabs. Latin-Christendom, as it fought against Islam, and as it was cut off from its original Mediterranean range of differing peoples, gradually "ethnicised" itself, becoming a Carolingian, Frankish/Gothic type of Euro-Christianity. It was this particularistic Euro-Christianity which provided the ideological basis for the Reconquest.

Both the *hidalgo* and the *limpieza* complexes carried by the settlers to the New World were therefore generated from a religious racism dynamically forged in the struggle against an Arab-dominated Islam, during which the aristocracy had come to play a central role. For the imperative of retaking the lands occupied and ruled by the Spanish Moors had placed a premium on the religio-military machine consisting of the great nobles, the military orders and the higher dignitaries of the Church. The additional fact that the Reconquest was sanctified as a Holy War and was quite clearly a "just war", i.e. an offensive/defensive war, legitimised the Spanish nobility's amassing of vast political and economic power. Even more crucially the model of the noble – the *hijo d'algo* or "son of someone", i.e. the hidalgo, whose fighting qualities were ascribed to the genetic superiority of his caste and lineage – became the normative model of identity of the society.

The complex of *hidalguía* generated from the deep rooted crusading spirit, linked to a modernised medieval warrior/complex,[13] was expressed in a two-caste system in which the socio-symbolic norm, those of predominantly noble and fighting lineage, looked down upon the agriculturalists (*labradores* and *campesinos*, i.e. peasants) as well as on the free artisan urban class. Manual labour or any connection with non-military or non-religious activities tended to be deeply stigmatised. To be lowly born – of peasant or of artisan origin – carried a stigma as powerful as that of Blackness in the pre-1938 Caribbean.

The symbolic material apparatus of valorisation/stigmatisation logically coded the normative desire. All Spanish skins wore *Don* masks (cf. Fanon's *Black Skins/White Masks*). However lowly-born, every Spaniard, like Cervantes's plain Alonso Quijana, aspired to reinvent himself as Don Quixote; aspired to be a *Don*.

The dominance of the aristocracy – through its control of what might be called the psychic desire/aversion apparatus of the order as a whole, was expressed at the economic level by its control of a new system –the *latifundium* system. For whilst the long centuries of the Reconquest had helped to undermine the feudal order by creating a more open and mobile frontier situation, it had also led to a situation in which vast expanses of the lands recaptured from the Moors had become concentrated in the exclusive ownership of the great nobles, the high clergy and the military orders. The *latifundium* complex was reinforced by the poverty of the soil, and the high prices paid in Northern Europe for Spanish wool, with both factors leading to the expansion of a nomadic pastoral system of sheep-rearing.[14]

This in turn led to a de facto form of enclosure system in which landlessness for a growing stratum of the dispossessed in the context of a demographic explosion became a fact of life. And since the ownership of land was the basis of wealth and the symbol of power in the *hidalguía* complex, the opening up of new world lands to Spanish settlers and the opportunity to become landed in the context of a new frontier provided a powerful psycho-economic motivation to emigration and settlement.

The Las Casas of before his conversion shared in this psycho-economic motivation. And since New World land without a steady labour supply was valueless, the Las Casas of the before saw nothing wrong in intra-Caribbean slave-raiding and trading nor in the *encomienda* system. In other words, his mode of perception was determined by this always already societally-coded motivation.

As a result, Las Casas found himself on the side of the settlers in December

1511, when the Dominicans in a famous sermon openly attacked and denounced both Indian slaving and the *encomienda* systems.

The attack was delivered in a Christian sermon by Fray Antonio Montesinos, a member of the Dominican order, but the position put forward was that of the Dominicans as a whole. Members of the order had only that year arrived in the island of Hispaniola and they were horrified at the disastrous effects on the Arawaks of the regimes of forced labour, slavery and *encomienda*.

His voice, Montesinos said, was the voice of one crying in the wilderness. By what right, he asked, or justice do you keep these Indians in such horrible servitude? ... Are these not men? Have they not rational souls? Are you not bound to love them as you love yourselves? All Spanish-Christians who were holders of *encomienda* Indian labour were in mortal sin, he warned, had condemned their immortal souls to hell. The settlers, led by Diego Columbus, were furious. For a while the lives of the Dominicans were in danger.

The Dominicans who had based their arguments on a consensually arrived at theological-juridical position, based both on their concepts of what were the "just titles" under which people could be enslaved, and on the conditions under which the Spanish sovereigns had a just title to the Indies, refused to retract. The Santo Domingo settlers sent (in 1512) a Franciscan, Alonso del Espinal, to argue against the Dominicans' position.

The Dominicans for their part sent Fray Alonso de Montesinos to defend their position. The crucial debates that were to determine the future mode of relations between the Spanish settlers and the New World peoples had begun.

Las Casas was, at that time, unhearing of the voice in the wilderness; unheeding too, when, not long after, he was refused absolution on the grounds that he was both a priest and an *encomendero*. At the time he saw nothing wrong in the *encomienda* since the setting up of an estate in the frontier conditions needed a steady and continuous supply of labour. And his position was at that time not only that of the majority but the State position. For the institutions of *encomienda* and of Indian-slaving provided the basis not only for settler-aspirations, but at the macro-level, for the commercial network called by the historians Pierre and Huguette Chaunu "Seville's Atlantic", a network which in turn provided the economic basis for the expansion of Spain as a world empire.

The new Spanish state, based on the juridical political system of absolute monarchy, was headed by the Catholic sovereigns Isabel of Castile and Ferdinand of Aragon. The earlier marriage of these two sovereigns had laid the basis for the monarchical revolution in Spain against the decentralised semi-feudal system which they inherited. With the help of a new cadre of jurists (*letrados*) learned in Roman law, they began to weld together a powerful modern state out of two separate entities, Castile and Aragon, and after 1492 to initiate the world's first global empire.

Between 1494 and 1560, Spain came to gain control of over half of the population in the western hemisphere. Between 1494 and 1670 when the *Treaty of Madrid* confirmed Spain's loss of Jamaica to the English, the landmass area under European control "went from about 3 million kilometres to about 7". This led to an unprecedented shift in the land-labour ratio. This shift was to provide the empirical conditions for the development of the mercantile system that the Chaunus call Seville's Atlantic; as well as for the historical rationale of the intra-Caribbean slave/trading and *encomienda* system.

The Chaunus have documented the putting in place of the new commercial network with its centre in Seville, Spain, where, as Braudel wrote, "the world's heart beats"; the putting in place of its mercantile, political and juridical structures, all of which, transported from the Mediterranean, were to be re-invented by Spain, leading to new and original structures which were to evolve "during the long passage of a century and a half".[15]

These new and original structures were to be at the same time the founding structures of what Immanuel Wallerstein has recently defined as the first economic world system in history. The structures of this emerging world system were integrated, in its first phase, by the formula of mercantilism, a politico-economic doctrine which although invented by the Spaniards, was soon to become, as Eric Williams wrote, the fundamental law of all Europe.[16] And the central tenet of this doctrine – that a trade balance based on the excess of exports over imports was the goal of national policy – led to the implementation of policies which could ensure the autarchic self-sufficiency of the network.

The town of New Seville after its founding by Juan de Esquivel in 1509 came to constitute one of the chain of settlements of the mercantile network of the Atlantic.[17] Its role was therefore determined by the overall logic of the system.

As the Chaunus point out, until about 1518 when some gold deposits were discovered on the island, Jamaica occupied a bottom-of-the-ladder role in the context of the gold cycle as contrasted with the gold-producing islands of Santo Domingo, Puerto Rico and Cuba. Because of its relative backwardness with respect to the gold cycle, Jamaica got off to a bad start under its founder Esquivel. Arawak Indians were at first exported as slave labour to the other islands to work in gold-mining and "washing" there; this export of Indian labour then led to the emigration of some of the original Spanish settlers.

It was soon to flower, however, once the Crown ordered a shift in its role and the governor and other officials were instructed to develop the island as a food supply and provision base. Esquivel, in pursuance of this instruction, had established two royal estates at Pimienta and Melilla on the basis both of the *encomienda* labour of the Arawaks and of their already cultivated lands (*conucos*). And what the Chaunus call New Seville's "brilliant beginning" was to be largely due to the rapid development of livestock rearing and food growing in its hinterland. Already in 1514, it had become the food provision supplier of the Caribbean.

Pedro de la Rentería's visit to Jamaica and to New Seville was caused by his and his partner's need for livestock and food supplies. For in 1512 Las Casas had gone with the expedition sent from Hispaniola under Diego Velázquez de Cuéllar to conquer and settle Cuba. However, as a friend of the governor Velázquez, Las Casas after taking part in the settlement of the town of Espíritu Santo, was assigned, together with his friend de La Rentería, a "good big" *encomienda* in "the nearby Ariamo River the richest in gold yet".[18]

In 1514 Las Casas's partner went off to Jamaica – his goal was to arrange to purchase and bring back a shipload of livestock and other foodstuffs both to feed their *encomienda* Indians, who were now engaged in washing the sands for gold, and to begin livestock rearing on their Cuban estate.

Whilst preparing a sermon to preach to the Spaniards of Espíritu Santo, Cuba, during the absence of his partner in New Seville, Jamaica, Las Casas was struck by the verse from Ecclesiastes (34:18) that read "stained is the offering of him that sacrificeth from a thing wrongfully gotten..." The verse led to a train of reflection in which he remembered the hard certainty with which he had rejected the Dominicans' position, and the logical sequence of his own behaviour which had been generated by the complex of *a priori* settler-assumptions.

At this moment, as Las Casas would later relate, he saw that no king nor indeed any earthly power whatsoever, could "justify our tyrannical entrance into the New World, nor these deadly allotments as is clear in Española, in San Juan and Jamaica, and in the Bahamas".[19] The actions of the Spanish settlers, and therefore of his before-conversion-settler-self, had brought a great evil on the Indians precisely because these actions were in explicit contradiction to the teachings of the Catholic Christian faith.

All that we did and do, he concluded sombrely, "go against the purpose of Jesus Christ and against the charity commanded in the Scriptures". Above all, the "deadly system of allotments", the *encomienda* system, was, in the context of Catholic Christian doctrines, "unjust and tyrannical".[20]

Following on his conversion, Las Casas went to see the governor, his friend, Velázquez, and stunned the latter by his decision to renounce the generous *encomienda* which had been allotted to him. In August 1514, he went public with his decision. Taking up the cry of Montesinos, Las Casas preached a sermon in which he told of his own conversion and set forth to the settlers of Espíritu Santo what he now saw as the mortal sin in which those Spaniards who held *encomiendas* were living. He announced his own giving up of the *encomienda* allotted to him, and urged on his fellow settlers the restitution they would have to make if they were not to lose their immortal souls.

Las Casas, in the meanwhile, had written his partner asking him to speed up his return. The latter concluded his arrangements in New Seville – a later document reveals that a shipload of provisions taken from the King's estates at Melilla and Pimienta had been handed over to one Salvador de la Rentería, de la Rentería's brother – and sailed from New Seville.

In his account of his conversion and its sequence, Las Casas records that as the caravel arrived off Cuba, he went out in a canoe to meet his partner at shipside. As they went back to the shore and then on to their estate on the Ariamo River, they recounted their experiences to each other. They both saw the parallelism of their conversions, their common turning away from the normative settler-mode of perception, almost at the same time, as a sign that the mission on which they were to embark had been divinely appointed.

Las Casas told his partner of the mission that he now saw before him, of the need that he would have to wage a struggle on two fronts. On the one front, his aim would be to save the Arawaks from the physical extinction which he saw taking place, because of the *encomienda* system which harnessed them to a regime of intensive labour undreamt of and unimaginable in the context of their former mode of life.

On the other front, he told de la Rentería his mission was to save the Spanish settlers from the *eternal damnation of their souls*. For Las Casas had an existential knowledge of how his former settler colleagues thought and felt, of how, spurred on by the wide open frontier of possibility which promised rapid enrichment and social ascension, the Spanish settlers, like his before-conversion-self, had become hardened and callous, trapped by the demands of a settler-psyche (*insensibles, hechos como hombres ciegos e inhumanos*, i.e. become insensible, transformed into blind and inhumane men). And Las Casas knew that the conversion experience for him had been an awakening from this spiritual and perceptual "blindness".

De la Rentería's conversion had followed similar lines. The latter, Las Casas tells us, had "always been a servant of God and very compassionate with respect to the calamitous state of the Indians". Spending the "Lenten season in a Franciscan monastery which at that time existed in the island" (of Jamaica), de la Rentería too experienced a process of reflection in which the thought of the "oppression of these people and of the miserable life they endured" brought to his mind the idea "that he ought to ask the king to grant him a licence and authority to establish a number of schools, in which all Indian children could be assembled and instructed (*doctrinarios*) so that the children at least could be freed from perdition and extermination (*mortandad*) and that *those whom God had elected to be saved could be saved*."[21]

With this aim in view, he was determined, after his return to Cuba, to go to Castille and to ask the King to give him leave to set up such a school.

De la Rentería's conversion centred about the theological concept of predestination, a concept central to the great disputes of the age. For the conflict between the Augustinian/Pelagian attitudes to human salvation, with St. Augustine insisting on God's grace as the true means to salvation, and on the predestining by God of some to be saved, others to be damned, and Pelagius to the contrary positing a strong role for human free will in the attaining of salvation, could almost be called *the* structuring controversy of Catholic Christianity. But both currents of this controversy had been maintained in a kind of dynamic equilibrium before first Luther, then Calvin – and the new historical forces in whose name and from whose perspectives they spoke, split the church on the basis of a now absolute either/or between Predestination/Faith/Grace on the one hand, and Free Will/Good Works on the other.

Both de la Rentería and Las Casas tended towards the predestination wing of the orthodox Catholic Christian continuum. And the spiritual universal egalitarianism generated by this attitude to predestination was to provide the key point of difference between Las Casas and Sepúlveda in the Valladolid dispute of 1550. However, even before the dispute with Sepúlveda, against a Dominican antagonist Fray Domingo de Betanzos who declared to the Council of the Indies that the Indians were "bestial", that God had prepared a specific reprobation for them, condemning them to extermination for their sins, Las Casas had insisted on a divine election and reprobation, specific to all men, universally applicable to all peoples.

All men, he warned his fellow Spaniards, were God's people and "it may be that once God has exterminated these people [the Indians] through our cruel hands, He will spill his anger over us all, ... inspiring other nations to do unto us what we have done unto them, destroying us as we destroyed them and it may be that more of those whom we hold in contempt will sit at the right hand of God than there will be of us, and this consideration ought to keep us in fear day and night".[20]

With this new way of seeing, the partners now agreed together that Las Casas should go to Castile to petition the King in both their names so that they attain the goals, now become the driving force in their lives, after the "joy and wonder" (*alegría y admiratión* – Las Casas) of their dual conversion experiences, one in Espíritu Santo, Cuba, the other in New Seville, Jamaica.

PART TWO

I put forward and proved many propositions that no one before me had touched upon nor written about, and one of them was that it was not against law and natural reason to offer men as a sacrifice to God, assuming their false god to be the true one.

Las Casas, commenting upon the Valladolid Dispute[22]

In another treatise Las Casas declared that all men are free 'if the contrary is not proved' and that freedom, which is natural, can be lost only *per accidens* [sic], that is, through special circumstances and not by nature, as Sepúlveda maintained.

Juan Freide[23]

With de la Rentería now in Cuba, the two friends translated their transformed mode of perception into practical action. They agreed that Las Casas should travel to Castile to petition the King in both their names, the one for the abolition of the *encomienda* and the Indian slave trade, the other for permission to set up a school in Cuba for the children of the Indians. In order to find sufficient money to pay the expenses of Las Casas's passage, as well as to "enable him [Las Casas] to remain at Court all the time necessary to find a remedy for the plight of these peoples"[24], the two men also agreed that they would pool the money that they had available and add to this whatever sums they could get from the sale of the shipload of livestock and provisions that de la Rentería had brought from New Seville.

Amongst these provisions, Las Casas tells us, were many pigs and much cassava bread and maize and other things, all of which were worth a great deal. For it was a seller's market in Cuba where the settlers' gold fever had drawn the majority of the Indians away from the food production which was their forte – and which had become central to the daily life of the goldless Jamaica – to the search for and washing and extraction of gold.

Las Casas was, therefore, able to finance the first two years of his lifelong mission in a great part with the proceeds from the sale of the livestock and provisions from New Seville. And, as a later letter from Pedro de Mazuela who had arrived in New Seville towards the end of 1514, newly appointed as treasurer and royal business manager suggests with a fine historical irony, the shipload of livestock and provisions, taken on credit from the royal estates at Pimienta and Melilla by one Salvador de la Rentería, Pedro's brother, who had later died in Santo Domingo, had not been repaid.

Yet from the perspective of contemporary Jamaica, and of our "individual national" history, the episode of the shipload of provisions from Seville, linked to the dual conversion experiences of the two friends, was to be involved in a greater and more far-reaching historical paradox. As the historian Peter Jones points out, the history of all post-Columbian New World societies can no longer be grasped as a "mere extension of European culture" but rather as part of a complex process in which whilst "European armies, European technologies and ideas and European diseases disrupted and sometimes destroyed traditional cultures [and] ... almost annihilated native populations" as they attempted to impose "a European way of life", after the conquest was over and settlement began, something else occurred:

> Once settlement was stabilised, it was not always clear who had conquered whom, and culture assimilated to each other in areas where the numerical advantage was not too heavily in favour of the invaders. Out of this cauldron of change, a variety of independent nations eventually emerged... as distinct from each other as Haiti is from Uruguay, the United States from Bolivia, or Canada from Brazil... [Their] individual national histories... have been moulded by particular geographic, climatic, and locational differences, by whatever existing native cultures were already there, and by the particular type, source and timing of the European invasion.[25]

Arriving in Spain in 1515, Las Casas had managed to secure an audience with the King in December. He had persuasively put the entire matter of the abuses inflicted on the Indians, and of their rapidly increasing death rate and possible extinction, to King Ferdinand in the context of a matter which needed to be dealt with if the royal conscience was to be absolved. After hearing the case put forward by Las Casas, the King arranged to see him again so that the issue could be dealt with in depth. However, the King, already ill at the time of the December meeting, died on 25 January 1516 before the second meeting could take place. He was succeeded by his grandson, Charles, the son of Isabella and Ferdinand's daughter Juana and her husband Prince Philip of Burgundy. Charles remained for a while still in the Low Countries and during his absence Spain was ruled by two co-regents, one, the cardinal of Spain, Ximénez de Cisneros, the other, sent by Charles from the Low Countries, a Flemish councillor of his, Adrian, the dean of the University of Louvain.

Las Casas obtained an interview with the co-Regents. Both men, deeply shocked at what they had heard, asked him to prepare a written proposal putting forward his ideas on what measures could be taken so as to remedy the situation and to stop the rapid rate of extinction of the Arawaks.

Las Casas presented his first memorial to the co-regents in 1516. The plan proposed measures by which to convert the Indians from their status as *encomienda* serfs and slave labour into that of free tribute-paying vassals, eventually the coequal subjects, with the Spanish settlers, of the Crown. The basic problem that had to be solved by the project was the provision of alternative mechanisms by which the following three key functions played by the *encomienda* system could continue to be implemented.

1.   The ensuring of a steady labour supply for the Spanish Christian settlers.

2.   The ensuring that the Indies venture yield rapid and regular revenues for the Spanish monarchy already embarked on a policy of imperial expansion in Europe.

3.   The ensuring of a regular extraction of gold, the regular provision of food supply products, in the context of the trading network of Seville's Atlantic.

To lay the basis for the abolition of the *encomienda* as the chief source of labour, Las Casas proposed in his 1516 plan that White and Black slaves be brought from Castile "to keep herds and build sugar mills, wash gold, and engage in other things which they know about and in which they can be occupied".

Two key points need to be noted here. The first is that slavery as it was then practised in Spain, and in the rest of the Mediterranean world, was credally rather than racially defined, i.e. based on a religious system of categorisation. Slaves in Spain were of all races. And this credal system was at the basis of another crucial concept: that of slaves won in a just war, or bought with "just title" as contrasted with those who were not.

The second point to be noted is therefore linked to the first: Las Casas is not here proposing the substitution of White and Black slaves for Indian slaves *per se*, but instead the substitution of enslaved men and women who can be categorised as "justly enslaved" within the system of classification legitimated by Catholic Christian doctrine, for a group of enslaved men and women who cannot be so classified.

Las Casas proposed that "communities" consisting of a Spanish town and a group of annexed Indian villages be set up. The Indians, freed from the *encomienda* system, should first be allowed to "rest and replenish their energies", then they were to be organised into a common pool with the Spaniards being assigned a certain number of Indians but no particular ones.[26]

In this transitional arrangement, the Indians were to live in large new settlements of a thousand souls each, near the mines and the Spanish town. Whilst they would still provide a labour pool for both, strict rules and regulations limited the hours to be worked, with ample leisure and vacation times enabling a work rhythm far closer to that to which the Arawak was culturally accustomed. The settlers were to be shareholders in the overall "company" and to receive a share in the profits. In exchange for this they would surrender to the community company suitable lands, livestock and farming tools.[27]

A single administrator was to oversee "a complete staff of Spanish officials and artisans", all of whom were to be employed in the enskilling and the instruction of the Indians. Among this group of teachers and trainers were to be included "priests, to minister to their religious requirement, and even a bachelor of letters (*bachiller de gramatica*) to teach reading and writing and Spanish".[28] Both the priests and the bachelor, one supposes, from a memorial that Las Casas wrote to the Pope in 1565, a year before his death, would, in order to teach the Indians, have to learn the latter's languages (the Pope, Las Casas would write then, should order all Bishops to learn the language of the Indians, and not to display the contempt for these languages that they so often did).

Wagner suggests that Las Casas had most likely seen the post of administrator as one for which he would have been more than suitable. And there is little reason to doubt that the proposed bachelor of letters for the first community school would have been de la Rentería; or at least that his idea of a school for the Indians, born out of his conversion experience, was here being incorporated into the overall plan.

The radical nature of Las Casas's proposal to provide large scale training in new agricultural and artisan skills, as well as the making literate of large sectors of the Indian population, along with their conversion to Christianity, in order to socialise them as free subjects, can be grasped if we observe the parallel "native" model that had been put in place in Granada, Spain. (After the Spanish Christians reconquered the last holdout of the Spanish Moors, Spanish Muslims were forced to convert to Christianity, and were subjected to a deliberate policy of what might be called "nativisation".)

Las Casas's counter-native model failed. The memorial was submitted to a *junta*, but the advice of the *junta* was for reform rather than for the radical organisation that Las Casas had proposed. The regents decided to send out a group of Heironymite friars as commissioners-at-large to oversee the government of the islands, and to reform conditions on the spot. Las Casas was also appointed as protector of the Indians, and sent out as a special witness to give the commissioners suitable aid and counsel. But the fine title could not hide the fact that the first memorial that had arisen directly out of the vividness of his and de La Rentería's transformed perceptions, had been rejected in favour of a "common sense" reform approach.

The common sense reform approach failed to stop the increasing mortality rate of the Indians and the abuse to which they were subjected by the settlers in the frontier situation. Las Casas came into sharp conflict with the commissioners who had begun to listen to the settlers' angry diatribes against him, and had begun to compromise with their powerful vested interests. By 1518 he was back in Spain to press for the abolition of the *encomienda* on the basis of a new scheme, which being of a more pragmatic nature, might find greater support in court circles.

The new scheme proposed that the type of settlers in the New World be changed. Spanish peasants and day labourers, accustomed to a degree of steady disciplined labour, and having no social aspirations which caused them to reject manual labour – as did the bulk of the settlers already there

– should be strongly encouraged to emigrate. The *encomienda* system should be abolished and the new type of settler should set the model for the Indians, teaching them the new skills and techniques of the Spanish system of agriculture.

To compensate the settlers who were already there for the loss of their *encomiendas*, each settler should be allowed a licence to import from Spain two Christianised Black Ladino slaves each, to help them with their urgent needs. Incentives should be offered to the peasant settler both to get him to settle in the Indies and to stimulate him to grow crops for food and export. One incentive was that any peasant who built a sugar mill should be allowed a licence to import 20 Black slaves directly from Africa as the labour complement of the mill.

This plan for the peasant migration was adopted and a royal decree issued. For various reasons, the plan as a plan was to fail. Three of its components, however, i.e. the idea of incentives for the growing of sugar and building of sugar mills, the idea of the importation of Black slaves directly from Africa into the Indies, and the justifying rationale that Black slaves should be imported in order to liberate the Indians, took on a historical dynamic of their own, going far beyond and in quite other directions to what Las Casas had intended.

Thus in 1518, as a direct result of his proposals, the Spanish Crown granted a licence to a Flemish courtier, Gouvenot, which gave him permission to import 4,000 African slaves (trade names *negros* and *negras*) into the Indies. Since this licence was also a form of negotiable currency, Gouvenot at once sold off a part of it to some Genoese merchants in Seville who were linked to the slave-trading houses in the Cape Verde islands off the Guinea coast.

Whilst the Flemish faction at court who strongly backed Las Casas had no vested interest in the New World *encomienda* and intra-Caribbean slave trading system, as did the Spanish councillors, Flemish capital had just begun to be invested in the slave trade out of Guinea, with the Portuguese supplying manpower and ships. In other words, at wider levels, historical processes were already at work in whose context, instead of the strictly regulated individual licences to be awarded to those peasant settlers who built sugar mills, the large scale importation of *negros bozales* directly from Africa had been set in motion.[29] Las Casas's protest at this distortion of his original intention was unavailing:

> I asked for and got permission from his Majesty [for the importation of African slaves into the New World] but I did not do so for them to be sold to the Genoese or to court favourites, but in order that they could be allotted to the new settlers.[30]

Opponents of Las Casas have attacked him for, among other charges, having been responsible for the introduction of African chattel slavery into the Americas, with the implication that he saw the Africans as "lesser beings" than the Indians.

Other historians, not so much defending Las Casas as setting the record straight, have pointed to the historical conjuncture by which, just as the source of White slaves was drying up from the Black Sea, with the Turkish capture of Constantinople, the source of Black slaves from the Guinea coast was opening up in the context of a general European expansion in which Black slavery and the agro-industry of the sugar cane were to be irrevocably connected from early in the fifteenth century.

The Portuguese arrived off the Guinea coast in 1441 and in 1470 had discovered the uninhabited island of São Tomé off the African coast. The island, rapidly settled by Portuguese traders and exiled Jews, soon developed a sugar plantation system based on African slave labour, much of it drawn from the Congo. São Tomé was an instant success, due not only to its soil and climate but also to the rapidly increasing European demand for sugar and the wholesale intensive use of slave labour. As Rolando Mellafe points out, in São Tomé sugar production increased 30-fold in 20 years (1530-1550) from 62.5 to 1,875 short tons a year.

The sugar cane plant had been taken to the Caribbean islands on the second voyage of settlement (1494). The first sugar mill was built in Juana (Cuba) in 1506. In 1510, the rising price of sugar on the emerging world market led to two others being built. By 1516, Francisco de Garay had built a sugar mill in New Seville, Jamaica, and would soon start another.[31] By 1520 some six mills had been built in Hispaniola and by 1521 sugar had begun to be exported in small quantities.

Indian slaves had at first been used for sugar production. For instance, in New Seville, Francisco de Garay, in partnership with King Ferdinand, had from 1515 exported food provisions to the settlers on the mainland in exchange for the Indian slaves that these settlers raided and captured. When these Indian slaves were sent to New Seville, Garay used some for his mill, but reshipped the majority for sale in Santo Domingo.

From 1518, with the arrival of the first batch of African slaves resulting from the Gouvenot *asiento*, the settlers began to turn more and more to sugar and to clamour for permission to import more and more *negros bozales*. And since some of the slaves from the Gouvenot *asiento* fell to the lot of Jamaica, the two mills of Garay in New Seville would most probably have used some African slave labour after 1518.

As the dynamic of sugar production began to displace the gold-washing complex in the islands, the compulsory work system based on African slavery began to gradually displace the slave trade in Indians, obeying increasingly a purely mercantile and commercial logic that from the fifteenth century (with the breakdown of the Catholic Church's prohibition against usury – that is against what an English contemporary of Las Casas called "making the loan of money a merchandise") had begun to displace the Catholic Christian ethic as the organising principle of secular life.

By another stroke of historical irony, New Seville as a capital town, indeed even as a town, had come to an end, partly due to the dynamic of the new commercial logic which linked the destiny of the Caribbean islands to sugar and African New World slavery, and partly due to those aspects of Las Casas's proposals which could be placed at the service of the new mercantile dynamic,

For in 1534, the treasurer, Pedro de Mazuela, obtained royal permission to shift the capital town from the north to the south coast. And the main reason for this granting of royal permission was Mazuela's plan to build the new town about the site of a sugar mill which he had already built there, and his plans to develop the new town around the sugar industry. To do this he also asked for and got permission for the incentive proposed by Las Casas, i.e. a licence to import twenty-five *negros bozales* as the labour complement for a sugar mill, which he had begun to build on the south coast near to his estate at Maymona. Mazuela had also been granted permission to arrange for the emigration of thirty Portuguese peasants from the Azores who were knowledgable in the making of sugar. But they were not to be the yeomen farmers of Las Casas's proposal. Rather they were part of an agro-business complex owned and organised by Mazuela, part then of a settler economy rather than of the peasant model of development (Spanish and Indian) dreamt of by Las Casas.

The town was shifted in 1534. New Seville would disappear from history, and with it the memory of the Franciscan monastery and of de la Rentería's experience there, of his plans for a school to instruct the Indians in Christian doctrine, making them literate in order to do so. The Arawak Indians, too, began to disappear from memory. For whilst sugar and the slave trade out of Africa would gradually displace the slave trade in Indians (by 1542 the Indians had been declared free men (*de jure*), it did not secure the abolition of the *encomienda* (the latter was to be simply, in time, shifted to the *hacienda* system) nor stop the extinction – the rationale of all Las Casas's proposals – of the Arawaks as a cultural-biological entity.

Las Casas had retired to the Dominican monastery at Puerto Plata in Santo Domingo after the defeat of his third scheme, i.e. his project for the peaceful conversion of the mainland Indians on the Paria coast. The intensive slave raiding and slave trading carried out on the coast by the settlers had so enraged the Indians that they had risen up and wiped out the settlement, killing all the friars during the brief absence of Las Casas. He had remained silent in the monastery until 1531 when the accelerated rate of Arawak mortality led to another memorial that year in which he urgently asked that the Arawaks be withdrawn from all forms of labour and that they be allowed to "rest and replenish themselves".[32] Except this were done, the islands would be depopulated of their presence. To replace their labour he again proposed that some 500 or 600 slaves imported from Africa should be allotted to the settlers in the different islands.

But the importation of Black slaves had already begun to respond to the economic dynamic of the expansion both of the slave trade itself and of the sugar industry rather than to what Las Casas saw as the categorical imperative of the Spanish presence in the Indies, i.e. that of the peaceful conversion mission on the model of the original Apostles. For Las Casas the importation of African slaves was intended to facilitate that Christian mission – doing all that I ought to as a Christian – as he had pledged to the head of the Dominicans before he left for Spain. However, the dynamic of a secular commercial-economic rationale, which had begun to use spiritual ends only as a means to the securing of temporal interests, was becoming increasingly determinant. And Las Casas had begun to sense this when he charged in his *History of the Indies* that the settlers and their ideologues had "inverted the spiritual end of this whole affair by making it the means; and the means – that is to say, temporal and profane things... have come to constitute the end of this Christian exercise".[32]

This inversion of the spiritual for purely temporal ends was linked to the fact that increasingly Charles V came to depend on the revenues from the Indies and the slave trade – the royal treasury received so many ducats a head for each *pieza* imported as well as the purchase prices of the *asiento* – to repay the exorbitant rates of interest of money-lending groups like the Fuggers with which he had financed both his election as Holy Roman Emperor (1519) and his policy of imperial expansion in Europe. This was to underlie the first documented appearance of the major African (in its cultural/ biological definition) component in the contemporary Jamaican ethos.

By 1520 the audiencia of Santo Domingo had seized on the rationale provided both by the Heironymite commission and by Las Casas that African slaves should be imported to replace the Indians and had asked for a licence to introduce more *negros bozales* into the island. They argued that "they would not be able to give full freedom to the Indians, nor to establish them in towns (as free tribute-paying vassals)" without African slaves as a substitute source of labour.[33] By 1536 the documented presence in Jamaica of some 38 Africans listed as *piezas* (23 men and 15 women, some with infant children) attest to the rapidity with which the Christian theological rationale of the substitution of slaves with a "just title" for those unjustly enslaved, had taken on a purely secular dynamic.

Of the 38 men and women listed by their Catholic Christian names as having been tallied at Pedro de Mazuela's south coast estate at Maymona, some eleven were auctioned off at the first documented auction which took place in the new south coast town that was transitionally called Seville on the River Caguaya. The prices were high. One African, the settlers wrote the Crown, was worth the labour of four Indians. The genetically tough and culturally flexible and adaptable rice farmers from the relatively harsher low lying swamplands, i.e. the cultural-agricultural bulom complex of the Upper Guinea coast[34] would, as a group, survive the rigorous intensive labour of a commercial mode of mass production, where the Arawaks would not. The Arawak mode of the human developed on the basis of the domestication of cassava (manioc) whose higher yield of starch per acre, higher than maize and potatoes, even wheat and barley, as well as its easy propagation, gave the opportunity for the creation of a leisure civilisation whose relative grace, gentleness and conviviality struck the more perceptive of their conquerors. It would disappear under the pressures of their abrupt acculturation to the cultural system of the highly aggressive mode of the human which had evolved in the geo-historical trajectory of the Mediterranean clash and conflict of multiple civilisations, empires, and of fiercely exclusive monotheistic creeds.[35]

It was not until ten years after the auction in Seville on the River Caguaya, that is, about 1546 at a conference on slavery held in Mexico, that Las Casas began to question his own position as he began to receive verified information that the assumptions on which he had based the justifying rationale for his proposal, i.e. that the African slaves had been justly captured in war – those who had become Muslims – and justly bought and traded, was a false assumption.

What one might call a second conversion experience of Las Casas begins after 1546 with this realisation. For once he knows of the "unjust methods by which the majority of the Africans too have been enslaved", his entire rationale for the substitution of one people by another falls to the ground. Las Casas now "sees" his former position as a result of his own blindness, and he implores God's forgiveness, since he considers that he himself has been guilty of complicity in "all the sins committed by the Portuguese on the Africans, not to mention our own sin of buying the slaves". For "the reduction of the Africans to slavery", he would write at this moment of awareness, "was as unjust and as tyrannical as the reduction to slavery of the Indians".[36] He had now to confront the possibility that in the face of the consequences of his proposal, not even the original purity of his motive nor his ignorance of the "unjust methods used" would sufficiently absolve him on that day of judgement when he found himself before the divine judge. Without such absolution, he would find himself excluded from the body of the spiritual elect, and would have failed to "have done all that he ought to as a Christian".

Yet the paradox here was that the "error" in which Las Casas had been involved went beyond his ignorance of the unjust methods used by the Portuguese to a more far-reaching "error" central to the symbolic logic of Catholic Christianity itself, and to the paradoxical nature of the "just/

unjust title" distinction. For as J.W. Maxwell has pointed out, the institution of slavery was approved doctrinally by the Catholic Church for some 1400 years until 1965, when it was officially corrected by the Second Vatican Council.[37]

And in the sixteenth century, with the shift from a traditional Mediterranean system of slavery – in whose geo-historical environment the "just/unjust title" distinction had been meaningful to the new purely secular mode of the mass-commercial slavery of the transatlantic trade, the paradox had become a truly tragic one. For the "just/unjust" distinction in the context of a now utterly changed geo-historical environment would gradually come to serve as the enabling rationalisation of the transatlantic slave trade; and the Catholic Church thus become the non-conscious yet tacitly very real accomplice, for some three and a half centuries, of the New World system of plantation slavery. And the paradox of the "just/unjust title" distinction and its consequences in history were only to be explained and absolved by the daring conceptual leap – "I put forward propositions no one had touched upon"[38] – made by Las Casas with respect to errors which had their origins in natural reason, in his historic dispute with Juan Ginés de Sepúlveda, at Valladolid.

Juan Ginés de Sepúlveda, a humanist scholar and a translator of Aristotle, as well as official royal historian, wrote a treatise in the form of a Latin dialogue in 1545, putting forward a closely reasoned defence of what he saw as the "just causes" which the Spaniards had for making war on the American Indians, and for the Spanish Crown to establish its sovereignty over the New World peoples by forcible conquest.

Las Casas, on hearing of the treatise, which was then circulating in manuscript form, promptly made moves to have its publication blocked on his return from the Indies. A struggle then began between the two men which came to a climax in a special *junta*, called officially by the Crown, to hear their opposing arguments with respect to the legality or illegality of all Spanish conquests in the New World.

The formal debate was held in Valladolid between 1550 and 1551. It dealt with the debating topic in the context of a more far-reaching question: what kind of relation – hierarchical or reciprocal – was to be established between the two modes of the human, one agro-artefactual, the other Neolithic, that now confronted each other on the Caribbean islands and mainland territories.

Logically linked to this question was another. Now that Columbus's discovery that the western antipodes hitherto classified as non-inhabitable in the medieval Euro-Christian episteme, were in fact *inhabited*, and by a people that quite clearly had never been reached by the original Christian gospel, what new system of classification was to be adopted for these people whose existence now placed in question the very universality of the Euro-

Christian figural scheme. Following upon Spain's incorporation of these new peoples and of their lands into a new Euro-American entity, was the system of classification to be that of an Empire [Sepúlveda]? Or was it to shift from that of a particularistic Euro-Christianity to that of a universal-Christian civilisation [Las Casas]?

At Valladolid, Sepulveda used a long-established doctrinal teaching of the Church, which laid down that those who were "incapable" should be ruled for their own good, to give a general ideological validity to a new thesis which went far beyond the original intention of the original thesis and to legitimate the Euro-Mediterranean mode of the human over, eventually, all other modes of the human. This new (in scale and intention) essentially secular system of classification, based on a represented essential difference between modes of the human, displaced the concept of the papal donation and the traditional just/unjust distinction with what may be called a *natural law charter*.

Not long after, Sepúlveda was to use this same natural law representation to legitimate the Portuguese Christians' capture and enslavement of Black Africans. The latter, he would write, were "disobedient by nature" and had as a consequence to be subjected to paternal rulership.

At Valladolid therefore, Sepúlveda made use of the very real geo-historically evolved differences between the neolithic mode of the human, as embodied in the American Indians, and the agro-artefactual/mode of the human, as embodied in the Spaniards, to represent an inherent and a natural system of difference between the two peoples.

Since, as Stephen J. Gould argues, "historical changes in classification are the fossilised indicators of conceptual revolutions",[39] the debate at Valladolid can be seen as the official occasion of the conceptual revolution that formally ushered in the modern world. It was a debate which Sepúlveda as the Spanish nationalist won (as O'Gorman argues, according to Phelan) precisely because his mode of reasoning corresponded to the great changes that were taking place in Europe, ushered in by the commercial revolution both before and after 1492. These changes were to lead to the organisation of human life on secular rather than on religious terms. Sepúlveda, in spite of his still hybrid use of religious terminology and concepts, can be said to have provided the first secular, operational self-definition of the human subject, one whose universally applicable verbal symbol was that of natural law rather than that of the Christian God, even where still couched in terms of the latter. In doing this he spoke to the reality of his times and to the rise of the nation-state and its reasons-of-state rather than the Christian Church as the regulatory system of an emerging world system at the level of everyday existence.

Las Casas, on the other hand, lost that debate because he was at once behind his time and ahead of his time. Yet the conceptual leap that he made from the very contradiction of his position, is a leap now resonantly in tune with our own, also transitional, times. For in providing a conceptual challenge to the new system of classification being put in place by Sepúlveda, the system that still provides the epistemic laws for our contemporary human system in its global dimension, Las Casas opened the way towards the evolution of a genuine science of human systems, in very much the same way as a science of natural systems followed in the wake of Columbus' challenge to the Mediterranean-centric classification of the earth's geography, and of Copernicus to the geocentric system of classification of the universe.

Columbus, with his empirical voyage, made possible a science of geography based on a purely encyclopaedic knowledge of the earth. Las Casas at Valladolid made the same leap (not to be followed up until our own century) with respect to the possibility of a science of human systems based on the encyclopaedic knowledge of their laws of functioning.

He did this in the context of what O'Gorman calls the "providential design".[40] In this he refused to accept Columbus's discovery – that the new world and all the earth was habitable and that therefore there were peoples in the world still unreached by the gospel – as a contradiction to the universality of the Christian figural schema. He saw it, rather, as a providential design of God, who had appointed Spain and her clergy now to fulfil that as yet unfulfilled universality by evangelising the new peoples, to make the Christian model of identity the unifying model for all the peoples of the earth, from whom in time, God would select the body of his spiritual elect.

Over against Sepúlveda's natural law thesis with its new secular concept of the Spaniards as constituting a natural body of the elect, Las Casas, both at Valladolid and in his *Apologética Historia* defined the human as being the same (*per esse*) everywhere, even *and* because of the fact that they were geo-historically different (*per accidens*).

Las Casas, as Phelan notes, was the first person to write comparative world history. Using the Christian schema of a single origin for humans, then tracing their separation and later isolation from each other, he argued that in this isolation, all groups of men – and there were never anywhere any race of monstrously deformed men – had lived according to what they held to be a system of virtues and vices. The practice of human sacrifice was only carried out because it seemed to some a virtue, because this was the offering to God that seemed to them an offering of the very best that they possessed – in other words because, to them, human sacrifice appeared positively as a rational act. As such, therefore, it was an error of natural reason and not its lack, since, as he later developed more fully in the Ciceronian definition of his book the *Apologética Historia*, all the peoples of the world are men: and all men are rational. It was their rationality which defined them.

Las Casas at Valladolid, in putting forward propositions that no one had put forward before, by introducing the novel conception that there was no inherent difference of rational substance between the Spaniards and the Indians, since the practices such as human sacrifice seen as rational by the Indians were an "error which had its origin in natural reason", made possible a science of human systems, as Columbus made possible a science of geography (by positing and proving that there was no difference of zonal substance, that the earth was the same everywhere, habitable in all five zones and in the western antipodes as well as in Jerusalem); and as Copernicus, Galileo, then Newton made possible a science of natural systems. For if Copernicus, as Hans Jonas points out,[41] made thinkable the quite novel conception that since the earth was a star and the planets "earths", and there was no difference between celestial and terrestrial substance as had been laid down in the geocentric Greek-Christian Ptolemaic view of the universe, then it meant that nature was the same everywhere and homogenous in substance.

This novel conception and its implication had then made possible Newton's new way of seeing or *theoria*[42] in which both earth and planets could be seen in the context of a universally applicable law of gravitation. In this new way of seeing, Newton was now able to conceive of the planets no longer in the Greek-Christian terms of their orbital circular (formal/spiritual) perfection, but rather in new terms – in that of "the rates of fall of all matter towards various centres". This new way of seeing then enabled prediction and conscious human control of natural forces that would lead eventually to the splitting of the atom, ushering in a new era of human history. For when, in this new way of seeing, David Bohm points out, "something was seen not to be accounted for in this way, one looked for and then discovered new and as yet unseen planets towards which celestial objects were falling".[43]

Las Casas at Valladolid, given his *a priori* conviction of a universal and potentially realisable system of human co-identification, in other words, the universal-Christian, and thereby refusing to accept "human sacrifice" or even cannibalistic rites as proof of a naturally determined difference in human rational substance, by a great conceptual leap made thinkable the possibility of a universally applicable law of human identification, in whose context the "errors" of specific forms of reason and of behaviours are lawlike and rule-governed.

For if, in doing "all that he ought to as a Christian", Las Casas continued to see as "rational", not the call for the abolition of slavery per se (that would be for another episteme, in another time, 150 years ago) but rather that slaves acquired with a "just title" should be substituted for slaves not so acquired, so, quite clearly, did the Aztec mode of the human see human sacrifice as supremely rational, doing all that he ought to as an Aztec.

And since in order to represent itself, each mode of the human must conceive itself in that specific mode – and this is the moment of human freedom, its discontinuity with the other natural species, its unique function as the medium through which consciousness enters the life of the planet – then the form of reason or episteme must as its primary function ensure the incorporation of the group as this specific group entity, by stabilising and disseminating this shared self-conception.

For we think in the mode of the symbolical self-representation, as we act upon the world in the mode of our hands. And both the insights and the oversights – Las Casas's errors – are always governed by our historically relative systems of self-representation.

The decoding of the "errors" of natural reason – of Las Casas, of the Portuguese, of their African partners, of the Catholic Church, of the Protestant sects and others – which made the "time on the cross" of our "unique individual history" (the dually tragic/creative origins of our history) possible, would seem to make our putting in place a science of human systems – by which we would make ourselves the paradoxical heirs to Las Casas's great argument at Valladolid – the fitting conclusion to a historical process that began with two conversion experiences and a shipload of provisions from New Seville.

It is not man, to paraphrase Paul Ricoeur, but his systems of representations that should be accused. We truly absolve Las Casas then when, putting an end to the prehistory of the Human, we take as the object of our metadisciplinary inquiry (because the present separation between the natural and the social sciences is itself a culture specific representation) the thousand representations out of which the Human has woven itself – and its Others.

Endnotes

1. Fray Bartolomé de Las Casas, *Historia de las Indias, Tomo III* in *Obras completas,* Vol. 5, Miguel Angel Medina, Jesús Angel Barreda, Isacio Pérez Fernández, eds. (Madrid: Alianza Editorial, 1994), 2191.
2. Ibid., 2324.
3. Lewis Hanke, *All Mankind is One...* (Dekalb: Northern Illinois University Press, 1974), 94-95.
4. The first town founded by the Spaniards in Jamaica 1509 was originally and officially called Seville. In 1518 the site of the town was moved and as was customary, the name New Seville seems to have been used to differentiate the new site from the old. We have used the latter name since this seems to have been customary in everyday usage.
5. See second epigraph at the beginning of the essay.
6. While the exact quote was not located, this is the central thematic of Las Casas's *Apologetica Historia*, where he spends substantial attention explaining their belief systems, which he compares to those of societies of Antiquity.

7. Las Casas, *In Defense of the Indians,* trans. by Stafford Poole (Dekalb: Northern Illinois University Press, 1974), 241-242.
8. One uses "African" here only in a geographical sense since the African system of identification was tribal-lineage and it was therefore as metaphysically "just" for the Christian to enslave the Muslim and vice versa.
9. John Francis Maxwell, *Slavery and the Catholic Church: The History of Catholic Teaching Concerning the Moral Legitimacy of the Institution of Slavery* (Chichester and London: Barry Rose Publishers, 1975).
10. Gerhard Hirschfeld, "Preface" to *History and the Idea of Mankind,* W. Warren Wagar, ed. (Albuquerque: University of New Mexico Press/Council for the Study of Mankind, 1971), vii. Emphasis added.
11. Henry Raup Wagner and Helen Rand Parish, *The Life and Writings of Bartolomé de las (sic) Casas,* (Albuquerque: University of New Mexico Press, 1967), 5.
12. J.H. Elliott, *Imperial Spain: 1469-1716* (London: Edward Arnold, 1963).
13. Frank Moya Pons, *Manual de Historia Dominicana* (Santiago: Universidad Católica Madre y Maestra, 1984), 12.
14. Huguette and Pierre Chaunu, *Séville et l'Atlantique, 1504-1560,* Tome 8, vol. 1 (Paris: Armand, 1955-59), 5.
15. Ibid.
16. See Eric Williams, *Capitalism and Slavery* (1944; London: Andre Deutch, 1964), 51-52.
17. Chaunu, *Séville et l'Atlantique.*
18. Wagner with Parish, *The Life and Writings of Bartolomé de las Casas.*
19. Las Casas, *Historia de las Indias,* 2087.
20. Ibid.
21. Las Casas, *Historia de las Indias,* 2398.
22. Las Casas, *Historia de las Indias,* 233.
23. Juan Friede, "Las Casas and Indigenism" in Friede and Keen, *Bartolomé de las Casas in History, Towards an Understanding of the Man and his Work* (Dekalb: Northern Illinois University Press, 1971), 165. As a Latin American historian Juan Freide has recently documented his claim that Las Casas was both the political and theoretical forerunner of all later anti-colonial struggles.
24. Las Casas, *Historia de las Indias,* 2088.
25. The quotation from Peter Jones could not be located.
26. Wagner and Parrish, *Life and Writings,* 22.
27. Ibid., 20.
28. Ibid., 20-21.
29. *Bozales:* the term for the lineage-cultural African slaves imported directly from Africa as distinct from the Christian-cultural Black slaves (*Ladinos*) born in Spain.
30. Wagner and Parrish, *Life and Writings,* 73.
31. The remains of one of these mills has been excavated at the New Seville site.
32. Las Casas, *Historia de las Indias, Tomo I* (Prólogo), in *Obras Completas,* Vol. 3, 343.
33. Exact quotation cannot be located, but use of the Hieronymite Commission's justification for the licence can be found in *Colleción de Documentos Ineditos...*

del *Archivo de Indias, Tome 1* (Madrid: Manuel B. de Quirós. 1864), 298-299.

34. Walter Rodney, *A History of the Upper Guinea Coast 1545-1800* (Oxford: Clarendon Press, 1970).

35. Colin Turnbull, "Rethinking the Ik: A functional Non-Social System" in *Extinction and Survival in Human Populations*, Charles D. Laughton and Ivan A. Brady, eds. (New York: Columbia University Press, 1978) notes the interrelation between the cultural systems or modes of the human and the physical environment in the case of Africa. Where the environment is abundant and the climate moderate, he notes it has never been necessary for a complex industrial technology to develop. Rather the African physical environment had demanded an "economic adequacy" which everywhere 'depends upon a sympathetic, adaptive response from the human population that must under these conditions function with the totality of fauna and flora as part of a natural world... Whereas other cultures for various reasons have had to develop an industrial technology and have sought increasingly to dominate the environment and control it, the African throughout the continent sees himself a part of the natural world, and adapts himself and his culture... to its varied demands. This leads to... as many cultural types as there are environmental types... The same correlation is highly significant also in any consideration of physical types.

36. Las Casas, *Historia,* Tomo III, 2324.

37. Maxwell, *Slavery and the Catholic Church.*

38. Source not located.

39. Stephen Jay Gould, *Hen's Teeth and Horses' Toes* (New York: Norton and Company, 1983), 67.

40. Edmundo O'Gorman, *La Idea del Descubrimiento de America: Historia de esa Interpretación* (Mexico: Centro de Estudios Filosoficos, 1951).

41. Hans Jonas, *The Phenomenon of Life: Towards a Philosophical Biology* (New York: Greenwood, 1979), 72.

42. David Bohm, *Wholeness and the Implicate Order* (London: Routledge and Kegan Paul, 1980), 4.

43. Ibid.

A NOTE ON DOCUMENTS

The references to the early history of New Seville are taken mainly from a series of documents relating to early Spanish Jamaica. They were transcribed by the historian Irene Wright who was commissioned by the Institute of Jamaica to do so and are now in the National Library of Jamaica.

The greatest insights into the daily life of New Seville during the period are given by a hitherto unpublished document, located by the Government's Research Mission to Spain in the summer of 1982. The document found bound in with some others relating to the early history of Cuba is labelled as *Accounts for the island of Santiago from it was settled until the year 1536,* Contaduria section No. 1174, Archives of Seville, Spain.

Bibliography

Balandier, Georges, *Daily Life in the Kingdom of the Kongo from the Sixteenth to the Eighteenth Century,* trans. H. Weaver (New York: Pantheon Books, 1966).

Bohm, David, *Wholeness and the Implicate Order* (London: Routledge and Kegan Paul, 1980).

Braudel, Ferdinand, *The Mediterranean and the Mediterranean World in the age of Philip II,* Vol. 1, (New York, Harper and Row, 1972).

Chaunu, Huguette and Pierre, *Séville et l'Atlantique, 1504-1560* (Paris: Armand, 1955-59).

Elliott, J.H., *Imperial Spain: 1469-1716* (London: Edward Arnold, 1963).

Freide, Juan, *Bartolomé de las Casas: Precurso de le Anti-Colonial is mo Su Lucha y Derrota,* Mexico: Siglo ventiuno. n.d.

— and Keen, Benjamin, (eds.) *Bartolomé de las Casas in History: Towards an Understanding of the Man and his Work* (Dekalb: Northern Illinois University Press, 1971.

Gould, Stephen Jay, *Hen's Teeth and Horses' Toes* (New York: Norton and Company, 1983).

Hirschfeld, Gerhard, "Preface" to W. Warren Wager (ed.), *History and the Idea of Mankind* (Albuquerque, N.M.: University of New Mexico Press, The Council for the Study of Mankind,1971), vii.

Hanke, Lewis, *All Mankind is One: A Study of the Disputation between Bartolome de Las Casas and Juan Ginés de Sepúlveda in 1550 on the Intellectual and Religious Capacity of the American Indians* (Dekalb: Northern Illinois University Press, 1974).

Jonas, Hans, *The Phenomenon of Life: Towards a Philosophical Biology* (New York: Greenwood, 1979).

Landström, Björn, *Columbus: The Story of Don Cristobal Colon* (New York: Macmillan, 1967).

Las Casas, Bartolomé de, *The History of the Indies,* trans. by Andree M. Collard (New York: Harper and Row, 1971).

— *Obras Escogidas de Bartolomé de las Cases. Historia de las Indies I* (Madrid: B.A.E. XCV, 1957).

— *Brevissima Relation de la Destrucción de las Indies* (Barcelona: Edition Fontanmara, 1979).

— *La Larga Marche de las Cases: Selección y Presentatión de Textos* (Lima: Centro de Estudios y Publicaciones, 1974).

Maxwell, J.F., *Slavery and the Catholic Church: The History of Catholic Teaching Concerning the Moral Legitimacy of the Institution of Slavery* (Chichester and London: Barry Rose Publishers, 1975).

Frank Moya Pons, *Manual de Historia Dominicana* (Santiago: Universidad Católica Madre y Maestra, 1984).

Mellafe, Rolando, *Negro Slavery in Latin America,* trans. J. Judge (Berkeley: University of California Press, 1975).

O'Gorman, Edmundo, *La Idea del Descubrimiento de America: Historia de esa Interpretación* (Mexico: Centro de Estudios Filosoficos, 1951).

Rodney, Walter, *A History of the Upper Guinea Coast 1545-1800* (Oxford: Clarendon Press, 1970).

Taviani, Paolo Emilio, *Cristobal Colon: Genesis del gran descubrimiento,* Vols. I and II (Barcelona: Editorial Tiede, 1974).

Wagner, Henry Raup with Parish, Helen, *The Life and Writings of Bartolomé de las Casas* (Albuquerque: The University of New Mexico Press, 1967).

Williams, Eric, *Capitalism and Slavery* (New York: Russell and Russell, 1961).

This article is abstracted from a book *The Rise and Fall of New Seville 1509-1536* being written for the New Seville Restoration Project by the author.

AGAINST A ONE-DIMENSIONAL DEGREE IN LITERATURE:
TOWARDS "RELEVANCE"

GENERAL ARGUMENT:

What, I have been asked to report, should be the place of Golden Age Literature in a degree in Spanish in the University of the West Indies? Has it any place at all? If so, which texts should be kept in, which thrown out? How approached, how ordered? A one-year course or two? Should it be made compulsory? Or left to that heterogenous "freedom of choice" which the new Degree structure offers?

It is my contention that these particular questions cannot be answered except in the context of wider and more central ones. Those relevant to our purpose are:

1. What place does the teaching of literature itself have in a University whose hinterland is an underdeveloped territory with scant resources and an exploding population with a rapidly increasing rise in material expectations?

2. What *relevance* does the teaching of literature have at a *time* when the written culture, of which the literature we teach is apart, is being superseded by the electronic media and the rise, barely as yet potential, yet clearly on the way to being actualised, of a neo-popular oral and visual culture.

3. What *validity* can the teaching of the literatures of the European peoples, politically the ex-colonisers, economically the neo-colonisers, have for West Indian students, politically the ex-colonised, economically the neo-colonised? Is not the teaching of these literatures but the continuance and development of that cultural colonisation which accompanied and was integral to the political domination of the past; the economic domination of the present?

4. More specifically, what *justification* can there be for teaching the literature of the Spanish Peninsula, when given our geopolitical situation, and our former formidable isolation from the Latin American territories, as well *as* the new urgency for mutual understanding and cooperation, our limited resources could better fulfil an immediate *function* through

the study of Latin American literature in Spanish; especially a literature that has begun to achieve a full national expression, valid in its own right, as well as of close relevance to us.

The approach to answering these four question, may well lie, we suggest, in the examination of a key concept – the concept of *relevance*. What *is* relevance? In an even wider context, this concept, this question is at the heart of the crisis of the University system in the Western pattern; a pattern on which we have been modelled. In an even wider context the crisis of the Western University system is a crisis of Western civilisation itself. We are then, a part of this crisis, and given our ambivalent relation to Western civilisation this crisis takes on extensions of meaning; or non-meaning in our context. Like other Universities in the Western, but specifically the English pattern a pervasive *functionalism* tended to marginalise genuine theory; to discourage the overall view and so lead to the *hypertrophy* of *specialisation* which reduced scholarship to a high level and narrow intellectual discipline; whilst it turned its back on the general purpose and being of mankind. And since theory, in its widest sense, is what a great teacher, Adorno, has claimed it to be 'a genuine form of practice', the retreat from theory and creative scholarship on the part of the British University system – and therefore of ours – has been a retreat from reality; a retreat into what C. Wright Mills has labelled as 'organised irresponsibility'.

The student revolt is the reaction to this irresponsibility; to this "rational" irrelevance. A young American lecturer in a recent interview perhaps best summed up the general unease, the feeling that our Universities are, on the whole,

> "hostile to… definitions of what's worth learning that go just beyond acquiring facts, techniques and theories, to include all of what a man or woman *is*. No university is really concerned with the student's feelings, their sense of self-respect or their ethical and political commitments; but these are the kind of things the black students care about. I don't know if a University can teach these things, but they are reluctant even to try".

What is suggested here is that in the Western University system the *immediate* relevance of facts, techniques, and theories, was pursued as *ends* in themselves; and were not related to the *real* relevance of the quest for knowledge; its possibility and ability to throw light on Man and his radical situation in this life. In Faculties of Arts all over the Western world, the Past – its fiction and reality, its literature and history was dissected in sealed compartments of abstract knowledge; no particle of dust from the torment of the present was allowed to distract. In this desert of accomplished irrelevance, a storm sprang up. What the students clamoured for, Unamuno – whose writing forms a part of that Spanish literature which they may have studied – had already posited: "La historia del pasado sólo sirve en

cuanto nos llega a la revelación del presente..." [*En torno al casticismo*, 1902].
From this focus I shall now examine the concept of relevance in each question.

1

Poor countries like ours, can least afford to dispense with creative thought;
with the transposition of creative theory into imaginative praxis. The creation
of a literature is central; it is literature as part of a creative culture which
releases the imagination from old colonial and traditional patterns, breaks
up the cake of custom, and creates new and dynamic patterns of identity.
As C.S. Lewis puts it:

> ... the transition from thinking and doing, in nearly all men, at nearly all
> moments, needs to be assisted by appropriate states of feeling...

A study of any literature is the study of the creation of these "appropriate
states of feeling" at "appropriate times". That is, a study of literature, which
relates it to the people and the society who made it; and who were "made"
by it. That is, literature should not be taught and studied as a fetish object,
in what Roland Barthes calls "a purely magical conception of the work".

It is this 'magical' approach to the teaching of literature which leads to the
unease of West Indian students, An object called literature, which was
presented as an inborn prerogative of the peoples of Europe, divided up into
totems such as 'the novel'; satire and criticism; Golden Age Literature;
dramatists and 'philosophes' in Eighteenth Century France', was thrust on
them, without any relation to their urgent questions about themselves, Soon
an advance was made, French Caribbean Literature, Spanish Caribbean
Literature, West Indian Literature were now *also* "offered". Here at least the
students, could relate their problems to parallel problems of fellow Caribbean
man, as formulated in three Languages; but the Spanish literature of Spain for
example and the Spanish literature of Cuba remained in compartments; an
either/or proposition, And so with English, their *'mother tongue'*; the ambivalence even in that phrase; and therefore the ambivalent relation of the two
literatures was not conceptually thought out; and reflected in the organisation
of the courses.

Then as a logical step forward, Dr. E. Brathwaite pointed out that the only
way to teach History to Caribbean students was to make the Caribbean their
Mediterranean; their central focus; to work out from there to that total history
with which our history relates. Dr. Irish of the Spanish Department has
followed this up with an as yet unpublished selection of texts which form the
basis of an approach to Practical Criticism. By the Caribbean focus that Dr.
Irish uses – his selections begins with Columbus's reaction to the Caribbean
islands and ends with short stories by men like Juan Bosch – all implicated in
the contemporary Caribbean reality – he transforms an exercise into a creative

approach to the study of literature. His quote from Jorge Luis Borges that very
'*culto*' writer of Argentina is instructive:

> "Let us begin our reading with writers close to us; soon we shall be able to
> explore the other world regions of the Divine Comedy, and the sound and
> fury of Macbeth... Let us at the outset steer clear of the old classics... whose
> language holds suggestion which are no longer our own".

Before the student can master the suggestions that are not his, he must
first come to terms with his own; not just to add to his knowledge; but
to transform his instinctive response to the appropriate states of feeling
that he finds in his own literature. It must become a conscious acceptance
of these feelings as being the motive force of his own "transposition" from
feeling to doing; to the recognition that the urgent task that after, as a
teacher of literature, he or she will be involved in, is not the building of
bridges or roads or schools which are part of the development process,
but instead the far more paradoxical and difficult task of *leading out* [educare];
rather than, as now too often, mutilating the central *dynamic* of the impulse
itself. The teaching of literature *can* help to fulfil this *real* need as distinct
from the manifold immediate needs, of a poor and unjust society which
must galvanise itself in order to affect the transformation of its reality.

But literature would have to be taught to answer to this imperative; and not
as of now, too often as an exercise with prepackaged answers for passing exams.
In fact, if literature is to be taught as a *real* need then the functional barbarism
of the exam system itself will have to be discarded. Our present examination
system does not allow students to *waste* time with thought; with the exploration of feeling. Yet what we must ask them to do, if literature is to be *relevant*
is not to dissect literature but to confront it; to explore it not as a mystic exercise
set aside from the secular business of living; but as an expression of man's
struggle to arrange the material bases of his existence, in order to attain to that
full creativity, that free play of the imagination that alone justifies living; to see
literature like all art as that promise of happiness without which we merely
exist; as that unceasing and utopian critique of a mutilated existence; of our
present barbaric reality.

By approaching the study of literature through a Caribbean focus, the
students take possession of their own sights and sounds; appropriate their own
interior landscape of the imagination. Then, having *experienced* the relevance
of literature to their own as yet unformulated fears and dreams; having
achieved some self-knowledge through comparison with their special island,
their place, their life, they are now ready to confront the more difficult and
more complex yet equally essential relevance of *all* the creative periods of art
or literature of whatever country or time. A perfect sonnet and an achieved
African mask are blood-brothers in the space-time of the imagination. They
embody the same "promesse de bonheur".

2

Hans Magnus Enzensberger, discussing the 'Consciousness Industry' (*New Left Review*, 64) has this to say:

> Written literature has, historically speaking, played a dominant role for only a few centuries. Even today the predominance of the book has an episodic air. An incomparably longer time preceded it in which literature was oral. Now it is being succeeded by the age of the electronic media which tend once more to make people speak... The revolutionary role of the printed book has been described often enough, and it would be absurd to deny it. From the point of view as its structure as a medium, written literature, like the bourgeoisie who produced it and whom it served, was progressive... Nevertheless almost everybody speaks better than he writes. Writing is a highly specialised technique... To this there corresponds the high degree of social specialisation that it demands. Professional writers have always tended to think in caste terms. The class character of their work is unquestionable, even in the age of universal compulsory education... Intimidation through the written word has remained a widespread and class-specific phenomenon even in advanced industrial societies."

As I said before, certain general problems common to our age have specific extensions of meaning in our particular context. The 'intimidation' of writing was an integral part of the apparatus of domination by which both the aboriginal Indians of the islands and the New World, as well as the blacks, the later neo-natives of our islands, were colonised and enslaved. As Professor Coulthard points out, the earliest justification of the enslavement of the Indians, put forward by Ginés de Sepúlveda, paid by the colon-settlers to defends their 'right' to the *encomienda* system which Las Casas opposed, was that the Indians were the natural inferiors of the Spaniards and had to serve them, because, as they lacked culture, *a system of writing* and they did not "preserve monuments of their history; they have the vaguest obscure memory of facts recorded in certain pictures, they lack written laws and have barbarous institutions and customs".

In one of the first pieces of "written literature" to come out of the traumatic clash between Indians and Spaniards – the *Comentarios Reales* – by the Inca Garcilaso de la Vega, half-Spaniard, half-Indian, acculturated to the dominant Spanish religion and culture; but still pervaded by the Indian legends, myths, memories and history that he had been *orally* taught by his Indian uncle, he tells us of the impact that *writing* had, of the superstitious awe which its power evoked in the Indians who were confused, thunderstruck, "diciendo quo con mucha razon llamaban dioses a los españoles con el nombre de Viracocha pues alcanzaban tan grander secretes." Lévi-Strauss, four centuries after, found that the leader of the Nambwikara Indians in the Brazilian jungle, at once grasped the use of writing – making wavy lines in simulacrum of – as a source of power over his fellow men. He points out how the scribe in largely illiterate societies tends to be both scribe and usurer at once; thus exercising a 'twofold empire' over other men; then goes on to show that writing was not one of the indispensable inventions of neolithic man, and concludes

> to say that writing is a double-edged weapon is not a mark of 'primitivism';
> the cyberneticians of our own age have rediscovered that truth.

In societies like our own, where the coloniser inhabited, for the most part a written literature; and the colonised an oral literature, the role of writing, and of written literature has played a more than usual dominating and oppressive role. Both the education system and the written literature of the colonising country have been used more often in their enslaving than in their liberating role. Redfield has pointed out that all cultures exist through an interaction between the folk of little tradition of the people; and the learned tradition of the priests or literary caste, the learned tradition takes from the ceaseless inventivity of the little tradition; and stylises, 'purifies', abstracts and universalises its concepts. The little tradition, in turn, takes back through the oral epics created by the learned tradition; or even through written literature returned to them orally, the abstract concepts of the learned tradition, later materialises them, parochialises them in myths, legends, beliefs etc.

When, however, an invading civilisation decapitates the learned tradition of another culture; and replaces it, then a disjuncture occurs between the "little" tradition and the "high" tradition. Where one is written and the other oral, the disjuncture is even greater. The lack of any real creative literature in a colonial society comes from the fact that the literate are educated to despise the oral tradition of the people; and to see the written tradition as the only vehicle of culture. The high tradition suffers from inanition; a lack of roots to feed on; the little tradition is alive and vigorous but suffers from the lack of a learned tradition to interact with. Caribbean writing has therefore sprung out of the first national movement where writers have broken the tabu and returned to the roots – the writing in "romance" in Spain, the beginning of their first national expression was also the popular response to Latin, the established language of the learned caste, Where the oral culture of the colonisers met the oral literature of the colonised however, a transculturation took place. The folk culture of the Caribbean is the result of this transculturation. That is to say, that the oral culture is more democratic, less caste-ridden; and in our present age, the oral tradition through the electronic media begins to break down the division between the-have-writing and the-have-not-writing. The electronic media are therefore instruments of potential liberation. But most of all, they present us with certain problems in the teaching of written literature which, far from making such teaching invalid, can creatively transform our approach.

Enzensberger points out that the "alienating factors" inherent in writing "cannot be eradicated from written literature", and continues:

> They are reinforced by the methods by which society transmits its writing

techniques. While people learn to speak very early, and mostly in psychologically favourable conditions, learning to write forms an important part of authoritarian socialisation by the school ('good writing' as a kind of breaking in).

The teaching of English as a standard written language in societies like ours where an oral Creole form of English is the norm, has led to the perpetration of incredible barbarisms. The deep and widespread concept of "good" English and "bad" English paralleling the idea of "good hair" (straight) and "bad hair" (tight-curled) has led to English language teaching throughout the schools which is authoritarian; and superstitious. Students are said to "lapse back" into "bad" English when they make "mistakes'. The majority of the teachers remain ignorant of the Creole as a logical pattern of speech which they need to learn if they are to teach English to Creole speakers. English is taught as something "magical" quite unconnected with the Creole they speak; rather than as a process in which transculturation between English and African languages has produced a Creole *variant* which differs from the Standard.

The teaching of language has been extended in a more sophisticated form to the teaching of literature. Literature became an object to be attained if one was to have culture, pass exams and get a degree; then in turn teach. Having been put through an obstacle race, the teachers then put their students through the same obstacles. The alienating factors in a written literature, although inferior to the liberating factors it embodies, were reinforced by the old approach to literature, and became pervasive. It was usually the literature which the student read on his own, that performed the true function of liberation; and subverted its alienating role. From time to time, the power of escape that great literature represents, broke through the system; often the truly creative teacher betrayed his caste and taught literature in what Marcuse calls its two-dimensional aspects; that aspect which is subversive of its reality. It is through this betrayal of the system that the Caribbean writer entered into a dialectical relationship with the literature of the coloniser; and adapting from their Universalist aspect, wrote novels out of a Caribbean reality. The creative living Caribbean reality was oral; the popular. Through this transculturation of the written literature of the coloniser and the oral culture of the colonised, the truly indigenous Caribbean writing has emerged. In no other period of literature can it be said, as it can be said of the Golden Age of Spain that it was the perfect realisation of the little and the learned tradition; of *lo popular* and *lo culto*. This is the same phenomenon to be seen in the Afro-Cuban and Afro-Antillean writing; in the later more achieved novels of Carpentier. The revaluation of *lo popular* in all literary culture can bring a new approach to literature inspired by the neo-populism of the literature of the film and the electronic media in general. As Enzensberger points out: "…we must… analyse the products of the traditional 'artistic' media from the standpoint of modern conditions of production."

A new transculturative process has begun in which the spoken language is breaking up the moulds of the literary language; which is itself coming closer to the language that people speak. An examination of the literature of the past, tracing their fusion and separation – e.g. Leavis shows the fusion still powerful in Bunyan, then the separation of the oral culture from the written language in later English prose; also much of the problematic of Caribbean and Latin American writing comes from the tension between the "literary language" and the language of "decir" and the creative synthesis to be made of the two – can open new avenues on literature, avenues which lead out from our own situation in time and place.

> America is the child of Europe and we must assassinate her in order to live. [Héctor Murena]

A statement of this sort by a Latin American writer poses the "problematic" of the relation opposition, imitation/rejection, acculturation/contra-acculturation which is basic to the culture which Redfield terms a "secondary civilisation". In this civilisation, literature and all other cultural forms of expression are not part of what Leavis calls an "organic" whole; the kind that we get in Elizabethan England, in Golden Age Spain. Instead literature becomes *not* the literary transposition of a reality whose cultural dynamic is both officially and unofficially accepted; but a weapon of transformation of that reality. In the complex process of transculturation between coloniser and colonised, it is the colonised, raging against his reality, that *reacts against* the "official" literature of the coloniser; but in his reaction in order to "assassinate" he absorbs certain universal aspects of the literature of the coloniser, to use as a weapon against him; in the process of fighting against, of rejecting, he becomes acculturated by that which he fights against. For if the official literature of the coloniser is an instrument of domination, through the official means of its dissemination, it also partakes in that revolutionary intention which is the particular characteristic of all art. For all art, by the principle of its structure, by the method of its creation, opposes to the *is* of reality, an imperative *ought* which criticises this reality; the two-dimensional universe as Marcuse calls it.

One critic points out that literature constitutes an opposition to the dictatorial law of language; that it represents a contradiction of all established systems and orders; that like all art it represents a confrontation with reality in all its dimensions, by creating a reality *sui generis*; not a reflection of reality but its transformation. The literature of the coloniser is therefore always potentially subversive of the coloniser as coloniser; since it is the actualisation of his human and creative potential. It is only through the written literature and the oral culture of the coloniser – folksongs, folk plays, folk religion – that his human visage comes through. This human visage, his Achilles heel as coloniser, is that which at once helps to destroy his colonising role; through its "critical" influence on a revolutionary national literature of the colonised; and his sole human contribution to that pragmatic cultural racism which he sees as his "civilising" mission. It is only art and literature which betrays his manifest destiny as a "civiliser"; in order to transform his destructive and exploitative mission into a partially humanising one.

But literature remained a weapon in the colonised countries by the way in which it was and is taught. It was and is still taught as a "ritualised invocation" which blocked its liberating potentiality by preventing any development of its implications. This was done by refusing to make any relation between the literature which was being taught and the reality of its relation, paradoxical and ambivalent to the *people* i.e. the students to whom it was taught. Students were seen in the passive role of *consumers*, and not as people participating from their point of view, both as human beings and as the colonised in a *process* called literature; a *process* which like life itself as Max Fischer points out, is a violation of the law of entropy – the tendency to convert matter into a disordered movement of molecules. The creation of life, the creation of art and literature represents an anti-tendency towards the improbable, towards the accumulation of energy which is itself a continuous accumulation of negative entropy. This accumulation leads in life and literature, to a "break in the order of things, an uprising against probability". An uprising against the tendency to chaos implicit in any system of domination, the literature of the coloniser is the uprising against himself as coloniser; it joins forces with the literature of the colonised in this common revolution against rational chaos.

The use of "literature" as proof of the *superiority* of the colonisers; as a sign of God's grace and their election to the Chosen and manifest destiny of a civilising mission, negates the liberating promise of literature. Even after the coloniser is gone, the Creole class who is his heir, and who occupies vis-à-vis the people, the same exploitative position, uses and utilises "literature and culture" in its mutilated form. The concept of "literature" as a part of the superior "civilisation", opposed to the native barbarism of the colonised masses; of "education" as the means of extending the "light" of this superior civilisation to the masses at once invalidates and negates the creative content of literature. The revolutionary role of "literature" is betrayed by the educators. Instead of being "human", literature becomes *civilised*. The epic treatment, which Ercilla gave to the Araucanian Indians-brave warriors as noble, even nobler than the Spaniards, parallels the revolutionary concepts of Rousseau and the vindication of Natural Man inherent in the Romantic Movement. These two influences produce the classic neo-epic in a Romantic version – the Martin Pierre which vindicates autochthonous values, exalts '*lo popular*' in a written form.

It is quite other with the obsession of a Sarmiento, who continuing in the footsteps of a Sepúlveda translated the fight for national fulfilment into a struggle between civilisation and barbarism-civilisation being the things, and literature of Europe; barbarism all that was not Europe, including the Indians whom he hated. Facundo gives form and expression to a *cultural racism*; its civilising mission is ultimately reduced to what Martínez Estrada another Argentinian has called, "la reiterada imitación de Vergilio, y la hypervaluación del cosmético cultural." Literature taught, as it is so often done, as an unrelated unmediated "cultural cosmetic" is irrelevant; and a poor country should find no money or time for it. Even more it is dangerous; it can lead to the mutilation of the imagination. Literature taught as "cultural cosmetics" creates an elite class with an elite sense of manifest destiny; that of civilising their fellow nationals. Implicit in this attitude is a cultural racism, a "racialisation" of thought that leads to an equally blind and racialised reaction. The teaching of literature is only relevant if it shatters the concept of a civilising mission and replaces it with the necessity of humanising oneself. The approach to the teaching of literature can well determine whether or not we turn out that dangerous and reactionary class of elites who see themselves – in González Prada's term – as *lazarillos* of the blind masses; or whether we infect our students with the creative impulse.

The addition of the literature of the Caribbean and Latin America to the syllabus is a step in the right direction. But the step will turn out to be two backwards, if the focus through which this literature is taught is not changed. Too often this literature is taught, and above all examined, as an *addition*, tacked on to the *real* literature which is that of Europe. In reaction to this attitude, still widely pervasive, is the cry that the only valid literature is that of the New World of which we are a part; since it is the only literature that is relevant. Why bother with Shakespeare and the Golden Age? The point to understand about these two attitudes is that they form part of the same general approach and world view. For both, literature is seen as a matter of texts strung together; as *objects* which can fulfil a *function*; for the "ancients" this function is that of obtaining a fetish called "*high standards*"; for the "moderns" the up-to-the-minute *function* is that of fulfilling the realisation of another fetish called *relevance*. Both respond to the functional pragmatism that is inherent in the present structure of the University. One makes a conservative gesture; the other makes a radical gesture. But the radicalism is the radicalism of a new one-dimensional reality. Marcuse describes this kind of gesture for what it is: Like the beatnik culture, like the new Afro movement, externalised in sandals, Dashiki, Afro haircut, the radical cry of relevance when imperfectly conceptualised, does not negate the status quo; is not contradictory to it. Instead:

> They are rather the ceremonial part of a practical behaviourism, its harmless negation, and are quickly digested by the status quo as part of its daily diet.

Indeed the division between "conservatives" and "radicals" is more apparent than real. Because of this, both will shift ground here and there, The "great objects" or texts of the literature of the past will be retained; the texts of the relevant new literature will become more numerous. The battle of the texts obscures the real issue; that if literature is to fulfil its liberating function, it must be taught as a *process*, at once universal and national; a process happening in historical time; a process which cannot be understood in its present manifestation if it is not explored in the past. Marcuse points out that *functionalism* "by the nature of its approach is hostile to history; to history as process".

The conservative functionalists teach both the reality and the fiction of the past – its history and literature – as objects in themselves unrelated to the present. The radical functionalists want to teach the fiction and the reality of the present, outside of its contradictory and ambivalent relation to the past. The literature of the present and near present, the literature immediately relevant to us, if not taught in its contradictory relation to the literature with which it exists in a dialectical process of reaction and response, converts the idea of relevance into mere utilitarianism. The given "functional form" of the approach to learning in the University, "remains as the ultimate frame of reference for theory and practise". Because of this the teaching of literature cannot fulfil its true role that of providing a critical theory of the approach to education itself as the instrument of the prevailing mutilating reality.

The radical functionalists have sprung up as a reaction to the conservative functionalists whose influence is still pervasive. In a paper presented on Practical Criticism and how it should be taught, we saw the rational irrelevance of the conservative functional approach. Extracts for practical criticism were to be selected without any reference to their authors; so that the students could bring no knowledge of the authors; no "emotional" reaction to the passages. They were to be "*in vacuo*" with that "misplaced abstractness" of functionalism, which is gained, by abstracting from its concepts, according to Marcuse, "the very qualities which makes the system an historical one and which give critical transcendent meaning to its function and dysfunction." The analysis of the style of a passage separated from the context of the reality of which this "style" was the reconciliation between the reality and its opposition in literature is a dangerous functionalist and behaviourist exercise.

It was in reaction to this type of irrelevance that the radicals cried-out for the teaching of a literature so relevant in its *content* that the escapism and rigid formality of the conservative approach could be combatted. But without a conceptualisation of relevance as itself a historical process, relevance is converted into a pragmatic utilitarianism; and in the context of our society teeters dangerously on the edge of becoming a synonym for an easy ride which makes it easier to pass exams; without having to be involved with the bother of thought; and imaginative enquiry. In fact, the exam system as a frame of reference compels students to this rationalisation; for the exam system as it now stands is itself part of the prevailing functionalism; in three hours one can organise competent cogent prepackaged answers to four questions; thought gets in the way of passing exams. With or without "relevant" texts, except the approach to literature and its teaching is radically changed, then the one-dimensional expansion of the *bureaucratisation* of learning continues as

> managerial modes of thought and research spreads into other dimensions of the intellectual effort... [Marcuse]

The new approach must be a change of perspective. Literature must be taught as a process. The literature of the New World most immediately relevant, the literature of the present even more so, must be the *radial centre*, the axis from which the process of literature is traced backwards in time; through the constant interaction/opposition/accommodation between the present reality and the past, Golden Age Literature of Spain can have no real relevance except taught in this way; equally the literature of Latin America today and yesterday can only be taught in its immediate rather than its real relevance if it is taught *outside* the process which led to its creation; and which it continues to create. Marcuse summarises:

> Recognition and relation to the past as present counteracts the functionalisation of thought by and in the established reality. It militates against the closing of the universe of discourse and behaviour; it renders possible the development of concepts which destabilise the closed universe by comprehending it as historical universe. Confronted with the given society as object of its reflection, critical thought becomes historical consciousness; as such it is essentially judgment. Far from necessitating an indifferent relativism, it searches in the real history of man for the criteria, of truth and falsehood, progress and regression.

The literature of the colonised can no more be explored and defined *in vacuo*, and vice versa, than can the term "proletariat" be conceived and examined as separate from the concept of the "bourgeoisie". Changes in the historical process of Spanish literature began with the discovery of the New World; and the reaction of the Spanish psyche to this discovery and conquest. Literature transposes the reality of its exaltation in a sonnet like that of Acuña "un Monarca, un Imperio y una espada": to the weariness of defeat; the mood of isolationism which Góngora displays in his *Soledades*, when attacking the discovery of the New World and the disruptive changes which this new and extended reality had brought, he seeks refuge in an idealised Golden Age set in the past; in equilibrium with an idealised Nature, and idealised peasants inhabiting it; the identity threatened by the rush of events finding refuge in a pastoral longing for the roots; providing a powerful critique of reality; of man's increasing alienation from and despoliation of nature. Equally the literature of Latin America was to be related to two central processes that came out of the interaction of several cultures. One was first defined by Sepúlveda as the civilising mission; the other by Las Casas as the humanising mission. Writers like Sarmiento and da Cunha belong to the first; others like González Prada and Martí to the second.

There can be no better illustration of the way in which the teaching has been approached than the rigid separation that has persisted in our University system between Latin Americanists, that is, lecturers who specialised in Latin America; and hispanists, those who specialised in Spain. After a long era when the conservative functionalists were in power, Spain was the centre of the Spanish Universe; and the Literature of Latin America regarded with contempt; Latin Americanists are now in power; and the tendency of the new functionalists is to marginalise the literature of Spain. On the banner of the one was *High Standards*: Look outwards and onwards: on the banner of the others *Relevance*: Look Inwards and Aroundwards! In the clash, a creative approach to the teaching of literature gets lost. Regionalism and relevance is opposed to cosmopolitanism and high standards. Yet as Unamuno argues:

> Conviene mostrar que el regionalismo y el cosmopolitismo son dos aspectos de una misma idea y los sostenes del verdadero patriotismo, que todo cuorpo se sostiene del juego de in *presión externa* con la *tensión interna*.

If for years, and even now the Conservative functionalists taught the lyric poetry of Europe, which emanated from the Provencal troubadours, as an Immaculate Conception, sprung like all European art from that Holy Ghost which had chosen Europe as the seedbed of the cultural destiny of man, the radical functionalists are ready to sweep away all those *texts* which embody such poetry and the romantic world view that went with it, without stopping to think how much of their all-or-nothing attitude is itself still conditioned by Western "passion", structured by a mode of feeling, which decaying in its own sphere, the sphere of love, still stretches its octopus tentacles out, so that those rejecting all that it stood for are still conditioned by what they reject in their very rejection. Like the terrorists of the bomb who must place a bomb not for the result but for the emotional feeling of the gesture, the terrorists of Literature must reject for the emotion of rejection; as the courtly lover loved in order to suffer; suffered in order to love; and dreaded nothing so much as fulfilment.

Yet research by Arabic scholars makes it certain that the influence of Arabic poetry of Andalusia as well of the Mozarabic cultural adaptation of Arabic poetry; plus a structure of feeling prevalent in Moslem Andalucía was a decisive influence, which leading to an adaptation reaction helped the rise of that *sui generis* hitherto Immaculate Conception called European lyric poetry. For Europe in the tenth century vis a vis the Arab word of Andalusia was very much in the position of the Third World today *vis-à-vis* Europe. It is this sense of history and literature as a historical process which led Lloyd Best to confront the intellectual revivalism of the Black Power Conference in Montreal to remind them of the historical parallel and roots of their own reaction:

> Its roots lie deep in our condition and I would guess some of them lie deep in the arrogance, in the blindness about self, "and in the indignation with which Western Europe burst during the 15th century on to the stage and

emerged as the controlling metropolis of the entire world.

Besieged for centuries by Islam, and subjugated by the Frankish Kings, the Europeans broke out crying Christian and merchant power. And before they knew the cause they were enmeshed in the greatest simplification of all: racial power. We are trapped now in this sickening syndrome where race and property provide the most convenient bonds of unity and are even said to express an essential inhumanity in man.

Awareness is all. The conservative functionalist sacralisation of European literature is essentially a worship of "cultural power"; in reaction; the radical functionalist exchange new shibboleths of power for the old. What gets lost is the process of literature, a process which is a sustained critique of the uses of power in reality; a process whose power to contradict reality lies in its powerlessness:

> Like technology, art creates another universe of thought and practice against and within the existing one. But in contrast to the technical universe, the artistic universe is one of illusion, semblance, *Schein*. However, this semblance is a resemblance to a reality which exists as the threat and promise of the established one. In various forms of masks and silence, the artistic universe is organised by the images of a life without fear – in masks and silence because art is without power to bring about this life and even without power to represent it adequately.

The justification for the teaching of literature does not depend only on whether we choose to abandon the *Don Quijote* and replace it with *Hombres de Maíz*; rather in our ability to trace in both the process of antagonistic contradiction to the established reality which both novels represent; and, by our teaching, to fulfil and disseminate their purpose; to strengthen their intention; and so become subversive of the present oppressive reality of our own function. We cannot as a University change the society in which we are enmeshed. But if there is any justification for a literary degree, then it must be that through the study of creative literature men and women go out into their one-dimensional world, equipped not to take their prescribed places within it; but through the compelling necessity to find themselves humanly at ease, to transform it.

LATIN AMERICAN OR HISPANIC OPTION

Students of either option would take year two as is. Also Latin American I as outlined. Hispanic Literature I would also remain compulsory for both as now. We shall outline our suggestions re this course below. It is in year three that the choice of option becomes effective. The courses as offered in Latin American literature, whilst perhaps subject to a greater degree of collaboration in order to unify themes and to prevent overlapping, already meet most of the requirements of a Latin American option. What we suggest is that a parallel Hispanic option needs to be worked out. Our suggestions are tentative – as far as texts are concerned. The emphasis is a parallelism of approach in order to attain coherence.

For what we would temporarily call a Hispanic Option – that is one that is more of a balance between Spain and Latin America – there is one change that would be necessary. If the texts of Latin American Literature II could be adjusted so that the students who choose the Hispanic Option would do Latin American Literature II in their Third Year *compulsorily*; but would in that course, be introduced to the *most* significant and paradigmatic novels and poetry; so that a few texts would touch on the most important developments. For example *Los Pasos Perdidos* of Carpentier would be taught in Latin American Literature II rather than "Under Race and Culture"; as would *Hombres de Maiz,* and so on. They would be introduced briefly to themes like *Race and Culture, Cultural and Political Ideas*, and the *Contemporary Narrative of L.A.* without having to do the Courses as such. The point of the Courses would be a deepening of the exploration of these aspects for those who choose a Latin American option.

Similarly in *Hispanic Literature One* an attempt will be made to introduce the students to the important themes of Hispanic Literature through paradigmatic texts also bearing in mind parallels and relationships with the literature of Latin America, The idea is that when the Third Year the student goes on to his Latin American Options – that is further courses which will supplement Latin American Two, he will be in a position to explore more of the literature of Spain on his own.

The students who choose the Hispanic Option will, in Year Three, be enabled to deepen and explore their knowledge of the Literature and culture of Spain; always with reference to Latin America; and we hope, vice versa. *Hispanic Literature One* is therefore seen as an introduction to the Literature of Spain, with the emphasis laid on its greatest creative period - the Golden Age.

HISPANIC LITERATURE I
POETRY:

"LO POPULAR Y LO CULTO EN LA POESIA DE ESPANA"

1. Ercilla's *La Araucana*: We begin with this as a central text – there is a recent edition that is quite good. We begin with this literary epic as it represents that interrelation of the two aspects of the Hispanic Course which is our aim. But we shall use this text to explore certain aspects of Spanish poetry. For example, the series of lectures would include:

a) The Sixteenth-Century Theory of Styles – the high style of the *literary* epic; its relation to the epic form in general; to Vergil's *Aeneid*; its relation to the Renaissance theories; its relation and differences to the "popular epic".

b) A lecture or two on the early epic, the *Poema de Mio Cid*; its versification that will lead to the popular ballads; its aspect of social protest where *popular* sentiment is on the side of the underdog as Julio Rodríguez Puértolas points out:

> Américo Castro ha senalado clue en el cantar cidiano 'la sociedad está vista desde abajo' El poema es en verdad, la gesta de los infanzones de tercerapugnan por ascender de categoría social…

This might also serve as a point of departure for a quick look, using extracts from the Anthology of Rodríguez Puértolas at the aspect of *popular* and social protest in the poetry of the Middle Ages in Spain; a current that will lead to the great revindication of *lo popular – Fuenteovejuna*.

These lectures could be given by say, Dr. Laurence at Mona; so that instead of one person teaching a course, a certain amount of collaboration takes place; where special areas can be welded into a synthesis.

The epic – the *Araucana* itself will be taught in Hispanic Literature at the same time as the Bernal Díaz and the Inca Garcilaso de la Vega and Felipe Poma de Ayala is being taught in Latin American I. The ideas about the epic – the truth of poetry and history will be brought out in the parallel relations Bernal Díaz's "true" account of a clash and conflict; and Ercilla's epic account. The universalisation in the epic which leads to Ercilla's noble treatment of the *Indian* as a worthy enemy; plus the prevailing Spanish current of "*lo popular*" which includes the Indians in that vein which in Spain gives rise to the exemplary and worthy peasant as in *Fuenteovejuna, Peribáñez*; and leads to the plays of Calderón. A quick glance at Lope De Vega's treatment of the Indians; in his *comedias*, a *popular* treatment in which Indians become idealised Spanish peasants, or pastoral figures.

In contrast with Ercilla's treatment of the Indian we have the epic of Pedro de Oña, a colon-settler on the same theme. In his epic there is the germ and seed of the later theories of Sarmiento. In the *Arauco Domado* – extracts used to compare with Ercilla's we get what Chevalier has called de Oña's Manichean "perspective". Ercilla inherits the universalist aspects of the literary epic which ennobles the enemy as well as the universalist aspect of Catholicism which sees the natural light of reason equally given to all men. With Pedro de Oña, Christianity becomes both national and imperial. In de Oña's epic, God is on the side of the Spanish battalions and protects the Spaniards who fight for his cause. In contrast the Indiana serve the designs of the infernal powers who are linked against the Christians. The epic struggle between Christianity and paganism in de Oña becomes that of Sarmiento between Civilisation and Barbarism. The religious and, cultural racism in de Oña poem is linked to the pervasive *limpieza de sangre*; that racialisation of Christian heresy which takes on new aspects in attitudes to the Indians.

The introduction to Golden Age poetry is therefore made through this link. After the epic a look at Spanish ballads; at their diffusion in America; at the popular poetry of Spain and Latin America and their relationship – as Torner shows in his investigations with *culto* poetry – See E. M. Torner: *Lirica Hispanica: relaciones entre lo popular y lo culto* (Castalia Madrid, 1965). The relationship of ballad and epic to history etc.

LYRIC POETRY:

Poesia de tipo tradicional a look at the beginnings of Spanish lyric poetry in the *'jarchas – judeo – españolas'*. Courtly love poetry, and the *Cancioneros*. The New Italianate Poetry: Garcilaso; the new innovations both as form and worldview. To conclude with the two poems of Fray Luis as paradigmatic of that *poesía de la soledad* which springs from the central important theme of Golden Age Literature – the theme of *Menosprecio de Corte y Alabanza de Aldea*, which in one of its aspects leads to the peoetry of solitude of interior reflexion, contemplation and mysticism. We hope to show in the poetry as well as in the play *Fuenteovejuna* that the topic *Menosprecio de Corte* etc, is, within the context of the official literature that Spanish Golden Age Literature was, the area of escape, the formulation of a critique of reality in literary terms. Indeed that unusual and revolutionary critique which *Fuenteovejuna* represents can only be understood within this literary revindication of Nature, *La soledad*, and *lo popular*, considered to be nearer to God. Its antithesis was the *Corte* which was in reality the centre of the organised Government; the establishment. The *"senda escondida"* of a Fray Luis becomes therefore a withdrawal from the official reality; the frequent obsessive *alabanza de aldea* and *menosprecio de Corte* transposes a powerful critique of "official" values on to a literary plane that, due to its venerable and detached literary lineage, made it safe from the Inquisition's attentions. Theocritus, Vergil, Horace, Ovid, had all provided the "academic" literary precedents and forms into which could be poured 'the content of contemporary preoccupations.

DRAMA

1. Lope de Vega's *Fuenteovejuna*.
2. Tirso de Molina's *El Burlador de Sevilla*.
3. Calderón's *El alcade de Zalamea*
Central theme: *Menosprecio de corte y alabanza de aldea* and the noble peasant conflict in Golden Age drama.

These three plays, apart from giving the high water mark of the Golden Age Spanish theatrical achievement, introduce important themes, which link with the preoccupations of the New World experience – concepts of justice; of Natural Law as being above man-made law, as being the touchstone of obligation and sanction of the *alabanza de aldea* as the critique of the powerful nobility of the day; and more so of the lower nobility, the hidalgo class, which with the revolution of prices brought by the influx of American treasure, found themselves ruined. For the exaltation of the peasant in Golden Age theatre is a transposition of the reality in which the wealthy peasants, the *kulaks*, profiting from the price rise in food, had begun to challenge the *hidalgo* class for posts in the municipal government, the lower nobility impoverished, and as the Lazarillo shows, increasingly hungry under the cloak of its pride became an object of satire. The exaltation of the peasant too, responded to the campaign for a return to the land waged in so many pamphlet as the peasants left for Madrid or the Indies and famine became a familiar reality. The exaltation of the peasant and *lo popular* also had it something of the exaltation of a Golden Age, an Arcadian ideal combined with a Christian ethic; and was partly due to the rise of the peasant class to positions of Nobility in the church on the strength of their *limpieza de sangre*; the denigration of the *hidalgo* class suspected of *converso* tendencies to intellectual speculation and commercial gain; and therefore of being the enemy within the gates the standard bearer not only of heretical religious beliefs, but of a new way of life, a *Weltanschauung*, only as yet dimly perceived as the rise of capitalism which would, of course, relegate Spain to a backwater, sweeping her religion and her pride, with a shove and a kick, into the dustbin of history.

The metaphysical concept of justice and order as the reflection of a harmony, which man, by living according to Natural Law and remaining in an equilibrium with Nature, implements, was being replaced by quite another concept not metaphysical at all; since Nature was to be desacralised so that Man could be her "Lord and Possessor". But the conquest of man over Nature was to mean the conquest of man by man. It is not surprising that a play like *Fuenteovejuna* was not to be found in any other European theatre for it embodies a metaphysical view of Nature which would only return with the concept of the Noble Savage; himself soon to be converted into Crusoe's man Friday as the conquest of Nature, symbolised most nakedly in the exploitation of the New World went on, and increased rapidly to the catastrophic climax of today.

The literary concept of the revindication of *lo popular* on a metaphysical and ethical plane was extended to the fictional reality of the New World. Indians and mulattos and Negroes alternated between being in the comic peasant tradition of the early Spanish Theatre; or in the tradition of the worthy and exemplary peasant of *Fuenteovejuna* and *El alcalde de zalamea*.

Opposed to the peasant harmony of dignity, work, equilibrium with natural and Christian laws is the figure of Don Juan, the archetypal reprehensible, anti-exemplary figure of the *Corte*. No measures, no bounds, no limits, no equilibrium, no "natural" concept of justice – a total irresponsibility; the reality of the *Corte*, the "is" of contemporary Spain compared with the idyllic Natural world of *Fuenteovejuna*. In these three plays it is possible to indicate the dynamics of the Spanish Golden Age Theatre; the way it incorporated the vision of the New World and the Indians of the New World; as well as the neo-natives, the blacks, into the coordinates of its literary reality. But the ideal universal attitude of the dramatist in Madrid could not be the attitude of the colon-settler whose relation to the New World Nature and to New World Man was one of domination; and one in which the Indian and black peasant had not as yet begun to challenge the supremacy of the dominant class in fact; or fiction.

THE NOVEL

The *Lazarillo*
The *Don Quijote*

The *Lazarillo* would serve as the exemplar of the picaresque novel in general even though Parker sees it as a precursor. The literature of the disrupted man, flocking into the city, marginal to the still dominant values, is reflected in the "culture of poverty" documentaries of today. The role of hunger, the quest for material survival in a world no longer ruled by age-old tradition and custom but by chance etc. If the *picaro* was subversive of the values of honour which he couldn't afford, the denizens of today's "culture of poverty" are subversive of the values of property, which they can't afford. As the *picaro* symbolised the breakup of an old system and the confused beginnings of a new, so do the disrupted marginal masses of today.

The *Quijote* of course is the compendium of all the important themes; it symbolises and sums them up. As such the *Quijote* will, by itself, span almost all the problematics of Spanish Literature. As the embodiment in literary terms of the clash between the *'ought'* and the *'is'* it is the tragedy of the attempt by Don Quijote to give power to the critique which literature represents; to actualise its critique in action. Yet literature retains its power only by its estrangement; its practice lies in its theory.

YEAR THREE: HISPANIC OPTION

The compulsory course for this option, we would suggest, would be transitionally, reworking of the present *Golden Age Literature II*. We propose that this course be called instead: *Hispanic Literature II*; and that a provisional theme title could be: LO POPULAT Y LO CULTO: EXPANSION AND DECLINE. It would begin with
   a) *Poema de mio Cid*
   b) *El libro de buen amor*
These texts, rather than seen as "medieval literature" as opposed to Golden

Age, would be envisaged as the early trajectory in which the "written" literature is still involved with and close to an "oral" culture. The frontier populist spirit of the *poema*; the vigour of a literature which reflects a reality of expansion leads into the *Libro de buen amor* where "culto" concepts of "love" are still embedded in a popular language; whose structure responds to popular reality of festivals and Catholic ritual; and, as Dr. Laurence has shown in a study parallels folk-festivals still pervasive in the largely oral reality of the Caribbean. For in the span of ages that our societies represent, we move from contemporary reality in the cities to structures of economy and structures of feeling which are far closer to medieval Europe's. Both the *Poema de mio Cid* and the *Libro de buen amor* are closer to certain pervasive Caribbean realities; than say a novel of the absurd by Camus. Yet such is the complexity that the novels of Camus do respond to the new reality of our cities; the reality of the marginal man; the "outsider" feeling of the disrupted majority; a feeling that Patterson groped towards in *The Children of Sisyphus*. To teach Literature at a University like ours is to understand, and come to terms with the fact that Caribbean man coexists in different centuries; in different areas of historical space-time. Like the Venezuelan singer who still sings of Charlemagne; the Brazilian Blacks, who still enact the popular ritual of Christians and Moors; the Caribbean man whose Carnival still contains "remote cultural influences" Catholic and African and Amerindian, the University student of the New World even those who come from the small elite class, still carry over from their childhood, echoes of an *oral* culture which by its nature is "popular". It is clear then that to be *relevant* in the context of out societies, cannot depend on whether or not one "cuts out" medieval literature and puts in Carlos Fuentes. In fact, depending on the approach the most contemporary reality can be made to seem irrelevant; and vice versa.

Following on the *Poema* and the *Libro de buen amor* would be the dramatic prose work: *La Celestina*. The Celestina, bawd and go-between, is still a familiar *type* and figure of Caribbean societies, the structure of whose economy is sometimes perilously near in character and marginality to the Celestina's precarious trade; the language close to spoken speech; the Celestina like the later picaro, herself a character a *lo popular*. The interaction and contradiction between the sordidness of La Celestina's reality; and the ideal sensual "passion" of the lovers reflects the contradiction between the reality of the marginal majority of Caribbean man – the culture of poverty – and the "ideal" property values of rights, freedom etc. of the upper and middle class who use the rhetoric of democracy to disguise privilege; and a relation of exploitation. Then, as now, tragedy springs from the tension and contradiction between the accepted rhetoric of a society; and its reality. The examination of *La Celestina* as a work of literature is extended and reinforced when the structure of the pattern of literature is shown to parallel the structure of the pattern of society.

This gives us the basic theme-title for the specifically Golden Age Litera-ture in this Course; we suggest a theme title such as: Patterns of Literature and Society in the Golden Age. The Theme of Desengano.

For this transitional stage the texts can remain very much the same as they are. As far as the *Novel* is concerned, Quevedo's *La Vida del Buscon* is the climax of exploration of a sick reality, The anti-heroism of the 'hero'; the reversal of outworn values; the gap between hypocritical rhetoric and reality; the gro-tesque of style, the caricature of "character" which etches the desengaño in bitter cruel tones. Perhaps here too, some of the Exemplary Novels of Cervantes – especially the *El licenciado vidriera*, could be taught; as the pattern of literature that parallels the patterns of society. In this year too, a further and more complex look could be taken at the Quijote.

DRAMA

Tirso de Molina's: *El Condenado por Desconfiado*

This play, which deals among other issues with the debate of predestination vs. free will, has proved a most popular play, creating discussion among a still largely and fundamentally religious student population. With this play an approach has been made to exploring the different coordinates of the sixteenth-and-seventeenth century Catholic ethic – as in most cases the students whether Catholic or Protestant, are totally conditioned by what Weber calls the Protestant Ethic. Some of the best discussions of this play have come from the occasional student who studies Sociology; and who has read Weber on the Protestant Ethic.

What this seems to suggest is the extent to which the exploration of structures of society can help to elucidate structures of feeling of a time and place so different from our own; what came out of the seminar discussion on this play, was usually an awareness on the part of those of us who took part in the discussion of the fact that our own structures of feeling which caused us to come down either on the side of free will or predestination were themselves conditioned by our time and place; and were therefore not a part of an irreversible human nature; also that several concepts which we took for granted were part of the superstructure of the pattern of our societies; that they were not necessarily right.

Since the aim and function of the Spanish theatre was didactic, very much along the lines of Brecht's concept of the theatre; the study of the play has lead often to the same examination of conduct according to certain moral criteria which the playwright originally intended. The theology behind the play, is a useful point of departure for a look at the theological writings of men like Domingo De Soto, Luis de Molina, Francisco Suárez, Francisco de Vitoria; and the way in which these structures of thought appear in the literature; and even in the political reality of the society. Calderón's *El medico de su honra*, a paradigmatic play about the "hypochondria of honour" which was the stage reflection of the *limpieza de sangre* neurosis which afflicted the society, perhaps touches on one of the most important single themes both in the theatre and in its reality. The theme of *desengaño* central to the era of decline, to the structure of feeling which accompany Spain's successive defeats, is made into a principle of moral behaviour in Calderón's play, *La vida es sueño*.

POETRY

The poetry of Quevedo draws with a baleful pen the fever-chart of the Spanish "malady". The *"conceptismo"* of his poems are the device which like the caricature-grotesque of his prose fills the vacuum, the hollow that yawns between reality and illusion. *Lo popular* in his ballads becomes cruel grotesque. His *culto* sonnets filled with images of decay and dissolution; with a "secularisation of belief" which leads to a confrontation with Death as the end terminus; rather than as the opening to eternal life; the frenzied sense of time, time passing; a world out of joint in which the modern sense of *alienation* comes across with force.

This *desengaño* of Quevedo will be compared and contrasted with that of Gracián and extracts from his *Criticón*. Lope de Vega, Góngora: their poetry studied as the two extremes; the *optimismo* of Lope, the "popular" and its uses in his poetry; the national patriotism of his epic poem like the *Dragontea*; the genuine religious feeling of his religious sonnets; the easy almost spontaneous feeling and style of his love poetry: compared to this, the studied use that Góngora makes of the "popular"; his stylisation of the "popular" even in the apparently simpler poems; his idealisation of *lo popular* and peasant life in the style of the epic; and therefore his revolutionary break with the theory of styles; his *Soledades* and its isolationist dream of a pastoral Golden Age in which Man lives in equilibrium with Nature; his attack on the New World, its discovery and exploitation; and therefore his anti-epic view of reality; his use of the *Menosprecio de Corte y alabanza de aldea* theme as a negation of the negation of the established official reality; the negation also expressed stylistically. The poetry of Sor Juana Inés de la Cruz – as the poetry of Spain in the New World – parallels with and divergences from Góngora the philosophical preoccupations of her Sueños; and her new World reality.

From the *Poema de mio Cid* to the *Soledades* of Góngora and the *Suenos* of Sor Juana Inés de la Cruz a trajectory of expansion, from the more *popular* to the most *culto* of cultismos, can be outlined. The texts chosen will be studied both as texts and as points of departure for the exploration of a structure of feeling, a structure of society which parallels the structure of a literature: of the culture of which it is the embodiment.

Note: C.f. A student's comparison of Góngora's idealised peasants with Carpentier's heroine of *Los pasos perdidos*; both justify "natural" razones de vivir as opposed to the artificiality of the Corte – i.e. Civilised official society.

Two additional courses which would, it seems be necessary for the Hispanic option could perhaps include the present Spanish Novel Course, perhaps extended even further into something like:

AFTER THE QUIJOTE: THE NOVEL IN SPAIN.

The relationship of *Costumbrismo* to *lo popular*; its similarities to and differences from *Criollismo* in the Latin American novel; comparison between the Indianist of L.A. and the Regionalist novels of Spain; the relation of these to the historical novel and nationalism; then down to the present day where the same cross referencing of themes and treatment between the novel in Spain and in Latin America (and vice versa) would begin to make the kind of interconnections that can break down the present Spain vs. Latin America either/or. In a sense the novel in Spain becomes part of a larger whole of the novel in Spanish.

Another necessary course, perhaps, for convenience sake called: 1898: Before and After, could attempt to trace the main line of ideas and their interaction with Literature from El Padre Feijoo, Luzán, and the eighteenth century spectrum to the beginnings and realisation of Romanticism; key figures like Larra and Bécquer, Zorilla; *costumbrismo* and realism in the theatre; "realism" in poetry; ideas and essays centred about *Krausismo* – Giner de los Rios, Cossío, Costa; the influence of these ideas; the precursors of 1898, Clarín and Ganivet; *Modernismo* in poetry; the 1898 fall out and the problematic of nationalism; the ideas and writings of Unamuno and others; their revindication of the *eterno paisajo castellano*; Ortega y Gasset, his *Meditaciones Sobre el Quijote* and its influence in Latin America; Maeztu's defence of 'la hispanidad'; Machado and his meaning; the movecentismo of Juan Ramón Jiménez; Lorca-apotheosis of *lo popular* y *lo culto*; the 1927 generation; the Civil War and its effect on Literature of the post war years: the contemporary approximation to a sense of crisis at once universal and national. These three Courses all offered in the Third Year would complete the requirements for the *Hispanic Option*; which is conceived to provide a coherent view of the literature and the reality of Spain and Latin America. The courses would themselves, become progressively less specialist and narrow; and more comprehensive and cross-referenced.

We suggest therefore that the system of examination, as a transitional measure pending a more fundamental change, could be supplemented by one Research Essay written on a specialised area of each Course. These Essays would form part of the assessment for the awarding of the Degree. Exam questions should become more general; that is, more comprehensive in scope so as to enable the assessment to be made on the student's ability to conceptualise his accumulation of dead erudition; rather than as too often now, to regurgitate it. Not more than two questions should be required in three hours – so that the handicap to thought as distinct from competent arrangement of material could be lessened; in this way the method of assessment would reflect the broadening more comprehensive and conceptual knowledge, inherent in the new degree structure; if the structure is to reflect an interrelated structure of meaning.

Note: "What is Development" and what is the role of Universities in Underdeveloped Country. In U.W.I. newsletter July/August 1971, p. 14.

PART THREE
THE DEGREE IN SPANISH: SPECIFIC PROPOSALS

What is exciting about the challenge of the new structure is the opportunity for a collaborative interdisciplinary planning of an approach to teaching: An approach in which the linking of disciplines should be like the interdependence of gears. The autonomy of each gear is not negated, but is in fact reinforced and extended, by the fact of its intrinsic usefulness not only as gear; but as a member of a whole mechanism, impelled by a central meaning. The aim of this interlinking should be to answer the question of a second-year Student who asked:

"What am I going to teach when I leave University? All I have is bits and pieces".

It is imperative therefore that a group from each Faculty should, before the beginning of the next Year, get together to work out clusters of combinations from each faculty; that these clusters be worked out around central and unifying themes; that each segmented lecturer know what is the approach and the basic assumptions in the other courses which the students who take these clusters are going to be faced with.

It is from this type of approach, helped by feedback from students as to the areas of difficulty which they encounter – the genuine difficulties, not the professional complaints designed to cut down on the work load – that lecturers will be able to reorient their course and lectures. The new degree structure cannot be implemented by the former segmented and specialist approach. The lecturer who knows nothing of sociology, or looks at it with disdain will resent sociological comment, brought into literary criticism by the student; and vice versa. As has already been pointed out, elements of social structure dealing with Asia, specifically, does not broaden the world view of a student of Latin American literature; except that a particular lecturer is able to make parallels with the social structure of Latin America; and *relate* the connections. If that lecturer can only specialise on Asia; and hugs his special area like an ikon isolated in time and space, then that lecturer cannot function in the context of the new structure; if the new formal structure is to have a structure of meaning. We have initiated what is in fact, a Reformation. We need now, the kind of collaborative machinery to be set up to examine and make proposals to meet the consequences.

The proposals we make here are limited in scope: transitional in nature. Until comprehensive interdisciplinary, inter-Faculty discussions get going; and get implemented we suggest that as a *first stage*, a stage only, the following proposals might be useful and valid. We limit our proposals only to where students choose to do an option in Spanish; but we remain fully aware of the need for the courses required for the *Option in Spanish* to be so planned; and so progressively transformed as to make them meaningful by themselves; and relation with Courses from other Modern Language Departments, Classics, History, Sociology etc. That is to say, the bits and pieces must have their own validity; which are then reinforced by their connection and role in a wider spectrum of meanings,

For students who would take a spread of courses that would amount to an option in Spanish, we propose that, as a transitional arrangement, student can be offered:

a) An Option in Hispanic Language and Literature
b) An Option in Latin American Literature

The central theme of both options will be the same. Courses will cluster about this central theme in such a way as to lead to a more integrated approach – one in which the dynamics of the literature taught, would be related in its complex contradiction to the history and the sociology of its reality; that is to say, the reality with which literature confronts would be explored as a frame of reference; in order to show how literature transcends its frame; transposes its reality. The students in any of our literature courses should therefore be able to see their related courses in say, History, Sociology, Politics as the extensions and deepening of their knowledge of that frame of reference with which their course in literature has already familiarised them. The connection is all.

YEAR TWO

LATIN + AMERICAN I:

As the course now stands (p. 10 of the pamphlet) it both extends and completes our suggestions for Year I. Its divisions, (a) Chronicles (b) Romantic and Independence writers (c) Gauchesque Literature (d) Afro-Cubanismo represent already that dialectic between coloniser, colonised, which we see as the central aspect in the New World reality between *lo popular* and *lo culto*. Instead of what Leavis would call "the organic" relation between the folk culture of the people and the *culto* or learned tradition that we find in the Golden Age of Spain, and later in Lorca, we get an essential disjuncture' on the one band, in that movement represented by Sarmiento and known as Civilisation in contrast to the "barbarism" of *lo popular*. The very formulation *civilización/barbarismo* i.e. the cultural descendant of Sepúlveda's assertion of the natural superiority of the Spaniard due to his civilised culture; and the natural inferiority of the Indian due to his "lack of a civilised culture", shows that the clash of culture is inherent in the coloniser/colonised relation.

The Chronicles, by giving two versions of the Spanish and the Indian past, from the side of the conquerors and the side of the conquered initiate this clash on one level. The *Comentarios Reales* revindicate the Incas and their culture but using the Spanish culture and religion as an insuperable framework of reference. On the other hand, Poma de Ayala's *New Chronicle* and *Good Government*, in the battle of the myths, assert the Indian past as a Golden Age; the pastoral longing in a time of stress, the revindication of the defeated becoming the revindication of an entire people. As Jean Franco puts it;

> Hence the tragic paradox that while for the Spaniard the conquest represented the possibility of Utopia, for the Indian it was the end of an era to which he would eventually look back as if to a Golden Age...

The age of glory for the Spaniards would be the age of defeat for the Indians as an anonymous Indian wrote: "Para quo su flor viviese, dañaron y sorbieron la flor de los otros…" This brilliantly expressed paradox could well become the theme of our approach to the literature, thought and culture of both countries.

From Year I, the students would have seen that on the whole in the Caribbean, the nationalist movement against Spain led to a revaluation of the Indian and the Negro. The "romanticisation" of Enriquillo's revolt is matched by the anti-slavery protest; the concept of Natural Law, the revaluation of Nature as an ideal critique of reality went hand in hand with the *culto* appreciation of the *popular*.

In the Argentine, with the group of writers under Romantic and Independence Writers, the reaction is more complex. With Echeverría, Jean Franco expresses the paradox like this:

> He expressed the dilemma of his time, the dilemma of a man whose artistic theories teach him to love the countryside and the 'folk' and whose living experience teaches him that the countryside and its inhabitants constitute threat to all values...

Therefore she argues, in *La Cautiva* and *El Matadero* Echeverría defends European values and attacks primitive native "barbarism". What is interesting here is that a European, Jean Franco sees the values defended by Echeverría as the only real values; since these are the values of her civilisation. This brings us to another aspect; another confrontation. The dialectic between the city and the country; the *ciudad campo*, another aspect of the *Popular-culto* which is a basic theme and dialectic in Hispanic literature.

The opposition, *ciudad campo*, translated into the colonial reality takes on a new dimension. Just as the Roman urbs were the focus of romanisation, Rome itself was overseas; and therefore existed in relation of internal colonialism with the *campo* even more, under the increasing capitalism of European imperialism, is the city in relation to the *campo* in the Latin American reality. As Martínez Estrada argues:

> Cuando la independencia Buenos Aires reemplazó a la metro oil. Se arado el virreinato del re, Buenos Aires suplanto al Monarca en la defenses de los fueros hispánicos ... Lo que en realidad se hizo, en vez que desprender America de Espana, fue desprender España; y quedo como un fragmento de ella Buenos Aires.
>
> El interior ha mirado siempre a la metropolí como a la metro soli; sus planes nacionalistas y los del resto han sido antagónicos y hasta disyuntiva.

The antagonism, between the city and the country rather than their complementarity rests on deep economic structures. Stavanhagen has shown that in Latin America the cities exist as the centre of an "internal colonialism" in relation to the rest of the country. The oligarchies of the city control the economy as the junior partners of the European economic oligarchies – as Martínez Estrada puts it: "Europa vino a resultar el punto ma's proximo a Buenos Aires, y éste su ciudad más a trasmano".

The Creole middle-class revolution headed by Bolívar would lead to a fight on two fronts – a fight against the Spanish colonisers and against the vast majority of the country – the Indians; the fight of the city against the *cameo*. There were therefore two strains of literature: that *criollismo* essentially middle-class, and external even where it glorified the Indian; as well as the savage anti-campo, anti-gaucho, anti-Indian, anti-Negro nationalism of Echeverría and Sarmiento.

Against this we have the *Martín Fierro* and the constant stream of literature whose revindication of the cameo and the Indian is in line with the political movement approach to the genuinely national and indigenous – *el indigenismo*.

In *Martín Fierro*, a masterpiece of Latin American national writing, although, not at first recognised as such by the hostile *cultos* of the city, we see that concept of idyllic Nature, which although in its romantic version descends from that "cultural universal" which is the single most important theme perhaps to be found in that great creative period of Spain's Literature – the Golden Age. That "cultural universal" we suggest was the classical topos – *Menosprecio de corte y alabanza de aldea*. It is the theme, we suggest, itself an expression of *lo popular y lo culto*, which may best introduce the literature of the

Golden Age of Spain in a parallel and dynamic relation with the literature of Latin America.

But before we look at that, a quick glance at Latin America II and Courses like Race and Culture, and Cultural Development and Political Ideas; as well as the Texts for Latin American Contemporary Narrative, show that these courses and texts as they stand can be unified around the central theme we suggest. The tragic dimensions of modern Latin American writing, as with Caribbean writing comes from this disjuncture of the economic, cultural, political elites from the masses who, even when they are disrupted to the cities, remain marginal to the dominant reality established by the city; that the centre of the Latin American reality imposed by the cities is external to itself; that the confrontation between *lo popular* the marginal disrupted masses and the small *creole-culto* class is the confrontation of the twentieth century; whether in Latin America; India, Africa; or the Third World *lo popular*, versus the small privileged portion of the world embodied in the U.S.A. and Europe.

PART TWO
THE DEGREE IN SPANISH: TOWARDS A NEW CONCEPTION

What we are trying to put forward is a new approach. The suggestions we shall make, suggestions which take into consideration the present structure as is, are therefore merely illustrative. If the main lines are accepted, then by the very nature of the approach itself, the practical applications will be best worked out through collaborative methods, constantly reviewed and discussed between staff and students. What we would like to see initiated is not a *change*, but the institutionalisation of a *process* of change in order to set up a dynamic tension between the need to formalise patterns; and the need to disrupt them.

We moved from one degree structure into another; but this changeover was not accompanied by any formulated philosophy of change. The pragmatic functionalist attitude prevailed. The justified cry of a need for relevance, of a broadening out from narrow specialist disciplines, met with the admirable response, implicit to the New Degree Structure. Admirable, in the sense that a decision was taken to break up the traditional cake of custom which we had inherited from the English university system; and a tradition which had well-tried and well-proven virtues. But the very validity of these virtues in a country and in a time so completely different from ours was itself proof that those virtues, chief of which was a high degree of specialisation, imposed on the totally different structure and dynamic of our own society were to be inadequate although they served a transitional purpose. Our difficulty is that we, moulded in this system, find it difficult to conceptualise outside the old patterns in which we were taught. Yet there has been little awareness of the fact that a New Degree Structure will imply new content and new approaches; and on the part of the educators the need to re-educate ourselves, to liberate ourselves as far as possible, from many of the assumptions that went with the old Degree Structure, assumptions the more tenacious, because they are so *implicit*; and because in *their time* they were so much what Antonio Machado has called *"la palabra a tiempo"* that they led to much that was of value. But values out of time and place negate their original purpose; and obstruct the creation of values *"a tiempo"*.

The old degree sStructure implied thorough specialisation on narrow areas of discipline; what J.H. Plumb has called the cultivation "of our minute gardens". The value of such a structure lay in its scrupulous exploration and accumulation of thoroughly documented facts. These facts did much to dissipate the mythologising of vague hypotheses, the lazy acceptance of half formulated and improperly conceived general truths. In the best representatives of the Old Degree Structure, teaching and research meant meticulous and objective concentration on the facts of narrow areas of discipline. The student learnt to be meticulous, organised, cogent, precise; to avoid waffle, hysterical praise in exclamation marks; emotional dispraise. All too often the techniques they were taught were techniques designed to help them in the accumulation of facts; but this technical knowledge was gained by a refusal. A refusal to try for the wider view, of to relate their specialised areas to the general experience of mankind. The old degree structure tended to become guilty-through-omission of a mythology of separate facts. Literature was to be taught as something having its own autonomy; its criticism became criticism for criticism sake. Although literature which is fiction exists in a dialectical relation with its fact which is history, the old degree structure insisted that history was history and should be taught by the History Department; and vice versa. Even where history had been taught in the Literature Department, we tended to teach history as history; rather than in its relation to the process of the creation of literature.

This is not to say that individual teaching did not transcend the imposition of the structural pattern. But the structure is the approach; the medium is the message; and the generality of teaching and learning reflected rather than contested the structure. The best of our students went out prepared to cultivate their minute gardens with scrupulous care and a straining after objectivity. But we sent out few prepared to take the risk that our modern conditions demand; the risk of attempting that new and imaginative synthesis which can begin the adventure of "taming" the twentieth-century technological and one-dimensional wilderness; few prepared to chart vistas from difficult peaks of Darien. Few prepared to bring an urgent purpose, and real relevance to the task of teaching, learning, living in the space time of their age and place. The greatest fault of the old structure was that it led to a capital accumulation of dead erudition; to what Noël Salomon called the "coquetry of myopic erudition... of attention paid to minute detail".

The *flexibility* of the New Degree Structure; as far as the form of its pattern is concerned; the attempt to broaden the vistas of the students by giving them the chance to combine a wider choice of specialised areas of disciplines represents a step forward. But it is a step that is made ambivalent by its lack of conceptualisation; by an inadequacy in the thinking through of the consequences of the change. For the change of form must mean a change of content. If this change is to be creative, it must mean a change of approach. And a change of approach of the part of lecturers must be a slow and painful process. Lecturers, highly specialised in narrow areas of discipline, each one shut away in his own segment, instructing the students in this segment *without any relation* to the other segment taught by other segmented lecturers cannot give students a broader and more related view, especially where courses offered *are not linked* by any thematic and structural concept. The vertical if irrelevant coherence of the old structure will be replaced not by a horizontal coherence but by a *heterogenisation* – to coin a term-of the mind. Without the necessary connections, parallels, and a total underlying coherence of relevant meaning and approach, the new degree structure will bring about – even more so than the old – the one-dimensional approach, the approach that is prevalent in the established reality where the desublimisation of art and literature has brought about their reduction to cultural consumer goods with:

> Bach as background music in the kitchen... Plato and Hegel, Shelley and Baudelaire, Marx and Freud in the drugstore. [Marcuse]

All unrelated, deprived of meaning they become anti-meaning.

If the new degree course is not to end up as an academic version of an Oxford pharmacy whose heterogeneous goods offered for sale make it paradigmatic of a totalitarian reality where:

> technology, culture, politics and the economy merge into an omnipresent system which swallows up or repulses all alternatives... [Marcuse]

If in fact, the teaching of literature and history is to continue and more fully develop its justifying value as the perennial offering of *alternatives* to the established reality, whether in the remembrance of the past which history offers; or in the "ought alternative" to the "is" which literature embodies, then a new concept of content, of approach must accompany a new form. The message must fully determine the medium; the medium must fully actualise the message. And if any one objects that neither the teaching of literature nor history has anything to do with a message, he is merely repeating the old message of the old medium, the old degree structure whose insistence that it was without ideology was merely the rationalisation of its liberal *Weltanschauung*. As that most *culto* writer of

Argentina, Borges, puts it: "Those who maintain that art must not propagate doctrines, refer only to those doctrines that are contrary to their own".

The actualisation of the potential inherent in the new Degree Structure will call for among other things a) Continous liaison and collaboration between the different departments so that *courses* can interweave parallel and contest one another so as to give students a unified critical approach to reality; an approach that springs from certain basic themes around which the courses, whether in literature or history, or sociology for example will revolve. Perhaps we can cite here an example already suggested – that the first year student in the Arts pursue the theme of *Caribbean 'Man': His radical situation in his time*. All teaching for the first year would fan out from that radial centre; all teaching of the history, literature and sociology of the past would be directed towards the *Revelation del presento*. This kind of thematic approach gives coherence and relevance; and in no way *reduces* the meaning of relevance to *utilitarianism*; nor circumscribes the area of his learning. As Dr. Brathwaite pointed out, the reality of Caribbean man's experience touches on the universal reality of all men. The literature, the history, the sociology of Caribbean man is that complex reality of which Carpentier's hero in *Los pasos perdidos* is the embodiment:

> Porque aqul no se habían volcado en realidad pueblos consanguíneos, como los que la historia malaxara en ciertas encrucijadas del mar, sino las grandes razas del mundo, las mác apartados, las masas distintas, las que durante milenios permanecieron ignorantes de su convivencia en el planeta.

It becomes an imperative then of a Caribbean university to begin to explore this new "*convivencia en el planeta*". Such an approach goes towards the kind of interdisciplinary studies that the new degree structure hints at. But if the hint is to be actualised it is clear that the specialisation of lecturers in particular segments of learning; plus the entire apparatus of narrow scholarship, of the exam system that is its concomitant, must come in for revaluation. To teach Caribbean literature in Spanish without some anthropological and sociological knowledge of the Nañigo cult, for example among other Afro Cuban religions and folk culture is to teach Caribbean literature in Spanish inadequately; equally for the lecturer in sociology to teach the sociology of the Nañigo cults without knowing something of the Afro-Cuban movements which they inspired is to teach sociology in the context of the new structure inadequately. To refuse to structure the course so that the student of literature in the Spanish department is taught in a parallel. (Members of staff are invited to suggest alternatives. This is just one possibility. To ignore the sociology of the popular culture from which the literature springs, is to negate the concept of the new structure.)

The excitement of a creative degree would come from the tension of teachers and students trying to make narrow areas of pure scholarship relevant to the needs of the *"revelación del presente"*; and from trying to synthesise these narrow areas, in the context of modern conditions, into a whole, in order to approach this dynamic, the old unreal division into peninsular and Latin America must be discarded; with its concomitant attitude that learning consists of areas of private property to be fenced against encroachers, instead of a collaborative exercise of a cross fertilisation of ideas, The private property concept is itself a reflection of a property-relation world in which learning is reduced to the naked form of a commodity. It is this property-relation world that the teaching of literature is supposed to negate; an established reality in which literature itself is reduced to a cultural consumer product. We cannot therefore proclaim in our practice, the acceptance of a commodity world whose irrationality, compartmentalises thought in order to deprive it of its subversive power, we can only justify the teaching of literature if we teach it in such as a manner as to reinforce and defend the antagonistic critical value of the literature taught; to prevent that cultural reconciliation of opposed truths which the established reality seeks through its heterogenisation of knowledge. We are most revolutionary in our approach when we seek to conserve against the prevailing odds, the critical implications of all great literature, which, like *Don Quixote*, takes issue with its reality; as we must now with ours, translating their critical content into present preoccupations.

PROPOSED APPROACH
THEME
LO POPULAR Y LO CULTO: A CENTRAL PROBLEMATIC IN THE LITERATURE OF THE CARIBBEAN, SPAIN AND LATIN AMERICA

The theme will be developed for both options, in Year I, through a Caribbean perspective. Our proposals here are fluid – a fairly hasty attempt to indicate a way of presenting the central problematic. Certain themes and accompanying texts are proposed; but no attempt is here made to divide into courses; although the present structure and the possibility of certain aspects being easily incorporated into existing courses, taken into consideration. What we are more concerned with here is the way in which a continuous and relevant exploration can be carried on from Year I to Year III.

1. HISTORY OF THE SPANISH LANGUAGE
How it began and developed

A general introduction to the internal and external history of the Spanish Language, from Vulgar Latin to Modern Spanish. In studying the principal factors which led to the implantation of Vulgar Latin, (the *popular* language *spoken* by the legionaries, traders, coloni, etc.), in the Iberian Peninsular and its subsequent predominance over the Pre-Roman languages, parallels as well as important differences will be seen between this language situation and the one that prevailed in the early period of Spanish colonisation in the Caribbean Examination of the oral process which led to the transformation of popular spoken Latin into Spanish Romance i.e. *lo popular* and its dialectical relation to *lo culto*, the *written* standard Latin; a similar process seen in the Caribbean, with *written* Spanish taking the place of Latin; and the *spoken* (and at times even the written) language continuing, in a more intensified form than in the peninsula, the tradition of 'popular' forms.

In the study of the principal developments of Spanish, constant reference will be made to the standardisation of Spanish forms, especially in *writing*, and to the persistence of nonstandard *popular* forms not only in the Peninsula but more particularly in America.

[Once this foundation has been laid it might be followed up by a course (e.g. Latin American Dialectology) which touches more directly on the regional Spanish of the Caribbean area. What are its characteristics? How do they resemble and differ from general American Spanish? African influence – what accounts from the relative absence of Spanish Creoles in the area? (Compare French, English). Is Caribbean Spanish a decreolised form?

At this stage, it would be useful to see once more points of similarity and divergence between the Caribbean language situation and the early Ibero-Romance situation.]

A CARIBBEAN INTRODUCTION TO LITERATURE IN SPANISH

Some of the literary works mentioned in this section are introduced for the sake of their content rather than for their literary merit, While an achieved literary work like Carpentier's *El reino de este mundo* should be done in its entirety, it might be adequate to deal with extracts from other technically weaker works. It might prove a useful exercise to use these less satisfactory works as points of comparison to show how, despite their relevance to our situation and the interest their subject-matter generates, they nevertheless fail as works of art.

Dr. Irish's *Voces del Caribe*, a selection of texts intended for Practical Criticism is the main inspiration for the thinking about this First Year Course. Indeed it is clear that his text can be used as part of the material needed for this introduction; and that Practical Criticism rather than being taught on its own can itself be taught "through" the teaching of the literature. Jean Franco has made the point that movements which were mainly movements in art and literature in Europe, were transformed into social, movements in Latin America and the Caribbean, The structure of Spain as an underdeveloped country brings her far nearer to Latin America than to Europe in this. As we have already argued close textual analysis of passages is a one-dimensional exercise, and Dr Leavis himself has seen the danger:

> For to insist that literary criticism is, or should be a specific discipline of
> the intelligence is not to suggest that a serious interest in literature can
> confine itself to the kind of intensive local analysis associated with 'Practical
> Criticism' – to the scrutiny of the 'word on the page' in their minute relations,
> their effects of imagery and so on...

That is not to say that the "words on the page" do not have their own
dynamic structure, a structure which is not a mere *reflection* of its reality;
and that such a study of the structure is not worthwhile. What we are
insisting is that the structure of literature cannot be taught as an examination
of techniques detached from the reality which these techniques transpose
into literature; that to attempt to do this is to fall into the trap of what we
called "Conservative functionalism".

Dr Irish's *Voces del Caribe*, by the very choice of his material, for its subjective
relevance to the students' experience, shows that in contradistinction to the
paper to which we referred, approaches to Practical Criticism have begun to
abandon the old type of functionalism; and that the teaching of Practical
Criticism is to be seen as an aspect of the Introduction to Literature, taught
through the literature, which is firmly associated with its reality.

The Caribbean experience is the experience of a relation between coloniser
and colonised, colons and Creoles, Creoles and the neo-autochthonous. The
literature parallels this relation. The First Year Course should use those texts
which can exemplify the dialectics of this relation. Dr. Irish begins his *Voces del
Caribe* with an extract from Columbus's *Diario de viaje*; and goes on with the
debate between Sepúlveda and Las Casas about the rights of the Colons vs. the
rights of the Indians. Borrowing from his example, we suggest that the
introduction of the Literature should begin with prose extracts centred about
the defence of Indians by Las Casas and the other theologians who use the
concept of natural law to uphold the rights of the Indians; and made the
Christianising mission a revindication of *lo popular*. This, in the Second Year,
will be connected with the Renaissance *culto* defence of the natural – and the
universalisation of this concept. The contrary view of Sepúlveda that the
Indians were without 'culture', had no writing and therefore were inferiors
and natural subjects, is the aspect of the *culto* which accepts its separation from
the *inculto*; will also be given to initiate the *complexity* of the relation between
lo popular y lo culto in the Caribbean where *lo popular* was of one race; and *lo culto*
mainly of another.

Extracts from Sahagún etc to show Indian's culture; from the Inca Garcilaso's
Comentario Reales to show the fusion of the popular ceremonial of the Catholic
Church with ancient pagan Indian rites.

Analysis of the Nañigo cult in Cuba to show this same transculturation of
Catholicism and African religions. Extracts from the essays and other writings
of Carpentier; especially from *La Música en Cuba* where he shows how the

Spanish popular song – the *guajiros* – have survived in Cuba, carrying on the same verbal tradition; but unlike the Afro-Cuban music, they have preserved a tradition rather than reinvented it.

An essay from Carpentier's Collection *Tientos y Diferencias* in which he stresses the importance of the oral tradition in the literature and culture of the Caribbean and Latin America; shows how this oral tradition has preserved and continued the *alta tradición cultural* of the different cultures it has inherited; a Venezuelan singer of today still sings stories of Charlemagne and the ruins of Troy, so that an oral tradition lost in Europe has become part of the *contexto ctónico* of the New World. Carpentier discusses what Unamuno describes as the *"Traditión eterna"*, this popular oral tradition carried on by the people who live outside history; whose tradition is continuous, non-exclusive, a tradition which according to Carpentier helps us to *"enlazar ciertas realidades presentes con esencial culturales, remotas cuya existencia nos vincula con lo universal sin tiempo"*. It is through this tradition that the song "Guantanamera", for example, carries on the melodic elements of the *Romance de Gerineldo*. This tradition fuses with the similar traditions of other peoples at those points, where certain cultural universals are expressed in different manifestations of religion and art. Out of this fusion one finds carved on a new World Church – an angel playing the maracas. Extracts of perhaps the whole texts of the original Spanish version of Esteban Montejo's *Autobiography of a Runaway Slave* where the complexities of the confrontation-fusion of the two strains of *lo popular* in the Caribbean – the Spanish coloniser and the Black colonised – are reflected even in their culture. For example:

> The *zapateo* was very graceful and not so indecent as the African dances – the dancers 'bodies hardly touched each other'.
> The *jota* was exclusively for the Spanish. They brought this dance to Cuba and would not let anyone else dance it.
> The *tumbandera* was another popular dance. This has vanished as well. The whites didn't dance it because they said it was a vulgar Negro dance. I didn't like it myself. I must admit the *jota* was more elegant.

His descriptions of the *Ñanigo* processions, the Santerías and the Santeros, the panoply of African gods worshipped to celebrate San Juan make it invaluable as a text for the exploration of *lo popular*. His book provides the knowledge of that secretive underground current which would largely influence Afro-Cuban poetry.

POETRY

The prose extracts give a frame of reference for the poetry; and so should the language. A general theme could link the poems selected for study perhaps as "Poetry and the growth towards National Expression in Caribbean literature". Under this general heading the approaches could be various, eg.

a)   The ballads, and ballad forms of the poetry of Martí – these as the point of departure for a glance at the ballad forms in Spain, the *romance traditional* and its wide diffusion throughout Latin America; an example of a *culto* or *artificioso* ballad by Lope or Góngora; a romantic patriotic ballad of the Duque de Rivas; the later ballad of Alvargonzález by Antonio Machado; Lorca's *Gipsy Ballads*. Martí used the ballad form, part of the national substance of Spain, as part of the Cuban national expression. The Indian ballads of González Prada can also be looked at here. *Lo popular* in the ballad form is used as an expression of national poetry.

b)   Romanticism; the movement which universalised the revaluation of the national, the indigenous; *lo popular*. Among these the poets selected by Dr. Irish with their themes of the *mulatas, the blacks, exile* etc. Cf, the same response in Spain with a poem by Bécquer, Espronceda; and an example from Blest Gana, Gómez de Avellaneda etc.

c)   Surrealism; Afro-Antillanism. The *negrismo* movement and its poetry; the deepening of national expression as the *culto* turns to revindicate lo popular.

d)   Modernismo, which in spite of its art for art's sake facet, is but another aspect of that ecumenical approach towards the autochthonous which Mariátegui sees as the actualisation of nationalism. As Federico de Onis describes it:

La primera face de creación de la poesía modernista fue un proceso de transformation y avance autóctono y original en lo esencial que nació espontaneoamente de la propia insatisfacción y necesidad interna de renovation, y se desarollo coetáneamente con el simbolismo frances y los demas... y independientes y semejantes se focundaron mutuamente.

Selections from Dr Irish's book with the focus on Darío who now reverses the influence, and influences Spain rather than Spain influencing Latin America. Cf. also poems of Unamuno, Juan Ramon Jiménez.

NOTE: For B.C.D. Dr. Irish's text is invaluable, and we have the needed anthology already made:

Among the Romantic Nineteenth-Century Poets whom he includes are:

a)   Francisco Muñoz del Monte (1800-1866) Santo Domingo. His poem 'La Mulata'

b)   José María Heredia (1803-1839) Cuba. Several Poems

c)   Gabriel de la Concepción Valdés alias Plácido 1809-1844 Cuba

d)   Bartolomé Crespo y Borbón: alias Creto Gangá (1811-1871)

e)   Some selections from Martí, including ballads

For Modernismo:

Selections from Ruben Darío, Andres Eloy Blanco (1897-1955), Candelaria

Obeso (1849-1884) a Negro poet of Colombia who published *Cantos populares de mi tierra*; and another Negro poet, Jorge Artel (1909) who published *Tambores en la noche*.

The selections from Afro-Antillano Poetry include poems from:

a) José Zacarías Tallet (1893-1962) Cuba
b) Regina Pedroso (1896-1983) Cuba
c) Luis Pales Mates (1878-1959) Puerto Rico
d) Nicolás Guillén (1902-1989) Cuba
e) Ramón Guirao (1908-1949) Cuba
f) Emilio Ballagas (1908-1954) Cuba

The usefulness of this is that Dr Irish's book could provide a text both for practical criticism and for the Year I Literature (part of it).

Professor Coulthard's *Raza y Color en La Literatura Antillana* provides a useful cross reference and cross comparison of a theme that is an aspect of the *popular/culto* dialectic. As one student wrote in an essay on Góngora, the longing for Black Roots of the present Black Power movement and the earlier negritude is another form of that "cultural universal" that gave birth to the pastoral form; the backward nostalgic glance at the Golden Age, a Utopia set in the past and used as a critique of a disruptive and stress filled contemporary reality. This perhaps is what Unamuno means when he says that the study of the past only has relevance when it leads us to: *"la revelación del presente"*.

E. CONTEMPORARY PROTEST, DESPAIR AND REVOLUTION

A few poems to show where we are at today

+ (Insert: Perhaps a look at the Argentinian gaucho folklore and legends, as well as the poetry of Hidalgo and Ascasubi, although this will be more fully done when the Martín Fierro is studied.)

THE NOVEL AND SHORT STORIES.
Romanticism, and the Novel as the vehicle for Nationalism.

In Spain the uprising of the Dos de Mayo against the French, called out a reaffirmation of nationalism, which was itself a popular uprising. The influence of Romanticism was itself a spur to nationalism; The Rousseauian influence tending 'to elevate Nature to the sphere of supreme Truth' with its stress on Natural Rights, reformulating in modern terms an aspect of the Natural law theory with which Las Casas had defended the Indians, leads to a revaluation of *lo popular* as an aspect of nationalism. Elements of the historical novel, *costumbrismo*, the exaltation of the *paisaje* were the national reactions against French Power; yet nationalist reactions pervaded by French Romanticism. As with Modernismo later, Romanticism however sprang up in answer to the indigenous needs of the different countries. The historical novel in Spain, springing out of the affirmation of Spanish nationalism was a parallel to the historical novel in the Caribbean, where nationalism was anti-imperialist and therefore anti-Spanish. Jean Franco sees the connection between the national struggle and social protest on behalf of the slaves *lo popular*:

> Nowhere was Romanticism associated with the struggle for freedom more fervently than in the Caribbean, and particularly in Cuba where the struggle for independence endured for the whole of the nineteenth century. As in the Argentine, literature and politics were linked and the novel, more than any other genre, became the vehicle for nationalism. And since no liberal could support national independence without taking up the cause of the Negro slave, the novel also became an anti-slavery document.

Again following the selections made by Dr. Irish, the novel *Enriquillo, Leyenda histórica dominicana* by Manuel de Jesús Galván, the Dominican writer, taught in comparison with the factual account of the *indio rebelde* given by Las Casas. Written in the same tradition as Las Casas who wrote his accounts primarily to bring about justice for the Indians, is the novel by Anselmo Suárez Romero: *Francisco: El serio o las delicias del campo*. This novel was intended to provide evidence for the tribunal set up by the British to bring about the abolition of the slave trade. Either that novel or extracts from Villaverde's *Cecilia Valdés*, in the same tradition, would reinforce the theme of the rise of national expression and the revindication of *lo opular*.

EL REINO DE ESTE MUNDO

Alejo Carpentier's* novel as a contemporary novel is an achieved national expression of the neo-baroque union/tension of the *culto* and the *popular*; since magical realism is itself a facet, an extension of the concept of *lo popular*; the oral imagination. For contemporary relevance, the three stories by Bosch and Otero and José Luis González in Dr Irish's selections, plus a more contemporary short story since the Cuban revolution, should introduce the student to the Literature in Spanish in the Caribbean; but in a framework of reference where parallel structures in Spain and Latin America are touched upon; so that these aspects can be extended in Year II and III.

* Note: His *Reino de este mundo* could be taught with reference to an extract from his early Afro-Cuban *costumbrista* novel *¡Ecue Yambo-O!*.
* Dr. Irish's extract, on the same theme, is from Antonio Zambrana: *El Negro Francisco: Novela de costumbres cubanas*. La Habana. 1951. Either could be used.

DRAMA.

Relatively little seems to have been done on Caribbean Drama. Dr. Irish refers to plays by the poet Bartolomé Crespo y Borbón (pseudonym Creto Gangá, 1811-1871) which seem to be *costumbrista* with a stage Afro-Spanish language. These may be looked at. On the other hand, the popularity of the plays of Lorca with First Year students comes from the fact that they are superb plays, which transpose the reality of a society still based on the *latifundio* stratification; and therefore whose conflicts can parallel our own; even where there are of course the differences of a Catholic background etc.

Until Caribbean drama has been explored to see if this form has achieved expression it would be wise to keep the *Bernarda Alba* and the *Bodas de Sangre*. The great advantage too of these plays is that Lorca in poetry and plays reflects in modern setting the same *popular-culto* interrelation which characterises the theatre of the Golden Age and his plays are a useful introduction to drama in Year II.

INTRODUCTION TO THE CULTURE AND CIVILISATION OF THE CARIBBEAN, SPAIN AND LATIN AMERICA

This is conceived as parallel to the course that Dr Noel now offers in Trinidad. It replaces the course in history which was taken out of the original course; but whose lack is now urgently felt by students who complain of the vacuum, the unrelatedness of the literature to the reality with which it is involved. A certain amount of reference can be made in Literature classes but not enough. In the history course, as given in the History Department, Spain is very much a poor relation; and history as history does not deal with the kind of history of cultural universals and ideas that our course demands. We need essentially a social and cultural history related to political facts; presented in its relation to literature – themes and styles. This course might well touch on areas which, while very important for every student of Spanish, could escape notice because of the range of courses open to students e.g. the theme of *desengaño* in Seventeenth-century Spain as reflected in its literature; the French Enlightenment in Spain and America; Romanticism; the Generation of 1898 etc.

UNIVERSITY OF THE WEST INDIES
DEPARTMENT OF SPANISH

INDEX

The original dynamic of Sylvia Wynter's creative and academic work has its origins in the structures of British colonialism implanted in Jamaica. The seismic effects of the anti-colonial and native labour uprisings in the late 1930s against the British imperial system that traversed her childhood and early adolescence were to determine the nature of her life and work.

Two years after Wynter's birth in Cuba in 1928, her parents returned with her to their native Jamaica, where she grew up. After attending St. Andrew High School for Girls, she was awarded the Jamaica Centenary Scholarship in 1946, which enabled her to attend King's College, University of London. There she received a BA with Honours (with Distinction on her exams) in 1951 and a MA with a thesis on Golden Age Spanish drama in 1953. During her BA studies, Wynter spent a year studying in Spain (1948-49) primarily at the University of Madrid, where she studied philology with Dámaso Alonso and Rafael Lapesa.

After her formal studies, Wynter began her first career as a writer and an artist, the latter of which included stints as an actress and a dancer in Rome. In the UK, she became part of the wave of Caribbean migrants who, as she wrote in her 1958 article in British *Vogue,* left "the slums of empire... in search of education, in search of a living, ...and in search of an identity". During this time, Wynter authored a series of pieces for the BBC's radio programme *Caribbean Voices* as well as stage plays, one of which translated (and adapted) García Lorca's *Yerma* to a Caribbean setting. In 1958, the same year of the creation of the short-lived West Indies Federation, (as she also noted in the *Vogue* article), Wynter's play *Under the Sun* was bought by the English Stage Company at the Royal Court Theatre, a work that became the basis of her 1962 novel, *The Hills of Hebron.*

Returning the following year to a newly independent Jamaica, Wynter embarked upon her second career as an academic. In 1963, she was appointed an assistant professor in the Department of Modern Languages at the University of the West Indies, Mona, where she subsequently received tenure in 1970. During this time, Wynter helped to found *Jamaica Journal,* an important Anglophone Caribbean journal of culture and critical analysis in which she published in 1968 the ground-breaking essay "We Must Learn to Sit Down Together and Talk about a Little Culture: Reflections on West Indian Writing and Criticism".

The Black movement which led to the call for Black Studies in high school and university curricula, led to Wynter being invited to teach in the United States, first in 1974, at the University of San Diego, as Professor of Comparative and Spanish Literature and Coordinator for the new interdisciplinary program, Literature and Society in the Third World; and in 1977, at Stanford University where she was dually appointed in the African and Afro-American

Studies Program and the Department of Spanish and Portuguese. She retired in 1994 from Stanford but nonetheless remained intellectually active and continued to publish major essays until 2015.

Wynter's prodigious *œuvre* encompasses multiple genres and registers, including drama, poetry, translations, children's literature, a novel, and an extensive series of distinctive essays of critical thought. All of her work, beginning with her early decolonising essays, has been directed toward what she later articulated as the imperative of the rewriting of knowledge beyond our present *episteme* of the figure of *Man,* initially brought into being during Renaissance humanism and then transformed in the wake of the Darwinian revolution. In this context, she has called for the New Studies that arose during the 1960s, and in particular Black Studies, to forge an ecumenical perspective of being human, on the basis of Frantz Fanon's concept of sociogeny, beyond the Word of Man.

ABOUT THE EDITOR

Demetrius L. Eudell began working closely with Wynter in early 1991, while he was a graduate student at Stanford University. Together with Carolyn Allen of the University of the West Indies, Mona, he co-edited in 2002 the first sustained engagement of Wynter's work in a special edition of the *Journal of West Indian Literature,* entitled, *Sylvia Wynter: A Transculturalist Rethinking Modernity.* Currently serving as Dean of Social Sciences, Eudell is also Professor of History at Wesleyan University, where he specialises in nineteenth-century U.S. history, intellectual history and the history of Blacks in the Americas. In addition to essays and articles on Black intellectual and cultural history, he is also the author of *The Political Languages of Emancipation in the British Caribbean and the U.S. South* and co-curator/co-editor of *Lichtenbergs Menschenbilder: Charaktere und Stereotype in der Göttinger Aufklärung.* As a member of the Sylvia Wynter Editorial Collective (with Jason Ambroise, Jack Dresnick, Jason Glenn, Patricia Fox, Greg Thomas), he is a part of a team of Wynter's former students who are preparing the publication of her later work for an edition entitled *"That the Future May Finally Commence": Essays for Our Ecumenically Human's Sake, 1984-2015.*